Microsoft®

DEVELOPING MICROSOFT® VISIO® SOLUTIONS

PUBLISHED BY
Microsoft Press
A Division of Microsoft Corporation
One Microsoft Way
Redmond, Washington 98052-6399

Library of Congress Cataloging-in-Publication Data
Developing Microsoft Visio Solutions / Microsoft Corporation.
p. cm.
Includes index.
ISBN 0-7356-1353-2
1. Computer graphics. 2. Microsoft Visio. I. Microsoft Corporation.

T385 .D474 2001
650'.0285'66869--dc21 2001030496

Printed and bound in the United States of America.

1 2 3 4 5 6 7 8 9 QWT 6 5 4 3 2 1

Distributed in Canada by Penguin Books Canada Limited.

A CIP catalogue record for this book is available from the British Library.

Microsoft Press books are available through booksellers and distributors worldwide. For further information about international editions, contact your local Microsoft Corporation office or contact Microsoft Press International directly at fax (425) 936-7329. Visit our Web site at mspress.microsoft.com. Send comments to *mspinput@microsoft.com*.

Acquisitions Editor: Juliana Aldous
Project Editor: Denise Bankaitis

Body Part No. X08-06277

Table of Contents

Preface **xix**

About this Guide xx

Assumptions xx

Conventions xx

New Features for Developers xxi

Online Reference Material, Samples, and Code xxiii

The *Developing Microsoft Visio Solutions* CD xxiii

The Microsoft Visio Developer Center xxiv

Part 1 **The Visio Development Environment**

1 Introduction to *Developing Microsoft Visio Solutions* **3**

About Visio Solutions 4

Modeling with Visio Shapes 4

Field Sales Automation: an Example of a Visio Solution 8

Using Visio Shapes to Create Solutions 10

Assembling Objects into Drawings 10

Shapes as Components 11

Using SmartShapes Technology to Develop Shapes 13

Using Automation in a Visio Solution 14

Automation and Visio Objects 15

Monitoring Events and Totaling Values: an Example 16

Planning a Visio Solution 18

Planning the Development Process 19

Planning Shapes and Stencils 21

Planning Templates 22

Automating Shapes and Templates 23

Integrating a Visio Solution with a Database 24

Choices for Implementing Automation 25

Migrating from Visual Basic to VBA 27

Part 2 Developing Visio Shapes

2 Creating Visio Shapes 31

Visio Shape Anatomy 32
- Closed and Open Shapes 33
- 1-D and 2-D Shapes 34
- Shape Handles 34
- Shapes in Groups 36

Drawing New Shapes 37
- Using the Drawing Tools to Create Shapes 37
- Drawing Closed Shapes 39
- Drawing Shapes by Repeating Elements 39
- Creating Groups 40
- Merging Shapes to Create New Ones 40

Importing Shapes from Other Programs 42
- Importing Graphic Images 42
- Editing Imported Metafiles and Bitmaps 43
- Converting Imported Metafiles to Shapes 44

Adapting Existing Visio Shapes 45
- Revising Existing Shapes 45
- Revising Existing Groups 46
- Shape Copyrights 49

3 Visio Masters, Stencils, Templates, and Documents 51

Creating Masters and Stencils 52
- Creating a Stencil 53
- Creating Masters on Stencils 55
- Editing Masters on Stencils 56

Creating Templates 57
- Creating a Template 58
- About Pages, Backgrounds, and Layers 60

Opening and Saving Visio Documents 62
- Components of a Visio Document 62
- Opening a Visio File 63
- Choosing the Right File Type for Your Solution 64

4 Visio Formulas **65**

The ShapeSheet Window 66

Displaying a ShapeSheet Window 66

Displaying Sections in a ShapeSheet Window 69

Examining a Shape in a ShapeSheet Window 73

Elements of Visio Formulas 76

Entering and Editing Formulas in a ShapeSheet Window 76

Functions and Operators in Visio Formulas 77

ShapeSheet Cell References 79

Rules for Cell References in Formulas 81

Units of Measure in Visio Formulas 83

Multidimensional Units 84

Specifying Units of Measure 85

Designing Visio Formulas 86

How Shapes Inherit Formulas 87

User-Defined Cells and "Scratch" Formulas 88

Protecting Formulas 90

Controlling Recalculation of Formulas 90

When to Supplement Visio Formulas with Automation 92

5 Controlling Shape Geometry with Formulas **93**

Shape Geometry 94

Describing Shapes in a Coordinate System 95

Representing Shape Geometry with Formulas 96

Representing a Shape's Position on a Page 98

Controlling How Shapes Stretch and Shrink 100

Height-based Formulas: an Example 100

Optimizing the Arrow Example 103

Controlling How Shapes Flip and Rotate 103

How Flipping Affects a Shape 103

How Rotating Affects a Shape 105

Designing Shapes that Flip and Rotate 106

Preventing Shapes from Flipping and Rotating 107

Controlling Curves in Shapes 108
Using Rounded Corner Styles 108
Understanding Arcs 109
Converting Line and Arc Segments 113
Useful Arc Formulas 113
Optimizing Shape Geometry 115
Using Locks to Limit Shape Behavior 116

6 Grouping and Merging Shapes 119

Groups versus Merged Shapes 120
Creating and Controlling Groups 121
Grouping and Ungrouping Shapes 121
Modifying a Group 122
How Grouping Shapes Affects Their Formulas 122
Controlling the Behavior of Groups 123
Controlling How Groups are Selected 124
Defining the Resizing Behavior of Grouped Shapes 125
Resizing Shapes in Only One Direction 126
Creating a 3-D Box: an Example 128
Protecting the Formatting of Shapes in Groups 131
Creating and Controlling Merged Shapes 131
Merging Shapes 132
Filling Merged Shapes 133
Hiding Shape Geometry 134

7 Enhancing Shape Behavior 135

Making Shapes Flexible with Control Handles 136
Adding a Controls Section to a Shape 136
Defining a Control Handle 137
Setting a Control Handle's Anchor Point 140
Setting a Control Handle's Behavior 140

Shortcut Menu Commands 142
Defining a Shortcut Menu Command 143
Controlling a Shortcut Command's Appearance on the Menu 144
Adding Check Marks to Commands on the Shortcut Menu 145
Dimming a Shortcut Command on the Menu 146
Hiding and Showing Commands on the Shortcut Menu 146
Using Shortcut Commands to Change Shape Geometry: an Example 147
Custom Properties 149
Using Custom Properties 150
Defining Custom Properties 151
Linking Custom Properties to a Database 155
Event Formulas 156
Using Cells in the Events Section 156
Simulating Events with the DEPENDSON Function 157
Functions that Perform Actions 158

8 Working with 1-D Shapes, Connectors, and Glue 161

How 1-D and 2-D Shapes Differ 162
Converting 1-D and 2-D Shapes 163
Examples of 1-D Shapes 164
Creating Routable and Other 1-D Connectors 165
Creating Routable Connectors 165
Creating Other 1-D Connectors 167
Controlling How Shapes Connect 172
Defining a Connector's Glue Behavior 173
Specifying What Can be Glued 174
Understanding Connection Points 175
Adding Connection Points to a Shape 178
Naming Connection Points 180
Designing Shapes for the Dynamic Connector 180

9 Designing Text Behavior **183**

About Text in Shapes and Masters 184

Viewing Text Attributes in the ShapeSheet Window 185

Controlling the Text Block's Position 186

Controlling Text in a Group 188

Resizing Shapes with Text 189

Controlling Text Block Size 189

Basing Shape Size on the Amount of Text 191

Basing Shape Size on Text Value 192

Changing the Font Size as a Shape is Resized 192

Writing a Formula to Resize Text 193

Controlling Text Rotation 194

Writing Formulas to Control Text Rotation 194

Gravity Formulas 195

Counterrotation Formulas for Level Text 196

Constraining Text Block Size 196

Working with Text Formulas 200

Displaying and Formatting Formula Results 200

Formatting Strings and Text Output 202

Protecting Text Formulas 204

Testing Text Block Formulas 204

10 Managing Styles, Formats, and Colors **207**

Working with Styles in the Drawing Page 208

Understanding Styles 208

Setting Default Styles for a Drawing 209

Creating a New Style 210

Editing a Style 211

Guidelines for Applying Styles to Shapes 212

Reformatting Shapes on the Drawing Page 213

Reformatting Masters in a Stand-alone Stencil 214

Reformatting All Instances of a Master 214

Using Styles in Stencils and Templates 216

Keeping Styles Consistent across Files 216

Using Naming Conventions for Styles 217

Guidelines for Defining Styles 217

Protecting Local Shape Formats 218
Preserving Local Shape Formatting through the User Interface 218
Preserving Local Shape Formatting through the ShapeSheet Spreadsheet 219
Managing Color in Styles, Shapes, and Files 219
Editing the Color Palette 220
Standardizing Color Palettes across Documents 221
Using a Formula to Define a Custom Color 221
Adding Transparency for Custom Colors 222
Custom Patterns 223
Creating a Custom Pattern 223
Developing Custom Fill Patterns 226
Developing Custom Line Patterns 228
Developing Custom Line Ends 230

11 Arranging Shapes in Drawings 233

Assigning Shapes and Masters to Layers 234
Using Layers Efficiently 234
Assigning Shapes and Groups to Layers 236
Designing a Grid 237
Setting the Grid for a Template's Drawing Page 237
Creating Masters that Work with a Grid 238
Using Formulas to Hold Grid Information 240
Aligning Shapes to Guides and Guide Points 241
Guidelines for Using Guides or Grids 241
Manipulating Guides and Guide Points 242
Guides in a Rotated Page 243
Grouping Guides with Shapes 243
Using Alignment Boxes to Snap Shapes to a Grid 244
Adjusting the Size of a Shape's Alignment Box 244
Updating an Alignment Box 247
Changing the Alignment Box for 1-D Shapes 247
Designing Shapes for Automatic Layout 248
Setting Layout Options for the Page 248
Setting Shape and Connector Behavior 250

12 Scaled Shapes and Measured Drawings 253
Choosing an Appropriate Drawing Scale 254
Understanding Drawing Scale and Page Scale 254
Factors to Consider in Choosing a Drawing Scale 255
Choosing a Scale for Masters 257
Determining an Appropriate Scale for a Master 257
Setting the Scale of a Master 259
Creating Shapes that Never Scale 260
13 Packaging Stencils and Templates 261
Designing Custom Shapes for Distribution 262
Shape Design Process Guidelines 262
Shape, Stencil, and Template Distribution Considerations 263
Testing Masters 264
Checking the Consistency of Masters 264
Checking the Master in the Master Drawing Window 265
Testing Masters with Different Page Scales 266
Adding Help for Your Custom Solution 268
Associating Help with a Master 268
Testing Shape Help 269
Adding HTML Help that is Integrated with the Microsoft Visio Help System 270
Finishing and Testing a Stencil 270
Creating Master Shortcuts 270
Cleaning up Masters in a Stencil 272
Cleaning up a Stencil File 273
Testing Stencils 274
Finishing and Testing a Template 276
Cleaning up a Template 276
Testing a Template 277
Installing Stencils and Templates 279
Moving Template Files 280
Protecting Stencils and Templates 280

Part 3 Extending Visio with Automation

14 Automation and the Visio Object Model 283
An Automation Overview 284
The Visio Object Model 284
Getting and Releasing Visio Objects 287
Declaring Object Variables 287
Accessing Visio Objects through Properties 287
Referring to an Object in a Collection 288
Iterating through a Collection 290
Releasing an Object 290
Using Compound Object References 291
Restricting the Scope and Lifetime of Object Variables 292
Using Properties and Methods 292
Declaring Variables for Return Values and Arguments 292
Getting and Setting Properties 293
Using an Object's Default Property 294
Using Methods 294

15 Programming Visio with VBA 295
Using the Visual Basic Editor 296
Starting the Visual Basic Editor 297
Navigating among Projects 297
Saving a Project 298
Enabling or Disabling VBA Project Creation 299
Creating a VBA Project 300
Inserting Modules and Class Modules into Your Project 301
Inserting User Forms into Your Project 303
Importing Files into and Exporting Files from Your Project 304
Using the Visio Type Library 305
Using the Object Browser 306
Setting References to Type Libraries 306
Using Visio Object Types 307
Using the Global and ThisDocument Objects 309
Using the Visio Global Object 309
Using the ThisDocument Object 311

Running VBA Code from Visio 312
Handling Errors 315
Running the Program in the Right Context 315
Verifying that Objects and Return Values Exist 315
Checking for Error Values 316
Managing a VBA Project 316
Removing Project Items 317
Protecting Your Solution's VBA Code 317
Using Digital Certificates to Produce Trusted Solutions 317
Using the Add-In Manager 323

16 Working with Visio Document, Page, and Shape Objects 325

Working with Document Objects 326
Getting a Document Object 326
Getting Information about Documents 328
Working with Styles in a Document 328
Creating a Style for a Document 329
Printing and Saving Documents 330
Displaying Pages of a Document 331
Working with Page Objects 332
Getting a Page Object 332
Getting Information about Pages 333
Adding Pages to a Drawing 333
Working with Shape Objects 334
Getting a Shape Object 334
Getting Information about a Shape 336
Creating and Changing Shapes 337
Adding Text to Shapes 339
Getting a Shape's Text 340
Identifying and Applying Styles to Shapes 341
Preserving Local Formatting 342
Creating Groups from a Program 342
Creating Masters 343
Creating a Simple Drawing: an Example 344

17 Automating Formulas **347**
Working with Formulas in Cells 348
Getting a Cell Object 349
Changing Cell Formulas Using the Formula property 351
Getting the Result of a Formula 351
Replacing a Formula with a Result 353
Overriding Guarded Formulas 353
Using Formulas to Move Shapes: an Example 354
Working with Sections and Rows 355
Adding Sections and Rows 355
Adding a Geometry Section to a Shape: an Example 356
Deleting Sections and Rows 358
Changing the Type of a Segment 359
Iterating through a Collection of Sections and Rows: an Example 360
Working with Inherited Data 361

18 Drawing with Automation **363**
Automating Drawing with Masters 364
Getting the Stencil 364
Getting the Master 365
Dropping the Master on the Page 365
Placing Shapes in a Drawing 367
Placing Shapes Using Automation: an Example 367
Placing Shapes in Relation to Other Shapes 369
Working with Selected Shapes 375
Getting Shapes that are Selected in a Window 375
Adding and Removing Shapes in Selections 376
Selecting and Deselecting Shapes in a Window 377
Performing Operations on Selected Shapes 377
Determining a Selection's Scope 378
Background Pages 378
Creating and Assigning Background Pages 378
Iterating through the Pages Collection: an Example 379
Setting up Pages and Backgrounds: an Example 379
Changing Page Settings 380

Layers 381
Identifying Layers in a Page or Master 381
Identifying the Layers to Which a Shape is Assigned 382
Assigning Shapes to and Removing Shapes from Layers 382
Adding Layers to and Deleting Layers from Pages and Masters 383
Changing Layer Settings 383

19 Automating Connections in a Visio Solution 385

Working with a Connect Object 386
Getting Information from a Connected Drawing 388
Determining Which Shapes are Connected 389
Determining Which Parts of Shapes are Connected 389
Getting the Cells in a Connection 391
Guidelines for Analyzing a Connected Drawing 392
Iterating through the Connections on a Page: an Example 393
Creating a Connected Drawing from a Program 395
What Can Be Glued to What 396
Gluing with Cell Objects 398
Gluing a Shape to Another Shape 398
Connecting Shapes in a Flowchart: an Example 400

20 Integrating Data with a Visio Solution 403

Associating Data with Shapes Using Automation 404
Adding Custom Property and User-Defined Rows 404
Generating and Using Unique IDs 405
Visio Properties for Storing and Retrieving Data 406
Storing and Retrieving XML Data in Your Solutions 407
Storing XML Data in and Retrieving XML Data from a Document 407
Storing XML Data in and Retrieving XML Data from a Cell 408
Writing Code to Extract Data from a Visio Drawing 410
Extracting Data from a Drawing: an Example 410
Examining the Code for Extracting Data from a Drawing 413
Writing Code to Create a Visio Drawing from Data 414
Creating a Drawing from Data: an Example 414
Examining the Code for Creating a Drawing from Data 417
Integrating a Visio Solution with a Database 418

21 Handling Visio Events **421**
An Event Overview 422
Writing Code Behind Events 423
Handling Events Fired by ThisDocument 424
Declaring an Object Variable Using the WithEvents Keyword 426
Defining a Class to Receive Events 428
Class Module that Responds to Events: an Example 430
Visio Event Objects 431
Defining Your Event Object 431
Filtering Your Event Object 433
Getting Information about an Event Object 436
Creating an Event Object that Runs an Add-on 436
Persistence of an Event Object that Runs an Add-on 437
Creating an Event Object that Sends a Notification 438
The VisEventProc Procedure: an Example 443
Event Objects that Send Notifications: an Example 444
Lifetime of an Event Object that Sends a Notification 445

22 Customizing the Visio User Interface **447**
Using CommandBar Objects to Customize the Visio User Interface 448
Working with the Command Bars Object Model 449
Creating a Command Bar 450
Getting Information about Command Bars 455
Deleting a Command Bar 455
Working with Command Bar Controls 456
Writing Code for a Command Bar: an Example 460
Preventing Users from Modifying Custom Command Bars 463
Preventing Users from Modifying All Visio Command Bars 464
Using Visio UIObject Objects to Customize the Visio User Interface 464
About Menu Objects 466
About Accelerator Objects 469
About Toolbar Objects 470
Planning User Interface Changes 472
Making User Interface Changes 475

Using Custom User Interface Files 486
About Custom.vsu 487
Saving a Custom User Interface File 487
Loading a Custom User Interface File 488
Restoring the Built-in Visio User Interface 489

23 Using COM Add-ins in a Visio Solution 491

Accessing COM Add-ins in Visio 492
Viewing a List of Available COM Add-ins 492
Using the COMAddIns Property to Get Information about COM Add-ins 493
Creating a COM Add-in for Visio 494
Working with Add-in Designers 494
Specifying Load Behavior 499
Writing Code in the Add-in Designer 500
Hooking a COM Add-in into a Command Bar Control 503
Writing Code for a COM Add-in: an Example 505
Making the DLL and Registering the COM Add-in 508
Distributing COM add-ins 509

24 Using ActiveX Controls in a Visio Solution 511

Adding ActiveX Controls to a Visio Solution 512
Working in Design Mode 512
Inserting a Control in a Drawing 513
Setting the Tabbing Order of Controls 515
Using the Visio Ambient Properties in Controls 515
Printing a Drawing Without its Controls 516
Protecting Controls from Changes 516
Handling a Control's Events 517
Working with Controls at Run Time 517
About Control Names 518
Getting a Control from the OLEObjects Collection 518
Distributing ActiveX Controls in a Visio Solution 519
ActiveX Controls that Interact with Shapes: an Example 520

25 Using the Visio Undo Manager in Your Program 523
The Visio Undo Manager 524
An Undo/Redo Overview 525
How the Visio Undo Manager Works with an Add-on 526
Creating Undo Scopes in Your Add-on 527
Creating an Undo Scope 527
Associating Events with an Undo Scope 528
Creating Undo Units 528
Creating an Undo Unit 529
Adding an Undo Unit in the Visio Undo Manager 530
Creating an Undo Unit that Maintains Non-Visio Data: an Example 531

26 Packaging a Visio Automation Solution 535
Installing a Visio Solution 536
Specifying Visio File Paths and Folders 536
How Visio Searches File Paths 538
Controlling when Your Program Runs 539
Distributing Your Program 544
Distributing Microsoft VBA Programs 544
Drawing File Size in a Microsoft VBA Solution 545
Using Universal Names in Your Solution 546
Important Licensing Information 546

27 Programming Visio with Visual Basic 549
Getting a Visio Instance 550
Creating an Application Object 550
Getting an Application Object 550
Releasing an Application Object 551
Using the Application Object in a Visual Basic Program: an Example 552
Working with an Instance's Window Handle 554
Interacting with Other Programs 554
Creating a Visio Document 555
Handling Errors in Visual Basic 556

Interpreting the Command String that Visio Sends to Your Program 558
Running the Program from the Macros Submenu 558
Running the Program when a Formula is Evaluated 558
Running the Program with Arguments 559
Running the Program from the Startup Folder 560
Parsing a Command String 560
Using the Visio Type Library in Visual Basic Projects 560

28 Programming Visio with C++ 563

How Visio Exposes Objects 564
C++ Support in Visio 566
Using the Wrapper Classes 566
The Interfaces Behind the Wrappers 568
Obtaining a Visio Application Object 570
Values Returned by Visio Methods 571
Arguments Passed to Visio Methods 573
Handling Visio Events in C++ Programs 574
Implementing a Sink Object 575
Using CVisioAddonSink 575
Visio Libraries 577
Advantages of Visio Libraries 578
The Architecture of a Visio Library 578
Declaring and Registering Add-ons 580
Running an Add-on 581

Part 4 Appendixes

Appendix A Properties, Methods, and Events by Object 587

Appendix B ShapeSheet Section, Row, and Cell Indices 609

Glossary 621

Index 637

Preface

About this Guide xx

New Features for Developers xxi

Online Reference Material, Samples, and Code xxiii

Developing Microsoft Visio Solutions is a complete guide to creating solutions with Microsoft Visio. This guide presents:

- An introduction to the Visio environment and conceptual information about Developing Microsoft Visio Solutions.
- Detailed information about using formulas to design SmartShapes symbols that model real-world objects and behavior.
- Information, tips, and techniques for using Microsoft Visual Basic for Applications (VBA) to extend Visio or to use Visio as a component in your own applications.
- An introduction to using the Microsoft Visual Basic and C++ programming languages to develop programs that use the Visio application as a component.

This Preface defines the guide's audience and conventions, introduces the top new features of interest to solution developers, and points to key online reference materials.

About this Guide

Developing Microsoft Visio Solutions provides assistance for anyone who wants to customize Microsoft Visio shapes or solutions, including application developers, systems analysts, programmers, architects, engineers, and users of computer-aided design (CAD) programs.

Assumptions

We assume you are already familiar with drawing techniques and with the Visio menus, tools, and commands. We also assume a high-school level knowledge of basic geometry and Cartesian coordinate systems. An understanding of transformations, trigonometry, and analytic geometry can also be helpful.

In the chapters that discuss controlling Visio with another programming language such as Microsoft Visual Basic for Applications (VBA) or C++, we assume you are familiar with the programming language you'll be using. Most of the examples in this book are written using VBA.

Conventions

This guide uses the following typographical conventions.

Typographical convention	Description
Bold	Programming terms in text.
Italic	Variables in text, formulas in text, or terms defined in text. In syntax, italic letters indicate placeholders for information you supply.
EmbeddedCaps	Capitalization for readability in Visio and VBA. Language terms are not case-sensitive in Visio or VBA, but they are case-sensitive in C++ and XML (Extensible Markup Language).
Title Caps	File names in text.
`Monospace font`	Code examples.

To enhance the readability of formula and code samples, these conventions are followed:

- Within formulas, we have inserted spaces before and after operators and equals signs (=). These spaces are not required and are removed by Visio if you enter them with your formula.
- In code examples, we have used numeric and string constants where you would ordinarily use variables or global constants, especially if you intend to localize your programs.

New Features for Developers

Microsoft Visio provides a powerful single platform for your custom drawing solutions. The new features and improvements in Microsoft Visio 2002 give you more options for defining the behavior of the elements in your solutions.

For details on new ShapeSheet cells and Automation events, methods, objects, and properties that have been added in Microsoft Visio 2002, see the Microsoft Visio Developer Reference (on the **Help** menu, click **Developer Reference**).

New features in Microsoft Visio 2002 for developers

Feature	Description
Object model changes that support new and improved Visio features	Experience more complete access to persisted document data and better access to a variety of commonly used areas in Visio with more than 90 new properties and methods in the Visio 2002 object model.
Native XML file format	Share your Visio drawings with a full-fidelity, XML-based, alternative file format. Based on Extensible Markup Language (XML) syntax, XML for Visio enables a more open exchange of Visio data with other applications.
Storage of XML data for solutions	Store well-formed, solution-specific XML data within your Visio documents. Your XML data can be associated with a document as a whole or stored in individual ShapeSheet cells.
Component Object Model (COM) add-in support	Develop Visio solutions using the new COM add-in technology that is available to many of the Microsoft Office applications.
Access to the command bar object model	Customize and create menus and toolbars in Visio using the command bar object model that is shared by all Microsoft Office applications.

New features in Microsoft Visio 2002 for developers *(continued)*

Feature	Description
Event filters	Use event filters to tailor the events you listen to, and prevent many of the events you don't want to hear from firing.
Digital signatures	Identify your VBA project code as a trusted source by digitally signing it.
New ShapeSheet cells and values	Use new cells to add transparency to any color attribute, set more concise glue type and behavior, set connectors as smooth curves, or flip shapes during placement. Set new values for more control in connected diagram solutions and for currencies.
Drop-down lists for ShapeSheet cells	Select values from drop-down lists in ShapeSheet cells that have a constant set of valid values.
GDI Plus for better graphic rendering and handling of file formats	Build graphically rich applications, manage raster image formats and metadata, and improve text readability with GDI Plus. Includes native support for JPEG, PNG, GIF, BMP, TIFF, EMF, and WMF files.
32-bit color and transparency	Take advantage of the ability to use over 16 million colors in this 32-bit color drawing environment. Produce professional-quality drawings when you add transparency, shadows, and semi-transparent objects to your documents.
Improved in-place behavior	Visio drawings embedded in other applications now run identically to drawings in the Visio application.
Ability to host add-ons inside of Visio windows	Support simultaneous docking of anchored windows, add-on windows, and stencils inside your Visio 2002 window. Windows can be docked or merged at the same time, and resized to suit your application.
Microsoft Visual Basic for Applications version 6.3	Use the same version of VBA as Microsoft Office XP.

For more details on features that are not discussed in this guide, see documentation updates and technical articles on the Microsoft Visio Developer Center on the MSDN Web site (msdn.microsoft.com/visio/).

Online Reference Material, Samples, and Code

Microsoft Visio 2002 includes a detailed Developer Reference with information on Visio Automation objects, methods, properties, and events and ShapeSheet sections, rows, cells, and functions. The Microsoft Visio Developer Reference is available from the **Help** menu in Visio (on the **Help** menu, click **Developer Reference**).

You can find shape samples and code on the *Developing Microsoft Visio Solutions* CD that is provided with this guide. Additional, related developer reference materials are on the Microsoft Visio Developer Center on the MSDN Web site (msdn.microsoft.com/visio/).

The *Developing Microsoft Visio Solutions* CD

Besides an electronic copy of this guide, you can find reference information, samples, and code on the *Developing Microsoft Visio Solutions* CD that correspond to each chapter in the guide.

Here's an overview of what is on the *Developing Microsoft Visio Solutions* CD:

- An illustration of the Visio object model
- Sample drawings and stencils that include a variety of shapes illustrating a wide variety of common shape behaviors
- Templates that contain a variety of useful Microsoft Visual Basic for Applications (VBA) macro samples
- Microsoft Visual Basic support files, along with C++ utility programs and source code described in Chapter 27, *Programming Visio with Visual Basic* and Chapter 28, *Programming Visio with C++*

System Requirements for the CD

To use the CD with this guide, you'll need the following:

- Microsoft Visio Professional 2002
- Microsoft Windows 98, Microsoft Windows 98 Second Edition, Microsoft Windows Millennium Edition, Microsoft Windows NT 4.0 with Service Pack 6 or later (requires Microsoft Internet Explorer 4.01 browser software with Service Pack 1 or later), or Microsoft Windows 2000 Professional or later operating system
- Microsoft Visual Basic 6.0 or later
- A C++ development tool, such as Microsoft Visual C++ 6.0 or later

The Microsoft Visio Developer Center

The Microsoft Visio Developer Center on the MSDN Web site (msdn.microsoft.com/visio/) contains current information for developers who are developing custom solutions for Visio, such as:

- Technical articles about different aspects of creating custom Visio solutions
- Developer support resources, including key reference materials that supplement the documentation in this guide, a knowledge base, and a library of downloadable files that includes sample code and applications
- Developer news, including developer-related events, upcoming online broadcasts, and the latest downloads
- Visio Newsgroups, a place for you to share information and get help from other Visio developers
- Information about developer training, including a course description and syllabus
- Real-world case studies so you can learn how companies are extending Visio technology to meet their specific needs
- Information about Visio Solution Providers and technical assistance

Point your browser to msdn.microsoft.com/visio/ to access the Microsoft Visio Developer Center.

Part 1

The Visio Development Environment

Chapter 1 Introduction to *Developing Microsoft Visio Solutions*

1

Introduction to *Developing Microsoft Visio Solutions*

About Visio Solutions 4

Using Visio Shapes to Create Solutions 10

Using SmartShapes Technology to Develop Shapes 13

Using Automation in a Visio Solution 14

Planning a Visio Solution 18

Migrating from Visual Basic to VBA 27

This guide is about developing *solutions*—combinations of Microsoft Visio shapes and programs that model the real world and solve specific drawing problems.

A software solution typically combines a custom program with one or more packaged software applications. Rather than developing functionality from scratch, the solution developer uses functionality that is built into a packaged product.

A Visio solution typically combines programmable shapes—either supplied with Visio or developed for the solution—with a template to create drawings in which the shapes are used. A Visio solution might also use Automation to control its shapes and drawings. A custom program in a Visio solution can be written in any programming language that supports Automation as a client, such as Microsoft Visual Basic for Applications (VBA), Microsoft Visual Basic, or C++. Visio provides an integrated development environment for convenient development of VBA projects.

This chapter introduces important Visio features and some concepts that will help you decide how to use them. To get the most out of this chapter and the rest of this guide, you should be familiar with Visio menu commands and tools. The best way to get acquainted with these is to create a drawing or two. If you haven't yet done this, we recommend that you do it now before continuing with this guide. Also, locate the Microsoft Visio Help and Developer Reference (on the **Help** menu, click **Microsoft Visio Help** or click **Developer Reference**), so you can find out more about Visio functionality, the ShapeSheet spreadsheet, and the Visio object model if you have questions about these areas while reading this guide.

If your solution will control the Visio engine with Automation, you should be familiar with the programming language you intend to use. Help for VBA is provided with Visio. For other programming languages, see their respective documentation.

About Visio Solutions

A Microsoft Visio solution is a combination of Visio shapes and programs that model the real world and solve specific drawing problems. A Visio solution usually includes *stencils* of master shapes, called *masters,* that a user can drag and drop onto the drawing page to create a drawing, without having to draw anything manually. A solution might also include *templates* that provide stencils of specific shapes such as title boxes, logos, or frames for use in new drawings, and that predefine the drawing scale, drawing size, and occasionally the paper size for printing.

Programs (either VBA code within the solution's Visio documents or standalone programs external to Visio documents) can help create the drawing, analyze the drawing, or transfer information between the drawing and external data sources. Shapes can have online Help to assist a user in using them correctly.

Modeling with Visio Shapes

A *model* helps you analyze and solve a problem using objects that resemble things in the domain of the model, whether that's the organization of people in your department, the arrangement of desks and chairs in a floor plan, the network you're selling to a customer, or a state diagram for an integrated circuit. Because a model resembles the real world, you can design and develop a solution in terms that users understand.

In a well-designed Visio solution, shapes correspond to objects in the domain of the model. Creating the drawing constructs the model. Shape behavior encourages correct modeling and correct graphical representation, while allowing the user to override certain attributes to create a readable representation.

For example, if you're planning the organization of a department, the domain of the model is the department, and employees are objects in the domain. A drawing that represents this model would be a simple organization chart of boxes with connecting lines that show who reports to whom.

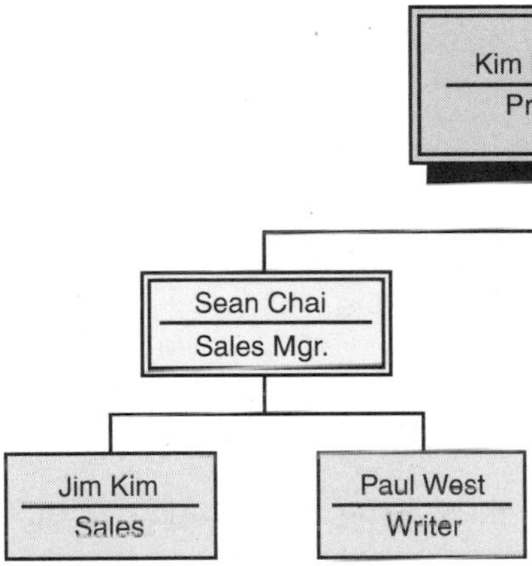

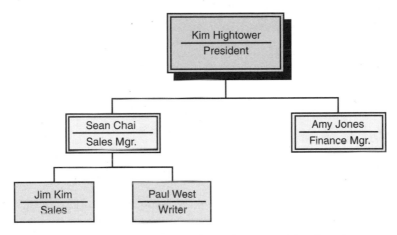

Figure 1-1 A user could reorganize a department by changing connections between employees.

Or, suppose you're creating a facilities plan to move your company to a new office building. The domain of the model is the building, and employees would be objects in this domain, but it would also include furniture, computing equipment, and so on. A drawing that represents this model would be an office layout diagram showing where each employee is located, and what furniture and equipment the employee has in an office.

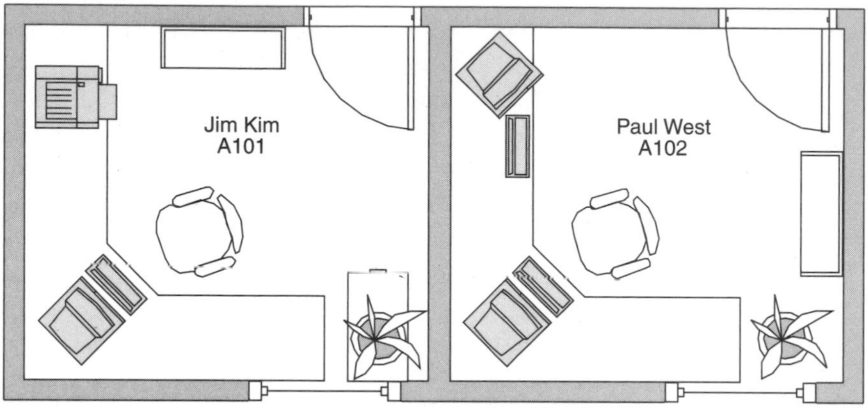

Figure 1-2 A user could create a moving plan by dragging employee, furniture, and computer shapes.

You can design Visio shapes as reusable components so that your users can create drawings without having to use drawing tools. Visio is an excellent tool for modeling, because not only can shapes resemble objects in the model domain, they can be designed to encourage development of a correct model.
For example:

- A user might reorganize a department by moving the connections between employees in an organization chart. Shapes could be designed to encourage correct organizational design by having predefined connection points, showing the user where to place connections (and subtly discouraging impractical arrangements, such as having one employee report to two managers).
- A user might create a moving plan by dragging employee, furniture, and computer shapes in an office layout diagram. Shapes could be designed to encourage correct layout by having control handles a user could drag to check clearances of doors and drawers, and shapes might be locked against resizing so a user couldn't inadvertently resize standard furniture so that it wouldn't fit in a real office.

Extracting data from a model

A Visio drawing is usually just a partial view of a model, and rarely the end product. A Visio solution is most valuable when drawings represent a model that data can be automatically extracted from. For example, in a process modeling solution, the drawing shows the steps of a process, but you might also need to know the cost per transaction of each process.

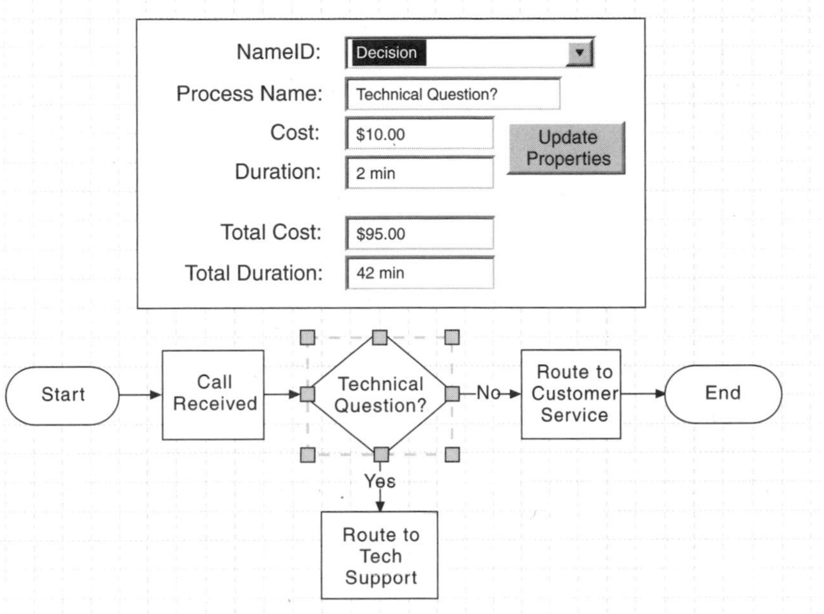

Figure 1-3 Data extracted from a process drawing.

Sometimes you can add enough data to a Visio drawing so that the complete model is stored in the drawing, but if you have many drawings that have to be consistent, part of the model can reside in a single shared database, such as specifications for kitchen cabinets, counters, and appliances, or tables of process inputs and outputs.

Validating a model

Models also have rules that dictate how objects should behave. Drawings must follow certain rules to be readable—for example, an organization chart with overlapping connectors and boxes is less effective than one where boxes are consistently spaced and connectors route around them.

However, creating a drawing that looks correct is not enough—shapes must be designed, and the drawing must be made, so that data it represents can be checked for accuracy. For example, in a moving plan, every employee should have a desk; multiple employees would rarely share a desk, and one employee would rarely have more than one desk.

A Visio solution can analyze data extracted from drawings to make sure it follows the rules of the model. Suppose many departments are being changed in a companywide reorganization. The reporting structures expressed in separate departmental organization charts can be automatically extracted and their separate structures merged into a global organization structure to check for consistency. For example, the solution could ensure that no employee reports to more than one manager, any employee not appearing in the proposed reorganization is being intentionally removed from the organization, and so on.

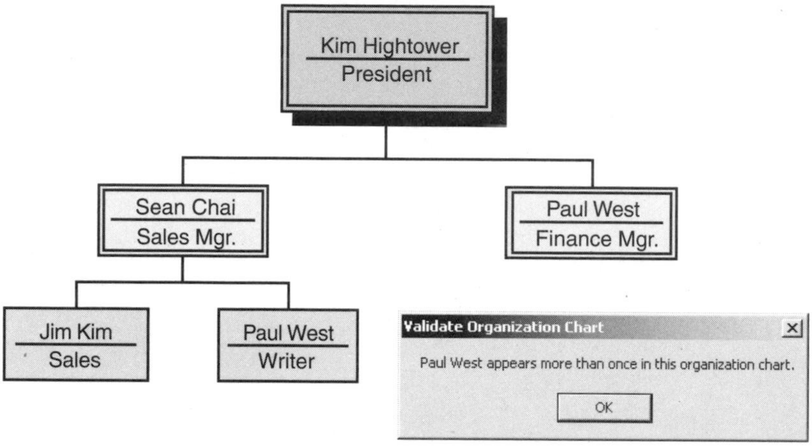

Figure 1-4 A Visio solution can analyze drawings to validate the model.

Field Sales Automation: an Example of a Visio Solution

To see how a Visio solution can model the real world, extract data from the model, and validate it, consider as an example a field sales solution for a company that designs and sells security systems.

Traditionally, a salesperson calls on a potential customer to discuss security needs, designs a system by looking up components in a parts catalog (which might include current prices) and sketching the proposed system with pencil and paper. The salesperson possibly gives the customer a rough estimate of cost, and then returns to the office to prepare a formal proposal. Back at the office, the sketch is re-created in a drawing program, prices are looked up and totaled for the bid, and a proposal document is written. If the customer accepts the proposal, the company prepares a contract for the customer to sign and a work order for the installation.

The traditional approach works well, assuming everything goes as planned. But suppose the original sketch omits some essential components, connects them incorrectly, or leaves something unconnected. Suppose the formal drawing doesn't match the sketch. If the salesperson's catalog is out of date, the proposed system might include components that are unavailable or more expensive. Creating each document manually increases the possibility of error at every stage in the process, up to and including installation at the customer site. Even if all goes well, at each stage it takes time to prepare each document, check for errors, and correct them.

Here's how a Visio solution can automate this process: The salesperson, carrying a laptop with Visio and the sales automation solution installed, calls on a potential customer. As they discuss security needs, the salesperson diagrams the proposed system by dragging shapes from a custom stencil to their correct locations in a Visio drawing of the installation site. The security system shapes are designed with connection points and control handles that make it easy for the salesperson to arrange them correctly, and the stencil is updated regularly so the salesperson doesn't have to worry about obsolete components.

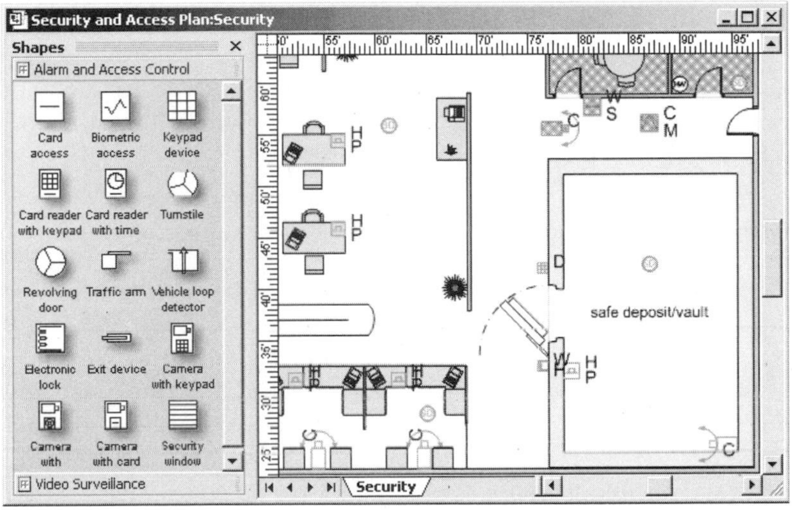

Figure 1-5 A security system designed with a Visio solution.

The security system shapes have custom properties that store data such as part numbers, and the solution includes a database of current prices and other detailed information about components, along with programs that can synchronize the shapes with the database. This allows the salesperson to do the following:

- Validate the proposed security system by checking the drawing to ensure that all components are correctly placed and connected, so the salesperson can correct errors before leaving the customer site.
- Look up current prices in the database to generate a bill of materials and an accurate estimate for the bid, so the customer knows what the cost will be.

Either in the field or back at the office, the Visio solution could generate the proposal, contract, installation work order, and invoice, all based on the salesperson's original drawing. The Visio solution creates more accurate documents in less time, freeing the salesperson to work with more customers.

Using Visio Shapes to Create Solutions

A Microsoft Visio solution almost always involves shapes. Visio offers the solution developer easy access to sophisticated graphics functionality with its drawing tools, and shapes can be programmed by means of formulas in the ShapeSheet window.

Every Visio shape includes an assortment of formulas that represent its attributes, such as its width and height, and its behavior, such as what the shape does when a user double-clicks it. Because Visio shapes are programmable through formulas, you can make them behave like the objects they represent in the real world. So, for example, you can associate important data—part numbers, names, manufacturers—with shapes representing office equipment. Your shapes can then become powerful components whose unique behavior within a larger solution is provided by the formulas you write.

Assembling Objects into Drawings

If you're accustomed to thinking about graphics as a collection of vectors, you can think about Visio graphics in a whole new way. Visio shapes are *parametric*. That is, a Visio shape can adjust its *geometry* and other attributes according to the values of certain parameters—some defined by the Visio engine, others by the shape developer. Instead of fixed geometry based on hard-coded *x,y* coordinates, a shape's geometry is based on formulas that recalculate dynamically as a user manipulates the shape. Instead of drafting with lines, you assemble intelligent objects to create the drawing you want.

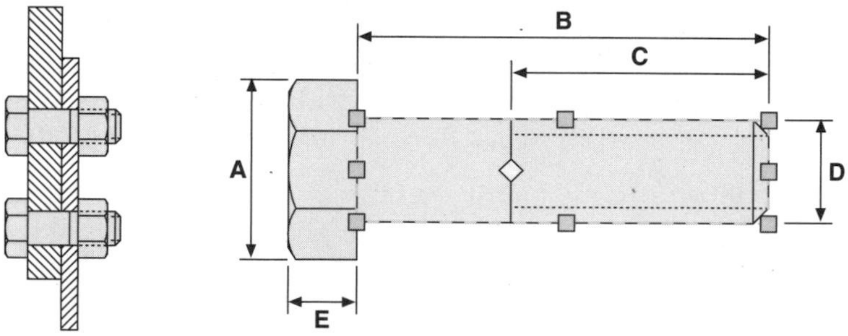

Figure 1-6 Visio shapes are parametric. (**A**) Head diameter. (**B**) Bolt length. (**C**) Thread length. (**D**) Bolt diameter. (**E**) Head thickness.

In the previous bolt shape, the bolt length, thread length, and bolt diameter are parameters that are controlled by formulas. The head diameter and head thickness are derived from these parameters.

These parameters are independent of each other, within practical physical limits. The user could set them by dragging the selection handles to change the bolt length or bolt diameter, or by dragging the control handle to change the thread length. A program could set them with numerical data from a manufacturer's database of available sizes.

Shapes as Components

Just as a procedure in a program encapsulates functionality so that it is easier to use and reuse, Visio shapes encapsulate behavior on the drawing page. Think of a Visio shape as a component whose default behavior is provided by the Visio engine, and whose unique behavior is provided by the formulas you write.

A solution rarely consists of a single shape. More often you'll develop a suite of shapes that support a particular kind of drawing, and you'll assemble these shapes as masters in a Visio stencil. A master appears as a shape in a stencil that you use to create instances, or shapes, based on the master. A master can be made of a single shape, multiple shapes, or a group. Instances inherit many of their characteristics from the master.

Users (or your programs) can drag masters from the stencil and drop them onto a Visio drawing. The stencil makes your custom shapes easy to reuse—the same shapes can be used by an engineer to simulate a product configuration, by a salesperson to show customers what they're buying, or by a graphic artist to create a catalog of your product line.

The first time a user drops a master onto a drawing page, Visio automatically creates an instance of the master on the drawing page and adds a copy of that master, or *document master*, to the drawing's document stencil. The document stencil is stored in the drawing file itself, which provides two major benefits:

- The drawing is entirely self-contained and portable. Once the user creates the drawing, they no longer need your stencil.
- Instances of a master inherit attributes from the master in the document stencil. A user can edit the master in the document stencil to change characteristics of all its instances in the drawing.

Because each instance of a master inherits from the document master, the instance can support a lot of complex behavior while remaining relatively small. Any formula can be overridden at the instance level, but global changes can be propagated to instances by altering the document master. And the drawing is portable because it contains copies of masters—the stencil or stencils that originally provided the masters are no longer required. All that's needed to view the drawing is a copy of Visio.

For example, the following network equipment shapes are designed to align and connect with the equipment rack shapes, so a network designer can create an accurate model of a server room. Individual shapes match the manufacturer's specifications for a precise fit, and the shape designer customized the shapes' alignment boxes and added connection points to make the shapes easier to use.

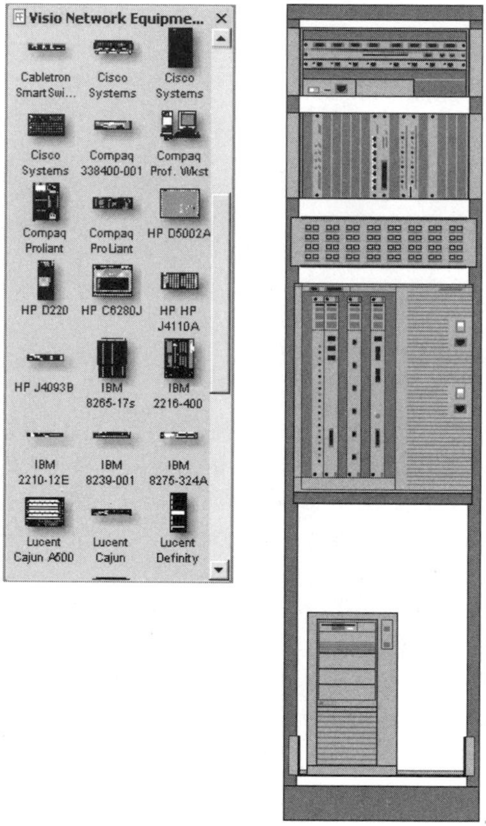

Figure 1-7 Network equipment shapes align and connect with equipment rack shapes.

To help the user create a drawing with your masters, you'll often provide a template. A template can provide shapes already on the drawing page, but more importantly, it can set up the drawing page with a uniform grid and scale, and include specific styles and layers. A template can also open one or more stencils. When the user creates a drawing based on a template, Visio opens the stencils and creates a new drawing file, copying the template's styles and other properties to the new file. As with the stencil, once the user creates the drawing, the template is no longer needed.

For details about the basics of creating Visio shapes, see Chapter 2, *Creating Visio Shapes*. For details about gathering shapes into stencils and providing templates with a solution, see Chapter 3, *Visio Masters, Stencils, Templates, and Documents*.

Using SmartShapes Technology to Develop Shapes

Using Microsoft Visio SmartShapes technology, you can develop shapes that behave like the objects they represent in the real world, modeling the characteristics that are meaningful for the kinds of drawings or diagrams you need to create. You do this by defining formulas that make the shapes behave the way they should according to the design rules, codes, or principles that apply to the corresponding objects.

Every Visio shape has its own ShapeSheet spreadsheet, which defines the shape's unique behavior and capabilities. Think of the ShapeSheet spreadsheet as the property sheet of a shape, in which each property is set by a value or formula that is recalculated dynamically as the user works with the shape. You can view and edit a shape's formulas in the ShapeSheet window.

Many features that you might expect to require external programming can be controlled through the ShapeSheet window. For example, you add menu items to a shape's shortcut menu by defining formulas for the shape in the ShapeSheet window. Formulas can control other attributes of a shape, such as:

- Geometry (flipping, rotation, visible or hidden paths)
- Color, pattern, and line weight
- Text, including font, paragraph formatting, and orientation
- Control handles that help users adjust the shape
- Connection points where other shapes can be glued
- Custom properties that can contain user data

The spreadsheet interface makes it easy to use cell references to link one shape property to another, which means that shape properties can influence each other in subtle and powerful ways. For example, you might link the color of a shape, such as a part in a mechanical drawing, to its dimensions to indicate whether the part is within tolerance.

This arrow shape is a classic example of controlling a Visio shape with formulas. Its formulas override the default behavior given to shapes by the Visio engine, which is to size proportionately when the shape is stretched horizontally or vertically. When this arrow shape is sized horizontally, its custom formulas allow the tail to stretch or shrink horizontally but leave the arrowhead unchanged.

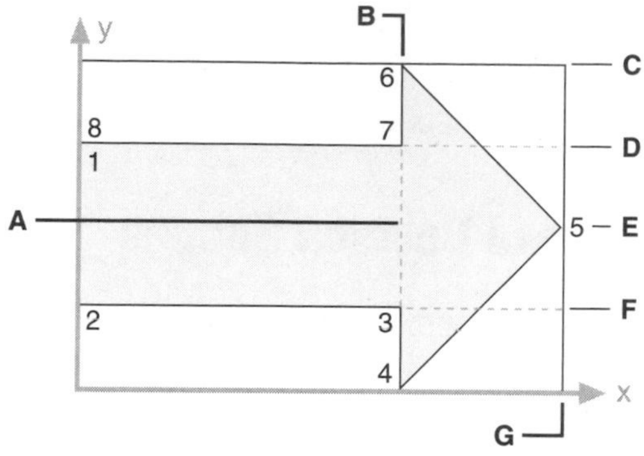

Figure 1-8 The arrow shape is controlled with Visio formulas. (**A**) The base of the arrowhead is defined as a fraction of Height. (**B**) All points on the base of the arrowhead have the same *x*-coordinate: Width - Height * 0.5. (**C**) Height. (**D**) Height * 0.75. (**E**) Height * 0.5. (**F**) Height * 0.25. (**G**) Width.

For details about working in the ShapeSheet window and controlling shapes with formulas, see Chapter 4, *Visio Formulas*. For a detailed discussion of the arrow shape example, see *Controlling How Shapes Stretch and Shrink* in Chapter 5, *Controlling Shape Geometry with Formulas*.

Using Automation in a Visio Solution

Some solutions require more than shapes, stencils, and templates. For example, you might need to create drawings based on data that changes from day to day, or perform routine shape development tasks over and over. You might support users who need to create drawings but don't want to become experts in Microsoft Visio, or you might use their drawings as a source of data for other purposes. You can automate such tasks by using Automation to incorporate the functionality of the Visio engine in a solution, simply by using its objects.

If you're familiar with Microsoft Visual Basic for Applications (VBA), you use objects all the time—controls such as command buttons, user forms, databases, and fields. With Automation, you can use other applications' objects as well. Drawings, masters, shapes, and even the Visio menus and tools can become components of your programs. A program can run within a Visio instance or start the Visio application and then access the objects it needs.

Visio includes VBA, so you don't need to use a separate development environment to write your programs. However, you can write programs that control the Visio engine in any language that supports Automation. Most of the examples in this guide are in VBA, but the principles apply to any programming language.

Automation and Visio Objects

Automation is the means by which a program written in VBA, Microsoft Visual Basic, C/C++, or another programming language that supports Automation can incorporate the functionality of an application such as Visio, simply by using its objects.

In Automation, the application that provides the objects (sometimes called the Automation server) makes the objects accessible to other applications and provides the properties and methods that control them. (This is sometimes called exposing the objects.)

The application that uses the objects (such as your program, sometimes called the Automation client) creates instances of the objects and then sets their properties or invokes their methods to make the objects serve the application. The server application and client application interact by making function calls through the Automation libraries, which are installed when any application that supports Automation—such as Visio, Visual Basic, or Microsoft Windows—is installed.

Unlike a scripting language, which simply automates the same actions you would perform in an application's user interface—choosing menu commands, pressing keys, typing, and so on—Automation accesses the application's objects. An object encapsulates data, behavior, and events with an interface that allows you to access them. Each Visio object has properties (data), methods (behavior), and events that you can use to take advantage of that object's capabilities in your program.

Visio objects reside in a Visio instance—a VBA program runs within an instance of the Visio application and then accesses the objects it needs. An external program runs outside an instance of Visio, so it starts Visio or accesses a Visio instance that is already running. Then it accesses the Visio objects it needs. Most objects in the Visio object model correspond to items that you can see and select in a Visio instance. For example, a **Page** object represents a drawing page; a **Shape** object represents a shape in a drawing. A shape's formulas are represented by **Cell** objects.

Many chapters in this guide describe how to incorporate Automation into a Visio solution. For an introduction, see Chapter 14, *Automation and the Visio Object Model*.

Monitoring Events and Totaling Values: an Example

To see how a solution might use Automation to access Visio objects, consider a solution that monitors events that are triggered as shapes are added to or deleted from a drawing. The solution keeps a running total of the power consumption represented by each shape, to make sure it doesn't exceed an established limit.

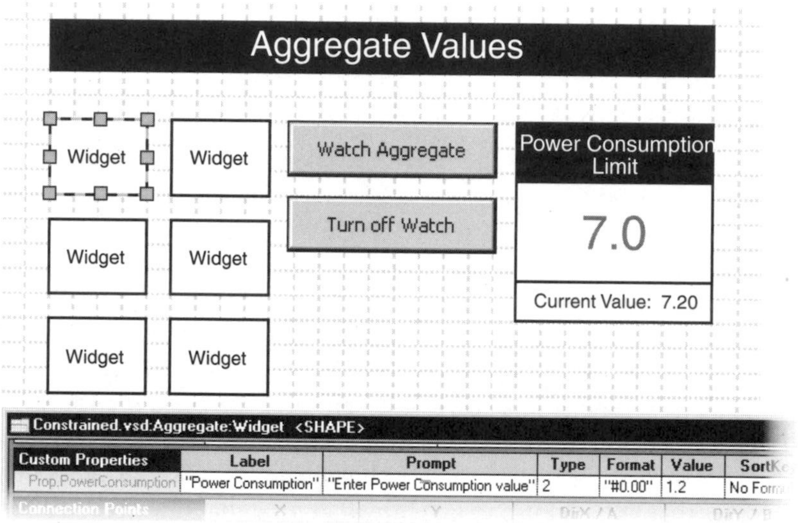

Figure 1-9 A solution that monitors power consumption represented by shapes in a drawing.

The example starts with an initialization procedure that checks all of the shapes in an existing drawing. The limit value is the text of a shape named "Limit," which the user can type in the Limit shape on the drawing. (The VBA **Val** function converts the text to a **Double** that can be used in subsequent calculations.) The solution keeps the running total in a user-defined cell named "PC" in a shape named "Current."

Each shape representing a device that consumes power stores its power consumption value in a custom property named "PowerConsumption," which the program accesses through the **Cells** property of a **Shape** object. The program iterates through the **Shapes** collection of the **Page** object passed to the **InitWith** procedure, checking the power consumption value of each shape that has a PowerConsumption property. If the total power consumption exceeds the limit set for the drawing, the solution alerts the user by setting the Color cell in the Character Format section of the Limit shape (Char.Color) to 2, which changes the color of the shape's text to red.

```
Option Explicit
Private WithEvents thePage As Page
Private theLimit As Double
Private theCurrent As Cell

Public Sub InitWith(aPage As Page)
    Dim i As Integer

    Set thePage = aPage
    theLimit = Val(aPage.Shapes("Limit").Text)
    Set theCurrent = aPage.Shapes("Current").Cells("User.PC")
    theCurrent.ResultIU = 0#

    For i = 1 To aPage.Shapes.Count
        With aPage.Shapes(i)
            If .CellExists("Prop.PowerConsumption", False) Then
                theCurrent.Result("") = _
                    theCurrent.Result("") + _
                    .Cells("prop.PowerConsumption").Result("")
                If theCurrent.Result("") > theLimit Then
                    aPage.Shapes("Limit").Cells("Char.Color"). _
                        Result("") = 2
                End If
            End If
        End With
    Next i
End Sub
```

Suppose the user adds a shape to the drawing. This action triggers a **ShapeAdded** event, which is handled by the following event procedure in the solution. Like the page initialization procedure, it adds the power consumption value of the newly added shape to the total, and checks whether it exceeds the limit for the drawing.

```
Private Sub thePage_ShapeAdded(ByVal Shape As Visio.IVShape)
    If Shape.CellExists("Prop.PowerConsumption", False) Then
        theCurrent.Result("") = theCurrent.Result("") + _
            Shape.Cells("prop.PowerConsumption").Result("")
        If theCurrent.Result("") > theLimit Then
            thePage.Shapes("Limit").Cells("Char.Color").Result("") = 2
        End If
    End If
End Sub
```

Deleting a shape triggers a **BeforeShapeDelete** event. Although a solution cannot cancel the deletion, it can perform operations that require the shape to be present before it is actually removed from the drawing. The following event procedure subtracts the power consumption value of the deleted shape from the total to keep it current and, if deleting the shape brings the total under the limit, changes the color of the Limit shape's text back to black (0).

```
Private Sub thePage_BeforeShapeDelete(ByVal Shape As Visio.IVShape)
    If Shape.CellExists("Prop.PowerConsumption", False) Then
        theCurrent.Result("") = theCurrent.Result("") - _
            Shape.Cells("prop.PowerConsumption").Result("")
        If theCurrent.Result("") <= theLimit Then
            thePage.Shapes("Limit").Cells("Char.Color").Result("") = 0
        End If
    End If
End Sub
```

For details about accessing a shape's formulas through Automation, see Chapter 17, *Automating Formulas*. For details about handling Visio events in a solution, see Chapter 21, *Handling Visio Events*.

Planning a Visio Solution

The easiest kind of solution to implement is a standardized drawing that uses the content supplied with Microsoft Visio, along with shapes, stencils, and templates that you create. If you want to provide more assistance to users for creating specific types of drawings, you might want to add programming with the solution in the form of Microsoft Visual Basic for Applications (VBA) code, a COM (Component Object Model) add-in, or a Visio add-on. If the drawings to be created follow a strict set of rules, a solution might include an application that uses data from another source to generate drawings that the user can modify. If a solution is to provide more than just drawings, it will involve integration with an external database and possibly with external applications (either off-the-shelf or developed in-house).

Planning the Development Process

One developer can often create a simple Visio solution that consists of custom shapes, a template, and a small amount of code. More elaborate solutions, however, can require a team of developers, each with particular skills. For example, the team could consist of the following members:

- A system architect, who understands software system design and has a good understanding of Visio, its architecture, and general capabilities. The system architect owns the technical vision and design of a Visio solution.
- Shape developers, who understand what makes shapes usable in the solution being developed and are thoroughly familiar with the Visio drawing tools and the ShapeSheet window. Shape developers need a solid understanding of mathematics and geometry, because much of their work will involve creating formulas to control shape behavior.
- Automation developers, who are skilled in the programming language that will be used to develop the solution (VBA, Microsoft Visual Basic, or C++, depending on the type of integration that the solution will require). Automation developers need a basic understanding of Visio shapes and formulas and should be thoroughly familiar with the Visio object model.
- Subject matter experts, who have extensive knowledge and experience in the domain of the solution. A subject matter expert advises the team on industry or corporate standards, processes, usability, and exceptions to the rules.

Once the team is assembled, the following steps are suggested for the development process:

- Interview users to understand their requirements and identify the objects in the domain of the solution.

  Ask users what steps they follow to accomplish their tasks. Collect examples of current drawings that your solution will automate or improve. In a large project, consider documenting requirements so that other users and developers can review them and understand what is needed.

- Develop the solution incrementally and involve the user at each stage to get feedback.

  Incremental development and integration of Visio capabilities in a solution usually leads to a better result. It allows the user to use the solution sooner, and is a good way to get feedback to improve the solution during development.

- Start by developing shapes and allowing your users to try them, and then revise the shapes based on users' feedback.

  The usability of a solution starts with how usable and relevant the shapes are going to be. For example, should you provide the user with many individual shapes, or schedule the time required to create multishapes (shapes that are designed to change appearance based on a setting)? Some users might find a few versatile shapes that can be manipulated into many different configurations more functional and less overwhelming than a stencil with many shapes to choose from; others might prefer a large assortment of single-purpose shapes.

- Once users are satisfied with the initial set of shapes, develop any drawing assistants or add-ons that the user might need to construct drawings, and, if necessary, fine-tune the shapes to work smoothly with them.

  Standardized drawings alone can deliver much of the benefit users are looking for. Beware of over-engineering a solution; just because Visio is programmable doesn't mean a solution must include programming.

- Finally, if your solution's shapes and add-ons will interact with a database or other applications, determine exactly how to make this work early in the development process, so you can design shapes and add-ons accordingly.

The approach to this step will depend on the kind of solution you are developing. For details, see *Integrating a Visio Solution with a Database* and *Choices for Implementing Automation* later in this section.

Planning Shapes and Stencils

Start developing your solution by building the shapes it will need, and put as much shape functionality as possible in formulas. There are two important reasons to start with shapes:

- Shapes can be smart—you can use the intrinsic capabilities of Visio shapes to handle much of the graphic functionality that you'd otherwise have to code.
- Shapes are independent of code that controls them. Once you develop the masters your solution will use, you can change the shapes without having to recompile your code, and vice versa.

If the shape behavior you want is predictable and can be accomplished with formulas (for example, automatic sizing or scaling), put it in the shape using the ShapeSheet. If the behavior changes dynamically at run time—for example, the text in a shape or the arrangement of shapes in a drawing may change—handle that behavior in a program such as in VBA code in a document, an ActiveX control, a Visio add-on, or a COM add-in. You can control the appearance and behavior of shapes with great precision by setting shape formulas. If you can create a stencil of masters to accompany your solution, users might not need to draw anything with the Visio drawing tools.

As you build masters for a program, test them in a Visio instance by manually creating the kinds of drawings you intend the program to automate. This will give you a good idea of the code you'll need to write and the data you'll need to provide. It will also show you if your shape is working the way you expect.

Finally, remember that the stencil that contains your masters is an important part of your solution's user interface. As such, you'll want to:

- Make sure masters are arranged in the stencil so that users can find them easily.
- Consider organizing related masters in different stencils, especially if you might use them in more than one solution.

For details about creating masters and stencils, see Chapter 3, *Visio Masters, Stencils, Templates, and Documents*. For details about distributing stencils in a Visio solution, see Chapter 13, *Packaging Stencils and Templates*.

Planning Templates

A template provides a common workspace for users. It facilitates standardization by making it easy for the user to create standardized drawings by choosing from sets of shapes.

A template can include styles and set up drawing pages using a uniform grid and measurement system. A template can set up drawing pages with shapes already on them and open one or more stencils so a user can add more shapes. A template can also provide drawings with their own user interface by including ActiveX controls, such as command buttons and text boxes, custom controls that perform special tasks, and VBA code that allows a user to interact with the drawing through the controls. Providing a template with a Visio solution can yield the following benefits:

- If your solution is designed to create new Visio drawings, you can save both programming effort and execution time by storing your program as VBA macros in a Visio template, or by providing a template as a stand-alone file with a Visual Basic or C/C++ program.
- When a template is used to create a document, Visio copies the template's styles, document properties, and VBA macros, modules, and user forms to the new document. You don't need to set the document properties or define styles with Automation unless you want them to differ from the template, nor do you need to distribute a separate VBA program unless your code is complex or you expect to update it in the future.
- If your solution customizes the Visio user interface, make those customizations in the template document rather than to Visio itself. That way, the user can use Visio for other tasks, and your solution's user interface will appear only when the user is actually using your solution.
- Using a template can prevent some translation difficulties if your program refers to styles and will be used with multiple languages.

Note Although providing VBA code in a template simplifies the files you need to distribute with a solution, it complicates fixing bugs or enhancing the code, because every document created from the template receives a copy of the code. For more flexibility, you might prefer to put the VBA code in a stencil or other document that accompanies your solution, so that you can distribute updates more easily. For details about creating templates, see Chapter 3, *Visio Masters, Stencils, Templates, and Documents*. For details about distributing templates in a Visio solution, see Chapter 13, *Packaging Stencils and Templates*.

Automating Shapes and Templates

After you develop your solution's masters and template (if any), you can use Automation to implement the rest of your solution. Exactly what this entails depends on the purpose of your solution and the context in which it will run. However, you'll typically use Automation to do the following:

- Implement your solution's user interface.

  Most stand-alone programs will need a dialog box or wizard page to advise the user what to do and prompt for any information that the program needs to execute.

- Store and retrieve data.

  Shapes can have custom properties, which can be configured to prompt the user to enter data or shape properties when, for example, a master is dropped on the drawing page. However, to preserve data types and protect data from unplanned changes, you might want your solution to store data in and retrieve it from an external database.

- Place shapes, set their properties, or connect them.

  If your solution creates a drawing, it will need to determine which masters to drop and where to drop them, set the shapes' text and apply styles, and connect shapes. If your solution reads drawings or works with existing shapes, it will need to find the shapes, make sure they're appropriate for the program, and get and set shape properties and formulas.

Remember that a shape can have formulas that resize or reorient it appropriately when your program moves or resizes it—just as if you moved or resized the shape yourself, using the mouse in a Visio drawing window. If you find yourself writing a lot of complex code that manipulates shapes, take a step back and think about whether that functionality can be handled by shape formulas.

For special considerations of distributing a Visio solution that includes Automation, see Chapter 26, *Packaging a Visio Automation Solution*.

Integrating a Visio Solution with a Database

Integrating a Visio solution with a database requires some planning to synchronize the drawings with the database. It's important to decide which database should be used, what should be changed and how, and when the changes should occur.

For example, in the security system solution described earlier in this chapter, each component (camera, sensor, control unit, and so on) is a numbered part in the manufacturer's catalog. By storing a part number as a custom property of each master, it is easy to look up part information in a version of the parts catalog stored as a database.

After designing the interactions between a solution and a database, a solution can make changes by:

- Handling Visio events that signal when the database should be updated or synchronized with the drawing.
- Creating an external program that queries the Visio drawing to extract the data when needed—for example, when the user requests it.
- Storing all of the solution's data in an external database and using data associated with Visio shapes, such as a custom property, as a key attribute to access records in the external database.

The Database Wizard provided with Visio can define user-defined cells and link custom property cells to database fields for simple solutions or for prototyping more complex solutions. You can use the DAO (Data Access Object) library provided by Microsoft to access databases through ODBC (Open Database Connectivity) or use the Jet database engine. Or, your Visio solution might call an Automation server that actually updates and synchronizes the database, which provides more control over the integrity of the database.

For details about Visio solutions and databases, see Chapter 20, *Integrating Data with a Visio Solution*.

Choices for Implementing Automation

The kind of program you write depends on what you're trying to do. You could write a VBA macro in a Visio document or another Automation controller application, or a stand-alone program in Visual Basic or C/C++. You could write a dynamic-link library (DLL) for a COM add-in, or another special kind of DLL that runs with Visio, called a Visio library (VSL). Users might run your program from the Microsoft Windows desktop or Windows Explorer, or they might run it from Visio, by choosing a command added to a Visio menu, a button added to its toolbar, or even by double-clicking or right-clicking a shape in a drawing. Or you could design your program to run automatically when a certain event happens, such as when a document is opened or created.

There are four basic ways to implement Automation in a Visio solution. You can implement the following:

- A stand-alone executable or EXE file, which is typically written in Visual Basic or C++, but can be written in any language that supports creation of an ActiveX Automation client.

  An EXE file is easy to build, can be written in many different languages, and is fairly robust. However, an EXE file must execute in a different process from the Visio instance it is controlling and must be loaded each time it is executed, which can affect performance.

- A Visio library, which is a standard Windows DLL with a prescribed Visio entry point and a .vsl file name extension.

  A VSL is much faster than an EXE file because it executes in the same process as a Visio instance and is loaded once, and then executed from memory. You can also determine, within context, when the VSL is visible to the user. However, a VSL is not as robust as an EXE file—if it crashes, the Visio instance usually does too—and it must be written in C++. Also, a VSL is faster than an EXE file only if most of its processing time is spent controlling the Visio instance; if the VSL spends half or more of its time controlling another application, then a program that executes in the process of the other application might be a better choice.

- VBA macros. VBA is included with Visio products and can be used to write macros, create dialog boxes, or create class modules. Other VBA clients, such as Microsoft Word and Microsoft Excel, can be used to control Visio also.

Like a VSL, VBA macros execute in the same process as a Visio instance and are easier to write, so programmers can accomplish more in less time. VBA macros are easy to distribute, which is both an advantage and a disadvantage. Every drawing contains a copy of the VBA code, which complicates fixing bugs and adding new features.

When you use VBA macros in Microsoft Visio 2002, be sure to consider security issues. You should plan on obtaining a digital certificate and signing your VBA project with it. For details on digital certificates and digital signatures, see *Using Digital Certificates to Produce Trusted Solutions* in Chapter 15, *Programming Visio with VBA*.

- A COM add-in, which is a standard Windows DLL that is specially registered to be loaded by Visio or any Microsoft Office or Office XP application.

  You can build COM add-ins with any of the Office applications in Microsoft Office Developer (version 2000 or later). If you have a Microsoft Office Developer license, you can also build COM add-ins using VBA in Visio. In addition, you can create COM add-ins with Visual Basic or C++. Like VSLs and VBA macros, COM add-ins execute in the same process as a Visio instance and are fairly easy to write.

- A hybrid approach that uses VBA in a Visio instance to load and execute Automation servers (either DLLs or EXE files) created in other languages.

  The hybrid approach supports in-process execution if the Automation server is created as a DLL, and it supports a wide range of architectures. However, a hybrid approach tends to require more careful system design.

Programming Visio with VBA is discussed in chapters 14 through 26 of this guide. For details about using Visual Basic with Visio, see Chapter 27, *Programming Visio with Visual Basic*. For details about programming Visio with C++ and writing VSLs, see Chapter 28, *Programming Visio with C++*.

Migrating from Visual Basic to VBA

If you are considering migrating from Microsoft Visual Basic to Microsoft Visual Basic for Applications (VBA), keep the following issues in mind:

- Who will use your solution and which version of Microsoft Visio they use.

  VBA programs are not compatible with earlier versions of Visio. If you open a document created with Visio 4.5 or later in Visio 4.0 or earlier, Visio opens the drawing, but the VBA programs are not accessible—there is no **Macros** submenu. Users will not be able to run your VBA program.

- Visio object types are not compatible with versions earlier than Visio 4.5. If your users are using earlier versions of Visio, you cannot use the Visio type library or Visio object types. To use Visio constants in your program, set a reference to the Microsoft Visio 2002 type library in Visio.

If you do decide to migrate your application from Visual Basic to VBA, you might want to check the following items in your program:

- Remove **CreateObject**, **GetObject**, and **vaoGetObject** references from your code.

  You do not need to get an **Application** object reference when programming in the VBA development environment in the Visio engine. If you are programming in another application's VBA development environment, such as Microsoft Excel, you still need these references to get or create a Visio instance, but when you are programming with the Visio engine, the Visio instance is already running.

- Transfer code.

  What components does your code use? Does it use custom controls that are not installed in VBA? Does it use Visual Basic forms? Find out if VBA supports the forms and the custom controls. If it does, you can import the forms from your Visual Basic projects into a VBA project and add any custom controls. If it does not, you could create a new user form in VBA and copy and paste between Visual Basic and VBA project items.

- Check for code that opens templates and stencils.

  VBA programs are stored in Visio files. If you store your VBA program with a template that opens the stencils containing the shapes you use in your program, you do not have to take the extra step in your program to open the template and stencils because they are already open, just as a Visio instance is already running.

- Digitally sign your VBA projects.

  VBA projects that are stored in your templates or stencils must be signed with a digital signature to work seamlessly in secure environments.

Part 2

Developing Visio Shapes

Chapter 2 Creating Visio Shapes
Chapter 3 Visio Masters, Stencils, Templates, and Documents
Chapter 4 Visio Formulas
Chapter 5 Controlling Shape Geometry with Formulas
Chapter 6 Grouping and Merging Shapes
Chapter 7 Enhancing Shape Behavior
Chapter 8 Working with 1-D Shapes, Connectors, and Glue
Chapter 9 Designing Text Behavior
Chapter 10 Managing Styles, Formats, and Colors
Chapter 11 Arranging Shapes in Drawings
Chapter 12 Scaled Shapes and Measured Drawings
Chapter 13 Packaging Stencils and Templates

2

Creating Visio Shapes

Visio Shape Anatomy 32

Drawing New Shapes 37

Importing Shapes from Other Programs 42

Adapting Existing Visio Shapes 45

The best Microsoft Visio solutions often begin on the drawing page, where you design shapes. Although you could define much of the custom behavior that a solution might need with programming, you'll get superior results faster by taking advantage of the built-in functionality of Visio shapes. If you design intelligence into your shapes, you can build a more flexible solution that requires less coding and maintenance in the long run.

Think of shapes as components that can be used to construct a diagram with little or no additional effort by the user. Each shape should, if possible, represent a real-world object; the user's main task will be to choose the shape from the stencil, and having it represent something familiar will help the user choose correctly. Put as much functionality into the shape as possible—within reason. A shape that does many things might be more confusing and harder to use than several shapes that each do one thing, and simpler shapes perform better in Microsoft Visio.

This chapter explores the different means of acquiring shapes for your solutions. Although drawing them yourself is always an option, you can also import graphics from other programs, convert metafiles into shapes, scan images to use as shapes, and adapt existing shapes for your own use. Later chapters provide greater detail about controlling shapes through formulas and other techniques.

Visio Shape Anatomy

Shape anatomy loosely refers to the geometry and user interface that make a shape appear and behave on the drawing page in particular ways. The term *shape* can refer to one line, arc, or spline; a series of segments; several shapes grouped together; or an object from another application. These shapes differ in their geometry in sometimes subtle and sometimes obvious ways that you need to know about, because these differences can affect how users work with your shapes. The four general shape anatomy considerations are as follows:

- Whether a shape is closed or open, which primarily affects how a shape can be filled
- Whether a shape is one-dimensional (1-D) or two-dimensional (2-D), a choice with fundamental impact on shape appearance and behavior
- The type of shape handles, which are user interface elements tied to shape geometry that tell users visually how to interact with a shape
- Whether the shape is a group, which affects how users edit the group and its member shapes, among other things

When you create new shapes for a solution, you define the shapes' anatomy to provide the visual clues your users will need to interact with your shapes. For example, shapes for doors, windows, desks—things that are built to standard industry sizes—can be locked against sizing so users don't accidentally stretch the shapes inappropriately as they are working with them.

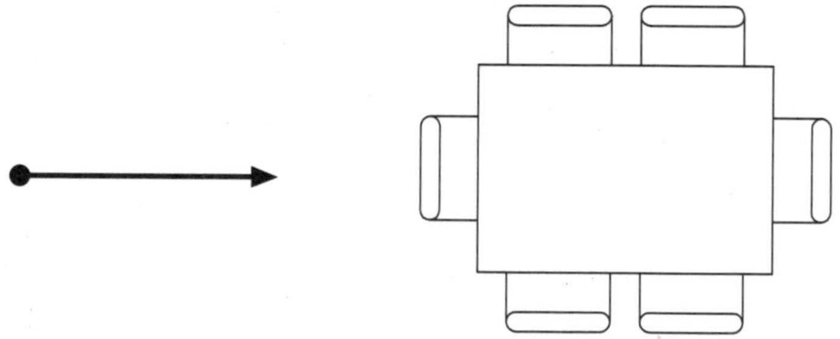

Figure 2-1 A single line is a shape, and so is the table with chairs, a Visio master shape composed of simpler shapes grouped together.

> **Note** A master is a shape in a stencil that you use to create instances, or shapes, based on the master. Instances inherit many of their characteristics from the master.

This section defines the elements of shapes that are the starting point for both designing your own shapes and revising existing ones.

Closed and Open Shapes

A shape can be made up of multiple line, arc, or spline segments called paths, each of which can be closed or open. Only a closed path can be filled with a color or pattern, and only an open path can be formatted with line ends.

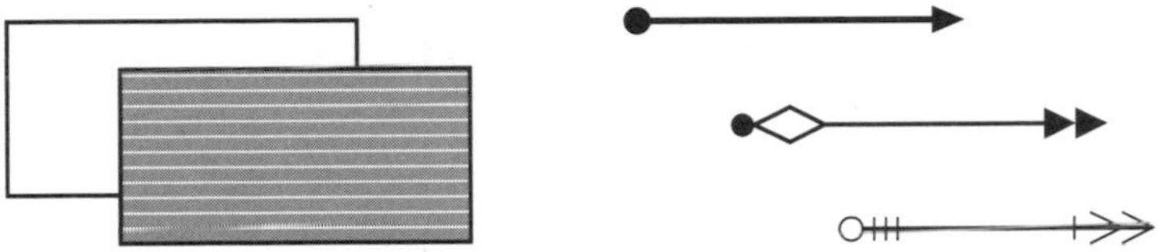

Figure 2-2 The rectangle represents four line segments in a closed path filled with a pattern. The lines represent open paths to which line ends have been applied.

Shapes can also have more than one path. An important consequence of this is that you can design a shape with multiple paths, some open and some closed, to create cutout regions (for example, a doughnut shape with a hole that cannot be filled with a color or pattern). Or you might create a shape, such as the recycle symbol below, composed of several paths.

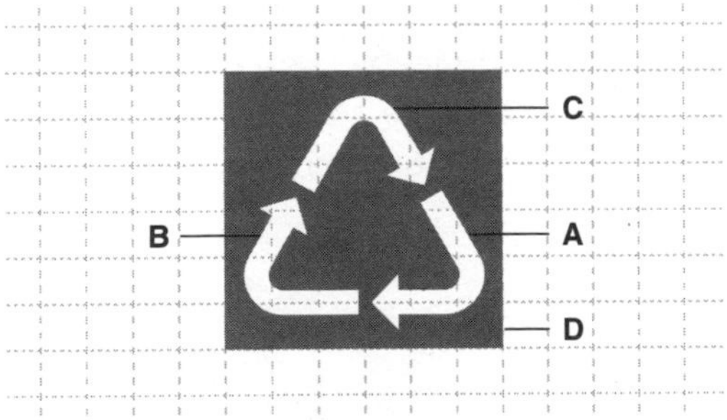

Figure 2-3 The recycle shape represents four paths, **A**, **B**, **C**, and **D**. Only the fourth path, **D**, is closed, indicated by the way color fills the shape. You can create similar shapes by combining geometry (on the **Shape** menu, point to **Operations**, and then click **Combine**).

For details about creating shapes with multiple paths, see *Creating and Controlling Merged Shapes* in Chapter 6, *Grouping and Merging Shapes.*

1-D and 2-D Shapes

A shape can be one-dimensional (1-D) or two-dimensional (2-D).

A *1-D* shape behaves like a line and displays endpoints that you can drag to resize the shape when you select it with the **Pointer** tool. You can glue the endpoints of 1-D shapes to the sides of 2-D shapes to create connecting lines that stay in place when the shapes are moved.

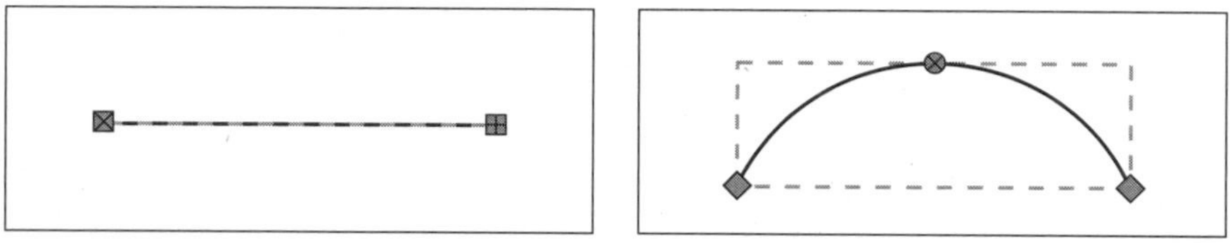

Figure 2-4 A 1-D shape has two endpoints. Some 1-D shapes also have other handles, such as this arc's control point.

A *2-D* shape behaves like a rectangle and displays selection handles that you can drag to resize the shape when you select it with the **Pointer** tool.

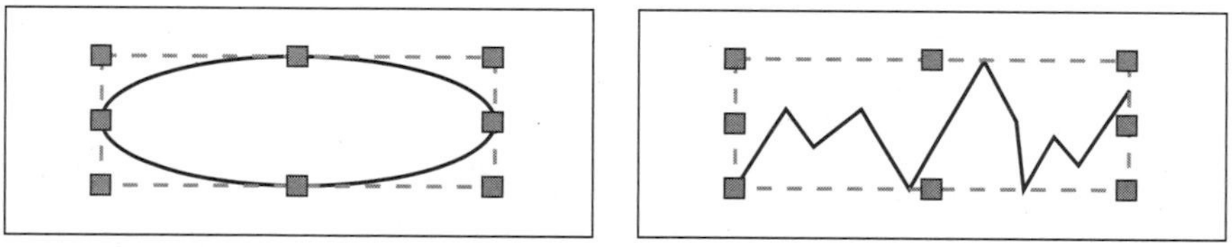

Figure 2-5 A 2-D shape has handles on all four sides and can be closed (like the ellipse) or open (like the zigzag line).

You can change 1-D shapes to 2-D and vice versa. For details, see *Converting 1-D and 2-D Shapes* in Chapter 8, *Working with 1-D Shapes, Connectors, and Glue.* For details about ways to control 2-D shape geometry, see Chapter 5, *Controlling Shape Geometry with Formulas.*

Shape Handles

Shapes come with a variety of handles, which provide you with methods of modifying shape appearance. A handle is a control that appears on a selected shape. Handles differ depending on the type of shape and the tool used to select it. For example, select a shape with the **Rotation** tool to display the rotation handles so that you can rotate the shape. The following table illustrates the most common shape handles used for editing shapes.

Overview of shape handles

Handle name	**Appearance**	**Behavior**
Selection handles	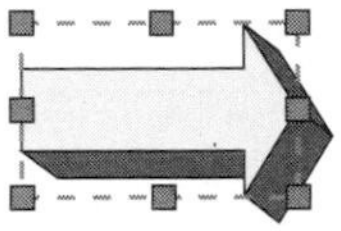	Appear when you select a 2-D shape with the **Pointer** tool. Drag *corner* selection handles to resize the shapes proportionally. Drag *side* selection handles to resize that side of the shape.
Endpoints	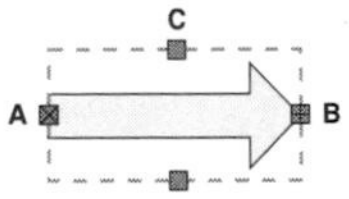	Appear when you select a 1-D shape with the **Pointer** tool. The direction of the shape (for routing purposes) is shown by a begin point (**A**) and end point (**B**). Some 1-D shapes also have selection handles (**C**). (For details, see *How 1-D and 2-D Shapes Differ* in Chapter 8, *Working with 1-D Shapes, Connectors, and Glue*.
Rotation handles	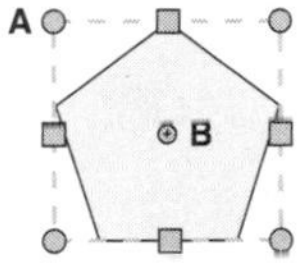	Round corner handles (**A**) that appear when you select a shape with the **Rotation** tool. The pin (**B**) marks the center of rotation. To rotate a shape, drag a corner handle. To change the center of rotation, drag the pin to a new location.
Vertices	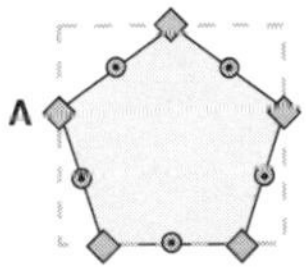	Diamond-shaped handles (**A**) that appear when you select a shape with the **Pencil**, **Line**, **Arc**, or **Freeform** tool. To reshape a shape, drag a vertex with the tool used to create the shape. The vertex turns magenta to indicate that it's selected. To add or delete segments, add or delete vertices using one of the previously mentioned tools.
Control points	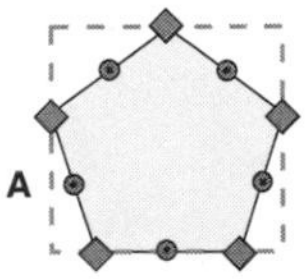	Appear on lines, arcs, and freeform curves when you select them with the **Pencil** tool. Drag control points (**A**) to change the curve or symmetry of a segment.
Eccentricity handles	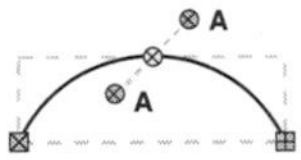	Adjust the angle and magnitude of an elliptical arc's eccentricity. To display eccentricity handles (**A**), first select an arc. Then select the **Pencil** tool and click the control point at the center.

You can add special-purpose handles to shapes to provide additional functionality, and program additional behavior for some handles, as the following table indicates.

For details about	See
Connection behavior and connection points	*Understanding Connection Points* in Chapter 8, *Working with 1-D Shapes, Connectors, and Glue*
Controlling rotation through formulas	*Controlling How Shapes Flip and Rotate* in Chapter 5, *Controlling Shape Geometry with Formulas*
Formulas used to program *control handles*	*Making Shapes Flexible with Control Handles* in Chapter 7, *Enhancing Shape Behavior*
Padlock handles and ways to protect shapes	*Using Locks to Limit Shape Behavior* in Chapter 5, *Controlling Shape Geometry with Formulas*

Shapes in Groups

Many Microsoft Visio masters are *groups*. At a glance, a group doesn't necessarily look much different from any other shape. However, groups have unique behavior that you need to know about to create your own and to anticipate how your users will interact with them. A key advantage of grouping is that you can work with a group as a single object, but independently format the member shapes of the group.

You can group any combination of shapes. Groups can also include guides, other groups, and objects from other programs.

> **Note** A master is a shape in a stencil that you use to create instances—or shapes—based on the master. Instances inherit many of their characteristics from the master.

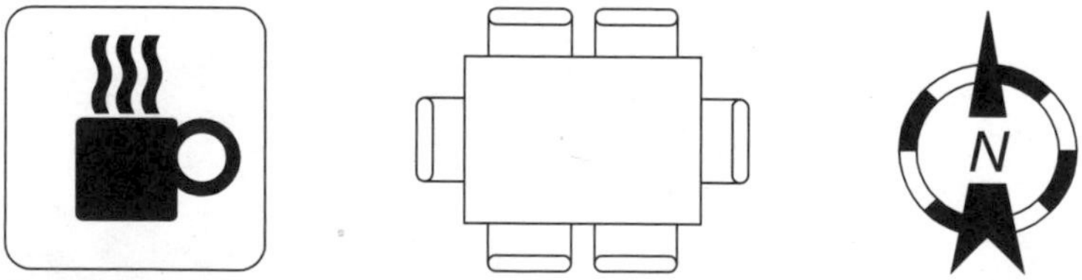

Figure 2-6 Some Visio shapes are groups—that is, sets of shapes grouped to form single shapes.

To find out if an object is a group

- Select the object. On the **Format** menu, click **Special**. If the object is a group, the dialog box indicates **Type: Group** below the master name.

  For details about working with existing Visio groups, see *Revising Existing Groups* later in this chapter. For details about group formulas, see *Creating and Controlling Groups* in Chapter 6, *Grouping and Merging Shapes*.

Drawing New Shapes

To represent custom objects that are particular to your business, or to apply your own copyrights, you must build shapes from the ground up. You can draw new shapes line by line, of course, but you can also take advantage of timesaving techniques developed by the Microsoft Visio shape creators.

One way to create your own shapes is to use the drawing tools in Visio. In addition, Visio includes unique commands and tools that simplify the process of creating more complicated geometry. For example, the **Union** and **Combine** commands create one shape from several other shapes, and the **Fragment** command breaks up shapes into smaller parts that you can rearrange, edit, or discard.

This section reviews the Visio drawing tools and key shape development techniques.

Using the Drawing Tools to Create Shapes

Drawing from scratch begins with the Visio drawing tools on the **Standard** toolbar. These tools resemble others you might have encountered, with some key additions. The **Pencil** tool is especially powerful because you can use it to draw both lines and arcs. As you begin to move the mouse, the Visio engine quickly calculates the path along which the pointer appears to be traveling. If the path of the mouse is straight, the **Pencil** tool draws a straight line segment. If the path curves, the **Pencil** tool draws an arc. As you draw, you'll see how Visio interprets the movements of the tool you're using.

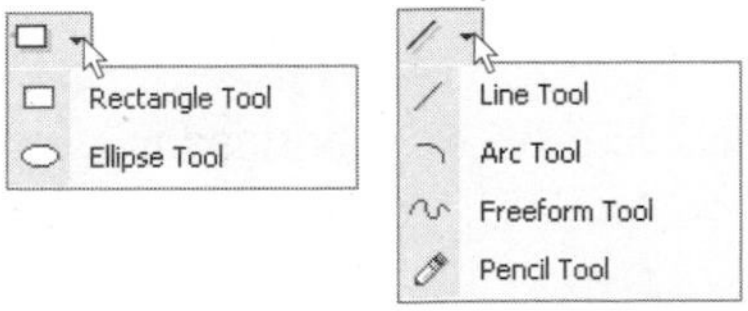

Figure 2-7 To draw a shape, use one or more of the drawing tools on the **Standard** toolbar.

Overview of drawing tools

To draw this	Use	Description
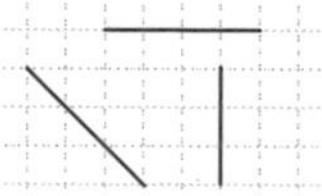		The **Line** tool is the best tool for drawing shapes composed only of straight lines. To constrain a line to any 45-degree angle, hold down the SHIFT key as you drag.
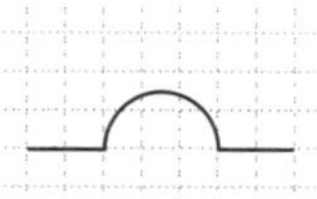		The **Arc** tool draws arcs that are always one-quarter of an ellipse. The direction you drag the mouse determines which way the arc bows.
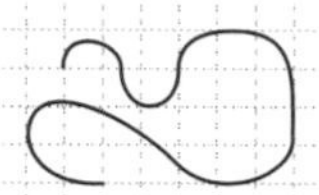		The **Freeform** tool works like a pencil on paper. Select it and drag to draw freeform curves (splines). For smoother curves, turn **Snap** off before you draw. (On the **Tools** menu, click **Snap & Glue**, and then clear the **Snap** check box. For other spline options, on the **Tools** menu, click **Options**, and adjust the **Freeform drawing** controls on the **Advanced** tab.)
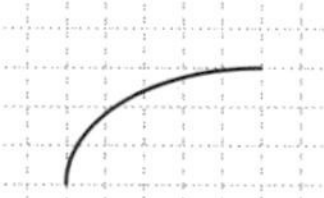		The **Pencil** tool draws both lines and arcs. If you move the pencil in a straight line, it draws a line. If you move it in a curve, it draws an arc. Each arc is a portion of a circle; its size is determined by the distance you move the mouse. The SHIFT key constrains this tool to either any 45-degree angle line, or to the current portion of a circular arc.
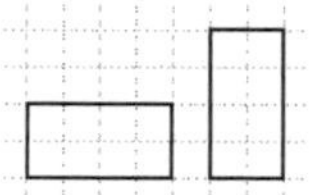		The **Rectangle** tool draws rectangles and squares. To draw a square, hold down the SHIFT key as you drag.
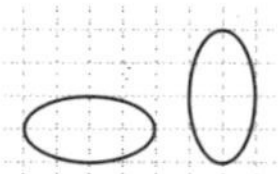		The **Ellipse** tool draws ellipses and circles. To draw a circle, hold down the SHIFT key as you drag.

Tip Using the **Pencil** tool to create a line or arc produces the same result as drawing with the **Line** tool or **Arc** tool. Using any of these tools, you can edit shapes after they are drawn by selecting and dragging an endpoint, control point, or vertex.

Drawing Closed Shapes

To create a shape that can be filled with a color or pattern, the shape must be closed.

To close a shape

- Drag the endpoint of the last segment you create over the vertex at the beginning of the first segment you create, and then release the mouse button.

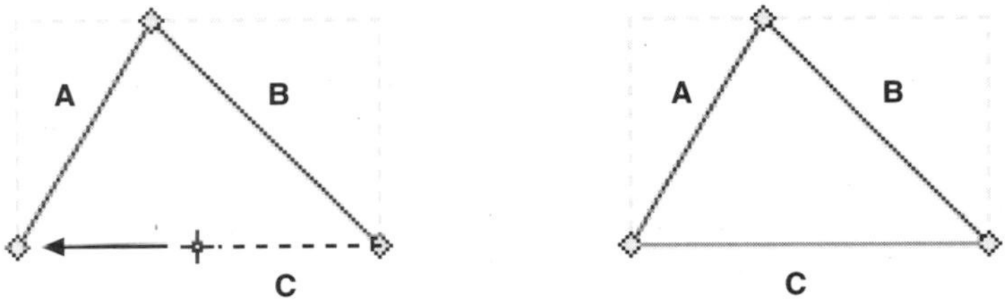

Figure 2-8 The process of drawing a closed shape: Line **A** is drawn first. Line **B** is drawn starting from the endpoint of line **A**. Line **C** is drawn from the endpoint of line **B** to the begin point of line **A**.

You might find it easier to connect the closing vertex if snapping is enabled (on the **Tools** menu, click **Snap & Glue**, and then select **Snap** on the **General** tab).

For details about using formulas to close shapes, see *Hiding Shape Geometry* in Chapter 6, *Grouping and Merging Shapes*.

Drawing Shapes by Repeating Elements

If you want to create a repeated series of lines or shapes with equal spacing, you can use the following technique.

To duplicate shape elements quickly

1. Select the elements.
2. To create the first copy, press the CTRL key while you drag the elements to the position you want.
3. Press F4 to repeat the creation of copies of the selected elements with the same offset value.

   This technique also works when more than one shape is selected.

Creating Groups

When you need to create shapes with complex geometry or that include multiple styles and formats, you can create a group. A group combines several individual shapes or other groups into a new Visio shape with components that can still be edited and formatted individually. Create a group when you want several shapes to move and size together, yet retain their individual formatting attributes.

To create a group

1. Select the shapes you want to group.
2. On the **Shape** menu, point to **Grouping**, and then click **Group**.

> **Note** If you want to create a master composed of several shapes, it's best to group the shapes. If you don't create the group, Visio groups the shapes when a user drags the master into a drawing—an additional step that can increase the time required to create an instance of the master.

For details about group behavior and formulas, see Chapter 6, *Grouping and Merging Shapes*.

Merging Shapes to Create New Ones

A great drawing technique you can use is to draw simple shapes, and then use one of the shape operation commands to merge the parts into a single shape. Using the **Operations** commands on the **Shape** menu, you can create shapes with cutout areas or fillable regions that you can format. Using whole shapes as a starting point can also be much more efficient than trying to draw something with many lines and arcs.

The following table describes the shape operation commands and gives examples of their results. For details about these operations and how they differ from grouping shapes, see *Groups versus Merged Shapes* in Chapter 6, *Grouping and Merging Shapes*.

Results of using the different shape operations

Command	Result	Example
Fragment	Creates new shapes from intersecting lines and 2-D shapes that overlap.	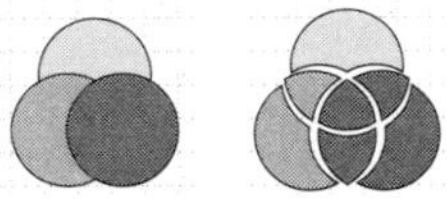
Combine	Creates a new shape from selected shapes. If the selected shapes overlap, the area where they overlap is cut out (discarded), creating a cookie-cutter effect.	
Union	Creates a new shape from the perimeter of two or more shapes. The shapes can be touching, overlapping, or nonadjacent. The new shape results from the mathematical union of the regions covered by the original shapes.	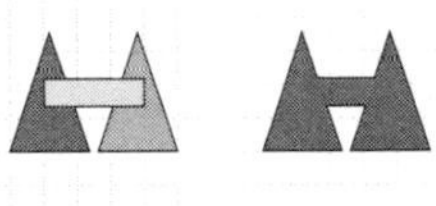
Subtract	Creates a new shape by subtracting the area where selections overlap the primary selection.	
Intersect	Creates a new shape from the area where the selected shapes overlap, eliminating nonoverlapping areas.	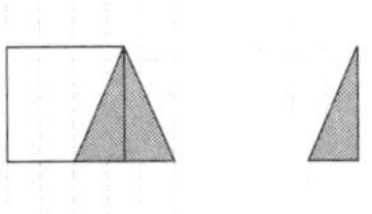
Join	Creates one shape of paths that are touching at their ends. **Join** assembles individual segments into one or more continuous paths, the number depending on the configuration of the selected shapes.	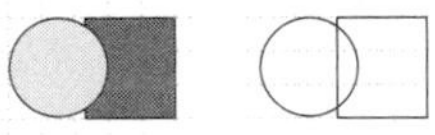
Trim	Splits selected objects at their intersections, including where a shape intersects itself. It creates a new shape for each piece. If shapes are split open, they lose their fill.	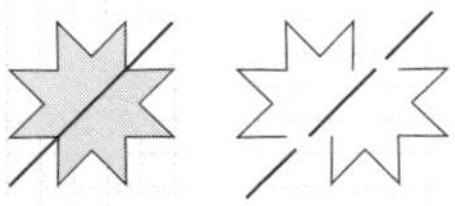
Offset	Creates a set of parallel lines or curves to the right and left of the original shape.	

Importing Shapes from Other Programs

If you wish, you could just create a shape out of your existing graphic files, clip art, or paper sketches, you can—by pasting a compatible image, importing a file, or scanning an image and then importing the scanned file. When you import an image, you create a Microsoft Visio graphic object. When you link or embed an image, you create an OLE object. On the drawing page, both graphic and OLE objects work on the whole like other Visio shapes, and you can use them to create masters.

Many files you import into Visio drawings as graphic or OLE objects are stored as Microsoft Windows metafiles, an exchange format used to store vector-based graphics. Raster-based graphics from BMP and DIB files are stored as bitmaps. You can edit both metafiles and bitmaps on the drawing page much like other shapes by moving, rotating, resizing, and adding text, geometry, or custom properties. And you can create a master from a metafile or bitmap. However, to provide additional editing capabilities, you can convert metafiles (but not bitmaps) to Visio shapes.

Importing Graphic Images

The simplest way to bring graphic images into a Visio drawing is to insert, or import, them. The result is a graphic object in either metafile or bitmap format, depending on the format of the original image.

To import a graphic image

- On the **Insert** menu, point to **Picture**, and then click **From File**. Select the file you want to import and then click **Open**.

  The image is imported as a new graphic object in metafile format (if the original graphic was vector-based) or bitmap format (if the original graphic was a BMP or DIB file).

You can also open graphic files directly by clicking **Open** on the **File** menu, and then choosing the appropriate format for **Files of type**.

For most files you import, an import settings dialog box is displayed, where you can specify how you want the imported file to appear in a drawing. For example, if you're importing a file in PCT format, you can specify whether to retain gradients and background and how to translate colors.

To find out if an imported graphic object is a metafile or a bitmap

- Right-click the object, point to **Format**, and then click **Special**. The dialog box indicates **Type: Metafile** or **Type: Bitmap**.

Because the data can go through up to two translations before it appears in the Visio drawing—one when you export from the other program, and one when you import into the Visio drawing—the picture might not look exactly the way it does in the original program.

With some vector-based graphics, such as Adobe Illustrator (.ai) and Encapsulated PostScript (.eps) files, lines might appear jagged in the Visio drawing. You may get better results with these file formats if you convert them to Visio shapes. For details, see *Converting Imported Metafiles to Shapes* later in this section.

> **Tip** You can import files in more than 20 formats. For a complete list, click **Open** on the **File** menu or click **Picture** on the **Insert** menu, and see the **Files of type** list.

Editing Imported Metafiles and Bitmaps

You can work with imported metafiles and bitmaps, as well as OLE objects, in much the same way you do any Visio shape. Type to add text, use the drawing tools to rotate and resize objects, and so on. You can apply a line style to change the appearance of the object's border. If the object includes some empty space, such as a background, you can also apply a fill style, color, or pattern.

Bitmap images have additional properties that you can set via the ShapeSheets window to control brightness, contrast, and other attributes.

To access image properties

1. Select the imported bitmap.
2. On the **Window** menu, click **Show ShapeSheet**.
3. In the ShapeSheet window, scroll to see the Image Properties section.

> **Note** If the Image Properties section is not visible, right-click the ShapeSheet window, click **View Sections**, select the **Image Properties** check box, and then click **OK**.

For details about each cell, select the cell, and then press F1.

Converting Imported Metafiles to Shapes

You can convert a graphic object in metafile format to a group or individual Visio shapes that can be formatted. Convert a metafile when you want to edit its component objects like individual shapes, apply fill color and patterns, or create intershape dependencies by writing formulas. Typically, you would convert a metafile to a group so that you could move it as a unit; however, if that's not an issue, convert it directly to shapes.

> **Note** If a metafile contains a bitmap as a component, it cannot be converted. Bitmaps cannot be converted to Visio geometry because, in a bitmap, Visio cannot determine what part of the object is a line, what is text, and so on.

To convert a metafile to a Visio group

1. Select the metafile.
2. On the **Shape** menu, point to **Grouping**, and then click **Convert to Group**.

To convert a metafile to Visio shapes

1. Select the metafile.
2. On the **Shape** menu, point to **Grouping**, and then click **Ungroup**.

To convert a shape back to a metafile

1. Select the shape, and then press CTRL+C to copy it.
2. On the **Edit** menu, click **Paste Special**, and then click **Picture (Enhanced Metafile)**.

Adapting Existing Visio Shapes

You don't have to start from scratch to create your own shapes. In fact, it's usually easier and faster not to. You can save time by finding an existing Microsoft Visio shape that resembles what you need and then modifying it.

There's an art to revising existing shapes and groups. This section provides tips for editing existing objects. For details about using the tools mentioned, see the Microsoft Visio Help (on the **Help** menu, click **Microsoft Visio Help**). For details about how the drawing page representation of a shape compares to its ShapeSheet representation, see *Examining a Shape in a ShapeSheet Window* in Chapter 4, *Visio Formulas*.

Revising Existing Shapes

To revise the geometry of almost any shape, select it with the **Pencil** tool, and then drag, add, or delete vertices. To change curves, drag a control point or a point's eccentricity handles.

> **Tip** You can select multiple vertices and move them as unit to easily preserve their relative position to each other.

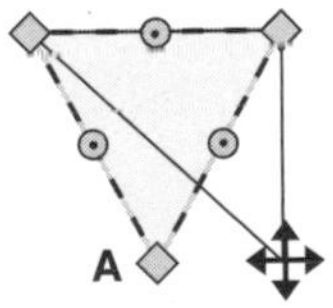

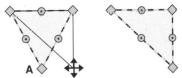

Figure 2-9 One way to reshape a shape is to drag a vertex (**A**) with the **Pencil** tool.

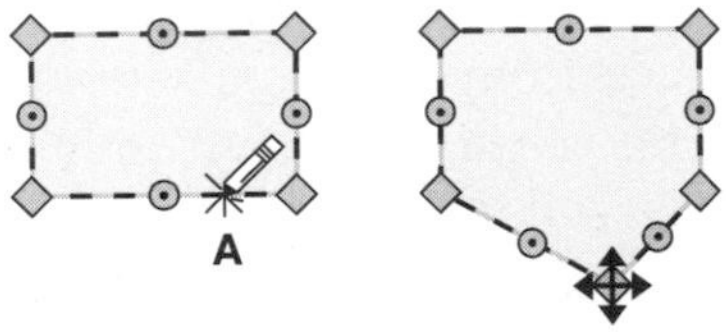

Figure 2-10 To add a segment, point to where you want to add the segment, hold down the CTRL key, and click with the **Pencil** tool (**A**). Then you can drag the new vertex with the **Pencil** tool to the position you want.

If you want fewer segments in a shape, delete the segments you don't want.

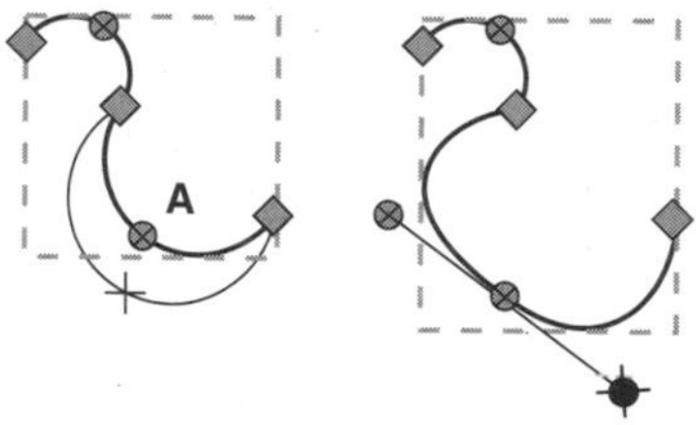

Figure 2-11 To delete a segment, select a vertex with the **Pencil** tool (**A**), and then press DELETE. The segment that the vertex is associated with is deleted. The remaining segments are reshaped accordingly.

How the Visio engine redraws the shape when you delete a vertex depends on whether the vertex is at the beginning or end of an open shape, the order that the segments were created in, and whether the segment that follows the vertex you delete is a line or arc. After you delete segments, you might need to adjust the shape by dragging vertices and control points until the shape appears the way you want.

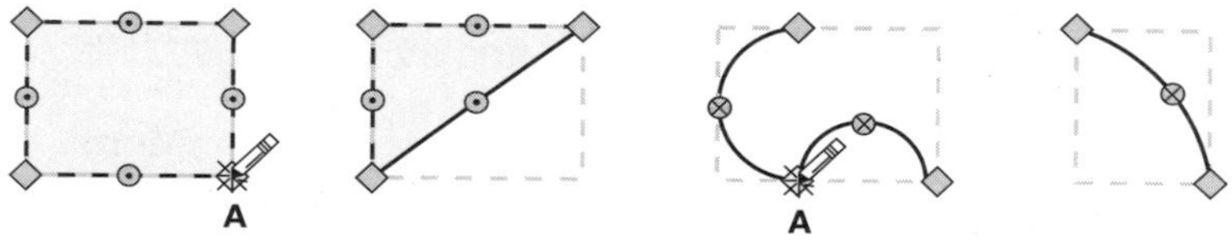

Figure 02-12 To change the curvature of an arc or freeform curve, drag a control point (**A**) until the segment appears the way you want.

Revising Existing Groups

You can take a group apart to see how it works and to revise it; however, you don't actually need to do this to revise a group. You can revise its member shapes by selecting each member shape in the drawing window.

A group can include guides and objects from other applications as well as shapes, and a group can include text and geometry independently of its member shapes. Each object in a group as well as the group has its own set of formulas, so when you ungroup shapes, you lose the group's formulas. However, if you ungroup a group that contains text or geometry, the Visio engine converts that text or geometry into a new shape.

Important If you convert a Visio drawing containing groups to a version of Visio earlier than Visio 2000, any text or geometry associated with a group (rather than its member shapes) will be lost.

You can edit a group and its member shapes directly on the drawing page by selecting the group or member shapes. You can also open a group in the group window.

Note When you select a group on the page, its selection behavior can vary. The group might be selected first, a group member might be selected first, or you might be able to only select the group and not its members.

To change the selection behavior for a group, click **Behavior** on the **Format** menu. Under **Group behavior**, in the **Selection** list, you can set the group to be selected as **Group first** (the group can be selected before its members), **Group only** (only the group can be selected, not its members), or **Members first** (the members of the group can be selected before the group).

If a group's selection behavior is set to **Group only**, users will be able to select the group, but not its members.

To open a group in the group window

1. Select the group.
2. On the **Edit** menu, click **Open Group**. (If you have named the group by using **Special** on the **Format** menu, the group name follows the command **Open**; otherwise, the command reads **Open Group**.)

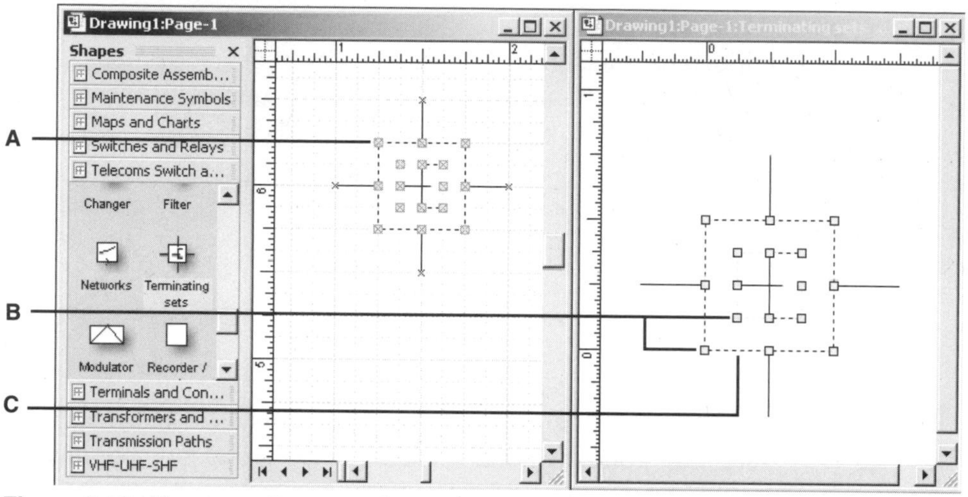

Figure 2-13 You can edit a group in the drawing window or the group window to work with its member shapes independently. Changes you make in the group window are also reflected in the drawing window. (**A**) The group in the drawing window with a member shape selected. You can edit the group's member shapes either on the drawing window or in the group window while preserving any formula dependencies among shapes. (**B**) Shapes in the group window appear as if they were independent, not grouped. (**C**) Moving a shape off the page in the group window moves it outside the group's alignment box.

> **Tip** After editing a group in the group window, you might need to re-adjust the width and height of the group so its selection rectangle tightly encloses all the group's shapes. To do this, select the group. On the **Shape** menu, point to **Operations**, and then click **Update Alignment Box**. For details, see *Using Alignment Boxes to Snap Shapes to a Grid* in Chapter 11, *Arranging Shapes in Drawings.*

For details about group behavior options, including the ability to drop shapes on top of a group to add them to the group (making the group a "drop target"), see *Modifying a Group* in Chapter 6, *Grouping and Merging Shapes.*

Ungrouping groups of shapes

Ungroup a group to end the association between member shapes and work with them independently. Ungrouping discards the group's formulas. If you ungroup an instance of a master, the shape no longer inherits characteristics from the master.

To ungroup shapes

1. Select the group.
2. On the **Shape** menu, point to **Grouping**, and then click **Ungroup**.

Shape Copyrights

Any shape that you create by revising a native Visio shape will retain the Visio copyright. If you distribute a master with this copyright to another user, that user must have a license to use a stencil that contains the original master.

If you want to distribute a shape free of copyright restrictions, you must create it from scratch. When you create shapes this way, you can apply your own copyright to it, either before or after you create a master from the shape.

To copyright a shape (or see if an existing shape has a copyright)

- Right-click the shape, point to **Format**, and then click **Special**.

> **Important** The copyright is a write-once field. Before adding a copyright, make a copy of the shape as backup in case of a typing error.

3

Visio Masters, Stencils, Templates, and Documents

Creating Masters and Stencils 52

Creating Templates 57

Opening and Saving Visio Documents 62

Whether you're planning a standardized drawing solution that includes new shapes you've developed or a custom application that integrates Microsoft Visio functionality into a larger system, you'll find that masters, stencils, templates, and documents are the primary components of most Visio solutions. As you design your solution, you'll want to consider how you use these components to best suit your needs.

You can distribute shapes you develop as reusable *masters* on a *stencil*. A stencil is like a software library in which you can collect the shapes you build for later reuse. You can also create a *template* that opens particular stencils and specifies page settings, layer information, styles, shapes, predrawn elements such as title boxes, and macros, which makes it simple to deliver a custom solution to users. The Visio documents you create contain the same common information, but the file name extension you use determines how the file appears to the user.

This chapter introduces these elements, and provides tips for making your solutions as efficient as possible.

Creating Masters and Stencils

A *master* is a shape, multiple shapes, a group, or an object from another application that is saved on a stencil, which can be opened in other drawings. You can create a shape on the drawing page, and then drag it into a stencil to create a new master. Or you can use commands available in the stencil window to create a new master. As you design masters, keep in mind that a common design goal is to create masters that allow the user to create drawings without having to draw anything by hand.

To reuse the masters you create, you save them on a stencil, which is a file with the extension .vss (or .vsx for XML format). You can save any Microsoft Visio file as a stencil. Unless otherwise specified, the term *stencil* refers to a stencil file. Stencil files exist autonomously from drawing files and template files; a stencil might open with a template because the stencils are saved as part of the template's workspace, but a stencil can be opened alone or with any drawing.

When a user drags a master from a stencil onto a drawing page, the Visio engine creates a copy of that master on the drawing's *document stencil* and creates an *instance* of the master on the drawing page. A drawing file always includes a document stencil that contains copies of the masters used in the drawing, even if the corresponding shapes are later deleted from the drawing page. An instance is linked to the copy of its master on the document stencil and inherits its behavior and appearance from that master.

Because a stencil contains the shapes from which users of your solution will construct a drawing, it is a primary user interface element in any drawing solution. The arrangement of shapes on the stencil, as well as shape behavior and performance, are all important usability considerations.

By default, the stencils that ship with Visio open in the Visio application as read-only. For you to work with a stencil or the masters it contains, the stencil must be editable.

> **Note** If you open the stencil while the drawing window is not active or no drawing window is open, the stencil opens as a stand-alone (in its own window). To make a stand-alone stencil editable, you must open the stencil file as **Original**.
>
> When you open a template that includes stencils in its workspace, or if you open a stencil with an open drawing window that is active, the stencils open in anchored windows (either docked or floating). To make a stencil in an anchored window editable, click the icon on the stencil title bar, and then click **Edit**.
>
> When a stencil in an anchored window is editable, a red asterisk appears on the upper-left corner of the icon on the stencil title bar.

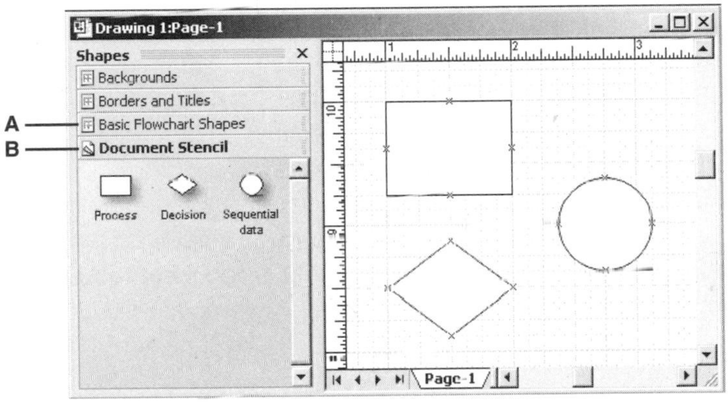

Figure 3-1 Stencils in a Visio drawing file. (**A**) Typically, when you open a template, its stencils open as read-only in anchored windows. (**B**) To display a document's stencil, on the **File** menu point to **Stencils**, and then click **Document Stencil**.

Creating a Stencil

One way to create a stencil is to open a new, empty file as a stencil. Because the new file's drawing page is empty, you can more easily keep file size to a minimum, and the file contains only the default styles until you add masters to the stencil.

To create a new, empty stencil file with write access

- On the **File** menu, point to **Stencils**, and then click **New Stencil**.

If you plan to base a new stencil on an existing one, you can add new masters to the existing stencil or edit the ones already there, and then save the revised stencil as a new file.

To open an existing stencil with write access

1. On the **File** menu, point to **Stencils**, and then click **Open Stencil**.
2. Select the stencil file you want to revise.
3. Click the arrow next to the **Open** button, click **Original**, and then click **Open**. Alternatively, you can click the icon on an open stencil's title bar, and then click **Edit** on the shortcut menu.

> **Note** The stencils, masters, templates, and source code provided with Microsoft Visio are copyrighted material, owned by Microsoft Corporation and protected by United States copyright laws and international treaty provisions. You cannot distribute any copyrighted master provided with Microsoft Visio or (continued) a Web-based subscription service, unless your user already has a licensed copy of Visio that includes that master, or your user has a valid subscription to the Web-based service, or you've signed an agreement that allows you to distribute individual masters to your users. This includes shapes you create by modifying or deriving shapes from copyrighted masters.
>
> To copyright your original shapes, select a shape, click **Special** on the **Format** menu, and then enter copyright information in the **Copyright** box. After you enter copyright information in the **Special** dialog box, it cannot be changed in a drawing, stencil, or template file.

You can quickly create a new stencil with masters already in it by saving the document stencil of a drawing file as a stencil file with the .vss file name extension (or .vsx for a stencil in XML format). This stencil will contain all the masters used during the drawing session, including masters with instances that you have since deleted from the drawing page. To save the cleanest and most user-ready version of the stencil, edit the document stencil and clean up the drawing page before saving it as a new stencil file.

To create a new stencil from a drawing's document stencil

1. On the **File** menu, point to **Stencils**, and then click **Document Stencil** to view or edit the masters before saving them.
2. On the **File** menu, click **Save As**.
3. For **Save as type**, click **Stencil (*.vss)** or **XML Stencil (*.vsx)**. Enter a name and location for the file, and then click **Save**.

Creating Masters on Stencils

Just as you can drag a master into a drawing to create a shape, you can drag a shape or group onto a stencil to create a master. To begin, the stencil must be editable. You can make a stencil editable either by opening it as **Original** or by clicking the icon on the stencil's title bar, and then clicking **Edit** on the shortcut menu.

You can create a master from an object that you have pasted or imported into Visio from another program. You can also create masters by adding new, blank masters to a stencil.

To create a master from a shape in a drawing

1. In the drawing window, display the page that contains the shape you want to use as a master.
2. Make sure the drawing window is active, and then drag the shape from the drawing window into the stencil window. Or hold down CTRL to drag a copy of the shape. If the stencil is open as **Read only**, a message is displayed, and you can dynamically change the stencil to make it editable.

   A default name and icon for the master is created in the stencil window.
3. To save your changes to the stencil file, click the icon on the stencil's title bar, and then click **Save** on the shortcut menu. If the stencil is in a stand-alone window, click Save on the **File** menu.

   If you are creating a new stencil, type a new name for the stencil. In the **Save As** dialog box, for **Save as type**, click **Stencil (*.vss)** or **XML Stencil (*.vsx)**. To protect the stencil from accidental changes the next time it is opened, click the arrow next to the **Save** button, and then click **Read only**.

   Click **Save**.

To create a new, blank master

1. Open a stencil.

   If the stencil to which you want to add the master is not editable, click the icon on the stencil's title bar (if the stencil is in an anchored window), and then click **Edit** on the shortcut menu.

   Alternatively, you can make a master editable by reopening the stencil as **Original**.

2. Right-click anywhere on the stencil window, and then click **New Master** on the shortcut menu.
3. In the **New Master** dialog box, for **Name**, type a name for the master, and then click **OK**.

A blank master is created in the stencil and represented by a blank square icon or by an icon with lines (continued) it. Edit the master and its icon by right-clicking the master and using the commands on the master's shortcut menu.

For details about other options in the **New Master** dialog box, click the **Help** button in the dialog box.

Editing Masters on Stencils

When you open a stencil with write access, you can edit the masters by opening the master drawing window as the following figure shows. To specify the attributes of masters and icons, right-click the master and choose commands from the shortcut menu.

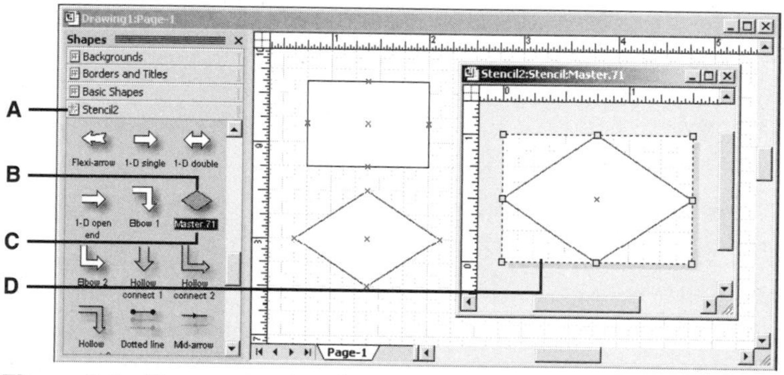

Figure 3-2 The master drawing window displays the drawing page for a master. (**A**) The red asterisk on the icon in the stencil title bar indicates that a stencil in an anchored window is editable. (**B**) You can add a new, blank master to a stencil, and edit the master and its icon. (**C**) You can rename a master quickly by double-clicking the master's text. (**D**) You can draw and edit on the master's drawing page using the same techniques you use on the document's drawing page.

To edit a master

1. In the stencil window, right-click the master you want to edit, and then click **Edit Master** on the shortcut menu.

The master drawing window appears, showing the drawing page associated with the master.

> **Note** If the stencil to which you want to add the master is not editable, click the icon on the stencil's title bar (if the stencil is in an anchored window), and then click **Edit** on the shortcut menu. Alternatively, you can make a master editable by reopening the stencil as **Original**.

2. When you are finished editing the master, close the master drawing window.

   If you've made any changes to the master, a message appears asking if you want to update the master. Click **Yes**. The master icon is also updated to reflect the changes you have made, unless the **Generate icon automatically from shape data** check box is cleared in the master's **Master Properties** dialog box.

Creating Templates

In general, to create a Microsoft Visio template, you open a new or existing drawing file, set options you want, open the stencils you want, and then save the file as a template.

A template can provide shapes already on the drawing page, but more importantly it can set up the drawing page with a uniform grid and scale and include specific styles and layers. A template can also open one or more stencils. When the user creates a drawing based on a template, Visio opens the stencils and creates a new drawing file, copying the template's styles and other properties to the new file. As with the stencil, once the user creates the drawing, he or she no longer needs the template.

The drawing page of a template file is typically blank, but you can choose to include shapes on the drawing page, such as a title block or a company logo, or your template may contain multiple drawing pages.

Creating a Template

You can save any Visio file as a template, and templates can include the following elements:

- A workspace list identifying one or more stencils, which are opened when you open a new drawing file with the template
- One or more drawing pages, including backgrounds; each page can contain a drawing and can use a different size and scale
- Microsoft Visual Basic for Applications (VBA) macros
- Print settings
- Styles for lines, text, and fill
- Snap, glue, and layering options
- A color palette
- Window sizes and positions

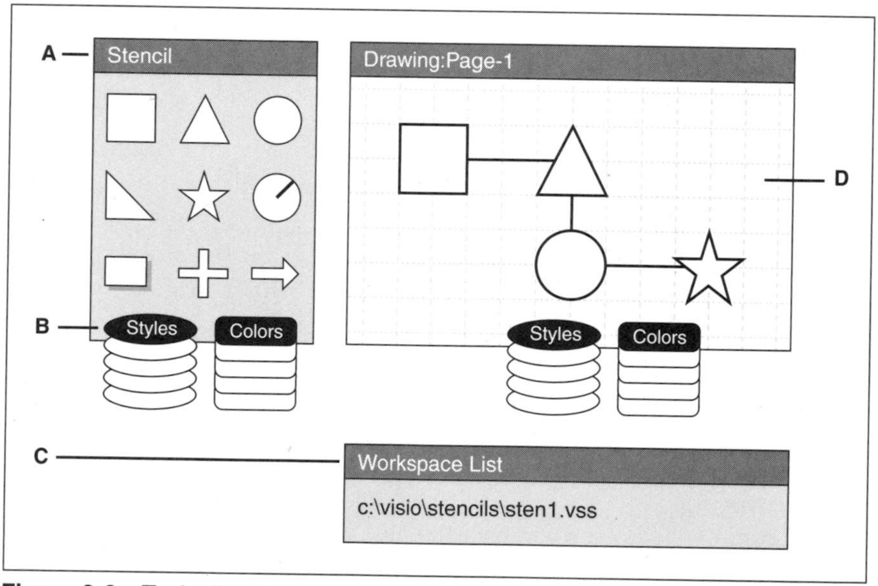

Figure 3-3 Typically, when you open a file as a template (.vst or .vtx for a template in XML format), you open at least two documents, a stencil file and a drawing file, which contain the elements shown. (**A**) One or more stencils, if specified in the template's workspace list. (**B**) Style definitions and colors used in the stencil file, which should match those of the drawing. (**C**) The template's workspace list, which specifies all the files and windows to open. (**D**) The drawing, which can have more than one page, and includes its own style definitions, color palette, and document stencil.

To create a template

1. Open the drawing file on which you want to base the template. Or open a new drawing file.
2. Open the stencil file (or files) that you want to open with the template.

   Open each stencil file as **Read only**. If you open the stencil file as **Original**, it will be saved that way in the template's workspace list.
3. Activate the drawing window, and then change or define options and settings that you want to include in the template.

   For example, you can define the styles you want to include, set page display options, and select a drawing scale.
4. If you want a drawing page to contain any standard elements, create the appearance you want. You can insert additional pages as either foreground or background pages.
5. Click **Properties** on the **File** menu. In the **Properties** dialog box, type information about the template, and then click **OK**.

   The text you type for **Description** appears when you pause your mouse pointer over a template icon in the **Choose Drawing Type** pane or over the name of a template in the file list in the **Open** dialog box.
6. On the **File** menu, click **Save As**.

   Click the arrow next to the **Save** button, and then click **Workspace**. In the **Save as type** list, click **Template (*.vst)** or **XML Template (*.vtx)**. In the **File name** box, type a name for the template, and then click **Save**.

Visio typically opens a template's stencils in anchored windows that are docked and read-only. However, a template can open some stencil files docked and others floating, some as read-only and others as original. A template's workspace list stores the names of the stencil files to open as well as the type, size, and position of window to display them in based on their appearance when you saved the template.

> **Note** If you are creating a template for scaled drawings, the page scale is set by the template's drawing page. The master scale is determined by the scale at which the shape is drawn. To avoid unexpected behavior, masters and drawing pages should use the same or a similar scale. For details, see Chapter 12, *Scaled Shapes and Measured Drawings.*

About Pages, Backgrounds, and Layers

As you design a Visio template, you should consider how you want to organize the information you plan to include. The Visio application provides display and organizational tools such as pages, backgrounds, and layers for arranging elements visually; you can use these tools to make your solutions work more effectively.

About pages and backgrounds

Templates and documents can contain multiple drawing pages, and each drawing page can have one or more background pages assigned to it. Background pages appear behind drawing pages, and usually contain shapes that you want to appear on more than one drawing page. You can use backgrounds to create visual layers of information. If you assign a background to another background, the newly assigned background appears behind both the original background and the drawing page.

Shapes on background pages cannot be modified from the foreground page; to modify background page elements, you must first navigate to the background page. As you develop a solution, you'll want to consider whether shapes will appear on both foreground pages and background pages, and whether your document templates should contain backgrounds.

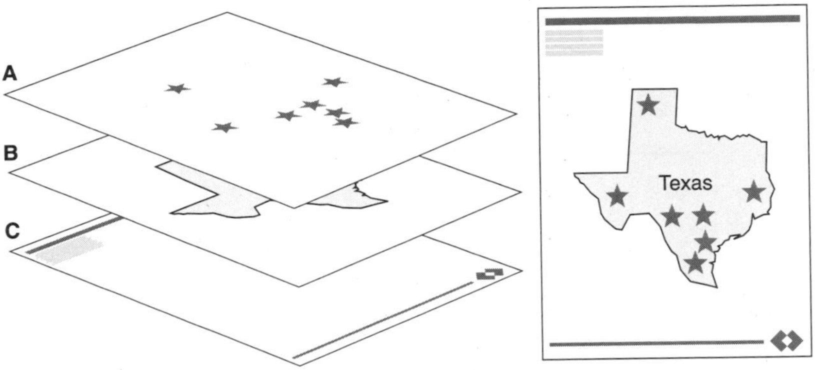

Figure 3-4 Backgrounds and pages work like stacked sheets of transparent paper. When you assign a background (**C**) to another background (**B**), it appears behind both the original background and the drawing page (**A**); the drawing page always appears on top.

About layers

You can use layers to organize masters and shapes into named categories within templates and drawings.

In other graphics programs, the term *layers* often refers to the stacking order (the front-to-back position) of objects on the page. In Visio, layers organize related shapes into named categories. A shape's membership in a layer has no effect on its position in the stacking order.

You can hide or show layers, print them or not, or protect layers from changes. Shapes can be assigned to more than one layer, and the layer information for a shape is independent of its display order and even its group membership. Additionally, each page in a document can have its own set of layers. When you design masters, you can assign them to layers; when users create instances of those shapes, they are automatically assigned to those layers.

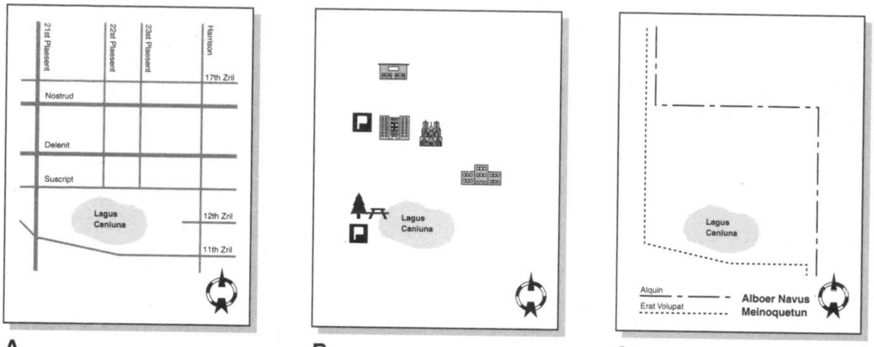

A B C

Figure 3-5 Shapes can belong to more than one layer. Here, the lake and compass shapes belong to the Streets layer (**A**), the Landmarks layer (**B**), and the Routes layer (**C**).

Opening and Saving Visio Documents

All Microsoft Visio files have the same format. However, a Visio document's file name extension determines how you open it and how you save any changes you make. A Visio document can be saved in binary or XML format and can be a drawing (.vsd or .vdx), stencil (.vss or. vsx), or template (.vst or .vtx). The Visio engine uses the file name extension to determine what to display on the screen when the document is opened. This means, for example, that you can save a drawing file (.vsd or .vdx) as a template (.vst or .vtx), which you can then open and work with as a template.

Components of a Visio Document

Each Visio document always has the following elements:

- At least one drawing page
- A document stencil that contains copies of any masters used on the drawing page (or, in the case of a .vss or .vsx file, a named stencil that displays the masters)
- A workspace list, which identifies all of the windows and files that are opened with the current file.
- A list of styles defined in the document, including at least the four default Visio styles (**No Style**, **None**, **Normal**, and **Text Only**)
- A color palette of 24 user-modifiable color slots and, beginning with Visio 2002, any number of additional colors defined by RGB (red, green, blue) or HSL (hue, saturation, luminosity) formulas in the document

- A Microsoft Visual Basic for Applications (VBA) project with a default (empty) class module called ThisDocument
- A document sheet that can store user-defined data

A document can also contain shapes on the drawing page, with styles and colors applied from those stored in the document, as well as a VBA project with modules, class modules, and user forms.

For details about defining custom colors in Visio, see *Using a Formula to Define a Custom Color* in Chapter 10, *Managing Styles, Formats, and Colors.*

For details about using VBA in Microsoft Visio, see Chapter 15, *Programming Visio with VBA*.

Opening a Visio File

You can open a Visio file with read/write access, with read-only access, or as a copy of the original document. When you click **Open** on the **File** menu, these options appear in a list under the **Open** button in the **Open** dialog box.

The Visio engine uses a document's file name extension to determine which windows should be active. For example, when you open a stencil file, only its document stencil is displayed. When you open a drawing file, only the drawing page is displayed. You can display the windows that aren't displayed by default for a Visio file:

- To display the document stencil for a file, on the **File** menu, point to **Stencils**, and then click **Document Stencil**.
- To display the drawing window for a stencil file, click **Show Drawing Page** on the **Window** menu. This option is available only when a stencil has been opened as stand-alone and no drawing window is open.

The following table describes how items appear by default for each file name extension when opened.

Default contents of different file types

File type	Document type	Contents
.vsd (binary format) .vdx (XML format)	Drawing	Opens all windows and files listed in the workspace, if the workspace was saved with the file. If not, Visio creates a drawing window and displays the page that was open the last time the file was saved.

Default contents of different file types *(continued)*

File type	Document type	Contents
.vss (binary format) .vsx (XML format)	Stencil	Opens the stencil as read-only (in a docked, anchored window, if a drawing window is active). If a drawing window is not active, Visio creates a stencil window and displays the file's stencil.
.vst (binary format) .vtx (XML format)	Template	Opens an untitled copy of the drawing in a drawing window, and opens all windows and files listed in the workspace list.

Choosing the Right File Type for Your Solution

You can take advantage of the different Visio file types to work more efficiently. Here are some tips for saving your work:

- Save a file's document stencil as a stencil file (.vss, or .vsx for a stencil in XML format) to create a new stand-alone stencil of frequently used shapes.
- To save a drawing with its current workspace view (so that the same windows appear in the same location when you reopen the file), use the **Workspace** option (click the arrow next to the **Save** button) in the **Save As** dialog box.

  To save your file and its workspace, on the **File** menu, click **Save As**. In the **Save As** dialog box, click the arrow next to the **Save** button, and then click **Workspace**. Type a name for the file, choose the folder to save it in, and then click **Save**.
- If you're saving stencil and template files that are meant to work together, make sure that their drawing page settings, styles, and colors are compatible. For details, see Chapter 10, *Managing Styles, Formats, and Colors*.
- If you're working on a document that you want others to review but not change, save the file as read-only. To do this, in the **Save As** dialog box, click the arrow next to the **Save** button, and then click **Read only**.

Users can open and edit a copy of a read-only file, but cannot edit the original. After you have saved a file as read-only, to make the file editable again, use the **Save As** command to save the file to another name.

For details on how to save different types of files, see the Microsoft Visio Help (on the **Help** menu, click **Microsoft Visio Help**).

4

Visio Formulas

The ShapeSheet Window 66

Elements of Visio Formulas 76

Units of Measure in Visio Formulas 83

Designing Visio Formulas 86

When to Supplement Visio Formulas with Automation 92

This chapter introduces basic concepts and terms about Visio formulas, such as the following:

- How to work with the ShapeSheet window for shapes and other Visio objects, and the behaviors that ShapeSheet sections control.
- Elements of a Visio formula—functions, operators, cell references, and units of measure—and how to edit formulas in a ShapeSheet window.
- General information about designing formulas, such as how shapes inherit formulas, when to add user-defined cells, how to protect formulas from changes a user makes in a drawing window, and how to control evaluation.
- Guidelines to help you decide when to use Automation to supplement the formulas in a solution.

The ShapeSheet Window

A Microsoft Visio object is stored internally as a set of formulas. For example, when you view a shape in a drawing window, you see it rendered graphically and see it behave according to its formulas. When you view the same shape in a ShapeSheet window, you see the underlying formulas that determine how the shape looks and behaves on the drawing page. These two windows simply provide different views of the same shape.

In a drawing window, some of the changes you make to an object affect its formulas. For example, when you move a shape with the **Pointer** tool, Visio changes and then reevaluates the formulas that define the shape's center of rotation, or *pin*, on the drawing page, because those formulas determine the shape's location on the page. However, a ShapeSheet window gives you more precise control over the appearance and behavior of the object, because you can edit the object's formulas to change its behavior. Whether you change an object in a drawing window or a ShapeSheet window, the modifications are automatically saved when you save the Visio document that contains the object.

Displaying a ShapeSheet Window

Most Visio objects—shapes, groups, masters, guides and guide points, pages, documents, styles, and linked or embedded objects from other applications—have underlying formulas that you can edit to change the object's behavior. To edit an object's formulas, you must first display a ShapeSheet window for the object.

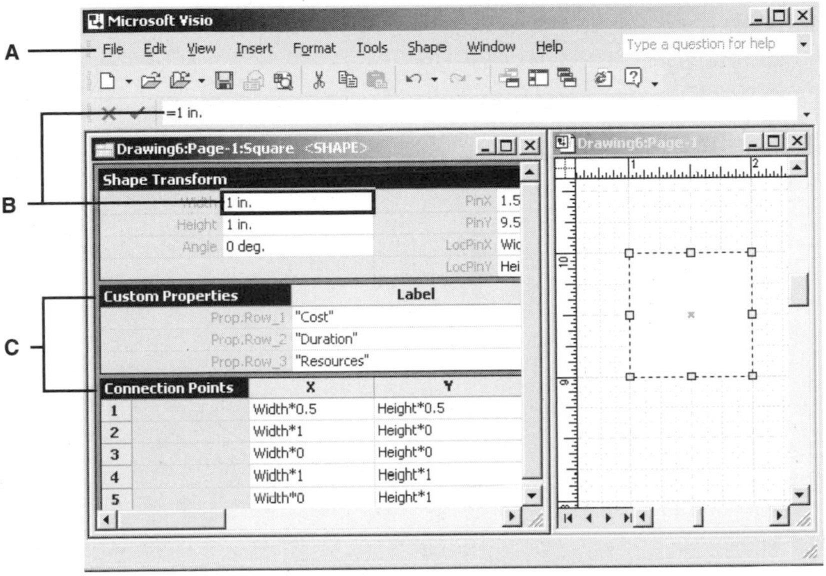

Figure 4-1 (**A**) When a ShapeSheet window is active, the menu bar contains commands for working with an object's formulas. (**B**) You can edit the formula in the selected cell or in the formula bar. (**C**) Each ShapeSheet section represents a set of related formulas.

To display a ShapeSheet window for an object on a drawing page

1. Select the object on the drawing page.

   To select a shape within a group (if its group behavior setting permits it), first select the group, and then select the shape. For more information about groups, see Chapter 6, *Grouping and Merging Shapes*.

2. On the **Window** menu, click **Show ShapeSheet**. Or click the **Show ShapeSheet** button on the **Developer** toolbar.

   To display the **Developer** toolbar, point to **Toolbars** on the **View** menu, and then click **Developer**.

> **Note** To add the **Show ShapeSheet** command to shapes' shortcut (right-click) menus, click **Options** on the **Tools** menu, click the **Advanced** tab, and select **Run in developer mode**. This option also adds the **Add-ons** submenu to the **Tools** menu.

Drawing pages, styles, Visio documents, and masters in stencils also have formulas that you can edit.

To display a ShapeSheet window for a page, master, style, or document

1. On the **View** menu, click **Drawing Explorer Window**.

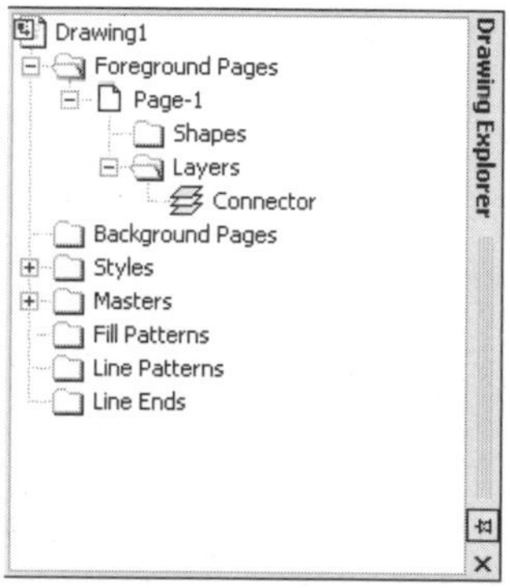

Figure 4-2 The **Drawing Explorer** window.

2. Click to open or close a folder.
3. In the **Drawing Explorer**, right-click the document, page, or style you want, and then choose **Show ShapeSheet** from the shortcut menu.

> **Tip** You can also display a ShapeSheet window for a page by clicking **Show ShapeSheet** on the **Window** menu with nothing selected on the page. Or, click the **Show ShapeSheet** button on the **Developer** toolbar.

To display a ShapeSheet window for a master in a stencil

1. If the master is in a stand-alone stencil, on the **File** menu, point to **Stencils**, click **Open Stencil**, and then select the stencil file that contains the master you want. Make sure **Original** or **Copy** is selected in the **Open Stencil** dialog box (click the arrow next to the **Open** button, and then click **Original** or **Copy**).

   If the master is in the document stencil of an open Visio document, on the **File** menu, point to **Stencils**, and then click **Document Stencil**.

2. In the Visio stencil window, right-click the master and click **Edit Master** on its shortcut menu.

   If the master is in the document stencil of an open Visio document, you can also display a master in its drawing window by right-clicking a master in the **Drawing Explorer** (under **Masters**) and clicking **Edit Master** on its shortcut menu.

3. In the master drawing window, select a shape, and then click **Show ShapeSheet** on the **Window** menu.

   If **Run in developer mode** is selected on the **Advanced** tab in the **Options** dialog box (click **Options** on the **Tools** menu), you can also right-click a shape or page in the master drawing window and click **Show ShapeSheet** on the shortcut menu.

Displaying Sections in a ShapeSheet Window

A ShapeSheet window is divided into sections of labeled cells that contain formulas that define related aspects of object behavior and appearance. Initially, Visio does not display all possible sections in a ShapeSheet window. Some sections are hidden simply to save space on the screen; others are present for an object only if they are needed and make sense for that type of object.

For example, to create a command that appears on a shape's shortcut menu, you must add an Actions section to the shape, either by clicking the **Section** command on the **Insert** menu while a ShapeSheet window is open and active, or through Automation. (For details about adding sections through Automation, see Chapter 17, *Automating Formulas*.)

To show or hide sections in a ShapeSheet window

1. Right-click in a ShapeSheet window, and then click **View Sections** on the shortcut menu.

2. In the **View Sections** dialog box, select the sections you want to show, or clear the sections you want to hide, and then click **OK**.

   If a section is dimmed, it is not available because it does not exist for this object.

To add sections using a ShapeSheet window

1. Right-click in a ShapeSheet window, and then click **Insert Sections** on the shortcut menu.

2. In the **Insert Section** dialog box, select the sections you want to add to the object, and then click **OK**.

Because Visio displays sections in a ShapeSheet window in a fixed order, you might have to scroll the ShapeSheet window to find the sections you added.

Geometry sections are unlike other types of sections in that an object can have more than one Geometry section, whereas it can have only one of other types of sections. Select **Geometry** in the **Insert Section** dialog box to add an empty Geometry section that contains a MoveTo and LineTo row; select **Ellipse** or **Infinite Line** to add a Geometry section that contains a single Ellipse or InfiniteLine row, respectively. For details about Geometry rows, see Chapter 5, *Controlling Shape Geometry with Formulas*.

> **Tip** You can expand or collapse a section in a ShapeSheet window by clicking the section name.

ShapeSheet Sections and What They Control

Each ShapeSheet section controls some aspect of a Visio object. As a solution developer, you need to know which section or sections control the behavior you want to modify.

This topic lists all possible ShapeSheet sections with a brief description of what the section does. For details about specific cells in a ShapeSheet section, search the ShapeSheet Reference in the Microsoft Visio Developer Reference (on the **Help** menu, click **Developer Reference**).

> **Note** Many of the sections you see in the ShapeSheet window interface are actually referred to as rows when you manipulate them through Automation. For a list of the sections, rows, and cells that appear in the ShapeSheet window, and for the corresponding index constants that you can use in a program to access sections, rows, and cells with Automation, see Appendix B, *ShapeSheet Section, Row, and Cell Indices* in this guide.

ShapeSheet sections

Section	Defines
1-D Endpoints	The *x*- and *y*-coordinates of the begin point and end point of a one-dimensional (1-D) shape.
Actions	Custom command names that appear on an object's shortcut menu and the actions that the commands perform.
Alignment	Alignment of an object with respect to the guides or guide points that the object may be glued to.
Character	Formatting attributes for an object's text, including font, color, transparency, text style, case, position relative to the baseline, and point size.
Connection Points	Connection points of an object.
Controls	*x*- and *y*-coordinates and behavior of an object's control handles.
Custom Properties	User-defined data associated with the object.
Document Properties	Document attributes, such as preview settings and output format.
Events	Formulas that evaluate when certain events occur, such as double-clicking a shape. **Note** ShapeSheet events are unique to the ShapeSheet; they are not the same as Automation events.
Fill Format	Fill formatting attributes for an object and its drop shadow, including pattern, foreground color and transparency, and background color and transparency.
Foreign Image Info	Width, height, and offset within its borders of an object from another application in a Visio drawing.
Geometry	Coordinates of the vertices for the lines and arcs that make up an object's geometry. If the object has more than one path, it has a Geometry section for each path.
Glue Info	Formulas that influence how a 1-D shape glues to other objects.
Group Properties	Behavior, selection, and display attributes for groups, including selection mode, display mode, and text, snap, and drop behavior.
Hyperlinks	Links between an object and a destination, such as another drawing page, another file, or a Web site.

ShapeSheet sections *(continued)*

Section	Defines
Image Properties	Bitmap attributes, such as image intensity (gamma), brightness, contrast, and transparency.
Layer Membership	Layers to which the object is assigned.
Layers	Layers of an object and the properties of each layer.
Line Format	Line formatting attributes, including pattern, weight, color, and transparency; whether the line ends are adorned (for example, with an arrowhead); the size of the adornments; the radius of the rounding circle applied to the line; and line cap style (round or square).
Miscellaneous	Properties that control various attributes, such as how the object looks when it is selected or dragged.
Page Layout	Page attributes that control automatic layout of shapes and routing of dynamic connectors, including default appearance and behavior of dynamic connectors and shapes.
Page Properties	Attributes such as drawing scale, page size, and offset of drop shadows.
Paragraph	Paragraph formatting attributes, including indents, line spacing, and horizontal alignment of paragraphs.
Protection	Status of locks set with the **Protection** command plus additional locks that can be set only in the ShapeSheet window.
Ruler & Grid	Settings of a page's rulers and grid, including density, origin, and spacing.
Scratch	A work area for intermediate formulas that are referred to by other cells.
Shape Layout	Placement and routing attributes, such as whether a connector can cross a shape or the style a connector should use when it jumps over another connector.
Shape Transform	General positioning information, such as width, height, angle, and center of rotation (pin); whether the object has been flipped; and how the object should behave when resized within a group.
Style Properties	Style attributes such as whether the style defines text, line, and fill formatting.
Tabs	Tab stop position and alignment.
Text Block Format	Alignment and margins of text in a text block. Also background color and transparency of the text block.
Text Fields	Custom formulas inserted in text using the **Field** command on the **Insert** menu.

ShapeSheet sections *(continued)*

Section	Defines
Text Transform	Positioning information about a shape's text block.
User-Defined Cells	Named cells for entering formulas and constants that are referred to by other cells and add-on tools. Unlike Scratch cells, user-defined cells are *portable*—for example, if a shape that refers to a user-defined cell in the page sheet is copied to another page that does not have the same user-defined cell, the cell is added to the page. If the page already has such a user-defined cell, the shape simply refers to that cell for its value.

Examining a Shape in a ShapeSheet Window

A good way to learn about Visio formulas and the ShapeSheet window is to view a shape with a drawing window and a ShapeSheet window side by side. This is a useful technique for taking apart existing masters so you can see how their behavior is controlled by custom formulas. It's also helpful to try changing the default formulas for a master to see the effect on the shape in the drawing window.

To examine a shape in a ShapeSheet window

1. Select the shape in the drawing window.
2. On the **Window** menu, click **Show ShapeSheet** to display the shape's ShapeSheet window.
3. On the **Window** menu, click **Tile** to arrange the ShapeSheet window and the drawing window side by side.

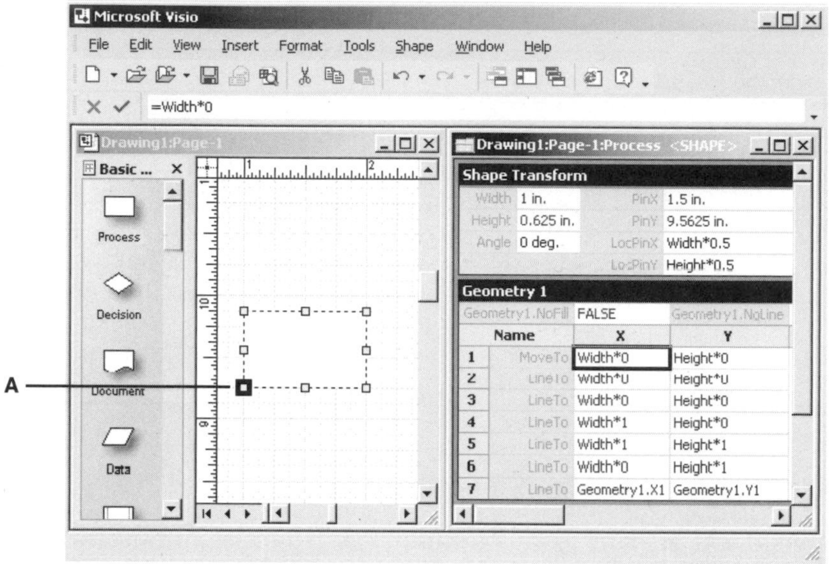

Figure 4-3 Examining a shape in a ShapeSheet window. (**A**) Selecting certairows or cells in a ShapeSheet window highlights the corresponding vertex in a drawing window.

To try this yourself, start by drawing a simple shape with straight line segments, such as a rectangle or other polygon, and display the ShapeSheet window as described in the previous procedure. In the ShapeSheet window, try any of the following suggestions and notice the effect on the shape in the drawing window.

- Change the values of the PinX and PinY cells in the Shape Transform section. The shape should move on the drawing page.
- Change the values of Width, Height, or Angle. The shape should shrink, grow, or rotate according to the new values.
- Click the label of a row in a Geometry section to select the row. In the drawing window, a black handle appears on the corresponding vertex.
- Select a row in a Geometry section. On the **Edit** menu, click **Delete Row**. The corresponding vertex is replaced by a straight line segment.
- Select a row in a Geometry section. On the **Insert** menu, click **Row** or **Row After**. Try entering your own values in the cells of the inserted row. A new vertex appears on the shape with the coordinates you specify.

If a ShapeSheet window displays values rather than formulas in cells, click **Formulas** on the **View** menu to display formulas instead.

To accept any change you make to a cell value, press the ENTER key.

You can display a section that is not visible, or you can hide a section you're not interested in. For details, see *Displaying Sections in a ShapeSheet Window* earlier in this section.

As you modify the shape, you might notice that some formulas are displayed in black text and others in blue. This indicates whether the formula is inherited or local, respectively. For details, see *How Shapes Inherit Formulas* later in this chapter.

In the drawing window, you can change the shape using the Visio drawing tools and commands to see the effect on the shape's formulas. Try any of the following suggestions:

- Move the shape with the **Pointer** tool. The shape's PinX and PinY formulas change to reflect its new position on the drawing page.
- Drag any selection handle to resize the shape. The shape's Width and Height formulas change to reflect its new size.
- Use the **Pencil** tool to select a vertex and delete it, or add a vertex and move it. Notice the effect on the shape's Geometry section.
- Change the shape's fill format or line format. The corresponding formulas in the shape's Fill Format or Line Format section change.
- On the **Format** menu, click **Protection** and select various options in the dialog box. The corresponding cells in the shape's Protection section change from zero (0) to 1. In the ShapeSheet window, try changing various Protection cells from a non-zero number to 0 (or from TRUE to FALSE) and notice the effect on the shape's padlock handles in the drawing window.

For a brief discussion of the Visio drawing tools, see Chapter 2, *Creating Visio Shapes*. For details about the Shape Transform and Geometry sections, see Chapter 5, *Controlling Shape Geometry with Formulas*.

For reference information about any ShapeSheet section or cell and for information on how to work in the ShapeSheet, see the ShapeSheet Reference in the Microsoft Visio Developer Reference (on the **Help** menu, click **Developer Reference**).

Elements of Visio Formulas

The key to controlling shape actions is to write formulas that define the behavior you want. A *formula* is an expression that can contain constants, functions, operators, and cell references. Microsoft Visio evaluates a formula to a result and then converts the result to the appropriate units for the cell that contains the formula. (Some formulas consist of a single constant, but all formulas go through this evaluation and conversion process.) In a ShapeSheet window, you can display cell contents as either values or formulas by clicking the appropriate command on the **View** menu.

> **Note** Much of what you do to shapes with Automation is done by getting and setting their formulas. For details, see Chapter 17, *Automating Formulas.*

Entering and Editing Formulas in a ShapeSheet Window

You can edit a cell's formula to change the value calculated for the cell and, as a result, change a particular behavior of a shape. For example, the Height cell in the Shape Transform section contains a formula that you can edit to change the shape's height. You enter and edit formulas in a ShapeSheet window much the same way you work in any spreadsheet program.

Visio regards anything in a cell—even a numeric constant, string, or cell reference—as a formula. Unlike a spreadsheet program, however, many Visio cells require a result of a specific type, such as a dimension, so anything you enter in them must imply a unit of measure, such as inches or centimeters.

The Visio engine automatically converts a formula's natural result into an equivalent result of the type required by the cell that contains the formula. For example, the FlipX cell in the Shape Transform section requires a Boolean result (TRUE or FALSE); in the FlipX cell, therefore, any formula that evaluates to a non-zero number is converted to TRUE, and any formula that evaluates to zero is converted to FALSE. For details, see *Units of Measure in Visio Formulas* later in this section.

To enter a formula, select a cell and then start typing either in the cell or in the formula bar, as the following figure shows.

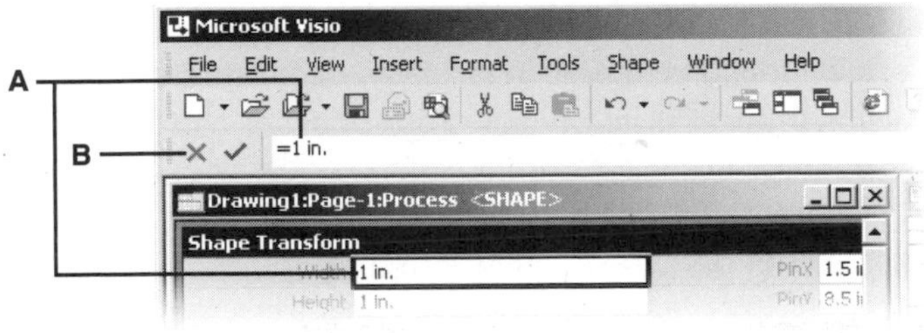

Figure 4-4 Entering a formula in a ShapeSheet window. (**A**) Select a cell, and then type or edit the formula and click the **Accept** button on the formula bar or press ENTER. (**B**) Click the **Cancel Change** button on the formula bar to cancel changes to a formula.

For details about entering and editing formulas or working in the formula bar, search the Microsoft Visio Developer Reference (on the **Help** menu, click **Developer Reference**).

> **Tip** Right-click a ShapeSheet cell to display its shortcut menu, which contains commands you can use to edit the cell.

Functions and Operators in Visio Formulas

If you've created formulas in a spreadsheet program, you've probably used functions and operators much like those you'll use in Visio formulas. This topic provides a brief overview of functions and operators and how they are used.

Functions

A *function* performs a single, well-defined task. Most functions take a fixed number of *arguments* as input, although some functions take none, some take a variable number of arguments, and some allow optional arguments. Although the type and number of arguments depend on the function, all functions have the same general syntax:

```
FUNCTION(argument1, argument2, ... argumentN)
```

Many functions that you can use in Visio formulas resemble those you've probably seen in spreadsheet programs: mathematical, such as SUM or SQRT; trigonometric, such as SIN or COS; or logical, such as IF or NOT. Many other functions are unique to Visio, such as GUARD, GRAVITY, or RUNADDON.

For details about functions, see the Microsoft Visio Developer Reference (on the **Help** menu, click **Developer Reference**).

> **Note** Certain functions appear in formulas generated by Visio, but are not listed in the **Insert Function** dialog box or described in the Microsoft Visio Developer Reference. These functions begin with a single underscore (for example, _ELLIPSE_THETA). They are reserved for internal use and should not be used in other formulas.

Operators

An *operator* performs an operation, usually by combining two *operands* to produce a result.

Many operators can be classed as arithmetic (addition, subtraction, multiplication, and so on) or logical (greater than, less than, or equal to). Other operators manipulate strings or perform actions such as running add-ons.

An operand can be a *constant* (a single value) or an *expression* (perhaps containing one or more functions) that evaluates to a single value. In a Visio formula (as in any spreadsheet program), an operand can also be a cell reference.

When a formula contains more than one operator, operators are evaluated in a certain order (sometimes called their *precedence*). For example, the multiplication operator (*) is evaluated before the addition operator (+). Consider the following expression:

```
4 + 5 * 6
```

Because multiplication has a higher precedence than addition, first *5 * 6* is multiplied to obtain 30, and then 4 is added to 30 to obtain a result of 34.

You can alter the order of evaluation by grouping expressions in parentheses. For example:

```
( 4 + 5 ) * 6
```

Because *4 + 5* is enclosed in parentheses, it is evaluated first and becomes 9. Then *9 * 6* is multiplied to obtain a result of 54.

If expressions in parentheses are nested, Visio starts with the expression in the innermost set of parentheses and works its way outward.

For a table of operators and their precedence in Visio formulas, search the Microsoft Visio Developer Reference (on the **Help** menu, click **Developer Reference**).

ShapeSheet Cell References

You can create interdependencies among Visio formulas by means of cell references. Cell references give you the power to calculate a value for one cell based on another cell's value. For example, a shape's Width cell might contain a formula that calculates the shape's width by referring to the value of its Height cell, so that when a user stretches the shape vertically its width stays in proportion.

A given formula can refer to any cell in a document, although it's most common with formulas for shapes to refer to cells of objects on the same page or particular cells in the same object.

> **Note** If you're planning to localize your solution for international markets, you might want to use universal names in formulas. In Visio, any object that can be assigned a name (for example, shapes or rows in a User-Defined Cells section) can actually have two names: a *local name* and a *universal name*. The local name is displayed to the user and must be translated if the solution is localized. The universal name is (for the most part) concealed from the user, does not need to be translated, and can be assigned only with Automation.
>
> You can enter universal names in formulas in a ShapeSheet window or set them with Automation, but once the formula is entered, it is displayed with local names in a ShapeSheet window. For details about using universal names in a solution, see Chapter 26, *Packaging a Visio Automation Solution* and the Microsoft Visio Developer Reference (on the **Help** menu, click **Developer Reference**).

References to cells in the same shape

A reference to a cell in the same shape needs to specify only the cell name, such as Height. If the cell is in a section with indexed rows, the section and row index are part of the cell name. For example, the following reference specifies the cell in column X, row 5, of the Connection Points section:

```
Connections.X5
```

> **Tip** You can quickly reference a cell in a formula by placing the insertion point in the formula bar or a cell, and then clicking the cell you want to reference. The name of the cell is inserted at the insertion point.

References to cells in other shapes or containers

A reference from one shape to a cell in another shape, page, master, or style requires a prefix that identifies the *container* of that cell. For example, a reference to a cell in another shape of the same page or master must include the shape's name or ID followed by an exclamation point and then the name of the cell, as shown in the following reference:

```
Armchair!Width
```

This reference specifies the Width cell in the Shape Transform section of the shape named Armchair.

If the shape is not named, or as an alternative to its name, a reference can include the shape's ID. For example, the following reference specifies the Width cell in the Shape Transform section of the shape whose ID is 2. This is recommended, because names are *scoped* to their containers (for example, two groups can each contain a shape that has the same name), but *Sheet.ID* is unique within that page, master, or style collection. For example:

```
Sheet.2!Width
```

> **Tip** An object on a drawing page always has an ID, whether or not it also has a descriptive name. Visio assigns the ID when the object is created. This ID does not change unless you move the object to a different page or document. To display an object's ID or give it a descriptive name, select the object, and then click **Special** on the **Format** menu.

A reference from the cell of a shape on the page to a cell that defines a property of that page requires the name ThePage followed by an exclamation point and the cell name. (In a master, a reference to ThePage refers to the object that defines properties of the master as a whole, such as its overall size and its drawing scale.) For example, the following reference specifies the PageScale cell of the page:

```
ThePage!PageScale
```

Rules for Cell References in Formulas

The syntax you use and whether you can refer to a shape by name depend on the relationship between the two objects. The following general rules apply:

- If a shape is a peer of the shape whose formula you are editing, you can refer to the peer shape by name. If the peer shape is a group, you can refer by name to the group, but not to its members. Neither can you refer by name to a shape's parent or its parent's peers.
- You can use Sheet.ID syntax to refer to any shape on the page, whether the shape is in a group or is a parent of a shape.
- If a shape contains a group shape, you must use Sheet.ID syntax to refer to it.
- Names that contain nonstandard characters must be enclosed in single quotation marks. Single quotation mark characters in a nonstandard name must be prefixed by a single quotation mark.

The following tables summarize rules for cell references in formulas, and the standard characters allowed in sheet names.

Summary of cell reference syntax

Cell	Cell reference syntax	Example
In the same object	`CellName`	`Width`
In a Geometry section	`Geometry`*n*`.ColumnnameRowIndex`	`Geometry1.X1`
In a named column with indexed rows	`Sectionname.Columnname[RowIndex]`	`Char.Font[3]`
In an unnamed column with indexed rows	`Sectionname.ColumnnameRowIndex`	`Scratch.A5`
In another named object in the same container	`Shapename!Cellname`	`Star!Angle`
In another object with the same name in the same container	`Shapename.ID!Cellname`	`Executive.2!Height`

Summary of cell reference syntax *(continued)*

Cell	Cell reference syntax	Example
In any object on the page	`Sheet.ID!Cellname`	`Sheet.8!FillForegnd`
In the page sheet	`ThePage!Cellreference`	`ThePage!PageWidth`
In a containing group	`Sheet.ID!Cellname`	`MyParentGroup!PinX`
In a named row	`Sectionname.Rowname [.Cellname]`	`User.Vanishing_ Point.Prompt`
A cell in the page sheet of another page in the document	`Pages[Pagename]! Shapename!Cellreference`	`Pages[Page-3]! ThePage!DrawingScale`
In a style sheet	`Styles!Stylename! Cellreference`	`Styles!Connector! LineColor`
In a master sheet	`Masters[Mastername]! Shapename!Cellreference`	`Masters[Door]!Sheet.5! Width`
In the document sheet of the current document	`TheDoc!Cellreference`	`TheDoc!OutputFormat`
A shape, page, master, document, or style with a nonstandard name	`'Sheetname'!CellName`	`'1-D'!LineColor`

Standard characters allowed in sheet names

Character position	Allowed characters
First	Any multibyte character Any alphabetic character Any of the following: ? ~ @ # _ (underscore)
Other than first	Any multibyte character Any alphanumeric-character Any of the following: ? ~ @ # _ (underscore) $. (period) Space

Specifying nonstandard sheet names in cell references

If you name a shape, page, master, document, or style using nonstandard characters (such as a dash), the Visio engine automatically delimits that name using single quotation marks ('). The Visio engine also prefixes any single quotation mark character in a nonstandard name with an additional single quotation mark. This adjustment allows Visio to correctly interpret the sheet name.

Keep this behavior in mind when you name various objects. If you want to use nonstandard characters in names, be sure that any references to nonstandard names include the required quotation marks. For example, if you name a shape *1-D*, you would refer to it in a formula using single quotation marks, such as *'1-D'!LineColor*.

Examples of how Visio handles nonstandard sheet names in formulas

Object	Name	Original formula	Adjusted formula
Shape	1-D	`=1-D!LineColor`	`='1-D'!LineColor`
Shape	One's	`=One's!LineColor`	`='One''s'!LineColor`
Style	Red!Bang	`=Styles!Red!Bang!LineColor`	`=Styles!'Red!Bang'!LineColor`

> **Note** Beginning with Microsoft Visio version 2002, the parser only makes this adjustment for nonstandard sheet names within the context of a formula. Nonstandard sheet names are not fully supported in previous versions of Visio.

Units of Measure in Visio Formulas

Microsoft Visio assigns the result of a formula differently depending on the cell in which you enter it:

- In general, cells that represent shape position, a dimension, or an angle require a *number-unit pair* that consists of a number and the qualifying units needed to interpret the number. For example, a formula in the Width cell might evaluate to 5, which might mean 5 inches or 5 centimeters, depending on the units of measure in effect for the drawing.

- Other cells have no intrinsic units of measure and evaluate to a string, to TRUE or FALSE, or to an index, depending on the nature of the cell. For example, the formula *=5* in the FillForegnd cell means color 5 from the drawing's color palette, whereas *=5* in the LockWidth cell means TRUE (only zero is FALSE) and locks the shape's width.

For best results, always specify the units of measure in your formulas, rather than relying on Visio to supply the correct units. If you don't specify units of measure with a number, it is evaluated using the internal units defined for the cell, which can be page units, drawing units, type units, duration units, or angular units:

- *Page units* measure sizes on the printed page, including typographic measurements. Page units are typically used for line thicknesses and font sizes that do not scale with the drawing.
- *Drawing units* specify the real-world measurement, such as a 50-meter pool (drawing units) that appears 10 cm long (page units) on paper. For example, if you enter the formula *=50* into the Width cell, which expects a number-unit pair in drawing units, Visio supplies the default drawing units currently set for the page and evaluates the formula accordingly.
- *Angular units* measure angular distances, such as a shape's rotation. Angles can be expressed in degrees or radians.

Internally, Visio uses inches for measuring distance, radians for measuring angles, and days for measuring durations.

For more details on units of measure, search the ShapeSheet Reference in the Microsoft Visio Developer Reference (on the **Help** menu, click **Developer Reference**).

Multidimensional Units

A Visio formula that multiplies or divides dimensional units produces a result in multidimensional units that can be stored in some cells. For example, if a shape is 5 feet wide and 10 feet high in drawing units, the formula *= Width * Height* evaluates to *50 ft ^ 2* (50 square feet). The following cells can store multidimensional results:

- The Value cell in a row of a Custom Property or User-Defined Cells section in the ShapeSheet.
- The A, B, C, and D cells in a row in the Scratch section in the ShapeSheet.

Use the FORMAT function to display multidimensional units using abbreviations such as *sq. in.* For details, see the FORMAT function in the Microsoft Visio Developer Reference (on the **Help** menu, click **Developer Reference**).

Be aware that most multiplication is intended to combine a value that has units with a value that has none. If such a calculation happens to multiply two values with units, the multidimensional result might not make sense. For example, if a color cell such as FillForegnd is set to the product of two cells in the Geometry section, the result would be a #DIM error because cells in the Geometry section always have units but the FillForegnd cell cannot contain a multidimensional value.

> **Note** In versions of Visio earlier than Visio 2000, formulas that multiplied or divided dimensional values could generate incorrect results. For example, the formula *=1 cm. * 1 cm.* was converted to 0.394 in. * 0.394 in. Multiplying just the constants and not the units, this formula evaluated to 0.155 in. Converting this result back to centimeters by multiplying it by 2.54 cm./in. produced an incorrect result of 0.394 cm. instead of the correct result of 1 cm.^2 (centimeters squared). Existing solutions that employ workarounds for this behavior should be changed to take advantage of multidimensional units in Visio versions 2000 and later.

Specifying Units of Measure

Because many drawings represent physical objects, you can specify units of measure in the imperial and metric systems, and you can specify angles in radians, decimal degrees, or degrees, minutes, and seconds of arc. You can also use standard typographical measurements such as picas, points, ciceros, and didots.

For best results, always specify a unit of measure when you enter a formula in a cell that expects a dimensional value, as shown by the examples in the following table.

Examples of number-unit pairs

Use	Don't use
`5 in.`	5
Width + 0.5 in.	Width + 0.5
7 in. * 1.5	7 * 1.5
`DEG(MODULUS(Angle, 360 deg.))`	`MODULUS(Angle, 360 deg.)`

Specifying units explicitly makes it easier to identify the number-unit pairs in your calculations, so that you don't inadvertently divide one number-unit pair with another number-unit pair or combine incompatible units, such as adding angles to lengths. In addition, specifying units of measure makes it easier to localize your formulas for international use.

You can identify units using a variety of strings (such as i, in, in., inch, inches) and you can use the FORMAT function to display results using popular formatting options.

> **Note** If you're planning to localize your solution for international markets, you might want to use universal names in formulas. The local name is displayed to the user and must be translated if the solution is localized. The universal name is (for the most part) concealed from the user, does not need to be translated, and can be assigned only with Automation.

For more details about units of measure and a list of the units supported in Visio, search the ShapeSheet Reference in the Microsoft Visio Developer Reference (on the **Help** menu, click **Developer Reference**).

Designing Visio Formulas

Designing good Microsoft Visio formulas requires more than correct syntax. A shape developer needs to understand where a shape obtains its default formulas, the advantages and disadvantages of storing formulas in certain cells, how to protect custom formulas against inadvertent changes, and how to control formula recalculation for best performance.

How Shapes Inherit Formulas

When you open a ShapeSheet window, a formula you see in a cell might be inherited from a master or a style. Rather than make a local copy of every formula for a shape, an instance of a master inherits formulas from the master and from the styles applied to it. This behavior has two benefits: It allows changes to the master's formulas or the style definition to be propagated to all instances, and it results in smaller Visio files because inherited formulas are stored once in the master, not once in each instance.

When you enter a formula in such a cell, you override the inherited formula with a local formula. The cell containing the local formula no longer inherits its formula from the master, changes to the master's formula are not propagated to that cell in the instance, and the shape occupies more storage in the document. (Style application is an exception—unless you choose to preserve local overrides when you apply a style, it always writes new formulas into the corresponding ShapeSheet cells. For details, see Chapter 10, *Managing Styles, Formats, and Colors.*)

You can tell whether a formula is local or inherited by the color of its text in the ShapeSheet. Black text in a cell indicates an inherited formula. Blue text indicates a local formula—either the result of editing the formula in a ShapeSheet window or some change to the shape (for example, resizing it in the drawing window) that caused the formula to change.

To restore an inherited formula to a cell, delete the local formula. Visio replaces it with the corresponding formula from the master.

Note In earlier versions of Visio, geometry formulas were always local. In Visio version 2000 and later, geometry formulas are inherited from masters. This means that any local change to a shape's geometry creates a copy of the inherited formula and causes the shape to occupy more storage. To keep Visio documents small in size, change inherited formulas in the master in the document stencil so that shapes can continue to inherit from the master. Solutions that use Automation to change geometry formulas in shapes should be redesigned to do the same.

User-Defined Cells and "Scratch" Formulas

Most ShapeSheet sections have a predefined purpose: Their cells control particular shape attributes or behaviors. However, you might need to simplify a formula with intermediate calculations, or store values to be used by other formulas or add-ons. You can store such formulas and values in an object's User-Defined Cells section or its Scratch section. To add these sections in a ShapeSheet window, click **Section** on the **Insert** menu, and then select the section you want to add.

The cells in User-Defined Cells and Scratch sections do not control specific shape attributes or behaviors, so you can use either or both to contain any formula. However, there are times when it makes more sense to use one or the other:

- You can provide a meaningful name for a user-defined cell, so it's a better place to store constants and values referred to in other formulas because references to a meaningful cell name make formulas easier to read.
- The Scratch section has X and Y cells, which are designated to contain a number-unit pair in drawing units. These cells are good places to put formulas involving shape coordinates.

> **Note** If a shape's cells will be accessed using Automation, place formulas in user-defined cells rather than Scratch cells. Any program can write to a Scratch cell and so overwrite formulas you place there. This is less likely to happen in a cell with a unique name.

User-defined cells

You can add a cell whose value and name you specify in the User-Defined Cells section. A user-defined cell can contain any formula, such as a constant referenced in other formulas or a calculation used by an add-on. For example, a master might refer to a user-defined cell in a page sheet. When an instance of the master is created, the instance refers to the user-defined cell of the page it is on—if the page already has that user-defined cell. If the page does not already have that cell, it is copied from the master. (The same is true for user-defined cells in document sheets.) This feature makes user-defined cells extremely portable, because the shape developer doesn't have to ensure that all possible destinations have that user-defined cell—if the shape needs the cell, it will be there.

The name you give to a user-defined cell must be unique within a section. To refer to the value of a user-defined cell in the same shape, use the syntax User.*name*. For example, User.Constant.

To refer to a user-defined cell in another shape, a page, or the current document, precede User.*name* with the appropriate scope. For example:

```
Sheet.2!User.Constant
ThePage!User.Constant
TheDoc!User.Constant
```

> **Tip** The User.Prompt cell, Action.Menu cell, Controls.Tip cell, and certain other cells are designated by default to contain strings. When you type in these cells in a ShapeSheet window, Visio automatically encloses the text in quotation marks. Begin the formula with an equals sign (=) to make the Visio application evaluate it as a formula. Visio does not automatically enclose text in quotation marks if you set the formulas of one of these cells using Automation.

Scratch cells

The Scratch section has six columns labeled X, Y, and A through D. The X and Y cells use the drawing's units of measure, so place calculations involving dimensions or shape coordinates in those cells. The A through D cells have no intrinsic units and are appropriate to use for any result type. To refer to cells in the Scratch section, specify the section name and the column and row label; for example, Scratch.A1.

Scratch cells are best suited for what their name implies—intermediate calculations that are local to a shape and not involved with Automation. Besides the fact that Scratch cells can't have meaningful names like user-defined cells, they also aren't as portable; if a shape refers to a Scratch cell in a page or document and you copy that shape to another page or document, the referring formula will fail with a #REF error because the Scratch formula from the source page or document is not copied to the destination.

Protecting Formulas

The only way to protect the formulas in individual ShapeSheet cells from change is to use the GUARD function. GUARD protects the entire formula in a cell; it cannot protect parts of formulas. Actions in the drawing window cannot overwrite formulas protected by the GUARD function. The GUARD function uses this syntax:

```
GUARD(expression)
```

where *expression* is the formula to protect. A formula protected with the GUARD function evaluates to exactly the same result as a formula not protected with GUARD.

When a shape is moved, resized, grouped, or ungrouped, Visio writes changes to ShapeSheet cells and can overwrite custom formulas. The cells most commonly affected by such actions are Width, Height, PinX, and PinY in the Shape Transform section. For example, to prevent a shape from being flipped, you can enter the formula:

```
FlipX = GUARD(FALSE)
FlipY = GUARD(FALSE)
```

A single action in the drawing window can affect several ShapeSheet cells. You must guard the formulas in each of these cells if you want to prevent unexpected changes to the shape. Of course, if a user deletes a ShapeSheet section, all the formulas in it, including guarded ones, will be deleted.

> **Note** The GUARD function prevents certain user actions via the drawing window; however, Visio does support Automation methods that you can use to overwrite guarded formulas programmatically.

Controlling Recalculation of Formulas

By default, a formula that refers to another cell is recalculated when the referenced cell changes. For example, if a formula refers to a shape's PinX cell and that shape is moved on the page, the formula is recalculated because PinX has changed. Most of the time this behavior is exactly what you want, and Visio formulas depend on it for much of their power and versatility.

Some recalculations might seem to result from simple cause and effect, but many factors influence the order in which formulas are recalculated. Formulas should be designed so that they do not depend on a particular order of recalculation.

However, not all recalculations are necessary. For example, the SETF function is a powerful function that can be used in a formula to set the formula of another cell. The SETF function only needs to be recalculated when the condition that triggers it occurs, but if the formula refers to cells that often change, it might frequently be recalculated unnecessarily. Recalculation takes time and affects shape performance.

To prevent unnecessary recalculations and improve the performance of your solution, enclose cell references in one of the following functions:

- Use GETREF(*cell reference*) to include a reference to another cell in a formula but not recalculate the formula if the value of that cell changes.
- Use GETVAL(*cell reference*) to use the value of another cell in a formula.

A big advantage of GETREF is that the target cell reference does not have to be enclosed in quotation marks. In earlier versions of Visio, a target cell reference used in a SETF function had to be enclosed in quotation marks, which required the formula to be translated for localized solutions.

Both GETREF and GETVAL allow a formula to track a cell reference if the reference changes—for example, if preceding rows are deleted or if the cell itself is deleted—but the referring formula is not recalculated when the referenced cell's value changes.

For example, the following formula is recalculated when Width changes, but not when PinX and PinY change:

```
= GETVAL(PinX) + GETVAL(PinY) + Width
```

The following formula is recalculated when the cell containing the SETF formula is triggered (for example, by a user choosing an action from a shortcut menu), but not when PinX changes:

```
= SETF(GETREF(PinX), 7)
```

When to Supplement Visio Formulas with Automation

One of the more important questions in developing a Microsoft Visio solution is this: When should you supplement formulas with Automation? Visio formulas can be extremely powerful, but the more complex formulas become, the more difficult they can be to design and test.

You might need to add Automation to your solution if your formulas:

- Use many SETF expressions to simulate flow of control (if-else, switch case, or loops). SETF is better used for onetime setup or initialization, not for setting a state machine.
- Depend on order of recalculation to get correct results. To provide the best performance, formulas are recalculated as needed, and the order is not guaranteed. Formulas that depend on other formulas to be recalculated first can produce inconsistent results.
- Produce inconsistent results that don't have an obvious cause. Complex formulas might depend on side effects that could change in a future release of Visio and cause the formulas to stop working. For example, formulas should not rely on a chain of circular references to loop a specific number of times.

For a discussion of how to divide functionality between Visio formulas and Automation, see Chapter 1, *Introduction to Developing Microsoft Visio Solutions*. For an introduction to Automation in the Visio product, see Chapter 14, *Automation and the Visio Object Model*.

5

Controlling Shape Geometry with Formulas

Shape Geometry 94

Controlling How Shapes Stretch and Shrink 100

Controlling How Shapes Flip and Rotate 103

Controlling Curves in Shapes 108

Optimizing Shape Geometry 115

Using Locks to Limit Shape Behavior 116

When you design a shape, you must decide how it will respond to a user action such as resizing or repositioning the shape. Microsoft Visio records the location of each shape vertex within the shape's coordinate space. These vertices, and the paths that connect them, define the shape's *geometry*. By writing formulas to control shape geometry, you determine how a shape looks and behaves in response to user actions.

This chapter defines shape geometry, describes how to control how shapes stretch, shrink, flip, and rotate, and describes how to control curves in shapes. It also offers suggestions for optimizing shape geometry and using locks to restrict what a user can do to a shape.

Shape Geometry

Most drawing programs are based on two-dimensional geometry. When you draw an object, the program records the object as a collection of horizontal and vertical locations. These locations, called *vertices* in Microsoft Visio, are measured from a point of origin on the page and are connected with line segments, just as if you were drawing the object on a piece of graph paper.

A sequence of line or curve segments that connect a shape's vertices is called a *path*. Each path corresponds to a Geometry section, which you can view in a ShapeSheet window or access through Automation. Each vertex defining a path corresponds to a row of its Geometry section. A path can be closed or open, and a shape can have more than one path (and therefore more than one Geometry section); for details, see Chapter 6, *Grouping and Merging Shapes*.

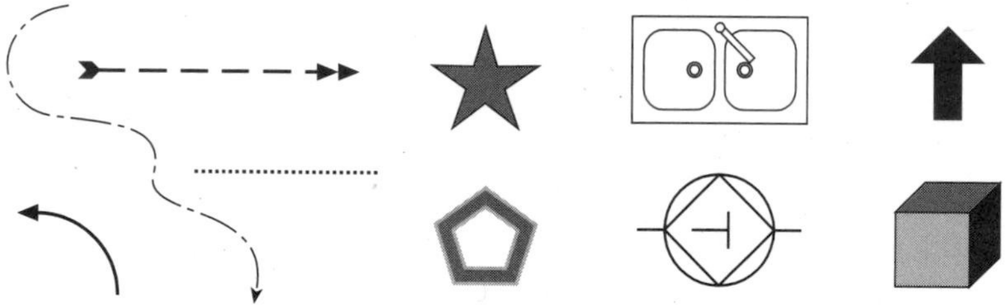

Figure 5-1 A sequence of line or curve segments that connect a shape's vertices is called a path.

What makes Visio different from other drawing programs is that you can use formulas to control vertex locations. Instead of simply recording a new position when a shape is moved or sized, Visio can calculate a vertex in relation to other vertices or other shapes, or constrain it to a fixed position on the page. The ability to describe shapes with formulas opens many possibilities for making shapes behave in complex and sophisticated ways.

The following illustration shows a simple example. In the rectangle on the left, width and height are independent of each other—changing one won't affect the other. However, in the rectangle on the right, height is calculated with a formula that refers to its width. Changing the shape's width will cause its height formula to be recalculated and the shape's height to change.

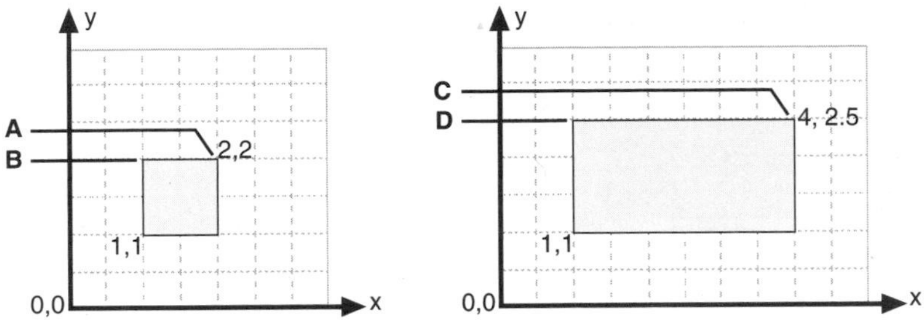

Figure 5-2 When you create a formula for a shape, Visio recalculates the shape's vertices on the basis of your formula. (**A**) Width = 1. (**B**) Height = 1. (**C**) Width = 3. (**D**) Height = Width * 0.5.

Describing Shapes in a Coordinate System

Among the most useful and powerful formulas are those that control a shape's size or position. Each vertex of a shape is recorded as a pair of *x,y* coordinates. When you move the shape or change its size, Microsoft Visio records the changes to the shape's vertices and redraws the shape at its new position or size. To move, flip, rotate, or resize a Visio shape with formulas, you must describe the shape in terms of the coordinate system.

Visio uses different coordinate systems to describe a shape. Depending on what you want to do to a shape, you might need to work with the following three coordinate systems.

Local coordinates A shape's width and height define the local coordinate system. The origin is the lower-left corner of the shape's width-height box. The Geometry section uses formulas to describe the local coordinates of the vertices for the paths that make up a shape. By modifying these formulas, you can control a shape's appearance, no matter where the shape is positioned on the drawing page.

Page coordinates The location of a shape or group on the drawing page is described in page coordinates, which have their origin at the lower-left corner of the page. Page coordinates are displayed on the ruler in the units of measure specified in the **Page Setup** dialog box (**Page Properties** tab).

Parent coordinates Visio also identifies the position of an object relative to its parent. For shapes on a drawing page, parent coordinates are equivalent to page coordinates. However, if a shape is in a group, its parent is the group, not the page, so its parent coordinates are the local coordinates of the group. In this case, the origin of the parent coordinate system is the lower-left corner of the group's width-height box.

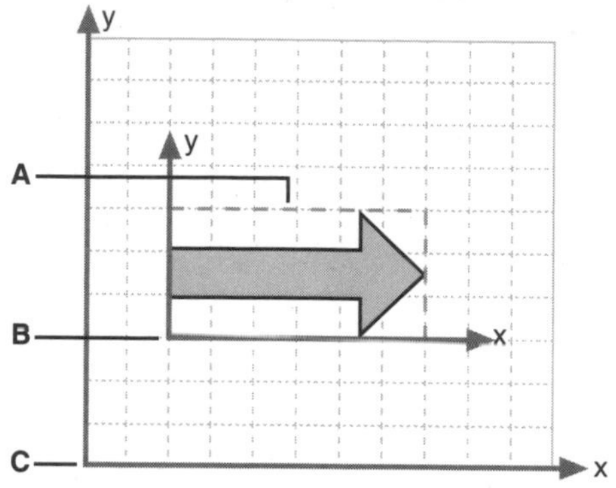

Figure 5-3 Visio uses different coordinate systems to identify shape vertices and position. (**A**) Width-height box. (**B**) Local coordinates. (**C**) Page coordinates.

> **Tip** You cannot move the origin of the page coordinate system. However, you can change the zero point of the coordinates displayed on the rulers by holding down CTRL and dragging the crossbar at the intersection of the two rulers. Moving the zero point has no effect on the page coordinate system, but it can be useful for measuring the distance between shapes.

Representing Shape Geometry with Formulas

Microsoft Visio represents a shape's width, height, and position on the page with formulas in its Shape Transform section. Visio usually expresses the value of each vertex in each shape's Geometry section as a fraction of the shape's width or height. When you move, resize, or rotate a shape, Visio writes new formulas in the Shape Transform section, and then reevaluates the vertex formulas in the Geometry section. When you edit a particular vertex, new formulas are generated for that vertex expressed in adjusted factors of Width and Height.

For example, consider the rectangle in the following illustration, shown with its Shape Transform and Geometry sections.

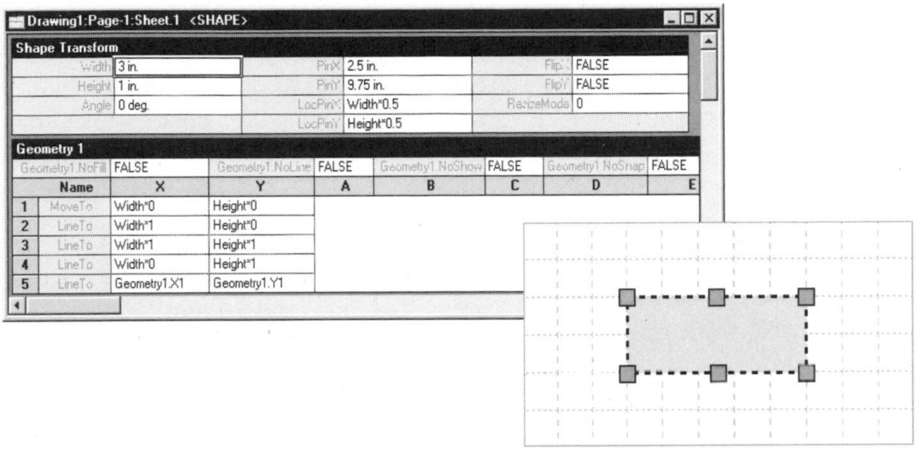

Figure 5-4 A rectangle with its Shape Transform and Geometry sections.

Notice that the rectangle has = *3 in.* in its Width cell and the formula =*Width* * *1* in two of its Geometry cells. If the shape is stretched horizontally on the drawing page, the value of the Width cell changes, which changes the value of the local coordinates specified in the Geometry section. The Geometry formula, however, remains = *Width* * *1*. The Geometry formulas that represent vertices of the shape are all local coordinates, expressed in terms of the shape's width and height.

Note Row types in the Geometry section describe how a segment of a path should be drawn. In the preceding example, the row types MoveTo and LineTo describe straight line segments. Imagine telling someone how to draw a rectangle on a sheet of paper. You would say something like "*Move* the pen *to* coordinates 0, 0, then draw a *line to* coordinates 3, 0..." and so on.

Row types that describe curves (especially curves drawn with the **Freeform** tool) are more complex than those describing straight lines, and certain row types can represent many vertices with a single row. For details about these Geometry row types and the Geometry section, see the ShapeSheet Reference in the Microsoft Visio Developer Reference (on the **Help** menu, click **Developer Reference**).

Representing a Shape's Position on a Page

The position of a shape on the page is described by its *pin*, or center of rotation. Microsoft Visio uses two coordinates (PinX, PinY and LocPinX, LocPinY) in the Shape Transform section to store the location of a shape's pin:

- The PinX and PinY cells store the pin's *x* and *y* locations with respect to its parent, which can be a group or page. That is, PinX and PinY are expressed in parent coordinates. PinX and PinY represent the shape's position with respect to its parent. If the shape is moved, the values of PinX and PinY change.
- The LocPinX and LocPinY cells store the pin's *x* and *y* positions with respect to the shape. That is, LocPinX and LocPinY are expressed in local coordinates. LocPinX and LocPinY represent the point around which the shape pivots if you rotate the shape. Like a shape's Geometry formulas, LocPinX and LocPinY are formulas that reference the shape's width and height. If the shape is moved, its LocPinX and LocPinY formulas don't change.

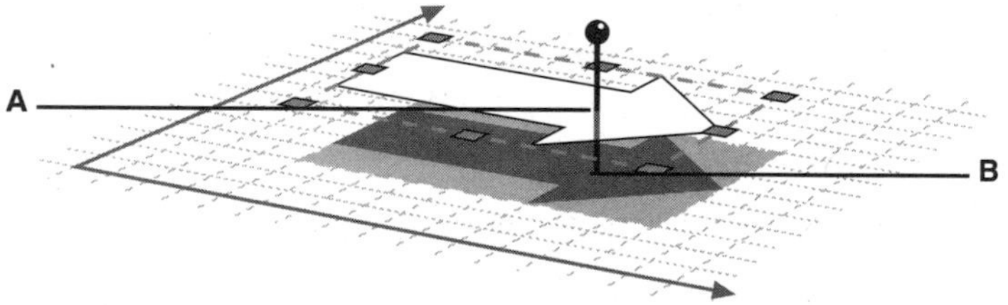

Figure 5-5 The pin describes a shape's position in local and parent coordinates. (**A**) The local coordinates of the pin describe this point (Width * 0.5, Height * 0.5). (**B**) The parent coordinates of the pin define this point.

To visualize how the pin works, imagine attaching a 3-by-5 index card to a sheet of paper by pressing a pin through the card and then through the paper. You can describe the location of the card on the paper with respect to the holes created by the pin.

That's how the pin works in Visio. The local coordinates of the pin (the hole in the card) are (*LocPinX, LocPinY*). The parent coordinates (the hole in the paper) are (*PinX, PinY*). If you pin the card to a different part of the paper—the equivalent of moving a shape on a page—the card's hole doesn't move with respect to the card. That is, the pin's local coordinates do not change. However, a new pinhole is formed on the paper, because the pin's parent coordinates have changed.

Using formulas to move a shape

When you move a shape on a page using the mouse, Visio updates the values of PinX and PinY to reflect the new position of the shape on the page. To use formulas to move a shape, you set the values of PinX and PinY. For example, to move the arrow in the following figure up the page by 1 inch, you might use this formula:

```
PinY = 1.5 in.
```

Or, you could tie the arrow's position on the page to the width of the page with a formula such as this one:

```
PinX = ThePage!PageWidth - 5 in.
```

By default, the pin is the center of the shape, which Visio expresses as formulas that use local coordinates (*Width*0.5*, *Height*0.5*). You can move a shape's pin in any of the following ways:

- Write new formulas in the LocPinX and LocPinY cells.
- Choose a **Pin Pos** option in the **Size & Position** window. To display this window for a selected shape, click **Size & Position Window** on the **View** menu, or right-click a shape, point to **View**, and then click **Size & Position Window** on the shortcut menu.
- Drag the pin with the **Rotation** tool in the drawing window.

If you move the pin by using the **Rotation** tool in the drawing window, the values of PinX and PinY also change so that the shape stays in the same position on the page.

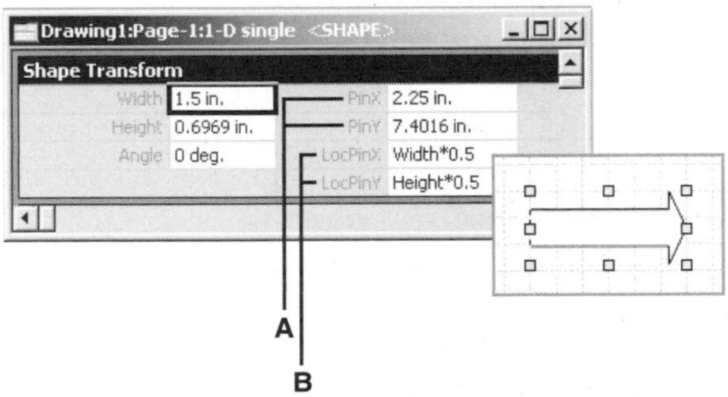

Figure 5-6 The Shape Transform section includes the local and parent coordinates of the pin. (**A**) The parent coordinates of the pin. (**B**) The local coordinates of the pin.

The values of the PinX and PinY cells correspond to the values shown in the **X** and **Y** options in the **Size & Position** window. You can change the values of PinX and PinY by changing values of **X** and **Y** in this window.

Preventing shape movement by protecting formulas

When a user moves or stretches a shape, Visio writes new values to the Shape Transform section and overwrites the affected cells' formulas, including those in the PinX and PinY cells. To protect a shape's formulas from being overwritten (thereby preventing a user from moving the shape), use the GUARD function.

For example, to guard the formulas shown in the previous section:

```
PinY = GUARD(1.5 in.)
PinX = GUARD(ThePage!PageWidth - 5 in.)
```

> **Tip** You can set the LockRotate, LockMoveX, and LockMoveY cells to prevent users from rotating or moving the shape and guard other formulas to protect shapes from other user actions. For details about protection locks and the GUARD function, see *Using Locks to Limit Shape Behavior* later in this chapter.

Controlling How Shapes Stretch and Shrink

You can use formulas to control the way a shape shrinks and grows in response to user actions in Microsoft Visio. Users generally resize a shape by moving its selection handles, but they might also edit a shape's vertices with the **Pencil** tool.

You can design a shape that uses different rules for stretching, depending on whether the user drags a width or a height handle. One such method is to use a *height-based* formula, so called because it preserves a shape's aspect ratio by defining its width in terms of its height. To do this for only part of a shape, you can place a height-based formula in the relevant cells in the Geometry section, depending on which part of the shape you want to control.

For details about using height-based formulas with a one-dimensional (1-D) shape, see Chapter 8, *Working with 1-D Shapes, Connectors, and Glue.*

Height-based Formulas: an Example

The following example, an arrow drawn with the **Line** tool, shows how to use formulas to control the way the arrow shrinks and grows. The default formulas that Visio generates for the arrow cause it to resize proportionately when stretched either horizontally or vertically.

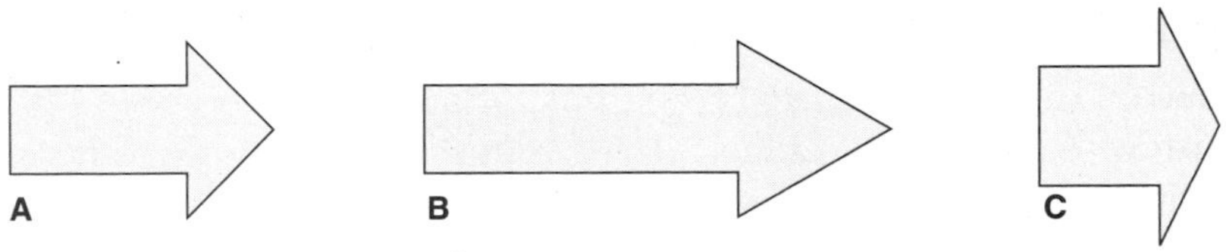

Figure 5-7 Resizing the original arrow changes the proportions of the shape. (**A**) Original arrow with default formulas. (**B**) Resized width. (**C**) Resized height.

With default formulas, arrows of different lengths have different-sized arrowheads, which looks inconsistent. If you were using the arrow in a drawing, you would probably prefer its tail to stretch and shrink horizontally, but the arrowhead to remain a constant size. However, if the shape is stretched vertically, you would probably prefer the arrowhead to resize proportionately.

Because the arrowhead's width is proportionate to its height, a height-based formula can describe the base of the arrowhead (the line connecting vertices 3, 4, 6, and 7 in the following figure) as a fraction of the shape's height.

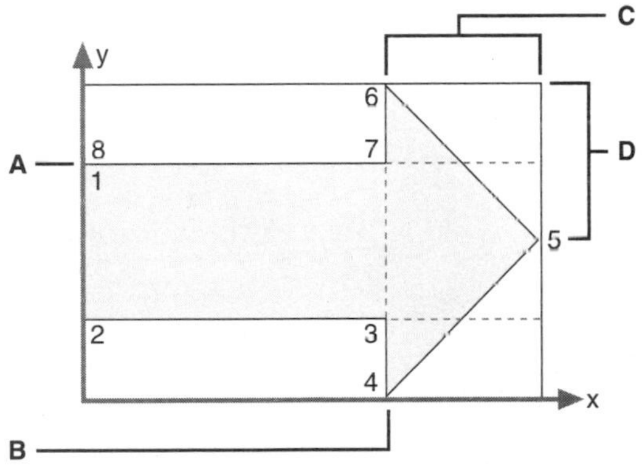

Figure 5-8 Each vertex corresponds to a row in the Geometry section. (**A**) All *y*-coordinates are by default multiples of Height. (**B**) All *x*-coordinates are by default multiples of Width. (**C**) Height * 0.5. (**D**) Height * 0.5

Vertex 5 falls exactly halfway between the top and bottom of the shape, so its *y*-position can be calculated as *Height * 0.5*. If the *x*-distance from vertex 5 to the base of the arrowhead is defined in terms of the height, the arrowhead will resize proportionately when the shape is stretched vertically, but it will not change when the shape is stretched horizontally.

The formula that produces this behavior keeps the base of the arrowhead equal to the width of the shape minus the distance from vertex 5 to the base, or:

```
= Width - Height * 0.5
```

The *x*-coordinate of each vertex along the base of the arrowhead (vertices 3, 4, 6, and 7) must be calculated using this formula. For efficiency, it's possible to place the formula only in the cell for vertex 3 and refer the other cells to this value. The *x*-coordinate of vertex 3 corresponds to the X3 cell of the Geometry1 section.

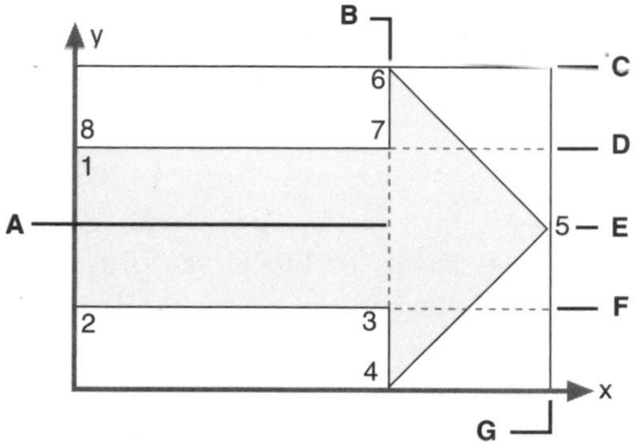

Figure 5-9 Vertices and formulas that describe the geometry of the arrow. (**A**) All points on the base of the arrowhead have the same *x*-coordinate: Width – Height * 0.5. (**B**) The base of the arrowhead is defined as a fraction of Height. (**C**) Height. (**D**) Height * 0.75. (**E**) Height * 0.5. (**F**) Height * 0.25. (**G**) Width.

The following illustration shows the resulting geometry of the proportionate arrow.

Drawing1.vsd:Page-1:Sheet.2 <SHAPE>

Geometry 1

	Geometry1.NoFill	FALSE	Geometry1.NoLine
	Name	**X**	**Y**
1	MoveTo	Width*0	Height*0.75
2	LineTo	Width*0	Height*0.25
3	LineTo	Width-Height*0.5	Height*0.25
4	LineTo	Geometry1.X3	Height*0
5	LineTo	Width*1	Height*0.5
6	LineTo	Geometry1.X3	Height*1
7	LineTo	Geometry1.X3	Height*0.75
8	LineTo	Geometry1.X1	Geometry1.Y1

Figure 5-10 Resulting geometry of the arrow.

Optimizing the Arrow Example

The height-based formulas in the previous topic, *Height-based Formulas: an Example*, produce the desired behavior, and work perfectly well. However, because the arrow is symmetrical, you can further refine its custom formulas by using cell references to reduce the number of calculations, making the shape easier to customize.

For example, the *Geometry1.Y1* and *Geometry1.Y7* cells both contain the same formula:

```
= Height * 0.75
```

This formula can also be expressed as:

```
= Height - Height * 0.25
```

The *Geometry1.Y2* cell already contains the formula *= Height * 0.25*, so you can simply refer to the cell for that part of the formula you want instead of repeating the entire formula. The formula in *Geometry1.Y1* and *Geometry1.Y7* therefore becomes:

```
= Height - Geometry1.Y2
```

Now the arrow requires only two custom formulas, *= Height * 0.5* and *= Height * 0.25*, to calculate its vertices. And you can alter the arrow's look by changing only one formula *(= Height * 0.25)*.

Controlling How Shapes Flip and Rotate

Will users flip and rotate your shapes? In some cases, you can design your shapes to accommodate these actions; in others, you might want to prevent them from doing so.

When you design a shape, you need to anticipate how the user will flip or rotate the shape and then design appropriate behavior. The Shape Transform section records a shape's orientation with respect to its parent. When a user flips or rotates a shape, its Shape Transform section reflects the actual transformation that occurs.

How Flipping Affects a Shape

When a shape is flipped, the value of its FlipX or FlipY cell changes to TRUE. The parent coordinates of the shape's origin change, but the location of the shape's pin doesn't change with respect to either its local or parent coordinates. In the following figure, the shape is rotated to show more clearly the interaction of the FlipX and FlipY cells.

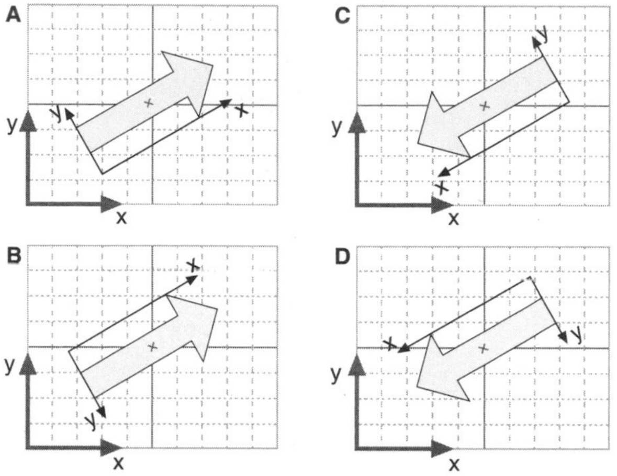

Figure 5-11 Local coordinates of a rotated shape as FlipX and FlipY values are changed. (**A**) FlipX = FALSE, FlipY = FALSE, Angle = 30 deg. (**B**) FlipX = FALSE, FlipY = TRUE, Angle = 30 deg. (**C**) FlipX = TRUE, FlipY = FALSE, Angle = 30 deg. (**D**) FlipX = TRUE, FlipY = TRUE, Angle = 30 deg.

If you are designing shapes that users can flip, you need to be aware of the different behaviors that result depending on the method that was used. To flip a shape, users can do the following:

- Click **Flip Vertical** or **Flip Horizontal** on the **Action** toolbar or **Shape** menu.
- Set the value of the FlipX or FlipY cell in the Shape Transform section.

Depending on which of the previous methods a user employs to flip a shape, two different shape transformations can result:

- When a user clicks **Flip Horizontal** on the **Action** toolbar or **Shape** menu, the shape appears to flip about a vertical line in the page coordinate system that passes through the shape's pin. The value of the FlipX cell is toggled between TRUE and FALSE. If the shape has been rotated, the value of the Angle cell becomes –*angle*, a different shape transformation, as the following figure shows.
- When a user edits the values of the FlipX cell in the Shape Transform section, setting the value of the FlipX cell to TRUE flips the shape horizontally by reversing the direction of the shape's local *x*-coordinate axis. The value of the Angle cell doesn't change.

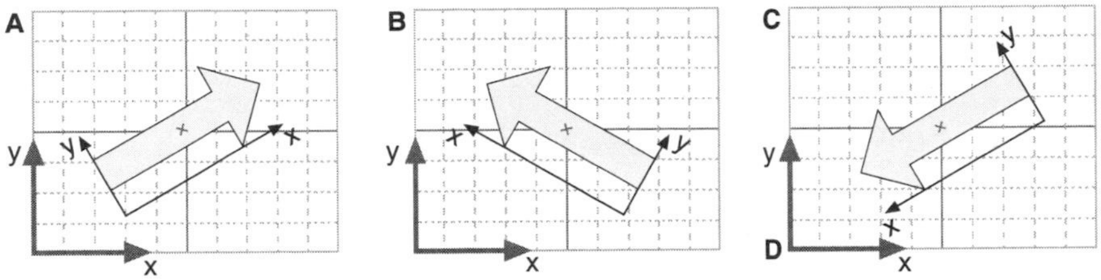

Figure 5-12 The **Flip Horizontal** command both flips and rotates the shape. (**A**) Original shape. (**B**) Effect of the Flip Horizontal command. (**C**) Effect of setting only FlipX = TRUE. (**D**) Page coordinate system.

Using **Flip Vertical** on the **Action** toolbar or **Shape** menu has the effect of toggling the value of the FlipY cell and changing the value of the Angle cell to *-angle*.

How Rotating Affects a Shape

To rotate a shape, a user can drag a shape handle with the **Rotation** tool or use the **Size & Position** window, which includes an editable **Angle** field (click **Size & Position Window** on the **View** menu). When a shape is rotated, the value in the shape's Angle cell describes the rotation of the shape's local coordinate system with respect to the parent coordinate system.

A shape rotates about its pin: The parent coordinates of a shape's origin change as the shape is rotated, but the location of the shape's pin does not change with respect to either its local or parent coordinates.

Note If page rotation is enabled, a user can rotate the views of a drawing page by dragging its corner with the **Rotation** tool. Although this causes existing shapes and guides to appear rotated as well, they are not—they maintain the same position and angle with respect to the origin of the page. Rotating a page doesn't affect the page's appearance when printed or the appearance of the rulers and grid in the drawing window.

To enable (or disable) page rotation in Microsoft Visio, click **Options** on the **Tools** menu, click the **General** tab, and select (or clear) **Enable page rotation**.

A page does not display a Shape Transform section in a ShapeSheet window, so you are unable to view or edit its Angle cell as you can for a shape. However, you can access it using Automation through the **PageSheet** property. For details about accessing formulas through Automation, see Chapter 17, *Automating Formulas*.

Designing Shapes that Flip and Rotate

If you expect users to flip and rotate your shape, you can design the shape to work at different angles and orientations. For example, you can change the way a shape flips or rotates by moving its local pin. In the following figure, when a user flips the transistor symbol vertically, the horizontal lead stays in position. When the shape is flipped horizontally, the vertical lead stays in position. This behavior makes the transistor flip appropriately in electrical schematics with cascaded transistors.

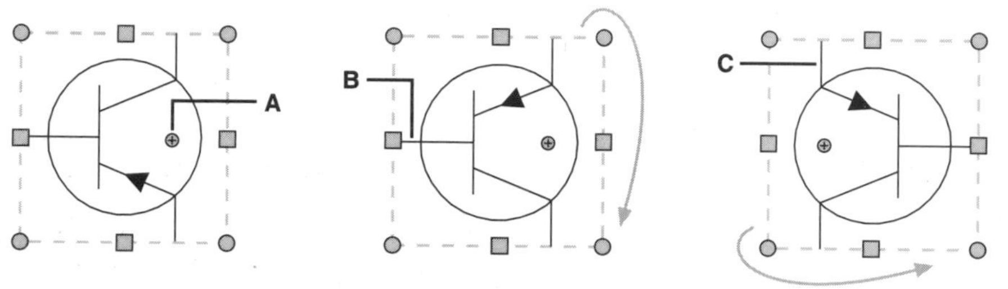

Figure 5-13 The transistor shape unflipped, flipped vertically, and then flipped horizontally. (**A**) The local pin is aligned with the vertical leads and with the horizontal leads. (**B**) The horizontal lead doesn't move. (**C**) The vertical lead doesn't move.

You can use the **Rotation** tool to drag the shape's pin to a new location. Doing this changes the values of PinX and PinY, but the LocPinX and LocPinY formulas also change to counteract the pin movement so that the shape doesn't jump on the page. You can also move the pin by changing only the formulas in the LocPinX and LocPinY cells. This changes the relationship between the local pin and the parent pin, so the shape also moves on the drawing page. For example, the transistor shape offsets the local pin with the following formulas:

```
LocPinX = Width * 0.75
LocPinY = Height * 0.5
```

Some shapes, such as the transistor shape shown in the following illustration, are commonly rotated by multiples of 90 degrees. If you design such a shape so that its alignment box coincides with the grid and its pin and any connection points lie on grid points, the shape will snap into alignment more quickly when a user flips or rotates it.

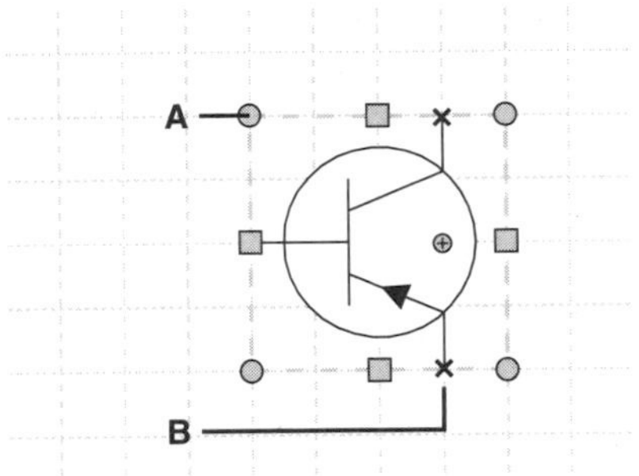

Figure 5-14 A transistor symbol designed to rotate in multiples of 90 degrees. (**A**) The alignment box is a multiple of the grid, and the pin is also on a grid point. (**B**) When the shape is rotated, the connection points always fall on grid lines.

For details about working with alignment boxes and the grid, see Chapter 11, *Arranging Shapes in Drawings*.

Preventing Shapes from Flipping and Rotating

You can prevent users from rotating a shape by guarding the formula in its Angle cell:

```
Angle = GUARD(0 deg.)
```

The shape can still be flipped, but users will not be able to use the **Rotation** tool or the **Rotate Left**, **Rotate Right**, or **Rotate Text** command on the **Shape** menu to rotate it unless they edit its Angle formula in a ShapeSheet window. This technique is easy but not ideal, because the shape still displays rotation handles when the **Rotation** tool is active, and the **Rotate Left**, **Rotate Right**, and **Rotate Text** commands are not dimmed on the menu—they simply don't do anything, which might confuse some users.

A better technique is to lock the shape against rotation by selecting **Rotation** in the **Protection** dialog box (on the **Format** menu, click **Protection**) or setting the LockRotate cell (in the Protection section) to a value other than zero. When the **Rotation** tool is active, padlocks appear on the shape's rotation handles, giving users a visual clue that is not provided when you guard the value of the Angle cell.

However, the lock doesn't prevent the shape from being flipped by means of the **Flip Vertical** and **Flip Horizontal** commands. To prevent a shape from being flipped, guard the formulas in its FlipX and FlipY cells:

```
FlipX = GUARD(FALSE)
FlipY = GUARD(FALSE)
```

There is no equivalent option in the **Protection** dialog box.

Controlling Curves in Shapes

When you want to create a shape with rounded corners, you can either apply a rounded corner style or create an arc, depending on how you want the shape to resize. The following figure shows the results of using these methods.

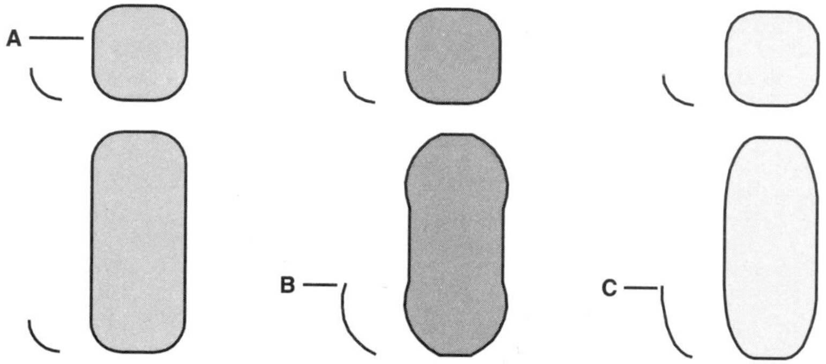

Figure 5-15 How shapes with different corners resize. (**A**) Rectangle with rounded corners stretches without affecting the curvature of its corners. (**B**) Circular arcs might distort the shape when it is resized. (**C**) Elliptical arcs resize smoothly with the shape, but the resulting corners might not be what you want.

If you draw a shape with the **Pencil**, **Line**, **Arc**, or **Rectangle** tool, you can connect the straight portions with an elliptical arc segment. As you stretch a shape, the beginning and ending vertices of a curve generally move in proportion to the stretching. Using arc segments for this purpose can give you more control over the shape, because arc segments don't depend on the line or corner style, and arcs can be controlled with formulas.

An elliptical arc can change its eccentricity to maintain smoothness. A circular arc tries to fit a circle between the beginning and ending vertices, which can result in a bulge or a sharp edge between a curve and a line. To prevent this distortion, you can control the bow of the arc with formulas. Creating a shape with rounded corners in this way ensures that the shape's corners span a set angle, so that the corners resize smoothly.

Using Rounded Corner Styles

When you use the **Corner Rounding** command on the **Format** menu, you are applying a rounded style to a line's corners. You can construct the shape with straight line segments, instead of a mixture of lines and arcs. The corner style does not change the shape's geometry, only the way it is drawn on the screen.

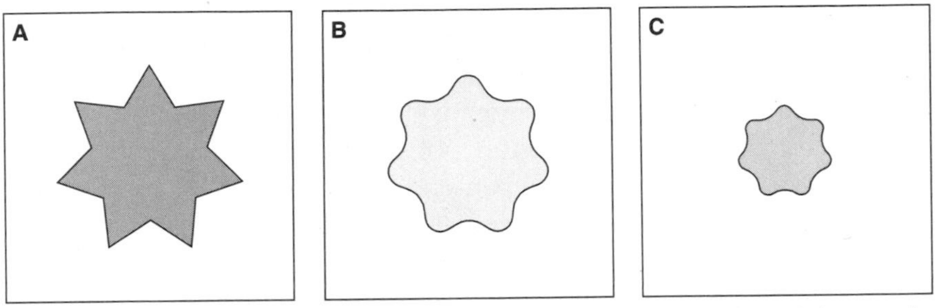

Figure 5-16 A polygon (**A**) formatted with rounded corners (**B**), and then resized (**C**).

Although a shape with a rounded corner style resizes as expected, applying a new line style that specifies different (or no) corner attributes can easily overwrite the rounded corner style. Therefore, you might want to protect the shape's formatting by setting its LockFormat cell to TRUE or guarding the formula in the Rounding cell of its Line Format section. For details about styles, see Chapter 10, *Managing Styles, Formats, and Colors.*

Understanding Arcs

A *circular arc* is a portion of a circle. An *elliptical arc* is a portion of an ellipse. An elliptical arc can appear to be circular, because a circle is simply a special case of an ellipse.

The arcs you draw with the **Arc** tool arc always a quarter of an ellipse, and those drawn with the **Pencil** tool are a portion of a circle. However, both are represented in a Geometry section as elliptical arcs, defined by EllipticalArcTo rows. To obtain a true circular arc, you must change its row type to ArcTo in its Geometry section.

Circular arcs

In a circular arc, the magnitude of the bow is the distance from the midpoint of the chord to the midpoint of the arc, as the following figure shows.

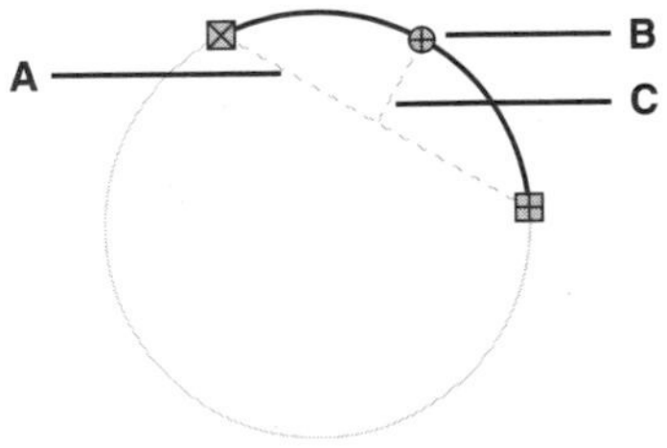

Figure 5-17 A circular arc. (**A**) Chord. (**B**) Control point. (**C**) Bow.

The bow's value is positive if the arc is drawn in the counterclockwise direction; otherwise, it is negative. A selected arc has a control point at the midpoint, which is always located along the perpendicular bisector of the chord. If you try to move the control point with the **Pencil** tool, the point moves freely, but it always snaps back to a position along the perpendicular bisector.

When you resize a circular arc, you change the radius of the circle of which the arc is a portion. The arc may flatten or bulge—appropriate resizing behavior for a circle, but perhaps not the expected behavior for your shapes. (To resize proportionately, you must use an elliptical arc as described later in this topic.)

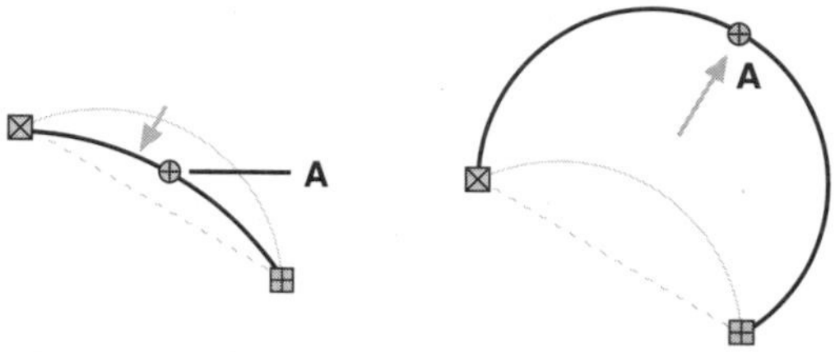

Figure 5-18 Resizing a circular arc. (**A**) Dragging the control point changes the bow value of the arc.

By default, all arcs created with the Microsoft Visio drawing tools are elliptical arcs. To create a circular arc, you must change the row type in its Geometry section.

To create a circular arc

1. Select an arc shape on the page. On the **Window** menu, click **Show ShapeSheet**.
2. In the Geometry section, select the LineTo or EllipticalArcTo row that you want to convert to a circular arc.
3. On the **Edit** menu, click **Change Row Type**.
4. Click **ArcTo**, and then click **OK**.

The following table shows what the cells of an ArcTo row represent.

Circular arc representation in the Geometry section

Row	Cell	Value
The row that precedes ArcTo row	X	The *x*-coordinate of the begin point of the arcthe
	Y	The *y*-coordinate of the begin point of the arc
ArcTo	X	The *x*-coordinate of the end point of the arc
	Y	The *y*-coordinate of the end point of the arc
	A	Size of the arc's bow

Elliptical arcs

When stretched, an elliptical arc's eccentricity changes in proportion to the stretching, so the arc maintains a smooth curve. *Eccentricity* controls how asymmetrical (lopsided) the arc appears.

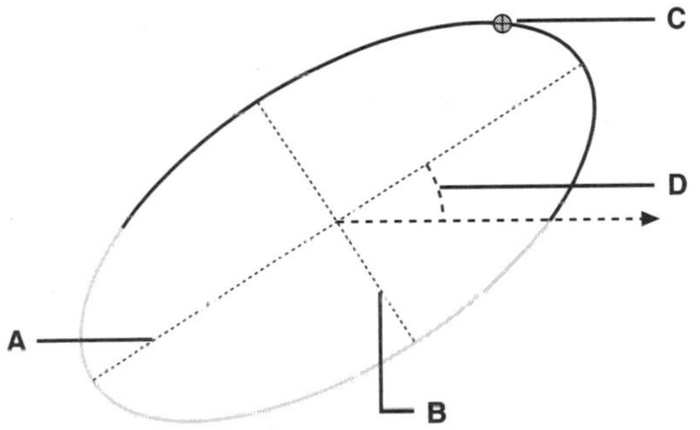

Figure 5-19 An elliptical arc. (**A**) Major axis. (**B**) Minor axis. (**C**) Control point. (**D**) Angle.

The eccentricity of an arc is the result of dividing its major axis by its minor axis.

In most cases, you'll probably want to use an elliptical arc in your shapes rather than a circular arc, because a circular arc's resizing behavior is constrained by the fact that it must remain circular.

Note In versions of Visio earlier than 2000, an ellipse was represented by two EllipticalArcTo rows. Beginning with Visio 2000, an ellipse is represented by a single Ellipse row.

For details on EllipticalArcTo and Ellipse rows, see the ShapeSheet Reference in the Microsoft Visio Developer Reference (on the **Help** menu, click **Developer Reference**).

To create an elliptical arc, do one of the following

- Draw an arc using the **Pencil** or **Arc** tool.
- In its Geometry section, change the row type of the LineTo or an ArcTo row that you want to convert to an elliptical arc to an EllipticalArcTo row.
- On the drawing page, use the **Pencil** tool to drag the control point of a straight line. This transforms the line into an elliptical arc.

An elliptical arc's geometry is described in an EllipticalArcTo row, as the following table shows.

Elliptical arc representation in the Geometry section

Row	Cell	Value
The row that precedes EllipticalArcTo	X	The *x*-coordinate of the begin point of the arc
	Y	The *y*-coordinate of the begin point of the arc
EllipticalArcTo	X	The *x*-position of the end point of the arc
	Y	The *y*-position of the end point of the arc
	A	The *x*-position of the control point of the arc
	B	The *y*-position of the control point of the arc
	C	Angle of the arc
	D	Eccentricity of the arc

You can move the control point of an elliptical arc to change the arc's eccentricity. An eccentricity of 1 represents a circular arc, and a value greater or less than 1 represents an arc with more or less eccentricity. For example, in an ellipse that is 2 inches wide and 1 inch tall, each elliptical arc has an eccentricity of 2. In an ellipse that is 1 inch wide and 2 inches tall, each elliptical arc has an eccentricity of $^1/_2$.

To change an elliptical arc's eccentricity

- Select the **Pencil** tool, and then press CTRL as you drag the control point to display the eccentricity handles, which you can stretch and rotate.

When you move an arc's eccentricity handles, Visio generates formulas in the C and D cells of the EllipticalArcTo row; these formulas record the current orientation and shape of the elliptical arc. If a shape with elliptical arcs is stretched, Visio changes the eccentricity and angle of the arcs, if necessary, so that the arcs resize consistently with the rest of the shape.

Converting Line and Arc Segments

You can convert a line or elliptical arc to a circular arc segment by changing the type of the corresponding row in the Geometry section. You can also change line and arc segments using various drawing tools.

To change a line or elliptical arc to a circular arc in the ShapeSheet window

- Right-click the LineTo or EllipticalArcTo row in the Geometry section that represents the segment you want to change. On the shortcut menu, click **Change Row Type**, and then click **ArcTo**. Or, select the row, click **Change Row Type** on the **Edit** menu, and then click **ArcTo**.

To change a line to an elliptical arc on the drawing page

- Select the **Pencil** tool, point to the line segment's control point, and then drag to form an arc.

To change either an elliptical or circular arc to a straight line on the drawing page

- Select the **Pencil** tool, point to the arc's control point, and then drag until it "snaps" into a straight line.

> **Note** Changing the row type can alter a shape's width-height box and overwrite proportional or height-based formulas. For this reason, you might want to set LockCalcWH to TRUE in the Protection section before changing a row type.

Useful Arc Formulas

You can control the resizing behavior of circular arcs using formulas that calculate the arc's bow and radius.

Calculate the bow from the radius and angle

If you know the radius of an arc and the angle that an ArcTo will subtend, you can calculate the bow with the following general equation:

```
|Bow| = radius * (1 - COS(angle/2))
```

If the bow is zero, the arc is a straight line. You can use this equation for any shape, open or closed, to create rounded corners that span a set angle, as shown in the following figure. The advantage of using circular arcs is that the corners resize smoothly. For example, if you know that the radius is 2 inches and the angle is 45 degrees, in an ArcTo row of the Geometry section, you would enter the following formula:

```
Geometryn.An = 2 in. * (1 - COS(45 deg. /2))
```

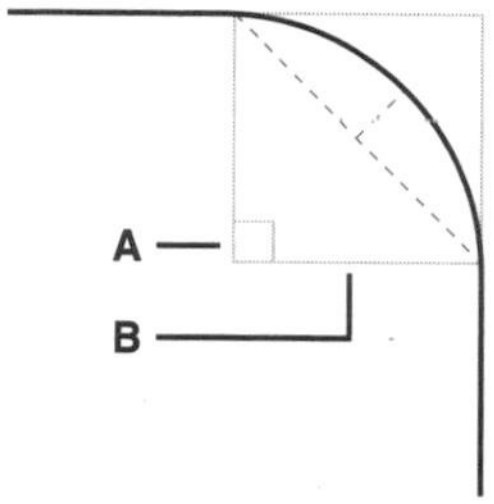

Figure 5-20 Using a circular arc segment for a rounded corner. (**A**) 90° angle. (**B**) Radius.

In a shape such as a rectangle where the value of *angle* won't change (it's always 90 degrees), you can reduce part of the formula to a constant. If *angle* is always 90 degrees, *(1–COS(angle/2)) = 0.2929*. So you can enter the formula as follows:

```
Geometryn.An = radius * 0.2929
```

Using this constant might speed up processing, but it limits flexibility if you later decide that the angle won't always be 90 degrees. For details about creating rounded corners, see *Using Rounded Corner Styles* earlier in this section.

Calculate the radius from the bow

If you know the bow of an arc, you can calculate its radius. To do this, find the magnitude of the chord—the distance between the arc's begin point and end point. In the following formula, X1, Y1 represent the arc's begin point, and X2, Y2 represent the arc's end point. The length of the chord, then, is:

```
Chord length = SQRT( (Y2 - Y1) ^2 + (X2 - X1)^2 )
```

And the radius is:

```
Radius = (4 * Bow ^2 + Chord ^2) / (8 * Bow)
```

Optimizing Shape Geometry

Shapes with simple geometry perform better than shapes with complex geometry. A shape with fewer rows in its Geometry section will render faster than a shape with many, and a shape with a single Geometry section will render faster than a shape with multiple Geometry sections. If you don't need to control a shape's vertices with formulas, consider simplifying its geometry. Here are some suggestions:

- As an alternative to creating a shape with multiple paths, skip segments in a single path by converting LineTo rows into MoveTo rows. A shape's Geometry section always starts with a MoveTo row, but after the first segment, it can have as many additional MoveTo rows as needed.
- Condense many line segments into a single PolyLineTo row. The X and Y cells of such a row define the *x,y* coordinates of the end point; however, a single POLYLINE formula in the row's A cell defines all of the vertices between the begin point (the X and Y cells in a prior row) and end point of the shape.

Any shape with more than three or four segments might perform better as a PolyLineTo row. However, it's easier to "read" a shape's geometry as a series of LineTo rows in a Geometry section rather than a series of arguments in a function. You can convert a PolyLineTo row into LineTo rows by right-clicking the row in the Geometry section and clicking **Expand Row**.

A POLYLINE formula can contain cell references or expressions. However, as soon as a user edits the shape with the **Pencil** tool, Microsoft Visio regenerates the formula, substituting constants for cell references and expressions. To prevent this, lock the shape against editing.

Visio creates PolyLineTo rows automatically when importing DWG files. For more information about PolyLineTo rows and POLYLINE formulas, see the Microsoft Visio Developer Reference (on the **Help** menu, click **Developer Reference**).

> **Note** Beginning with Visio 2000, the **Freeform** tool creates a *nonuniform rational B-spline*, or NURBS, represented by a NURBSTo row in the ShapeSheet. (A spline is a freeform curve that is based on a polynomial equation.) In versions of Visio earlier than Visio 2000, the **Freeform** tool created splines. Visio 2000 and later versions support spline row types (SplineStart and SplineKnot) for backward compatibility.

Using Locks to Limit Shape Behavior

Most actions in the drawing page change a shape's formulas and so can affect the specialized behavior and custom formulas you have designed for the shape. You can set constraints on shape behavior, called *locks*, that prevent particular actions on the drawing page.

For example, consider a grand piano. Pianos come in different sizes, but they are built only one way—the shorter strings are always to the right as you face the keyboard. To protect this characteristic, you would lock a grand piano shape against horizontal flipping. A user could still rotate the piano shape—as you could if you were pushing a real piano around the room—but not flip it.

One of the simplest ways to protect your shapes is to set the lock cells in the Protection section of the ShapeSheet window. Some cells in the Protection section correspond to options in the **Protection** dialog box (on the **Format** menu, click **Protection**); others can be set only in a ShapeSheet window. For details about Protection cells, see the Microsoft Visio Developer Reference (on the **Help** menu, click **Developer Reference**).

Setting locks prevents accidental changes to a shape. For example, if your shapes represent items with standard dimensions, such as building materials, you can lock their resizing handles, because users shouldn't be able to stretch the shapes in all directions. Setting some locks causes a padlock symbol to appear in place of some or all selection handles on the shape, indicating that the feature cannot be changed.

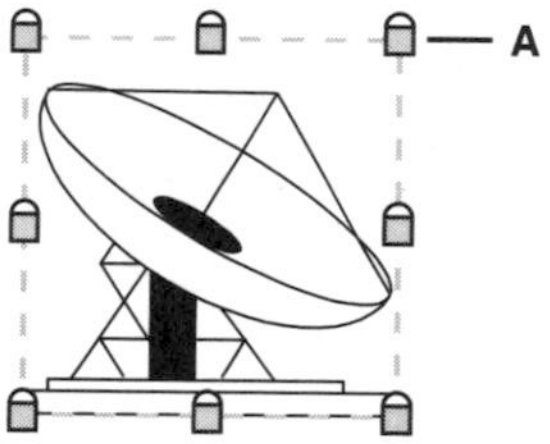

Figure 5-21 Setting protection locks gives the user visual feedback. Padlocks (**A**) indicate that you cannot resize the shape.

To lock a feature, set the appropriate cell in the Protection section to a nonzero number. To unlock a feature, enter *0* in the cell.

Setting locks doesn't affect the menu commands that are enabled and doesn't protect other formulas from change. For example, if you lock the width and height of a shape that is in a group, and then scale the group, the width and height of the shape can change. Locking prevents the user only from scaling the shape with the mouse. For more information about controlling what users can do with groups, see Chapter 6, *Grouping and Merging Shapes*.

> **Note** You can also use the GUARD function in your custom formulas to prevent them from being overwritten by user or Visio actions. The GUARD function and protection locks protect your shapes in complementary ways. The GUARD function prevents formulas from changing, but it allows user actions. By contrast, setting locks in the Protection section prevents user actions without protecting cell formulas.
>
> For example, if you set a shape's Width formula to *= GUARD(5 pica)*, users can drag the shape's side selection handles to stretch the shape, but the shape snaps back to its original width as soon as Visio reevaluates its Width formula. However, if you set the LockWidth cell to TRUE (1), users cannot drag the side selection handles in the first place.

For details about GUARD, see *Designing Visio Formulas* in Chapter 4, *Visio Formulas*. Also see the ShapeSheet Reference in the Microsoft Visio Developer Reference (on the **Help** menu, click **Developer Reference**).

6

Grouping and Merging Shapes

Groups versus Merged Shapes 120

Creating and Controlling Groups 121

Controlling the Behavior of Groups 123

Protecting the Formatting of Shapes in Groups 131

Creating and Controlling Merged Shapes 131

You can group or merge component shapes to create shapes with complex geometry or to control the behavior of multiple shapes. The method you choose affects how you can work with the shapes that result, and might also affect performance.

This chapter describes the key differences between grouped and merged shapes, how to create groups, how to create merged shapes, and how to control the behavior of merged shapes and groups using ShapeSheet formulas.

Groups versus Merged Shapes

Grouped and merged shapes behave differently. How you want the completed shape to behave should determine whether you group or merge the shapes from which it is created.

When to use groups

- To create a complex shape that contains more than one text block or that has multiple styles or formats applied to it.
- To maintain user-defined formulas for the component shapes.
- To allow users to subselect and modify shapes within a complex shape.

When to use merged shapes

- To create a shape with transparent holes in its fill.
- To combine component shapes into a single shape that cannot be unmerged by the user.
- To create a shape that responds more quickly to user actions than a group.
- To create a shape with Geometry sections that can be conditionally hidden or shown.

Characteristics of groups

- A group can be ungrouped to recover the individual shapes.
- A group allows several shapes to move and size together, yet retain their individual formatting attributes, including user-defined formulas.
- Different styles and text formats can be applied to the shapes that make up the group.
- Component shapes in a group can be subselected and directly moved or resized.
- Each component shape retains its own ShapeSheet spreadsheet, *plus* the group has its own ShapeSheet spreadsheet.

Characteristics of merged shapes

- A merged shape is represented by a single ShapeSheet spreadsheet that contains multiple Geometry sections.
- A merged shape overwrites user-defined formulas of the component shapes.
- A merged shape is limited to a single text block, and a single set of formatting attributes.
- A merged shape can have "holes" in its fill.

Creating and Controlling Groups

You should create a group when you want several shapes to move and size together, yet retain their individual formatting attributes or multiple text blocks. When you group items, a new ShapeSheet spreadsheet is created for the group, each member of the group maintains its own ShapeSheet spreadsheet, and the group becomes the parent coordinate system for each original item. Additionally, formulas for shapes included in the group, such as 1-D Endpoint or Shape Transform values, are modified to refer to the group rather than the page.

Figure 6-1 Groups can contain shapes with different formatting attributes.

Grouping and Ungrouping Shapes

It's a good idea to group shapes before adding connection points or defining custom formulas because these elements generally must reference the group to work properly.

- To create a group, select shapes for the group. On the **Shape** menu, point to **Grouping**, and then click **Group** to combine the selected shapes or other groups into a new Microsoft Visio shape with components that can still be edited and formatted individually.
- To ungroup a group, select the group. On the **Shape** menu, point to **Grouping**, and then click **Ungroup.**

Modifying a Group

Users can add shapes to a group or remove shapes from a group. Depending on the solution you're developing, the ability to modify a group might be desirable, or it might cause your shapes to work in unexpected or undesirable ways. You can prevent a group from being modified by setting the LockGroup cell in the Protection section of the group's ShapeSheet spreadsheet to TRUE.

You or your solution users can automatically add shapes to unlocked groups in the following two ways:

- Drag a shape that is designated to be added to a group on drop, and drop it onto a group that is designated to accept dropped shapes.

  To designate a group to accept dropped shapes, select **Accept dropped shapes** under **Group behavior** in the **Behavior** dialog box (with the group selected, click **Behavior** on the **Format** menu). Or enter TRUE in the IsDropTarget cell in the Group Properties section of the group's ShapeSheet spreadsheet.

  To designate a shape to be added to a group on drop, select **Add shape to groups on drop** under **Miscellaneous** in the **Behavior** dialog box. Or enter TRUE in the IsDropSource cell in the Miscellaneous section of the shape's ShapeSheet spreadsheet.

- Select both the group and shape(s) to be added to the group. On the **Shape** menu, point to **Grouping**, and then click **Add to Group**.

You or your solution users can remove a shape from a group in one of two ways:

- Subselect a shape in a group. On the **Shape** menu, point to **Grouping**, and then click **Remove from Group**. The shape remains, but it is no longer a member of the group.
- Subselect a shape in a group, and then press DELETE.

How Grouping Shapes Affects Their Formulas

When you add a shape to a group, its parent coordinate system switches from the page's coordinates to those of the group. When you ungroup shapes or remove the last shape from a group, the group is no longer the parent, and the group ShapeSheet spreadsheet is deleted. Formulas that refer to parent coordinates change when you group or ungroup the shape, and custom formulas that you define for a shape can be overwritten.

The following table shows the cells that are reset with new formulas when you group or ungroup shapes.

How formulas change when a shape is grouped or ungrouped

Section	Cell	What happens
Shape Transform	Width, Height	After grouping, formulas reference the group to define the shape's size in proportion to the group's size. After ungrouping, formulas reference the width and height of the new parent or are constant if the new parent is a page. Formulas protected with the GUARD function are not affected.
Shape Transform	PinX, PinY	Formulas base the pin coordinates on the group's or new parent's coordinate system. After grouping, formulas define the pin's location in proportion to the group width and height.
1-D Endpoints	BeginX, BeginY, EndX, EndY	Formulas base the coordinates of the begin and end points on the parent's coordinate system. After grouping, formulas define the endpoints' position in proportion to the group width and height.
Alignment	[all cells]	After grouping, formulas base the position of the alignment guide on the group's or new parent's coordinates.

When you group shapes that are connected to other shapes, the connections are maintained, unless a shape is connected to a guide that has—or as a result of the grouping will have—a different parent. If a shape is glued to a guide and you add the shape but not the guide to a group, the shape's connection to the guide is broken. The reverse is also true: If you add a guide to a group, but don't also add shapes that are glued to that guide, the shapes' connections to that guide are broken. If you include both the guide and the shapes that are glued to it, the Visio engine maintains the connections.

Controlling the Behavior of Groups

If you're designing shapes for a custom solution, you can precisely control numerous aspects of a group's behavior. For example, you might want to prevent users from subselecting items in a group, or you might want to prevent shapes contained in a group from being resized.

When you work with formulas in grouped shapes, you can use local coordinates, parent coordinates, or page coordinates, as the following illustration shows. Defining different resize behavior for a grouped shape can involve converting coordinates from one system to another.

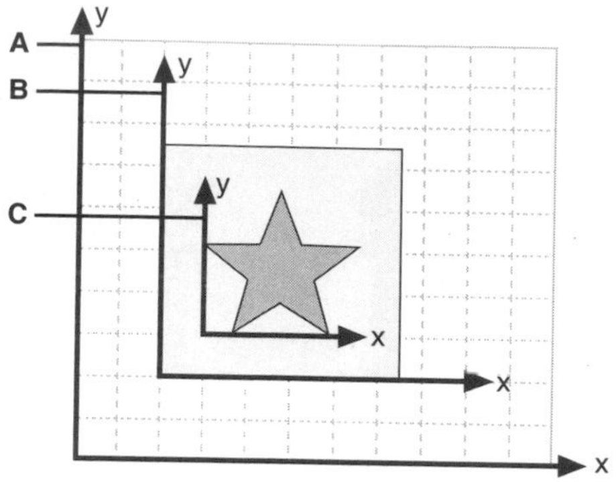

Figure 6-2 A shape in a group in the Visio coordinate system. (**A**) Page coordinates. (**B**) Parent coordinates. (**C**) Local coordinates.

Controlling How Groups are Selected

Microsoft Visio supports three types of behavior for selecting groups:

- Group selection only (group members cannot be selected)
- Group selection first (second click selects group member)
- Group member first (second click selects entire group)

In addition, you can prevent the immediate children of a group from being moved by setting the DontMoveChildren cell in the Group Properties section to TRUE. You can determine the selection behavior of the grouped shapes you create by modifying the SelectMode cell in the Group Properties section of the group's sheet. When groups are nested, the group selection behavior of the currently selected group is respected.

Settings for the SelectMode cell (Group Properties section)

Value	Description
0	Click selects the group only. Subsequent click deselects the group. Corresponds to **Group only** in the **Selection** list in the **Behavior** dialog box.
1	Click selects the group first. Subsequent clicks select group members. To reselect the group, you must first deselect it. (This is the default.) Corresponds to **Group first** in the **Selection** list in the **Behavior** dialog box.
2	Click selects a group member first. Subsequent click selects the group. If the group contains stacked component shapes, subsequent clicks select the next shape in the stacking order, and then the group. Corresponds to **Members first** in the **Selection** list in the **Behavior** dialog box.

> **Note** Clicking in quick succession can be interpreted as a double-click and might open the group's text box rather than select the next shape in the selection order. To prevent this, pause briefly between clicks.

Defining the Resizing Behavior of Grouped Shapes

When you are defining the resizing behavior of a group, you need to consider how the size and position of the group members should change within the group. As a group is resized, its component shapes are typically stretched and repositioned to maintain their proportions in the group coordinate system. However, some shapes represent objects with fixed physical dimensions. When the group changes size, you can define these shapes to change position, but not change their size or proportions. In some cases, that will mean when a group is resized, some component shapes will be resized and others will not. The ResizeMode cells in the Shape Transform sections for member shapes control their resizing behavior.

For example, in the following figure, the kitchen island group contains a countertop, range, and sink. The range and sink represent physical objects of industry-standard size that should not resize with the island. A countertop, however, can be constructed to any size and should resize with the island.

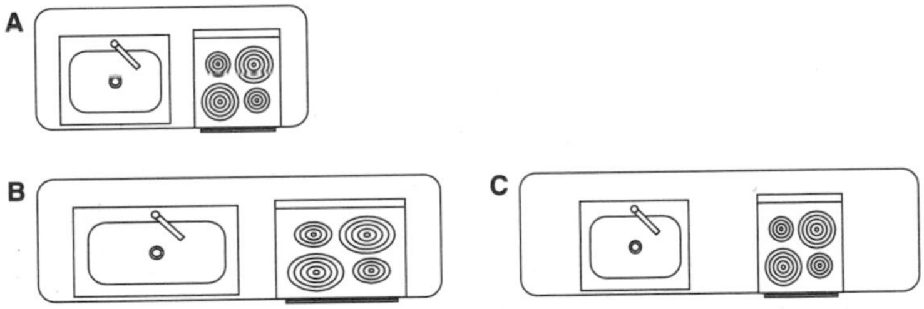

Figure 6-3 Resizing shapes in a group. (**A**) Original group. (**B**) By default, component shapes resize when the group is resized. For shapes with fixed dimensions such as the sink and range, this results in undesirable behavior. (**C**) To reposition the sink and stove rather than resize them, enter the value 1 in the ResizeMode cell in the sheets for those shapes.

You can control a component shape's or group's resizing behavior with its ResizeMode cell (Shape Transform section). To control how a component shape behaves when the group that contains it is resized, set the value of the ResizeMode cell for the component shape. To control how a group is resized when it is nested within another group, set the value of the ResizeMode cell for the group. Using the preceding example, you would set ResizeMode to 1 for the sink, and then group the sink with the countertop. The following table shows the resizing options you can use.

Settings for the ResizeMode cell (Shape Transform section)

Value	Description
0	Shape resizes according to the group's ResizeMode setting. Corresponds to **Use group's setting** under **Resize** behavior in the **Behavior** dialog box. (This is the default.)
1	Shape keeps its size when the group is stretched; only its location within the group changes. Corresponds to **Reposition only** under **Resize** behavior in the **Behavior** dialog box.
2	Shape resizes proportionally when the group is stretched. Corresponds to **Scale with group** under **Resize behavior** in the **Behavior** dialog box.

When you set a different resizing behavior, do it for the highest-level shape possible—for example, set the resize behavior for the stove rather than each burner. To keep users from accidentally resizing a shape in a group, either by resizing the group or by subselecting the shape and resizing it individually, set the ResizeMode cell to 1, and also set the LockWidth and LockHeight cells to 1 in the Protection section of the ShapeSheet. If you set locks for a shape's width, height, or aspect ratio and then add the shape to a group, the shape's resizing behavior takes precedence over any locks you've specified for the group.

Resizing Shapes in Only One Direction

When you want to control how shapes in a group resize, you can customize the component shapes' resizing behavior with formulas. For example, the three-dimensional (3-D) box shape in the following figure is a group made up of three shapes: one for the face of the box, one for the top, and one for the side, each of which resizes differently. When you resize the face, it stretches proportionately in width and height, but the top stretches only in width, and the side stretches only in height. This way, the shape maintains its 3-D look as it is stretched.

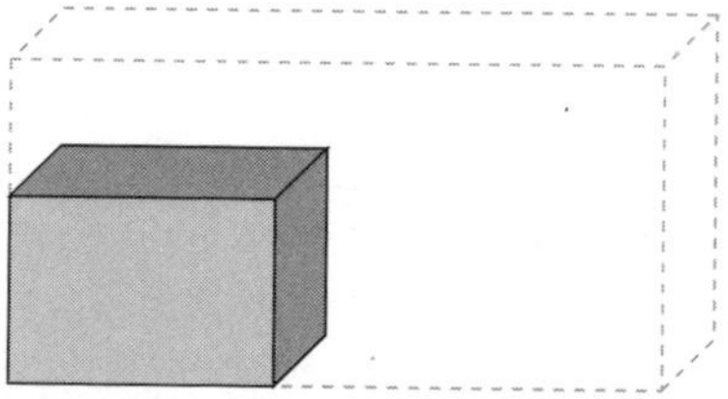

Figure 6-4 The top and side of the 3-D box stretch in only one direction when the box is resized.

You use two key techniques to get this kind of resizing behavior in a group:

- Define the dimension of the component shape that doesn't resize as a constant value and the dimension of the shape that does resize in terms of the corresponding group dimension.
- Move the pin of the component shape to the origin in its local coordinate system (the lower-left corner of the local *x*- and *y*-axis). Then define the shape's parent pin in terms of the group's width or height, so that the location of the component shape is always fixed with respect to the group. Otherwise, the component shape moves with respect to the parent coordinate system when the group is resized.

In the 3-D box shape, the top's height and the side's width are both constant values, because they shouldn't resize when the group is resized. The top's width is defined in terms of the group width, so the top can resize in the direction of width. Similarly, the side's height is defined in terms of the group height, so the side resizes in the direction of height.

The face shape defines the alignment box for the group, because its size and position determine the size and position of the top and side. The parent pin defines each component shape's position at the appropriate edge of the group alignment box. For the top, the *x*-coordinate of the parent pin is 0 in., and its *y*-coordinate is the same as the group's height. For the side, the *x*-coordinate of the parent pin is equal to the group's width, and its *y*-coordinate is 0 in.

It's easiest to see the relationship between the component shapes' width and height and the group's width and height if you draw the shape without angled vertices, as shown in the following figure.

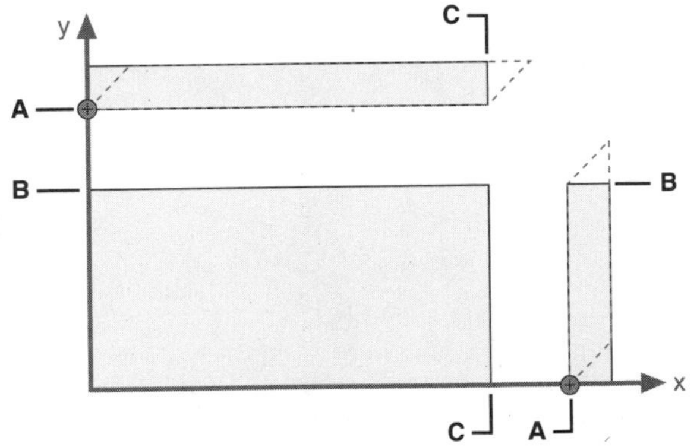

Figure 6-5 Exploded view of the 3-D box shape. (**A**) Pin. (**B**) <group sheet id>!Height. (**C**) <group sheet id>!Width.

Creating a 3-D Box: an Example

Using the techniques described in the previous topic, you can create a shape with resizing behavior similar to the three-dimensional (3-D) box. One shape defines the alignment box for the group, and the component shapes are fixed in position with relation to the alignment box. In addition, the component shapes resize in only one direction as the group is resized.

To draw the actual 3-D box group, do the following:

- Define the group's custom alignment box by drawing the face of the 3-D box first, grouping it, and then locking the alignment box.
- Roughly draw the top and side shapes as simple rectangles, and then add them to the group.
- Modify the vertices of the top and side to give them a 3-D look.
- Customize the formulas in the Width cell, Height cell, and PinX and PinY cells of the top and side shapes to control their resizing behavior.

As the following figure shows, vertex 2 of the top and vertex 3 of the side are skewed. The *y*-position of the top's vertex 2 is equal to that shape's height. The *x*-position of the side's vertex 3 is equal to that shape's width. Top height and side widths are a constant value, 0.125 in. By adding this constant to the appropriate vertex formulas, the shapes are skewed.

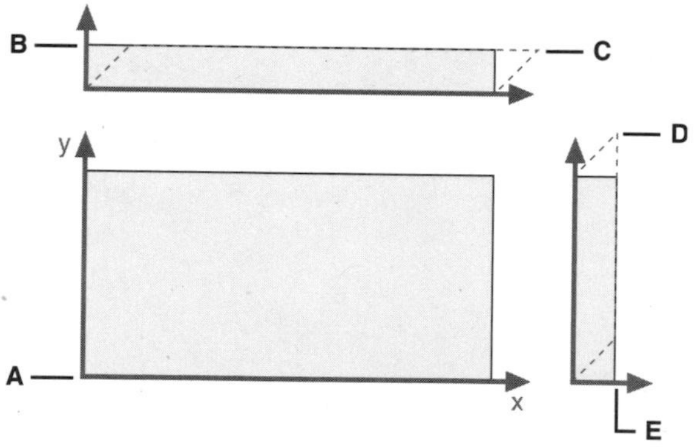

Figure 6-6 Local coordinates for the component shapes of the 3-D box. (**A**) Local coordinates of the group. (**B**) Height = 0.125 in. (**C**) Width + 0.125 in. (**D**) Height + 0.125 in. (**E**) Width = 0.125 in.

To draw the 3-D box as a group

1. Use the **Rectangle** tool to draw rectangular boxes representing the face, top, and side in approximately the right position. Don't worry about making the top and side look 3-D for now.
2. Select just the face, and group it.
3. Select the group. On the **Window** menu, click **Show ShapeSheet**, and then set the formula for the LockCalcWH cell (Protection section) to 1.

   This preserves the face's alignment box. Otherwise, the group alignment box will grow when you add the top and side shapes.
4. With the group still selected, on the **Edit** menu, click **Open Group** to open the group window. Then select the top and the side shapes on the drawing page and drag them into the group window to add them to the group. Close the group window.
5. Right-click in the group's ShapeSheet window. On the shortcut menu, click **Insert Section**, and then click **Scratch** to add a Scratch section. In the Scratch section, enter the following formulas:

   ```
   Scratch.X1    = .5 in.
   Scratch.Y1    = .5 in.
   ```

   Scratch.X1 sets a constant that determines the width of the side. Scratch.Y1 sets a constant that determines the depth of the top.
6. Set the top and side shapes to reference the constants you defined in the group's ShapeSheet window.

   To do this, in the drawing window, select the top shape. On the **Window** menu, click **Show ShapeSheet**, and add a Scratch section (as described in step 5). Do the same for the side shape. In the top's and side's Scratch sections, enter these formulas:

   ```
   Scratch.X1    = <group sheet id>!Scratch.X1
   Scratch.Y1    = <group sheet id>!Scratch.Y1
   ```

   You must supply the group's ID in these formulas. For example, if the group's ID is Sheet.4, the formula for the X1 cell would be *Sheet.4!Scratch.X1*.
7. Define the skew for the vertices in the top and side shapes.

   To do this, you customize formulas in the Geometry section, as the following tables show.

Custom formulas in the Geometry section for the top

Row (Name)	X	Y
1 (MoveTo)	= 0 in.	= 0 in.
2 (LineTo)	= Scratch.X1	= Height
3 (LineTo)	= Width + Scratch.X1	= Height
4 (LineTo)	= Width	= 0 in.
5 (LineTo)	= Geometry1.X1	= Geometry1.Y1

Custom formulas in the Geometry section for the side

Row (Name)	X	Y
1 (MoveTo)	= 0 in.	= 0 in.
2 (LineTo)	= 0 in.	= Height
3 (LineTo)	= Width	= Height + Scratch.Y1
4 (LineTo)	= Width	= Scratch.Y1
5 (LineTo)	= Geometry1.X1	= Geometry1.Y1

8. Define the resizing behavior for the top and side shapes.

To do this, you customize the Width, Height, and Pin formulas in the Shape Transform section. For the top, use the following formulas:

```
Width       = <group sheet id>!Width
Height      = Scratch.Y1
PinX        = 0 in.
PinY        = <group sheet id>!Height
LocPinX     = GUARD(0 in.)
LocPinY     = GUARD(0 in.)
```

In the Shape Transform section for the side, use the following formulas:

```
Width       = Scratch.X1
Height      = <group sheet id>!Height
PinX        = <group sheet id>!Width
PinY        = GUARD(0 in.)
LocPinX     = GUARD(0 in.)
LocPinY     = 0 in.
```

9. Prevent users from selecting the component shapes by entering 0 (group only) in the SelectMode cell (Group Properties section) of the group's sheet.

Protecting the Formatting of Shapes in Groups

When you apply local formatting to a group by clicking a command on the **Format** menu, you also apply the format to all of the shapes in the group. The formatting applied to the group can overwrite any local formatting of the shapes within the group; if you've used formulas to change the formatting of the component shapes, those formulas are also overwritten. To avoid this effect, you can do the following:

- Protect specific formatting cells with the GUARD function.
- Lock a group against formatting changes.
- Selectively prohibit application of styles to some or all of the shapes in the group master.

To protect specific formulas from changing when a user locally formats a shape, use the GUARD function.

You can lock a group against formatting with the LockFormat cell in the Protection section of the group's sheet. This lock prevents a user from applying a style or local format to the group. When a user tries to do so, a message appears indicating that the action isn't allowed.

When you lock a group against formatting, the shapes in the group can still be subselected and individually formatted unless you set the LockFormat cell for individual shapes in the group. You can also selectively lock against formatting in a group when you want to allow users to format some shapes but not others.

Creating and Controlling Merged Shapes

A merged shape has all the standard ShapeSheet sections for a single shape, but instead of a single Geometry section, the merged shape contains a Geometry section for each separate path (a sequence of line or curve segments that connect a shape's vertices). Because you can work with a single ShapeSheet spreadsheet, setting attributes for a merged shape with multiple geometries is far more efficient than working with shapes that have been grouped, where each shape in a group has its own ShapeSheet spreadsheet.

When a shape has multiple Geometry sections, you can hide and show individual sections conditionally. For example, you might hide a path when another path in the shape is unfilled, and make it visible when the path is filled. A merged shape has only one text block and one set of formatting attributes, as the following figure shows. If you're merging multiple shapes that contain text or special formatting, the merged shape retains the text and formatting of the first shape you selected.

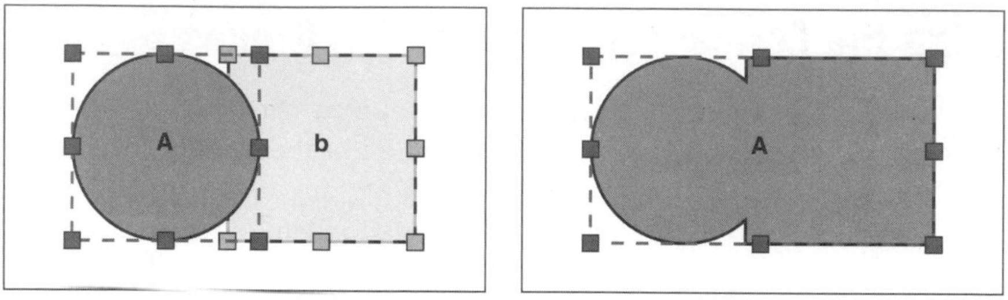

Figure 6-7 When you merge shapes with different formats and text labels, the resulting shape retains the text label and attributes of the first shape you selected. The selection handles for the first object you select are green, while those on subsequently selected objects are blue.

Merging Shapes

When you want to merge several shapes into one shape that contains multiple Geometry sections, you merge component shapes using the **Combine**, **Join**, or **Union** command on the **Operations** submenu of the **Shape** menu. Unlike the **Group** command, these commands merge several shapes to create a single shape that contains multiple paths represented by multiple Geometry sections.

To merge several shapes that overlap each other into a single shape that combines all of the shapes' geometry information into one Geometry section, use the **Union** command.

To combine multiple selected shapes into a single new shape

- On the **Shape** menu, point to **Operations**, and then click **Union**, **Combine**, or **Join**. The resulting shape contains multiple Geometry sections corresponding to the paths of the original component shapes. For **Union**, the resulting shape will contain multiple Geometry sections if the original shapes did not overlap on the page.

When you merge shapes, the original shapes and any custom formulas in them are not retained, and you cannot recover them by ungrouping as you can do with grouped shapes.

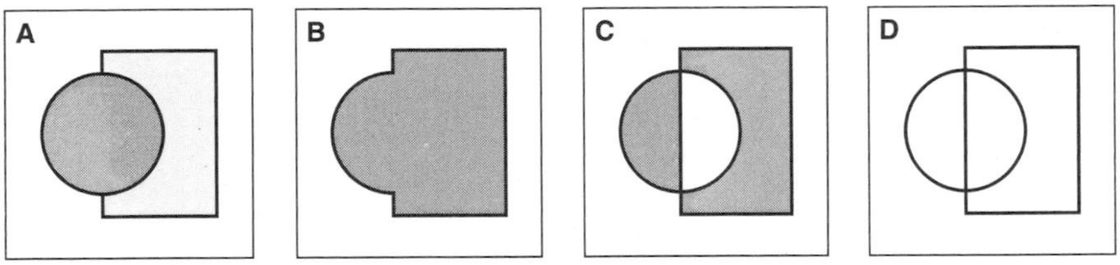

Figure 6-8 Merging shapes. (**A**) Before merging shapes. (**B**) **Union** merges overlapping shapes into a single geometry. Using **Union** on shapes that don't overlap maintains the geometry of each original shape. (**C**) **Combine** merges selected shapes, while maintaining the geometry of each original shape. If the selected shapes overlap, the area where they overlap is cut out (discarded), creating a cookie-cutter effect. (**D**) **Join** creates a new shape from the perimeter of two or more shapes, while maintaining the geometry of each original shape. The new shape results from the mathematical union of the regions covered by the original shapes.

Filling Merged Shapes

A Geometry section includes a NoFill cell that controls whether the associated path is filled, as well as a NoLine cell that controls whether the stroke associated with the path appears. If the NoFill cell is set to TRUE, the shape appears hollow. Because merged shapes can have only one set of formatting attributes applied, you can use this setting to selectively control the appearance of individual Geometry sections within shapes that have been merged.

When filled regions in any shapes overlap, the overlaps created by merged paths are considered to be outside of the filled paths and therefore are not filled, as in the following example on the left. If one path is completely contained by another, as in the following example on the right, it is not filled—even if its NoFill cell is set to FALSE. To fill the shape, set the NoFill cell for that shape to TRUE.

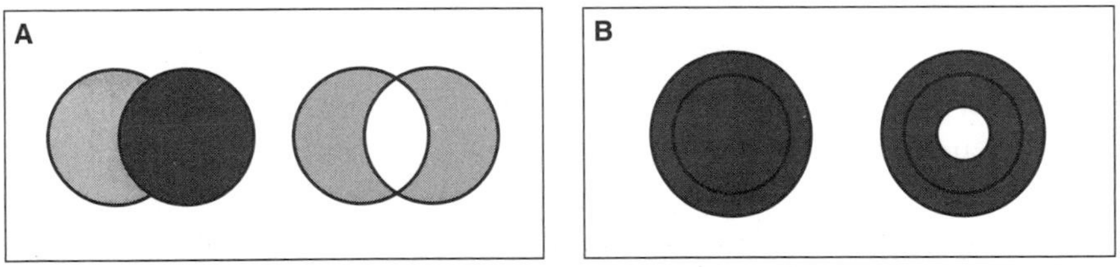

Figure 6-9 Merging filled shapes and shapes contained within another shape. (**A**) When merged shapes that have been filled overlap, the overlapping areas are considered by Visio to be outside of the shapes and are not filled. (**B**) The same principle applies when shapes are contained within another shape. Setting the NoFill cell for the smaller shape to TRUE causes the shape to be filled, though if another shape were contained inside of it, the new shape would appear hollow.

Hiding Shape Geometry

A Geometry section includes a NoShow cell that controls whether a shape's geometry is visible. To hide a shape described in a Geometry section, set the NoShow cell that corresponds to that shape to TRUE. You can use this cell to design shapes for which the geometry is not visible or is visible only at certain times.

For example, you might create a merged shape representing a subsystem that has multiple Geometry sections representing different components. Depending on the state of the subsystem, you can hide individual components by setting their NoShow cells to TRUE in the ShapeSheet spreadsheet. You might choose to edit directly in the ShapeSheet window, or you might add shortcut commands that allow users to selectively hide or show parts of the shape. For details about adding a shortcut command that controls whether shape geometry is visible, see *Shortcut Menu Commands* in Chapter 7, *Enhancing Shape Behavior.*

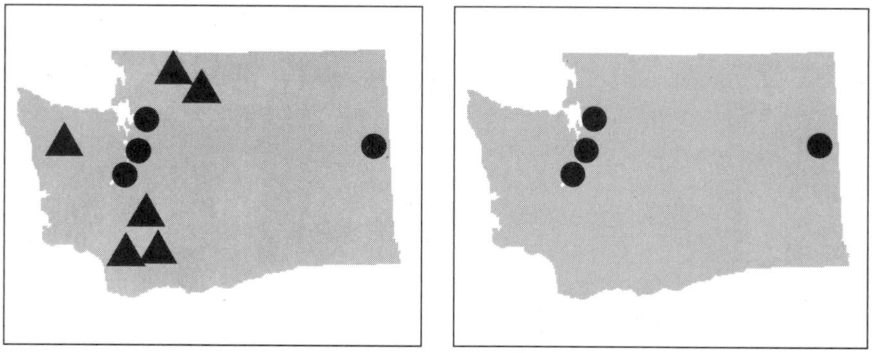

Figure 6-10 This merged shape represents a shape with two possible states; when the triangle shapes are hidden, only the dots remain visible.

7

Enhancing Shape Behavior

Making Shapes Flexible with Control Handles 136

Shortcut Menu Commands 142

Custom Properties 149

Event Formulas 156

You can write any number of Microsoft Visio formulas to control the appearance or position of a shape on a page, but there's more to shape behavior than geometry and location. A shape can provide information to users in the form of visual feedback, such as control handles with tool tips or custom commands on a shortcut menu. Moreover, users can associate information with a shape in the form of custom property data or layer assignments. These enhancements to shape behavior can make a shape better model the real-world object it represents.

Making Shapes Flexible with Control Handles

One way to control shape behavior while providing your users with greater flexibility is to add *control handles* to a shape. Control handles appear as small yellow diamonds that users can select and move. A shape responds to changes in the control handle's position according to your formulas. The real strength of control handles is that they let you design a shape to take advantage of user input.

For ideas about using control handles, look at the shapes that come with Microsoft Visio. Each shape with a control handle includes tool tip information describing the handle's behavior. The following figure shows different uses for control handles in a shape.

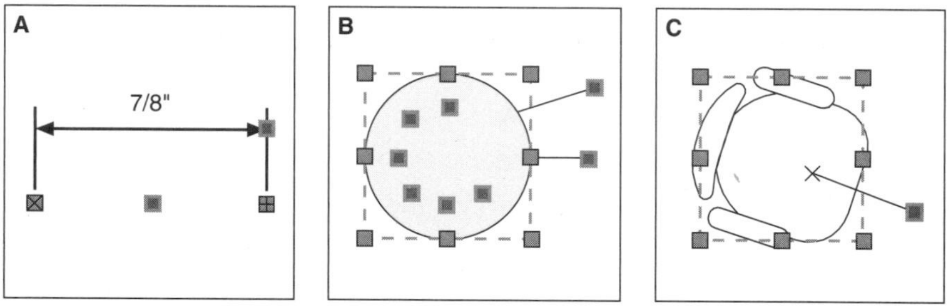

Figure 7-1 Visio masters with control handles. (**A**) Users can drag out dimension lines and adjust line heights. (**B**) Users can drag out lines of any length to connect the token ring. (**C**) Users can orient the chair in relation to another shape.

Adding a Controls Section to a Shape

To add a control handle to a shape, you add a Controls section in its ShapeSheet spreadsheet, and then modify formulas in the appropriate row of the Controls section. The Controls section defines control handle attributes. Each row in a shape's Controls section corresponds to a control handle, and cells in each row determine aspects of the control handle's behavior. For example, the Can Glue cell determines whether a control handle can be glued to other shapes, and you can use the Tip cell to define a descriptive tool tip that appears when a user pauses the pointer over a control handle. After adding the Controls section, you can write formulas in other ShapeSheet cells that refer to a row in the Controls section to define that handle's behavior.

For details about adding a control handle to a text block, see *Controlling the Text Block's Position* in Chapter 9, *Designing Text Behavior.*

Defining a Control Handle

You use the cells in the Controls section to define the location and behavior of a shape's control handles. For example, you might create a word balloon with a mouthpiece that can be repositioned by adding a control handle that controls a vertex of the shape, as the following figure shows. In this example, you want the word balloon to be a two-dimensional (2-D) shape with an alignment box around the rectangle part only so that the position of the control handle doesn't affect the rest of the shape.

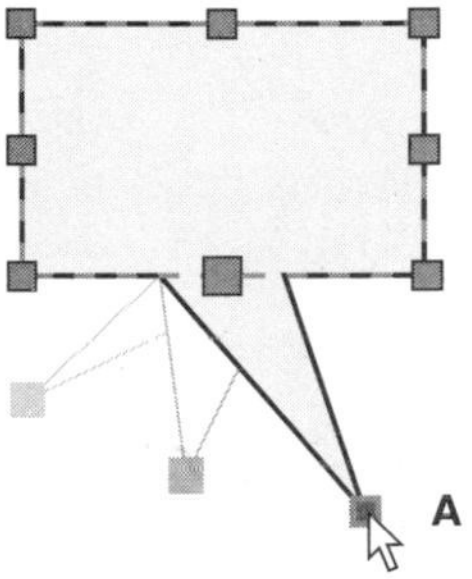

Figure 7-2 Control handle (**A**) defined for a vertex of a word balloon. Use a control handle to reposition the mouthpiece.

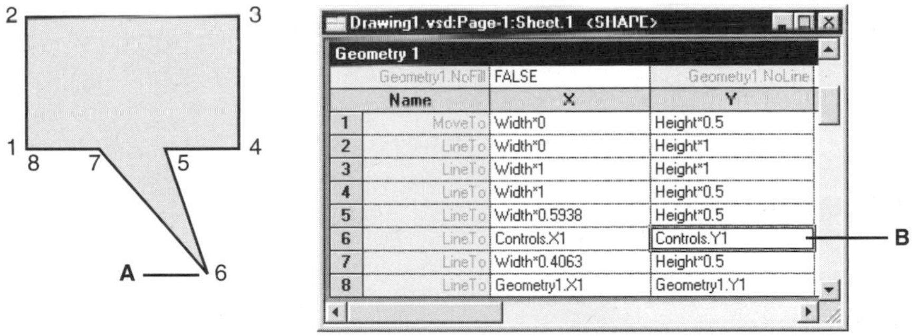

Figure 7-3 The location of the control handle is defined by the formula in a cell in the Geometry section. To attach the sixth vertex to a control handle (**A**), enter the control handle reference in this Geometry cell (**B**).

To draw the word balloon shape

1. Use the **Line** tool to draw the rectangle with the mouthpiece inverted, as illustrated below.

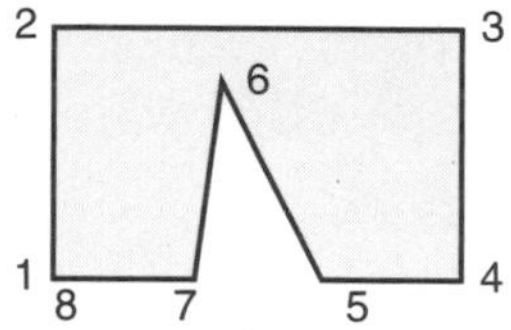

Figure 7-4

2. Protect the shape from width/height recalculation by setting the LockCalcWH cell in the Protection section of the shape's sheet to TRUE (or 1). This maintains the rectangle's original alignment box when the mouthpiece is moved using the control handle.

In the following procedure, you'll add a Controls section and formulas to associate the control handle with the mouthpiece vertex.

To add a control handle to the word balloon shape

1. Open the **ShapeSheet** window for the word balloon shape. On the **Insert** menu, click **Section**, select the **Controls** check box, and then click **OK**.

> **Note** To add a control handle to a shape that already has a Controls section, select a row in the Controls section, right-click, and then click **Insert Row** on the shortcut menu.

When you add the Controls section to a shape, a control handle with the coordinates *Width*0,Height*0* is created in the section and added to the shape on the drawing page. You can move the control handle with the mouse, but it won't do anything until you associate the shape's geometry with it in some way—typically you would associate it with the vertex you want the handle to control.

2. Put references to the control handle's position (the Controls.X*n* and Controls.Y*n* cells) in the cells in the Geometry section that correspond to the vertex you want to control with the handle.

In general, you enter a formula that refers to the *x*-coordinate of a control handle in an X cell of the Geometry section and a formula that refers to its *y*-coordinate in a Y cell. If you drew the word balloon segments in the order shown in the preceding figure, the mouthpiece vertex is controlled by Geometry row 6. For this example, you would enter the following formulas:

```
Geometry1.X6   = Controls.X1
Geometry1.Y6   = Controls.Y1
```

The mouthpiece seems to vanish, because you have temporarily assigned its vertex to the local coordinates 0,0 (the result of the control handle's default formulas *Width*0,Height*0*).

3. Drag the control handle in the drawing window to make the mouthpiece reappear.

   Or, position the mouthpiece by changing the control handle's default formulas (for example, to *Width*0.75,Height*-0.5*).

4. The X Dynamics and Y Dynamics cells describe the control handle's anchor point, which is connected to the control handle with a dynamically drawn black line when live dynamics has been turned off. For details, see *Setting a Control Handle's Anchor Point* later in this section. For this example, leave the default values unchanged.

5. In the X Behavior and Y Behavior cells, enter a constant from zero (0) to 9 to determine how the control handle repositions as the shape resizes. For this example, enter the following constants:

   ```
   X Behavior    = 4
   Y Behavior    = 2
   ```

   For details, see *Setting a Control Handle's Behavior* later in this section. For constants that you can use in the cells of the Controls section, see the cell topics associated with the Controls section in the Microsoft Visio Developer Reference (on the **Help** menu, click **Developer Reference**).

6. The Can Glue cell of a control handle determines whether a control handle can be glued to other shapes. For this example, leave the default value unchanged.

7. In the Tip cell, enter a string for the control handle tool tip.

   The string is automatically enclosed in quotation marks. For this example, you might enter:

   ```
   Tip    = "Reposition mouthpiece"
   ```

Setting a Control Handle's Anchor Point

Each control handle you define has an *anchor point* on the shape in relation to which it is drawn. The anchor point is defined by the formulas in the control point's X Dynamics and Y Dynamics cells.

Live dynamics functionality updates shape geometry as a user moves a control handle. When live dynamics is disabled, a black "rubber-band" line stretches between the anchor point and the control handle as the user drags the handle. This rubber-band line serves as a visual aid to help users determine where the control handle is being moved to and what will happen to the shape as a result. The location of the anchor point does not affect how the shape appears on the page, but only how the rubber-band line appears as the user moves the control handle.

When live dynamics is enabled, the anchor point has no visible effect and the control handle moves with the mouse pointer. To disable live dynamics for a drawing (it is enabled by default), click **Options** on the **Tools** menu, click the **General** tab, and clear the **Enable live dynamics** check box.

You can set the anchor point at any position in relation to the shape using the X Dynamics and Y Dynamics cells. By default, the anchor point appears at the position of the control handle. However, you can position the anchor point in a fixed location relative to the shape. For example, to set a control handle's anchor point at the bottom of a shape, enter the following formula:

```
Y Dynamics  = Height * 0
```

To set the anchor point at the center of a shape, enter the following formulas:

```
X Dynamics  = Width/2
Y Dynamics  = Height/2
```

> **Note** The live dynamics feature is not available in versions of Visio earlier than Visio 2000.

Setting a Control Handle's Behavior

When a user stretches a shape that has a control handle, you can specify how the handle behaves when the shape is stretched—whether the control handle moves in proportion to the shape or stays in the same place relative to the shape. If you want to fix the position of a control handle, you can hide it so a user cannot drag it.

To change display properties for control handles, you can set the following values in the shape's sheet:

- Set the NoCtrlHandles cell in the Miscellaneous section to TRUE to prevent control handles from appearing when a user selects a shape. This has the same effect as using the X or Y Behavior cell to make a handle hidden, but overrides X and Y Behavior settings that make the handles visible. For details on settings for X Behavior and Y Behavior cells, see the following table.
- Set the UpdateAlignBox cell in the Miscellaneous section to TRUE to cause a shape's alignment box to recalculate whenever a user moves a vertex. When a vertex is associated with a control handle, this causes the alignment box to be updated when the control point is moved. If the LockCalcWH cell (Protection section) is set to TRUE (or 1), UpdateAlignBox has no effect until LockCalcWH is set to FALSE.

You can also use the values of the X Behavior and Y Behavior cells in the Controls section to define a control handle's position and behavior, as the following table describes. The X Behavior and Y Behavior cells operate independently of each other.

Settings for X Behavior and Y Behavior cells

Visible	Hidden	Control handle behavior when shape is stretched
0	5	Moves in proportion with the shape when the shape is stretched.
1	6	Moves in proportion with the shape, but cannot be moved horizontally (X Behavior) or vertically (Y Behavior).
2	7	Offsets a constant distance from the shape's left side (X Behavior) or bottom (Y Behavior).
3	8	Offsets a constant distance from the center of the shape.
4	9	Offsets a constant distance from the shape's right side (X Behavior) or top (Y Behavior).

For example, the following figure shows a word balloon with a control handle whose X Behavior value is 4 and Y Behavior value is 2.

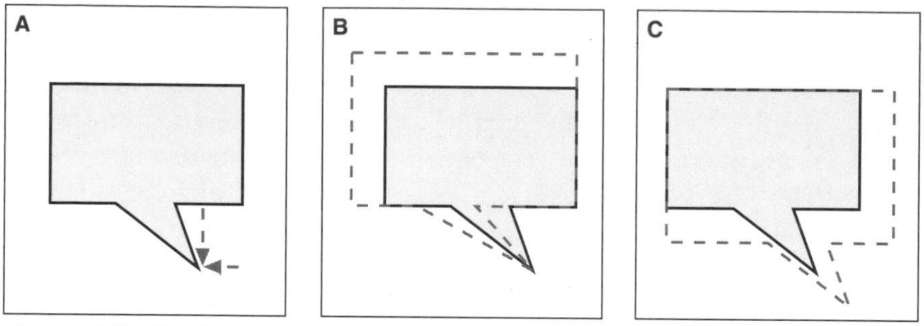

Figure 7-5 The X and Y Behavior cells control the position of the control handle relative to the shape's outline. (**A**) The control handle is offset a constant distance from the shape's right and bottom. (**B**) If the shape is stretched using the handles on the left or top, the control handle stays anchored. (**C**) If the shape is stretched using the bottom or right handles, the control handle moves to retain the offset.

Shortcut Menu Commands

When a user right-clicks a shape on the drawing page, a shortcut menu appears that includes commands that apply to the selection. You can define commands that appear on a shape's shortcut menu and on the **Actions** submenu of the **Shape** menu. A row in a shape's or page's Actions section defines a command name and action provided by that shape or page.

For example, you could define an action called **Run Program** for a shape that evaluates this formula when performed:

```
Action = RUNADDON("my_prog.exe")
```

When a user right-clicks the shape, **Run Program** appears on the shortcut menu. If the user clicks **Run Program**, Microsoft Visio evaluates the formula. In this case, My_prog.exe starts.

> **Note** Action cells, like Event cells, are evaluated only when the action occurs, not when you enter the formula.

This section describes using formulas to work with shortcut menu commands. You can also customize the user interface, including shortcut menus, using Automation. For details, see Chapter 22, *Customizing the Visio User Interface.*

Defining a Shortcut Menu Command

You can create shortcut menu commands for almost any shape behavior that is controlled by a ShapeSheet cell. For example, you might create shortcut commands for turning on and off various cells in the Protection section for a shape, or you might define commands that modify a shape's formatting cells.

To define a shortcut menu command for a shape or page

1. Select a shape. On the **Window** menu, click **Show ShapeSheet**.

   To display the page's sheet, make sure that nothing is selected, and then click **Show ShapeSheet** on the **Window** menu.

2. If the Actions section is not already present, click **Section** on the **Insert** menu. In the **Insert Section** dialog box, select **Actions**, and then click **OK**.

   If the Actions section is present but not visible, click **Sections** on the **View** menu. In the **View Sections** dialog box, select **Actions**, and then click **OK**.

   To add additional actions, select a cell in the Actions section, right-click, and then click **Insert Row** on the shortcut menu.

3. In the Action cell, enter the formula that you want to be evaluated when the user chooses the Action command.

   For example, you might create two parallel actions that use the SETF function to lock and unlock the text in the shape using the following formulas:

   ```
   Action 1      = SETF(GetRef(LockTextEdit), TRUE)
   Action 2      = SETF(GetRef(LockTextEdit), FALSE)
   ```

4. In the Menu cell, enter a command name as you want it to appear on the shortcut menu.

   For example, you might enter the text "Lock Text" for Action 1 so that the command **Lock Text** appears on the shortcut menu, and the text "Unlock Text" for Action 2 so that the command **Unlock Text** appears below it.

   You can use the Checked cell to add a check mark to a selected command; use the Disabled cell to dim a command. For details on using these cells, see *Controlling a Shortcut Command's Appearance on the Menu* later in this section.

To test the new command, right-click the shape or page to display its shortcut menu, and then choose the Action command you defined.

> **Tip** After you've added an Actions section to the ShapeSheet window for a shape or page, you can define common actions quickly by using the **Action** command on the **Edit** menu. The command is dimmed until you select a cell in an Actions section. In the **Action** dialog box, type a name for the menu item in **Menu**, select an action, and click **OK**. The corresponding cells of the Actions section are updated. If you choose an action in the dialog box such as **Go to page**, the appropriate formula is entered in the Action cell.

Controlling a Shortcut Command's Appearance on the Menu

The actions you add appear by default at the top of the shortcut menu in the order that they are listed in the Actions section. To control the appearance and position of your action command in the shortcut menu, you can use a prefix before the name you type in the Menu cell. To display your command at the bottom of the shortcut menu, use the following syntax:

```
= "%Menu item"
```

To display a divider bar above the command, use the following syntax:

```
= "_Menu item"
```

To create a keyboard shortcut for the command, place an ampersand (&) before the desired shortcut letter, as follows:

```
= "&Menu item"
```

In addition, you can write formulas that place check marks next to commands to indicate that they've been selected, dim commands that aren't relevant for a particular context, and toggle between two mutually exclusive commands on the shortcut menu by hiding and showing the relevant command.

Adding Check Marks to Commands on the Shortcut Menu

When you define several shortcut menu commands for a shape, you can show which one has been applied to the shape by placing a check mark beside it on the menu. To do this, you set the Checked cell of the selected Actions row to TRUE. You can also use a logical expression to check and uncheck the command by referencing a user-defined cell.

For example, you might want to check either the **Lock Text** or **Unlock Text** commands added in the previous example. To do so, you would enter the following formula in the Checked cell of the **Lock Text** action:

```
Checked 1   = LockTextEdit=TRUE
```

In this case, when the value of the LockTextEdit is TRUE, the Checked cell evaluates the formula as TRUE, and a check mark is placed beside the command name to indicate that the text is locked, as shown in the following figure.

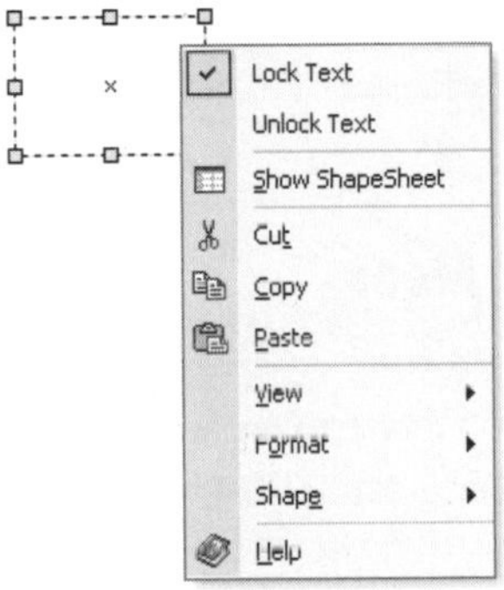

Figure 7-6 You can place a check mark beside the commands you define in the Actions section.

You could also enter a similar formula for the second action to check the **Unlock Text** command as follows:

```
Checked 2   = LockTextEdit=FALSE
```

In this example, the **Unlock Text** command would be checked on the shortcut menu when LockTextEdit is FALSE.

Dimming a Shortcut Command on the Menu

To refine the shape, you can dim commands that don't currently apply to the shape. For example, when a user chooses the **Lock Text** command, the text is locked so that only the **Unlock Text** command needs to be available on the menu. To do this for the **Lock Text** example, you would enter the following formula in the Disabled cell of the Actions section for the **Lock Text** action:

```
Disabled 1  = LockTextEdit=TRUE
```

You could enter a similar formula in the Disabled cell for the **Unlock Text** action as follows:

```
Disabled 2  = LockTextEdit=FALSE
```

The result of any formula in the Disabled cell is evaluated as either TRUE or FALSE. When the **Lock Text** command is chosen, the value of LockTextEdit is TRUE, so the expression in the Disabled cell evaluates to TRUE, and the **Lock Text** command is dimmed. If the **Unlock Text** command is chosen, LockTextEdit is FALSE, so the expression in the Disabled 2 cell is TRUE and the **Unlock Text** command is dimmed.

Hiding and Showing Commands on the Shortcut Menu

Whenever a shape has only two states or attributes that represent an either/or situation, such as the **Lock Text** and **Unlock Text** examples we've been working with, you can create the appearance of hiding and showing command names by conditionally changing the text that appears on the menu. For example, you might prefer to streamline your user interface by displaying only one command on the menu at a time: If the text is locked, the command on the shortcut menu is **Unlock Text**. If the text is unlocked, the command is **Lock Text**.

To create a command that changes on the shortcut menu, you need only one row in the Actions section. You write two logical expressions: one in the Action cell to toggle the value of LockTextEdit, and another in the Menu cell to determine which command to display based on the value of LockTextEdit:

```
Action = SETF(GetRef(LockTextEdit),NOT(LockTextEdit))
Menu = IF(LockTextEdit,"Unlock Text","Lock Text")
```

If the value of LockTextEdit is TRUE, SETF sets it to FALSE; otherwise, the value of LockTextEdit is FALSE, so SETF sets it to TRUE. The formula in the Menu cell also refers to the LockTextEdit cell: If it is TRUE, the **Unlock Text** command appears, and if it is FALSE, the **Lock Text** command is visible.

When a shape has more than two states or menu commands, users will find it less confusing if you use the Checked or the Disabled cell to indicate which commands are available.

> **Tip** You can use the SETF function in an Event or Action cell to toggle the value of another cell between two options, or to increment values in another cell. Because the formula in an Event or Action cell is evaluated only when the event occurs, you can write a self-referential formula using the SETF function that doesn't cause a loop. For example, to toggle the value of CellA depending on the value of CellB, use the following syntax in an Events or Action cell:
>
> ```
> SETF(GetRef(CellA), IF(CellB=FALSE, TRUE, FALSE) )
> ```
>
> To increment the value of *cell* by one, use this syntax:
>
> ```
> SETF(GetRef(cell), cell + 1 )
> ```

For details about the syntax of the SETF function, see the Microsoft Visio Developer Reference (on the **Help** menu, click **Developer Reference**).

Using Shortcut Commands to Change Shape Geometry: an Example

You can use shortcut menu commands to control shape geometry, so that users can choose a command to change the shape's appearance. For example, you can create a single shape that represents two states: on or off, open or closed, engaged or disengaged. To do this, you create a merged shape that contains multiple Geometry sections in its ShapeSheet spreadsheet using the **Combine** command. Then, in the Actions section of the merged shape, you can define shortcut menu commands that control the visibility of the Geometry section that represents one state. To demonstrate, we'll create an office chair with arms that can be shown or hidden as the following figure shows.

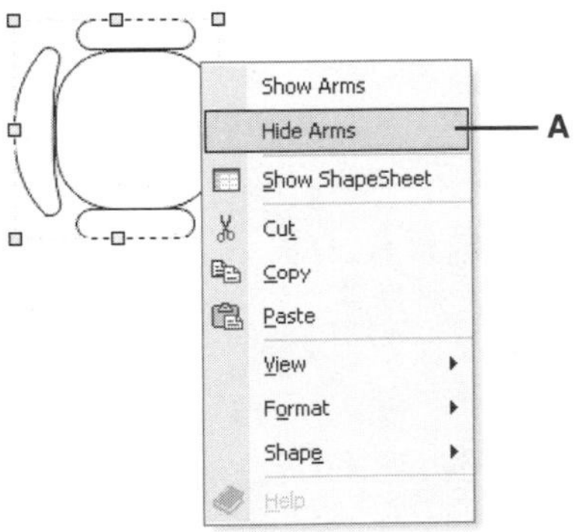

Figure 7-7 You can define shortcut commands that appear when you right-click the merged shape. In this example, choosing the command (**A**) hides the geometry of one of the merged shape's component shapes.

To combine shapes into a merged shape

1. Create the shapes you want to use in your merged shape.

   For example, to create a chair, draw a rectangle or oval for the seat, one for the chair back, and one for each arm. These shapes should touch, but not overlap when you place them to make the shape of the chair.

2. Select the chair shapes. On the **Shape** menu, point to **Operations**, and then click **Combine**.

   A single shape that contains one Geometry section for each original shape is created. The Geometry sections are numbered in the order in which you selected the shapes.

For details about merging shapes, see *Creating and Controlling Merged Shapes* in Chapter 6, *Grouping and Merging Shapes*.

To add an Actions section to the merged shape and define shortcut commands

1. Select the merged shape. On the **Window** menu, click **Show ShapeSheet**.
2. On the **Insert** menu, click **Section**. Select **User-defined cells** and **Actions**, and then click **OK**.
3. Type a name for the user-defined cell.

   For example, type *State* to create the user-defined cell User.State.
4. Enter the value *TRUE* in the user-defined cell. The initial value is TRUE so that the chair arms are visible.
5. Select the first row in the Actions section, and then click **Row** on the **Insert** menu to create a total of two rows in the Actions section.
6. To define the command names and corresponding actions, enter these formulas:

```
Action[1]     = SETF(GetRef(User.State),TRUE)
Menu[1]       = "Show Arms"
Action[2]     = SETF(GetRef(User.State),FALSE)
Menu[2]       = "Hide Arms"
```

7. In the two Geometry sections that correspond to the arms of the chair, enter this formula:

```
Geometryn.NoShow      = NOT(User.State)
```

For example, if the arms of the chair correspond to the Geometry3 and Geometry4 sections, you would enter:

```
Geometry3.NoShow     = NOT(User.State)
Geometry4.NoShow     = NOT(User.State)
```

The Action cell formula uses the SETF function to set the value of User.State to TRUE when the **Show Arms** command is clicked or FALSE when the **Hide Arms** command is clicked. The Menu cell defines these command names.

To hide and show paths, you enter formulas in the NoShow cell of the appropriate Geometry section that refer to the value of the User.State cell. The NoShow cell controls whether the path defined by that Geometry section is shown or hidden. In this case, the arms are both shown or both hidden, so the same formula is used in the NoShow cells of the two corresponding Geometry sections.

The NOT function returns TRUE if an expression is FALSE, and if TRUE, returns FALSE. When a user clicks **Hide Arms**, User.State is set to FALSE. The NOT function then returns TRUE so that the value of the NoShow cell is TRUE and the path and fill for the corresponding component are hidden.

Custom Properties

The appearance of a shape in a drawing, however sophisticated, is rarely the whole story. The real-world object that a shape represents often has important data associated with it—part numbers, prices, quantities ordered or in the warehouse; names, dates, addresses, telephone numbers; manufacturers, suppliers, customers; dimensions, materials, tensile strength. Having this kind of data in a drawing makes it a powerful tool for analysis and communication.

You can associate data with a Microsoft Visio shape by defining custom properties in its ShapeSheet spreadsheet, or by working in the **Custom Properties** window or dialog box or in the **Define Custom Properties** dialog box. You give each custom property a unique name and optionally define other characteristics, such as data type, format, and default value.

This section introduces using ShapeSheet formulas to define and edit custom properties. You can also use Automation to integrate information from other sources into your Visio drawings. For details, see Chapter 20, *Integrating Data with a Visio Solution*.

Using Custom Properties

Custom properties open a world of possibilities for making your solutions richer and more reflective of the real-world systems they describe. Some of the things that you can do with data that is associated with your shape include the following:

- **Add data when you create a shape** For example, you might define custom properties for resistance, voltage, and amperage and enter data for them in masters that represent electronic components. When the user drops one of the shapes in a drawing, the data accompanies the shape.
- **Collect data from a user** Microsoft Visio can prompt the user to fill in custom properties of a master each time it is dropped in a drawing, encouraging the user to enter the data that your solution needs. The user can also display and edit a shape's custom properties from its shortcut menu.
- **Display data in a shape's text** You can insert a text field in the shape's text to display the result of a custom property's formula. A text field can display a value, the result of a formula, or any global value that the Visio engine provides, such as file summary information or the current date and time.

Sometimes data stays behind the scenes, but often you'll want to display data in a drawing or change the drawing as the data changes. You can use a shape's custom properties to do the following:

- **Control a shape's behavior** Because custom properties are stored in ShapeSheet cells, they can play a role in other formulas—for example, a shape's geometry can be linked to its custom properties, allowing the shape to respond to user input.
- **Extract data from a drawing** You can obtain data from a shape's custom properties and write it to an external destination such as a spreadsheet or database. For details, see Chapter 20, *Integrating Data with a Visio Solution.*
- **Transfer data from an external source** You can set custom properties to use data from an external source, such as a spreadsheet or database, by writing a program that uses Automation to direct the flow of data. For details, see Chapter 20, *Integrating Data with a Visio Solution.*

Custom properties can serve as containers for data from an external source, or they can provide a data-entry interface for shapes in a drawing. Whether custom property data resides in only the shape or interacts with an external source is up to you.

For example, you can use custom properties to update an inventory control list. You can create a stencil containing masters that represent the parts in inventory. For each master, you might define the custom properties **Name**, **Price**, and **Quantity**. You can set the value of these properties when you create the shapes, or you can allow the shapes' users to enter the name, price, and quantity for a given part, even prompting users to do so.

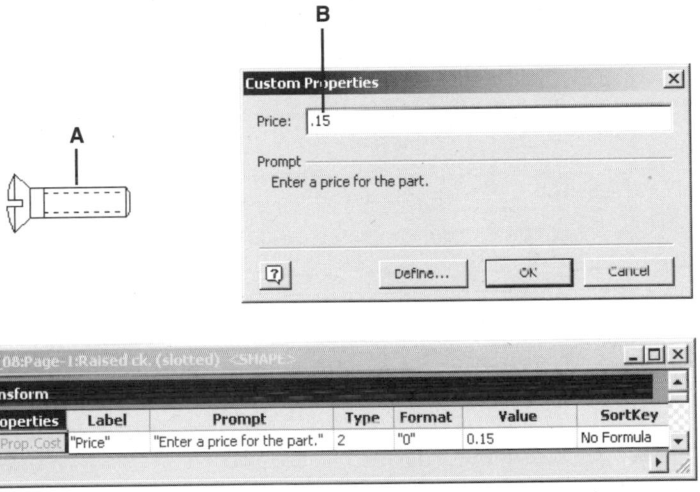

Figure 7-8 Custom properties for an inventory control list (**A**) Shape with custom properties. (**B**) The value typed here is the value of the Prop.Cost cell.

Defining Custom Properties

You can define a custom property to store string, numeric, Boolean, date or time, duration, currency, fixed list, or variable list data with any object represented by a sheet, such as a shape, group, master, guide, page, or document. A custom property is stored as a ShapeSheet row whose name and cells you define. You can view and modify custom properties through the Visio menu commands, as well as create reports from the information or refer to the values in other ShapeSheet cells. Custom properties are a way to associate database-like fields with a shape or a page.

If you want to create a custom property to hold data, but you do not want that data to be visible in the **Custom Properties** window or dialog box, you can set a shape's Invisible cell (Custom Properties section) to TRUE. The GUARD function cannot protect the data in the Value cell of a Custom Property row.

You can define custom properties for a single shape or a page by adding a Custom Properties section to its sheet or by working in the **Custom Properties** window or dialog box. If you're editing a stencil, a more efficient method is to define custom properties for the stencil's masters so that their instances also contain the properties.

The **Custom Properties** window provides a convenient at-a-glance view of the custom properties associated with a page or a selected shape, as well as an interface for entering new values for those properties.

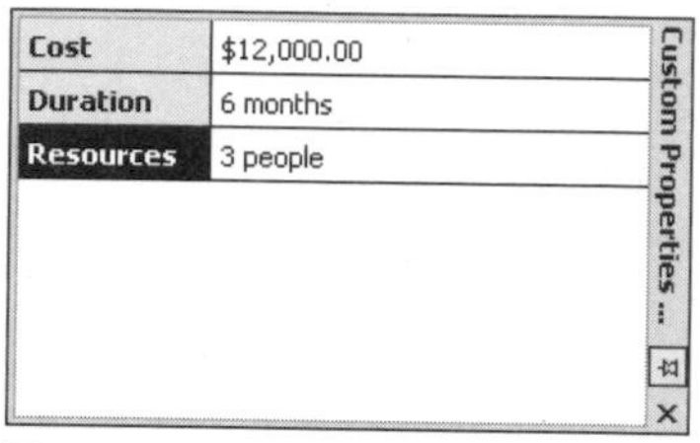

Figure 7-9 You can enter new values for custom properties in the **Custom Properties** window.

To add custom properties to a shape, master, or page using the Custom Properties window

1. On the **View** menu, click **Custom Properties Window**.
2. Choose the shape, master, or page to which you want to add custom properties by selecting the shape on the page, selecting the shapes in a master in its drawing window, or clicking on the page.

> **Note** To edit a master in its window, make its stencil editable by opening it as **Original**. Then, right-click the master in its stencil and click **Edit Master** on the shortcut menu.

3. Right-click in the **Custom Properties** window, and then click **Define Properties** on the shortcut menu.
4. In the **Define Custom Properties** dialog box, enter values for the settings that you want to use.
5. Click **New** to add the custom property and continue adding more properties, or click **OK** to add the custom property and close the dialog box.

To add custom properties to a shape, master, or page using the ShapeSheet window

1. Select a shape on the page, select the shapes in a master in its drawing window, or click an empty portion of the drawing page.

> **Note** To edit a master in its window, make its stencil editable by opening it as **Original**. Then, right-click the master in its stencil and click **Edit Master** on the shortcut menu.

2. On the **Window** menu, click **Show ShapeSheet**.
3. If the Custom Properties section is not already present, click **Section** on the **Insert** menu. In the **Insert Section** dialog box, select **Custom Properties**, and then click **OK**.
4. In the Custom Properties section, select the Row label Prop.Row_1, which appears in red text. In the formula bar, type a descriptive name.

   For example, type *Unit_Cost* and press ENTER to create the custom property Prop.Unit_Cost. The name that appears in the Row label is the cell name for the Value cell in that row. Use this name (for example, *Prop.Unit_Cost*) in cell references.
5. In the Label cell, type the label that appears to users in the **Custom Properties** window or dialog box for this property.

   For example, type *Cost Per Unit*. Visio automatically encloses the string in quotation marks.
6. In the Prompt cell, type descriptive or instructional text that appears to users in the **Custom Properties** window or dialog box when the property is selected.

   For example, type *Enter the cost per unit for the part*. Visio automatically encloses the string in quotation marks.
7. In the Type and Format cells, enter a data type and format for your custom property's value.

   For details, see the following table.
8. Optional: Set the Invisible cell to a non-zero number (TRUE) to prevent the custom property from appearing in the **Custom Properties** window or dialog box. Set the Ask cell to a non-zero number (TRUE)

to display the **Custom Properties** window or dialog box whenever an instance of the shape is created.

To see the custom property you have defined, select the shape on the drawing page or cancel all selections if you want to view the page's custom properties. Then click **Custom Properties** on the **Shape** menu.

Custom property types and format

Type	ShapeSheet cell formula	Description
String	`Type = 0` `Format = "<picture>"`	This is the default. Use a valid format picture* in the Format cell to format strings as number-unit pairs, dates, times, and so on.
Fixed list	`Type = 1` `Format = "Item 1;Item 2"`	Displays the list items alphabetically in a drop-down list box in the **Custom Properties** dialog box. Specify the list items in the Format cell. Users can select only one item from the list.
Number	`Type = 2` `Format = "<picture>"`	Use a format picture* in the Format cell to specify units of measure and other number formats.
Boolean	`Type = 3`	Displays FALSE and TRUE as items users can select from a drop-down combo box in the **Custom Properties** dialog box.
Variable list	`Type = 4` `Format = "Item 1;Item 2"`	Displays the list items in a drop-down combo box in the **Custom Properties** dialog box. Specify the list items in the Format cell. Users can select a list item or enter a new item; new items are added to the list.
Date or time	`Type = 5` `Format = "<picture>"`	Use a format picture* in the Format cell to specify days, months, years, hours, minutes, seconds, or other date formats; time formats; or combination of date and time formats.
Duration	`Type = 6` `Format = "<picture>"`	Use a format picture* in the Format cell to specify elapsed time in hours, days, weeks, months, or other duration formats.
Currency	`Type = 7` `Format = "<picture>"`	Use a format picture* in the Format cell to specify currency formats.

* For example, `[Format = "# #/10 UU"]` formats the number 10.92 cm as "10 9/10 CENTIMETERS" (specifying the use of "10" in the denominator and the uppercase, long form of the units). For details about valid format pictures, see *Formatting Strings and Text Output* in Chapter 9, *Designing Text Behavior*. Or search for "format function" in the Microsoft Visio Developer Reference (on the **Help** menu, click **Developer Reference**).

Linking Custom Properties to a Database

After you have defined custom properties for a shape, you can link the data to a database. By establishing connections between shapes and database records, you can create Visio drawings that function as visual representations of data. For example:

- From a personnel database, you can generate an organization chart.
- From a parts-specifications database, you can generate masters for your employees to use in drawings.
- By connecting an inventory database to an office space plan, you can track furniture and equipment. If you delete a chair from the office plan, you also delete a record from the database.

The **Database Wizard** can automate this process for you. It links the values of ShapeSheet cells in the Custom Properties section to a database created in an application compliant with the Open Database Connectivity (ODBC) standard, such as Microsoft Access 7.0 or later, or Microsoft SQL Server. If you revise the database, you can refresh the values in the ShapeSheet cells to reflect the revisions. Once you've established a shape-record connection, you can pass information back and forth between your Visio drawing and the database and keep the two versions of the data synchronized.

When it links a shape to a database, the **Database Wizard** adds the Custom Properties and User-Defined Cells sections to the shape's sheet. The wizard stores information about the primary key for the database, the database fields that are linked to ShapeSheet cells, and the last valid data retrieved from the database in user-defined cells.

To run this wizard, on the **Tools** menu, point to **Add-Ons** (or point to **Macros** if you're not running in developer mode), point to **Visio Extras**, and then click **Database Wizard**. For details about options, click **Help** in the wizard.

Event Formulas

The Microsoft Visio engine has numerous ways of triggering and responding to events. You can put formulas into ShapeSheet cells that perform an action, such as running a macro or navigating to another drawing page, in response to an event. These formulas can be used in the Events section, which handles a select group of events, or in other cells. You can also use the DEPENDSON function to simulate other events. In addition to the DEPENDSON function, there are several built-in functions that are particularly useful in event handling because they perform actions.

Visio also supports the use of Automation for writing code to handle events. With Automation, you can develop powerful solutions that use Microsoft Visual Basic for Applications (VBA) programs, stand-alone programs, and other more advanced approaches to handling events. For details, see Chapter 21, *Handling Visio Events.*

Using Cells in the Events Section

You can define how a shape responds to specific user actions by writing Visio formulas that handle events. Whenever the user performs one of the four actions described in the following table, the formula in the corresponding ShapeSheet cell is evaluated. The Events section of a ShapeSheet window contains the following cells; when a user performs any of these actions, the formula in the cell is evaluated.

Events section cells

Cell	Event that triggers the formula
TheText	The shape's text or formatting is changed, or the text requires recomposition.
EventXFMod	The shape's position, size, or orientation on the page is changed.
EventDblClick	The shape is double-clicked.
EventDrop	A new instance is created by pasting, duplicating, or CTRL+dragging a shape, or by dragging and dropping a master.
TheData	Reserved for future use.

By entering formulas in the Events section cells, you define how the shape responds to each event. Unlike most ShapeSheet formulas, event formulas are evaluated only when the event happens, not when you enter the formula or when cells referenced by the formula change. This means that Events cells behave somewhat differently than other ShapeSheet cells, as follows:

- The value displayed in an Events cell may appear to be out-of-date or inconsistent with the cell's formula. For example, suppose you entered this formula in the EventDblClick cell:

  ```
  = Width > 1 in.
  ```

  This formula returns TRUE or FALSE. However, the formula is evaluated when the user double-clicks the shape, not when the shape is resized, so the value displayed in the cell reflects what was true for the shape the last time it was double-clicked.

- The order of evaluation and the number of times an event is evaluated are unpredictable. For example, if a shape is resized, both TheText and EventXFMod are evaluated, but the order in which these events trigger evaluation is undefined. However, Visio evaluates each cell at least once in the order it chooses.

Simulating Events with the DEPENDSON Function

You can use the DEPENDSON function to simulate events in other ShapeSheet sections such as the Scratch section. Using this function enables you to respond to events other than those provided in the Events section, and it also provides finer control over your event handling.

For example, if you put the following formula in a Scratch cell for a shape, the Visio engine opens the shape's text block whenever the shape is moved:

```
OPENTEXTWIN() + DEPENDSON(PinX, PinY)
```

In another example, if you put the following formula in a Scratch cell, the add-on Myprog.exe is launched whenever the shape is flipped in either direction:

```
RUNADDON("my_prog.exe") + DEPENDSON(FlipX, FlipY)
```

> **Note** The DEPENDSON function has no effect when used in an Events or Action cell. For details, see the DEPENDSON function in the Microsoft Visio Developer Reference (on the **Help** menu, click **Developer Reference**).

Functions that Perform Actions

Microsoft Visio includes built-in functions that perform actions rather than produce a value, making them especially useful in event formulas. The following table shows a partial list of functions; for a complete list as well as details about function syntax, see the Microsoft Visio Developer Reference(on the **Help** menu, click **Developer Reference**).

Functions to use in event formulas

Function name	Description
`CALLTHIS("procedure", ["project"], [arg1,arg2,...)`	Calls a procedure in a VBA project and passes the procedure a reference to the **Shape** object that contains the CALLTHIS formula being evaluated, along with any arguments specified in that formula. For example: `CALLTHIS("ThisDocument.myProc",,`*`Height, Width`*`)`
`GOTOPAGE("pagename")`	Displays the indicated page in the currently active window. A URL can also be used here. For example: `GOTOPAGE("Page-2")`
`OPENFILE("filename")`	Opens a file in a new window. If multiple files are listed, the requests are queued and executed in order of evaluation, with the last named document receiving final focus. If the current Visio document is activated for visual (in-place) editing, a new Visio instance is launched with the requested file name.
`OPENSHEETWIN()`	Opens and displays a ShapeSheet window showing the shape that contains this formula.
`OPENTEXTWIN()`	Opens the text block for the shape that contains this formula.
`PLAYSOUND("filename"|"alias", isAlias, beep, synch)`	On systems with a sound card, plays the sound recorded in filename, or plays the system alias for a sound if *isAlias* is a non-zero number. If the sound cannot be played, Visio can beep to indicate an error. Sounds can be played asynchronously or synchronously. For example: `PLAYSOUND ("chord.wav", 0, 0, 0)` Plays the wave audio file chord.wav synchronously with no warning beep.

Functions to use in event formulas *(continued)*

Function name	Description
`RUNDADDON("string")`	Launches the specified macro or add-on, or executes VBA code. Any statement that can be entered in the VBA **Immediate** window can be specified as a RUNADDON argument.
`RUNADDONWARGS ("filename","arguments")`	Launches an add-on and passes it the given argument string.
`SETF(GetRef(cell), formula)`	When evaluated, the result of the expression in formula becomes the new formula of the specified cell. If formula is enclosed in quotation marks, the quoted expression is written to the cell. For example: `SETF (GetRef(Scratch.A1),` Evaluates the formula *=Scratch.A1+1* and sets the Scratch.A1+1) formula of the Scratch.A1 cell to the result, which is its previous value incremented by 1.

Performance Considerations for Event Formulas

Because event formulas are evaluated each time the event occurs, they can affect the usability and performance of your shapes. Follow these general guidelines:

- **Use event formulas sparingly** Avoid event formulas for frequent events such as moving or sizing the shape (EventXFMod) or editing its text (TheText). Handling these events can interrupt the user's workflow and make shapes awkward to use.
- **Keep event formulas simple** A complex formula takes longer to evaluate, which slows the performance of the shape.
- **Be aware that some actions take longer than others** Even a simple event formula may trigger a time-consuming action. For example, it takes longer to launch a stand-alone executable add-on than to run a macro, and longer to navigate to a Web page than to navigate to another page in the same Visio document.

8

Working with 1-D Shapes, Connectors, and Glue

How 1-D and 2-D Shapes Differ 162

Creating Routable and Other 1-D Connectors 165

Controlling How Shapes Connect 172

Should a shape behave like a box or a line? When you're designing a Microsoft Visio shape, that's one of the questions you need to ask. A shape that behaves like a box—that is, a two-dimensional (2-D) shape—can be stretched vertically or horizontally. A shape that behaves like a line—a one-dimensional (1-D) shape—can be stretched and rotated in one operation. You can use 1-D shapes to join other shapes together, and in this capacity they are often called *connectors*. The attribute of a shape that causes it to stay joined to another shape is called *glue*. You can glue a 1-D or 2-D shape to other shapes.

This chapter explains the differences between 1-D and 2-D shapes and describes how to create different types of 1-D shapes. It also explains how to work with the glue that holds shapes together.

How 1-D and 2-D Shapes Differ

When the size or length of a line shape is less important than the connection it represents, create a 1-D shape. Because 1-D shapes are often used to connect other shapes, they are often called connectors. For example, in a flowchart, circuit diagram, or mechanical illustration, 1-D shapes can be used to connect other components. However, not all 1-D shapes are connectors. Some behave as lines, such as callouts or dimension lines, or are simply easier to work with as 1-D shapes, such as the wedge of a pie chart.

Most shapes when you first draw them are 2-D. Their width-height boxes have eight handles for resizing. When you draw a single arc or line, however, the result is a 1-D shape that has handles for begin and end points and for height adjustment. Not only do 1-D and 2-D shapes look different, they behave differently on the drawing page.

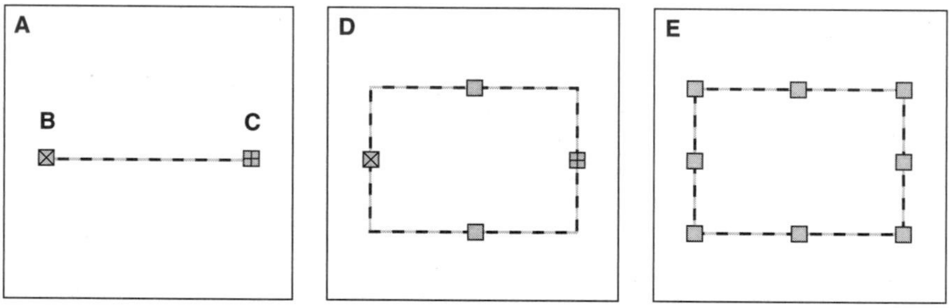

Figure 8-1 Selection handles on 1-D and 2-D shapes. (**A**) 1-D shape. (**B**) Begin point. (**C**) End point. (**D**) 2-D shape converted to 1-D. (**E**) 2-D shape.

When a user drags a 2-D shape onto the drawing page, the outline of its alignment box appears rectangular. When a user drags a 1-D shape onto the drawing page, its alignment box appears as a straight line. This can make the 1-D shape easier for users to align, as with a 1-D wall shape in a space plan.

Two of the 1-D shape's handles have a special purpose. The starting vertex of a 1-D shape is its *begin point*, and the handle that represents the end of the line formed by the shape is the *end point*.

You can glue the begin or end point of a 1-D shape to a guide, guide point, connection point, shape vertex, or selection handle. If you glue one end, the other end stays anchored on the page, and the 1-D shape stretches as the glued end moves with the shape to which it is glued.

Converting 1-D and 2-D Shapes

A shape that looks like a box can behave like a line because you can convert a 2-D shape to 1-D and vice versa. Converting a shape in this way dramatically changes the sections it displays in the ShapeSheet window.

A key difference between a 1-D and 2-D shape is that a 1-D shape includes the 1-D Endpoints section in its ShapeSheet window; a 2-D shape does not have this section. Converting a 2-D shape to 1-D adds this section and its default formulas. Converting a 1-D shape to 2-D removes this section, regardless of any protection (including GUARD functions) you might have set.

When you convert a 2-D shape to a 1-D shape, the Alignment section is deleted, and the formulas in the Shape Transform section's Width, Angle, PinX, and PinY cells are replaced with default 1-D formulas. Converting a shape does not remove its connection points, but its connections to other shapes or guides are broken.

To convert a shape between 1-D and 2-D

1. Select the shape.
2. On the **Format** menu, click **Behavior**.
3. Under **Interaction style**, select **Line (1-dimensional)** to specify a 1-D shape. Select **Box (2-dimensional)** to specify a 2-D shape.
4. Click **OK**.

   Visio modifies the shape and adjusts the alignment box according to the behavior you chose.

> **Note** One way to create a 1-D shape is to draw the shape as a 2-D shape, convert it to 1-D, and then adjust the vertices and define custom formulas. You can save time and effort when you initially draw the shape by orienting it horizontally—that is, by dragging left to right or right to left in the direction you want the line to go. Visio places 1-D endpoints on the left and right sides of the shape you draw, so a horizontally drawn shape will be closer to what you want after it is converted to 1-D.

Examples of 1-D Shapes

1-D shapes can vary greatly in their appearance and functionality. A 1-D shape might look like a line, or might appear to be a 2-D shape. However, as a 1-D shape, you can take advantage of its endpoints. By adding custom formulas, you can make the shape behave intelligently when the user drops it on the page, such as a window snapping into place on a wall in an office layout.

However, not all 1-D shapes require special formulas to be useful. Because a 1-D shape looks like a line as it is being dragged, it can be faster to position in a drawing. Consider using 1-D shapes whenever you want to create masters that your users will align precisely in a drawing. For example, a text callout or annotation shape is easier to position accurately if users can see exactly where the line will point.

The 1-D shapes shown in the following figure have custom formulas that create smart behavior.

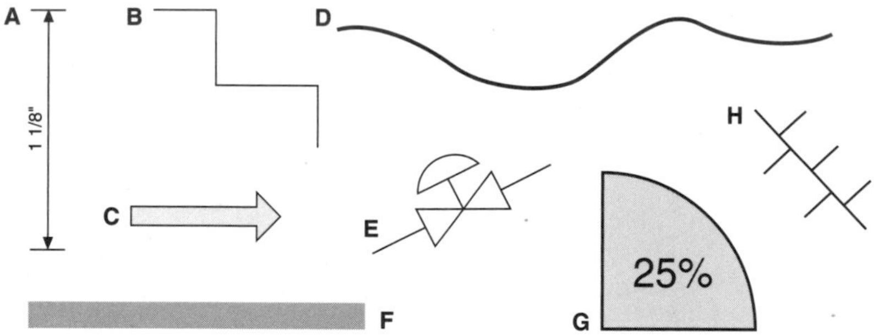

Figure 8-2 Examples of 1-D shapes. (**A**) Vertical dimension line. (**B**) S-connector. (**C**) Arrow. (**D**) Drip line. (**E**) Diaphragm valve. (**F**) Wall. (**G**) Pie wedge. (**H**) Bus.

The formulas for the S-connector keep the connector right-side up. As its endpoints are moved, the shape resizes in a way that keeps it upright by stretching its horizontal or vertical segments.

The formulas for the diaphragm valve shape give it height-based resizing behavior. As a user moves an endpoint the line stretches, but the middle details remain the same size. If a user increases the shape's height, the middle details resize proportionately, but the line does not change.

The arrow shape shown in the figure could also be a 2-D shape. Whether such a shape should act like a line or a box depends on how it will be used: If you intend the arrow to be used in an up-down, left-right manner only, then making it a 2-D shape can make horizontal and vertical positioning easier. In addition, 2-D shapes must be rotated using the **Rotation** tool, whereas it is very easy to accidentally change the angle of a 1-D shape by nudging one of its endpoints. However, to allow the arrow shape to connect other shapes through the Visio user interface (rather than programmatically), it must either be a 1-D shape or have an outward connection point. For details about outward connection points, see *Understanding Connection Points* in *Controlling How Shapes Connect* later in this chapter. For details about connecting shapes programmatically, see Chapter 19, *Automating Connections in a Visio Solution*.

Creating Routable and Other 1-D Connectors

If you are designing solutions for connected diagrams, you must decide whether your users will use the connector tools built into Microsoft Visio to connect your shapes or to design your own connectors.

The **Connector** tool, **Connect Shapes** command (**Shape** menu), and **Dynamic Connector** shape create *routable connectors* between *placeable shapes*. A routable connector is a 1-D shape that draws a path around other shapes rather than crossing over them on the drawing page. A placeable shape is a shape (usually 2-D) that works with the routable connector. Whether shapes are placeable and routable in a drawing determines how Visio reacts when changes occur, such as when shapes are added, deleted, resized, or repositioned. In response to such changes, Visio automatically repositions shapes that are placeable and reroutes shapes that are routable.

Routable connectors can save users time when they revise complex connected diagrams. In some cases, however, you might want a connector with more predictable behavior—that is, one that does not automatically reroute. For example, if your drawing type requires connecting lines that always form a 90-degree angle or that connect shapes with a curved connector, you can create your own 1-D connector that is not routable.

Creating Routable Connectors

You can create a routable connector from any 1-D line by setting its ObjType cell in the Miscellaneous section to 2.

The value specified in the ObjType cell controls whether objects are placeable or routable in diagrams when users lay out shapes using the **Lay Out Shapes** command (**Shape** menu).

The following table provides related values for the ObjType cell.

Values for a shape's ObjType cell

Value	Meaning
0 (or &H0)	Default. Visio decides whether the shape is placeable or routable based on the drawing context.
1 (or &H1)	Shape is placeable.
2 (or &H2)	Shape is routable. Must be a 1-D shape.
4 (or &H4)	The shape is not placeable, not routable.
8 (or &H8)	Group contains placeable/routable shapes. (Reserved for Visio use.)

When you create a new 2-D shape, by default Visio sets its ObjType to No Formula, which evaluates to zero (0), meaning that Visio determines whether the shape can be placeable depending on its context. For example, if you draw a simple rectangle, the value of its ObjType cell is 0 by default. If you then use the **Connect Shapes** command or the **Connector** tool to connect the rectangle to another shape, Visio decides that the rectangle can be placeable, and sets the rectangle's ObjType cell to 1 (placeable).

> **Note** Using the ShapeSheet, you can also create a placeable 1-D shape, which can be beneficial when the shape is not a connector and will be used in a drawing with automatic layout. Setting a 2-D shape to routable, however, has no effect on its behavior.

If you are creating shapes that you do not want to work with routable connectors, set the ObjType cell to 4. Connectors can glue to connection points on the shape, but in a diagram that contains placeable and routable connectors, the nonplaceable shape is ignored—that is, routing lines behave as if the shape does not exist.

To control the path taken by a routable connector, you set its behavior, which corresponds to the value of the ShapeRouteStyle cell in the Shape Layout section. By default, the value of this cell is No Formula, which evaluates to 0, meaning the connector uses the behavior set for the page.

Controlling the layout of connectors

The **Lay Out Shapes** command (**Shape** menu) and the **Layout and Routing** tab in the **Page Setup** dialog box (click **Page Setup** on the **File** menu) provide numerous choices of behavior you can specify for selected shapes or for the page by combining different connector styles with different directions. You can also specify behavior for a shape or the page by setting ShapeSheet cells:

- For example, setting a connector's ShapeRouteStyle cell to 7 creates a routable connector that always routes as if it's contained in a tree diagram in top-to-bottom orientation. (This is equivalent to choosing **Flowchart/Tree** for **Style** and **Top to Bottom** for **Direction** in the **Lay Out Shapes** dialog box under **Placement**.)
- To define this behavior as the page default, set the RouteStyle cell to 7 in the page's Page Layout section. (This is equivalent to choosing **Tree** for **Style** and **Top to Bottom** for **Direction** on the **Layout and Routing** tab in the **Page Setup** dialog box).

For details about other settings for the ShapeRouteStyle and RouteStyle cells, search for those cells in the Microsoft Visio Developer Reference (on the **Help** menu, click **Developer Reference**).

When you create a template for a diagram that uses routable connectors and placeable shapes, you can customize the default values that Visio uses to route and place shapes. By specifying values with the **Lay Out Shapes** command (**Shape** menu), you define the default values for the page. Users can edit shapes on the page to override the page settings; however, when users create or add placeable shapes, by default, the settings for the page are used.

For details about creating diagrams that use routable connectors and placeable shapes, search for "layout" in the Microsoft Visio Help (on the **Help** menu, click **Microsoft Visio Help**).

Creating Other 1-D Connectors

When your solution calls for a connector with behavior that you can control programmatically, you can create one that does not automatically route. You can control how a connector extends from its begin point to its end point with formulas.

Creating an angled connector: an example

The following figure shows an angled connector with two right-angle bends. The custom formulas for this connector are included in this section as a demonstration of the type of formulas you need to control 1-D shapes. You can find other 1-D connectors in the **Connectors** stencil (on the **File** menu, point to **Stencils**, point to **Visio Extras**, and then click **Connectors**).

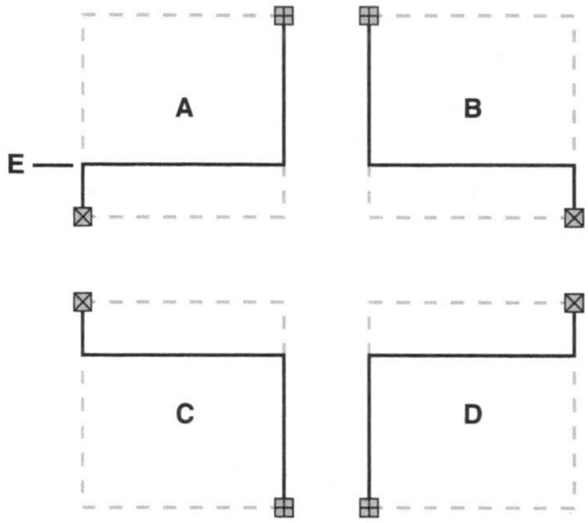

Figure 8-3 The four ways an angled connector can bend when a user moves it. (**A**) BeginY <= EndY. (**B**) BeginX > EndX. (**C**) BeginX <= EndX. (**D**) BeginY > EndY. (**E**) The connector always bends 0.25 in. (vertically) from the begin point.

With its two bends in the middle, the angled connector has two vertices that require custom formulas. To calculate the coordinates of the first vertex after the begin point, remember that its *x*-coordinate is the same as that of the begin point. The *y*-coordinate is 0.25 in. if the shape is drawn from the bottom up. If it is drawn from the top down, its *y*-coordinate is calculated as:

```
= Height - 0.25 inches
```

The *x*-coordinate for the next vertex is the same as the *x*-coordinate for the last LineTo row, which specifies the shape's end point and so is always Width or zero (0). Its *y*-coordinate is the same as the preceding vertex.

To create an angled connector

1. Select the **Line** tool and draw a straight 1-D line from left to right.
2. On the **Window** menu, click **Show ShapeSheet**.
3. Enter the following formulas in the Shape Transform section:

```
Width = GUARD(ABS(EndX - BeginX))
Height = GUARD(ABS(EndY - BeginY))
Angle = GUARD(0 deg.)
```

4. On the **Insert** menu, click **Section**, and then select **User-Defined Cells**.
5. In the User-Defined Cells section, enter a name for the cell, such as *yOffset,* and then enter *0.25 in.* in the Value cell.

6. Select the last row in the Geometry section, and then click **Row After** on the **Insert** menu. Repeat to add a total of two rows.

   Each row corresponds to a vertex of the shape.

7. In the Geometry section, enter the formulas shown in the following table.

Custom formulas in the angled connector

Row	X	Y
MoveTo	`= IF(BeginX <= EndX,0,Width)`	`= IF(BeginY <= EndY,0,Height)`
LineTo	`= Geometry1.X1`	`= IF(BeginY <= EndY, User.yOffset. Height - User.yOffset)`
LineTo	`= Geometry1.X4`	`= Geometry1.Y2`
LineTo	`= IF(BeginX <= EndX,Width,0)`	`= IF(BeginY <= EndY,Height,0)`

8. In the Protection section, set the LockHeight cell and LockVtxEdit cell to 1.

   Setting LockVtxEdit protects the geometry formulas by preventing users from editing the shape vertices. Setting LockHeight protects the height formula and removes the top and bottom handles, which aren't needed for a connector.

9. Drag the begin point or end point of the connector on the drawing page to see the angle and the offset.

If you want to allow users to change the position of the bend in the angled connector, you can add a control handle by linking User.yOffset to a control handle, and then locking the handle's *x*-position so that it moves only in the *y* direction.

Creating a height-based 1-D shape

Some shapes, such as the 1-D pipe-and-valve shape in the following figure, can stretch between two points to connect other shapes. You can create this type of 1-D shape as a single shape with multiple geometry components that have different resizing behaviors. In a 1-D shape, the endpoints control the shape's width. In the pipe-and-valve shape, when a user drags an endpoint, only the line component stretches. When a user drags a top or bottom handle, only the valve component resizes, and it does so in a way that maintains its aspect ratio.

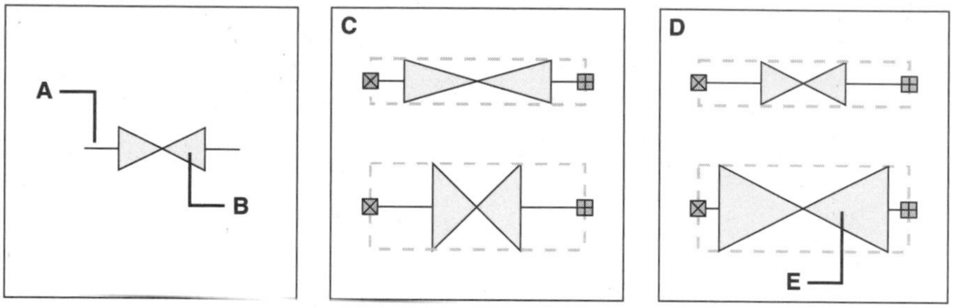

Figure 8-4 A pipe-and-valve shape with default formulas versus height-based formulas (**A**) Pipe. (**B**) Valve. (**C**) Using default formulas, the valve shape becomes distorted when stretched in either direction. (**D**) Using height-based formulas, only the pipe increases in length when the valve shape is stretched horizontally. (**E**) Using height-based formulas, the valve grows proportionately when stretched vertically.

To make the valve shape stretch and shrink the way it should, you use a height-based formula to define the width of the valve component in terms of the shape's height. To create this connector as a single shape, draw two line segments at either end of a valve shape, point to **Operations** on the **Shape** menu, and then click **Combine**.

To maintain the valve's proportions when the shape is resized, define the *x*-coordinates of the valve's vertices in relation to the center and height of the shape, as shown in the following figure. Doing so also serves to keep the valve centered in the width-height box. This approach requires that you set formulas in the X cell of the Geometry section.

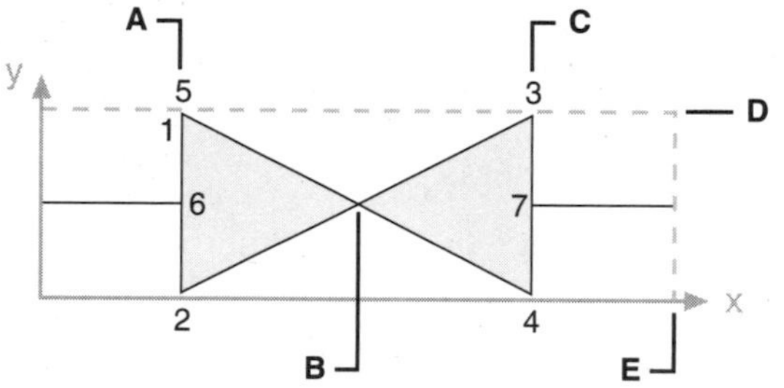

Figure 8-5 Height-based formula for a 1-D shape with multiple geometry components. (**A**) Width * 0.5 - Height * 1. (**B**) Width * 0.5. (**C**) Width * 0.5 + Height * 1. (**D**) Height. (**E**) Width.

To create this shape in a way that ensures your Geometry rows match the figures and tables shown here

1. Select the **Line** tool and draw a straight line from left to right to form the left segment of the pipe.
2. Use the **Line** tool to draw the valve, starting at point 1 as shown in the preceding figure.
3. Use the **Line** tool to draw the right segment of the pipe from left to right. Then draw the left segment of the pipe from left to right.
4. Press and hold the SHIFT key while you select the shapes in this order: valve, left line, right line.
5. On the **Shape** menu, point to **Operations**, and then click **Combine**.
6. On the **Format** menu, click **Behavior**.
7. On the **Behavior** tab, click **Line (1-dimensional)**, and then click **OK**.

To control the valve portion of the shape, open the ShapeSheet window for the combined shape and enter the formulas shown below in the Geometry1 section.

Custom formulas in pipe-and-valve shape's Geometry1 section

Row	X	Y
MoveTo	`= Width * 0.5 - Height * 1`	`= Height * 1`
LineTo	`= Geometry1.X1`	`= Height * 0`
LineTo	`= Width * 0.5 + Height * 1`	`= Height * 1`
LineTo	`= Geometry1.X3`	`= Height * 0`
LineTo	`= Geometry1.X1`	`= Geometry1.Y1`

To control the point where the left pipe segment meets the valve (vertex 6 in the preceding figure), enter the following formula:

```
Geometry2.X2        = Geometry1.X1
```

To control the point where the right pipe segment meets the valve (vertex 7 in the preceding figure), enter the following formula:

```
Geometry3.X1        = Geometry1.X3
```

Tip When you draw 1-D shapes such as the pipe-and-valve shape, you often draw several shapes and then either group or combine them. Using the **Combine** command results in a more efficient shape. If a user doesn't need to subselect component shapes, you don't need to group them, which adds a group sheet. However, you need to make sure that the endpoints of the resulting 1-D shape are in the right place.

Visio always places the begin point on the left end of a 1-D shape and the end point on the right. If you draw a shape from top to bottom and then convert it to 1-D, the endpoints might not be where you want them. So draw the component parts from left to right.

You shouldn't add any custom formulas to the component shapes before you combine them, because the **Combine** command removes them anyway.

Controlling How Shapes Connect

The behavior that allows part of a shape to stay connected to another shape is called *glue*. You can specify the part of a shape to which another shape can be glued by defining a *connection point*.

You can glue the begin or end points of a one-dimensional (1-D) shape to a guide, guide point, shape vertex, selection handle, or connection point. You can also glue the begin or end point of a 1-D shape to the pin (a shape's center of rotation) of a 1-D or 2-D shape to create walking glue (also known as *dynamic* glue). If you've enabled users to glue shapes to vertices or handles, Microsoft Visio automatically creates an inward connection point on a shape when you glue another shape to its vertices or handles.

When an endpoint of a 1-D shape is glued to another shape, you can move the glued-to shape, and the glued endpoint stays attached, stretching the 1-D shape as the unglued endpoint stays anchored. When a 2-D shape is glued to another shape and you move the glued-to shape, the 2-D shape moves with it.

Defining a Connector's Glue Behavior

You can choose the type of glue behavior a 1-D connector shape uses, *static* or *dynamic*:

- If the endpoint of a 1-D shape remains fixed to a particular connection point, it is said to use static glue. Static glue is point-to-point glue: The connection is always between the same two points, no matter how the shapes move. The default behavior for a shape you draw or any shape that is not placeable or routable is static glue.
- If the 1-D shape's endpoint "walks" from connection point to connection point (or from side to side) to improve the visibility of the connection as the other shape moves, it is said to use dynamic glue. This is how routable connectors glue placeable shapes. You can think of dynamic glue as shape-to-shape glue: It connects two shapes between the shortest route allowed by a particular routing style, simplifying a drawing.

When you create a connector, you can set it to use dynamic glue so that its endpoints can move from one connection point to another as a user moves the shapes to which the connector is glued. Visio redraws the connector so it connects the shapes at their two closest connection points.

If the connector's endpoint is glued with static glue, the selection handle displays the default begin point or end point symbol in dark red. If the connector's endpoint is glued with dynamic glue, its selection handle is solid red.

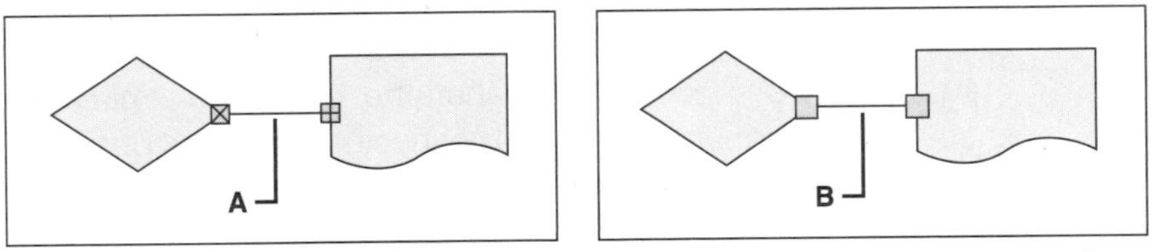

Figure 8-6 A connector defined to use dynamic glue can create a connection with static or dynamic glue. (**A**) Drag an endpoint to connect with static glue. (**B**) Drag an endpoint to the middle of a shape or press CTRL and drag an endpoint to connect with dynamic glue.

To define static or dynamic glue for a connector

1. Select the shape, and then click **Show Shapesheet** on the **Window** menu.
2. If the Glue Info section is not displayed, click **Sections** on the **View** menu. In the **View Sections** dialog box, select **Glue info**, and then click **OK**.
3. In the Glue Info section of the ShapeSheet spreadsheet, enter *0* in the GlueType cell to specify static glue, or enter *2* to specify dynamic glue.

By default, dynamic glue connects via the shortest route allowed by a particular routing style between two connection points or midshape selection handles. You can set a preference so that a shape with dynamic glue walks to a side, top, or bottom connection point when the glued endpoint is moved. To do this, set the WalkPreference cell in the Glue Info section. Routable connectors ignore the setting of the WalkPreference cell; their routing behavior is controlled by the value of the ShapeRouteStyle cell. For details about WalkPreference and ShapeRouteStyle settings, see the Microsoft Visio Developer Reference (on the **Help** menu, click **Developer Reference**).

> **Note** When a user glues a 1-D connector with dynamic glue to another shape, Visio generates a formula that refers to the EventXFMod cell of the other shape. When that shape is changed, Visio recalculates any formula that refers to its EventXFMod cell, including the formula in the BegTrigger and EndTrigger cells. These two cells contain formulas generated for a 1-D shape by Visio when the 1-D shape is glued to other shapes. Other formulas for the 1-D connector refer to the BegTrigger and EndTrigger cells and move the begin or end point of the connector or alter its shape as needed.

Specifying What Can be Glued

You can specify the parts of a shape to which another shape can be glued on a page in the **Snap & Glue** dialog box. For example, most Visio templates enable users to glue 1-D shapes only to guides, guide points, and connection points. On the **Tools** menu, click **Snap & Glue** and select additional **Glue to** options that are appropriate for your drawing or template.

Although 1-D shapes are usually used to connect 2-D shapes, you can glue the following parts of 2-D shapes:

- An entire side of a shape (shape geometry) to a guide or a guide point
- An edge of the alignment box to a guide
- A selection handle to a guide point
- A control handle to a connection point
- An outward or inward/outward connection point to an inward or inward/outward connection point on another shape

Understanding Connection Points

When you design a shape, you indicate locations where it can glue or be glued by adding connection points to the shape. As you create masters, consider which points users will most likely need and avoid creating additional points, because they can make a shape respond less efficiently.

A connection point's type influences whether other shapes can be glued to it or whether the shape that has the connection point can be glued to other shapes:

- Other shapes can be glued to an *inward* connection point. Inward connection points behave like connection points in versions of Visio products earlier than Visio 2000. An inward connection point attracts endpoints of 1-D shapes and outward or inward/outward connection points of other shapes. Diagrams such as flowcharts and organization charts that consist of 2-D shapes and 1-D connectors need only inward connection points on 2-D shapes.
- A shape with an *outward* connection point can be glued to an inward connection point on another shape. An outward connection point is attracted to inward and inward/outward connection points of other shapes. Office layout diagrams and CAD diagrams that consist almost exclusively of 2-D shapes can take advantage of outward connection points.
- An *inward/outward* connection point behaves like an inward connection point when you glue the endpoint of a 1-D shape or a shape with an outward connection point to it. It behaves like an outward connection point when you glue it to another shape. Inward/outward connection points are useful for shapes that might be glued together in any order. For example, if wall segment shapes have an inward/outward connection point at each end, either end of one wall segment shape could be glued to either end of another wall segment shape,

in any order. If such a shape had an outward connection point on one end and an inward connection point on the other, you would be forced to glue an outward end to an inward end, which would be less convenient.

> **Note** Beginning with Visio 2000, Visio imports connection points created in earlier versions of Visio as inward connection points with no preferred direction. Any scratch formulas in the A, B, C, and D cells of such rows are imported without change.

The following illustration shows a paving tile shape that has all three kinds of connection points.

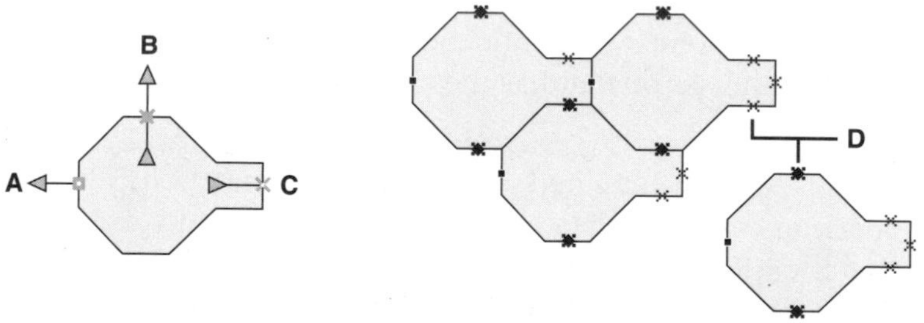

Figure 8-7 A paving tile shape with inward, outward, and inward/outward connection points. (**A**) Outward connection point. (**B**) Inward/outward connection point. (**C**) Inward connection point. (**D**) An inward/outward connection point snaps to the closest inward or inward/outward connection point.

To glue outward and inward/outward connection points, the **Connection Points** check box must be selected under **Glue to** in the **Snap & Glue** dialog box on the user's system. When a user drags a shape with outward or inward/outward connection points, the shape snaps to the nearest inward or inward/outward connection point. If a shape has more than one outward connection point, Visio snaps the connection point closest to the mouse pointer.

A connection point can have a direction, or vector, which determines whether shapes rotate when they are glued together. Initially, if a connection point is placed on a shape's geometry, its vector is perpendicular to the segment in which the connection point is placed. Otherwise, the connection point has a vector of 0 (that is, no direction). When an outward connection point is glued to an inward (or inward/outward) connection point and both connection points have a non-zero vector, Visio aligns the vectors of both, rotating the shape as needed. If either connection point has a vector of 0, the shapes are not rotated.

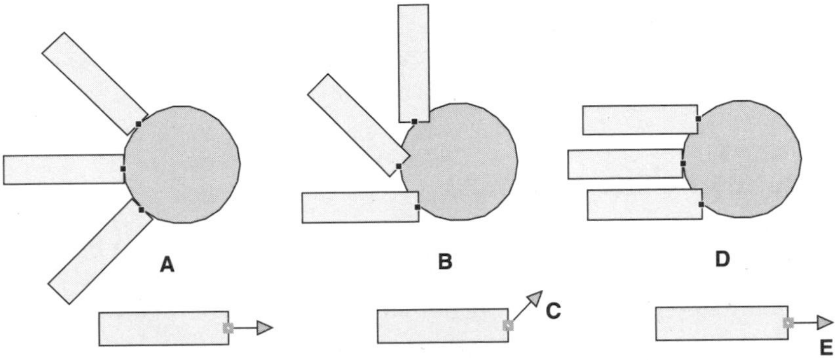

Figure 8-8 A connection point's vector determines how a shape rotates when it is glued. (**A**) Perpendicular vector (the default). (**B**) Angled vector. (**C**) To change a connection point's vector, select the connection point and drag the green direction handle to the angle you want. (**D**) No vector. (**E**) To prevent a shape from rotating when it is glued, drag the direction handle onto the connection point. The green direction handle turns gray, which indicates that the connection point has no vector.

When a shape with an outward connection point is glued, Visio generates formulas in its PinX, PinY, and Angle cells representing that shape's connection with the shape to which it is glued. For example, these are the formulas generated for one of the shapes glued along a perpendicular vector. Circle1 is the name of the shape to which it is glued; references to the EventXFMod cell of the circle shape and the page ensure that the glued shape moves or rotates as needed to preserve the connection. The following LOCTOPAR and ANGLETOPAR formulas convert local coordinates of the glued shape to the coordinate system of the shape to which it is glued (Circle1).

```
PinX = LOCTOPAR(PNT(Circle1!Connections.X2+-0.3536 in.,
           Circle1!Connections.Y2+0.3536 in.),
           Circle1!EventXFMod,ThePage!EventXFMod)

PinY = LOCTOPAR(PNT(Circle1!Connections.X2+-0.3536 in.,
           Circle1!Connections.Y2+0.3536 in.),
           Circle1!EventXFMod,ThePage!EventXFMod)

Angle = ANGLETOPAR(-45 deg.,Circle1!EventXFMod,EventXFMod)
```

Compare the following PinX and PinY formulas of a shape with a vector of 0. If the inward or outward connection points don't have a direction vector, Visio doesn't generate an Angle formula.

```
PinX = PNTX(LOCTOPAR(PNT(Circle3!Connections.X2,
          Circle3!Connections.Y2),
          Circle3!EventXFMod,ThePage!EventXFMod))+-0.5 in.

PinY = PNTY(LOCTOPAR(PNT(Circle3!Connections.X2,
          Circle3!Connections.Y2),
          Circle3!EventXFMod,ThePage!EventXFMod))+0 in.
```

Adding Connection Points to a Shape

Microsoft Visio automatically creates an inward connection point at the vertex or selection handle of a shape when a connector is glued at that position, so you must manually add connection points only when you need an inward connection point in a nonstandard location, or when you need an outward or inward/outward connection point.

You can add a connection point to a shape by using the **Connection Point** tool. To add outward connection points or change a connection point's type, on the **Tools** menu, click **Options**, click the **Advanced** tab, and then ensure **Run in developer mode** is selected under **Developer Settings**.

To create a connection point

1. Select the shape.
2. Click the **Connection Point** tool.
3. Do one of the following:
   - To create an inward connection point, hold down CTRL, and then click where you want to add the connection point.
   - To create an outward connection point, hold down CTRL+ALT, and then click where you want to add the connection point.
   - To create an inward/outward connection point, select an existing connection point, right-click, and click **Inward & Outward** on the shortcut menu.

Note You can change the connection point "gender" by right-clicking a connection point and clicking **Inward**, **Outward**, or **Inward/Outward** on the shortcut menu.

When you add a connection point, Visio adds the Connection Points section to the ShapeSheet window with a row describing the point's *x*- and *y*-local coordinates, the *x*- and *y*-coordinates of its direction, and its type (inward, outward, or inward/outward). By changing the formulas for a connection point's coordinates, you can control how the location of the connection point changes when a shape is resized.

If you add a connection point to a shape's geometry, Visio orients the direction vector perpendicularly to the segment in which the connection point was added—inward for an inward connection point, outward for an outward connection point, or both inward and outward for an inward/outward connection point.

Tip If the **Glue To** setting for **Shape geometry** is selected in the **Snap & Glue** dialog box (**Tools** menu) and the user drags a shape with an outward connection point to another shape, Visio automatically creates an inward connection point with the appropriate vector and glues the shapes together. If the shapes are dragged apart, breaking the glue, Visio automatically deletes the connection point it created.

To prevent other shapes from being glued to a shape's geometry, set the NoSnap cell in the shape's corresponding Geometry section to TRUE. This disables snapping to geometry, gluing to geometry, nudging 1-D shapes to geometry, 2-D snap and glue, and snapping to shape extensions. For example, you might do this to prevent a window shape from connecting to an electrical outlet, or a chair from connecting to another chair. Setting NoSnap causes shapes to rotate less as the user drags them across potential snap points, and filters out geometry extensions that aren't useful.

Naming Connection Points

You can rename the Connections Points row to create a more meaningful reference for the value contained in the X or Y cell of the same row. The cell name you enter must be unique within the section. When you create a name for one cell in this section, Microsoft Visio names all the cells in the section with the default name, Connections.Row_*n*. If no rows in the section are named, the name cell is blank.

For example, to rename the cell for the first row, enter *Custom* in the formula bar to create the cell name Connections.Custom. Visio creates the name Connections.Row_2 for the cell in the second row. To refer to the X cell of the first row, use Connections.Custom.X1 or Connections.X1. To refer to the Y cell of the first row, use Connections.Custom.Y1 or Connections.Y1. To refer to the X cell of the second row, use Connections.Row_2.X or Connections.X2, and to refer to its Y cell, use Connections.Row_2.Y or Connections.Y2.

Designing Shapes for the Dynamic Connector

The dynamic connector can extend inside a shape's bounding box to intersect the shape's geometry. (A shape's bounding box is the smallest nonrotated rectangle that encloses the shape's alignment box.)

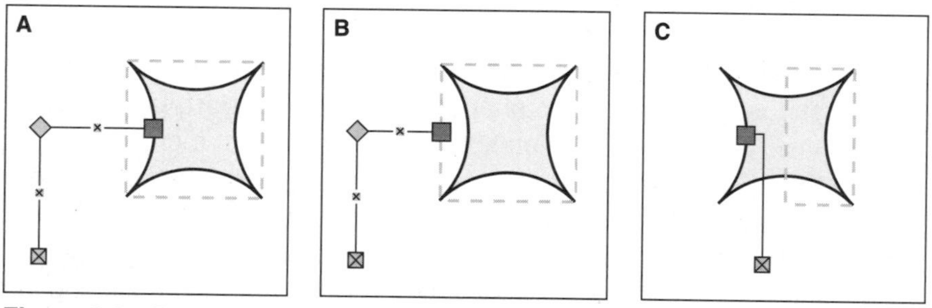

Figure 8-9 Dynamic intersection with shape geometry. (**A**) Dynamic intersection enabled. (**B**) Dynamic intersection disabled. (**C**) Dynamic intersection enabled for a shape with geometry outside of its alignment box. The dynamic connector "finds" the outermost geometry on the side to which it is glued.

The dynamic connector can also extend into groups to intersect the geometry of a shape in a group.

Note In versions earlier than Visio 2000, the dynamic connector did not extend into the shape's bounding box or into groups.

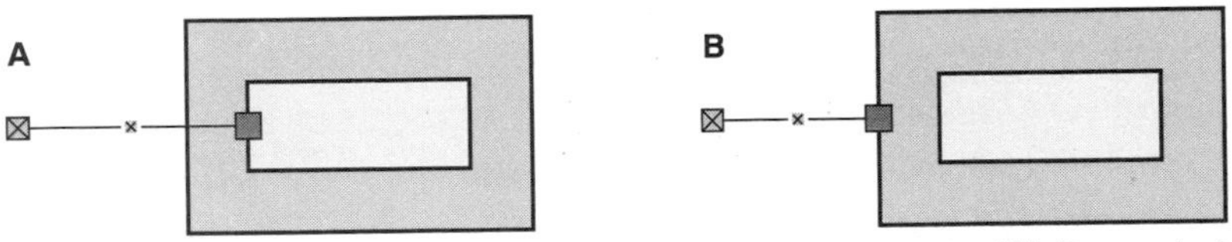

Figure 8-10 Dynamic intersection with shapes in groups. (**A**) Dynamic intersection enabled. (**B**) Dynamic intersection disabled.

Dynamic intersection is enabled for shapes by default. However, dynamic intersection causes the Visio engine to perform complex calculations that can affect shape performance when a connector is dynamically glued to a shape, especially in shapes that have multiple or complex geometries, or in groups that contain many shapes.

Dynamic intersection for a shape is controlled by the ShapeFixedCode cell in its Shape Layout section. ShapeFixedCode contains an 8-bit integer in which each bit controls a different dynamic connection behavior. To disable dynamic intersection for a shape, set the value of its ShapeFixedCode cell to its current value plus 128. To reenable dynamic intersection for that shape, subtract 128 from the current value of its ShapeFixedCode cell. For details about setting ShapeFixedCode to other values, see the Microsoft Visio Developer Reference (on the **Help** menu, click **Developer Reference**).

To develop usable shapes that perform well with the dynamic connector, consider the following suggestions:

- Design the shape so that all of its geometry is within its alignment box. This yields the best-looking results when a dynamic connector is glued to the shape.
- Provide connection points on the shape if you want the dynamic connector to glue to specific locations. If a shape has a connection point on the side that the dynamic connector "walks" to, the connector glues to the connection point rather than the shape's geometry, thus avoiding the potentially time-consuming calculations involved in dynamic intersection.
- If you want to prevent the dynamic connector from intersecting a shape's geometry under any circumstances, disable dynamic intersection by setting the shape's ShapeFixedCode cell. This is especially recommended for shapes enclosed within other shapes, as often occurs in groups.

9

Designing Text Behavior

About Text in Shapes and Masters 184

Resizing Shapes with Text 189

Controlling Text Rotation 194

Working with Text Formulas 200

By default, users can add text to any Microsoft Visio shape. When you design shapes, it's important to consider the position and appearance of the text block attached to a shape. Should the text rotate with the shape? Should the text resize with the shape? Should the shape be allowed to have text at all?

The variety of possible text behaviors is endless, but in practice only a limited number prove useful. After all, the goal is to produce good-looking, readable text. Because smarter text behavior usually involves larger, slower, and more complex formulas, you must balance the text block's sophistication with the expected uses for the shape. There is no single, simple answer, but consistency is important: Similar shapes should have similar text behavior.

About Text in Shapes and Masters

The text of a shape or a master has a coordinate system defined by an origin and axes relative to the shape's local coordinate system. This coordinate system is called the *text block*. When you create a shape or master, by default its text block is exactly the same size as the shape's or master's width-height box: It has the same width and height and has zero rotation in relation to the shape. The default text block pin is in the center.

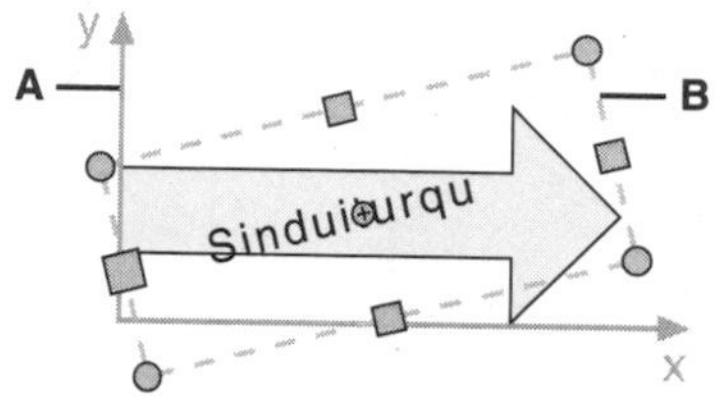

Figure 9-1 The local coordinate systems of a shape and its text block. (**A**) Local coordinates of the unrotated shape. (**B**) Text block rotated with respect to the shape's local coordinate system.

The following table outlines some of the questions that you should consider when you design the text behavior for a shape or a master.

Factors to consider when designing text behavior

Item	Questions to ask
Text block position	Location in shape or master?
	Should the shape or master have multiple text blocks?
Text block size	Limit to a minimum or maximum size?
	Grow text block as more text is added?
	Should text determine shape size?
	Affected by shape resizing, rotating, or flipping?
Text block appearance	Should text use opaque background or transparent color?
User interaction	Should the user be prevented from adding or changing the text in a shape?
	Should the user be able to move the text block in relation to the shape?

Viewing Text Attributes in the ShapeSheet Window

A shape's Text Transform section defines a text block's size, location, and rotation within the shape's local coordinate system, just as the Shape Transform section positions a shape within its group or page. To view the Text Transform section: Open the ShapeSheet window for the shape or master, click **Section** on the **Insert** menu, select **Text Transform**, and then click **OK**. By default, the Text Transform section contains the values shown in the following table.

Text Transform section default values for a new shape

Cell	Formula
TxtAngle	`= 0 deg.`
TxtHeight	`= Height * 1`
TxtLocPinX	`= TxtWidth * 0.5`
TxtLocPinY	`= TxtHeight * 0.5`
TxtPinX	`= Width * 0.5`
TxtPinY	`= Height * 0.5`
TxtWidth	`= Width * 1`

Options in the **Text** dialog box correspond to cells in the shape's Character, Paragraph, Tabs, and Text Block Format sections. When a user applies a formatting command on the **Format** menu, Microsoft Visio updates cells in these sections of the shape's sheet.

The row numbers displayed in these sections reflect the number of bytes of text that use the formatting defined in that row, as shown in the following figure. The number of bytes and the number of characters in a text block are often the same; however, in a multi-byte character set such as Japanese, the byte count and the character count might be different. For example, in a Character section with the row numbers 18, 16, and 13, the first 18 bytes of text in the text block have the format described in the first row. The next 16 bytes of text have the format described in the second row, and so on.

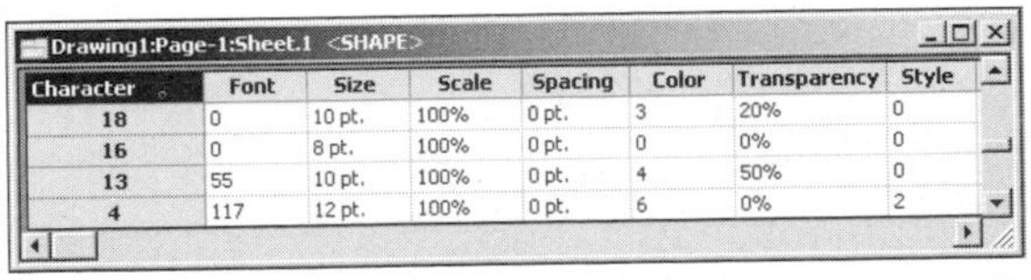
Drawing1:Page-1:Sheet.1 <SHAPE>

Character	Font	Size	Scale	Spacing	Color	Transparency	Style
18	0	10 pt.	100%	0 pt.	3	20%	0
16	0	8 pt.	100%	0 pt.	0	0%	0
13	55	10 pt.	100%	0 pt.	4	50%	0
4	117	12 pt.	100%	0 pt.	6	0%	2

Figure 9-2 The Character section for a shape with several different font formats.

In general, if you write custom formulas in the Character, Paragraph, Tabs, or Text Block Format sections, be sure you consider user actions that could overwrite your work. For example, if a user locally formats characters in a text block, a new row is added to describe the formatting of those characters. When a user cuts text, the affected rows are deleted. If you want to write a custom formula in a cell of the Character section, copy the formula into that cell in each row of the section. That way, as rows are added and deleted, the formula remains intact.

> **Note** If the shape is a group, formulas that refer to the Width and Height cells might need to be modified to access the group's values rather than those of a component shape.

Controlling the Text Block's Position

As you develop a shape, it often makes sense to move the text block from its default position to more easily accommodate readable text. For example, in many Visio shapes, the text block appears below the shape by default so that typing in it doesn't obscure the shape.

Moving a text block manually

You can easily move a shape's text block manually by selecting the shape using the **Text Block** tool.

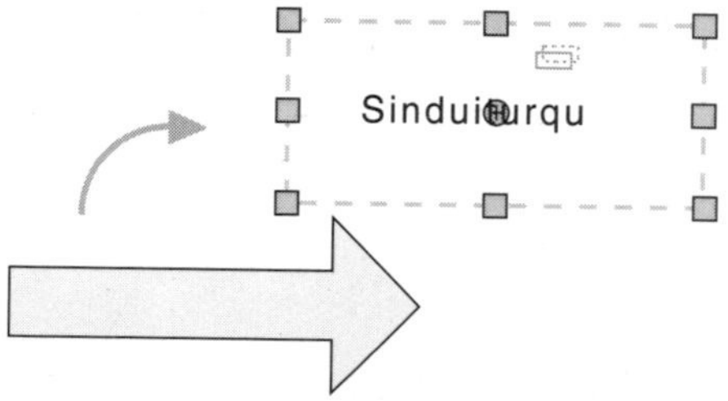

Figure 9-3 To move the text block manually, select a shape with the **Text Block** tool, and then drag. The **Text Block** tool turns into a double box when you select a shape's text block.

When you select a shape's text block using the **Text Block** tool you can also quickly resize it by dragging a side selection handle, or rotate it by dragging a rotation handle. If you are designing shapes to distribute to other users, make sure that the text block is big enough for users to select and adjust easily. For example, the default size of a one-dimensional (1-D) shape's text block may be too small for a user to select and adjust with the **Text Block** tool.

Adding control handles to a text block

If you want to provide the users of your shapes with a more obvious method of adjusting text position, you can add a control handle that moves the text block.

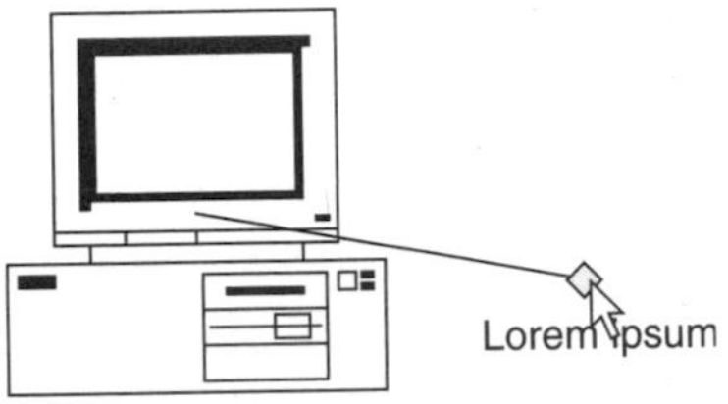

Figure 9-4 Adding a control handle to a shape's text block makes it easy for users to reposition it.

You can set the text block position and define a control handle for the block's pin by adding a Controls section in the ShapeSheet for the shape, and entering formulas in that row. A control handle is added for each row that you add to the Controls section. The formulas in the control handle's row can vary depending on the position you choose for the text block. The following steps describe how to add a control handle for a text block that is centered below the shape.

To add a control handle to a text block

1. Draw a shape on the page and then select it.
2. On the **Window** menu, click **Show ShapeSheet**.
3. On the **Insert** menu, click **Section**, select **Controls**, and then click **OK**.
4. Add these formulas in the Controls section to center the text block below the shape with a control handle that appears in the center of the text block:

```
X = Width * 0.5 + TxtWidth * 0
Y = Height * 0 + TxtHeight * - 0.5
X Dynamics = Width/2
Y Dynamics = Height/2
X Behavior = (Controls.X1 > Width/2) * 2 + 2
Y Behavior = (Controls.Y1 > Height/2) * 2 + 2
```

5. Add these formulas to the Text Transform section:

```
TxtPinX = Controls.X1
TxtPinY = Controls.Y1
```

> **Note** To view the Text Transform section, open the ShapeSheet window for the shape or master, and then on the **Insert** menu, click **Section**, select **Text Transform**, and then click **OK**.

The formulas in the X and Y cells in the Controls section specify the position of the control handle in relation to the shape's local coordinates. The formulas in the X Dynamics and Y Dynamics cells set the position of the control handle's anchor point at the center of the shape. For details about control handle anchor points, see *Setting a Control Handle's Anchor Point* in Chapter 7, *Enhancing Shape Behavior*. The X Behavior and Y Behavior cells define the behavior of the control handle after it is moved or after the shape is resized.

Controlling Text in a Group

When you group shapes, a text block is created for the group; you can also work with the text blocks for individual shapes contained in the group. By default, the group's text block opens when a user presses the F2 key, selects the **Text** tool A, or begins typing. To add text to any other shape in the group, a user must first subselect the shape.

It's a good idea to use a group's text block to contain text in a master that represents a group that you want users to edit easily. For example, you might create a master for a road sign indicating a speed limit. To allow users to edit the speed limit value easily, you could use the group's text block to contain the speed limit number, while a shape contained in the group might contain the "Speed Limit" label.

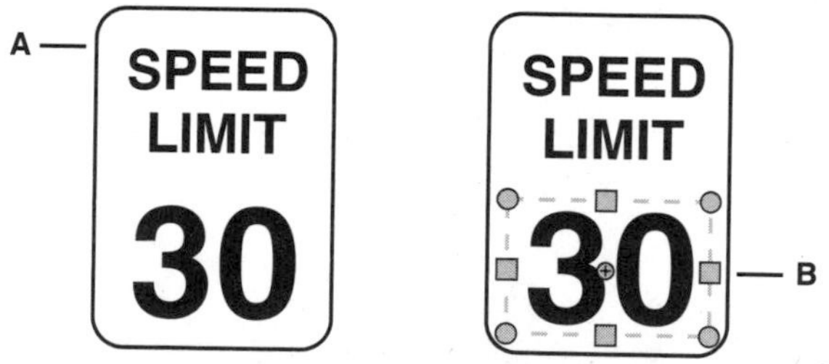

Figure 9-5 Using a group's text block makes it easy for users to edit text in masters you create. When a master is a group (**A**), the group's text block (**B**) can contain the text that users are most likely to edit.

You can prevent a group's text block from being edited either by clearing **Edit text of group** under **Group behavior** in the group's **Behavior** dialog box (on the **Format** menu, click **Behavior**) or by changing the value of the group's IsTextEditTarget cell from TRUE to FALSE.

If the group's text block cannot be edited, the text block of the topmost shape in a group is opened when a user presses F2, selects the **Text** tool, or begins typing. If a group's text block cannot be edited and the topmost shape in a group is itself a group, the text block settings for that group determine whether the group's text block or that of the topmost shape in the group is opened.

For details about grouping shapes, see Chapter 6, *Grouping and Merging Shapes*.

Resizing Shapes with Text

Text associated with your shapes should look good after users edit the text or resize the shape. You can control text behavior and appearance with formulas that correlate shape geometry and text. You add text formulas by editing the cells in the ShapeSheet window.

This section describes how to control the size of a shape's text block as a user types in it, base a shape's size on either the amount or value of its text, and proportionately change a shape's font as the shape is resized.

Controlling Text Block Size

When you customize text block behavior, you'll often want the text block to expand as users add text. You can add formulas that control text block size by setting the initial boundaries of the text block and then ensuring that the text block can resize to encompass added text.

To control the text block size, use the MAX function to define the maximum allowable size and the TEXTWIDTH and TEXTHEIGHT functions, which evaluate the width and height of the composed text (theText) in a shape. Add these formulas to the shape's Text Transform section to create a text block that expands as the user types more text:

```
TxtWidth = MAX(TEXTWIDTH(theText), 8 * Char.Size)
TxtHeight= TEXTHEIGHT(theText, TxtWidth)
```

> **Note** To view the Text Transform section, open the ShapeSheet window for the shape or master. On the **Insert** menu, click **Section**, select **Text Transform**, and then click **OK**.

You can modify the previous formula, or enter your own formulas to specify different behavior.

Controlling text block width

By default, the width of the text block is set to whichever value is greater: the longest text line terminated by a hard return, or eight times the font size (which ensures that the text block is at least wide enough to hold a word or two). If the text block contains text formatted with more than one font size, this formula uses the size of the first font used in the text block at the time the formula was created.

To tie the width of a text block to a variable You can enter formulas that tie the width of a text block to a different variable, such as the width of the shape or the font size of the text, or you can specify a fixed width for the text block. By default, the text block width is the same as the width of the shape. If you wanted the text block to be half the width of the shape instead, you would enter this formula in the Text Transform section of the shape's sheet:

```
TxtWidth = Width/2
```

Or, if you wanted the text block to be 20 times the width of the font size, you would enter this formula:

```
TxtWidth = 20 * Char.Size
```

To set a minimum text block width You can also set a text block's width to a minimum size by using the MIN function. For example, this formula ensures that when a shape is resized, its text block doesn't stretch wider than 4 inches or resize narrower than 0.5 inch:

```
TxtWidth = MIN(4 in., MAX(0.5 in., Width))
```

In this case, the value for maximum text block width will be the larger of either 0.5 inch or the width of the shape. The minimum width for the text block is calculated in turn by comparing the maximum value with 4 inches, and choosing whichever is smaller.

To prevent a text block from resizing If you want to prevent the text block from resizing if the shape is resized, you can enter a fixed width for the text block. For example, to set a text block's width to 2 inches, you would enter this formula:

```
TxtWidth = 2 in.
```

Controlling text block height

Normally, you want the height of a text block to expand when users add text to it. When you're designing the behavior of text blocks, you want to build in as much flexibility as possible so users aren't prevented from adding text to a shape. By default, TxtHeight is equal to the height of the shape. Adding the following TxtHeight formula returns the height of the shape's composed text where no text line exceeds TxtWidth:

```
TxtHeight = TEXTHEIGHT(theText, TxtWidth)
```

This formula returns a value that represents the height of the text in the shape, including line spacing and space before and after each paragraph in the block, assuming that no line in the block is longer than the maximum value for TxtWidth. This formula delivers good results in most cases, allowing the height of the text block to expand as users add text.

Basing Shape Size on the Amount of Text

You can create a shape whose size depends on the amount of text it contains. If you want a shape that is just big enough to fit the text typed into it, such as a word balloon or text callout shape, use the TEXTWIDTH and TEXTHEIGHT functions as part of the formulas for the shape's width and height.

For example, the following formula in the Shape Transform section limits a shape's width to the length of the text lines it contains plus a small margin.

```
Width = GUARD(TEXTWIDTH(theText) + 0.5 in.)
```

The function returns the width of all the text in the shape (theText). The shape's width is limited to that value plus 0.5 inch; when the text block is empty, the shape's width is 0.5 inch. The GUARD function prevents the user from stretching the shape's width with selection handles, which would cause new values to overwrite the formula in the Width cell. To make it more obvious to users that they cannot stretch the shape manually, you could also set the LockWidth cell in the Protection section.

This related formula limits a shape's height to the number of lines of text it contains:

```
Height = GUARD(TEXTHEIGHT(theText,Width))
```

> **Tip** The TEXTWIDTH and TEXTHEIGHT functions cause Microsoft Visio to recompose the shape's text with each keystroke. To maximize performance, you can include a minimum-size test in your formula so the text grows only after the text reaches a given width or height. Beyond that width or height, Visio still must recompose the text with each keystroke. For example, you can create a 2-inch by 0.5-inch box that grows in height to accommodate additional text. To offset potential performance problems, the box doesn't resize until the text height reaches 0.5 inch. To create this behavior, add these formulas to the Shape Transform section:
>
> ```
> Width   =  2 in.
> Height  =  GUARD(MAX(.5 in. TEXTHEIGHT(TheText, _
>            Width)))
> ```

Basing Shape Size on Text Value

You can create a shape whose size is controlled by the value of the text it contains. For example, in a bar chart, you can ensure that the size of a bar depends on the value it represents. With the EVALTEXT function, you can create simple charting shapes or other shapes into which users type a value that determines the shape's width or height. For example, to associate a shape's width with its text value, put the following formula in the Shape Transform section:

```
Width = GUARD(EVALTEXT(TheText))
```

The EVALTEXT function evaluates the text in the shape's text block as if it was a formula and returns the result. For example, if you type *10 cm,* the shape's width changes to 10 cm. If there is no text or the text cannot be evaluated—for example, a nonnumeric value is typed—the shape's width is zero. You can further refine the shape by resizing it only in the direction of growth, such as for a bar that grows to the right. To do this, use the **Rotation** tool to move the shape's pin to the stationary end.

Changing the Font Size as a Shape is Resized

By default, when a user resizes a shape, its geometry and text block change, but the font size does not. You can make font size a function of shape geometry by writing formulas in the Character section of the ShapeSheet. The formulas discussed in this section adjust only the character size. If you want to change text indents or line spacing, you must use similar formulas in the cells that control those attributes.

> **Note** If a shape is to be used in scaled drawings, you should take the drawing scale into account when you make font size a function of shape height.

Writing a Formula to Resize Text

You can make font size a function of a shape's size so that when a user resizes the shape, its text increases in proportion to the value of its height. To create a shape whose size and text font size resize proportionately, use the following general formula in the shape's Character section:

```
Size = (Height/<original height>) * (<original font size>)
```

For example:

```
Size = (Height/1 in.) * 12pt
```

The third value in the formula is a ratio derived from dividing the original text size by the height of the shape. For example, if you use the **Triangle** shape from the **Basic Shapes** stencil at its default size, this value will range from 0.037 for text that was originally 4 points to 1.1852 for text that was originally 128 points.

To improve shape performance, you could store the proportional formula in a user-defined cell. For example, assume the original shape height is 3 cm and the original font size is 10 pt. Insert the User-Defined Cells section in the ShapeSheet window, and then add the following formulas:

```
User.FontSize       = Height/3cm * 10pt
Char.Size           = User.FontSize
```

> **Note** To insert the User-Defined Cells section in the ShapeSheet window: Select the shape, click **Show ShapeSheet** on the **Window** menu, click **Section** on the **Insert** menu, select the **User-defined cells** check box, and then click **OK**.

If you want to ensure that the font size is always readable, you can limit the range of acceptable sizes. For example, to limit font size from 4 to 128 points, you would use the MIN and MAX functions in conjunction with the proportional formula previously mentioned:

```
User.FontSize = MIN(128pt, MAX(4pt, Height/3cm * 10pt))
```

For details about the MIN and MAX formula syntax, see the Microsoft Visio Developer Reference (on the **Help** menu, click **Developer Reference**).

Be sure to use minimum and maximum font sizes that are supported by the expected printers and drivers. To ensure consistency if the Character section for a shape contains more than one row, the Size cells in subsequent rows should use similar formulas.

Controlling Text Rotation

You can control the appearance of rotated text so that users don't have to read upside-down text. By default, when a shape is rotated, the text block rotates, too—which can cause readability problems for shapes rotated from 90 to 270 degrees. If you are designing shapes for use in drawings where readability is an issue, you can customize text rotation behavior using one of the following methods:

- To prevent upside-down text as a shape is rotated, use the GRAVITY function, which orients the letter baseline toward the bottom or right edge of the page.
- To prevent text from rotating under any circumstances, use a counterrotation formula to keep the text block level with respect to the bottom of the page as a shape is rotated.

Writing Formulas to Control Text Rotation

You can use the GRAVITY function to prevent upside-down text or to ensure that text blocks are always level with respect to the bottom of the page with a counterrotation formula.

In addition, you can choose whether the gravity or level text block is centered over the shape or offset from it. For example, a text pointer like those shown in the following figures is formatted with a solid color background and remains centered on the shape. By contrast, if you were designing street shapes for a map, you might want to offset the street names from the lines that represent the streets.

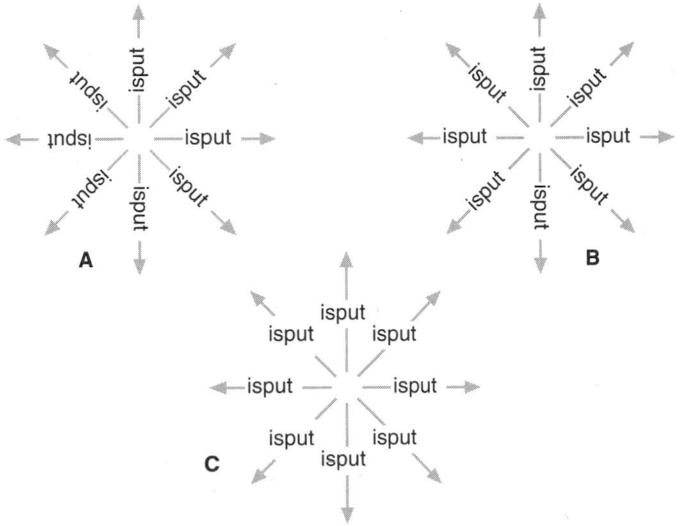

Figure 9-6 Text can rotate with a shape, or not. Default behavior can result in upside-down text (**A**). Gravity formulas adjust text block orientation for readability (**B**), while level text formulas counterrotate the text block to keep it upright (**C**).

Rotation is cumulative. If you rotate a shape's text block, and then rotate the shape, the amount of the shape's rotation is added to the amount of the text block's rotation.

Gravity Formulas

The GRAVITY formula calculates the text block rotation for the indicated shape rotation. Angle is a reference to the Angle cell of the shape and represents the shape's current rotation. The syntax for the GRAVITY formula is:

```
GRAVITY(Angle, limit1, limit2)
```

To specify gravity behavior for a shape's text, you add the GRAVITY formula to the Text Transform section in the shape's ShapeSheet spreadsheet. For example:

```
TxtAngle = GRAVITY(Angle, -60deg., 120deg.)
```

If the value of Angle falls within the range defined by the following two angles, in this case –60 deg. and 120 deg., the formula returns a value of 180 degrees and the text block is rotated 180 degrees to read correctly. If the Angle doesn't fall within the range, the formula returns a value of zero (0) degrees, and the text block is not rotated. Using this formula, the text is upright for most angles of rotation. For details about GRAVITY formula syntax, see the Microsoft Visio Developer Reference (on the **Help** menu, click **Developer Reference**).

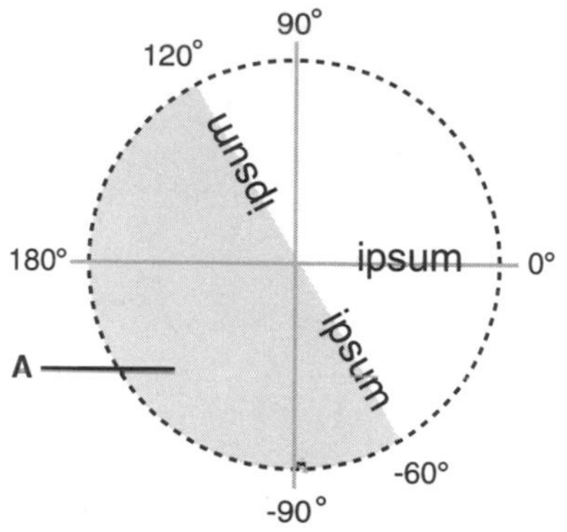

Figure 9-7 Without GRAVITY behavior, text rotated from 120 to 300 (or –60) degrees (**A**) appears upside down.

Counterrotation Formulas for Level Text

To counterrotate a text block as a shape is rotated, add the following formula to the Text Transform section in the shape's ShapeSheet:

```
TxtAngle = IF(BITXOR(FlipX, FlipY), Angle, -Angle)
```

This formula checks to see if the shape has been flipped, and determines the angle to use based on that information. If the shape has been flipped in both dimensions or has not been flipped at all (if FlipX and FlipY are either both TRUE or both FALSE), the BITXOR formula returns a value of FALSE and the IF formula returns the value –Angle. The original angle is maintained if the shape has been flipped in only one dimension (if either FlipX or FlipY is TRUE). The Microsoft Visio engine writes only the values FALSE (0) or TRUE (1) into the FlipX and FlipY cells, so you can safely assume these are the only values present.

If the shape will never be flipped, you can use a simpler formula to counterrotate the text block:

```
TxtAngle = -Angle
```

If you rotate a shape's text block (such that TxtAngle > 0 degrees), and then rotate the shape, the apparent text angle is the sum of the value of TxtAngle and Angle.

Constraining Text Block Size

When you're designing level text for a small shape, the shape can become obscured by the text if a user types a lot of text or rotates the shape to certain angles. You can constrain the width of the text block to accommodate shapes using the formulas described in this section.

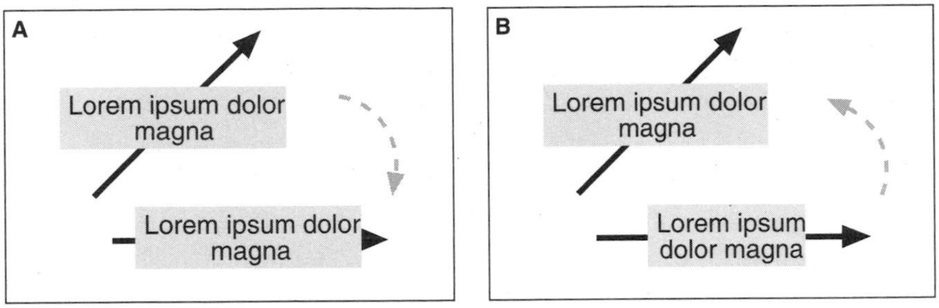

Figure 9-8 When you design a shape's text behavior, you want to prevent the text from obscuring the shape. (**A**) Centered, level text can obscure the shape when rotated, and by default constrains the text block width. (**B**) You can write formulas to widen the text block if the shape is rotated out of the way.

Constraining the width of a level text block

With some shapes, such as one-dimensional (1-D) arrows or short shapes, counterrotating text to keep it level isn't enough. As the shape rotates, the level text can obscure portions of the shape, as in the preceding figure. This is especially likely to happen when the text block is centered horizontally and vertically on the shape and has an opaque background. You can write formulas that keep the text block level and adjust its width as necessary when a user rotates the shape or adds text.

When you use the counterrotation formula described in *Counterrotation Formulas for Level Text* earlier in this section, the text block stays level as the shape rotates. The default Text Transform formulas constrain text block width to shape width, which might not be useful or attractive if the shape is rotated and stretched. To constrain the text block width to the shape width only if the shape is within 15 degrees of horizontal, use the following formulas in the Text Transform and Scratch sections:

```
Scratch.A1   = DEG(MODULUS(Angle, 180 deg.))
Scratch.B1   = AND(Scratch.A1 >= 15 deg., Scratch.A1 <= 165 deg.)
TxtWidth     = MAX(0.5 in., IF(Scratch.B1, 2.5 in., Width - 0.25 in.))
TxtHeight    = 0.25 in.
TxtAngle     = IF(BITXOR(FlipX, FlipY), Angle, -Angle)
```

Note To add the Scratch section to a ShapeSheet spreadsheet, right-click the ShapeSheet window, click **Insert Section**, select **Scratch**, and then click **OK**.

The formula in the TxtWidth cell mentioned previously keeps the text block at least 0.5 inch wide for readability. If the shape is rotated beyond the limit defined in the B1 cell of the Scratch section, text block width is set to 2.5 inches; otherwise, it is set to the shape's width minus 0.25 inch to prevent the text from obscuring the shape. The formula in the Scratch.B1 cell performs the rotation test, returning FALSE if the text block width is constrained by the shape width, or TRUE if the text width is unconstrained. The formula in the A1 cell yields a shape angle normalized to a value from 0 degrees to 180 degrees to determine deflection from horizontal.

These formulas work most of the time, but they fail for short shapes that are close to the horizontal limit and have wide text. A more sophisticated solution would take the width of the shape and the composed width and depth of the text into account. However, you should balance the advantage of improved behavior with the adverse effect it could have on your solution's performance.

Controlling the width of an offset level text block

Depending on the alignment of a text block, the shape's rotation, and the amount of text, the text block can obscure the shape. For cases where you want to customize a shape's text block so that it remains level and is also offset from the shape, you can write formulas so that the text block always stays offset from an imaginary boundary defining the shape's sides.

For example, in a space plan, you might want to move and rotate furniture but keep the labels right-side up as viewed on the page, as the following figure shows.

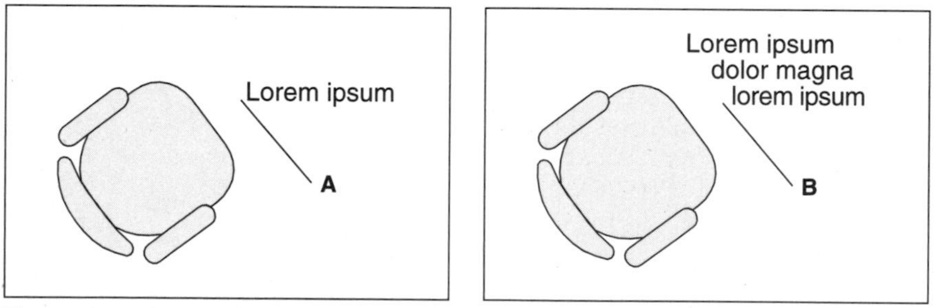

Figure 9-9 Level text offset from a shape. (**A**) The nearest corner of the text block is offset from the shape's side. (**B**) As text is added, the offset shifts so the text block won't overwrite the shape.

Add the following formulas to the Text Transform section of a shape to create this behavior:

```
TxtWidth     = MAX(8 * Char.Size, TEXTWIDTH(theText))
TxtHeight    = TEXTHEIGHT(theText, TxtWidth)
TxtAngle     = IF(BITXOR(FlipX, FlipY), Angle, -Angle)
TxtPinX      = Width + (TxtWidth/2 * ABS(COS(Angle)) + TxtHeight/2 *
               ABS(SIN(Angle)))
TxtPinY      = Height/2
```

The TxtWidth and TxtHeight cells allow the text block to grow as text is added. In the TxtAngle cell, the counterrotation formula levels the text. The text block's pin (TxtPinX) offset is calculated by requiring that, in the shape's local coordinate system, the side of the text block be to the outside of the edge of the shape. The following figure shows that the offset is the sum of line 1 and line 2.

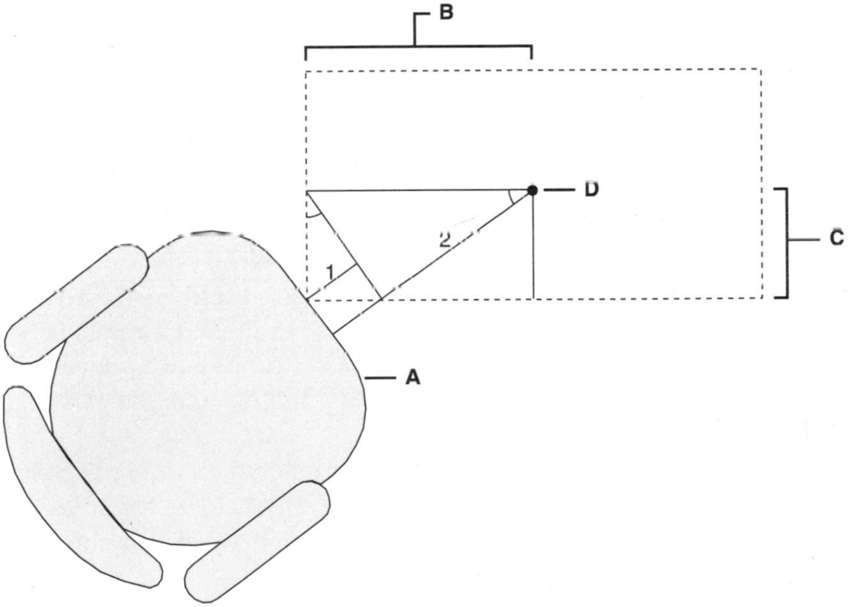

Figure 9-10 Calculating the text block offset (**A**) Edge of shape. (**B**) TxtWidth/2. (**C**) TxtHeight/2. (**D**) TxtPinX offset = 1 + 2.

Line 1 is the leg of a right triangle whose hypotenuse equals TxtHeight/2, so its length is calculated using the Angle cell in the Shape Transform section in this formula:

```
Line 1 = (TxtHeight/2) * ABS(SIN(Angle))
```

Line 2 is a leg of a right triangle whose hypotenuse equals TxtWidth/2, so its length is calculated using this formula:

```
Line 2 = (TxtWidth/2) * ABS(COS(Angle))
```

The offset is always a positive value, even when the shape is rotated at a negative angle, because we use the ABS function to return the absolute value for lines 1 and 2. Calculating the offset this way means additional formulas are not needed to keep the text block from overwriting the shape as it rotates.

Working with Text Formulas

Modifying a shape's text formulas allows you to define sophisticated behavior for shapes in the solutions you develop. You can display the values from the formulas you enter, as well as format the values to better reflect the shape's role. This section outlines some of the more advanced approaches you can use when modifying a shape's text formulas, and it also provides information on protecting the formulas you create and testing your shapes to ensure that they behave as you intend.

Displaying and Formatting Formula Results

You can display the results of a formula and format the output appropriately. When you select the text block, and then click **Field** on the **Insert** menu, the text field created is really the value from the evaluated formula in a ShapeSheet cell converted to text. You can use the same techniques to develop custom text fields as those you use in the ShapeSheet window, and you can display the formatted results in the shape itself.

When you create a formula for a text field, the formula appears in the Text Fields section of the shape's ShapeSheet window. The formulas are displayed in the order they were inserted in the text, not necessarily the order in which they appear in the text.

Displaying a shape's width in different units

You can use text fields to show a shape's current width in inches, centimeters, points, or other units. To do this, you can use the FORMATEX function to specify the units you want to display for the result.

The FORMATEX function takes this syntax:

```
FORMATEX(expression, "formatpicture" [,"inputunit"] [,"outputunit"])
```

This function returns the result of *expression* evaluated in *inputunit* as a string formatted according to *formatpicture* expressed in *outputunit*. The *formatpicture* is a code that indicates how the result should be formatted. If you specify the optional *inputunit* and *outputunit*, use a numerical value or a valid spelled-out or abbreviated unit of measure (in, in., inch, and so on). If you don't specify *inputunit*, the units of the expression are not converted. If you don't specify *outputunit*, the input unit is used.

To use the FORMATEX function to display the shape's width in a text field

1. Select a shape.
2. On the **Insert** menu, click **Field**.
3. In the **Field** dialog box, under **Category**, click **Custom Formula**.
4. In the **Custom Formula** box, enter an expression using the FORMATEX function, specifying the desired format picture, and input and output units.

   For example, if Width is in inches and you want to display it in centimeters, enter:

   ```
   = FORMATEX(Width,"0.00 u", "in.", "cm.")
   ```

5. Click **OK**.

   The Microsoft Visio engine formats the value of Width using two decimal places, abbreviates the units, and converts inches to centimeters. For example, if Width is 1.875 in., Visio displays 4.76 cm.

For details about valid format pictures, search the Microsoft Visio Developer Reference (on the **Help** menu, click **Developer Reference**).

Displaying normalized angular values

You can design a shape that displays the current angle of rotation as part of its text. For example, shapes representing lines of bearing on a nautical chart or slope indicators in a property line diagram display the current angle. By default, the Visio engine returns angular values from –180 to +180 degrees. You can use the ANG360( ) function to convert the value of the shape's angle to a value from 0 to 360 degrees (or from 0 to 2pi radians), and then display the value in the shape.

To display the value of a normalized angle in a text field

1. Select a shape.
2. On the **Insert** menu, click **Field**.
3. In the **Field** dialog box, under **Category**, click **Custom Formula**.
4. In the **Custom Formula** box, enter:

```
= ANG360(Angle)
```

5. Under **Format**, click **Degrees**.
6. Click **OK**.

Formatting Strings and Text Output

When you display strings, such as formula results in a text field or custom property values, you can specify a format for the output. Text output can be formatted as a number-unit pair, string, date, time, duration, or currency. The Visio engine recognizes a set of *format pictures* that format the text as you want it to appear. For example, the format picture `"0 #/10 uu"` formats the number-unit pair 10.9cm as `"10 9/10 centimeters"`.

Format pictures appear in the list of formats when you use the **Field** command (on the **Insert** menu, click **Field**), as arguments to the FORMAT and FORMATEX functions, and as formulas you can use in the Format cell of the Custom Properties section of the ShapeSheet window. For details about all the format pictures that you can use, including date, time, duration, currency, and scientific notations, search for "format pictures" in the Microsoft Visio Developer Reference (on the **Help** menu, click **Developer Reference**).

Using the FORMAT function

In any formula that resolves to a string, including custom text field formulas, you can use the FORMAT function to format the output. The FORMAT function uses the following syntax:

```
FORMAT(expression, "formatpicture")
```

The result of *expression* is formatted according to the style specified by *formatpicture*. The function returns a string of the formatted output. The format picture must be compatible with the type of expression used, and you cannot mix expression types. For example, if you combine the formatting of a date and a number by using the number and date format pictures together `("#.## mmddyy")`, the Visio engine ignores the `"mmddyy"` portion and tries to evaluate the expression using the first part `("#.#")` of the format picture.

To use the FORMAT function in a text field, specify a custom formula as described in *Displaying and Formatting Formula Results* earlier in this section. In the **Custom formula** box, include the FORMAT function in your formula. (To enter a formula in the **Custom formula** box, open the shape's text block, click **Field** on the **Insert** menu, select **Custom Formula** under **Category**, and then type the formula in the **Custom formula** box.)

The following table provides examples for formatting common number-unit pairs.

Custom text formats for number-unit pairs

Syntax	Display output
`FORMAT( 0ft. 11.53in., "0.## U")`	0 FT. 11.53 IN.
`FORMAT( 260.632 cm, "0.## u")`	260.63 cm.
`FORMAT( 0 ft. 11.53 in. , "# #/# u")`	11 5/9 in.
`FORMAT( 260.632 cm, "0 #/# uu")`	260 5/8 centimeters
`FORMAT( 260.632 cm, "0 #/5 uu")`	260 3/5 centimeters
`FORMAT( 0ft. 11.53in., "0.000 u")`	0 ft. 11.530 in.

Displaying formatted custom properties

You can format the displayed value of a custom property so that it appears the way you want in the **Custom Properties** dialog box. To do this, you use a format picture in the Format cell in the Custom Properties section of the shape's ShapeSheet window. For example, a project timeline shape can have a custom property called Cost that measures the cost of a process. To format "1200" as currency, you can specify the following format picture in the Format cell of the shape's Custom Properties section:

```
Format = "$###,###.00"
```

The Visio engine uses the current **Regional Options** settings in **Control Panel** to determine the currency symbol, decimal character, and thousands separator to display. Under the U.S. English version of Microsoft Windows, the value is displayed in the **Custom Properties** dialog box as `"$1,200.00"`.

In addition, you can display the value of a custom property in a text field. By clicking **Field** on the **Insert** menu when the shape is selected, you can specify a custom property and a format picture for the value of that property. In the **Field** dialog box, you can specify a custom property under **Category**. The Visio engine displays a list of appropriate format pictures based on the custom property's data type. The value of the custom property is then displayed in the shape's text block using the format picture you assigned.

If you intend to perform calculations with custom properties, you can define a data type other than string for the property value, such as number, currency, date or time, and duration. For details, see *Custom Properties* in Chapter 7, *Enhancing Shape Behavior.*

Protecting Text Formulas

You can protect custom text formulas you create for a shape so that user actions cannot overwrite them. Many common user actions on the drawing page—applying a font, setting margins, applying a text style—affect the values of the Text Transform, Text Block Format, Character, Paragraph, and Tab sections. If you write formulas to customize these text attributes, you can do the following:

- Protect the formula using the GUARD function
- Prevent users from making changes using a protection lock

Use GUARD to protect formulas in cells that control the position or location of the text block. For example, protect formulas that customize text width and text height so that resizing a shape won't overwrite your formulas. When you use GUARD to protect a formula in a cell that controls text formatting, users cannot locally format the text. For details about how applying styles affects the shape's formulas, see Chapter 10, *Managing Styles, Formats, and Colors.*

Use a protection lock to prevent users from formatting a shape or typing in it. Set the LockFormat cell in the Protection section to 1 to keep users from applying any formatting or styles. Set the LockTextEdit cell in the Protection section to 1 to keep users from typing in a shape (but to allow them to apply a text style). It's best to use LockTextEdit only in cases where entering text would cause the shape to behave in unexpected ways (as can happen with very small shapes).

You can hide text completely by setting the HideText cell to TRUE in the Miscellaneous section. You can still type in the shape: The text is visible as you type, but it won't show in the shape when you're finished typing.

Of course, the more protection you use, the less your users can modify a shape. You want to be able to give users enough flexibility to accomplish their tasks while preserving customized shape formulas.

Testing Text Block Formulas

Use the following steps to test the positioning and resizing of a shape's text block. To ensure that the position of the text block remains correct as a user manipulates the shape, you need to test all combinations of flipping, rotating, and reversing ends.

To test a shape's text block positioning

1. Create an instance of the master you want to test, and then type some text in it.
2. Duplicate the instance seven times. Rotate each instance by increments of 45 degrees. Arrange the eight instances in a rosette. Group the instances for easier handling.

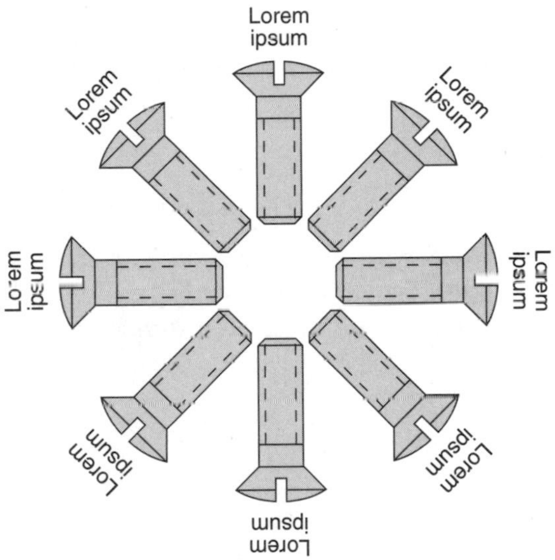

Figure 9-11 This is a test set, and illustrates how the shape normally behaves under various rotations.

3. Duplicate the test set two times (for 2-D objects) or five times (for 1-D objects), and arrange as rows with three columns.
4. If testing a 1-D shape, select the three groups in the bottom row. On the **Shape** menu, point to **Operations**, and then click **Reverse Ends**.
5. Select the group(s) in the middle column. On the **Shape** menu, point to **Rotate or Flip**, and then click **Flip Vertical**.

6. Select the group(s) in the right column. On the **Shape** menu, point to **Rotate or Flip**, and then click **Flip Horizontal**.
7. Print the results and examine them in detail. Fix any problems and test again as needed.

Next, test your shape's ability to handle text. To do this, you replace the test text in every shape, and then check the results.

To tcst how a shape resizes as text is added

1. Select one of the shapes, and then type new text.

   Type enough text to stretch the text block in a manner appropriate to the intended use of the shape.
2. Click away from the shape, and then press CTRL+A to select all the shapes.
3. Press F4 to repeat the new text in all the selected shapes.
4. Print the results and examine them. Fix any problems and test until you get the results you want.
5. As a final test, resize each group. Try both moderate and extreme sizes.

Do the shapes work the way you expected? Does the text still look good? Can you at least read it? If not, maybe you should specify a minimum text width. For details, see *Constraining Text Block Size* in *Controlling Text Rotation* earlier in this chapter.

10

Managing Styles, Formats, and Colors

Working with Styles in the Drawing Page 208

Guidelines for Applying Styles to Shapes 212

Using Styles in Stencils and Templates 216

Protecting Local Shape Formats 218

Managing Color in Styles, Shapes, and Files 219

Custom Patterns 223

As a shape developer, you apply styles to the shapes you draw to ensure consistency. You also define the styles and custom options, such as custom fill patterns, that will appear in the templates you create for your users. Styles in Microsoft Visio work a little differently from styles you might have used in other software, such as word-processing or spreadsheet programs. In Visio, you can define styles that apply formatting attributes to text, lines, and fills all at once. Or, you can define styles that apply formatting to text only, to lines only, to fills only, or to any combination of the three.

This chapter explains how to apply and create styles when you're working with shapes; provides guidelines for designing the styles that appear in your templates; explains how to change formatting attributes of the masters you work with and how to protect the styles of the masters you create; and describes how to create custom line patterns, fill patterns, and line ends that users can apply just like in any Visio format.

Working with Styles in the Drawing Page

Styles are named collections of formatting attributes that you can apply to a shape. In Microsoft Visio, a single style can define text, line, and fill attributes, so applying a style can be an efficient way to promote consistency in your shapes.

When you apply a style to a shape, you format the following attributes:

- **For text** The font, size, style (such as bold or italic), color, transparency, and character spacing; text block alignment, margins, and background color; paragraph alignment, indents, and spacing; tab spacing; and bullet formatting.
- **For lines** The line weight, color, transparency, pattern, cap, arrowhead style, and corner style.
- **For fills** The pattern and the foreground and background colors and transparency for a shape's interior (its *fill*) and for its shadow, if there is one.

Understanding Styles

You can apply a style to a shape, or you can apply *local formatting* using the commands on the **Format** menu to achieve the same effect. If many of your shapes have the same format, styles provide a more efficient use of computer resources than local formatting. A style definition is stored in only one place in a Visio document, and several shapes can refer to it. With local formatting, all the formatting instructions are stored separately with each shape. Shapes formatted using styles respond faster than locally formatted shapes when they are created, moved, scaled, and rotated.

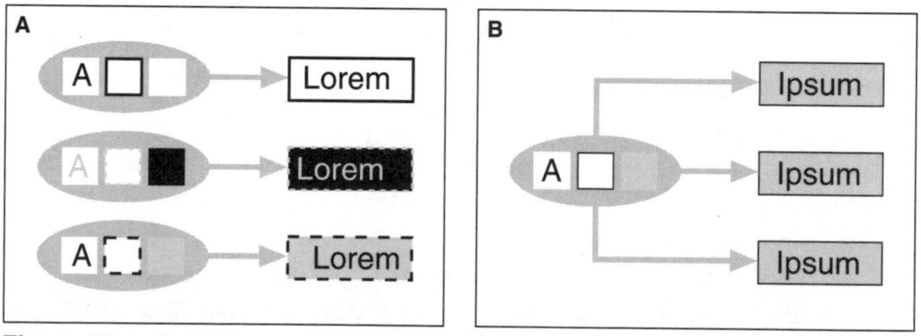

Figure 10-1 Local formatting attributes are stored with each shape (**A**). When you apply a style to multiple shapes, the style's definition stores the formatting information in one place (**B**).

A style can contain various attributes from three main style attribute classes: Text, Line, and Fill. Each attribute class corresponds to a ShapeSheet section:

- Line Format for the Line attribute class
- Fill Format for the Fill attribute class
- Character, Text Block Format, Paragraph, Bullets, and Tabs for the Text attribute class.

Each style attribute within an attribute class corresponds to a ShapeSheet cell, such as FillForegnd and FillPattern in the Fill Format section. A single style can define attributes in one or more of the attribute classes of Text, Line, or Fill.

In the documents you create, you can separately define styles for text, line, or fill, or you can define styles that apply a combination of attributes from these attribute classes. You can find the styles displayed in the following places in the user interface:

- Styles that apply to text appear in the **Style** list on the **Formatting** toolbar or the **Text Style** list on the **Format Text** toolbar.
- Styles that apply to fills and lines are listed in the **Line Style** and **Fill Style** lists on the **Format Shape** toolbar.
- Styles that apply to text, lines, and fills are listed in the **Style** dialog box (on the **Format** menu, click **Style**).
- All styles in a document are listed in the **Styles** folder in the **Drawing Explorer** (on the **View** menu, click **Drawing Explorer Window**).

When a user applies a style to a shape that has local formatting, any cells in the shape that correspond to the enabled attribute classes in the style inherit attributes from the style instead of the master.

For example, if a shape's line is locally formatted and you apply a style that specifies only text and fill formatting, the local formatting of the line remains intact. By right-clicking a shape, pointing to **Format**, and then clicking **Style** on the shortcut menu, users can also apply styles independently for text, line, or fill. For example, suppose that local formatting has been applied to a shape's text, but the user wants to apply a style just for the fill and line that normally applies attributes for the fill, line, and text. By choosing fill and line styles in the **Style** dialog box, those attributes are applied, while the text formatting is untouched. For details, see *Protecting Local Shape Formats* later in this chapter.

Setting Default Styles for a Drawing

When you are drawing a number of shapes, you can ensure consistency by specifying the styles that you use most often as the document's default styles. The Visio engine applies the default text, line, and fill styles currently set for a drawing page when you draw using any of the tools on the **Standard** toolbar.

You can also set default styles for a template's drawing page to help its users draw consistently or according to particular standards.

To change a document's default styles

1. Make sure nothing is selected and that the drawing page window is active. On the **Format** menu, click **Style**.
2. In the **Text style**, **Line style**, and **Fill style** boxes, select the new default styles you want, and then click **OK**.

The new default styles affect any shapes you subsequently draw with the drawing tools. Instances of masters dragged onto the drawing page are not affected—they inherit their styles from the master. The new default styles remain in effect for a drawing page until you change them.

Creating a New Style

You can create a new style to include in your template or to quickly and consistently format several shapes. The styles you define in your templates appear to the user in the **Drawing Explorer**, in the **Style** and **Define Styles** dialog boxes, and, if they apply text formatting, in the **Style** list on the **Formatting** toolbar.

You can create a new style from scratch or base it on an existing one. For example, say you have created a line and entered a formula that evaluates to 3 mm in the LineWeight cell. If you are drawing many 3 mm lines, it's efficient to create a style that you can reuse. The advantage of creating new styles based on existing ones is that you can then develop a hierarchy of styles, in which the changes made to one style are inherited by all of the styles that are based upon it, as the following figure shows. You must be careful, however, not to inadvertently edit a series of styles—and all the shapes formatted with those styles—when you mean to edit only one.

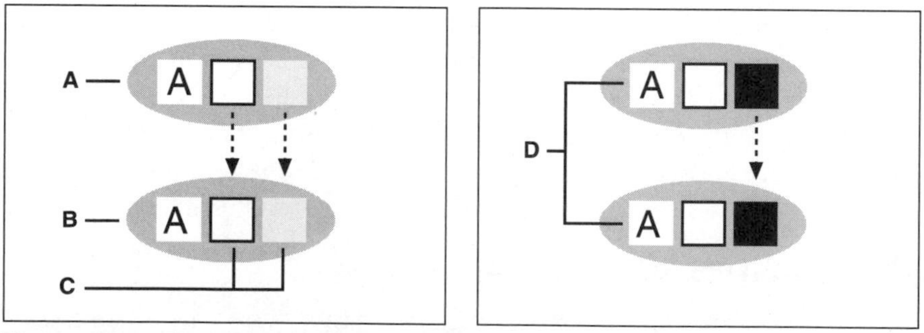

Figure 10-2 Deriving a new style from an existing base style. (**A**) Base style definition. (**B**) Derived style definition. (**C**) The derived style inherits its line and fill from the base style. (**D**) Editing the base style changes the derived style.

When you create a new style, settings are inherited depending on whether the style is created from scratch or based on an existing one. Consider the following:

- A style that you base on another style inherits the base style's attributes.
- A style that you create from scratch inherits the default document settings as a starting point for the attributes that you check under **Includes** in the **Define Styles** dialog box. You can change some or all of these settings to define your style.

To create a style, click **Define Styles** on the **Format** menu. The **Based on** option controls whether the style is based on another. For details about using the **Define Styles** dialog box, search the Microsoft Visio Help (on the **Help** menu, click **Microsoft Visio Help**).

If you define a style for a drawing and want to use it in another drawing, you can copy the style. To do this, drag a shape formatted with the style into the file to which you want to add the style. (Alternatively, copy and paste the shape.) Then delete the shape. The style definition remains in the file. If the file already contains a style with the same name, the existing definition takes precedence, and the style will not be copied into the file.

> **Note** If you use the technique of copying a shape into a different drawing file to create a style, be aware that a copy of the master for that shape instance will be created on the document stencil. If you are using the drawing file to create a template, you'll probably want to delete the master from the document stencil before you save the file as a template.

Editing a Style

You can edit a style in two ways:

- On the **Format** menu, click **Define Styles**, select an existing style from the **Style** list in the **Define Styles** dialog box, and then change the style's **Text**, **Line**, or **Fill** attributes.
- Make changes to the style's formulas in the ShapeSheet window.

Making changes in the **Define Styles** dialog box is a straightforward and user-friendly method. However, not all of the options available in a style's ShapeSheet window can be accessed through the **Define Styles** dialog box. For example, you can define formulas related to a style by editing cells in the style's sheet.

To edit a style's formulas

1. On the **View** menu, click **Drawing Explorer Window**.
2. In the **Drawing Explorer**, open the **Styles** folder, right-click the style, and then click **Show ShapeSheet** on the shortcut menu.
3. Make changes to the formulas in the style's sheet.

Guidelines for Applying Styles to Shapes

Whether you're designing shapes for your own stencils or working with existing masters, using styles is an efficient way to format shapes. Microsoft Visio offers several techniques for applying and editing styles. The technique you use depends on whether you want to reformat all shapes that use a particular style, reformat the master itself and so all subsequent instances of it, or change the instances currently on a drawing page, as follows.

Techniques for applying styles to shapes

To change or reformat this	Do this
Appearance of all instances of a master currently on the drawing page as well as those you add later	Edit the drawing file's styles.
Appearance of a master in a stencil	Apply different styles in the stand-alone stencil.
Only the instances of a master on the drawing page	Edit the copy of the master in the document stencil.

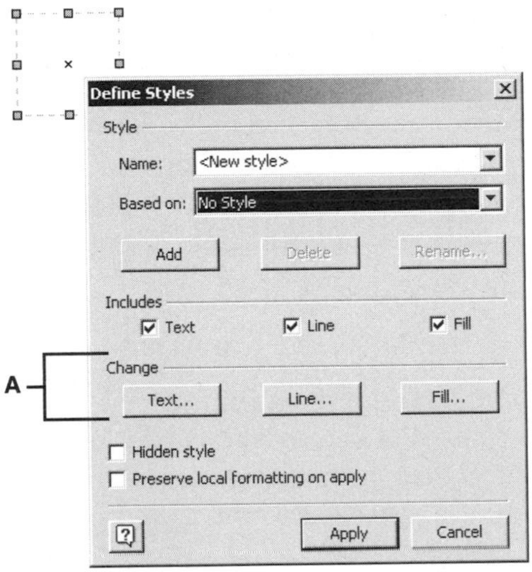

Figure 10-3 When you define a style, you can modify the text, line, and fill settings independently (**A**).

Reformatting Shapes on the Drawing Page

You can edit a style to change the appearance of all shapes in a document that use the style. To do this, use the **Define Styles** command on the **Format** menu to revise the text, line, or fill attributes of an existing style. All shapes formatted with the edited style are changed.

For example, suppose that you're working with the **Basic Flowchart Shapes** stencil, but you want text to appear in 10-pt italic, Times Roman type. Shapes from this stencil are formatted with the **Flow Normal** text style. You can use the **Define Styles** command to change the style definition for **Flow Normal** to format text in the font you want. The new definition affects all shapes in the document to which the style is applied, as well as any new shapes you add that are formatted with that style.

A new style definition is saved only with the current drawing file. The standalone stencil and its masters are not changed, as the stencil file has its own style definitions.

Reformatting Masters in a Stand-alone Stencil

You can reformat masters in a stand-alone stencil by choosing new styles, and thus reformatting any instances subsequently created from those masters. Unlike editing a style to reformat the shapes that use it, this procedure changes the definition of the master in a stencil and saves the changes to the stencil. Use this procedure to edit masters in stencils you use in many different drawings.

To reformat a master with a different style

1. Open the stencil file containing the master you want to edit.

   To make the stencil editable, click the icon on the stencil's title bar, and then click **Edit** on the shortcut menu. Alternatively, on the **File** menu, point to **Stencils**, and then click **Open Stencil**. In the **Open Stencil** dialog box, click the arrow next to the **Open** button, click **Original**, and then click **Open**.

2. In the stencil window, right-click the master you want to edit, and then click **Edit Master** on the shortcut menu to open it in the master drawing window.

3. Select the shape you want to modify, or subselect the shape you want if the master is a group, and then reformat the shape as you want it to appear.

   For example, on the **Format** menu, click **Style**, choose a text, line, or fill style to apply, and then click **OK**.

4. Close the master drawing window.

   When you are prompted to update the master, click **Yes**.

5. Make sure the stencil window is active, and then on the **File** menu, click **Save**. Or, click the stencil icon on its title bar and click **Save** on the shortcut menu.

   The edited master is saved in the stencil. If you need to revert to the previous version of the master, you can edit it again to reformat it using the original styles. Or if it is a Visio stencil, you can reinstall the original from Microsoft Visio.

Reformatting All Instances of a Master

You can quickly reformat all instances of a master in a document without changing either the master or its style definition by editing the copy of the master in the document stencil.

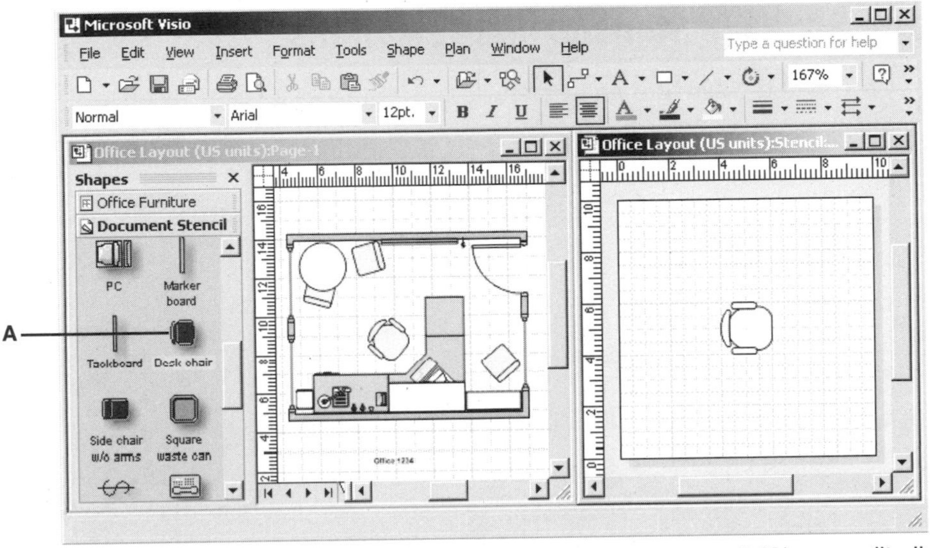

Figure 10-4 By editing the copy of a master in the document stencil (**A**), you edit all of its instances on the drawing page.

To reformat all instances of a master

1. On the **File** menu, point to **Stencils**, and then click **Document Stencil**.
2. For each instance of the master that you want to reformat, right-click the master in the **Document Stencil**, and then click **Edit Master** on the shortcut menu.
3. In the master drawing window, reformat the master as you want.
4. Close the window and, when prompted, save your changes to see the effects on the drawing page.

> **Note** This technique works only if the instances of the master retain their original formatting. Shapes to which you've applied a different style or local formatting are not affected.

Using Styles in Stencils and Templates

When you're designing stencils and templates for others to use, your styles should be consistent and easy to apply. Users can perceive styles as the only formatting options available, so it's often better to include a larger number of styles in your templates than your user might need.

Figure 10-5 The **Style** list on the **Formatting** toolbar makes styles that apply text formatting easily accessible.

Keeping Styles Consistent across Files

When you create a stencil that will be used with a template, the style definitions should be the same in both the stencil and template files. When a user creates an instance of a master, the instance inherits the master's styles, which are applied as follows:

- If a style of the same name does not already exist in the drawing file, it is copied from the stencil file and added to the drawing file.
- If a style of the same name already exists in the drawing file, the existing style is used.

If the style's definition in the drawing file differs from the definition in the stencil file, the drawing's definition is used, and the shape's appearance in the drawing is different from that of the master. This behavior is sometimes referred to as the "home team wins" rule, because the style on the drawing page "wins" over the formatting attributes of a style with the same name in a master.

If you plan to save the drawing page as a stencil or template, you'll save file space by deleting any styles that are not used by your shapes. To do this, use the **Define Styles** command on the **Format** menu and delete styles that you haven't used. Alternatively, you can open a new drawing file that contains only the default styles, and then drag the shapes formatted with the styles you want to copy into the new file. For details about cleaning up stencils and templates, see Chapter 13, *Packaging Stencils and Templates*.

If a shape on the drawing page or on the document stencil uses a style that you delete, the following occurs:

- If the style was based on another style, the shape assumes the base style.
- If the style wasn't based on another style, the shape assumes the **No Style** style, a default Microsoft Visio style that cannot be edited or deleted.

Using Naming Conventions for Styles

The styles you create for your stencils and templates will be easier to use if you consistently follow a naming convention. Explicit style names, such as "Quarter-Inch Black Line" or "8-pt Arial Left," are more expressive and understandable than abbreviated names, such as "Line2" or "T8L." Styles appear in alphabetic order in the toolbar list and in the **Style** and **Define Styles** dialog boxes.

Good naming conventions keep related styles together in the lists, making it easier for users to find the styles they need. Line, fill, and text styles with similar attributes should have similar names. For example, if you name a 1-pixel-wide line style "1 Pixel Line," you should name a 3-pixel-wide line style "3 Pixel Line" rather than "Line3." It's a good idea to name styles based on how you expect them to be used:

- Name styles specific to a shape or stencil according to the shape (or shapes) they're applied to, such as "Flow Connector Text."
- Name general-purpose styles according to their formatting attributes, such as "Black Line" or "Arial Centered."

> **Tip** To make a style appear at the top of the **Style** list, preface the style's name with a character that has a low ASCII value, such as a hyphen (-). For example, "- Standard Line" or "- Corporate Blue."

Guidelines for Defining Styles

Visio developers follow these guidelines when defining styles. The following guidelines may be helpful as you define styles for the solutions you create:

- Text styles should use the TrueType fonts provided with the Microsoft Windows operating system.

  Limit font choices to those you know everyone using the Windows operating system will have. If you know that your users will have other fonts installed (especially those designed for specialized markets, such as cartographic symbols), you can also safely use those fonts in the styles you define.

- Fill and line styles should use colors supported by a standard 256-color VGA monitor.

Limit color choices to the most basic graphics system your users might have. Depending on the audience for your solution and the audience's typical hardware configuration, you might be able to offer a more expansive selection.

- Base styles on **Normal**, rather than on each other.

  When you have a hierarchy of styles based on each other, changing one style automatically changes all styles that are based on it. This behavior might confuse inexperienced users, so you might choose to define styles that are not based on other styles. For a more experienced audience, however, you could take advantage of this powerful feature in your solutions.

- Design styles to apply only one formatting attribute class (fill, line, or text), or all three.

  Multiple-attribute styles can be confusing to new users. You might find, however, that your users always use one fill, one line, and one text style for a specific shape you're designing. If so, you can develop a style containing all three formatting types.

Protecting Local Shape Formats

Applying a style can change the formulas in the Line Format, Fill Format, Text Block Format, Character, Paragraph, and Tab ShapeSheet sections for a shape. If they are not protected, local (custom) formulas in the related ShapeSheet cells can be overwritten. For example, you might have written a custom formula in the Size cell of the Character section of a shape in a master to dynamically change the font size of your master based on its text block height. If a user applies a different text style to the shape, the custom formula is overwritten.

You can protect local shape formats by using the **Preserve local formatting** option in the **Style** dialog box, by setting the LockFormat cell, or by using the GUARD function to protect formulas.

Preserving Local Shape Formatting through the User Interface

You can protect local shape formatting by selecting the **Preserve local formatting** check box in the **Style** dialog box when applying a different style.

When you select **Preserve local formatting**, the style is applied, but local formatting is maintained. If **Preserve local formatting** isn't selected, the new style is applied, and any local formatting is overwritten.

Preserving Local Shape Formatting through the ShapeSheet Spreadsheet

Setting the LockFormat cell to 1 in the Protection section of a shape's sheet protects a shape from both formatting and style changes. Using the GUARD function in a formula prevents that cell from changing when a user applies formatting or styles. If you protect a group using the LockFormat cell, you automatically protect the shapes and other groups within it from inheriting formatting; however, users can subselect shapes in the group that are not explicitly locked and change their formatting. For details about protecting formatting in a group, see Chapter 6, *Grouping and Merging Shapes*.

Use the LockFormat cell and the GUARD function with care. When a shape is locked against formatting, Microsoft Visio automatically displays a message when a user tries to format the shape. In contrast, the GUARD function works without any notification or user messages. Either behavior can confuse or annoy users who want to format a protected shape. As you develop shapes, you must find the appropriate balance between limiting shape behavior and increasing user flexibility in your solution.

Managing Color in Styles, Shapes, and Files

When you are designing masters, you need to consider how the color of the master will look on different user systems. You can apply color to a shape using either the Microsoft Visio color palette or a custom color that you define. The method you choose affects how the shape appears if used in another document. You can apply color to a shape in the following ways:

- By applying a color from the Visio color palette, you choose an index of one of the palette's colors. The Visio engine records only the index to the color palette, not the color itself.
- By defining an RGB (red, green, blue) or HSL (hue, saturation, luminosity) value, either in the **Colors** dialog box or as a formula, you apply a custom color to a shape.

In Microsoft Visio 2002, you can also apply transparency as part of the setting for foreground and background fill and shadow colors, and line, character, text block, or layer colors.

> **Note** Beginning with Visio 2002, the Visio engine uses a 32-bit color model, which makes over 16 million colors available in a Visio drawing. This true-color model also makes it possible for transparency to be applied to various color settings such as fill color, line color, text, and shadows.
>
> Earlier versions of Visio support a palette-based color model. In the palette-based color model, as many as 253 different colors could be chosen for a given document—24 of these colors belong to the Visio logical color palette, and the remaining 229 are available for custom colors. Colors are stored by index in a color table that is part of the document.
>
> In Visio 2002, colors are stored with each shape as RGB values; each cell for a shape can explicitly store a 24-bit color in the form of an RGB formula. For backward compatibility, Visio 2002 still maintains a document color table (maximum of 253 indexed colors) in addition to the explicit RGB color values.
>
> The ShapeSheet window displays cell color formulas exactly as they are entered. In Visio 2002, values are displayed as the index value for logical colors (the first 24 entries in the color table are reserved for the logical color palette) and as the RGB values for custom colors. This is a change from Visio 2000, which displays the index values for all colors, both logical and custom.

Editing the Color Palette

The color palette appears in the **Color Palette** dialog box, as well as in the drop-down list of colors in the **Fill**, **Line**, **Font**, **Text Block**, and other dialog boxes. For any document that uses the default Visio palette, a color index refers to the same color: 0 is black, 1 is white, 2 is red, and so on.

However, users can choose the color they want to appear at any index by editing the color palette. If they do, any color property mapped to that index can change color. For example, if you apply a fill color to a master by clicking red in the palette, the shape's fill color is recorded as 2. If a user creates an instance of the red master in a document in which the second index in the color palette has been edited, the shape's fill color will change to whatever color appears at index 2.

Most users do not edit a document's color palette, so colors are not likely to shift. But you can ensure that a shape's color never changes, regardless of a document's color palette, by using a custom RGB or HSL color. To specify a custom color as a formula, use either the RGB or HSL function. For details about using these functions, see *Using a Formula to Define a Custom Color* later in this section.

Standardizing Color Palettes across Documents

When you're designing stencils that you intend to open with a template, you should use the same color palette in all documents. If the color palettes do not match, the colors defined by an index in a master's styles can change when an instance is dragged into a document that has a different color value at that index. To standardize the color palette used in documents that are intended to open together, such as stencils and templates, you can copy the color palette used in one file to another.

If you edit the color palette in a stencil file, you can copy the color palette to a template.

To copy a stencil's color palette to a template

1. Open the template file.
2. On the **Tools** menu, click **Color Palette**.
3. For **Copy colors from**, select the stencil whose color palette you want to copy to the template file, and then click **OK**.
4. Save the document.

Using a Formula to Define a Custom Color

You can define shape color using a function that specifies an RGB or HSL value. For example, to ensure that a stop-sign shape is always red, you can enter the following formula in the Fill Format section:

```
FillForegnd = RGB(255,0,0)
```

The RGB function's three arguments specify the red, green, and blue components of the color. Each can have a value from 0 to 255. To specify the color using an HSL value, you could instead use the formula HSL(0,240,120) in the FillForegnd cell. For details about function syntax, see the HSL function or RGB function topics in the Microsoft Visio Developer Reference (on the **Help** menu, click **Developer Reference**).

Rather than specifying color constants as the argument to these functions, you can use the RED, GREEN, and BLUE or HUE, SAT, and LUM functions to return the value of a color constant from the document's color palette or from another cell. For example, using RED(FillForegnd) with a stop-sign shape might return 255, the value of the red component in the fill color for that shape.

You can use the RGB and HSL function together with the other color functions to define a color based on another cell's color in the same or a different shape. This is particularly useful in a group containing shapes of related but not identical colors. You can define the grouped shape's colors in terms of one shape's color in the group. For example, if the topmost shape in a group is Star 7, you could enter the following in Star 7.2:

```
FillForegnd = RGB(RED(Sheet.7!FillForegnd),0,0)
```

If a user applies a new color to the group, the topmost shape changes color, but Star 7.2 changes only the proportion of red in its fill color.

When you specify a custom color using the RGB or HSL function, the color is added to the color list in the **Fill**, **Line**, **Font**, and other dialog boxes in which you can assign color. If you create a master from a shape to which a custom color has been assigned, and then drop an instance of it in another Visio document, the custom color is added to that document's color lists as well.

Adding Transparency for Custom Colors

Beginning with Visio 2002, you can specify transparency independent of color settings. As the following table shows, each transparency cell is located next to its corresponding color cell in the ShapeSheet spreadsheet. Transparency is specified as a positive percentage value from 0% (completely opaque) to 100% (completely transparent).

Corresponding Color and Transparency cells

Section	Color cell	Transparency cell
Fill Format	FillForegnd	FillForegndTrans
	FillBkgnd	FillBkgndTrans
	ShdwForegnd	ShdwForegndTrans
	ShdwBkgnd	ShdwBkgndTrans
Line Format	LineColor	LineColorTrans
Character	Char.Color	Char.ColorTrans
Text Block Format	TextBkgnd	TextBkgndTrans
Image Properties		Transparency
Layers section (Page)	Layers.Color	Layers.ColorTrans

Custom Patterns

You can create your own fill patterns, line patterns, and line ends. For ease of discussion, these styles are collectively termed *custom patterns* and appear to users as options in the **Fill** and **Line** dialog boxes. To design a custom pattern, you create a master pattern that represents one instance of the pattern, such as a dot that, when applied as fill, looks like a complete pattern, such as polka dots. A *master pattern* is a special type of master that appears to end users only as an additional fill pattern, line pattern, or line end.

When you create a master pattern, you set its properties to specify the following:

- The master pattern name
- The type of custom pattern—fill pattern, line pattern, or line end
- The pattern's behavior—how the custom pattern is applied to a shape and how it changes as the shape is stretched or formatted
- The custom pattern's use in scaled or unscaled drawings

A custom pattern is always saved as a master pattern, though it is not visible in the stencil. Master pattern names appear in alphabetic order at the bottom of the appropriate list of options in the **Fill** or **Line** dialog box. Users can then apply the custom pattern by clicking the **Line** or **Fill** command on the **Format** menu, and then selecting the master pattern name from the appropriate list. Custom patterns appear in the **Drawing Explorer** when a stencil containing them is open and they have been applied to shapes in the drawing.

For other useful information on patterns, search the Microsoft Visio Help (on the **Help** menu, click **Microsoft Visio Help**).

Creating a Custom Pattern

When a user applies a custom pattern, its master pattern is copied to the document stencil. The custom pattern then remains available in the active document, even if the stand-alone stencil containing the original master pattern is closed. The Microsoft Visio engine records the choice by inserting the USE function in the FillPattern, LinePattern, BeginArrow, or EndArrow cell. For example, if a user applies a custom line end called "Star" to the begin point of a line, the BeginArrow cell of the line will contain the formula `USE("Star")`. The Visio engine applies the custom pattern based on the size of its alignment box.

If a user does not apply a particular custom pattern from a stencil while the stencil is open, it no longer appears in the **Fill** and **Line** dialog boxes after the stencil containing it is closed.

If a user copies a shape formatted with a custom pattern to another document, the usual inheritance rules apply. The master pattern is copied to the new document, unless the new document already contains a master pattern of the same name, in which case the document master of that name is applied.

Many of the techniques that you use to develop master shapes also apply to developing master patterns. For example, you—and your users—will have more predictable results if you use a single shape or a group in your master (shape or pattern). You can always combine multiple geometries to create a single shape using the commands on the **Operations** submenu of the **Shape** menu. In addition, you should create a master pattern as a single instance of the minimum design to repeat as intended.

> **Note** Do not use text or gradient fills in a master pattern. They do not appear when the pattern is applied to a shape.

To create a custom pattern

1. Open a new document or stencil.
2. On the **View** menu, click **Drawing Explorer Window**. In the **Drawing Explorer**, right-click the **Fill Patterns**, **Line Patterns**, or **Line Ends** folder, and then click **New Pattern** on the shortcut menu.
3. In the **Name** box, type the custom pattern name as you want it to appear in the **Fill** and **Line** dialog boxes.
4. Under **Type**, click **Line Pattern**, **Line End**, or **Fill Pattern**.
5. Under **Behavior**, click an option to specify how the pattern is applied to a shape.
6. Select **Scaled** if the custom pattern models an object with real-world dimensions.

   For example, if you're creating a fill pattern of 4-inch-square kitchen tiles, select **Scaled** to preserve the pattern dimensions when the pattern is applied to a shape on a scaled drawing page.
7. Click **OK** to create a new, empty master pattern.

8. Open the appropriate folder, and then right-click the name of the pattern you just added. Click **Edit Pattern** on the shortcut menu to open the master drawing window, where you can draw the custom pattern.

   If you want users to be able to change the color of a pattern or line end after it's applied to a shape, design the master pattern in black and white, as described in in *Developing Custom Fill Patterns* later in this section.

9. With the master drawing window for the pattern still open, click **Page Setup** on the **File** menu. On the **Page Size** tab, click **Size to fit drawing contents**, and then click **OK**.

> **Tip** You'll want to adjust the size of your pattern drawing depending on how you want the pattern to appear inside a shape or line. Repeat step 9 each time you change the pattern drawing size.

10. After you create the pattern, close the master drawing window, and save the document as a stencil.

    Although the icons for the patterns you create are not visible when you save a pattern in a stencil, the patterns you defined appear at the bottom of the appropriate lists in the **Fill** and **Line** dialog boxes when that stencil is open. When a custom pattern is applied to a shape, the pattern name is added to the list in the current **Drawing Explorer** window.

> **Note** Beginning with Visio 2002, you can create a custom pattern that is based on a bitmap and apply that custom pattern to line ends, fills, and line patterns. You can use only one bitmap object to create a custom pattern. If you attempt to create custom pattern that includes more than one bitmap, only the first bitmap in the pattern is used and the remaining bitmaps are ignored when the custom pattern is applied to a shape. Added geometry and any transforms or transparency applied to the bitmap are also ignored.

Developing Custom Fill Patterns

You can design custom fill patterns that fill a shape in one of three ways, depending on the behavior you choose in the master's **Pattern Properties** dialog box. The most common type of fill pattern behavior is tiled, where instances of the pattern are repeated to fill the shape from the lower-left corner outward, as shown in the following illustration.

You can also create a centered or stretched fill pattern. In a centered pattern, a single instance of the pattern fills the shape. The pattern's pin is aligned with the shape's pin. In a stretched pattern, a single instance of the pattern is stretched horizontally and vertically to fill a shape. The position of the pattern's pin is disregarded. As you resize the shape, the pattern resizes, too, unlike tiled or built-in patterns.

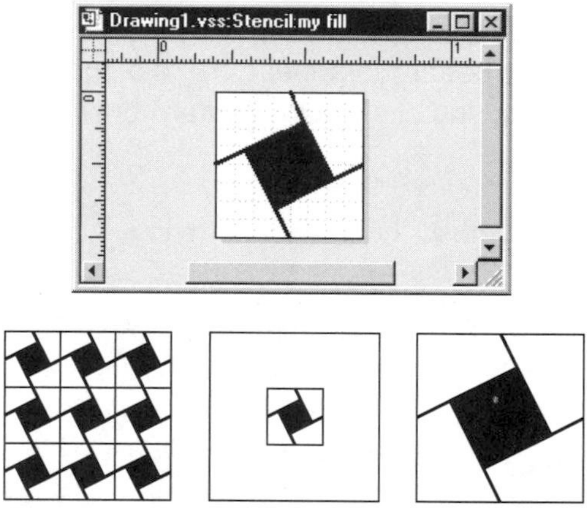

A B C

Figure 10-6 When you create a custom fill pattern, you can also specify how that pattern is applied to shapes. You can choose to fill the shape with instances of the pattern from the lower-left corner outward (**A**), center one instance of the pattern on the shape (**B**), or stretch one instance of the pattern to fill the shape (**C**).

Fill pattern colors

If you design your fill pattern in black and white, users can set the pattern color when they apply it to a shape as they can any Visio pattern. White areas (line or fill) in your pattern inherit the foreground fill color of the shape to which the pattern is applied; black areas (line or fill) in your pattern inherit the shape's background fill color. If your pattern contains any colors other than black and white, the pattern retains those colors when applied to a shape.

Designing tiled patterns

The most common fill pattern behavior is tiling, in which the pattern is tiled by the edges of its alignment box. You can get different tiling effects by creating a pattern with a larger or smaller alignment box (as the following figure shows) or by placing the pattern off-center within its alignment box. For details about creating a custom-size alignment box, see *Adjusting the Size of a Shape's Alignment Box* in Chapter 11, *Arranging Shapes in Drawings*.

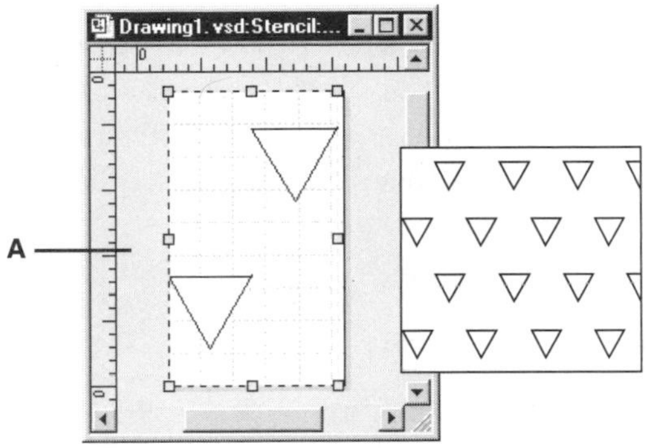

Figure 10-7 In this example, the master pattern includes two offset triangle shapes in a large alignment box (**A**). Tiled fill patterns fill the shape from the lower-left corner.

When your tiled pattern represents a real-world object, select **Scaled** in the master pattern's **Pattern Properties** dialog box. For example, a 1-ft by 1-ft ceramic floor tile should always be the same size, regardless of the drawing scale in which it is used. The default fill pattern behavior is unscaled, which means the pattern behaves like the built-in Visio patterns: They always print at the same size, regardless of drawing scale.

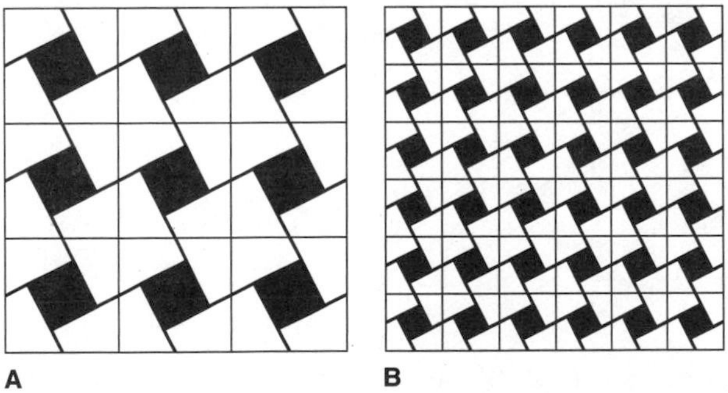

Figure 10-8 On a drawing page that uses an architectural scale, an unscaled pattern (**A**) looks the same as on a page with no scale, but a scaled pattern (**B**) retains its dimensions.

Developing Custom Line Patterns

By applying a custom line pattern, a user can reformat a line as railroad tracks, a garden path of stepping-stones, or any other line pattern. When you design a line pattern, consider how the pattern repeats along the length of the line and around curves and corners. Consider also whether the pattern should be resized when the line weight changes. These considerations—the pattern's behavior—determine how the Visio engine applies the pattern to a line and can dramatically affect the line's appearance.

You choose a **Behavior** option in the master pattern's **Pattern Properties** dialog box to control how a line pattern is applied to a line. You can design line patterns to behave in one of four ways, as the following illustrations show.

To create a railroad track, each instance of the pattern is bent to fit around curves as it repeats along the length of the line.

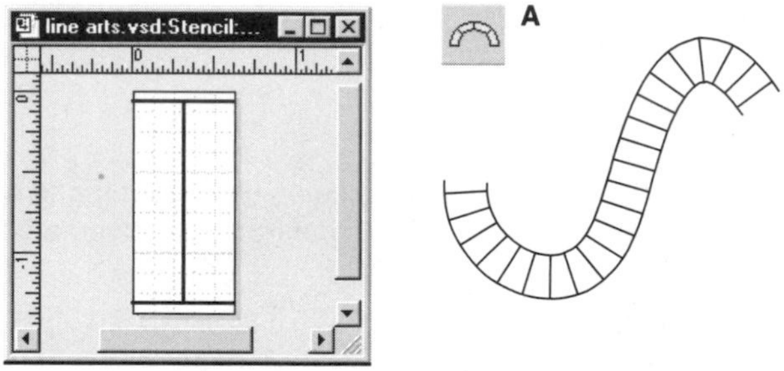

Figure 10-9 Choose this option (**A**) to bend instances of the pattern to fit a curved line.

To create a garden path, each instance of the pattern is positioned and rotated as it is repeated along the length of a line.

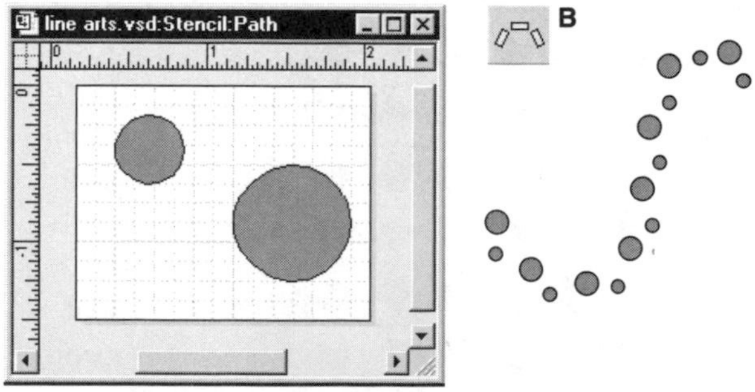

Figure 10-10 Choose this option (**B**) to repeat instances of the pattern to fit a line without bending around curves.

To create a tapered line, a single instance of the pattern is stretched along the entire length of a spline.

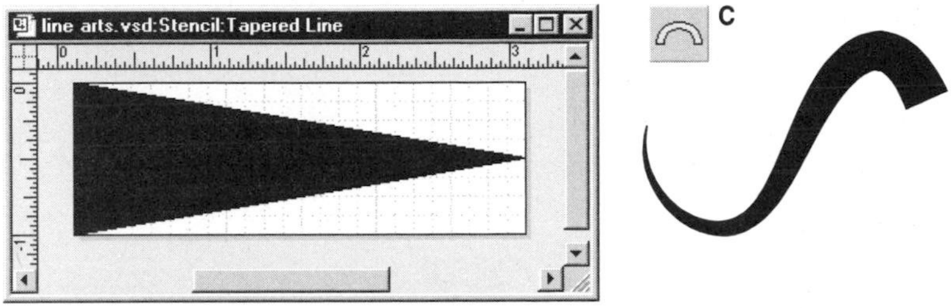

Figure 10-11 Choose this option (**C**) to stretch a single instance of the pattern along the length of a line.

To create a flow line, the pattern is repeated on top of the line, fitting whole instances of the pattern between corners. The alignment box in this example is larger than the arrowhead to control the spacing between instances of the pattern.

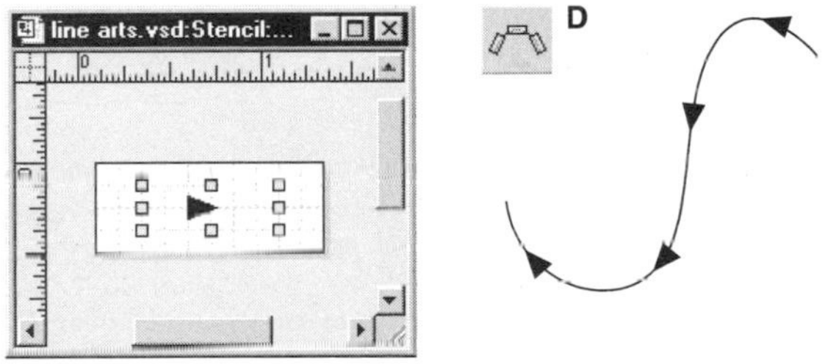

Figure 10-12 Choose this option (**D**) to repeat instances of the pattern on top of a line for a "string of beads" effect.

Customizing the alignment box and pin

To design an effective line pattern, you must consider the size of the alignment box and pin position as well as the shape of the pattern. In fitting a pattern to a line, the pattern's pin is aligned to the line and repeats or stretches the pattern by the edges of its alignment box. If the alignment box is larger than the pattern, spaces appear between pattern instances as they repeat on the line. If the alignment box is smaller than the pattern, you'll get an overlapping effect when the pattern is applied. For details about creating a custom-size alignment box, see *Adjusting the Size of a Shape's Alignment Box* in Chapter 11, *Arranging Shapes in Drawings.*

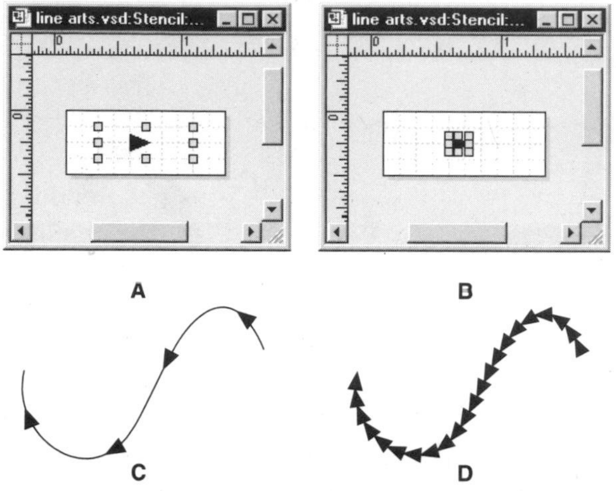

Figure 10-13 By changing a line pattern's alignment box, you can control how instances of a pattern repeat along a line. (**A**) The flow arrow line pattern alignment box is larger than the pattern instance. (**B**) The overlap arrow line pattern alignment box is smaller than the pattern instance. (**C**) Line with flow arrow pattern applied. (**D**) Line with overlap arrow pattern applied.

Scaled versus unscaled line patterns

If you design an unscaled line pattern (that is, the **Scaled** option is cleared in the master pattern's **Pattern Properties** dialog box), when a user applies the line pattern, the Visio engine resizes its alignment box until its height equals the line weight. Scaled line patterns keep their dimensions regardless of the drawing scale or the line weight.

Color in line patterns

When you design a line pattern, apply black to the areas (line or fill) that you want users to be able to change by choosing a new color in the **Line** dialog box. Apply white or any other color to the areas you don't want users to be able to change. Set the fill of your line pattern to **None** if you want the fill area to be transparent when applied to a line.

Developing Custom Line Ends

A custom line end is the simplest type of custom pattern to create—it's simply a shape that can attach to the endpoint of a line. When you design a line end, you determine whether it can adjust to the direction of the line to which it's attached and whether it resizes as the line weight changes. You can design a line end to do the following:

- Orient itself with respect to the line. If you move the line, the line end adjusts to point in the same direction.
- Orient itself with respect to the page. If you move the line, the line end remains upright as viewed on the page.

The Visio engine attaches the pin of the line end to the endpoint of a line. If the line end behavior is to orient with respect to the line, the line is trimmed between its endpoint and the bounding box of the line end for a seamless look. Otherwise, the line is not trimmed. As you design a line end, consider where to place the pin to achieve the right effect. For example, to design an arrowhead, you would draw a triangle, and then move the pin to the pointing tip.

> **Note** A line end must point to the right; otherwise, it won't be applied properly.

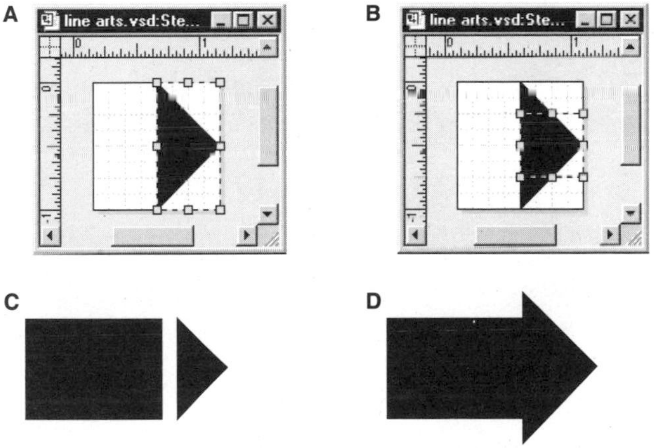

Figure 10-14 (**A**) This simple arrowhead is a right triangle with black fill. (**B**) This refined arrowhead is a group with an alignment box that is slightly narrower than the triangle. The pin was moved to the arrowhead's point. (**C**) The simple arrowhead line end applied to a 36-pixel line. (**D**) The refined arrowhead line end applied to a 36-pixel line.

> **Tip** To move a 2-D shape's pin, right-click the shape, point to **View**, click **Size & Position** on the shortcut menu, and then choose an option from the drop-down list in the **Pin Pos** field. Or select the shape with the **Rotation** tool, and then drag the pin to a different position.

Another consideration in designing a line end is whether its size should be affected by the weight of the line to which it is applied. If you design an unscaled line end (that is, leave **Scale** cleared in the master pattern's **Pattern Properties** dialog box), the height of the line end's alignment box is set to equal the line weight as long as the user sets **Begin size** and **End size** to **Medium** (the default) in the **Line** dialog box. However, on a 1-pixel line, the line end might not be visible. To ensure that your line end works at any line weight, you can customize its alignment box. If a user sets **Begin size** and **End size** to something other than **Medium**, the line end resizes in the same way any line end resizes. For details about creating a custom-size alignment box, see *Adjusting the Size of a Shape's Alignment Box* in Chapter 11, *Arranging Shapes in Drawings*.

If your line end represents an object with real-world dimensions, such as a fitting at the end of a pipe, select **Scaled** in the master pattern's **Pattern Properties** dialog box. The **Begin size**, **End size**, and **Weight** settings in the **Line** dialog box will have no effect on the size of a scaled line end.

11

Arranging Shapes in Drawings

Assigning Shape and Masters to Layers 234

Designing a Grid 237

Aligning Shapes to Guides and Guide Points 241

Using Alignment Boxes to Snap Shapes to a Grid 244

Designing Shapes for Automatic Layout 248

As you design Microsoft Visio stencils and templates, you'll want to give careful consideration to defining behavior for how the shapes in your stencils interact with the drawing page and each other, and as a result how they are arranged on the page.

You can organize shapes on the drawing page using layers; other tools for helping to arrange shapes on the page include the grid and ruler guides. Both the document's snap behavior settings and the alignment boxes of individual shapes can also affect how shapes align on the page.

Additionally, the Visio engine includes powerful functionality for automatic layout. By setting parameters for this feature, you can more easily control how shapes are positioned relative to one another when automatic layout is used.

Assigning Shapes and Masters to Layers

In Microsoft Visio, you can organize related shapes in a drawing into named categories called layers.

In other graphics programs, the term *layers* often refers to the drawing order (the front-to-back position) of objects on the page. However, in Visio, shapes can be assigned to more than one layer, and the layer information for a shape is independent of the shape's display order and even its group membership. You can hide or show layers, print them or not, or protect layers from changes. Additionally, each page in a document might have its own set of layers. When you design masters, you can assign the shapes in the masters to layers; when users create instances of those masters, the shapes are automatically assigned to those layers.

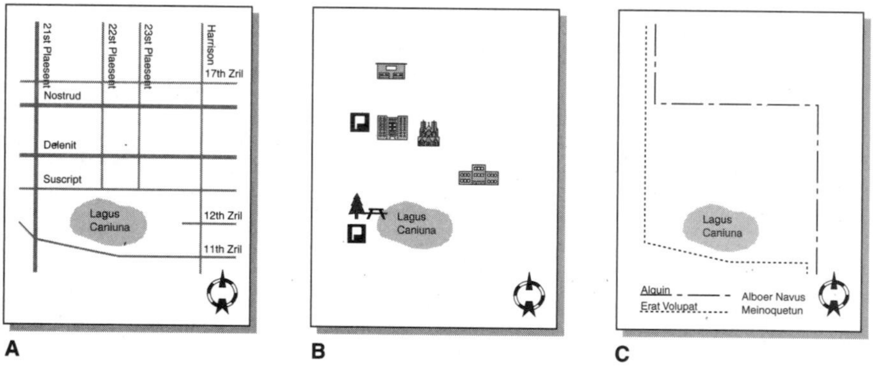

Figure 11-1 Shapes can belong to more than one layer. Here, the lake and compass shapes belong to the Streets layer (**A**), the Landmarks layer (**B**), and the Routes layer (**C**).

Using Layers Efficiently

When a user drags a master onto the drawing page, the new shape instance inherits layer information from the master. If a shape is assigned to a layer that doesn't exist on the page, Microsoft Visio automatically creates the layer. When shapes include layer assignments, users can highlight shapes by showing layers in different colors, print shapes by layer, lock all shapes on a layer, or hide all shapes on a layer. A shape can belong to more than one layer, so you can create shapes that reflect complex, real-world usage.

For example, if you're creating shapes for an office plan stencil, you can assign the wall and door shapes to one layer, window shapes to a second layer, electrical outlet shapes to a third layer, and furniture shapes to a fourth layer.

To prevent unwanted changes, you might lock the wall layer while editing shapes on the window layer.

Layers belong to pages; every page (either a page in the drawing window or in a master drawing window) has a list of layers associated with the page. Shapes are assigned to layers and can belong to more than one layer. By hiding or locking different layers on a page, you can control which shapes are visible or editable.

A master might contain multiple shapes, so various shapes in a master can be assigned to different layers or belong to more than one layer. In this way, you can control the appearance and behavior of an instance of the master using layers.

Each page in a drawing file can have a different set of layers. Both foreground and background pages can have layers to organize the shapes that appear on them. A shape can belong to any and all layers on the current page. If you have a shape that belongs to a layer and copy that shape to another page in the drawing, the associated layer is added to the destination page if that page doesn't already have a layer with the same name.

To create, remove, or rename a layer

- On the **View menu**, click **Layer Properties**. Click **New** to create a layer and name it, select a layer name and click **Remove** to delete the layer, or select a layer and click **Rename** to rename the layer. Click **OK** to accept the settings.

To control the behavior of each layer

- On the View menu, click **Layer Properties**. In the **Layer Properties** dialog box, click in the property columns to select the properties that you want the layer to have (selected properties are indicated by check marks in the layer's row). Click **OK** to accept the settings.

To remove unreferenced layers

- On the **View** menu, click **Layer Properties**. In the **Layer Properties** dialog box, select **Remove unreferenced layers**, and then click **OK**.

  Removing all layers that have no shapes assigned to them from the drawing page reduces a document's file size, which is helpful when you're designing a stencil or template for others to use.

Assigning Shapes and Groups to Layers

When you create layers in the **Layer Properties** dialog box (on the **View** menu, click **Layer Properties**), each layer is represented by a row in the Layers section of the page's ShapeSheet spreadsheet.

A shape or group you assign to a layer using the **Layer** dialog box (with the shape or group selected, click **Layer** on the **Format** menu) is automatically listed by index number in the Layer Membership section in the shape's or group's ShapeSheet spreadsheet. The index number indicates the row order of the layer in the Layers section of the page's sheet.

> **Note** Layers are listed alphabetically in the **Layer** and **Layer Properties** dialog boxes, so the order of layers in the dialog boxes does not necessarily correspond to the layer index numbers.

To assign a shape or group to a layer

1. Select the shape or group on the page or in a master.

   > **Note** If you're assigning a shape in a master to a layer, the stencil containing the master must be opened as either **Original** or **Copy**. To select a shape or group in a master, right-click the master in the stencil window, and then click **Edit Master** on the shortcut menu. The master opens in its drawing window.

2. Click **Layer** on the **Format** menu.
3. If no layers currently exist, the **New Layer** dialog box appears. Type a name for the layer to which you want to assign the shape or group, and then click **OK** to display the **Layer** dialog box, where the new layer appears in the list.

   If the page in the drawing window or the master drawing window already has layers, the **Layer** dialog box appears instead of the **New Layer** dialog box.

> **Note** You can also add, delete, or rename layers by clicking **Layer Properties** on the **View** menu in either a page or master drawing window.

4. Click each layer name that you want to assign the shape or group to. Press CTRL while clicking to select multiple layers.

   To create a new layer and assign the shape or group to it, click **New** and repeat step 3.

5. Click **OK** to close the **Layer** dialog box, and then save any changes that you made to the master or page.

6. To control the behavior of the layers, click **Layer Properties** on the **View** menu. In the **Layer Properties** dialog box, click in the property columns to select the properties that you want the layer to have (selected properties are indicated by check marks in the layer's row).

   Click **OK** to accept the settings.

For more information about working with layers on the drawing page, such as assigning color and transparency to a layer, see the Microsoft Visio Help (on the **Help** menu, click **Microsoft Visio Help**).

For details about editing masters and stencils, see Chapter 3, *Visio Masters, Stencils, Templates, and Documents*.

Designing a Grid

By default, the Microsoft Visio drawing page displays a grid. If you design the scale of your shapes and drawing pages with the grid in mind, your users can quickly snap a drawing into place. Not all shapes need to snap to a grid, and not all templates require a customized grid. For most technical drawings, however, you should consider the grid when designing your masters.

For additional information about using grids in scaled drawings, see Chapter 12, *Scaled Shapes and Measured Drawings*.

Setting the Grid for a Template's Drawing Page

When you set up the drawing page in a template, you can decide whether the grid is variable or fixed. With a variable grid, the grid increments change as you zoom in and out. A fixed grid displays the same increments at every magnification. With either type, you can set how finely the grid and rulers are subdivided.

In any view, users should be able to easily snap to a grid that works with the grid spacing used for the masters.

Grid settings you select in the **Ruler & Grid** dialog box are stored in the page's Ruler & Grid section in its ShapeSheet spreadsheet. The variable grid settings are stored in the XGridDensity and YGridDensity cells. The fixed grid settings are stored in the XGridSpacing and YGridSpacing cells.

To set the grid spacing

- On the **Tools** menu, click **Ruler & Grid**.

To show or hide the grid

- On the **View** menu, click **Grid**.

To view a page's Ruler & Grid formulas

- With nothing selected on the drawing page, click **Show ShapeSheet** on the **Window** menu, and then scroll to the Ruler & Grid section.

Creating Masters that Work with a Grid

If you design masters so their dimensions are multiples of an underlying grid spacing, users can take advantage of the snap-to-grid feature to drag shapes into precise positions quickly. When a user drags a master from the stencil, the instance is easily aligned on grid lines when dropped.

When snapping to grid lines is enabled, the edges of a two-dimensional (2-D) shape's alignment box snap to visible grid lines, showing the user the exact position of the shape. For a 2-D shape, the snap-to-grid action is most useful if both the width and the height of the shape are multiples of the spacing of the currently displayed grid, as the following figure shows. If this is not the case, opposite edges of the object snap separately, the dragging behavior of the shape is jerky, and the user must pay attention to whether the left or right edge snaps to the grid.

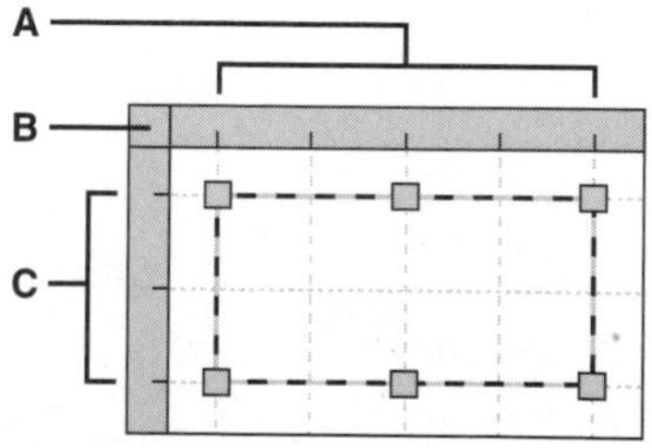

Figure 11-2 Designing a shape with width and height as multiples of the grid's units. (**A**) Width = 1 inch (4 * grid). (**B**) Grid spacing = ¼ inch. (**C**) Height = ½ inch (2 * grid).

To ensure that shapes snap to the correct position on the grid, masters should use the same units of measure as the drawing page. When you set up the drawing page for your template, specify the grid using the same units of measure as those used for the masters you design to be used with that template.

To set the units of measure for a master

1. Right-click the master, and then click **Edit Master** to open the master drawing window.

> **Note** The stencil containing the master must be opened as either **Original** or **Copy**. If the stencil was opened as **Read only**, you can click the icon on the stencil's title bar, and then click **Edit** on the shortcut menu to make it editable.

2. On the **File** menu, click **Page Setup**, click the **Page Properties** tab, and then select a **Measurement units** option. Then, save the stencil.

For details about editing stencils, see Chapter 3, *Visio Masters, Stencils, Templates, and Documents*. You can also search for "masters" or "stencils" in the Microsoft Visio Help (on the **Help** menu, click **Microsoft Visio Help**).

To set the units of measure for a page or template

- On the **File** menu, click **Page Setup**, click the **Page Properties** tab, and then select a **Measurement units** option.

If you want something other than a shape's edge to snap, you can adjust the shape's alignment box. For details about customizing the alignment box, see *Using Alignment Boxes to Snap Shapes to a Grid* later in this chapter.

> **Tip** If you are designing two masters that are likely to be connected, position their connection points so that when the masters are both snapped to the grid and appear to be aligned, the connector will travel a straight path between the two closest connection points. For details about connection points, see Chapter 8, *Working with 1-D Shapes, Connectors, and Glue*.

Using Formulas to Hold Grid Information

To create masters based on a grid that you might later change, you can store the basic grid spacing used for a shape as a formula in a master. Grid spacing information isn't normally stored with masters, but by writing custom formulas, you can easily edit the masters in a stencil to work with different grids.

Creating formulas for a variable grid

When you're working with a template, you might change the document's units of measure. Doing so changes the document grid units, which in turn affects the way shapes snap to the grid. If you know a template's units of measure are likely to change, you can define the masters used in that template to work with different systems.

For example, you might want to adapt a template and stencil designed for a ¼-inch grid for use with different measurement units, such as centimeters. If you've defined the width and height of the masters in the stencil in terms of a variable (specified in a user-defined cell) based on the grid spacing, you can simply change the variable for each master to reflect the new units of measure. When you do so, the masters are automatically sized to work with the new grid. You can name the user-defined cell so it's easy to understand its function.

For example, the following formulas create a shape for a 1-cm grid:

```
User.GridUnit        = 1 cm.
Width                = 6 * User.GridUnit
Height               = 4 * User.GridUnit
```

You can specify any unit you want in the user cell's formula. To make the shape work in a grid based on inches, simply edit the value of the User.GridUnit cell and specify *0.25 in.* instead of *1 cm.*

Creating formulas for a fixed grid

If your template's drawing page uses a fixed grid, you can define the shape formulas in terms of the grid spacing stored in the page; if the unit for the fixed grid changes in a new document, the shapes in the stencil automatically reflect the change. Instead of storing the grid spacing as a user-defined variable, the following width and height formulas refer to the grid information in the page:

```
Width       = 6 * ThePage!XGridSpacing
Height      = 4 * ThePage!YgridSpacing
```

Aligning Shapes to Guides and Guide Points

When you design a template, you can help your users work more efficiently by including guides or guide points on the drawing page. *Guides* are the nonprinting lines on the Microsoft Visio drawing page used for alignment, as the following figure shows. Defined as *infinite lines*, guides behave much like regular lines in that they can have associated text and they support the use of styles. A *guide point* is the crossbar-shaped guide dragged from the intersection of the two rulers. Users can quickly align and move shapes by gluing them to a guide or guide point—when a guide is moved, all shapes glued to it also move.

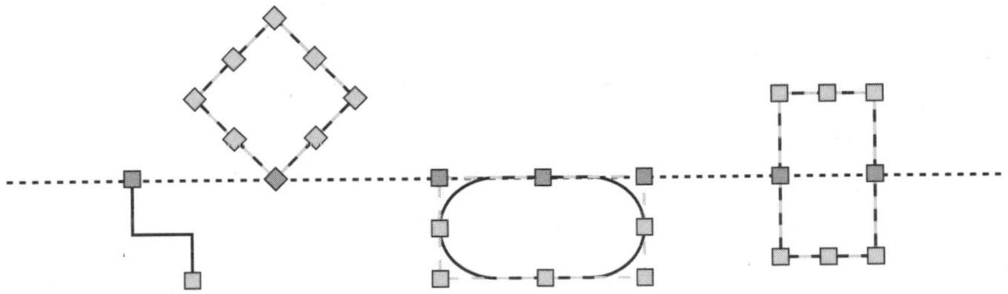

Figure 11-3 You can glue a point, a side, or the middle of a two-dimensional shape to a guide.

Guidelines for Using Guides or Grids

Guides and grids offer different approaches to aligning shapes on a page. Generally, guides offer more flexibility than grids. The following table offers some tips for deciding whether to use grids, guides, or both for your design goals.

For details about using grids for aligning shapes, see *Designing a Grid* earlier in this chapter, and *Using Alignment Boxes to Snap Shapes to a Grid* later in this chapter.

Comparison of guides and grids

Guide or grid feature	Guide support	Grid support
Discrete objects	Guides and guide points are discrete objects whose appearance and behavior can be controlled by formulas.	Grid lines are not discrete objects, and therefore you cannot set properties or write formulas for them.
Rotation	Guides can be rotated with respect to the page by entering a value for **Angle** in the **Size & Position** window (on the **View** menu, click **Size & Position Window**).	Grid lines always appear horizontal and vertical with respect to the window, not the page.

Comparison of guides and grids *(continued)*

Guide or grid feature	Guide support	Grid support
Grid and guide intervals	Guides can be manually positioned at any interval.	Grid lines are always displayed in even intervals.
Printing	Guides can be printed by clearing the **Non-printing shape** check box in the **Behavior** dialog box (on the **Format** menu, click **Behavior**).	Grid lines cannot be printed.

Manipulating Guides and Guide Points

The geometry of a guide is represented as a single InfiniteLine row in its ShapeSheet spreadsheet. Like regular lines, you can apply styles to guides; by default, guides use the predefined **Guide** style. You can easily manipulate guides on the page.

When you create a guide, it is parallel to the ruler from which you dragged it. Rulers are always vertical and horizontal with respect to the window, not the page, so if you create a guide in a rotated page, the guide might be rotated with respect to the page you place it on.

To create a guide

- Point to either the horizontal or vertical ruler with the mouse. The pointer changes to a two-headed arrow. Drag to where you want the guide on the drawing page and release the mouse button.

To create a guide point

- Drag from the intersection of the two rulers (not two guides).

To select a guide on the drawing page

- Click the guide with the **Pointer** tool. The guide turns green. You can then move it, delete it, display the **Size & Position** window (on the **View** menu, click **Size & Position Window**) to rotate it or specify its position and orientation, or open a ShapeSheet window showing its properties.

To position a guide precisely on the page

- Use formulas. For example, in a drawing on A5 paper at a 1:500 scale, the page width represents 74 meters. You can position the guide with respect to page width with a formula such as the following:

```
PinX   = ThePage!PageWidth-5m
```

To turn the display of guides for a document on or off

- On the **View** menu, click **Guides**.

To disable snapping to guides for a document

1. On the **Tools** menu, click **Snap & Glue**.
2. On the **General** tab, under **Snap to**, clear the **Guides** check box.

Guides in a Rotated Page

When you create a guide, it is always parallel to the ruler you dragged it from. Rulers are always vertical and horizontal with respect to the window, not the page, so if you create a guide in a rotated page, the guide appears rotated with respect to the page you place it on.

To specify a guide's angle of rotation

- With the guide selected, display the **Size & Position** window (on the **View** menu, click **Size & Position Window**), and then enter a value for **Angle**. Alternatively, you can select the guide, select the **Rotation** tool  , and then rotate it.

Like shapes, a guide's Shape Transform section records the point around which the guide rotates in the PinX and PinY cells and the angle of rotation in the Angle cell. A shape that is glued to a guide has an Alignment section, which refers to the guide with a formula that includes the INTERSECTX or INTERSECTY function.

Grouping Guides with Shapes

You can use guides or guide points to align shapes and groups as you develop masters. For example, you can group a shape and a guide. When you open the group window to edit the group (to do so, select the group, and then on the **Edit** menu, click **Open Group**), the guide appears. The guide makes it easy to align additional shapes relative to the other shapes in the group.

If a shape is glued to a guide and you add the shape (but not the guide) to a group, the shape's connection to the guide breaks. The reverse is also true: If you add a guide to a group, but don't also add the shapes that are glued to it, the shapes' connections to that guide break. If you include both the guide and the shapes that are glued to it in the group, the connections are maintained.

Using Alignment Boxes to Snap Shapes to a Grid

When a user drags a shape into the drawing window, by default the shape's selection rectangle, or alignment box, is snapped to the nearest grid line. (If snapping is turned off for a document, Microsoft Visio positions the shape where it was dropped.) All shapes have an alignment box, which by default is the same size as the shape's width-height box. If a shape is asymmetrical or composed of odd-sized components, users might find it harder to predict its alignment and snapping behavior. Or you might want parts other than the outer edges of the shape to snap to the grid. You can customize a shape's alignment box to clarify its intended use.

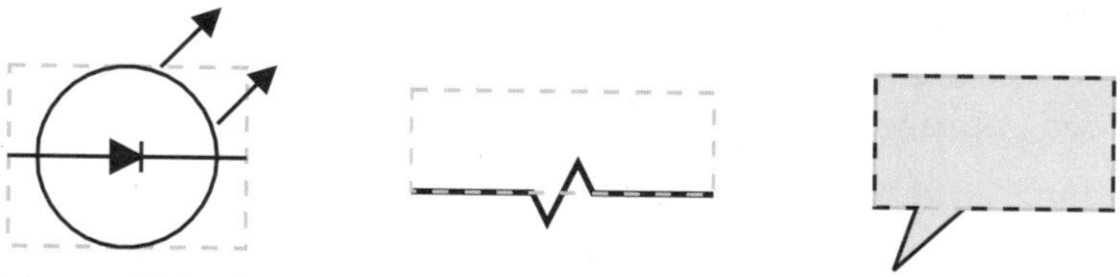

Figure 11-4 An alignment box can be larger or smaller than the shape it represents, and is displayed when a shape is selected or moved.

If a shape is rotated at an angle that is not a multiple of 90 degrees, the alignment box is the smallest upright rectangle that contains all of the paths of the shape as if their line thickness were set to zero.

Adjusting the Size of a Shape's Alignment Box

You can customize the size of an alignment box for a shape. For example, you can design a series of different shapes with same-sized alignment boxes so that they snap and align correctly, as the following figure shows.

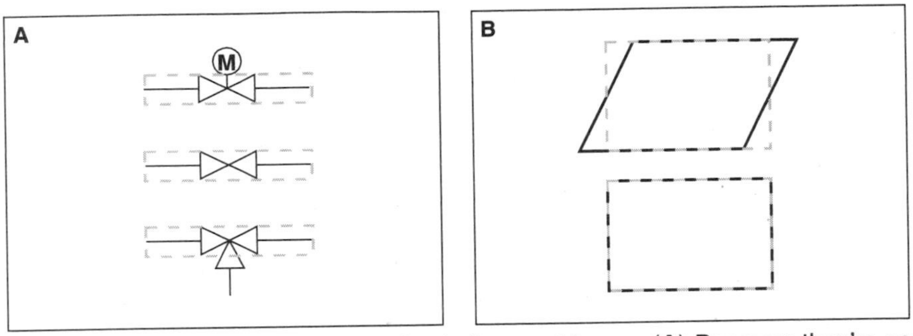

Figure 11-5 Masters with customized alignment boxes. (**A**) Because they're used to connect other shapes, the alignment boxes for these 1-D valves are the same height. (**B**) To make alignment easier, the Data shape's alignment box (top) is the same size as the Process shape (bottom).

To create an alignment box that is distinct from a shape's geometry, you draw the alignment box first, and then prevent Visio from changing it as you create and edit the shape's geometry.

To define an alignment box that differs from the width-height box

1. Draw your shape.
2. Select the shape, and then click **Show ShapeSheet** on the **Window** menu.
3. In the Protection section, set the formula for the LockCalcWH cell to TRUE (or 1).

   This setting preserves the current alignment box so that it won't change as you define the shape's geometry.
4. Use the **Pencil**, **Line, Arc**, or **Rectangle** tool (not the **Pointer** tool) to add to or modify the shape's geometry.

Enclosing a shape in a larger alignment box

You can enclose a shape in an alignment box that's larger than its width-height box. This can make the shape easier for users to snap to the grid. For example, the symbol for an electrical outlet is a rectangular shape enclosed in a larger, square alignment box to make it easier to position the shape.

To enclose a shape in a larger alignment box

1. Draw one shape, and then draw another shape that is the size you want for the larger alignment box.
2. Select the two shapes. On the **Shape** menu, point to **Grouping**, and then click **Group**.

3. Select the alignment box shape in the group, and then delete the alignment box shape from the group.

> **Note** You can alternatively edit the group in the window. On the **Edit** menu, click **Open Group**, and then delete the alignment box shape from the group.

Customizing a group's alignment box

You can customize the size of a group's alignment box to make your master easier for users to snap and align. When a master is a group of one or more shapes, the group supplies the alignment box. For some shapes, the default group alignment box would not align the shape appropriately. In the following figure, the shape is a group with a custom alignment box.

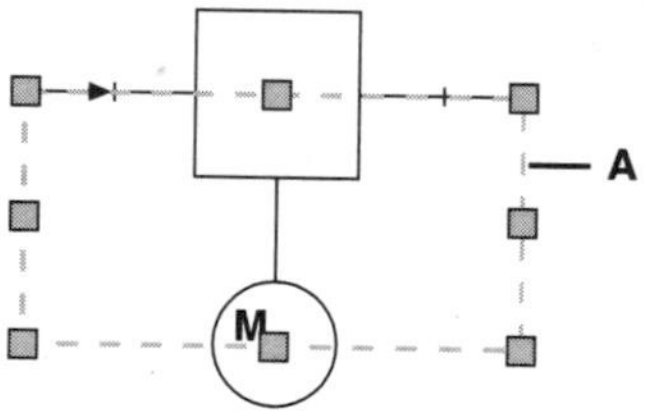

Figure 11-6 This custom alignment box (**A**) is smaller than the group and doesn't encompass the group's label shape.

To create a group with a custom-sized alignment box

1. Construct the separate shapes that will make up the group in the master. Don't customize formulas for these shapes yet.
2. Use the **Rectangle** tool to create a shape the size and position of the desired alignment box relative to the other shapes in the master.
3. Select the alignment box only and group it (press SHIFT+CTRL+G), and then click **Open Group** on the **Edit** menu to open it in the group window.
4. Select the other shapes you want to add to the group, drag them into the group window, and position them relative to the alignment box.
5. Delete the alignment box shape, and then close the group window.
6. Add custom formulas to the shapes as desired.

Updating an Alignment Box

A shape's alignment box might no longer coincide with its width-height box after you edit its vertices or, in a group, after you resize a shape, or add a shape to or delete one from the group. To explicitly realign the alignment box with the width-height box, on the **Shape** menu, point to **Operations**, and then click **Update Alignment Box**. (The LockCalcWH cell in the Protection section must be set to FALSE or 0 for this command to work).

If a shape vertex corresponds to the position of a control handle that you defined, moving the control handle also changes the shape's geometry so that the alignment box no longer coincides with the width-height box. In this case, you can set the UpdateAlignBox cell in the Miscellaneous section to TRUE so that the alignment box always resizes as the control handle is moved.

Changing the Alignment Box for 1-D Shapes

By default, a one-dimensional (1-D) shape's endpoints are centered horizontally in its alignment box. By moving the begin point and end point within the shape's local coordinate space, you can change the alignment box and make it easier for users to align your shape. For example, the following figure shows a 1-D wall shape with endpoints at the wall's edge, rather than its center. When users drag the shape, the line of the alignment box follows the edge rather than the center of the wall.

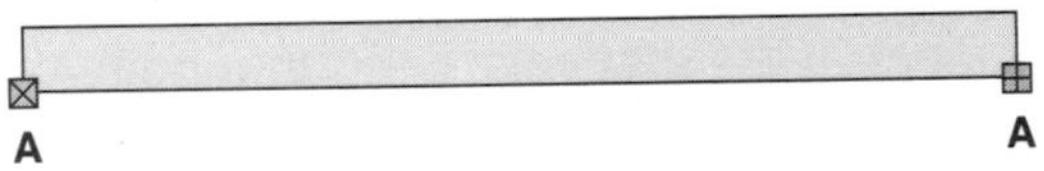

Figure 11-7 This customized alignment box for a 1-D wall shape includes endpoints (**A**) aligned with the wall's edge that make it easier to place.

To move the alignment box for a 1-D shape

1. With the **Rectangle** tool, draw the shape.
2. Select the shape. On the **Format** menu, click **Behavior**.
3. On the **Behavior** tab, select **Line (1-dimensional)**, and then click **OK**.
4. On the **Window** menu, click **Show ShapeSheet**.
5. In the Shape Transform section, type *0 in.* in the LocPinY cell.

   Moving the *y*-position of the local pin aligns the endpoints with the shape's edge.

> **Tip** You can hide the alignment box of a 1-D shape such as a connector if displaying it would interfere with the shape's function. On the **Format** menu, click **Behavior**, and then clear the **Show alignment box** check box. Or set the NoAlignBox cell to TRUE in the Miscellaneous section.

Designing Shapes for Automatic Layout

Microsoft Visio provides powerful automatic layout capabilities that position shapes and reroute the connectors between shapes based on user-selected layout options. You can control how the shapes and connectors in your solutions interact as the drawing is manipulated or in response to the **Lay Out Shapes** command by customizing the default parameters for the pages in your templates. You can also override the placement and routing behavior for individual shapes and connectors in masters of the stencils you design.

Setting Layout Options for the Page

When a user manipulates a drawing or uses the **Lay Out Shapes** command (**Shape** menu), Microsoft Visio uses the values of cells in the Page Layout section of the page's sheet to determine the default routing and placement behavior for the connectors and shapes in the drawing. You can modify the values of cells directly, or by selecting options on the **Layout and Routing** tab in the **Page Setup** dialog box (on the **File** menu, click **Page Setup**).

You can also specify placement behavior for individual shapes and routing behavior for connectors in the Shape Layout section in the ShapeSheet. Several of the cells in the Shape Layout section duplicate those in the Page Layout section, so you can specify shape-specific overrides for certain global behaviors.

In general, specifying global layout options for the page and limiting the number of shape-specific overrides makes the routing behavior in your solution more consistent, and therefore more predictable for users. For example, you might specify that placeable shapes move away when another shape is dropped on the drawing as a global setting, but modify the Shape Layout section of a shape in a particular master to prevent instances of the shape from moving. Or you might specify that instances of a connector shape use a certain line style, or jump in a particular direction.

Following is a table that lists cells in the Shape Layout section that override default settings in the Page Layout section.

Shape Layout cells that override Page Layout settings

Shape Layout cell	Applies to	Determines
ShapePlowCode	Placeable shapes	Whether placeable shapes on the drawing page move away when this shape is dropped near those shapes. Override page defaults with **Plow no shapes** (1) or **Plow every shape** (2).
ConLineJumpCode	Routable shapes	When a connector jumps. Override page defaults with **Never** (1), **Always** (2), **Always to other** (3), or **To neither** (4).
ConLineJumpStyle	Routable shapes	The style for a connector jump. Override the page defaults with **Arc** (1), **Gap** (2), **Square** (3), **Triangle** (4), or multisided jumps (5-9). For details, see the ConLineJumpStyle cell in the ShapeSheet Reference in the Microsoft Visio Developer Reference (on the **Help** menu, click **Developer Reference**).
ConLineJumpDirX and ConLineJumpDirY	Routable shapes	The horizontal (X) or vertical (Y) direction for a connector jump. For horizontal jumps, override the page defaults with **Up** (1) or **Down** (2). For vertical jumps, override the page defaults with **Left** (1) or **Right** (2).
ConLineRouteExt	Routable shapes	The appearance of a connector. Override the page defaults with **Straight** (1) or **Curved** (2).
ShapePlaceFlip	Placeable shapes	The orientation of a placeable shape toward the next placeable shape it is connected to. Override the page defaults with FlipX (1), FlipY (2), FlipRotate (4), or FlipNone (8). For details, see the ShapePlaceFlip cell in the ShapeSheet Reference in the Microsoft Visio Developer Reference (on the **Help** menu, click **Developer Reference**).
ShapeRouteStyle	Placeable and routable shapes	The style and direction for a connector on the drawing page. For details about values for this cell, see the ShapeRouteStyle cell in the ShapeSheet Reference in the Microsoft Visio Developer Reference.

> **Note** This is only a partial list of cells that you can control in the Page Layout and Shape Layout sections. See the Microsoft Visio Developer Reference for detailed information about the functions of each cell in these ShapeSheet sections (on the **Help** menu, click **Developer Reference**).

Setting Shape and Connector Behavior

When you create a new master, its Shape Layout settings reflect the current page settings. You can modify these settings to define how instances of a master interact with other shapes when a user manipulates a drawing or clicks the **Lay Out Shapes** command (**Shape** menu). For example, you might want to allow shapes to be placed on top of a certain shape, rather than moving away from it. Or you might want to allow connectors to route through certain shapes rather than around them.

The same applies to connector shapes: You can modify the behavior of dynamic connectors to provide more custom interactions during automatic shape layout. For example, you might want to prevent certain connectors from jumping, or you might want to specify a certain line jump style for connectors that are allowed to jump.

When you design masters, you might also want to specify custom behavior for connection points. Connection points can have an associated direction, which controls how connectors attach to the shape. By manipulating the direction of a connection point, you can control even more closely how connectors attach to that shape.

> **Note** Connection point direction options are available only when you are running Microsoft Visio in developer mode (on the **Tools** menu, click **Options**, click the **Advanced** tab, and then select **Run in developer mode**).

To change the direction of a connection point

1. Choose the **Connection Point** tool ⨯ from the **Standard** toolbar, and then click to select a connection point.
2. Right-click the connection point and select a direction from the shortcut menu. **Outward** cannot be used for point-to-point connections.
3. Click and drag the gray triangle attached to the connection point to specify a direction. When the connection point has been activated, the triangle turns green.

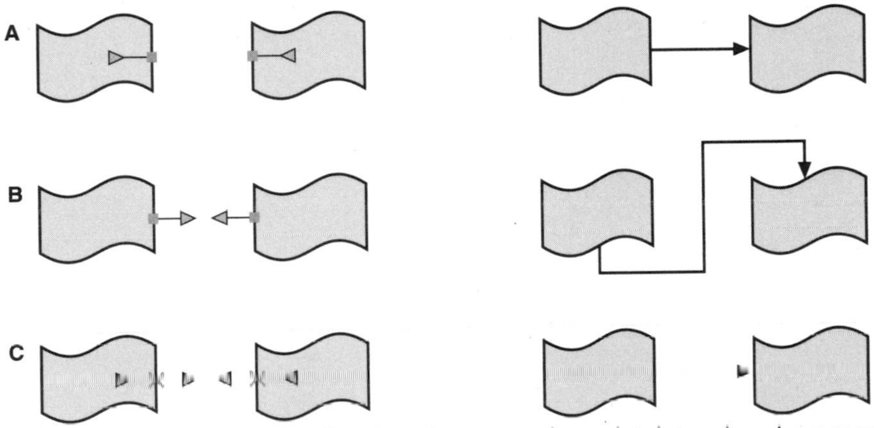

Figure 11-8 Changing the direction of a connection point determines how connectors attach to that shape. (**A**) If you want the connector to attach to the outside of the shape, drag the Inward connection point circle inside the shape. (**B**) **Outward** connection points cannot be connected to, and serve only as points for snapping the shape to another shape. (**C**) **Inward & Outward** connection points provide versatile connection options.

12

Scaled Shapes and Measured Drawings

Choosing an Appropriate Drawing Scale 254

Choosing a Scale for Masters 257

Creating Shapes that Never Scale 260

When the drawings your users create represent real-world objects, the drawings need shapes and templates that draw to scale. You can design masters that size appropriately when users drag them into a drawing page with a scale, such as ¼ inch = 1 foot. If you design the *template* as well, you can ensure that the scale of the drawing page works with the scale of the masters you provide and thereby simplify a complicated drawing task for your users.

This chapter explains how to choose an appropriate scale for drawings and shapes that need scaling; the chapter also describes how to prevent shapes from scaling even in a scaled drawing. For details about designing a grid for both scaled and unscaled drawings and creating shapes that snap to a grid, see Chapter 11, *Arranging Shapes in Drawings.*

Choosing an Appropriate Drawing Scale

Any drawing that depicts physical objects that are too small or too large to be drawn easily, or are larger than the paper size, must be scaled to fit on the page. For example, in an architectural rendering of a house, ¼ inch on the drawing page might represent 1 foot of the actual house. Schematic diagrams, such as flowcharts and organization charts, depict abstract objects; therefore, these types of drawings are unscaled.

In Microsoft Visio, *drawing units* are sizes in the real world. In the previous example of a house, 1 foot is the drawing unit. *Page units* are sizes on the printed page—¼ inch in the house example. The ratio of page units to drawing units is the *drawing scale*.

ShapeSheet cells that describe object size or position—that is, most cells—are expressed in drawing units. Cells that represent measurements on the printed page, such as text format and indents, are shown in page units. If the drawing scale is changed, all ShapeSheet cells that are expressed in drawing units remain constant, but the shape is redrawn to the new scale.

Understanding Drawing Scale and Page Scale

To understand how drawing scale and page scale relate to each other, consider the swimming pool in the following figure. The pool is 40 feet long and 20 feet wide, drawn using a 1-point line, and labeled using 8-point type.

With a drawing scale of ¼ inch = 1 foot (1:48), the picture of the pool is drawn 10 inches long by 5 inches wide. If you change the drawing scale to ⅛ inch = 1 foot (1:96), the pool is still 40 feet long and 20 feet wide; however, the picture of the pool is now only 5 inches by 2½ inches. Regardless of the scale, the line size remains 1 point and the font size 8 points.

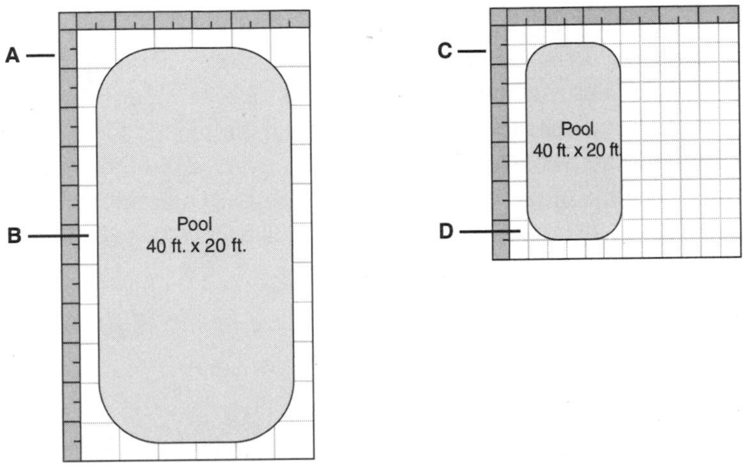

Figure 12-1 The pool is 40 ft by 20 ft in drawing units, regardless of the drawing scale. (**A**) Drawing scale: 1/4 in. = 1 ft (1:48). (**B**) In page units, the pool is 10 in. by 5 in. in this drawing scale. (**C**) Drawing scale: 1/8 in. = 1 ft. (1:96). (**D**) In page units, the pool is 5 in. by 2-1/2 in. in this drawing scale.

Factors to Consider in Choosing a Drawing Scale

To choose the appropriate drawing scale to include in a template, consider the following:

- The expected size of the drawing, in drawing units
- The paper size on which users will print their drawings
- The industry or drawing conventions that apply to the drawing type users create with your template, such as margins or title blocks

For example, a user can print a house plan on an 8½-inch by 11-inch sheet of paper, in landscape orientation. If the drawing scale is ¼ inch = 1 foot, the drawing page represents 34 feet by 44 feet (assuming no margins are set for the printed page). An area of 34 feet by 44 feet might not be large enough to accommodate the house and its landscape design. Instead, you might choose a smaller scale, such as ⅛ inch = 1 foot or 1 inch = 10 feet.

Tip Drawing units can represent measurements other than distance. You can use elapsed time rather than distance for a page scale by setting the drawing units to hours, days, weeks, months, and so on. For example, you can use elapsed weeks (abbreviated "ew" in ShapeSheet formulas) as the drawing units for the diagram of a project timeline. For a complete list of units, see the Microsoft Visio Developer Reference (on the **Help** menu, click **Developer Reference**).

To set the drawing scale for a page

1. On the **File** menu, click **Page Setup**, and then click the **Page Properties** tab.
2. For **Measurement units**, select the drawing units you want, and then click the **Page Size** tab.
3. Under **Page Size**, choose the orientation and size of paper on which the drawing will be printed.

   The values in the **Page Size** tab show you the drawing unit measurements of your page according to the selected scale and paper size.
4. Click the **Drawing Scale** tab, and then under **Drawing scale**, choose a predefined scale from the list:
   - Click **Architectural**, **Civil Engineering**, or **Mechanical Engineering** to select from among the built-in industry-standard scales for these professions.
   - Click **Metric** to set a standard metric page scale ratio.

   Or, click **Custom scale** and enter a scale ratio to define a different scale.

Tip To ensure that a master you create matches the drawing scale for a template's page, edit the master and repeat the preceding procedure in the master drawing window. For details, see *Setting the Scale of a Master* later in this chapter.

Choosing a Scale for Masters

You can scale masters as well as drawing pages. A shape's appearance on the drawing page depends on both the master's scale and the drawing page's scale. If a shape is scaled, and the page is unscaled or has a very different scale (or vice versa), the shape might behave in ways the user does not expect when the shape is dropped onto the page. If users aren't aware of scaling differences, they might become frustrated when they try to use shapes on a page with an incompatible scale.

Although you can't prevent users from creating a new drawing of any scale and dragging your shapes onto it, you can ensure that the drawing pages you provide with your templates have drawing scales that match those in your masters. You can also create masters that work in as many different drawing scales as possible.

Determining an Appropriate Scale for a Master

It is always best if the drawing scale of a master matches the drawing scale of the page on which it is dropped. This is not always possible; so within certain limits, Microsoft Visio handles differences of scale by ensuring that the shape, as drawn, is the same size, *in drawing units*, as the master:

- If the scale of the shape differs from that of the drawing page by a factor of eight or less—that is, if the drawing scale of the master is no more than eight times greater or smaller than the drawing scale of the page—Visio calculates the shape's size in drawing units and scales it appropriately on the drawing page. This behavior prevents a shape from becoming so large that it obscures the drawing page or so small that you can't see it.
- If the difference in scales exceeds a factor of eight, Visio *antiscales* the shape; the shape is drawn in the same size, *in page units*, as the size of the master. The user can resize the shape once it is dropped. For example, in the following figure, when the table shape is dragged into a drawing whose scale is outside the range of eight, the shape appears at the same size, in page units, as the master (2 inches), but Visio recalculates its width using the drawing scale of the page.

Visio uses a factor of eight when antiscaling a shape, so this is sometimes called the "range of eight" rule.

For example, you can create a master of a table that can be used in space-planning templates that vary in scale from ½ inch = 1 foot (a drawing scale of 1:24) to 1 inch = 10 feet (a drawing scale of 1:120). In the following figure, when a 48-inch table shape is dragged onto a drawing whose scale doesn't differ by more than a factor of eight, the table is properly scaled. The Shape Transform section shows its width is still 48 inches.

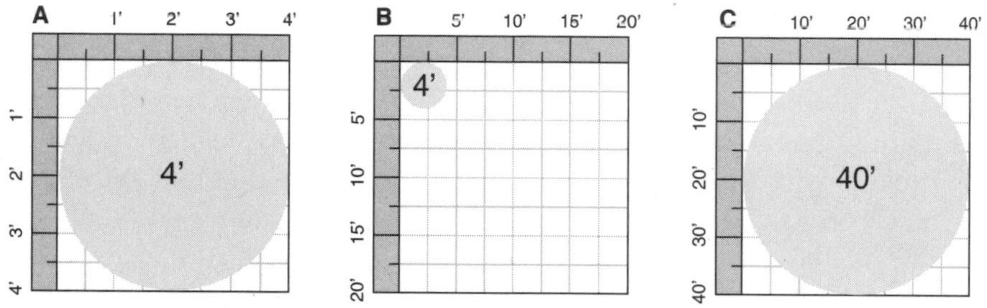

Figure 12-2 How shapes are redrawn at different scales according to the range of eight rule. (**A**) Master scale: 1/2 in. = 1 ft. Scale ratio: 1:24. Size (drawing units): 4 ft. Printed size (page units): 2 in. (**B**) Drawing scale: 1 in. = 10 ft. Scale ratio: 1:120. Size (drawing units): 4 ft. Printed size (page units): 0.4 in. Scale ratio: (1/24) / (1/120) = 5. 5 is within the range of 8, so the shape is scaled. (**C**) Drawing scale: 1 in. = 20 ft. Scale ratio: 1:240. Size (drawing units): 40 ft. Printed size (page units): 2 in. Scale ratio: (1/24) / (1/240) = 10. 10 is outside the range of 8, so the shape is antiscaled.

Visio applies the "range of eight" rule only to width and height values. Constants in formulas are not adjusted. So, for example, typing the following formula in a cell of the Geometry section might cause unexpected results:

```
Width - 1 ft
```

Because Visio changes the shape's width, the Width reference will be scaled, but a 1-foot measurement will remain 1 foot in drawing units, so the shape might still look incorrect even after it has been correctly scaled.

To take advantage of the "range of eight" rule in designing your masters, follow these guidelines:

- Set the scale of a master in between the largest and smallest scales in which the master is likely to be used. This way, the master works with the greatest range of drawing scales within the range of eight. This "middle scale" can be calculated as the square root of the largest drawing-scale ratio times the smallest drawing-scale ratio.

- If you want a shape never to scale, set the scale of the master to an extreme measurement, so that the shape always antiscales when dropped on the page. For example, use a scale such as 1000 inches = 1 inch, which is well outside the range of the "range of eight" rule. For details, see *Creating Shapes that Never Scale* later in this chapter.

Setting the Scale of a Master

In general, set the scale of a master equal to the scale of the drawing page with which the master will be used. By default, a master uses the scale of the drawing page on which it was created, before the shape was dragged into a *stencil*. Or, if you use the **New Master** command to create a master directly on the stencil, by default the master is unscaled.

> **Note** To edit a master, you must open the stencil file as **Original**. If you open the stencil as **Read only**, you cannot edit its masters. If the stencil was opened as **Read only**, click the icon on the stencil's title bar, and then click **Edit** on the shortcut menu to make it editable.

To set the scale for a master

1. Right-click a master in your stencil, and then click **Edit Master** on the shortcut menu.
2. On the **File** menu, click **Page Setup**, and then click the **Drawing Scale** tab.
3. Under **Drawing scale**, choose a predefined scale from the list:
   - Click **Architectural**, **Civil Engineering**, or **Mechanical Engineering** to select from among the built-in industry-standard scales for these professions.
   - Click **Metric** to set a standard metric page scale ratio.

   Or, click **Custom Scale** and enter a scale ratio to define a different scale.

Creating Shapes that Never Scale

You can create antiscaled masters; that is, shapes that are the same size in page units for all drawing scales. For example, a title block in an architectural drawing or a legend in a map should remain the same size regardless of the scale. To maintain the size of a title block shape, its dimensions must be converted to page units even though they are expressed in drawing units.

Microsoft Visio has two page formulas that allow you to determine the scale: *ThePage!PageScale* and *ThePage!DrawingScale*. You can write an antiscaling formula that uses the ratio of these two values to convert a value expressed in page units to its equivalent in drawing units.

To convert a page unit value into the equivalent drawing unit value, multiply by the following ratio:

```
ThePage!DrawingScale / ThePage!PageScale
```

If you write a custom formula for a master using this ratio, users can drag the shape into any drawing scale, and the shape's scale does not change. For example, to create a shape that is always 5-cm wide on paper and cannot be resized, enter this formula in the Shape Transform section:

```
Width = GUARD(5 cm * (ThePage!DrawingScale / ThePage!PageScale))
```

If you want users to be able to resize the shape, do not use the GUARD function. When a user creates an instance from this master on a page that has a scale of 1 cm = 1 m, the Width formula is reevaluated for the scale of the destination page:

```
= 5 cm * (1 m / 1 cm)
= 5 cm * 100
= 500 cm
```

When the shape is printed or displayed on the screen at actual size, Visio scales the 500-cm shape to 5 cm.

If you are creating a number of antiscaled masters, you might find it more efficient to store the antiscaling formula in a user-defined cell of the page sheet, such as *ThePage!User.Antiscale*. That way, you can quickly edit the antiscaling formula by changing values in only one place, the page sheet. The formula of any antiscaled master becomes:

```
Width       = 5 cm * ThePage!User.AntiScale
```

13

Packaging Stencils and Templates

Designing Custom Shapes for Distribution 262

Testing Masters 265

Adding Help for Your Custom Solution 268

Finishing and Testing a Stencil 270

Finishing and Testing a Template 276

Installing Stencils and Templates 279

Masters, stencils, and templates make up the package that a graphic solution comes in. Not every solution requires all three, but your solution might if it includes many new or customized shapes, and you plan to distribute them to users. In addition, you can include your own Help files to assist your users. Before you distribute your masters, stencils, and templates to others, it's important to test them thoroughly. Only by testing can you ensure that every component of your Microsoft Visio solution is easy for users to understand and use.

This chapter explains how to put the finishing touches on masters, stencils, and templates. It also describes how to add Help for shapes and includes detailed lists for testing your work based on the methods used by the Visio quality assurance staff.

Designing Custom Shapes for Distribution

If you are taking the time to develop your own shapes, you probably plan to reuse them or distribute them in stencils and templates for others to use. The goal of good shape design is to create shapes that work the way users expect them to. Like any creative work, developing shapes is an iterative process that benefits from experimentation and review.

What works on your system may not work as well on someone else's system. Not all installations of the Microsoft Windows operating system are exactly alike. You can design more usable shapes, stencils, and templates for others to use if you know your users' hardware configurations. Even if you create shapes for only your own use, knowing the characteristics of your computer environment saves design time by helping you create shapes that work the first time.

On any given system, the speed of the processor or the amount of memory affect the usability of your stencils and templates. Shapes with many complex formulas recalculate and redraw more slowly than simple shapes and take up more storage. Be sure to test your stencils on all the systems your users might have.

Shape Design Process Guidelines

To ensure a professional shape solution, consider using the following design process guidelines:

1. Make notes about a shape's intended function. What requirements must it satisfy? How must it behave to meet those requirements? If the shape will be one of a collection in a stencil, how must it behave to be consistent with other shapes?

2. Draw a prototype of the shape and format it to look the way you want, and then experiment with the shape using the Visio drawing tools. How does the shape behave when you move it, size it, rotate it, or group it with other shapes? What happens when you lock parts of the shape? Which behaviors do you want to change?

3. Identify the ShapeSheet cells that influence the behavior you want to change. Which cells need custom formulas, and to which cells should the formulas refer?

4. Create one formula at a time and check its effect on the shape's behavior. Keep notes as you go, either on paper or in text blocks on the drawing that contains your prototype shape. If you're trying different alternatives, you might want to copy the shape each time you try something new and keep the copies, so you can return to an earlier version if needed.

5. Write Help for the shape, so your users will understand the shape's intended function.

6. Test the shape for usability by giving it to co-workers to see if the shape meets their expectations as well as your own.

When you know exactly what you want the shape to look like, how you want it to behave, and what formulas you need to accomplish what you want, re-create the shape from the beginning. This might seem like unnecessary work, but it's the best way to ensure that no obsolete formulas remain in ShapeSheet cells and that the shape itself is drawn and formatted cleanly.

Shape, Stencil, and Template Distribution Considerations

When you design stencils and templates for distribution, keep the following shape distribution considerations in mind:

- **The resolutions of different video systems** If you design for the system with the lowest resolution and fewest colors, your layouts and shapes will likely appear even better on more sophisticated systems. However, a stencil designed for higher resolution or more colors probably won't look as good on a less sophisticated system.
- **The possible or likely output devices that a user might use to print your shapes** Know the capabilities and limitations of your user's output devices. You should test your shapes by printing them on the output device you expect your users to have to make sure the lines and fills look the way you want.
- **Whether to copyright your shapes** The stencils, masters, templates, and source code provided with Microsoft Visio are copyrighted material, owned by Microsoft Corporation and protected by United States copyright laws and international treaty provisions. You cannot distribute any copyrighted master provided with Microsoft Visio or through a Web-based subscription service, unless your user already has a licensed copy of Visio that includes that master, or your user has a valid subscription to the Web-based service, or you've signed an agreement that allows you to distribute individual masters to your users. This includes shapes that you create by modifying or deriving shapes from copyrighted masters.

  You can, however, copyright your own original shapes.

To copyright your own shapes

- Select a shape. On the **Format** menu, click **Special**.

  Add copyright information as a final step in your shape development. Once you have entered copyright information in the **Special** dialog box, it cannot be changed in a drawing, stencil, or template file.

Testing Masters

You should test all the masters on a stencil together for consistency and then test each master individually. After performing the following tests, spend a few minutes to construct the kind of diagram or chart the shapes are intended to produce. This is the best way to evaluate their interaction, accuracy, and usefulness and to discover limitations or missing elements.

Checking the Consistency of Masters

You need to ensure that a stencil contains all the masters it should, that the names and formats are understandable, and that the icons appear in a predictable order on the stencil. If you have a written specification for master standards, be sure to check each shape against the specification.

To check the consistency of masters on a stencil, open the stencil file as **Original**, and then verify the items shown in the following table.

Verifying the consistency of masters on a stencil

Item	What to verify
Expected number of masters are on the stencil	Verify this number against the specification, if you have one. If the stencil is later modified and you test it again, you will know whether masters have been added or removed.
Master name and prompt	Check for correct spelling, punctuation, capitalization, grammar, content, and spacing, and that these are consistent with other shapes.
	Remove trailing spaces in the master name that would cause highlighting to extend farther than needed when the icon is selected.
	Align names in the same way for each master on the stencil.
Icons	Ensure that each icon is a meaningful, clear representation of its master. To check, right-click the master and click **Edit Icon** on the shortcut menu.

Verifying the consistency of masters on a stencil *(continued)*

Item	What to verify
Icons *(continued)*	Arrange icons logically, align them consistently, and ensure that they appear in the order you want on the stencil. Set icons to the correct size. **Normal** is the most commonly used setting (use the **Icon size** box in the **New Master** or **Master Properties** dialog box). Icons with custom graphics are set to update automatically. To check, right-click the master and click **Master Properties** on the shortcut menu. In the **Master Properties** dialog box, select the **Generate icon automatically from shape data** check box.

Checking the Master in the Master Drawing Window

To test a master in the master drawing window, open the stencil file as **Original**. In the stencil window, double-click a master icon or right-click the master and click **Edit Master** on the shortcut menu; this will open the master's drawing window. You can then verify the following items.

Verifying items in a master

Item	What to verify
Scale used by shape	Shape should use the appropriate scale. To check, on the **File** menu, click **Page Setup**, and then click the **Drawing Scale** tab. For example, an office layout solution might use an architectural scale where 1/2" = 1'0". An office shape would need to use the same drawing scale.
1-D or 2-D interaction style	Interaction style should be appropriate for shape. To check, select the master on the page and click **Behavior** on the **Format** menu.
Information about the master in the **Special** dialog box is correct	For example, verify that the **Data** boxes contain information and the shape is linked to shape-specific Help. To check, select a shape in the master drawing window and click **Special** on the **Format** menu.
Appropriate protection options are set	Open the ShapeSheet window for a shape or the page in the master drawing window and check the Protection section. Or select a shape in the master drawing window and click **Protection** on the **Format** menu to verify the protection settings.
Connection points are visible	On the **View** menu, click **Connection Points**.

Testing Masters with Different Page Scales

Because a stencil and a drawing page are opened with each template you provide, you should test each shape on all the different page scales with which the shape is intended to work. It's also helpful to test a shape on a page with a very different scale.

To test a shape in a drawing of the same scale

1. On the **File** menu, click **Open**.
2. For **File name**, select a template file containing a stencil with masters to test and a drawing page that uses the same scale as the masters.
3. Click the arrow next to the **Open** button, click **Read only**, and then click **Open**.
4. Drag a master onto the drawing page to create the instance to test.

Verify the items in the following table.

Verifying an instance of a master in a drawing of the same scale

Item	What to verify
General shape behavior	The shape is aligned appropriately within its alignment box as you drag it.
	The shape behaves as expected when connected to other shapes; for example, a connector shape uses the appropriate glue type.
	The shape acts as expected when you double-click it. Check the settings by selecting the shape on the page, clicking **Behavior** on the **Format** menu, and then clicking the **Double-Click** tab.
	The shape can be deleted.
	The shape looks the way you want it to when you print it on expected output devices. For example, some fill patterns affect performance on some printers.
Snap and glue behavior	The shape and the alignment box snap to the grid. The instance snaps to other shapes and to the grid or guides as expected.

Verifying an instance of a master in a drawing of the same scale

(continued)

Item	What to verify
Shape text	The shape's text box appears in the correct place, and text you type in it wraps and aligns appropriately. The shape and its text act as you expect when you do the following: ■ Apply a fill style. ■ Resize the shape vertically, horizontally, and proportionately. This test is particularly important if you have programmed the shape to resize in a unique way—for example, in only one direction. ■ Rotate the shape using the **Rotate Left** and **Rotate Right** commands and the **Rotation** tool. ■ Reverse ends and flip the shape vertically and horizontally. ■ Ungroup the shape. If it is not a group, the **Ungroup** command is dimmed.
Shape customization	If the shape has custom properties, they appear as expected. To check, select the shape and click **Custom Properties Window** on the **View** menu. Or, click **Custom Properties** on the **Shape** menu. If the shape has customized actions on its shortcut menu, they work as intended. To check, right-click the shape and click the action command (or commands). The prompt and shape-specific Help provide useful information about the shape. The **Special** dialog box contains appropriate information. To check, select the shape and then click **Special** on the **Format** menu.

To test a shape in a drawing of a different scale

1. Create a new drawing page with a much different scale from the shape you want to test.

   For example, if the master was created at a scale of 1:1, create a drawing page with a scale of ¼ inch = 1 foot.

2. Drag a master onto the drawing page to create the instance to test.

3. Verify the following:
   - The shape is aligned appropriately within its alignment box as you drag it.
   - The shape and the alignment box snap to the grid.
   - The shape and its text act as you expect when you resize the shape vertically, horizontally, and proportionately.
   - The shape and its text act as you expect when you rotate the shape using the **Rotate Left** and **Rotate Right** commands and the **Rotation** tool.

Adding Help for Your Custom Solution

You can provide online Help that displays general guidelines for using the masters in a stencil or the subtleties of a shape's behavior. Microsoft Visio supports both HTML Help (.chm files) and WinHelp (.hlp files). This section assumes that you are familiar with the techniques and terminology used in creating Microsoft Windows online Help files. For details, see the Microsoft Platform SDK in the *MSDN Library*.

Associating Help with a Master

You can associate Help with any shape in a drawing, but typically you'll associate Help with masters in a stencil. A user displays Help for a shape from the shortcut menu of the shape or master.

Microsoft Visio locates a shape Help topic using the context identifier (ID) number that is specified in the .hpj file that is used to compile .hlp files, or the .hhp file that is used to compile .chm files. To associate a particular Help topic with a shape, you must provide the context ID number for that topic.

To associate Help with a master on a stencil

1. Open the stencil as **Original** or click the icon on the stencil title bar, and then click **Edit** on the shortcut menu so you can edit its masters.
2. Double-click a master to open its drawing window, and then select the shape.
3. On the **Format** menu, click **Special**.
4. In the **Help** box, use the following syntax to enter the Help file name and keyword:

   `filename.hlp!#n` or `filename.chm!#n`

The name of your Help file is *filename.hlp* or *filename.chm* and *n* is the context ID number defined for the topic you want to associate with this shape. For example, Shape.hlp!#63 or Shape.chm!#63.

If you want to display the contents topic of your Help file, do not specify a context ID number. Use the following syntax:

`filename.hlp` or `filename.chm`

5. Click **OK**.

When a user clicks the **Help** command, the indicated topic appears as follows, depending on the Help system you're creating:

- In a standard window that is part of the master Help system for HTML Help.
- In a pop-up window that is not linked to a parent Help system for WinHelp.

If you do not define a Help topic for a shape, the **Help** command is dimmed on the menu.

> **Note** Pressing F1 displays the Microsoft Visio Help, not a particular shape's topic.
>
> For Visio to find your Help file, you must place it in the correct folder. By default, Visio first looks for a shape Help file in the default folder for Help files (usually the Help folder under the correct language folder in the Visio product folder). You can change the default folder by changing the **Help** path setting on the **File Paths** tab (on the **Tools** menu, click **Options**).

Testing Shape Help

Make sure your shape Help is as thoughtfully designed as the shape itself. Test the Help and its jumps for consistency and accuracy.

To test shape Help

1. Right-click a master on the stencil, or create an instance of the shape and right-click the instance on the page. Click **Help** on the shortcut menu and check that the correct Help topic appears.

2. Create another instance of the shape, point to the instance, and click the right mouse button. Click **Help** on the shortcut menu and check that the correct Help topic appears.
3. Test all jumps to make sure they display the correct topics.
4. Check each topic for spelling, grammar, consistency, and accuracy of its content.

Adding HTML Help that is Integrated with the Microsoft Visio Help System

To create a custom Help system that is integrated with the Microsoft Visio Help system, use the **InvokeHelp** method. The arguments passed to the **InvokeHelp** method correspond to those described in the HTML Help API. For a list of *command* values, see the HTML Help API Reference on the Microsoft Developer Network (MSDN) Web site. Microsoft Visual Basic programmers can use the numeric equivalent of the C++ constants defined in the HTML Help API header files.

For example, use the following code to show the default Visio Help window:

```
Application.InvokeHelp "Visio.chm", 15, 0
```

Use this code to hide the Visio Help window:

```
Application.InvokeHelp "", 18, 0
```

For more information on **InvokeHelp**, see the Microsoft Visio Developer Reference (on the **Help** menu, click **Developer Reference**). For more information about the HTML Help API, search for "HTML Help API Overview" on the MSDN Web site.

Finishing and Testing a Stencil

After you have created a stencil containing your masters, a few tasks remain to prepare your stencil for distribution. For example, the stencils you create will be easier to use if the masters look as if they belong together and each conveys the corresponding shape's purpose.

Creating Master Shortcuts

You can create shortcuts to masters in the same stencil or in other stencils. To create master shortcuts, the masters must be in a stencil that has been saved. These shortcuts look and behave exactly like a master, but they are references to a master that can reside on any stencil. Master shortcuts contain no shape data—only a reference to the original master. When the shortcut is dragged onto the drawing page, the original master is retrieved and used to create the new shape.

By creating mastser shortcuts in your stencil, you can:

- Reduce the size of your stencils by referencing, rather than duplicating, masters.
- Simplify maintenance of your masters by keeping the shape data in a single location.
- Provide multiple shortcuts to a single master and define actions for each shortcut (called Drop actions) that affect the appearance of the shape when it is dropped onto the page.

To create a master shortcut, do one of the following

- Right-click the master, and then click **Create Shortcut** on the shortcut menu. The shortcut appears in the same stencil as the master; you can then drag the shortcut to another stencil. A stencil must be editable to create a master shortcut on the same stencil as the master.
- Right-click the master, and then click **Copy**. Right-click the stencil where you want to place the shortcut, and then click **Paste Shortcut**. The shortcut appears in the same stencil as the master.
- Drag the master to another stencil while holding down CTRL+SHIFT. Instead of creating a copy of the master in the destination stencil, Microsoft Visio creates a shortcut to that master.

To define actions that occur when a master shortcut instance is dropped on the page

1. Make sure the stencil with the master shortcut is editable by opening the stencil as **Original**, or by clicking the icon in the stencil title bar and clicking **Edit**.
2. Right-click the master shortcut, and then click **Master Shortcut Properties**.
3. In the **Drop actions** box in the **Master Shortcut Properties** dialog box, enter any cell names set equal to a valid formula or value that you want to apply to the instance of the master. For example, to apply a red fill color to a shape when it is dropped on the drawing page, enter the following:

```
FillForegnd = 2
```

You can enter any number of cell values separated by a semicolon. For example:

```
FillForegnd = 2 + 3; LockFormat = 1
```

Cleaning up Masters in a Stencil

You can edit the master name and icon to make your masters easier for users to identify. You can also add a prompt that appears as a tool tip when a user pauses the pointer over the master in the stencil window and explains the master's purpose.

By default, a master's name is the identifier that Microsoft Visio assigns, and its icon is a miniature version of the master. When you edit a new master, the icon is updated to reflect the shape you draw unless you specify otherwise.

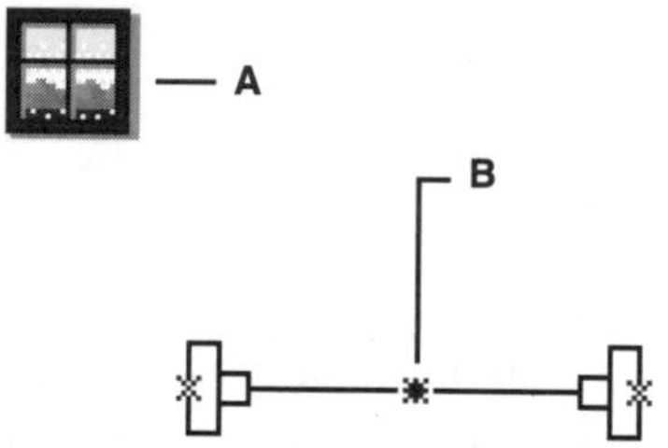

Figure 13-1 To help users identify your master, you can design a custom image for its icon. (**A**) Window master icon. (**B**) Window shape as it appears in the drawing window.

To specify a master name and prompt

1. Open the stencil as **Original**. Or click the icon on the stencil's title bar, and then click **Edit**.
2. In the stencil window, right-click a master, and then click **Master Properties** on the shortcut menu.
3. In the **Name** box, type a name for the master. If you want to align the master name under the icon in some fashion other than centered, click an **Align master name** option.
4. In the **Prompt** box, type the text you want to appear in the tool tip when the user points to the icon.
5. For **Icon size**, select the size that you want.

To create a custom master icon

1. In the stencil window, right-click a master, and then click **Edit Icon** on the shortcut menu.
2. Use the drawing tools in the icon editing window to edit the icon or create a new design.
3. When you are finished, close the icon editing window.
4. To protect your custom icon, right-click the master, and then click **Master Properties**. Verify that the **Generate icon automatically from shape data** check box is cleared.

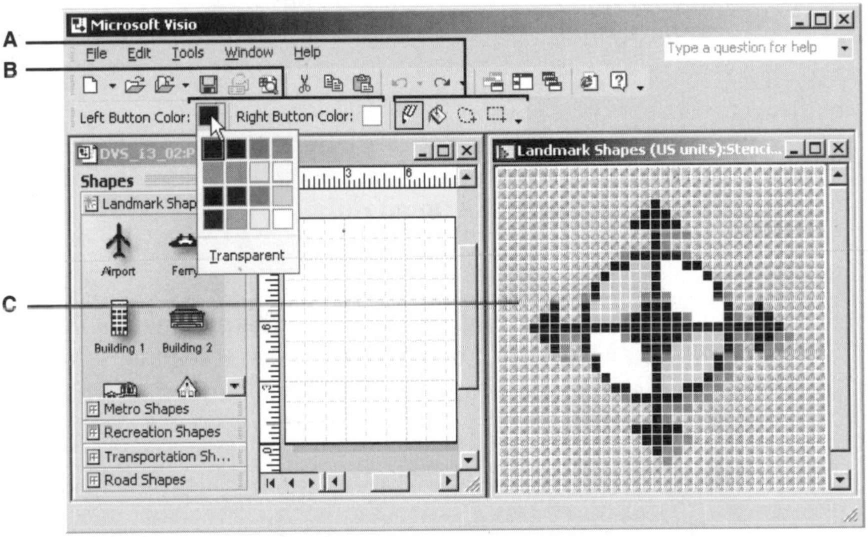

Figure 13-2 The icon editing window and tools. (**A**) Editing tools. (**B**) Click the left or right mouse button to apply the current color, or to choose another color from the color palette. (**C**) Icon editing window.

Cleaning up a Stencil File

Before you save a finished stencil, you should do the following cleanup tasks to enhance performance:

- Arrange the icons in the stencil windows to ensure that they appear on the screen in order from left to right, top to bottom, when the file is opened.
- Include file summary information for the stencil. To do so, make the stencil window active, and then click **Properties** on the **File** menu.

- To save file space, make sure your stencil file contains only the required single drawing page and that there are no shapes on it.
- Delete any styles from the drawing page that are not used by the masters in the stencil. A stencil file should contain only masters and their styles.
- Verify that the style definitions in a stencil match those for styles of the same name in any templates that open the stencil. For details about working with styles, see Chapter 10, *Managing Styles, Formats, and Colors*.
- Use the **Save As** command to save your stencil file. In the **Save As** dialog box, click the arrow next to the **Save** button and make sure that **Workspace** is *not* selected. A stencil's workspace list should be empty.

Testing Stencils

You test stencils by reviewing the **Open** dialog box information and opening the stencil as **Original**, **Copy**, and **Read only**.

> **Tip** To protect your original stencil, create a copy that contains the shapes you want to test and use the copy for testing. After you test, incorporate changes in the original stencil and make a new copy for additional testing.

To test the stencil in the Open dialog box

1. On the **File** menu, point to **Stencils**, and then click **Open Stencil**.
2. For **File Name**, select a stencil file.
3. Verify the following:
   - The default setting is **Read only** (under the **Open** button).
   - When you pause the mouse pointer over the name of a stencil in the file list, a tool tip appears with a title and description of the stencil.

To test the original version of a stencil

1. Open the stencil file as **Original**.
2. Verify the following:
   - The file opens with its name displayed correctly in the title bar. For example, the name should look like this: Basic Shapes.vss. (If the stencil is open in a docked, anchored window you will not see the .vss extension.)
   - The stencil window occupies the left quarter of the screen.
   - Property information for the stencil is provided. To check, click the icon on the stencil's title bar, and then click **Properties** on the shortcut menu. Verify that the spelling, grammar, content, spacing, capitalization, and punctuation for the text in the various boxes on the **Summary** tab are correct for the stencil.

To test a copy of a stencil

1. Open a stencil file as **Copy**.
2. Verify the following:
   - The file opens with a generic name, such as Stencil1.
   - File property information is blank except for the **Author** box; the **Author** box displays the user name specified in the **Options** dialog box (**Tools** menu) or when Visio was installed on the computer.

To test the read-only version of a stencil

1. Close all other files (including drawing files) and open the stencil file as **Read only**.
2. Verify the following:
   - The file name in the title bar appears in braces.
   - On the **File** menu, the **Save** command is dimmed.
   - On the **Edit** menu, the **Cut**, **Clear**, and **Duplicate** commands are dimmed.
   - On the **Master** menu, all commands are dimmed.

Finishing and Testing a Template

Before you save a template, check the following items:

- The workspace should contain only the files you want to be opened.
- All the windows are in appropriate positions.
- Any window you want to be minimized is minimized.

You create a workspace for a template by selecting **Workspace** under the **Save** button in the **Save As** dialog box and saving the template file. After that, unless you clear the **Workspace** option, Microsoft Visio updates a template's workspace list each time the original file is saved—adding files that are open and eliminating files that are closed.

Cleaning up a Template

To make your template as efficient and easy to use as possible, you should clean up the windows and workspace in your template as well as include summary information in your template. Begin by opening up your template as **Original**.

To delete unnecessary masters from the template's document stencil

1. Make sure the drawing window is active.
2. On the **File** menu, point to **Stencils**, and then click **Document Stencil**.
3. Delete only those masters that do not have instances in the template's pages.

To make sure the size of windows and stencils appears correctly on different systems

1. Open the template on a system with a display resolution your users are most likely to have.
2. On the **Window** menu, click **Tile** to help position windows correctly.
3. Open the template again on systems with different display resolutions to ensure that the window positions still work.

To provide summary information for your template

1. On the **File** menu, click **Properties**, and then click the **Summary** tab.
2. Provide any summary information you want to include with your template.

Testing a Template

You test a template by verifying the information about it that appears in the **Open** dialog box, and then testing how the template acts when it is opened as **Original**, **Copy**, or **Read only**.

If you create a template by saving an existing Visio file as a new template (.vst) file, the new template may inherit an irrelevant workspace list. Be sure to test your template to make sure its workspace list opens the files and windows you want before you release the template to users.

> **Tip** To protect your original template, create a copy that contains the shapes you want to test and use the copy for testing. After you test, incorporate changes in the original template and make a new copy for additional testing.

To test template information in the Open dialog box

1. On the **File** menu, click **Open**.
2. For **Files of type**, click **Template**.
3. Pause your mouse pointer over the template file that you are testing.
4. Verify that a title and description appear for the file.

   If the title and description don't appear, be sure to add these later to the original file by clicking **Properties** on the **File** menu.

To test the original version of a template

1. Open the template file as **Original**.
2. Verify that the template opens correctly using the following criteria:
   - The file opens with its name displayed correctly in the title bar. For example, if the template file is Organization Chart.vst, the name in the title bar should also be Organization Chart.vst.
   - All stencil (.vss) files associated with the template open as **Read only**, unless intended to open as **Original** files.
   - The drawing page window opens in **Whole Page** view, unless you explicitly specify another option. **Whole Page** view is the best option for most monitors. (On the **View** menu, point to **Zoom**, and then click **Whole Page**.)

- The stencil and drawing windows are positioned correctly. Click **Tile** on the **Window** menu to verify the window positions, unless you have already repositioned them during the current work session.
- The template includes the correct number of pages. Check the **Page** tabs at the bottom of the drawing page. Templates should have only one page unless you have intentionally created additional pages.
- The content of each page (including each background) is correct.
- Nothing unintentional appears on the area outside the drawing page. To check, display each page at 5% magnification. To ensure all the shapes are visible, click **Select All** on the **Edit** menu.

3. Verify that the template's settings are correct using the following criteria:

- Each page scale is compatible with the shapes intended for use with the template. To check, for each page, click **Page Setup** on the **File** menu, and then click the **Page Properties** tab.
- The page size corresponds to the page orientation used for printing. Unless you specifically want pages to tile when they are printed, the settings should correspond as follows: If the page size is taller than it is wide, the orientation should be portrait. If the page size is wider than it is tall, the orientation should be landscape.
- No masters remain on the document stencil, unless you have created instances of the master on the template's drawing page, in which case no other masters should appear. To check, point to **Stencils** on the **File** menu, and then click **Document Stencil**.
- File property information is filled out. To check, click **Properties** on the **File** menu and verify the spelling, grammar, content, spacing, capitalization, and punctuation.
- The template settings for each page are as expected. To check, on the **Tools** menu, click the **Options**, **Snap & Glue**, and **Ruler & Grid** commands. On the **File** menu, click **Page Setup** and then click the **Page Size**, **Drawing Scale**, and **Page Properties** tabs. Check the style lists on the **Format** toolbars.

- The template display options are set appropriately: rulers, grid, guides, connection points, and toolbar.
- Make sure the template's color palette matches that of any stencils that open with the template.

To test a copy of a template

1. Open the template file as **Copy**.
2. Verify that the file opens with a drawing page name that looks like this: Drawing1:Page1.
3. Verify that the drawing page, and any pages you have added, look the way you expect.
4. Verify that all stencil files (.vss) associated with the template open as **Read only**.
5. On the **File** menu, click **Properties** and verify that all file properties are blank except for the **Author** box; the **Author** box displays the user name specified using the **Options** dialog box (on the **Tools** menu, click **Options**) or the name specified when Visio was installed on the computer.

To test the read-only version of a template

1. Open the template file as **Read only**.
2. Verify that the file name in the drawing window title bar appears in braces and starts with the template name.
3. Verify that on the **File** menu, the **Save** command is dimmed.

Installing Stencils and Templates

For Microsoft Visio to find your stencil and template files, as well as any add-ons you intend to work with these files, place them in the Solutions folder (under the correct language folder in the Visio product folder). By placing your files in this folder, your stencil and template files will appear when the user clicks the **Choose Drawing Type** command (on the **File** menu, point to **New**, and then click **Choose Drawing Type**) or the **Open Stencil** command (on the **File** menu, point to **Stencils**, and then click **Open Stencil**). They'll also appear when the user starts Microsoft Visio 2002 and then chooses to create a new drawing in the **Choose Drawing Type** pane (on the **View** menu, click **Task Pane**).

If you want to install your stencil and template files elsewhere, you can change the default folder where Visio searches for files. To do this, click **Options** on the **Tools** menu, click the **File Paths** tab, and then specify the default path you want.

Moving Template Files

The file name for each stencil and drawing that opens with a template is stored in the template's workspace list as a fully qualified path and name. Problems can arise when files are moved to different computers where local or network drives are configured differently. To prevent some of these problems, Microsoft Visio checks the path as follows:

1. When Visio is about to open a file from the workspace list, it first examines the file's stored path.
2. If the path is exactly the same as the stored path for the file that contains the workspace list, Visio assumes that these files were meant to be in the same folder.
3. Visio uses the current workspace file's folder to locate files.

   As long as you copy stencils and templates to the same folder when you must move files, Visio can locate and open all the files in a workspace list.

Protecting Stencils and Templates

The easiest way to protect stencils and templates from accidental changes is to make the files read-only. If a stencil or template is read-only, modifications cannot be saved to the file. When you create a template, open the stencil files you want to include as **Read only** and save the template. That way, Microsoft Visio automatically opens the stencils as read-only when a user opens the template.

When you use the **Save** or **Save As** command, you can click the **Read only** option (under the **Save** button) to save a Visio file with Microsoft Windows read-only protection. If you save a file in this way, your users cannot open it as an original—only as a copy.

Another way to protect a document is to use the **Protect Document** command. This command prevents a user from changing any background pages in a template; the command also protects all masters in a stencil, all shapes on the drawing, and all styles in the template if the user tries to change them. If you enter a password, a user must type the password before editing any of the checked items.

To protect a document, click **Drawing Explorer Window** on the **View** menu, right-click the document name in the **Drawing Explorer**, and then click **Protect Document** on the shortcut menu.

Part 3

Extending Visio with Automation

Chapter 14 Automation and the Visio Object Model
Chapter 15 Programming Visio with VBA
Chapter 16 Working with Visio Document, Page and Shape Objects
Chapter 17 Automating Formulas
Chapter 18 Drawing with Automation
Chapter 19 Automating Connections in a Visio Solution
Chapter 20 Integrating Data with a Visio Solution
Chapter 21 Handling Visio Events
Chapter 22 Customizing the Visio User Interface
Chapter 23 Using COM Add-ins in a Visio Solution
Chapter 24 Using ActiveX Controls in a Visio Solution
Chapter 25 Using the Visio Undo Manager in Your Program
Chapter 26 Packaging a Visio Automation Solution
Chapter 27 Programming Visio with Visual Basic
Chapter 28 Programming Visio with C++

14

Automation and the Visio Object Model

An Automation Overview 284

The Visio Object Model 284

Getting and Releasing Visio Objects 287

Using Properties and Methods 292

Automation is the mechanism that enables you to extend the functionality of Microsoft Visio or to include the Visio engine as a graphics engine for your own program. With Automation, you can use the Visio engine to create or update drawings based on data from an external source, to read drawings and gather information from them, or simply to extend the behavior of a drawing with a Microsoft Visual Basic for Applications (VBA) macro.

This chapter describes Automation and the Visio object model—the objects that the Visio engine exposes through Automation. It shows how to access these objects from a program and briefly covers the VBA syntax for using Visio objects, properties, and methods, and includes some sample code.

For details about handling events in your program, see Chapter 21, *Handling Visio Events*.

For details about creating an external Microsoft Visual Basic program, see Chapter 27, *Programming Visio with Visual Basic*. For comparable information about C++ syntax, see Chapter 28, *Programming Visio with C++*.

An Automation Overview

Automation is a means by which a program written in Microsoft Visual Basic for Applications (VBA), Microsoft Visual Basic, C/C++, or another programming language that supports Automation can incorporate the functionality of Microsoft Visio simply by using its objects.

The way that objects in an application are related to each other, along with each object's properties (data), methods (behavior), and events, is called the program's *object hierarchy* or *object model.* In the Visio object model, most objects correspond to items that you can see and select in the Visio user interface. For example, a **Shape** object represents a shape in a drawing.

In Automation, the application that provides the objects (such as Visio, sometimes called the *Automation server*) makes the objects accessible to other applications and provides the properties and methods that control them. This is called *exposing* the objects.

The application that uses the objects (such as your program, sometimes called the *Automation client*) creates instances of the objects and then sets their properties or invokes their methods to make the objects serve the application.

The Automation server and Automation client interact using COM (Component Object Model) services, which are installed when any version of the Microsoft Windows operating system later than Windows 95 is installed.

Visio (versions 4.5 and later) includes VBA, so you don't need to use a separate development environment to write your programs. However, you can write programs that control Visio in any language that supports Automation clients. The examples in this guide are written in VBA, but the principles apply to any programming language.

The Visio Object Model

The Microsoft Visio object model represents the objects, properties, methods, and events that the Visio engine exposes through Automation. More important, it describes how the objects are related to each other.

Most objects in the model correspond to items you can see and select in the Visio user interface. For example, a **Shape** object can represent anything on a Visio drawing page that you can select with the pointer—a shape, a group, a guide, a control, or an object from another application that is linked, embedded, or imported into a Visio drawing.

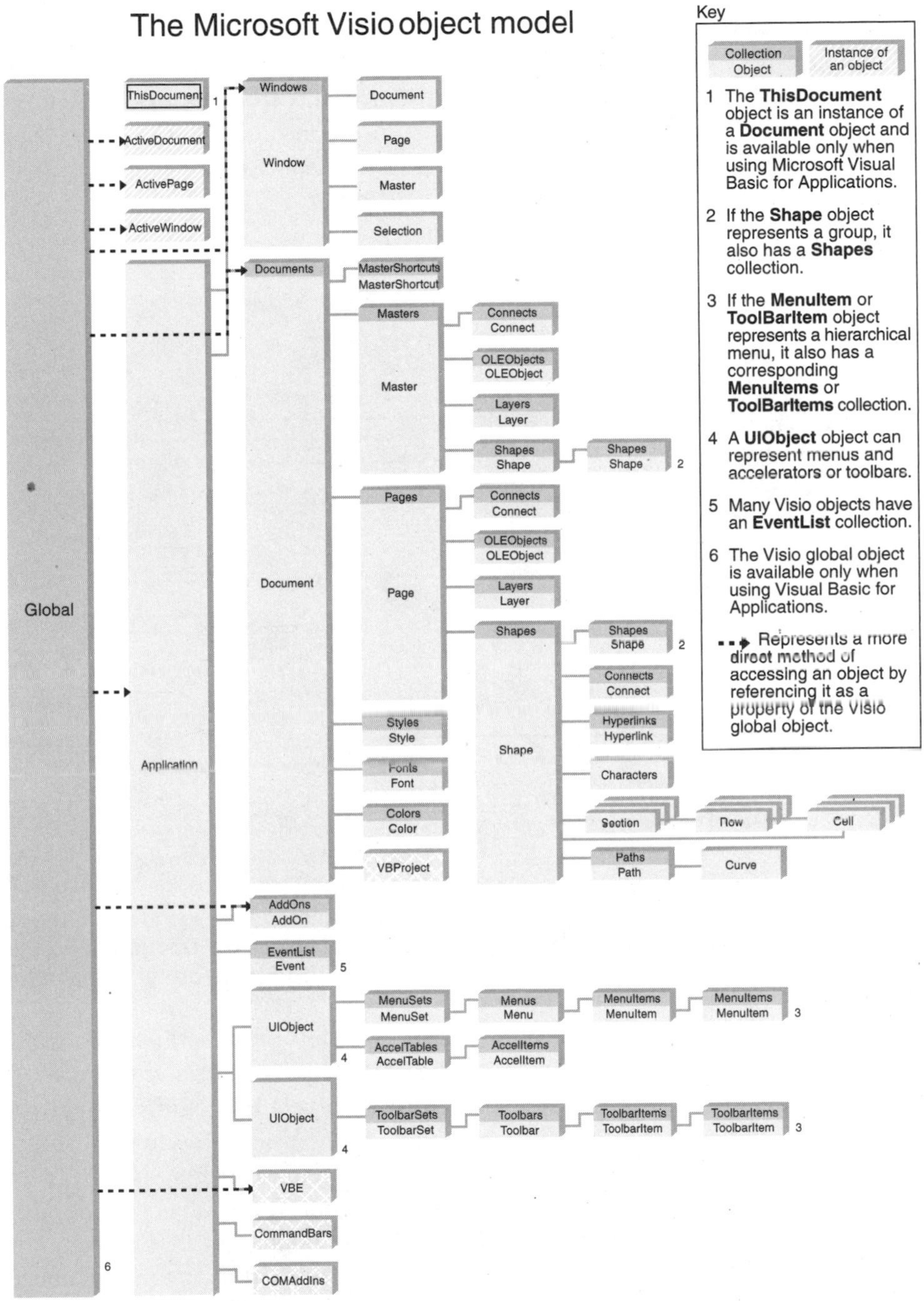

Figure 14-1 The Visio object model.

Some objects represent collections of other objects. A *collection* contains zero or more objects of a specified type. For example, a **Document** object represents one open document in a Visio instance; the **Documents** collection represents all of the documents that are open in the instance. For a more detailed discussion of collections, see *Referring to an Object in a Collection* in *Getting and Releasing Visio Objects* later in this chapter.

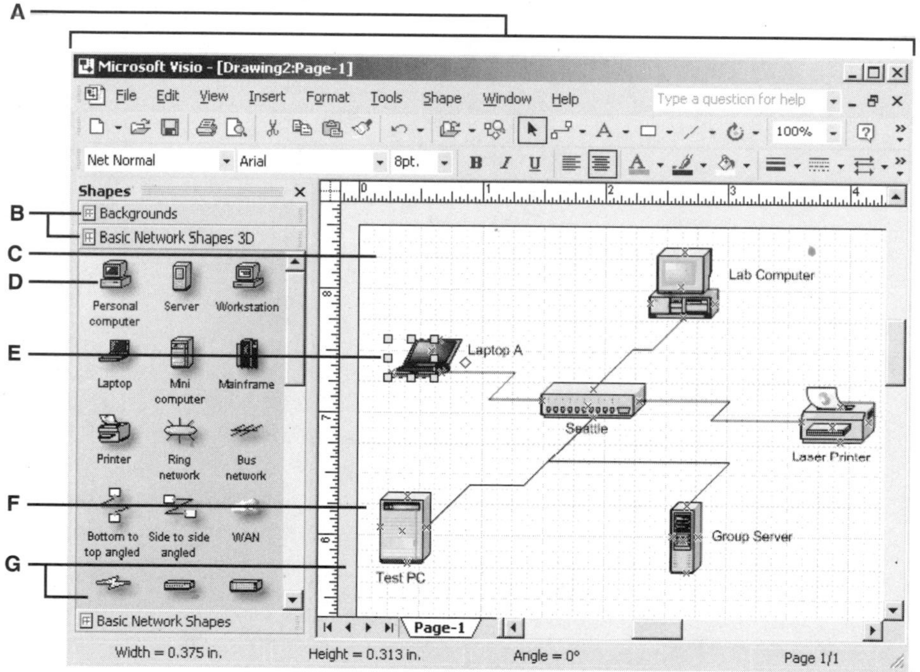

Figure 14-2 Many objects in the Visio object model correspond to items you can see in the Visio user interface. (**A**) **Application/global** object. (**B**) **Document** objects. (**C**) **Page** object. (**D**) **Master** object. (**E**) **Selection** object. (F) **Shape** object. (**G**) **Window** objects.

Using a Visio object is really a two-step process: First you get a reference to the object, and then you use the object's properties and methods to do something. You usually get a reference to an object by getting a property of an object higher in the Visio object model. Many of the objects are used primarily to access other objects. For example, to get a reference to a **Shape** object, you must get references to the objects that are higher in the object model; for example, the page that contains the shape, and the document that contains the page.

For a summary list of Visio objects, properties, methods, and events, see Appendix A, *Properties, Methods, and Events by Object.*

Getting and Releasing Visio Objects

You get an object by declaring an object variable, navigating through the object model to get a reference to the object you want to control, and assigning the reference to the object variable. Once you have a reference to an object, you can set and get the values of its properties or use methods that cause the object to perform actions.

Declaring Object Variables

A variable that stores a reference to a Visio object should be declared as a Visio object type such as *Visio.Page* or *Visio.Document* as defined in the Visio type library. Once you have gotten an object you want to control, use the **Set** statement to assign the reference to the object variable.

You don't have to assign all object references to variables, but it's almost always a good idea, especially if your program refers to an object more than once. For example, most programs have at least one object variable to store a reference to the **Page** object that represents the page that your program will manipulate. The objects you reference depend on the purpose of your program. You can't store the value of an object variable between program executions.

A variable can be declared as the more general **Object** data type, but using Visio object types will increase the speed of your program as well as eliminate possible confusion or conflicts in object and property names when programming with other applications and Visio. For example, when declaring an object variable for a Visio page use the following syntax:

```
Dim pageObj As Visio.Page
```

You could eliminate *Visio* and just use *Page*, but other applications may have a **Page** object. For example, Microsoft Excel has a **Cell** object, as does Visio, but the two objects are different and cannot be used interchangeably. It is good practice to refer to the object and the application specifically.

You can declare a variable as local, module-level, or global. The scope you choose depends on how you plan to use the variable in your program. For complete details about declaring variables, see the Microsoft Visual Basic Help.

Accessing Visio Objects through Properties

Most Visio objects have properties whose values refer to other objects. You use these properties to navigate up and down the layers of the object model to get to the object you want to control.

Let's say the object you want to control is the **Shape** object. You first gain access to the object model through the top-level object, the **Application** object.

The **Documents** property of an **Application** object returns a **Documents** collection. You would continue stepping through the object model in the following manner:

- The **Documents** property of an **Application** object returns a reference to the **Documents** collection.
- The **Item** property of a **Documents** collection returns a reference to a **Document** object.
- The **Pages** property of a **Document** object returns a reference to a **Pages** collection.
- The **Item** property of a **Pages** collection returns a reference to a **Page** object.
- The **Shapes** property of a **Page** object returns a reference to a **Shapes** collection.
- The **Item** property of a **Shapes** collection returns a reference to a Shape object.

Conversely, most objects have a property that refers to the object above it in the hierarchy, such as the **Document** property of a **Page** object, which returns a reference to the **Document** object that contains the **Page** object.

Referring to an Object in a Collection

A collection is an object that represents zero or more objects of a particular type. You can iterate through a collection to perform the same operation on all of its objects, or to get a reference to a particular object in the collection. Each collection has two properties you can use to refer to the objects in it:

- The **Item** property returns a reference to an object in the collection. This is the default property for most collections.
- The **Count** property returns the number of objects in the collection. For details about the **Count** property, see *Iterating through a Collection* later in this section.

The **Item** property takes a numeric argument that represents the object's *index,* or ordinal position, within the collection. The first item in most collections has an index of 1. For example, if a **Document** object's **Index** property returns *5*, that **Document** object is the fifth member of its **Documents** collection.

The following collections, however, are indexed starting with zero (0) rather than 1: **AccelTables**, **AccelItems**, **Colors**, **Hyperlinks**, **MenuSets**, **Menus**, **MenuItems**, **ToolbarSets**, **Toolbars**, and **ToolbarItems**. If the **Index** property of an object in one of these collections returns *5*, that object would be the sixth member of its collection.

To get an object by specifying its index, use code such as the following (where *pagsObj* represents a **Pages** collection and *shpsObj* represents a **Shapes** collection):

```
Set appObj = Visio.Application
Set docsObj = appObj.Documents
Set docObj = Documents.Item(1)
Set pagsObj = docObj.Pages
Set pagObj = pagsObj.Item(1)
Set shpsObj = pagObj.Shapes
Set shpObj = shpsObj.Item(1)
```

Assuming at least one shape is on the page, this statement returns a reference to the first **Shape** object in the **Shapes** collection. If the collection is empty, this statement causes an error.

> **Tip**   You might want to check the **Count** property of a collection before using **Item**, to make sure **Count** is not 0.

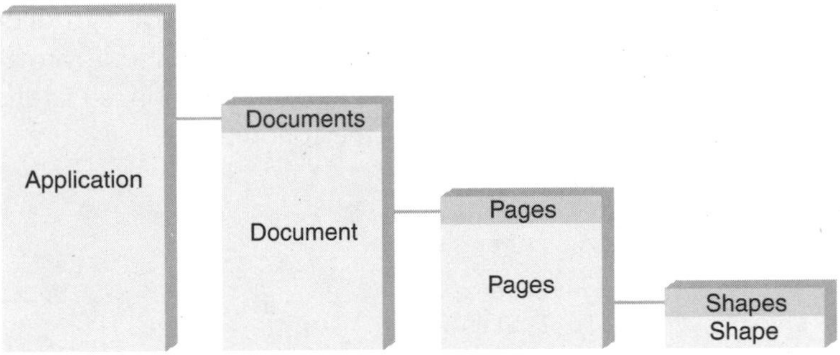

Figure 14-3   Shape object and related objects higher in the Visio object model.

For certain collections—**Documents**, **Pages**, **Masters**, **Shapes**, or **Styles**—the **Item** property can also take a string argument that specifies the object's name, which can be more convenient than referring to the object by its index. For example, the following code gets the **Master** object named **2-D Double** in the **Masters** collection.

```
Set mastObj = mastsObj("2-D Double")
```

Iterating through a Collection

A collection's **Count** property returns the number of objects in the collection. If the **Count** property is zero (0), the collection is empty. For example, the following statement displays the number of documents that are open in a Visio instance:

```
MsgBox "Open documents = " & Str$(Documents.Count)
```

Most often, you'll use the **Count** property to set the limit for an iteration loop. Notice the use of **Count** in the **For** statement of the following example. The **For** loop iterates through a **Documents** collection, checking the last three characters of each **Document** object's file name. If the last three characters are *vss* or *vsx* (indicating that the document is a stencil), its name is added to the list in a combo box.

```
Set docsObj = Application.Documents
For i = 1 To docsObj.Count
     Set docObj = docsObj.Item(i)
     If UCase(Right(docObj.Name, 3)) = "vss" Then
            ComboBox1.AddItem docObj.FullName
     End If
Next i
```

The code inside a loop such as the previous one should not change the number of objects in the collection (for example, by adding or deleting objects). Otherwise, the value of **Count** changes after each iteration of the loop.

To delete objects from a collection using a loop, you can decrement the counter rather than increment it. Each time an item is deleted from a collection, **Count** decreases by 1 and the remaining items shift position, so an incrementing loop will skip items. Use a loop such as the following:

```
Dim shpsObj As Visio.Shapes
Dim i As Integer

Set shpsObj = ActivePage.Shapes
For i = shpsObj.Count To 1 Step -1
     shpsObj.Item(i).Delete
Next i
```

Releasing an Object

An object in a program is automatically released when the program finishes running or when all object variables that refer to that object go out of scope. If an object variable is local to a procedure, it goes out of scope as soon as that procedure finishes executing. If the object variable is global, it persists until the program finishes executing, unless the object is explicitly released.

Releasing an object in a program does not affect the corresponding object in the Visio instance. For example, releasing a **Document** object does not close the corresponding Visio document. The document remains open, but your program no longer has access to it.

To release an object explicitly, set its object variable to the Visual Basic keyword **Nothing**. For example:

```
Set docObj = Nothing
```

If you assign the same object reference to more than one variable, be sure to set each variable to **Nothing** when you release the object.

Don't release an object until you're finished using it. Once you release the object, the program can no longer refer to the corresponding object in the Visio instance. For example, if you release a **Document** object, the program can no longer manipulate that Visio document using that variable, so it is unable to save or close the document or retrieve other objects from it.

However, if an object reference becomes invalid, you might have to release the object explicitly in your program. For example, if the user closes the Visio document or deletes a shape, references to those objects become invalid. Attempting to use any object variable that contains an invalid object reference will cause an error. To determine when to release objects from your program, you could write event handlers that release objects in response to events such as **BeforeShapeDelete**. For details on handling events, see Chapter 21, *Handling Visio Events*.

Using Compound Object References

You can concatenate Visio object references, properties, and methods in single statements, as you can with Microsoft Visual Basic for Applications (VBA) objects. However, simple references are sometimes more efficient, even if they require more lines of code.

For example, the following statement refers to the first shape on the third page of the first open document in a Visio instance:

```
Set shpObj = Documents(1).Pages(3).Shapes(1)
```

Executing this statement retrieves one object—the **Shape** object assigned to *shpObj*. Compare the following series of statements that use simple object references:

```
Set docObj = Documents.Item(1)
Set pagsObj = docObj.Pages
Set pagObj = pagsObj.Item(3)
Set shpsObj = pagObj.Shapes
Set shpObj = shpsObj.Item(1)
```

Running these statements retrieves five objects: a **Document** object, a **Pages** collection, a **Page** object, a **Shapes** collection, and a **Shape** object. References to these objects are assigned to variables and are available for other uses, unlike the previous example. If your program will eventually need access to these intermediate objects, your code will be easier to read and maintain if you retrieve them all in this way.

Restricting the Scope and Lifetime of Object Variables

Because an object reference exists independently of the item to which it refers, object references can become invalid as a result of user actions that are beyond your program's control. For example, if you have a reference to a **Shape** object and the user deletes the corresponding shape, the reference still exists in your program, but it is invalid because it refers to a nonexistent shape.

You can prevent invalid references by restricting the scope and lifetime of an object variable. For example, when your program resumes execution after giving control to the user, you can release certain objects and retrieve them again to make sure the objects are still available and your program has references to the objects in their current state.

A more robust means of maintaining valid object references is to capture the events raised by the object that you are referencing. For example, if you have a reference to a **Shape** object, you can handle any events that might cause your variable to become invalid—for example, the **BeforeShapeDelete** event. For details about handling events in your program, see Chapter 21, *Handling Visio Events*.

Using Properties and Methods

Once you have a reference to an object, you can get and set the values of its properties or use methods that cause the object to perform actions. For properties and methods that have return values or arguments, you must declare variables in your program. These variables can be object references, or they can be values such as strings or numbers. For example, the value of a **Shape** object's **Text** property is a string—the text of the shape.

Declaring Variables for Return Values and Arguments

When declaring a variable for a return value from a property or method, declare the variable with either an explicit data type or the Visual Basic **Variant** data type, and use a simple assignment statement to assign the value to the variable.

When declaring a variable for an argument to a property or method, the same rules apply: Use an object variable for an object (using a specific type of object is preferable), and use either the **Variant** data type or the appropriate explicit data type for other kinds of values.

For details about declaring object variables, see *Declaring Object Variables* in *Getting and Releasing Visio Objects* earlier in this chapter. In addition, all property and method arguments are described in the Automation Reference in the Microsoft Visio Developer Reference (on the **Help** menu, click **Developer Reference**).

Getting and Setting Properties

Properties often determine an object's appearance. For example, the following statement *sets* the **Text** property of a **Shape** object:

```
shpObj.Text = "Hello World!"
```

The following statement *gets* the text of this shape:

```
shpText = shpObj.Text
```

Some properties take arguments. For example, the **Cells** property of a **Shape** object takes a string expression that specifies a particular cell in the corresponding shape. When a property takes arguments, enclose them in parentheses. For example, the following statement sets the formula of the PinX cell.

```
shpObj.Cells("PinX").Formula = "1.25 in"
```

The following statement gets the formula of the PinX cell and stores it in *strPinX*:

```
strPinX = shpObj.Cells("PinX").Formula
```

Most properties of Visio objects are *read/write*, which means you can both get and set the property's value. Certain properties are *read-only*—you can get them, but you cannot set them. For example, you can get the **Application** property of an object to determine the Visio instance that contains the object, but you cannot set the **Application** property to transfer the object to a different instance.

A few properties are *write-only*—you can only set their values. Such properties usually handle a special case for a corresponding read/write property. For example, you change the formula in a cell by setting its **Formula** property, unless the formula is protected with the GUARD function. In that case, you must use the **FormulaForce** property to set the formula. However, you cannot get a cell's formula by using **FormulaForce**; you must use **Formula**, whether the cell's formula is protected.

For details about properties and methods, including whether a property is read/write, read-only, or write-only, see the Microsoft Visio Developer Reference (on the **Help** menu, click **Developer Reference**).

Using an Object's Default Property

Most objects have a default property that is used if you don't specify a property when referring to that object. For example, the default property of a **Document** object is **Name**, so the following two statements return the same value:

```
'Long format
docName = Documents.Item(5).Name
'Short format
docName = Documents.Item(5)
```

The default property for most collections is **Item**, so you can use a statement such as the following to specify an object from a collection:

```
'Long format
Set shpObj = shpsObj.Item(1)
'Short format
Set shpObj = shpsObj(1)
```

To determine the default property for any Visio object, search for that object in the Microsoft Visio Developer Reference (on the **Help** menu, click **Developer Reference**). The default property for a Visio object is also marked with a blue dot in the **Object Browser**. For details about the **Object Browser**, see *Using the Object Browser* in Chapter 15, *Programming Visio with VBA*.

Using Methods

Methods often correspond to Visio commands. For example, a **Shape** object has a **Copy** method that performs the same action as selecting the shape and clicking the **Copy** command on the **Edit** menu in Visio. Other methods correspond to other actions. For example, a **Window** object has an **Activate** method that you can use to make the corresponding window active, which is the same as clicking that window with the mouse.

The syntax for using a method is similar to that for setting a property. If a method creates an object, like a **Page** object, the method returns a reference to the newly created object, as in the following example. (Methods that don't create objects typically don't return values.)

```
Dim pagObj As Visio.Page
Set pagObj = pagsObj.Add
```

15

Programming Visio with VBA

Using the Visual Basic Editor 296

Creating a VBA Project 300

Using the Visio Type Library 305

Using the Global and ThisDocument Objects 309

Running VBA Code from Visio 312

Handling Errors 315

Managing a VBA Project 316

Any programming language that supports Automation can be used to write programs that access Microsoft Visio objects, get and set properties, invoke methods, and receive events. Visio provides a standard integrated development environment (IDE) for convenient development of Microsoft Visual Basic for Applications (VBA) projects.

If your solution will use Automation to control shapes and drawings, read or write data to or from external sources (such as a database), or interact with other applications, you can write VBA code in Visio to accomplish these tasks. The Visio VBA IDE is consistent with the IDE in all VBA-enabled applications, for example, Microsoft Office or Office XP applications. If you've used VBA in any of these applications, the Visio environment will be familiar to you.

This chapter provides a brief overview of some common tasks using VBA in Visio. For complete details about using the VBA development environment and writing VBA code, see the Microsoft Visual Basic Help.

Using the Visual Basic Editor

To build your Microsoft Visual Basic for Applications (VBA) program, you create a VBA project using the Visual Basic Editor. Every Microsoft Visio document, or file, can contain a project that you can add modules and forms to, depending on what your solution requires. At a minimum, every project contains a **ThisDocument** class module. This class module represents the properties, methods, and events of a specific document associated with your Visio VBA project.

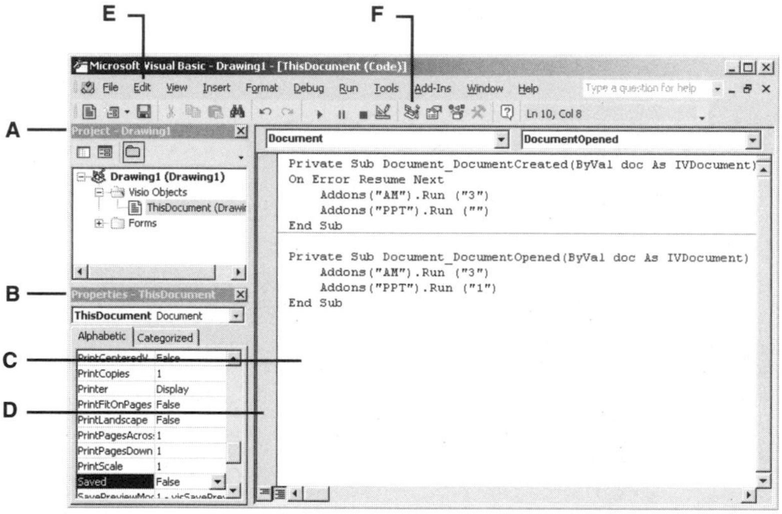

Figure 15-1 Visual Basic Editor: the VBA development environment. (**A**) The **Project Explorer** displays a list of projects and project items in Visio documents. (**B**) The **Properties** window displays a list of the properties for the selected item. (**C**) The **Code** window. (**D**) The programming workspace displays all open modules, class modules, and user forms during design time. You build your program in this area. (**E**) The menu bar displays the commands you use to build, run, and debug your program. (**F**) The toolbar provides quick access to commonly used commands in the development environment.

In the **Code** window, you can write, display, and edit code in new procedures or in existing event procedures. You can open any number of code windows on different modules, class modules, or user forms, so you can easily view the code and copy and paste between windows.

Starting the Visual Basic Editor

You can start the Visual Basic Editor without opening a Visio document, but you must first open a document to see the VBA project for that document. A Visio instance adds projects only to documents that are opened as **Original** or **Copy**; however, if the document already has a project, you can view the project for a document that is opened as **Read only**. A project is added to a document only if VBA project creation has been enabled in Visio. For details, see *Enabling or Disabling VBA Project Creation* later in this section.

To start the Visual Basic Editor

1. Start Visio and open a template (.vst or .vtx), stencil (.vss or .vsx), or drawing (.vsd or .vdx) as **Original** or **Copy**, not **Read only**.
2. On the **Tools** menu, point to **Macros**, and then click **Visual Basic Editor**. Or, click the **Visual Basic Editor** button on the **Developer** toolbar.

You can customize your working environment in VBA by setting options such as font size, code color, syntax error options, and variable declaration requirements.

To set environment options in the Visual Basic Editor

- On the **Tools** menu, click **Options**, click the **Editor** or **Editor Format** tab, and then set the options you want.

By default, projects will have the same name as the document with which they are associated. However, each project has a **Project Properties** dialog box where you can rename your project and provide additional information such as a project description. You can also lock your project.

To open the Project Properties dialog box

- On the **Tools** menu, click ***Project Name*** **Properties**, and then set project properties. Or, right-click the project name in the **Project Explorer**.

Navigating among Projects

To navigate among projects in the Visual Basic Editor, use the **Project Explorer**. It lists modules, class modules, and user forms for the projects in all open Visio files. You can double-click on any module, class module, or user form in the **Project Explorer** to open its **Code** window.

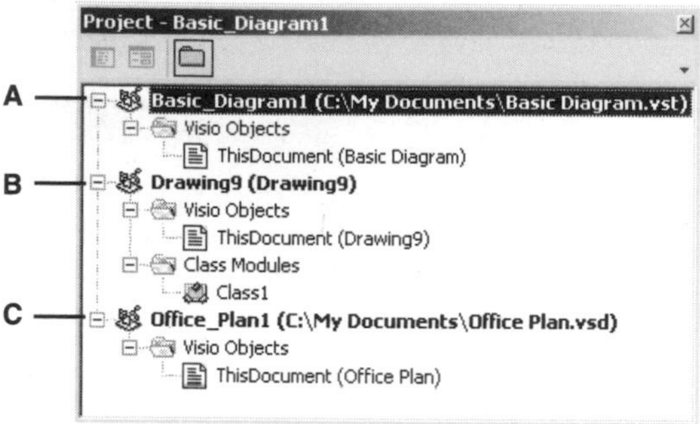

Figure 15-2 The **Project Explorer** displaying three Visio files that are open in a Visio instance. (**A**) An example of a template and the items in its project. (**B**) An open Visio drawing and the items in its project; this drawing hasn't been saved. (**C**) An open Visio drawing, saved as Office Plan, and the items in its project.

> **Note** If you do not see the **Project Explorer** when you open the Visual Basic Editor, click **Project Explorer** on the **View** menu.

Saving a Project

A VBA project is stored in the Visio document that contains it. A Visio document can be saved as one of the following file types:

- Template (.vst or .vtx)
- Stencil (.vss or .vsx)
- Drawing (.vsd or .vdx)

When a user creates a new Visio document from a template, the Visio instance copies the VBA project and its items to the new document.

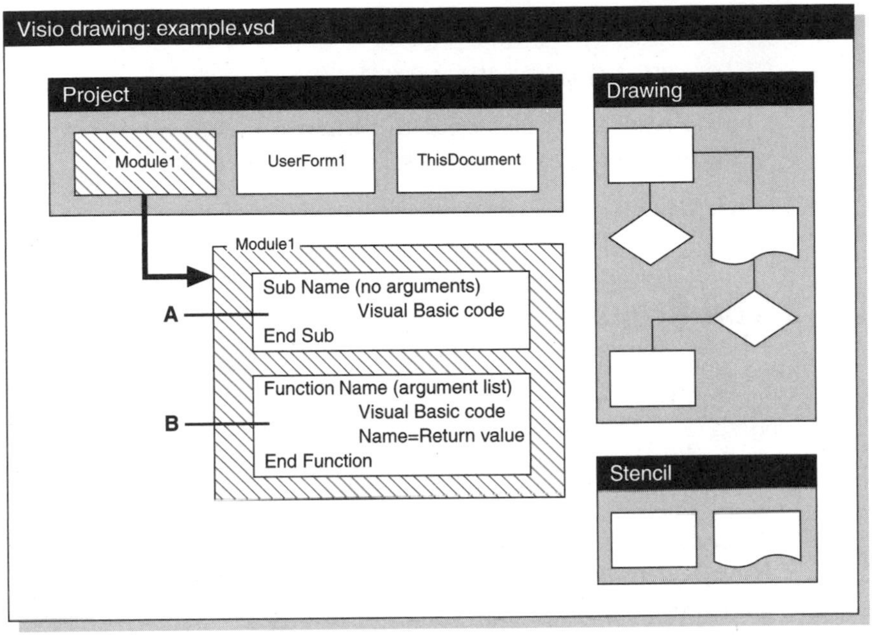

Figure 15-3 An example of how a Visio drawing might look after adding items to the default project and saving the drawing. (**A**) First **Sub** procedure in the module (macro). (**B**) First **Function** procedure in the module (user-defined function).

To save your Visio document and its VBA project

- In the Visio user interface, click **Save** on the **File** menu. Or, in the Visual Basic Editor, click **Save *File Name*** on the **File** menu.

  The document's file name and location are displayed in parentheses after the project name in the **Project Explorer** in the Visual Basic Editor.

Enabling or Disabling VBA Project Creation

In Visio, a VBA project gets created in your document whenever you open a new document (or a document that doesn't already have a project) while the Visual Basic Editor is open in Visio. Beginning with Microsoft Visio 2002, you have the option to suppress the creation of VBA projects while the Visual Basic Editor is open in Visio.

You enable or disable VBA project creation using the **Enable Visual Basic for Applications project creation** option on the **Advanced** tab in the **Options** dialog box. When this check box is selected, VBA projects are not automatically created for documents that don't already have VBA projects; however, VBA projects are still accessible in documents with VBA projects.

To disable VBA project creation

1. On the **Tools** menu, click **Options**.
2. On the **Advanced** tab, clear the **Enable Visual Basic for Applications project creation** check box.
3. Click **OK**.

Creating a VBA Project

A Microsoft Visual Basic for Applications (VBA) project consists of modules, class modules, and user forms.

- A *module* is a set of declarations followed by procedures—a list of instructions that a program performs.
- A *class module* defines an object, its properties, and its methods. A class module acts as a template from which an instance of an object is created at run time. Every Visio-based VBA project contains a class module called **ThisDocument**; this class module represents the properties, methods, and events of the Microsoft Visio document that contains the VBA project.
- A *user form* contains user interface controls, such as command buttons and text boxes.

A simple project might require a single user form or module, although more complex projects might contain multiple modules, class modules, and user forms. For example, a solution that generates a drawing could include a user form to gather information from the user. It could also include code, organized in one or more modules and/or class modules, that does the following:

- Validates the user's input
- Translates the code into data that could be used to generate a drawing
- Uses Automation to create the drawing in the Visio drawing window

If the solution should run in response to an event, such as opening a document, the solution could include code that would run when that event occurred.

You can add existing modules, class modules, or user forms to your project by importing files; or, you can export project items for use in other projects. You can also insert an ActiveX control into your Visio document. For details about ActiveX controls, see Chapter 24, *Using ActiveX Controls in a Visio Solution*.

Inserting Modules and Class Modules into Your Project

Many VBA programs contain one or more modules—a set of declarations followed by procedures. Every Visio VBA project contains the class module **ThisDocument**, which is an object that represents the project's document. You can create additional class modules to define custom VBA objects in your project.

To insert a module or class module

- In the Visual Basic Editor, on the **Insert** menu, click **Module** or **Class Module**.

  The **Code** window will display an empty module where you will insert procedures that create templates into which you enter VBA code.

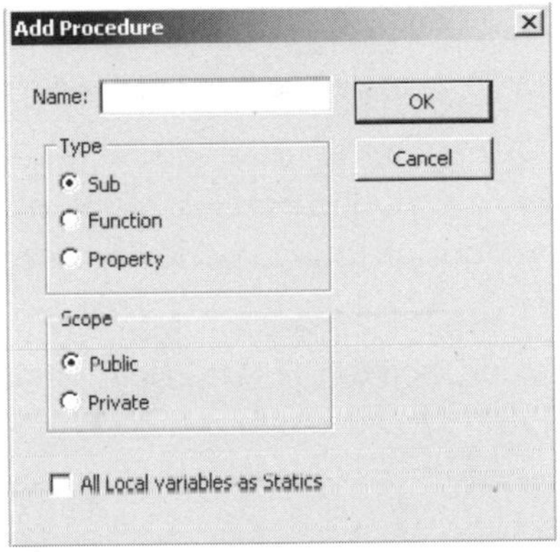

Figure 15-4 The **Add Procedure** dialog box.

To add procedures to modules and class modules

1. In the Visual Basic Editor, on the **Insert** menu, click **Procedure** to open the **Add Procedure** dialog box.
2. In the **Name** box, name the procedure.

   The procedure's name is displayed on its module's submenu on the Visio **Macros** submenu on the **Tools** menu. A procedure name cannot include spaces or reserved words (such as **MsgBox**, **If**, or **Loop**) that VBA uses as part of its programming language.
3. Under **Type**, choose the type of procedure: **Sub**, **Function**, or **Property**.

   Modules and class modules can contain more than one type of procedure.

- To write a procedure that takes no arguments, insert a **Sub** procedure.
- To write a function that takes arguments and returns a value, insert a **Function** procedure.
- To add properties to a class module, insert a **Property** procedure.

4. Under **Scope**, choose **Public** or **Private**.

   Scope is the extent to which a procedure can be accessed by other modules and programs.

   - A procedure with a *private* scope can be accessed by only the module that contains it; only a procedure within the same module can call a private procedure, and a private procedure does not appear on any menus or in any dialog boxes.
   - A procedure with a *public* scope can be accessed by other programs and modules. Visio displays public procedures of modules and the **ThisDocument** class module that take no arguments on the **Macros** submenu.

5. To declare all local variables as static, select the **All Local variables as Statics** check box.

   You can declare the variables in your procedure as local or static (global).

   - *Static* variables exist for the lifetime of your entire program.
   - *Local* variables exist only while the procedure that they are declared in is running. The next time the procedure is executed, all local variables are reinitialized. However, you can preserve for the lifetime of your program the value of all local variables in a procedure by making them static, which fixes their value.

6. Click **OK**.

   VBA inserts a *procedure template* into the item's **Code** window into which you can enter code. The template contains the first and last lines of code for the type of procedure you insert.

For details about procedures, see the Microsoft Visual Basic Help.

Inserting User Forms into Your Project

If you want your program to prompt the user for information, you can build a user interface by inserting user forms. A *user form* contains user interface controls, such as command buttons and text boxes. When you add a user form to your project, VBA automatically opens the **Toolbox** of controls. A *control* is an object you place on a user form that has its own properties and methods; a control also fires events that you can respond to. You use controls to receive user input, display output, and trigger event procedures.

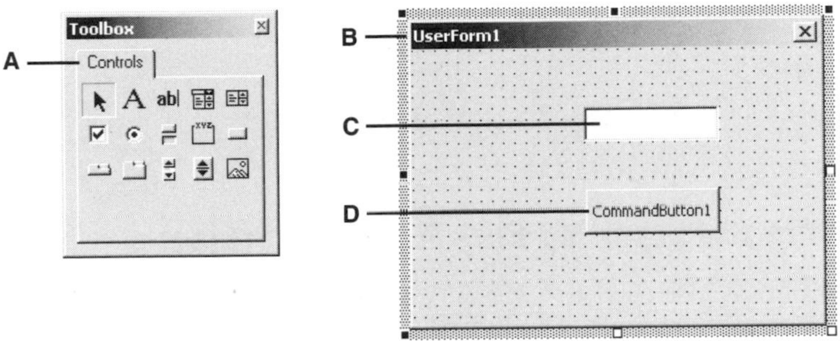

Figure 15-5 **Toolbox** and user form containing controls. (**A**) **Controls** tab in the **Toolbox.** (**B**) User form. (**C**) Text box control. (**D**) Command button control.

To add a user form to your project

1. On the **Insert** menu, click **UserForm**.
2. From the **Toolbox**, drag the controls that you want onto the user form.

   For details about adding controls, such as command buttons and text boxes, see the Microsoft Visual Basic Help.
3. Double-click a user form or control to display its **Code** window.
4. Click the event that you want to respond to in the drop-down list of events and procedures in the **Code** window; you can then start typing your code. Or, insert a procedure and start typing your code in the procedure template.

> **Tip** This guide uses the VBA default user form and control names for clarity, but it is considered good programming technique to change the default names to something more descriptive. Many programmers use the following naming conventions:
>
> ```
> User form default name = UserForm1
> Revised name = frmGetDocName
> ```
>
> Notice the use of *frm* in the revised name of the user form. In the control name, many programmers use *frm* (form), *txt* (textbox), *lbl* (label), *cmd* (command button), and so on, so you can quickly recognize the type of object.

Importing Files into and Exporting Files from Your Project

To import an item into your project, on the **File** menu, click **Import File**. You can choose any VBA module (files with a .bas extension), user form (files with an .frm extension), or class module (files with a .cls extension) to add a copy of the file to your project. To export an item from your project so that it will be available for importing into other projects, select the item you want to export in the **Project Explorer**, then on the **File** menu, click **Export File** and enter the location in which you want to save the file. Exporting an item does not remove it from your project.

You can also drag projects or project items between Visio files by selecting the project or project item you want to move in the **Project Explorer** and then dragging its icon onto a Visio project icon. A project item is automatically stored in the correct project folder. A project is referenced in the References folder, because a Visio file can contain only one project, but that project can reference other projects.

> **Note** You cannot drag the **ThisDocument** class module between Visio files, but you can drag (or copy and paste) code from **ThisDocument** into other project items.

Using the Visio Type Library

The Microsoft Visio *type library* contains Automation descriptions of the objects, properties, methods, and events that the Visio engine exposes. Microsoft Visual Basic for Applications (VBA) projects that belong to Visio documents automatically reference the Visio type library, which you use to define Visio object types in your program. Using the Visio object types that are declared in the Visio type library increases the speed of your program because VBA interprets Visio objects at compile time rather than run time. When you compile a program during design time, VBA checks for syntax and programming errors and matches object types against type libraries. If you use a general variable type, such as *Object*, VBA doesn't interpret it until run time; at that time, VBA queries the Visio engine about object references. This extra querying step decreases the speed of your program.

The type library also contains the global symbolic constants defined for arguments and return values of properties and methods. Because most arguments to properties and methods are numeric values, using these constants can make your code easier to write and to read. For example, suppose you want to find out what type of window a **Window** object represents. The **Type** property of a **Window** object returns an integer that indicates the window's type. If you set a reference to the Visio type library in your project, you can use a constant instead of an integer to check the window's type, in this example, **visDrawing** instead of 1.

For a list of constants used by a particular method or property, see that method or property in the Developer Reference in Microsoft Visio (on the **Help** menu, click **Developer Reference**).

You can view the contents of the Visio type library using the VBA **Object Browser**.

> **Note** The examples in this guide assume that you have a reference set to the Visio type library. To verify this, on the **Tools** menu, click **References**, and then make sure the Microsoft Visio 2002 type library is selected.

Using the Object Browser

You can use the **Object Browser** to view the Visio type library. The **Object Browser** displays constants, classes (objects), and class members (properties, methods, and events) of type libraries referenced by open projects.

The **Object Browser** displays Visio properties, methods, events, and constants as *members* in the **Members of** list. The **Details** pane displays each member's syntax as a code template that you can copy and paste or drag into a module; you can then substitute your own variables and arguments. Using code templates decreases the chance of typing errors.

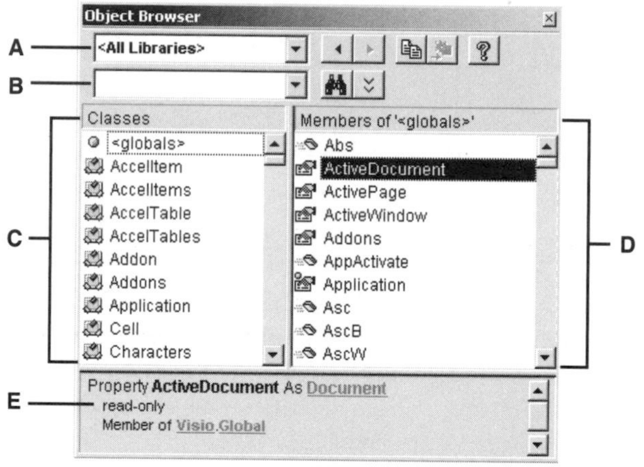

Figure 15-6 The **Object Browser**. (**A**) **Project/Library** box. (**B**) **Search Text** box . (**C**) **Classes** list. (**D**) **Members of** list. (**E**) **Details** pane.

To use the Object Browser

1. On the **View** menu, click **Object Browser**. Or click the **Object Browser** button on the toolbar.

2. To browse or search for a Visio object, property, method, event, or constant, type its name in the **Search Text** box, or click any member in the **Members of** list.

Setting References to Type Libraries

Applications that support Automation provide a type library to describe the objects that they expose to Automation. If you want to access the objects of another application from your Visio solution, click **References** on the **Tools** menu, and then select the type library you're looking for in the **Available References** list. You can also use this procedure to set a reference to the Visio application from any other application that supports Automation. For example, you can set a reference to Visio from a Microsoft Word application to enable you to use Visio objects in your Word application.

Any type libraries that are checked in the **Available References** list will appear in the **Project/Library** box for your project. You can also set a reference to any open Visio documents or browse to any unopened Visio documents in the **References** dialog box.

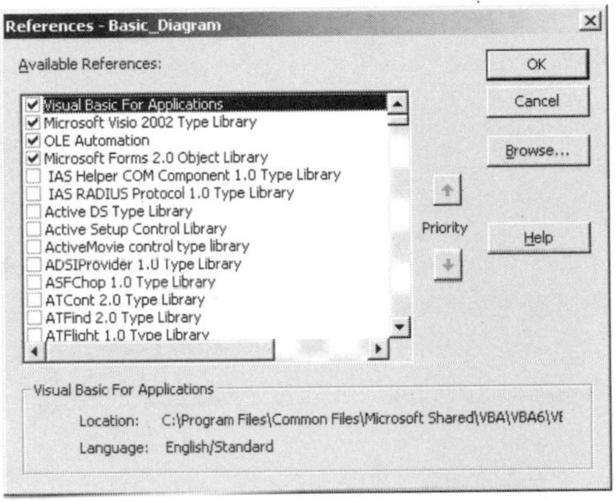

Figure 15-7 An expanded **Available References** list.

> **Note** To view only the class and members in the Visio type library, click **Visio** in the **Project/Library** box in the **Object Browser**.
>
> Visio does not automatically reference the Microsoft Office Object library; you will need to set a reference to this library if you plan on accessing objects such as command bars and COM add-ins.

Using Visio Object Types

You can take advantage of the Visio type library to write code more effectively. By using Visio object types declared in the Visio type library, you can declare variables as specific types, such as *Visio.Page:*

```
Dim pagObj as Visio.Page
```

Using a Visio object type, such as *Visio.Page,* enables your program to check the type of object it is referencing in the Visio type library at compile time. This is called *early binding*. This example uses *Visio* to inform the program that it is

referencing Visio object types in the Visio type library, and it uses *Page* to inform it that the *pagObj* variable is a **Page** object. For details about using Visio objects, see Chapter 14, *Automation and the Visio Object Model.*
Here are a few common object types:

```
'A Documents collection
Dim docsObj As Visio.Documents
'A Document object
Dim docObj As Visio.Document
'A Shapes collection
Dim shpsObj As Visio.Shapes
'A Shape object
Dim shpObj As Visio.Shape
'A Master object
Dim mastObj As Visio.Master
```

When you type a period after an object or library type, a list of available object types, properties, and methods for the preceding object or variable type appears automatically in the Auto List window. To insert an object type from the list in your code, double-click the type in the list.

> **Tip** If the list of available object types, properties, and methods for an object doesn't automatically appear when you're typing in the **Code** window, on the **Tools** menu, click **Options**, click **Editor**, and then select the **Auto List Members** check box.

In this example, the appropriate object type is **Page**.

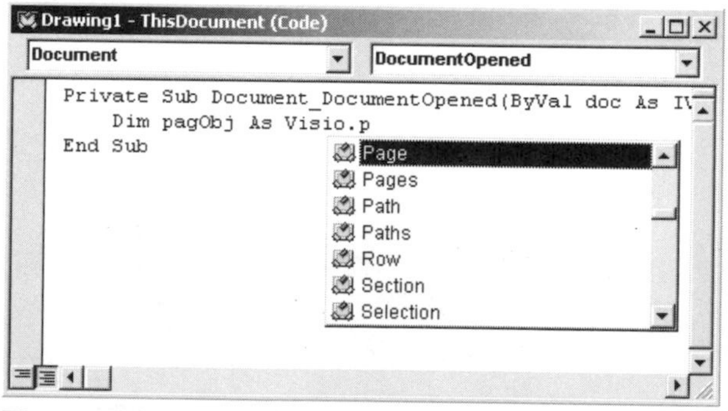

Figure 15-8 The Visio type library Auto List window.

Using the Global and ThisDocument Objects

Unlike a stand-alone program, which needs to obtain a reference to the Microsoft Visio **Application** object by creating or getting it, code in a Microsoft Visual Basic for Applications (VBA) project executes in a running Visio instance so you don't need to obtain a reference to the **Application** object. The Visio engine provides the global object, which represents the Visio instance. The Visio engine also provides the **ThisDocument** object, which represents the Visio document associated with your project.

Using the Visio Global Object

The *global object* represents the instance and provides more direct access to certain properties. The properties of the Visio global object are not prefixed with a reference to an object.

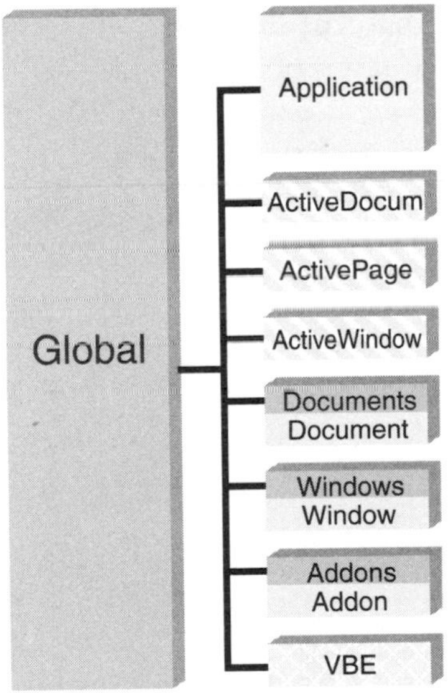

Figure 15-9 The Visio global object and its properties.

The **Application** object is a property of the Visio global object, so you can access any of the **Application** object's properties by directly referencing the **Application** property of the Visio global object.

The following three examples of code get the first document in a **Documents** collection—all three use different syntax.

This first example creates an **Application** object. This code is typically used when writing an external program:

```
Dim appVisio As Visio.Application
Dim docsObj As Visio.Documents
Dim docObj As Visio.Document
Set appVisio = CreateObject("visio.application")
Set docsObj = appVisio.Documents
Set docObj = docsObj.Item(1)
```

This second example uses the **Application** property of the Visio global object:

```
Dim docsObj As Visio.Documents
Dim docObj As Visio.Document
Set docsObj = Application.Documents
Set docObj = docsObj.Item(1)
```

This third example directly accesses the **Documents** property of the Visio global object:

```
Dim docObj As Visio.Document
Set docObj = Documents.Item(1)
```

Notice in the second and third examples that **Application** and **Documents** are not preceded by an object. When you are referencing any property or method of the Visio global object, you don't need to declare a variable for the global object or reference it as the preceding object of a property—the global object is implied. The third example is the most direct method of accessing the **Documents** collection from a VBA project.

The following examples show code for commonly used properties of the Visio global object:

```
Set docObj = ActiveDocument
Set pagObj = ActivePage
Set winObj = ActiveWindow
```

For details about the Visio global object's properties and methods, see the Automation Reference in Microsoft Visio (on the **Help** menu, click **Developer Reference**).

> **Note** The Visio global object is available only when you are writing code in the VBA project of a Visio document.

Using the ThisDocument Object

Every VBA project in your Visio application contains a default class module called **ThisDocument**, which represents the properties, methods, and events of the document associated with the project. Like any class module, other programs can access **ThisDocument** at run time.

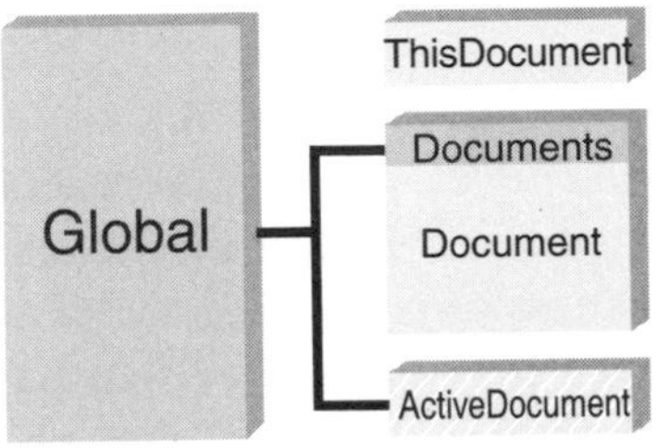

Figure 15-10 Use the **ThisDocument** object to manipulate the document associated with your VBA project

If you want to manipulate a document, but not necessarily the document associated with your VBA project, get the **Document** object from the **Documents** collection. If you want to manipulate the document associated with your VBA project, use the **ThisDocument** object.

For example, to reference the first page of the drawing Hello.vsd, you could get the **Document** object from the **Documents** collection of the global object. The following example gets the first page of Hello.vsd from the **Pages** collection of the document:

```
Set docObj = Documents.Item("hello.vsd")
Set pagObj = docObj.Pages.Item(1)
```

If Hello.vsd is the document associated with your VBA project, you could just use the **ThisDocument** object as the following example does:

```
Set pagObj = ThisDocument.Pages.Item(1)
```

Once you have a reference to a **Document** object, you retrieve other Visio objects by getting properties of the **Document** object, and then of other objects in the object hierarchy.

You can add properties and methods to the **ThisDocument** object because it is an *extensible object*—an object whose functionality you can extend. The **ThisDocument** object is the only extensible object the Visio engine provides. You can also select **ThisDocument** in the **Project Explorer** and change its properties, such as page settings and default styles; in the **Properties** window, you can also change the document properties, such as title, creator, and subject.

For details about properties, methods, and events for **ThisDocument**, select the **ThisDocument** object in the **Project Explorer** for the project you are interested in, open the **Object Browser**, view the Visio project containing **ThisDocument** in the project list, and browse the members of **ThisDocument**.

Running VBA Code from Visio

You can run your Microsoft Visual Basic for Applications (VBA) code within the Visual Basic Editor to test and debug it during development. This section discusses several ways to run your code in the Visual Basic Editor. For details about debugging a VBA program, such as adding breakpoints, adding watch expressions, and stepping into and out of execution, see the Microsoft Visual Basic Help.

A user can run your finished macros in the Microsoft Visio user interface by choosing it from the **Macros** submenu on the **Tools** menu. A *macro* is a VBA procedure that takes no arguments. Procedures that take arguments will not appear on the **Macros** submenu.

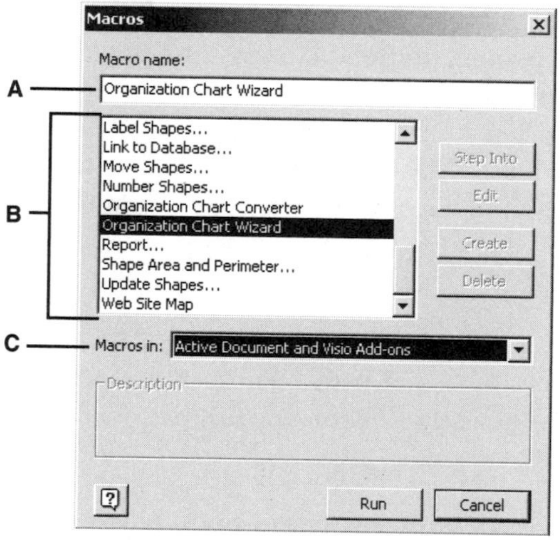

Figure 15-11 **Macros** dialog box. (**A**) Name of the selected macro. (**B**) List of available macros and add-ons. (**C**) List of accessible projects, modules, and drawings.

A program can also run in response to events or in other ways that you design. For details about running a program in response to events, see Chapter 21, *Handling Visio Events*. For other ways to run a program, see Chapter 26, *Packaging a Visio Automation Solution*.

To run a macro from the Visual Basic Editor

1. On the **Tools** menu, click **Macros**.
2. In the **Macros** list, select the macro you want and click **Run**.

   If the macro you want is not listed, make sure you've chosen the correct project, module, or drawing in the **Macros In** list. Private procedures do not appear in any menus or dialog boxes.

Or,

1. In the **Project Explorer**, open the module that contains the macro.
2. In the **Code** window, click to place the insertion point inside the macro.
3. On the **Run** menu, click **Run Sub/UserForm**.

   The macro that contains the insertion point runs.

To run a macro from the Macros dialog box in Visio

1. In Visio, on the **Tools** menu, point to **Macros**, and then click **Macros**.
2. In the **Macros** list, select your program and click **Run**.

> **Note** From a user's point of view, it doesn't matter if the program the user runs is an add-on or a macro, so the Visio application combines these programs in dialog boxes. For example, you can run an add-on or macro from the **Macros** dialog box or from the **Macros** submenu.

To provide a description of your macro that appears in the Macros dialog box

1. In the Visual Basic Editor, open the **Object Browser**.
2. In the **Project/Library** list, click the project that contains the macro.
3. In the **Classes** list, click the module that contains the macro, then right-click the macro in the **Members of** list and click **Properties**.
4. Enter a description in the **Description** box.

To run your macro from the Visio Macros submenu

1. On the **Tools** menu, click **Macros**.
2. On the **Macros** submenu, point to the project that contains your macros, and then click the macro you want to run.

The following illustration shows how a module might appear on the Visio **Macros** submenu, with its macros displayed on the module's submenu.

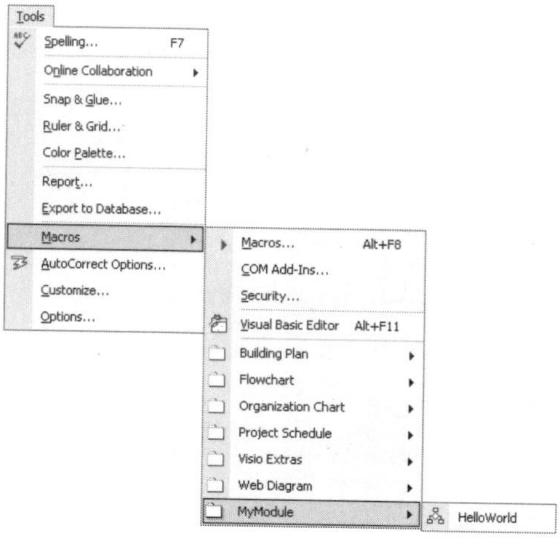

Figure 15-12 Visio **Macros** submenu.

If you want your macros to appear on the **Macros** submenu, but not the module that contains your macros, name your module *ShowInMenu*. The **ShowInMenu** module does not appear on the Visio **Macros** submenu, but its macros do, as shown in the following illustration.

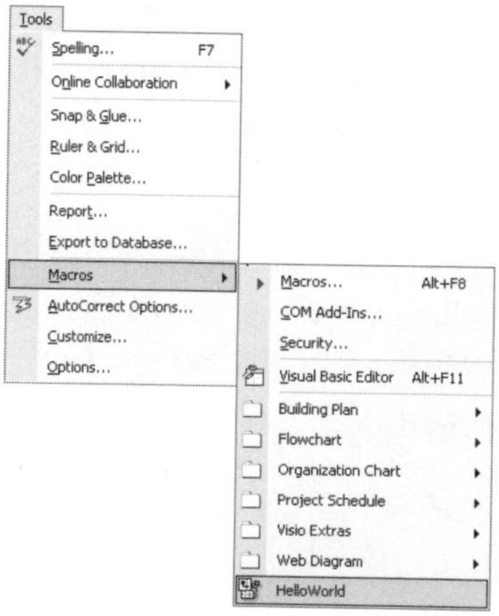

Figure 15-13 **Macros** submenu showing a macro from the **ShowInMenu** module.

Handling Errors

When an error occurs during program execution, Microsoft Visual Basic for Applications (VBA) generates an error message and halts execution. You can prevent many errors by testing assumptions before executing code that might fail if the assumptions aren't valid. You can trap and respond to errors by using the **On Error** statement in your program. For details about **On Error**, see the Microsoft Visual Basic Help.

Errors can arise from a variety of situations. This section lists some common error situations and suggests ways of preventing them.

Running the Program in the Right Context

If you've determined the context in which your program will run, you can make some assumptions about the environment. For example, if you're writing a VBA program to handle double-click behavior, you can probably assume that a document is open and that the double-clicked shape is selected in the active window. However, there are limits to a program's ability to control user actions. For example, nothing stops a user from attempting to run a VBA program designed to handle a double-click event from the **Macros** dialog box instead of double-clicking the shape.

If your program requires a selected shape, check the **Selection** property of the active window to make sure it contains at least one object.

```
Dim selectObj As Visio.Selection
Set selectObj = ActiveWindow.Selection
If selectObj.Count = 0 Then
     MsgBox "You must select a shape first." , , "Select shape"
Else
     'Continue processing
End If
```

Verifying that Objects and Return Values Exist

It's wise to test whether a collection contains objects before attempting to access them. The following example checks to see if a document has masters before attempting to iterate through the **Masters** collection, which would cause an error if the collection were empty.

```
If ThisDocument.Masters.Count = 0 Then
     MsgBox "Document has no masters."
     'Go to an error handler
End If
```

If a property or method is supposed to return something, it's a good idea to make sure it actually did. For example, if your program formats a shape's text, you might want to verify that the **Shape** object contains text. For example:

```
Dim shpObj As Visio.Shape
Dim strText As String
Set shpObj = ActivePage.Shapes.Items(1)
strText = shpObj.Text
If strText = "" Then
     MsgBox "The selected shape has no text to format." , , "Format
Shape Text"
Else
     'Continue processing
End If
```

Checking for Error Values

VBA has an **Error** function that returns a string. When an error occurs in the Microsoft Visio application, it returns an error code and a string that describes the error. Use the **Error** function to obtain the string associated with the error code returned by Visio.

The Visio **Cell** object has an **Error** property, which indicates whether an error occurred when a cell's formula was evaluated. If your program alters ShapeSheet formulas, check this property to make sure the formula works as expected. Constants for valid error codes are declared by the Visio type library and begin with **visError**.

Managing a VBA Project

To work effectively and to minimize maintenance tasks later, use these project management practices:

- Remove project items that are no longer needed to reduce file size and make the project easier to maintain.
- Protect your code, if necessary, from being viewed or modified by users.
- Digitally sign your Microsoft Visual Basic for Applications (VBA) projects to show that your solution is from a trusted source.
- Design modules, class modules, and user forms for reuse, to save time writing code. In addition, VBA versions 6.0 and later allow you to run add-ins that can be shared across applications.

For details about reusing project items, see *Importing Files into and Exporting Files from Your Project* in *Creating a VBA Project* earlier in this chapter.

Removing Project Items

When you remove an item, you permanently delete it from the project list—you cannot undo the **Remove** action. Make sure remaining code in other modules and user forms doesn't refer to code in the removed item.

To remove a project item

1. Select the item in the **Project Explorer**.
2. On the **File** menu, click **Remove *name***.
3. You will be asked if you want to export the item before removing it.
    - Click **Yes** to open the **Export File** dialog box.
    - Click **No** to delete the item.

Protecting Your Solution's VBA Code

To protect your code from being viewed or modified by users, you can *lock* a project. When you lock a project, you set a password that must be entered before the project can be viewed in the **Project Explorer**.

To lock your VBA project against viewing

1. On the **Tools** menu, click ***Drawing Name* Properties**.
2. Click the **Protection** tab and select the **Lock project for viewing** check box.
3. Enter a password and confirm it.
4. Save your Visio file and close it.

The next time you open the Visio file, the project is locked. Anyone who wants to view or edit the project must enter a password.

Using Digital Certificates to Produce Trusted Solutions

Like other Microsoft Office or Office XP products, Microsoft Visio uses Microsoft Authenticode technology to allow you to digitally sign VBA projects in your documents by using a digital certificate that identifies you as a trusted source. Visio has security-level settings that allow users to identify code produced by trusted sources and to prevent unsigned VBA projects from running in Visio.

To produce a trusted solution, you need to obtain and install a digital certificate that you can use to digitally sign your VBA projects in Visio documents. When opening a signed document, Visio can verify if an authentic digital signature exists and determine if the signed VBA project has been altered in any way since it was signed. Depending on the security level, Visio either automatically disables macros that might have been altered, or lets the user decide whether to enable or disable these macros.

> **Note** The security settings for Visio apply specifically to VBA projects within Visio documents. Visio does not provide security for Visio add-ons, COM add-ins, and any ShapeSheet functions that cause external code to run.

As a Visio solution developer, digitally signing your VBA projects can help to ensure that your solution users will be able to run the solution without being blocked by security settings. However, there are some security options in the control of users and administrators that can potentially interfere with your solution. For details, see *Security and policy settings that can affect your solution's VBA code* later in this section.

Setting security levels for Visio

A Visio document opens in run mode by default unless the macros in the document have been disabled. Macros are enabled or disabled depending on the security level setting for Visio and whether the VBA project has been digitally signed. The following table describes the possible ways that security settings, signed and unsigned projects, and trusted and untrusted sources can interact when a document opens.

How security levels and digital signatures work together

Type of document and verification result	High security	Medium security	Low security
No project	Document is opened.	Document is opened.	Document is opened.
Unsigned project	Macros are automatically disabled without notification and the document opens.	User is prompted to enable or disable macros.	No prompt. Macros are enabled.
Signed project from a trusted source. Verification succeeds.	Macros are automatically enabled and the document opens.	Macros are automatically enabled and the document opens.	No prompt or verification. Macros are enabled.

How security levels and digital signatures work together *(continued)*

Type of document and verification result	High security	Medium security	Low security
Signed project from an unknown author. Verification succeeds.	A dialog box is displayed with information about the certificate. Macros can be enabled only if the user chooses to trust the author and certifying authority by selecting the **Always trust macros from this author** check box in the **Security Warning** dialog box. A network administrator can lock the trusted sources list and prevent the user from adding the author to the list and enabling the document's VBA project's macros.	A dialog box is displayed with information about the certificate. The user is prompted to enable or disable macros. Optionally, the user can choose to trust the author and certifying authority by selecting the **Always trust macros from this author** check box in the **Security Warning** dialog box.	No prompt or verification. Macros are enabled.
Signed project from any author. Verification fails, possibly due to a virus.	User is warned of a possible virus. Macros are automatically disabled.	User is warned of a possible virus. Macros are automatically disabled.	No prompt or verification. Macros are enabled.
Signed project from any author. Verification not possible because public key is missing or incompatible encryption methods were used.	User is warned that verification is not possible. Macros are automatically disabled.	User is warned that verification is not possible. User is prompted to enable or disable macros.	No prompt or verification. Macros are enabled.

How security levels and digital signatures work together *(continued)*

Type of document and verification result	High security	Medium security	Low security
Signed project from any author. The signature was made after the certificate had expired or been revoked.	User is warned that the signature has expired or been revoked. Macros are automatically disabled.	User is warned that the signature has expired or been revoked. User is prompted to enable or disable macros.	No prompt or verification. Macros are enabled.

If the user selects the **Always trust macros from this source** check box in the **Security Warning** dialog box, the certificate is listed on the **Trusted Sources** tab of the **Security** dialog box.

The **Trusted Sources** tab in the **Security** dialog box lists all digital certificates that have been previously accepted by a user or that have been previously installed by a network administrator. A user doesn't add trusted sources directly to this dialog box, but can add a new certificate to the list by selecting the **Always trust macros from this author** check box upon opening a signed document from a new source for the first time. An administrator can lock the trusted sources list so that no new sources can be added to the list by users. Therefore, only macros signed by using approved certificates currently in the list will run.

> **Note** Visio does not support the **Trust all installed add-ins and templates** option that some Microsoft Office and Office XP applications support.

To change the security level for macro virus protection

1. On the **Tools** menu, point to **Macros**, and then click **Security**.
2. Click the **Security Level** tab, and then choose the security level you want to use.

   High Runs code only from trusted sources.

   Medium Permits users to choose whether to run potentially unsafe code.

   Low Runs all code, trusted or not.
3. Click **OK**.

> **Note** To disable macros programmatically when a document opens, use the **visOpenMacrosDisabled** flag in the **OpenEx** method of a **Documents** collection.

Digitally signing a VBA project

To digitally sign VBA projects in your solution, you must first obtain a digital certificate for software publishing. You can get a digital certificate in three ways:

- Create a digital certificate for your own use.
- Obtain a digital certificate from your organization's internal certification authority.
- Obtain a digital certificate from a commercial certification authority such as VeriSign, Inc.

For more information about digital certificates and digital signatures, search on these terms in the MSDN Library: "digital signature," "digital certificate," "Authenticode," and "security."

To digitally sign a VBA project

1. Open the document or template that contains the VBA project you want to sign.
2. Open the Visual Basic Editor (on the **Tools** menu, point to **Macros**, and then click **Visual Basic Editor**).
3. In the **Project Explorer**, select the project you want to sign.
4. On the **Tools** menu, click **Digital Signature**.
5. Do one of the following:
   - If you haven't previously selected a digital certificate, or want to use another one, click **Choose**, select the certificate, and then click **OK** twice.
   - To use the current certificate, click **OK**.

   If a VBA project has been signed previously, clicking **Choose** and selecting a new digital certificate replaces the previous signature. To remove a signature from a previously signed project, click **Remove**.

Security and policy settings that can affect your solution's VBA code

Be aware that administrators and users can set security levels, installation options, or run-time options for VBA projects that might interfere with your solution's ability to run VBA code in Visio.

Users can set Visio security levels and whether VBA is enabled or disabled in Visio at run time in the Visio application. Administrators can set security policies using a Policy Editor or logon scripts, or by manually updating the registry. Settings that affect security and the ability to run code in a solution include the following:

- **Security level settings** In addition to user control over security level settings, administrators can also set policies that determine the minimum allowable security level for a user or a group. The highest security level setting (user or administrator) is enforced.
- **Disabling VBA in Visio** Visio users can temporarily disable VBA in Visio by clearing the **Enable Visual Basic for Applications** check box on the **Advanced** tab of the **Options** dialog box (on the **Tools** menu, click **Options**). Administrators can set a policy (user or group) for this option to disable VBA.

  Visio users and administrators can also disable VBA in Visio by choosing not to install VBA. If another application installs VBA, it will then become available to Visio. In that case, users and administrators would still have the option to disable VBA temporarily using the methods previously mentioned.
- **Denying access to the Visual Basic object model from Visio** An administrator can set a policy that denies access to the Visual Basic object model from Visio. When access to the Visual Basic object model is denied, the **Application.VBE** property and the **Document.VBProject** property are disabled. This setting provides security against viruses that use these properties to replicate themselves into projects of other documents. This is an administrator setting only; users cannot set this property through the Visio user interface.

Additional details for administrators on setting security policies can be found in the Microsoft Visio Resource Kit, available from the Microsoft Visio Web site (http://www.microsoft.com/office/visio/).

Using the Add-In Manager

In the Visual Basic Editor, you can use the **Add-In Manager** to manage add-ins that extend the VBA development environment. These add-ins are COM-based and provide the developer with a way to use a single add-in to add functionality to any VBA host application (VBA version 6.0 and later), including Visio. For more information about add-ins, see the Microsoft Visual Basic Help.

To display the Add-In Manager from the Visual Basic Editor

- On the **Add-Ins** menu, click **Add-In Manager**.

  The **Add-In Manager** dialog box appears with a list of add-ins that have been registered with Visio.

> **Note** The add-ins described in this section apply specifically to extending the VBA development environment. For details on using COM add-ins to extend Visio, see Chapter 23, *Using COM Add-ins in a Visio Solution*.

16

Working with Visio Document, Page, and Shape Objects

Working with Document Objects 326

Working with Page Objects 332

Working with Shape Objects 334

Creating a Simple Drawing: an Example 344

In the Microsoft Visio object model, the most fundamental object you work with is the **Shape** object. To navigate to the **Shape** objects, you commonly work with the **Document** and **Page** objects that precede them in the object hierarchy.

This chapter describes techniques for working with **Document**, **Page**, and **Shape** objects—getting and setting their properties, and invoking their methods. You can apply many of these techniques when working with other Visio objects in the object model.

For details about these objects or any objects, properties, methods, and events in the Visio object model, see the Microsoft Visio Developer Reference (on the **Help** menu, click **Developer Reference**). For a summary list of Visio objects, properties, methods, and events, see Appendix A, *Properties, Methods, and Events by Object*.

> **Note** Beginning with Visio 2000, any object that can be assigned a name (for example, a page or a shape) can have two names: a local name and a universal name. If you are developing solutions that will be localized, see *Using Universal Names in Your Solution* in Chapter 26, *Packaging a Visio Automation Solution*.

Working with Document Objects

A **Document** object represents a drawing file (.vsd or .vdx), stencil file (.vss or .vsx), or template file (.vst or .vtx) that is open in a Microsoft Visio instance. When working with an existing drawing from a program, you'll often simply work with the active page of the active document—that is, the drawing displayed in the active drawing window. However, in some circumstances, your program might open a document for the user or retrieve a document that is open but not active.

Getting a Document Object

To get information about a document, you need to get a reference to a **Document** object.

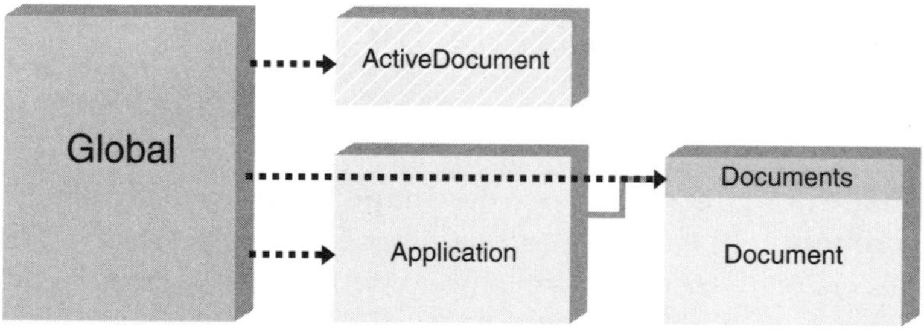

Figure 16-1 **Document** object and related objects higher in the Visio object model.

Depending on the design of your solution, you can get a reference to the **Document** object in several ways. The following examples all assume that you have defined an object variable *docObj* (Dim docObj As Visio.Document).

- The global and **Application** objects have an **ActiveDocument** property that refers to the document in the active window regardless of the window's type. The following statement retrieves the active document in a Visio instance and assigns it to *docObj*:

  ```
  Set docObj = ActiveDocument
  ```

As an alternative, if you've retrieved the active window, you can get the **Document** property of that **Window** object; it refers to the same **Document** object as does **ActiveDocument**.

For details about the global object, see *Using the Visio Global Object* in Chapter 15, *Programming Visio with VBA*.

- If you know an open document's file name, you can retrieve it from the **Documents** collection, whether the document is active. For example:

  ```
  Set docObj = Documents.Item("Hello.vsd")
  ```

  The previous statement retrieves the document Hello.vsd from the **Documents** collection. If Hello.vsd is not open, attempting to retrieve it causes an error.

- You can use the **Open** method of a **Documents** collection to open a document if you know its path and file name:

  ```
  Set docObj = Documents.Open("c:\Visio\Drawings\Hello.vsd")
  ```

  This statement opens the document Hello.vsd as an original and adds it to the **Documents** collection.

You can open any Visio document—stencil, template, or drawing file—with the **Open** method, but this is not recommended for stencils and templates. The **Open** method opens the document as an original, rather than as a copy or read-only. An original document can be changed, which is undesirable for stencils and templates because nothing prevents the user from editing masters, altering the template's workspace, or making other potentially unwelcome changes.

To open a Visio document as read-only, use the **OpenEx** method. You can also use **OpenEx** to open:

- A copy of a document
- A copy of a document without adding its name to the Visio **File** menu
- A stencil docked in a drawing window
- A stencil minimized
- A document with Microsoft Visual Basic for Applications (VBA) macros disabled

For details, see **OpenEx** in the Microsoft Visio Developer Reference (on the **Help** menu, click **Developer Reference**).

Getting Information about Documents

You can get information about a document by retrieving properties, such as **Description**, **Keywords**, **Subject**, and **Title**. These properties correspond to text boxes in the **Properties** dialog box for the document (on the **File** menu, click **Properties**).

A **Document** object has three properties you can use to get a document's file name:

- **Name**, which returns only a document's file name—for example, Hello.vsd. Until a document is saved, **Name** returns the temporary name of the document, such as Drawing1.
- **FullName**, which returns the drive, path, and file name of a document. For example, c:\Visio\Drawings\Hello.vsd. Like the **Name** property, until a document is saved, **FullName** returns the temporary name of the document.
- **Path**, which returns only the drive and path of a document's full name. For example, c:\Visio\Drawings\. Until the document is saved, **Path** returns a null string ("").

These properties are read-only. To change the name, drive, or path of a document, use the **SaveAs** method to save the document under a different name or to a different drive or path.

You can get the status of a document by getting its **ReadOnly** or **Saved** property:

- **ReadOnly** returns **True** if a document is opened as read-only.
- **Saved** returns **True** if all of the changes in the document have been saved.

You can also get information about a **Document object by getting the DocumentSheet** property of the **Document** object. This property returns a **Shape** object whose **Cells** property returns **Cell** objects that contain the document's formulas. These **Cell** objects correspond to cells shown in a document's ShapeSheet window. For details about working with formulas, see Chapter 17, *Automating Formulas.*

Working with Styles in a Document

To determine what styles are available in a document, get the **Styles** property of a **Document** object. The **Styles** property returns a **Styles** collection, which represents the set of styles defined for a document. The **Name** property of a **Style** object returns the style name that appears in style lists and in the **Define Styles** dialog box (on the **Format** menu, click **Define Styles**).

The following example iterates through the document's **Styles** collection and lists the style names in a listbox on a user form:

```
Sub ListStyles ()
    Dim stylsObj As Visio.Styles
    Dim stylObj As Visio.Style
    Dim styleName As String

    Set stylsObj = ThisDocument.Styles
    UserForm1.ListBox1.Clear

    For Each stylObj In stylsObj
          styleName = stylObj.Name
          UserForm1.ListBox1.AddItem styleName
    Next

    UserForm1.Show
End Sub
```

> **Tip** You can change the default styles for a **Document** object in the Visual Basic Editor. Select the **ThisDocument** object in the **Project Explorer** and change the styles listed in the **Properties** window. The styles in the **Properties** window are: **DefaultFillStyle**, **DefaultLineStyle**, **DefaultStyle**, and **DefaultTextStyle**.

Creating a Style for a Document

To create a style from a program, use the **Add** method of a **Styles** collection and specify the name of the new style. You can optionally specify the name of a style on which to base the new style and whether the style includes text, line, and fill attributes.

For example, to create a new style named **Caption** based on the **Normal** style that includes only text attributes:

```
Set stylObj = stylsObj.Add("Caption", "Normal", 1, 0, 0)
```

To create a new style that is not based on another style, with text, line, and fill attributes:

```
Set stylObj = stylsObj.Add("Street Sign","", 1, 1, 1)
```

You can change the style's name by setting its **Name** property, or change whether it includes text, line, or fill attributes by setting its **IncludesFill**, **IncludesLine**, or **IncludesText** property. For details about creating styles, see the Microsoft Visio Help (on the **Help** menu, click **Microsoft Visio Help**).

A **Style** object has a **Cells** property you can use to set formulas for ShapeSheet cells that define the style. This property returns a **Cell** object that corresponds to a cell in a style.

For example, to change the font size of a style:

```
Set fontsizeCellObj = stylObj.Cells("Char.Size")
fontsizeCellObj.Formula = "18 pt"
```

For details about working with formulas, see Chapter 17, *Automating Formulas*.

Printing and Saving Documents

Your program can print or save the drawing it creates. For users who are comfortable with the Visio menu commands, you'll probably create the drawing from your program and leave printing and saving to the user. If not, you can handle these steps from your program.

Printing documents and pages

You can print a document or a page in a document by using the **Print** method.

To print all of the pages of a document, use **Print** with a **Document** object. This is equivalent to clicking **All** in the **Print** dialog box (on the **File** menu, click **Print**). To print just one page, use the **Print** method with a **Page** object. This is similar to displaying that page and clicking **Current page** in the **Print** dialog box.

When printing from Microsoft Visual Basic for Applications (VBA) or Visual Basic, you must:

- Apply the method to a variable of type **Object**. You cannot use a specific Visio object type.
- Apply the **Print** method's result to a dummy variable.

For example, to print a document:

```
Dim docObj As Visio.Document
Dim docObjTemp As Object
Dim dummy As String
Set docObj = ThisDocument
Set docObjTemp = docObj
dummy = docObjTemp.Print
```

Saving documents

To save a document from a program, use the **Save** or **SaveAs** method of a **Document** object.

Use the **SaveAs** method and supply a file name and path to save and name a new document, to save a copy of an existing document under a different name, or to save an existing document to a different drive or path. For example:

```
ThisDocument.SaveAs  "c:\visio\drawings\myfile.vsd"
```

Use the **Save** method only if the document has already been saved and named. For example:

```
ThisDocument.Save
```

Unlike the **Save** menu command in the Visio user interface, which displays the **Save As** dialog box if a document is unnamed, using the **Save** method on an unnamed document won't invoke the **SaveAs** method—it will cause an error.

To find out whether a document has ever been saved, check its **Path** property, which returns the drive and path of the document's full name or a null string ("") if the document hasn't been saved. To find out whether a document has been saved since changes were made to it, check its **Saved** property.

Displaying Pages of a Document

In Visio, the pages of a document are displayed in a window. To display a particular page using Automation, you might expect to use a method or property of a **Document** object. However, to change the page that is being displayed by Visio, you actually use the **Page** property of the **Window** object. For example:

```
ActiveWindow.Page = NameOfPageToDisplay
```

where *NameOfPageToDisplay* is the valid name of a page in the document.

> **Note** You do not have to display a page in Visio in order to access it through Automation. All pages of a document are accessible from the Pages collection of the Document object regardless of whether they are displayed.

The following example displays the last page of the active document in the active window:

```
Sub TurnToLastPage()
    Dim szPageName As String
    Dim iPageCount As Integer

    'Get the page count
    iPageCount = ActiveDocument.Pages.Count

    'Get the name of the last page
    szPageName = ActiveDocument.Pages(iPageCount).Name

    'Display the last page in the ActiveWindow
    'i.e. "Turn" the page
    ActiveWindow.Page = szPageName

End Sub
```

Working with Page Objects

A **Page** object represents a drawing page, which can be either a background or a foreground page. Once you have a reference to a document, you need to get a **Page** object for the drawing page you want to work with.

If you expect your user to create or display a drawing and then run your program, it's reasonable to assume that the active page contains the drawing you want. You can either get the active page in the Microsoft Visio instance, or you can get the active document and retrieve a page from its **Pages** collection.

Getting a Page Object

To work with a drawing page, you need to get a reference to a **Page** object.

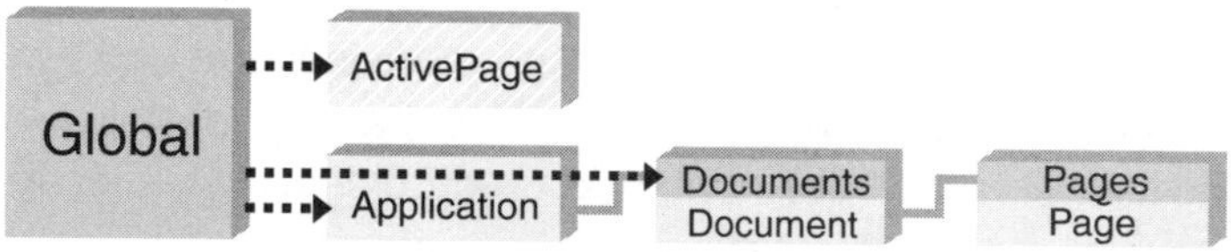

Figure 16-2 **Page** object and related objects higher in the Visio object model.

To get a page from a document, get the **Pages** collection of the **Document** or **ThisDocument** object and get a **Page** object from the collection. You can get a page by its index within the collection, or if you know the name of the page, you can get it by name. For example, to retrieve a page named Engineering:

```
Set pagObj = ThisDocument.Pages.Item("Engineering")
```

To get the active page of an application, you can get the **ActivePage** property of the global or **Application** object. For example, using the global object:

```
Set pagObj = ActivePage
```

For details about the global object, see *Using the Visio Global Object* in Chapter 15, *Programming Visio with VBA*.

Getting Information about Pages

You can get information about a page by retrieving properties, such as **Name** and **Background**, that are displayed in text boxes on the **Page Properties** tab in the **Page Setup** dialog box (on the **File** menu, click **Page Setup**). The **Document** property of a page returns the **Document** object that contains the page.

A **Page** object also has properties you can use to identify the contents of a drawing page:

- **Shapes** returns a collection of all the **Shape** objects on a page.
- **Connects** returns a collection of all the **Connect** objects on a page.
- **OLEObjects** returns a collection of all the OLE 2.0 linked objects, embedded objects, and ActiveX controls on a page.

You can also get information about the dimensions and appearance of a drawing page by getting a **Page** object's **PageSheet** property. This property returns a **Shape** object whose **Cells** property returns **Cell** objects that contain the page's formulas. These **Cell** objects correspond to cells shown in a page's ShapeSheet window.

For example, the following statements return the width of the page:

```
Set shpObj = pagObj.PageSheet
Set celObj = shpObj.Cells("PageWidth")
dWidth = celObj.Result("inches")
```

For details about working with formulas, see Chapter 17, *Automating Formulas*.

Adding Pages to a Drawing

A Visio document can contain more than one page. Each page of a document can contain a unique drawing, and some pages can serve as backgrounds to other pages.

You can create multiple-page documents from a program by adding pages and assigning backgrounds to them. You can also change page settings, such as the drawing scale and page width and height.

Initially, a new document has one page. To create another page, use the **Add** method of the document's **Pages** collection. For example:

```
Set pagObj = ThisDocument.Pages.Add
```

Once you have added a new page to the collection, you can use the **Name** property of the **Page** object to name your page.

> **Note** In Visio, the pages of a document are displayed in a window. For details on displaying a particular page using Automation, see *Displaying Pages of a Document* in *Working with Document Objects* earlier in this chapter.

Working with Shape Objects

The most fundamental Microsoft Visio object that you will work with is the **Shape** object. A **Shape** object represents a basic shape, a group, a guide or guide point, or a linked or embedded object. A **Shape** object can also represent the formulas of a page, master, or document. A **Shapes** collection represents all of the **Shape** objects on a drawing page, in a group, or in a master.

Getting a Shape Object

To get information about a shape, you need to get a reference to the **Shape** object. To do this, you must first get a reference to the **Shapes** collection of the object that contains the shape in which you are interested.

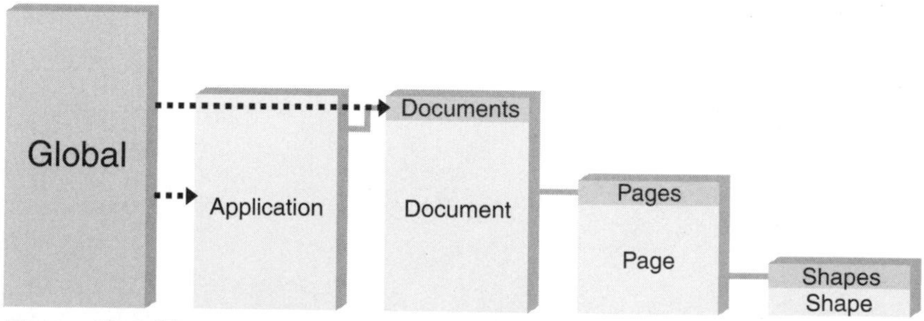

Figure 16-3 Shape object and related objects higher in the Visio object model.

To get a **Shapes** collection of a page, get the **Shapes** property of the **Page** object. To get a **Shapes** collection of a master, get the **Shapes** property of the **Master** object. If a **Shape** object represents a group or the sheet for a page or master, that **Shape object also has a Shapes** property.

You can get a **Shape** object from a **Shapes** collection by its index within the collection, by its name, or by its unique ID.

Getting a shape by its index

The order of items in a **Shapes** collection is the same as the order in which the shapes were drawn. The first item in a **Shapes** collection is the shape farthest to the back on the drawing page (the first shape drawn), and the last item is the shape closest to the front (the last shape drawn). For example, to get the shape closest to the front on the page:

```
shpIndex = shpsObj.Count
Set shpObj = shpsObj.Item(shpIndex)
```

Getting a shape by name or unique ID

A **Shape** object has three properties that identify the shape—**Name**, **NameID**, and **UniqueID**.

Name returns *shapeName[.nnnn]*. The name of the shape is *shapeName*; you can set this name either by using the **Name** property or by typing a name in the **Special** dialog box (on the **Format** menu, click **Special**).

If you do not assign a name to a shape, the **Name** property returns one of the following values:

- If the shape is the first or only instance of a particular master on a page or in a group, *shapeName* is the name of the master with no ID number. For example, Decision.
- If the shape is a second or subsequent instance of a particular master on a page or in a group, *shapeName* is the name of the master followed by the shape's ID number. For example, Decision.43.
- If the shape is not an instance of a master, *shapeName* is Sheet followed by the shape's ID number. For example, Sheet.34. In this case, the **Name** and **NameID** properties of the shape return the same string.

  A shape's name can be from 1 to 31 characters in length and is usually descriptive of the shape, such as Desktop PC. For example, to get a shape named Desktop PC:

  ```
  Set shpObj = shpsObj.Item("Desktop PC")
  ```

NameID returns *Sheet.n* where *n* is an integer ID of the shape—for example, Sheet.34. This ID is assigned to the shape when it is created on a drawing page and is guaranteed to be unique within the shape's page or master. For example, to get a shape whose ID is 5:

```
Set shpObj = shpsObj.Item("Sheet.5")
```

UniqueID(visGetGUID) returns the shape's unique ID if it has one. You can work with unique IDs only from a program—you can't access them in the Visio user interface. Most often, unique IDs identify shapes that have corresponding records in a database. For example, an office floor plan might have dozens of identical desk, chair, and PC shapes, but you can use the unique ID of each shape to associate a particular shape in the floor plan with a particular record in a facilities database.

A shape doesn't have a unique ID until a program generates one for it. By contrast, a master always has a unique ID, generated by the Visio engine. A unique ID is stored internally as a 128-bit value, but the Visio engine returns this value as a string. You can pass the unique ID string with the **Item** property to get a shape by its unique ID. For example:

```
Set shpObj = shpsObj.Item("{667458A1-9386-101C-9107-00608CF4B660}")
```

For more details about unique IDs for shapes and masters, see Chapter 20, *Integrating Data with a Visio Solution*.

Getting Information about a Shape

Because a **Shape** object can represent more than just a basic shape, you might need to determine its type. A **Shape** object has a **Type** property that indicates the type of shape it is. The values returned by the **Type** property are represented by the following constants defined in the Microsoft Visio type library:

- **visTypeShape** identifies a shape that is not a group, such as a line, ellipse, or rectangle, including shapes with multiple paths.
- **visTypeGroup** identifies a group. A group can contain shapes, groups, foreign objects, and guides.
- **visTypeForeignObject** identifies an object imported, embedded, or linked from another application.
- **visTypeGuide** identifies a guide or guide point.
- **visTypePage** identifies a shape containing properties of a page or master.
- **visTypeDoc** identifies a shape containing properties of a document.

An instance of a master can be a basic shape or a group, depending on how the master was created.

In the **Shapes** collection of a **Page** object, each group counts as a single shape. However, a group has a **Shapes** collection of its own. The following function counts the shapes on a page, including those in groups (but not the groups themselves), by iterating through the **Shapes** collection of a **Page** object. The following function also checks the **Type** property of each **Shape** object to see whether the shape is a group. If **Type** returns **visTypeGroup**, the example retrieves the number of shapes in the group and adds that number to the total number of shapes.

```
Function ShapesCount (root As Object) As Integer
    'Return value
    Dim iCount As Integer
    'Shapes collection
    Dim shpsObj As Visio.Shapes
    'Shape object
    Dim shpObj As Visio.Shape

    iCount = 0
    'Assumes root.Shapes is a group or a page
    Set shpsObj = root.Shapes
    For Each shpObj In shpsObj
        If shpObj.Type = visTypeGroup Then
            iCount = iCount + ShapesCount(shpObj)
        Else
            iCount = iCount + 1
        End If
    Next
    ShapesCount = iCount
End Function
```

Creating and Changing Shapes

Most of the work your program does will be with shapes—creating new shapes or changing the way shapes look. You'll often create shapes by dropping masters onto a drawing page, as described in Chapter 18, *Drawing with Automation*.

Creating new shapes

You can draw lines, ellipses, and rectangles from a program by using the **DrawLine**, **DrawOval**, and **DrawRectangle** methods of a **Page** object. When you draw lines, ovals, and rectangles instead of dropping a master, you supply coordinates for the two opposite corners of the width-height box for the new shape.

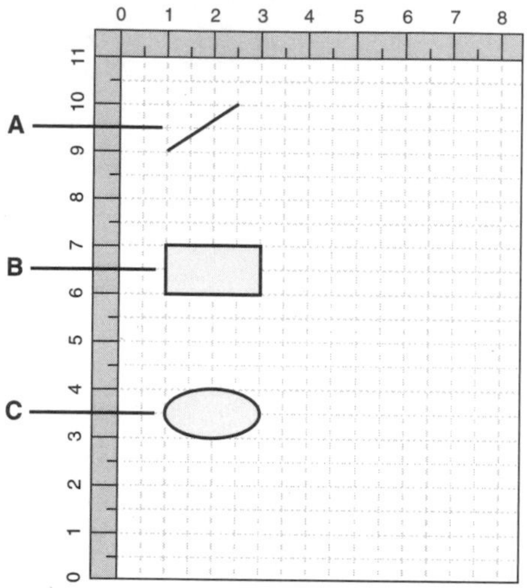

Figure 16-4 Creating shapes with the **DrawLine**, **DrawRectangle**, and **DrawOval** methods. (**A**) pagObj.DrawLine 1,9,3,10. (**B**) pagObj.DrawRectangle 1,6,3,7. (**C**) pagObj.DrawOval 1,3,3,4 .

The order in which you specify the corners doesn't really matter when you draw ellipses and rectangles. However, the order does matter for lines. It's often important to know which end of a line is the *begin point* and which is the *end point*.

For example, you might want to apply a line style that formats a line's end point with an arrowhead, or glue a line's begin point to another shape. When you draw a line from a program, the first *x,y* coordinate pair determines the line's begin point, and the second *x,y* coordinate pair determines the line's end point—the same as when you draw a shape with the mouse.

You can also draw shapes using the **DrawBezier**, **DrawNURBS**, **DrawPolyline**, and **DrawSpline** methods. For details about these methods, see the Microsoft Visio Developer Reference (on the **Help** menu, click **Developer Reference**).

Modifying shapes

You can also draw original shapes and modify existing shapes, or change a shape's appearance and behavior, by setting its formulas. A **Shape** object has a **Cells** property that returns a **Cell** object containing a formula.

For example, to hide the text of a shape:

```
Set celObj = shpObj.Cells("HideText")
celObj.Formula = "True"
```

For details about working with formulas, see Chapter 17, *Automating Formulas*.

Copying, cutting, deleting, and duplicating shapes

You can copy, cut, delete, and duplicate shapes using the **Copy**, **Cut**, **Delete**, and **Duplicate** methods of a **Shape** object. These methods work in the same way as the corresponding menu commands in the Visio user interface. You can use these methods with a **Shape** object whether or not the corresponding shape is selected in the drawing window.

To duplicate a shape at a particular location on the page, use the **Drop** method for a **Page** object. You supply a reference to the shape you want to duplicate and to the coordinates where you want to position the shape's pin. For example:

```
Set shpObj = pagObj.Shapes("Sheet.1")
pagObj.Drop shpObj,1,2
```

To paste shapes from the Clipboard, use the **Paste** method of a **Page** object. For details about pasting from the Clipboard, see the **Paste** method in the Microsoft Visio Developer Reference (on the **Help** menu, click **Developer Reference**).

Adding Text to Shapes

You'll often set a shape's text from the program rather than provide it as part of a master. You can add text to a shape or change existing text by setting the **Text** property of a **Shape** object to a string expression. For example:

```
shpObj.Text = "Twinkle"
```

To include quotation marks in the text, use two quotation mark characters ("") to enclose the string. For example:

```
shpObj.Text = """Are you currently a customer of XYZ?"""
```

To control where lines break in text, use the Microsoft Visual Basic **Chr$** function to include an ASCII linefeed with the string. For example:

```
shpObj.Text = "Twinkle," & Chr$(10) & "twinkle" & Chr$(10) _
    & "little star"
```

Figure 16-5 Set the **Text** property of a **Shape** object to add text to the corresponding shape.

To work with part of a shape's text, get the shape's **Characters** property, which returns a **Characters** object. You set the **Begin** and **End** properties of the **Characters** object to mark the range of text with which you want to work.

A shape's text is contained in its text block and is positioned in its own coordinate system relative to the shape. You can control the size and position of a shape's text block by setting formulas in the shape's Text Transform section. For details about working with formulas, see Chapter 17, *Automating Formulas*. For techniques you can use in Visio to change a shape's text block and control text behaviors, see Chapter 9, *Designing Text Behavior*.

Getting a Shape's Text

The **Text** property of a **Shape** object returns a string containing the text displayed in the shape. If a shape's text contains fields, such as a date, time, or custom formulas, the string returned by the shape's **Text** property contains an escape character (hex 1E, decimal 30), not the expanded text that is displayed for the fields.

If you want the shape's text with fields fully expanded to what they display in the drawing window, get the shape's **Characters** property and then get the **Text** property of the resulting **Characters** object. You can also get a subset of the shape's text by setting the **Begin** and **End** properties of the **Characters** object.

Fields in a shape's text evaluate to the results of formulas you can view in the shape's Text Fields section. Use the **FieldFormula** and related properties of the **Characters** object to control fields in a shape's text.

> **Note** In versions earlier than Visio 2000, the string returned by a shape's **Text** property contained a 4-byte field code that began with an escape character. The next three bytes contained the **FieldCategory**, **FieldCode**, and **FieldFormat** values for the field. Beginning with Visio 2000, only a single escape character is stored and **FieldCategory**, **FieldCode**, and **FieldFormat** are stored in the Fields.UICat[*i*], Fields.UICod[*i*], and Fields.UIFmt[*i*] cells in the shape's Text Fields section. (These cells do not appear in the ShapeSheet window.) Field code constants are defined in the Visio type library under **visFieldCodes**.

In addition to the text displayed in the shape, there are other parts of a shape that may contain text:

- A shape may contain text in user-defined cells or custom properties. To access this text, use the **Formula** property of the **Cell** object that contains the text.
- A shape may contain text in its **Data1**, **Data2**, and **Data3** fields, which appear in the **Special** dialog box for that shape (on the **Format** menu, click **Special**). To access this text, use the **Data1**, **Data2**, and **Data3** properties of the **Shape** object.

Identifying and Applying Styles to Shapes

A **Shape** object has properties that identify the text, line, and fill styles applied to that shape:

- **TextStyle** identifies a shape's text style.
- **LineStyle** identifies a shape's line style.
- **FillStyle** identifies a shape's fill style.

You can get these properties to determine a shape's text, line, or fill style, or you can set these properties to apply styles to the shape.

You can also set the **Style** property to apply a multiple-attribute style to a shape. If you get a shape's **Style** property, however, it returns the shape's fill style, because a property cannot return multiple objects. For more details, see the Microsoft Visio Developer Reference (on the **Help** menu, click **Developer Reference**).

Preserving Local Formatting

Your program or your user can apply specific formatting attributes to a shape in addition to its text, line, or fill styles. This kind of formatting is called *local formatting*. If you apply a style to that shape later, the style overrides the local formatting unless you preserve it.

To preserve local formatting when applying a style from a program, use one of the following properties instead of **FillStyle**, **LineStyle**, or **TextStyle**:

- **FillStyleKeepFmt**
- **LineStyleKeepFmt**
- **TextStyleKeepFmt**
- **StyleKeepFmt**

These properties correspond to selecting the **Preserve local formatting** check box in the **Style** dialog box (on the **Format** menu, click **Style**).

Creating Groups from a Program

A group is a shape composed of other shapes. To create a group from a program, use the **Group** method of a **Window** object or a **Selection** object. The following statement creates a group from the selected shapes in a drawing window:

```
winObj.Group
```

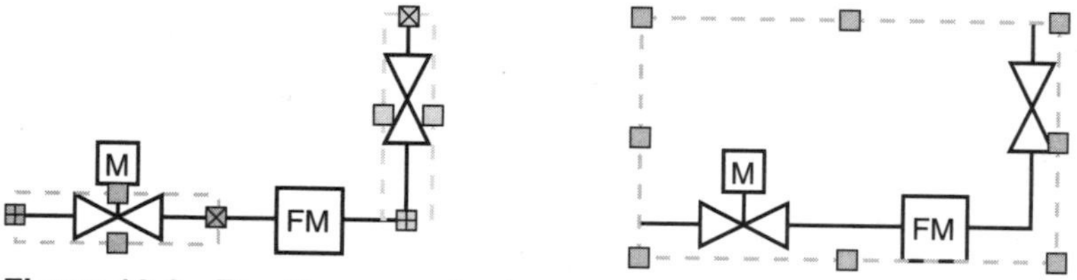

Figure 16-6 The **Group** method creates a group from selected shapes.

To add a shape to a group, use the **Drop** method of a **Shape** object that represents the group, with a reference to the shape you want to add and to a position inside the group. For example:

```
grpObj.Drop shpObj, 0.375, 0.125
```

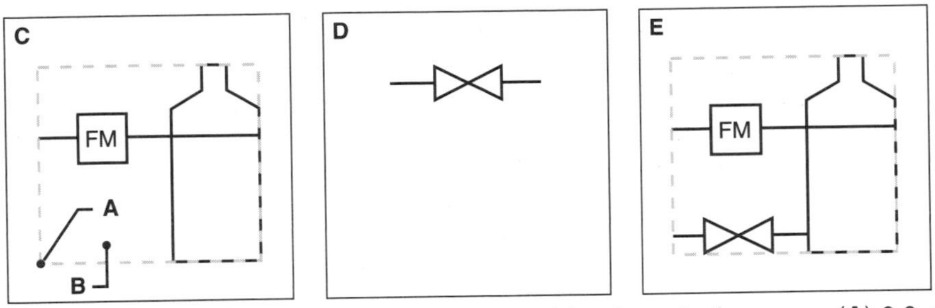

Figure 16-7 Use a group's **Drop** method to add a shape to the group. (**A**) 0,0. (**B**) 0.375, 0.125. (**C**) grpObj. (**D**) shpObj. (**E**) grpObj after grpObj.Drop.

The coordinates 0.375, 0.125 are expressed in local coordinates of the group. If the shape that's being dropped is a **Master** object, the pin of the master is positioned at those coordinates. If the shape that's being dropped is a **Shape** object, the center of the shape's bounding box is placed at these coordinates.

You can control the behavior of a group by setting formulas in the shape's Group Properties section. For details about working with formulas, see Chapter 17, *Automating Formulas*.

Creating Masters

To create masters from a program, you drop a shape from a drawing page into a document (often a stencil), as you do when creating a master with the mouse. Supply a reference to the **Shape** object that you want to make into a master using the document's **Drop** method. Before you can drop a **Shape** object in a stencil, the stencil must be opened as an original rather than read only, as is typically the case when a stencil is opened by a template (.vst or .vtx) file. To open a stencil as an original, use the **Open** method. For example:

```
Dim stnObj As Visio.Document
Dim shpObj As Visio.Shape
Set stnObj = Documents.Open("Basic Shapes.vss")
stnObj.Drop shpObj, 0, 0
```

A master often consists of several components, which, for best performance, should be grouped. You are not required to group components of a master in a stencil. However, if they are not, the Visio engine automatically groups the shapes when the master is dropped in a drawing. This increases the time required to create an instance of the master.

> **Note** In addition to **Shape** and **Master** objects, the **Drop** method accepts **Selection** objects, or any object that provides an **IDataObject** interface. For details about the **Drop** method, see the Microsoft Visio Developer Reference (on the **Help** menu, click **Developer Reference**).

Creating a Simple Drawing: an Example

Here's a program that demonstrates how you can traverse the object model using **Document**, **Page**, and **Shape** objects to create a drawing. This example *creates* Microsoft Visio objects as opposed to referring to Visio objects that already exist. This program follows these steps:

1. Gets the first page in the **Pages** collection of the document associated with the Microsoft Visual Basic for Applications (VBA) project.
2. Adds the stencil **Basic Shapes.vss** to the **Documents** collection.
3. Drops an instance of the **Rectangle** master from the stencil onto the drawing page.
4. Sets the text of the rectangle shape on the drawing page to "Hello World!"
5. Saves the document.

```
Sub HelloWorld ()
    'Stencil document that contains master
    Dim stnObj As Visio.Document
    'Master to drop
    Dim mastObj As Visio.Master
    'Pages collection of document
    Dim pagsObj As Visio.Pages
    'Page to work in
    Dim pagObj As Visio.Page
    'Instance of master on page
    Dim shpObj As Visio.Shape

    'Get the first page in the document associated with the VBA
    'program.
    'A new document always has one page, whose index in the Pages
```

```
    'collection is 1.
    Set pagsObj = ThisDocument.Pages
    Set pagObj = pagsObj.Item(1)
    'Get the stencil from the Documents collection and set the
    'master.
    Set stnObj = Documents.Add("Basic Shapes.vss")
    Set mastObj = stnObj.Masters("Rectangle")
    'Drop the rectangle in the middle of a US letter-size page.
    Set shpObj = pagObj.Drop(mastObj, 4.25, 5.5)
    'Set the text of the rectangle.
    shpObj.Text = "Hello World!"
    'Save the drawing. The message pauses the program so you know the
    'drawing is finished.
    ThisDocument.SaveAs "Hello.vsd"
    MsgBox "Drawing finished!", , "Hello World!"
End Sub
```

The drawing created by this program looks something like this.

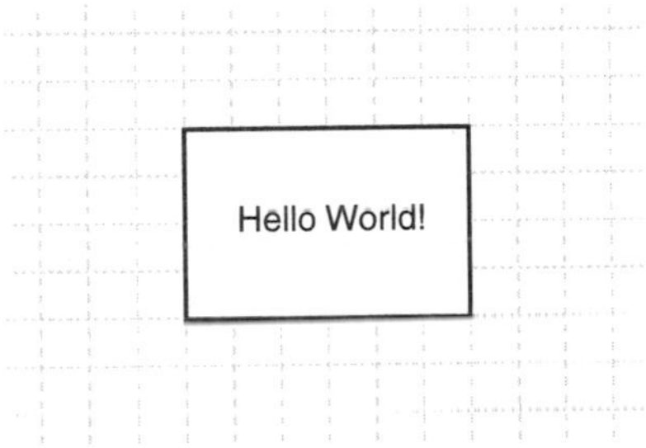

Figure 16-8 The drawing created by the Hello World program.

This program uses the Visio object types, such as *Visio.Document*, *Visio.Master*, *Visio.Pages*, *Visio.Page*, and *Visio.Shape*, defined in the Visio type library. Using Visio object types instead of the general *Object* variable type increases the speed of your program.

This program uses object variables to hold references to the Visio objects. Each **Set** statement assigns an object reference to an object variable, starting with the **ThisDocument** object. Notice the progression from **ThisDocument** object to **Pages** collection to **Page** object.

Set pagsObj = ThisDocument.Pages uses the **ThisDocument** object, which is equivalent to the specific **Document** object associated with a VBA project. If you want to reference the **Document** object of the file associated with your VBA project, you don't need to get it from the **Documents** collection; just begin by referencing the **ThisDocument** object.

Set stnObj = Documents.Add("Basic Shapes.vss") doesn't reference an object higher in the Visio object model preceding **Documents**. **Documents** is a property of the Visio *global object*. The Visio global object has properties and methods you can reference with no qualifying object. For details about the Visio global object, see Chapter 15, *Programming Visio with VBA*.

Set shpObj = pagObj.Drop(mastObj, 4.25, 5.5) uses the **Drop** method to drop a master on the page represented by the *pagObj* variable. (Although you can draw shapes from scratch in a program, dropping a master is a far easier and more common technique.) The *mastObj* argument specifies the master to drop; *4.25, 5.5* are the page coordinates of the location to drop the pin (its center of rotation) of the new shape. These coordinates are measured from the lower-left corner of the drawing page in drawing units expressed as inches. The **Drop** method returns a reference to a **Shape** object—the new rectangle—that is assigned to the variable *shpObj*.

shpObj.Text = "Hello World!" assigns the string "Hello World!" to the **Text** property of the **Shape** object, which causes Visio to display that string in the rectangle. This is similar to selecting a shape with the pointer in a Visio drawing window and typing *Hello World!*

ThisDocument.SaveAs "Hello.vsd" uses the **SaveAs** method to save the **ThisDocument** object under the file name Hello.vsd. Because no folder path is specified, the document is saved in the working folder (probably the folder that contains the program). The **MsgBox** statement simply lets you know the drawing is finished. When you click **OK** in the message box, the program finishes.

To get details about any Visio object, property, method, or event, see the Microsoft Visio Developer Reference (on the **Help** menu, click **Developer Reference**). To find information about VBA programming, see the Microsoft Visual Basic Help, which is accessible from the **Help** menu in the Visual Basic Editor.

17

Automating Formulas

Working with Formulas in Cells 348

Working with Sections and Rows 355

Working with Inherited Data 361

In addition to the properties that are exposed in the Microsoft Visio object model, you can control **Shape**, **Style**, **Page**, **Master**, and **Document** objects by working with the formulas that are contained in **Cell** objects. Just as you can view, enter, and edit formulas in cells in a ShapeSheet window, you can get and set formulas contained in the **Cell** objects that belong to a shape. For this reason, it is essential for an Automation developer to understand the functionality that the Visio engine provides with its SmartShapes technology. Anything you can do with a formula in a ShapeSheet window you can also do in your program.

You can alter a shape even more dramatically by working with whole sections and rows of its formulas. For example, you can add Geometry sections, delete vertices, or change the row type of segments, converting them from lines to arcs or arcs to lines.

> **Important** For a complete list of sections, cell reference names, and section, row, and cell index constants, see Appendix B, *ShapeSheet Section, Row, and Cell Indices.* You can also find index constants and their values by searching the Visio type library for **VisSectionIndices**, **VisRowIndices**, and **VisCellIndices**.

This chapter introduces you to automating formulas of **Cell** objects that belong to **Shape**, **Style**, **Page**, **Master**, and **Document** objects. It also discusses working with sections and rows from your program. For more information about working with Visio formulas, see Chapter 4, *Visio Formulas*.

Working with Formulas in Cells

In the Microsoft Visio object model, a Shape object has many cells—each cell contains a formula whose value determines some aspect of an object's appearance or behavior.

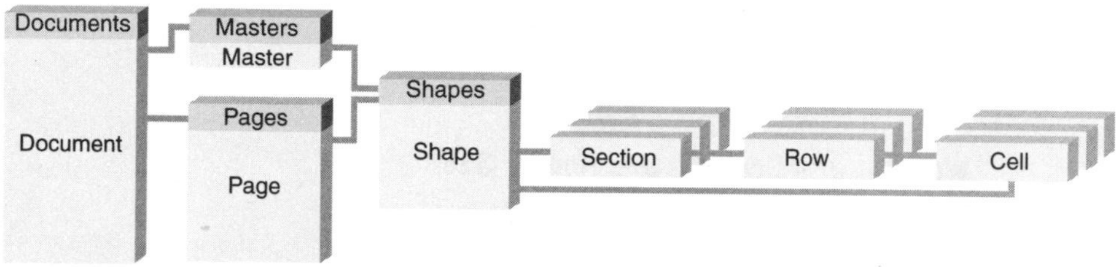

Figure 17-1 Cell object and related objects higher in the Visio object model.

Let's say you want to change the width of a **Shape** object from your program. A **Shape** object in the Visio object model does not expose a width property. However, the **Shape** object does contain a **Cell** object that defines the shape's width. You can modify the shape's width by referring to the shape's width cell and changing its formula. In this way—referring to the appropriate **Cell** objects—all of the functionality available to you in an object's ShapeSheet window is also available to you through Automation.

- To work with formulas of a **Shape** or **Style** object, use the **Cells** or **CellSRC** property of the object to get a particular **Cell** object.
- To work with formulas of a **Page** or **Master** object, use the **PageSheet** property of the object, which returns a **Shape** object. You can then use the **Cells** or **CellSRC** property of that **Shape** object to work with its formulas.
- To work with the formulas of a **Document** object, use the **DocumentSheet** property of the object, which returns a **Shape** object. You can then use the **Cells** or **CellSRC** property of that **Shape** object to work with its formulas.

Getting a Cell Object

You can get a **Cell** object from a collection either by name, or by its section, row, and cell indices. After you retrieve a **Cell** object, you can use its methods and properties to get or set the cell's formula or its value.

Getting a Cell object by name

To get a **Cell** object, use the **Cells** property of a **Shape** object and specify the cell name. You can use any valid cell reference with the **Cells** property.

For example, to get the PinX cell of a shape:

```
Set pinXCellObj = shpObj.Cells("PinX")
```

To get the *y*-coordinate of the shape's fourth connection point:

```
Set conYCellObj = shpObj.Cells("Connections.Y4")
```

In these examples, we are getting **Cell** objects from a collection by name. These cell names are the same names you see in the shape's ShapeSheet window.

> **Note** The **Cells** property uses a local name. If you plan to localize your solution, use the **CellsU** property to specify a universal name.
>
> For more details on local and universal names, see *Using Universal Names in Your Solution* in Chapter 26, *Packaging a Visio Automation Solution.*

Getting a Cell object by section, row, and cell indices

You can use the **CellsSRC** property to retrieve any cell by its section, row, and cell indices.

For example, to get the Font cell in the first row of a shape's Character section:

```
Set fontCellObj = shpObj.CellsSRC (visSectionCharacter, _
    visRowCharacter + 0, visCharacterFont)
```

If a section contains more than one row and you want to refer to a cell in the second row or beyond, add an integer offset to the row constant for that section. Although you can use a row constant without an offset to get the first row of a section, it's good practice to use the row constant as a base and add an integer offset to it, starting with zero (0) for the first row. For example:

```
'First row of the Scratch section
visRowScratch + 0
'Second row of the Scratch section
visRowScratch + 1
'Third row of the Scratch section
visRowScratch + 2
```

The position of a section or row can change as a result of operations that affect other sections and rows. For example, if a Scratch section contains three rows and you delete the second row, the third row shifts to become the second row. As a result, **visRowScratch** + 2 is no longer a valid reference because the section no longer has a third row.

You can also use section and row indices to add or delete sections or rows from a shape or to iterate through rows in a section.

Note In Visio 5.0, the Geometry*n*.NoFill and Geometry*n*.NoShow cells appeared in a ShapeSheet window in the third and fourth cells in the Start row of a Geometry section, and were named Geometry*n*.A1 and Geometry*n*.B1 (Geometry*n*.X0 and Geometry*n*.Y0, respectively, in Visio versions earlier than 5.0). You can refer to these cells by either name.

Getting a user-defined or custom properties cell

Certain shapes might have cells named by the user or the shape developer. User-defined cells are defined in the shape's User-Defined Cells section; custom property cells are defined in the shape's Custom Properties section. Each row in the User-Defined Cells or Custom Properties section has a Value cell that contains the value of the user-defined cell or property, and a Prompt cell that can contain a string. A custom property row has additional cells that control how the custom property can be used.

The Value cell is the default for a user-defined or custom property row, so you can get the Value cell by specifying just the section and name of the row. For example, to get the Value cell of a user-defined cell named Vanishing_Point:

```
Set celObj = shpObj.Cells("User.Vanishing_Point")
```

To get any other cell in a user-defined cell or custom property row, you must include the name of the cell you want. For example, to get the Prompt cell for a custom property named Serial_Number:

```
Set celObj = shpObj.Cells("Prop.Serial_Number.Prompt")
```

For details about defining custom properties in a ShapeSheet window, see *Custom Properties* in Chapter 7, *Enhancing Shape Behavior.*

Changing Cell Formulas Using the Formula property

To change a cell's formula, set the **Formula** property of a **Cell** object to a string that is a valid formula for that cell. For example, to set the formula of a shape's LocPinX cell to = *2 * Width*:

```
Set celObj = shpObj.Cells("LocPinX")
celObj.Formula = "2 * Width"
```

If you omit the equals sign from a formula string, the Visio engine automatically adds it to the formula.

If the formula string contains quotation marks—for example, if inches are specified as " rather than *inches* or *in.*—use two quotation mark characters ("") to pass one quotation mark to the Visio engine. Or, if you want to assign a string constant—for example, to set the formula of the Prompt cell of a custom property row, use the following:

```
shpObj.cells("prop.row_1.prompt").Formula = """Enter property"""
```

Note Formulas set using the **Formula** property are processed using local syntax (localized names, decimal- and list-separators defined by the local regional settings). To provide a solution that works in multiple locales, use the **FormulaU** property and universal syntax.

For more details on local and universal names, see *Using Universal Names in Your Solution* in Chapter 26, *Packaging a Visio Automation Solution.*

Getting the Result of a Formula

Every cell has a formula, and every formula evaluates to a result. You can see this in a ShapeSheet window by clicking **Formulas** or **Values** on the **View** menu. If you're viewing formulas, a cell might display *Width * 0.5*. If you're viewing values, and if Width is 5.0 in., the same cell would display 2.5 in.

The following properties get the result of a formula:

- **Result** returns the formula's result as a floating point number in the units you specify.

- **ResultIU** returns the result as a floating point number in Visio internal units, inches, radians, or elapsed days.
- **ResultInt** returns the result as an integer in the units you specify.
- **ResultStr** returns the result as a string in the units you specify.
- **GetResults** returns the results of multiple cells in the units you specify.

For example, the formulas that determine local coordinates of a shape's center of rotation are stored in its LocPinX and LocPinY cells. The following statements get the result of the formula in the LocPinX cell:

```
Set celObj = shpObj.Cells("LocPinX")
localCenterX = celObj.Result("inches")
```

When getting the results of certain shape formulas, especially those that determine a shape's dimensions or vertices, you'll probably want to preserve the level of precision that floating point numbers provide.

If you plan to use the floating point numbers returned by **Result** or **ResultIU** to re-create shapes in other Visio drawings, assign the results to **Variant** or **Double** variables to reduce the possibility of rounding errors and maintain the same level of precision.

You can specify units using an integer constant (such as **visInches** or **visMeters**) or any string that the Visio engine accepts.

To specify the Visio internal units (inches or radians), specify a zero-length string ("") for the units, or use the **ResultIU** property instead of **Result**.

As an alternative to specifying units as a string, use the unit constants (defined by **VisUnitCodes**) in the Visio type library. For example, you can specify centimeters by using the constant **visCentimeters**.

```
localCenterX = celObj.Result(visCentimeters)
```

> **Note** Passing units as integers is more time- and space-efficient than passing units as strings. Passing integers is also preferable because it helps avoid localization issues (for example, "inches" is not localized as "inches" in all languages.)

Use **visPageUnits** to specify the units defined for the page or **visDrawingUnits** to specify the units defined for the drawing. **ResultStr**, like any other result property, takes a units argument, effectively giving you a way to convert between any units. You might use **ResultStr** specifically to access cell formulas that contain strings, such as the Prompt cell in a custom property row, or to retrieve a string to populate a control in the user interface.

Replacing a Formula with a Result

Occasionally you might want to replace a formula with its result expressed as a constant, either to improve the performance of a shape or because you no longer need to preserve its formulas. The Visio engine evaluates formulas any time you make a change to a shape that affects its formulas. Depending on how often this occurs while your program is executing, it can have a noticeable effect on performance. To replace a formula with its result, use the cell's **Result** property to set its formula. This is similar to setting the cell's **Formula** property—it's a shortcut for evaluating the formula and replacing it with the equivalent constant as the cell's new formula.

For example, suppose a shape's LocPinX formula is = *3 in.* + *1 ft/2*, which evaluates to 9 inches. To replace that formula with its result, use the following statement:

```
celLocPinX.Result("inches") = celLocPinX.Result("inches")
```

After this statement executes, the LocPinX cell's formula is = *9 in.*

You can also improve performance by reducing the number of dependencies in your formulas. For details about designing formulas, see *Controlling Recalculation of Formulas* in Chapter 4, *Visio Formulas.*

Overriding Guarded Formulas

Microsoft Visio has a GUARD function that protects a cell's formula from changes. If a cell's formula is protected with GUARD, attempting to set the formula with the **Formula**, **Result**, or **ResultIU** property causes an error. You can, however, change the cell's formula as follows:

- Use **ResultForce** or **ResultIUForce** instead of **Result** or **ResultIU**.
- Use **FormulaForce** instead of **Formula**.

> **Important** Be cautious when overriding guarded formulas. Often a shape developer guards the formulas of a master to protect its smart behavior against inadvertent changes by a user. If you override these formulas, the shape might no longer behave as originally designed.

Using Formulas to Move Shapes: an Example

This sample program moves selected shapes in the active window by setting formulas for the pin of a two-dimensional (2-D) shape, or the begin and end points for a one-dimensional (1-D) shape. The program uses a user form with four buttons that call the **Nudge** subroutine with the arguments shown.

```
Sub Nudge (dx As Double, dy As Double)
     'Call Nudge as follows:
     'Nudgc 0, -1 (Move down one unit)
     'Nudge -1, 0 (Move left one unit)
     'Nudge 1, 0 (Move right one unit)
     'Nudge 0, 1 (Move up one unit)
     On Error GoTo lblErr
     Dim selObj As Visio.Selection
     Dim shpObj As Visio.Shape
     Dim unit As Double
     Dim i As Integer

     'Establish a base unit as one inch
     unit = 1
     Set selObj = ActiveWindow.Selection
     'If the selection is empty, there's nothing to do
     'Otherwise, move each object in the selection by the value of
     'unit
     For i = 1 To selObj.Count
            Set shpObj = selObj(i)
            Debug.Print "Nudging " ; shpObj.Name; " _
                   ("; shpObj.NameID; ")"
            If (Not shpObj.OneD) Then
                   shpObj.Cells("PinX").ResultIU = (dx * unit) + _
                          shpObj.Cells("PinX").ResultIU
                   shpObj.Cells("PinY").ResultIU = (dy * unit) + _
                          shpObj.Cells("PinY").ResultIU
            Else
                   shpObj.Cells("BeginX").ResultIU = (dx * unit) + _
                          shpObj.Cells("BeginX").ResultIU
                   shpObj.Cells("BeginY").ResultIU = (dy * unit) + _
                          shpObj.Cells("BeginY").ResultIU
                   shpObj.Cells("EndX").ResultIU = (dx * unit) + _
                          shpObj.Cells("EndX").ResultIU
                   shpObj.Cells("EndY").ResultIU = (dy * unit) + _
                          shpObj.Cells("EndY").ResultIU
            EndIf
     Next i
     Exit Sub
lblErr:
End Sub
```

Working with Sections and Rows

You can change certain characteristics of a shape, style, page, master, or document by adding and deleting sections and rows. You can also iterate through sections or rows to perform the same operation on each item, such as listing all of a shape's Geometry formulas.

Adding Sections and Rows

In many cases, you'll want to add an entire section to a shape. For example, you might add a Geometry section to create a shape with multiple paths, or a Scratch section to serve as a working area for building complex formulas. Before you can use a newly added section, you need to add at least one row to the section. Depending on the kind of row you add, you might also need to set the formulas of cells in the row.

To add a section, use the **AddSection** method of a **Shape** object. For example, to add a Scratch section to a shape:

```
shpObj.AddSection visSectionScratch
```

To add a row to a section, use the **AddRow** method and specify the section, row, and row tag. When you add a row to a Geometry section, the row tag indicates the type of row to add—for example, **visTagLineTo** indicates a LineTo row. The row tag argument is primarily used to add rows to the Geometry section. For most other sections, use a row tag of zero (0) as a placeholder. For example, to add a row to a Scratch section:

```
shpObj.AddRow visSectionScratch, visRowScratch + 0, 0
```

Row tag constants are defined in the Visio type library in **VisRowTags**.

Row tags and the rows they represent in a Geometry section

Row tag	Represents this row in Geometry section
visTagComponent	First row. Determines display properties of the component defined by the Geometry section.
visTagMoveTo	MoveTo row (X and Y cells in a Start row)
visTagLineTo	LineTo row
visTagArcTo	ArcTo row
visTagEllipticalArcTo	EllipticalArcTo row
visTagSplineBeg	SplineStart row
visTagSplineSpan	SplineKnot row
visTagEllipse	Ellipse row

Row tags and the rows they represent in a Geometry section *(continued)*

Row tag	Represents this row in Geometry section
visTagInfiniteLine	InfiniteLine row
visTagPolylineTo	PolylineTo row
visTagNURBSTo	NURBSTo row

A shape can have only one of each kind of section except for Geometry. If a shape already has a particular section and you attempt to add it, you'll get an error. You can use the **SectionExists** property to find out whether it has a section, and then add one if necessary.

> **Note** You cannot add or delete rows from **visSectionCharacter**, **visSectionParagraph**, **visSectionTextField**, or **visSectionTab**.

Adding a Geometry Section to a Shape: an Example

A basic shape in a Visio drawing consists of zero or more components, or paths. Each path is a sequence of connected segments. In most shapes, a segment is either a line segment or an arc segment, which can be an elliptical arc. Each path is represented by a Geometry section, and each segment is represented by a row in a Geometry section.

To add a Geometry section to a shape, use the **AddSection** method with **visSectionFirstComponent** to insert the section before existing Geometry sections, or **visSectionLastComponent** to append the section after existing Geometry sections. For example, to add a Geometry section after existing Geometry sections:

```
shpObj.AddSection visSectionLastComponent
```

After adding a Geometry section, you must add at least two rows (rows are not added automatically to a section added from a program). Use the **AddRow** method with the following row tags:

- **visTagComponent** determines display properties of the component defined by the Geometry section. This should be the first row of every Geometry section.
- **visTagMoveTo**, **visTagEllipse**, or **visTagInfiniteLine** determines the first vertex, or starting point, of the component. This should be the second row of every Geometry section. A **visTagEllipse** or

visTagInfiniteLine row will also be the final row because ellipses and infinite lines are represented by single-row sections.

You can add additional vertex rows using the row tags **visTagLineTo**, **visTagArcTo**, **visTagEllipticalArcTo**, **visTagMoveTo**, **visTagPolylineTo**, or **visTagNURBSTo**. Each vertex row defines the local coordinates of a vertex and the type of segment that connects the vertex with the previous one.

You can add spline rows using the row tags **visTagSplineBeg** and **visTagSplineSpan**. Precede the spline start row (**visTagSplineBeg**) with a start row (**visTagMoveTo**) or a vertex row, and use **visTagSplineSpan** to add spline knot rows.

The following procedure inserts a Geometry section before other existing Geometry sections of a shape. It adds the component row, the MoveTo row, and four LineTo rows. (These are the rows you typically need to define a straight line.) It then sets cell formulas in each row to draw the line diagonally across the shape's width-height box.

```
Sub AddGeometry ()
    Dim shpObj As Visio.Shape
    Dim iSection As Integer
    Dim i As Integer

    'Set an error handler to catch the error if no shape is selected
    On Error GoTo errNoShp
    Set shpObj = ActiveWindow.Selection(1)
    On Error GoTo 0

    iSection = shpObj.AddSection(visSectionFirstComponent)
    shpObj.AddRow iSection, visRowFirst + 0, visTagComponent
    shpObj.AddRow iSection, visRowVertex + 0, visTagMoveTo
    For i = 1 To 4
           shpObj.AddRow iSection, visRowVertex + i, visTagLineTo
    Next i
    shpObj.CellsSRC(iSection, visRowVertex + 0, visX).Formula = _
           "Width * 0.25"
    shpObj.CellsSRC(iSection, visRowVertex + 0, visY).Formula = _
           "Height * 0.5"
    shpObj.CellsSRC(iSection, visRowVertex + 1, visX).Formula = _
           "Width * 0.5"
    shpObj.CellsSRC(iSection, visRowVertex + 1, visY).Formula = _
           "Height * 0.25"
    shpObj.CellsSRC(iSection, visRowVertex + 2, visX).Formula = _
           "Width * 0.75"
    shpObj.CellsSRC(iSection, visRowVertex + 2, visY).Formula = _
           "Height * 0.5"
```

```
    shpObj.CellsSRC(iSection, visRowVertex + 3, visX).Formula = _
          "Width * 0.5"
    shpObj.CellsSRC(iSection, visRowVertex + 3, visY).Formula = _
          "Height * 0.75"
    shpObj.CellsSRC(iSection, visRowVertex + 4, visX).Formula = _
          "Geometry1.X1"
    shpObj.CellsSRC(iSection, visRowVertex + 4, visY).Formula =
          "Geometry1.Y1"
    'Exit the procedure bypassing the error handler
    Exit Sub
errNoShp:
    MsgBox "Please select a shape then try again.", vbOKOnly, _
          DVS_TITLE
End Sub
```

The following illustration shows the shape before and after inserting the Geometry section.

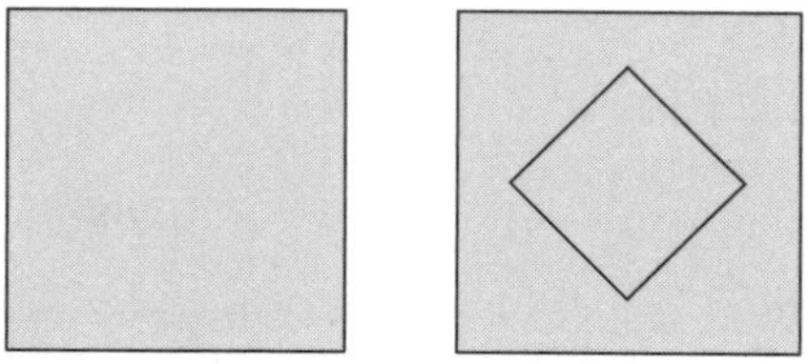

Figure 17-2 Inserting a Geometry section in a shape.

Notice that **visRowVertex** with no offset, or with an offset of zero (0), refers to the MoveTo row. When adding vertex rows, always add an offset of 1 or more to **visRowVertex** so you don't inadvertently replace the MoveTo row, which can cause the shape to behave in unexpected ways. You can insert additional MoveTo rows in a single Geometry section to create a gap. For details about working with formulas in the Geometry section, see Chapter 5, Controlling *Shape Geometry with Formulas* or search for "Geometry section" in the Microsoft Visio Developer Reference (on the **Help** menu, click **Developer Reference**).

Deleting Sections and Rows

Deleting a section automatically deletes all of its rows and cells. You can delete any section except **visSectionObj**, although you can delete rows in that section. To delete a section, use the **DeleteSection** method of a **Shape** object. For example, the following statement deletes the Scratch section of a shape:

```
shpObj.DeleteSection visSectionScratch
```

Deleting a nonexistent section does not cause an error.

You can also delete a row from a section. For example, you can remove a vertex from a shape by deleting the row that defines the vertex from the shape's Geometry section. The following statement deletes the last vertex of a rectangle:

```
shpObj.DeleteRow visSectionFirstComponent + 0, visRowVertex + 3
```

> **Note** You cannot add or delete rows from **visSectionCharacter**, **visSectionParagraph**, **visSectionTextField**, or **visSectionTab**.

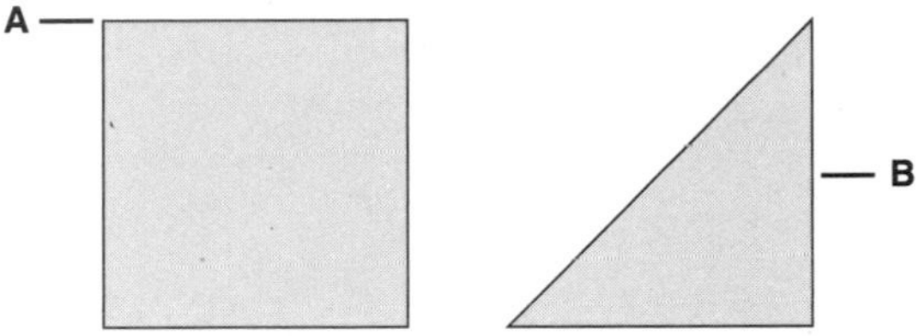

Figure 17-3 Deleting a vertex row. (**A**) This vertex is represented by **visRowVertex** + 3. (**B**) After deleting the vertex row, the shape changes in appearance.

Changing the Type of a Segment

You can define a segment as a line, arc, elliptical arc, spline, ellipse, infinite line, polyline, NURBS (nonuniform rational B-spline), or MoveTo row by setting the type of row or rows that represent the segment. From a program, you can do this by setting the **RowType** property of a **Shape** object.

For example, the following statement converts the first segment of a shape to a line segment.

```
shpObj.RowType(visSectionFirstComponent + 0, visRowVertex + 1) = _
    visTagLineTo
```

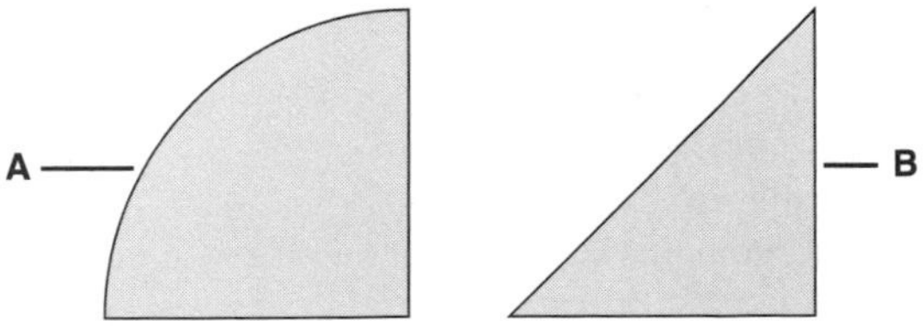

Figure 17-4 Changing the row type of a vertex row. (**A**) This arc segment is represented by **visRowVertex** + 1. (**B**) After the row type is changed, the shape changes in appearance.

Iterating through a Collection of Sections and Rows: an Example

You can perform the same operation on multiple sections or rows by iterating through them, using the following **Shape** object properties to limit the iteration loop:

- **GeometryCount** represents the number of Geometry sections for a shape.
- **RowCount** represents the number of rows in a section.
- **RowsCellCount** represents the number of cells in a row.

The following example iterates through the rows and cells in a shape's Geometry section and uses the **CellsSRC** property to retrieve each cell. It then displays each cell's formula in a listbox on a user form.

```
'This example assumes the active
'page contains a shape
Sub IterateGeometry ()
    'Shape object
    Dim shpObj As Visio.Shape
    'Section number for accessing Geometry section
    Dim curGeomSect As Integer
    'Loop variable for Geometry sections
    Dim curGeomSectIndx As Integer
    'Number of rows in section
    Dim nRows As Integer
    'Number of cells in row
    Dim nCells As Integer
    'Current row number (0 based)
    Dim curRow As Integer
    'Current cell index (0 based)
    Dim curCell As Integer
    'Number of Geometry sections in shape
    Dim nSects As Integer

    Set shpObj = ActivePage.Shapes(1)
    UserForm1.ListBox1.Clear
    nSects = shpObj.GeometryCount
    For curGeomSectIndx = 0 To nSects - 1
        curGeomSect = visSectionFirstComponent + curGeomSectIndx
        nRows = shpObj.RowCount(curGeomSect)
        For curRow = 0 To (nRows - 1)
            nCells = shpObj.RowsCellCount(curGeomSect, curRow)
            For curCell = 0 To (nCells - 1)
                UserForm1.ListBox1.AddItem _
                    shpObj.CellsSRC(curGeomSect, curRow, _
                        curCell).LocalName & _
```

```
                    ": " & shpObj.CellsSRC(curGeomSect, _
                        curRow, curCell).Formula
            Next curCell
            Next curRow
    Next curGeomSectIndx
    UserForm1.Show
End Sub
```

For a list of logical position constants, see Appendix B, *ShapeSheet Section, Row, and Cell Indices.*

Working with Inherited Data

A shape (that is, an instance of a master) inherits much of its data from its master and from styles. Rather than make a local copy of every formula for a shape, an instance of a master inherits formulas from the master and from the styles applied to it. This behavior has two benefits: It allows changes to the master's formulas or the style definition to be propagated to all instances, and it results in smaller Microsoft Visio files because inherited formulas are stored once in the master, not once in each instance.

No local copy of the shape's data exists until you change some part of its data. Everything you do when adding, modifying, or deleting shape data affects the local formulas for the shape, not the master. If the data your program is trying to work with doesn't exist locally—that is, if the shape inherits the data from a master or style—Microsoft Visio first creates a local copy of the data, and then performs the requested action. Once data exists locally, inheritance for that data is severed, and changes to the data in the master no longer affect the shape's local data.

Be aware when you are writing programs that a shape might not have a local copy of all of the data that appears in its ShapeSheet window or that you can access from a program. The shape might behave as if the data were local, but some data might be local and other data might be inherited from a master or a style.

For example, if a shape is an instance of a master that has connection points, the shape inherits the master's connection points. The shape has the same connection point behavior as the master and displays the inherited Connection Points section in its ShapeSheet window. However, the shape doesn't have a local copy of the Connection Points data—instead, it inherits that data from the master. If you attempt to delete this shape's Connection Points section, the Connection Points data doesn't change because there is no local copy to delete, and the shape continues to inherit its Connection Points data from the master.

Overriding or restoring inheritance

To override inheritance for an entire section, either delete each row in the section, or delete the entire section and add a new, empty section of the same type. In the latter case, you delete the section to make sure no local copy already exists, which would cause an error if you attempted to add the section.

To restore an inherited section, delete the local copy. The shape inherits that section again from the master or style.

> **Note** In earlier versions of Microsoft Visio, Geometry formulas were always local. Beginning in Visio 2000, shapes inherit their geometry formulas from the master, which results in smaller and faster shapes. Any local overrides to these geometry formulas will cause the shape to get a local copy and increase in size. For this reason, you might want to consider making broad changes to the master.

18

Drawing with Automation

Automating Drawing with Masters 364

Placing Shapes in a Drawing 367

Working with Selected Shapes 375

Background Pages 378

Layers 381

No matter what kind of drawing you create, you'll typically follow certain steps in your program. You'll add shapes to the drawing, often by dropping masters from a stencil. You'll need to determine where to place the shapes, and you may calculate their positions using data gathered from another source.

This chapter explains basic techniques for programmatically creating drawings, including working with shapes, background pages, and layers. If your drawings will include connected shapes, see Chapter 19, *Automating Connections in a Visio Solution*. For details about associating data with the shapes in your drawing, see Chapter 20, *Integrating Data with a Visio Solution*.

Automating Drawing with Masters

The most convenient means of creating shapes from a program is to drop masters from a stencil. A master is essentially ready to use in a drawing, requiring very little additional processing by your program. You can use masters from a stencil you develop and provide with your program or from any of the stencils provided with Microsoft Visio.

To drop a master on a page

1. Create a **Document** object that represents the stencil containing the master you want.
2. Create a **Master** object that represents that master.
3. Create a **Page** object that represents the drawing page where you want to drop the shape and drop the master onto the drawing page.

Getting the Stencil

You can get a reference to any stencil that is already open by retrieving it from the **Documents** collection of the **Application** object. For example:

```
Set stnObj = Documents("Basic Shapes.vss")
```

The example uses the variable name *stnObj* rather than *docObj* to distinguish among the stencil and other kinds of files. This naming convention can prevent confusion later.

As with any file-related operation, it's prudent to make sure the stencil is actually available before attempting to use it. The **Set** statement above would return an error if Basic Shapes.vss was not open. To check for this, use the following code:

```
'If the file is not open, open it
On Error Resume Next
'Get a reference to the Stencil object
Set stnObj = Documents("Basic Shapes.vss")
'The stencil was not open, we need to open it
If stnObj = Nothing Then
    'OpenEx could not open the file
    On Error Go To errorhandler
    Set stnObj = Documents.OpenEx ("Basic Shapes.vss",visOpenRO)
End If
```

Typically a stencil is opened as a read-only file to protect it from changes, but it's always possible for the user to open it as an original and alter its workspace or move or delete a file, which could affect which stencils are opened when the template is used.

Getting the Master

To get a reference to a master, you need to get the **Masters** collection of a stencil file that contains the master you want. A **Document** object has a **Masters** property that returns the **Masters** collection for a document's stencil. You can refer to a **Master** object by its name or by its index within the **Masters** collection. For example:

```
Set mastObj = stnObj.Masters("Star 5")
```

A common pitfall in this process is to get the **Masters** collection of the drawing file rather than that of the stencil file. Every Visio document has a stencil, which means that every **Document** object has a **Masters** collection. However, the **Masters** collection of a drawing file contains only the masters that have already been dropped onto the drawing; the **Masters** collection of a new document is usually empty. In either of these cases, this particular **Masters** collection often won't contain the master you're trying to get. If your program fails to get a **Master** object, make sure you're getting it from the stencil file and not the drawing file.

Dropping the Master on the Page

To drop a master on the page, you first need to get the **Page** object that represents the drawing page, and then use the **Drop** method of the **Page** object. The **Drop** method is equivalent to dragging and dropping a shape with the mouse.

Drop takes three arguments: a reference to an object and a pair of coordinates. If the object being passed to the **Drop** method is a master, the coordinates indicate where to position the object's pin on the drawing page. If the object being passed is an instance of a master, the pair of coordinates indicate the center of the object's width-height box.

```
Set pagObj = ThisDocument.Pages(1)
Set shpObj = pagObj.Drop(mastObj, 4.25, 5.5)
```

Coordinates are measured from the lower-left corner of the page. In this example, 4.25, 5.5 positions the shape's pin in the center of an 8½-in. by 11-in. drawing page in an unscaled drawing. (In a scaled drawing, you specify coordinates in drawing units expressed in inches. For example, if the drawing scale is 1 in. = 1 ft., you would specify the coordinates 51, 66 to drop the shape in the center of the page.) For details about shape coordinates, see Chapter 2, *Creating Visio Shapes*.

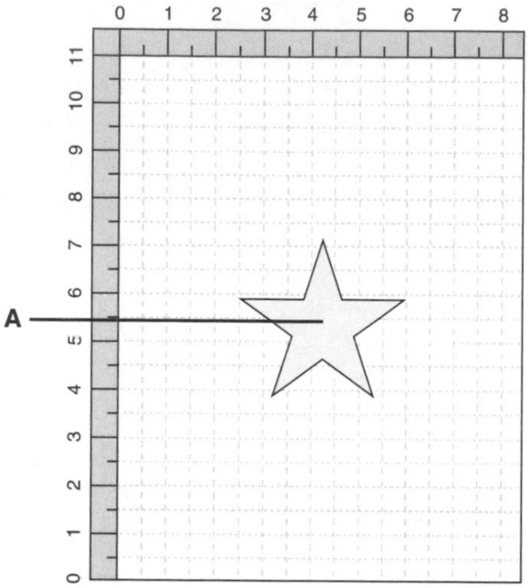

Figure 18-1 The shape's pin is positioned at the coordinates 4.25, 5.5 (**A**) specified with the **Drop** method.

For simplicity's sake, this example drops a single shape in the exact center of the drawing page, and uses constants to indicate its position. However, determining where to place shapes in a real-world drawing can be a challenge, especially in a connected diagram with more than a few shapes. For an example of one approach, see *Placing Shapes in a Drawing* later in this chapter.

In addition to dropping masters onto a drawing page, you can use the **Drop** method to:

- Make a shape from an existing shape.
- Add a shape to a group.
- Create a master on the fly by dropping a shape into a stencil (the stencil file must be open as **Original**, not **Read only**).
- Modify a master by dropping an object into an open master.

To drop multiple shapes, use the **DropMany** method, which is equivalent to dragging and dropping multiple shapes with the mouse.

> **Note** When a program draws or drops a shape in a scaled drawing, it must convert the coordinates from drawing measurements to inches. For example, the following statement draws a rectangle from 3 ft 4 ft to 5 ft, 6 ft on a drawing scaled in inches:
>
> ```
> PagObj.DrawRectangle(36, 48, 60, 72)
> ```

Placing Shapes in a Drawing

Determining where to place shapes can be one of the more challenging tasks for a program that creates Microsoft Visio drawings, especially in connected diagrams or other kinds of drawings with complex relationships between shapes. The ultimate goal is the same: You'll need to calculate a pair of page coordinates for each shape you place on the drawing page. The approach you take will depend on the kind of drawing you're trying to create and the data on which the drawing is based.

In addition, Visio provides automatic layout capabilities that control how the shapes and connectors between shapes in your drawing interact. You can view the default layout settings in the Page Layout and Shape Layout sections in a ShapeSheet window. You can customize these settings in your program by working with the formulas in these sections. For details about shapes and automatic layout, see *Designing Shapes for Automatic Layout* in Chapter 11, *Arranging Shapes in Drawings*. For details about the Page Layout and Shape Layout sections, see the Microsoft Visio Developer Reference (on the **Help** menu, click **Developer Reference**).

Placing Shapes Using Automation: an Example

The following **CreateDrawing** procedure provides an example of placing shapes in a simple network diagram. The example reads data from a two-dimensional array—the first element in the array describes the name of a master in the Basic Network Shapes 3D stencil, and the second element of the array is a shape label. **CreateDrawing** places a hub in the middle of the page, and then places the components in a circle around the hub.

This example demonstrates several techniques for placing shapes, including the following:

- To place the hub in the middle of the page, the program uses the values in the **PageHeight** and **PageWidth** cells of the page sheet.
- To place shapes evenly around the hub, the variable *dblDegreeInc* was calculated based on the number of elements in the array. This variable was then used to identify the *x*- and *y*-coordinates for dropping the shape.

```
Public Sub CreateDrawing(arrNetData As String)
    Dim shpObjHUB As Visio.Shape
    Dim shpObjNodes As Visio.Shape
    Dim mstObj As Visio.Master
    Dim stnObj As Visio.Document
    Dim dblX, dblY As Double
    Dim dblDegreeInc As Double
    Dim dblRad As Double
    Dim dblPageWidth, dblPageHeight As Double
    Dim i As Integer
    Const PI = 3.1415
    Const CircleRadius = 2

    'Divide the circle by the number of objects in the array so they
    'are spaced evenly
    dblDegreeInc = 360 / UBound(arrNetData)
    'Read the PageWidth and PageHeight properties
    dblPageWidth = ActivePage.PageSheet.Cells("PageWidth").ResultIU
    dblPageHeight = ActivePage.PageSheet.Cells("PageHeight").ResultIU
    'Open the Basic Network Shapes 3D stencil
    Set stnObj = Application.Documents.OpenEx("Basic Network Shapes _
          3D.vss", visOpenDocked)
    'Process the hub shape
    Set mstObj = stnObj.Masters(arrNetData(0, 0))
    Set shpObjHUB = ActivePage.Drop(mstObj, dblPageWidth / 2, _
          dblPageHeight / 2)
    'Set the text of the hub shape
    shpObjHUB.Text = arrNetData(0, 1)
    'Process the nodes
    For i = 1 To UBound(arrNetData)
          Set mstObj = stnObj.Masters(arrNetData(i, 0))
          'Determine X, Y location for placement (in circle
          'around hub)
          dblRad = (dblDegreeInc * i) * PI / 180
          dblX = CircleRadius * Cos(dblRad) + (dblPageWidth / 2)
          dblY = CircleRadius * Sin(dblRad) + (dblPageHeight / 2)
          'Add shape to drawing in proper location
          Set shpobj = ActivePage.Drop(mstObj, dblX, dblY)
          'Set shape text
          shpobj.Text = arrNetData(i, 1)
    Next
End Sub
```

Notice the use of page sheet properties to get information about positioning on the page. Shapes are spaced evenly around the hub by using the *dblDegreeInc* variable to calculate the *x*- and *y*-coordinates based on the number of elements in the array.

> **Note** To calculate page coordinates that are visible in the drawing window, use the **GetViewRect** method of a **Window** object. You can use these coordinates to place shapes in the middle of a window. For details, see the **GetViewRect** method in the Microsoft Visio Developer Reference (on the **Help** menu, click **Developer Reference**).

Placing Shapes in Relation to Other Shapes

If you want to find shapes based on whether they are located on or near other shapes, or modify a shape's behavior relative to another shape, you can use these properties: **SpatialRelation**, **SpatialNeighbors**, **SpatialSearch**, **DistanceFrom**, **DistanceFromPoint**, and **HitTest**.

You can use these properties to create shapes that change their settings based on the other shapes they are dropped on or near. For example, in an office layout solution, you could create smart furniture shapes such as a cabinet shape that attaches itself to a wall when dropped next to it, and takes on the style of a cabinet that is located nearby. Or, you can prevent a user from placing a shape near or on certain other shapes, such as not allowing a user to drop a fire extinguisher near any type of heat source in a building layout.

Properties or methods that determine spatial relationships between shapes

Property or method	Description
SpatialRelation property	Returns an integer that represents the spatial relationship of one shape to another shape. Both shapes must be on the same page or in the same master. Use this property to determine whether one shape contains, is contained by, overlaps, or touches another shape.

Properties or methods that determine spatial relationships between shapes *(continued)*

Property or method	Description
SpatialNeighbors property	Returns a **Selection** object that represents the shapes that meet certain criteria in relation to a specified shape. Use this property to find a set of shapes that contain, are contained by, overlap, or touch a specific shape.
SpatialSearch property	Returns a **Selection** object whose shapes meet certain relationship criteria in relation to a point that is expressed in the coordinate space of a page, master, or group. Use this property to find a set of shapes that contain, are contained by, overlap, or touch a specific coordinate space.
DistanceFrom property	Returns the distance from one shape to another. Both shapes must be on the same page or in the same master. Use this property to determine if one shape is within a required distance of another shape.
DistanceFromPoint property	Returns the distance from a shape to a point. Use this property to determine if a coordinate on a shape is within a required distance of a point.
HitTest property	Determines if a given *x,y* position hits outside, inside, or on the boundary of a shape. Use this property to check one shape against criteria for a limited set of other shapes.

Using the SpatialRelation property: an example

The **SpatialRelation** property of a **Shape** object returns the relationship between the calling shape and another shape (passed as an argument with the property).

The Microsoft Visual Basic for Applications (VBA) code in the following example assumes the user can drop any shape from the document stencil onto a page with existing shapes. The text of each shape on the page changes to display the relationship between the dropped shape and each shape in the drawing.

```
sPrivate Sub Document_ShapeAdded(ByVal Shape As IVShape)
    Dim ShapeOnPage As Shape
    Dim dblTolerance As Integer
    Dim iSpatialRelation As VisSpatialRelationCodes
    Dim strSpatialRelation As String

    On Error GoTo errHandler

    'Try setting different tolerance values
    dblTolerance = 0.25

    For Each ShapeOnPage In ActivePage.Shapes
        If Shape = ShapeOnPage Then
            'The shape being tested is the shape that was added
            'Display the shape name
            Shape.Text = Shape.Name
        ElseIf ShapeOnPage.Name <> "Abstract" Then
            'Get the relation between the added shape, and the
            'iterated shape on the page
            iSpatialRelation = Shape.SpatialRelation(ShapeOnPage, _
                dblTolerance, 0)
            'Convert return code to text
            Select Case iSpatialRelation
                Case VisSpatialRelationCodes.visSpatialContain _
                        strSpatialRelation = "Contains"
                Case VisSpatialRelationCodes.visSpatialContainedIn _
                    strSpatialRelation = "is Contained in"
                Case VisSpatialRelationCodes.visSpatialOverlap _
                    strSpatialRelation = "overlaps"
                Case VisSpatialRelationCodes.visSpatialTouching _
                    strSpatialRelation = "is touching"
                Case Else
                    strSpatialRelation = "has no relation with"
            End Select
            'Put relation on shape
            ShapeOnPage.Text = Shape.Name & " " & _
                strSpatialRelation & " " & ShapeOnPage.Name
            End If
        Next
        errHandler:

    End Sub
```

Using the SpatialNeighbors property: an example

You can use the **SpatialNeighbors** property of a **Shape** object in your program to determine the relationship between the shape of interest and the rest of the shapes on the page. The property returns the set of shapes (as a **Selection** object) that meet the criteria set by the arguments passed with the property. For details about using the **Selection** object, see *Working with Selected Shapes* later in this chapter.

The VBA code in this example assumes the user will drop a shape within the boundaries of a square, circle, or both, already provided on the drawing page. The text of the dropped shape displays the results of the property being called.

```
Private Sub Document_ShapeAdded(ByVal Shape As IVShape)
    Dim ShapeOnPage As Shape
    Dim dblTolerance As Integer
    Dim ReturnedSelection As Selection
    Dim strSpatialRelation As String
    Dim iSpatialRelation As VisSpatialRelationCodes

    On Error GoTo errHandler

    strSpatialRelation = ""

    'Try setting different tolerance values
    dblTolerance = 0#

    'Try setting different spatial relationships
    iSpatialRelation = visSpatialContainedIn

    Const ISRELATED = " is contained by "
    Const ISNOTRELATED = " is not contained."

    'Get the set of spatially related shapes
    'that meet the criteria set by the parameters
    Set ReturnedSelection = _
        Shape.SpatialNeighbors(iSpatialRelation, dblTolerance, 0)

    'Evaluate the results
    If ReturnedSelection.Count = 0 Then
        'No shapes met the criteria set by the
        'parameters of the method
        strSpatialRelation = Shape.Name & ISNOTRELATED
    Else
        'Build the positive result string
            For Each ShapeOnPage In ReturnedSelection
                strSpatialRelation = strSpatialRelation & Shape.Name _
                    & ISRELATED & ShapeOnPage.Name & Chr$(10)
```

```
        Next
    End If

    'Put the results on the added shape
    Shape.Text = strSpatialRelation

    errHandler:

End Sub
```

Using the DistanceFrom and DistanceFromPoint properties: an example

The VBA code in this example demonstrates the **DistanceFrom** and **DistanceFromPoint** properties of a **Shape** object. These properties are used to determine the distance from the calling shape, and a shape passed as an argument with the property. Use **DistanceFromPoint** to determine the distance from a specific point on the shape.

The VBA code in this example expects the user to drop various shapes onto the page at various distances from a base shape. A message box appears to inform the user if the dropped shapes are too close to the base shape. The minimum acceptable distance is defined by *dblMinimumDistance*.

To test this example, paste the following code in the **ThisDocument** code window of a new drawing, save the drawing and close it, reopen the drawing, and then drop shapes onto the page.

```
Public objBaseShape As Visio.Shape

Public Function MeetsClearanceRequirements(BaseShape As Shape, _
    ShapeToCheck As Shape, dblMinimumDistance As Double) As Boolean
    Dim bRetVal As Boolean
    On Error GoTo errHandler
    'Check distance from specific point
    'Use the DistanceFromPoint property
    dblDistance = _
          ShapeToCheck.DistanceFromPoint(BaseShape.Cells("PinX"), _
                BaseShape.Cells("PinY"), 0)
    'To check distance from closest points use DistanceFrom property:
    'dblDistance = ShapeToCheck.DistanceFrom(BaseShape,0)
    If dblDistance < dblMinimumDistance Then
          bRetVal = False
    Else
          bRetVal = True
    End If
```

```
        MeetsClearanceRequirements = bRetVal
        Exit Function

        errHandler:
                bRetVal = False
End Function

Private Sub Document_DocumentOpened(ByVal doc As IVDocument)
        'Draw a rectangle on the page; this will be the
        'shape that all added shapes are compared to
        Set objBaseShape = ActivePage.DrawRectangle(3, 7, 4, 6)
End Sub

Private Sub Document_ShapeAdded(ByVal Shape As IVShape)
        Dim strMsg As String
        Dim dblMinimumDistance As Double

dblMinimumDistance = 2

        'Because the objBaseShape is set when the document is opened,
        'attempt to compare shapes on different pages
        If objBaseShape.Parent = Shape.Parent And (objBaseShape <> _
                Shape) Then
                If MeetsClearanceRequirements(objBaseShape, _
                        Shape, dblMinimumDistance) Then _
                        strMsg = "Distance requirements met"
                Else
                        strMsg = "Too close"
                End If
                'Display message
                MsgBox strMsg
        Else
                'Do nothing, shapes are on a different page, or
                'BaseShape = Added Shape
        End If
End Sub
```

Working with Selected Shapes

You can access a shape's properties and methods from a program whether the shape is selected or not. You can also create a **Selection** object to work with multiple shapes. A **Selection** object is similar to a **Shapes** collection in that it represents a set of **Shape** objects and has an **Item** and a **Count** property. Unlike a **Shapes** collection, a **Selection** object represents only shapes that are selected.

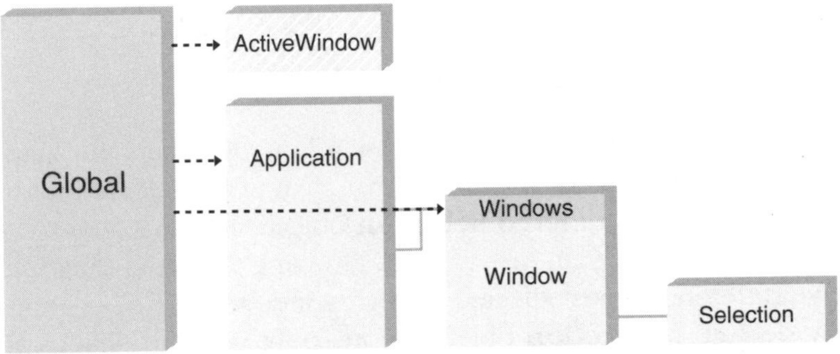

Figure 18-2 **Selection** object and related objects higher in the Visio object model.

You can get a **Selection** object that represents shapes that are selected in a window, or create a **Selection** object that represents shapes you specify from any **Shapes** collection. The order of items in a **Selection** object follows the order in which the items were selected. The first item returned is the first shape selected.

Getting Shapes that are Selected in a Window

To work with shapes the user has selected in a window, get the **Selection** property of that **Window** object.

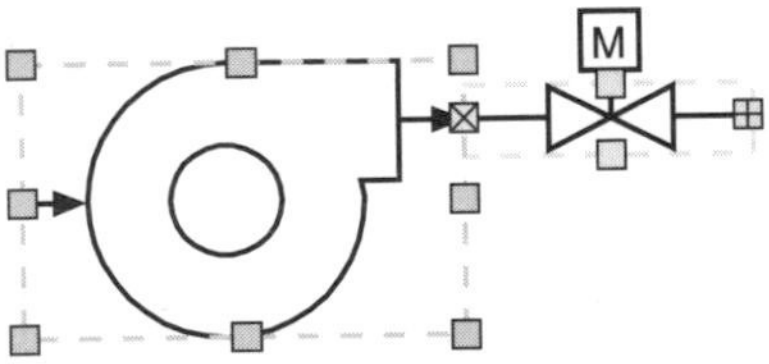

Figure 18-3 **Window.Selection** represents shapes selected in a drawing window.

The following example gets the **Selection** object of the active window:

```
selectObj = ActiveWindow.Selection
```

If all of the shapes on a page are selected, the **Selection** object of the window and the **Shapes** collection of the page are the same set of shapes. If nothing is selected, the **Selection** object is empty and its **Count** property returns zero (0). If your program requires a selected shape, you might check the **Selection** property of the active window to make sure it contains at least one object, such as in the following example:

```
Set selectObj = ActiveWindow.Selection
If selectObj.Count = 0 Then
    MsgBox "You must select a shape first."
Else
    'Continue processing
End If
```

A **Selection** object retrieved from a window represents the shapes selected in the window. Subsequent operations that change the selection in the window have no effect on the retrieved **Selection** object.

If you have more than one window showing the same drawing page, you can have different shapes selected in each window.

By default, a **Selection** object reports only selected shapes and groups; shapes subselected within a group are not included. To report subselected shapes (a shape that is a child of a group) or a group that is a parent of a subselected shape, you can modify the default settings of a **Selection** object's **IterationMode** property. For details about the **Selection** object and its properties, see the Microsoft Visio Developer Reference (on the **Help** menu, click **Developer Reference**).

Adding and Removing Shapes in Selections

To add an item to a selection, use the **Selection** object's **Select** method and specify the **Shape** object to select. You can add a shape to a selection or remove it from the selection of a shape without affecting the other selected shapes.

The constants **visSelect** and **visDeselect**, defined in the Visio type library, control the action that is performed. For example, the following statement adds a shape to those already in the **Selection** object:

```
selObj.Select shpObj,visSelect
```

The following statement removes a shape from a selection:

```
selObj.Select shpObj,visDeselect
```

The following statement makes a selection include exactly one shape:

```
selObj.Select shpObj, visSelect + visDeselectAll
```

Selecting and Deselecting Shapes in a Window

To select a shape in a window from a program, use the **Select** method of a **Window** object and specify the **Shape** object to select. You can add a shape to a selection or remove a shape from a selection without affecting the other selected shapes. For example, the following statement adds a shape to those already selected in a drawing window:

```
winObj.Select shpObj,visSelect
```

To select all the shapes on a drawing page, use the **Window** object's **SelectAll** method; to deselect all selected shapes, use the **DeselectAll** method. If you get a **Selection** object after using **SelectAll**, the new **Selection** object includes a **Shape** object for each shape on the drawing page displayed in that window. If you get a **Selection** object after using **DeselectAll**, the new **Selection** object is empty.

Performing Operations on Selected Shapes

After you have a **Selection** object, you can perform operations on the selected shapes, similar to the actions you can perform in a drawing window.

For example, you can use the **Copy**, **Cut**, **Delete**, or **Duplicate** method of a **Window** or **Selection** object to copy, cut, delete, or duplicate selected shapes:

```
selectObj.Delete
```

Or you can perform Boolean operations such as union, combine, and fragment using the **Union**, **Combine**, and **Fragment** methods. These methods correspond to the **Union**, **Combine**, and **Fragment** commands in Visio, which create one or more new shapes that replace the selected shapes:

```
selectObj.Union
```

Before using **Union**, **Combine**, or **Fragment**, make sure that only the shapes you want to affect are selected. These methods delete the original shapes, so any smart formulas in the original shapes are lost and the **Selection** object that represents the shapes is no longer current.

For details about what you can do with a **Selection** object as well as any of the objects, properties, or methods discussed here, see the Microsoft Visio Developer Reference (on the **Help** menu, click **Developer Reference**).

Determining a Selection's Scope

To find out whether a **Selection** object gets its shapes from a **Page** object, a **Master** object, or a **Shape** object (group), check the **Selection object's ContainingPage**, **ContainingMaster**, and **ContainingShape** properties.

- If the shapes are on a page, the **ContainingPage** property returns that **Page** object, and **ContainingMaster** returns **Nothing**.
- If the shapes are in a master, the **ContainingMaster** property returns that **Master** object, and **ContainingPage** returns **Nothing**.
- If the shapes are in a group, the **ContainingShape** property returns a **Shape** object that represents the group. Otherwise, this property returns a **Shape** object that represents the page sheet of the master or page that contains the shapes.

Background Pages

A Microsoft Visio document can contain more than one page. Each page of a document may contain a unique drawing, and some pages can serve as backgrounds to other pages.

You can create multiple-page documents from a program by adding pages and assigning backgrounds to them. You can also change page settings, such as the drawing scale and page width and height.

Creating and Assigning Background Pages

When you want the same arrangement of shapes to appear in more than one drawing, you can place the shapes on a background page. For example, if your program creates drawings on multiple pages, you might create a background page with header and footer shapes, or title block and border shapes.

The same background page can be assigned to any number of foreground pages. And although a foreground page can have only one background page, a background page can have its own background page, so it's possible to construct a drawing of many background pages. To create a background page, add a page to the drawing and set its **Background** property to **True**. For example:

```
backPagObj.Background = True
```

To assign the background page to another page so that the background's shapes appear in the drawing window when that page is displayed, set the foreground page's **BackPage** property to the name of the background page. For example:

```
pagObj.BackPage = "Floor Plan"
```

Iterating through the Pages Collection: an Example

The items in a **Pages** collection are indexed starting with foreground pages in the order they are listed in the **Reorder Pages** dialog box, followed by background pages in arbitrary order. (To view the **Reorder Pages** dialog box, right-click any page tab in the drawing window, and then click **Reorder Pages**.)

The following example iterates through the **Pages** collection of the active document and lists the names of all foreground pages in a listbox on a user form.

```
Sub IteratePages ()
    Dim pagsObj As Visio.Pages
    Dim pagObj As Visio.Page

    Set pagsObj = ThisDocument.Pages
    UserForm1.ListBox1.Clear
    For Each pagObj In pagsObj
        If pagObj.Background = False Then
            UserForm1.ListBox1.AddItem pagObj.Name
        End If
    Next
    UserForm1.Show
End Sub
```

Setting up Pages and Backgrounds: an Example

The **CreateAndAssignBackground** procedure creates one foreground page and one background page and then assigns the new background page to the new foreground page.

```
'Paste CreateAndAssignBackground in the ThisDocument
'code window and then run the procedure

Public Sub CreateAndAssignBackground()

    Dim pgForeGround As Visio.Page
    Dim pgBackGround As Visio.Page
    Dim szBackGroundPageName As String

    'Add new page to active document
    Set pgForeGround = ActiveDocument.Pages.Add

    'Add new page for background to active document
    Set pgBackGround = ActiveDocument.Pages.Add

    'Set the Background property to True
    pgBackGround.Background = True
```

```
        'Get the background page name
        szBackGroundPageName = pgBackGround.Name

        'Assign the background page to
        'the foreground page
        pgForeGround.BackPage = szBackGroundPageName

    End Sub
```

Changing Page Settings

For Visio solutions, Microsoft Visual Basic for Applications (VBA) programs usually use a Visio template to create a drawing. The template can provide the correct settings for the drawings created by your program, so you might not need to change settings such as the drawing scale or page scale. If you need to change these settings, or if you create a drawing without using a template but don't want to use the Visio defaults, you can change the page settings by changing page formulas.

To change a page formula, get the **PageSheet** property of a **Page** object, which returns a **Shape** object that represents a page's formulas. You then use the **Cells** property of this **Shape** object to retrieve a page cell by name, as you would retrieve cells for shapes on the drawing page.

A **Master** object also has a **PageSheet** property that you can use to get the same settings—drawing scale, page scale, and so on—for the master as you can for the page. You might do this, for example, to determine whether the scale of a master is appropriate for the drawing page before you drop the master onto the drawing page.

> **Note** You can also access page settings by getting a special shape called **ThePage** from both the **Page** and **Master** objects' **Shapes** collections. This is the equivalent of getting the **PageSheet** property of a **Page** or **Master** object.

For example, suppose your program allows the user to change the scale of a space plan from your program rather than from the Visio engine. The following statements set the scale of *pagObj* so that 1 foot in the drawing equals 1/8 inch on the drawing page:

```
Set pagSheetObj = pagObj.PageSheet
Set pagCelPageScale = pagSheetObj.Cells("PageScale")
Set pagCelDrawScale = pagSheetObj.Cells("DrawingScale")
pagCelPageScale.Result("in") = 0.125
pagCelDrawScale.Result("ft") = 1.0
```

The page cells you're mostly likely to work with are those that control the drawing's size and scale. Other page cells control the fineness of the rulers and the grid, the layers defined for the page, actions, and user-defined cells. For a list of page sections and cells, see Appendix B, *ShapeSheet Section, Row, and Cell Indices*.

Layers

A page can have *layers*, which you can use to organize the shapes on a page. You assign shapes to a layer to work with named categories of shapes—to show them or hide them, print them or not, or protect them from changes—without having to place the shapes on a background page or incur the overhead of grouping them. A shape's layer is independent of its stacking order or even its membership in a group.

A master can be associated with layers. When a master with layers is dropped in a drawing, the instance of that master is assigned to those layers on the page. If the layers don't already exist, the Microsoft Visio instance creates them.

When you work with layers from a program, you can find out which layers are available in a drawing page or master, and which layers a shape is assigned to in a drawing. You can assign shapes to layers, add layers, and delete layers. You can also show or hide a layer, make it printable or editable, and change other layer settings, similar to the way you set layer properties in the **Layer Properties** dialog box or the Layers section of a ShapeSheet window.

Identifying Layers in a Page or Master

To identify the layers defined for a page or master, get its **Layers** property. This property returns a **Layers** collection, which contains a **Layer** object for each layer defined for the page or master. If the page or master has no layers, its **Layers** collection is empty. A **Layer** object has a **Name** property that returns the name of the layer as a string. This is the default property of the object.

You access a **Layer** object from the **Layers** collection by name or by index. For example, to get a **Layer** object for the layer named "Plumbing":

```
Set layerObj = layersObj.Item("Plumbing")
```

The following example gets all the layers in a collection of the active page and prints their names in the Visual Basic Editor **Immediate** window:

```
Sub GetLayers ()
    Dim layersObj As Visio.Layers
    Dim layerObj As Visio.Layer
    Dim layerName As String
    Set layersObj = ActivePage.Layers
    For Each layerObj In layersObj
        layerName = layerObj.Name
        Debug.Print layerName
    Next
End Sub
```

As in most collections, objects in the **Layers** collection are indexed starting with 1. Each layer in the collection is represented by one row in the Layers section of the page or master.

A **Layer** object's **Index** property tells you the index of a layer in the **Layers** collection. A **Layer** object's **Row** property tells you the corresponding row in the Layers section of the page sheet. These are usually different numbers.

Identifying the Layers to Which a Shape is Assigned

Use the **LayerCount** property of a **Shape** object to get the total number of layers to which the shape is assigned, and then use the **Shape** object's **Layer** property to get a particular layer. For example, the following statement gets the second layer to which the shape is assigned:

```
Set layerObj = shpObj.Layer(2)
```

Check the properties of the **Layer** object, such as **Name**, to find out more about that layer.

If the shape is not assigned to any layer, its **LayerCount** property returns zero (0), and getting its **Layer** property causes an error.

Assigning Shapes to and Removing Shapes from Layers

To assign a shape to a layer, use the **Add method of the Layer** object. For example:

```
layerObj.Add shpObj, preserveMembersFlag
```

The **preserveMembersFlag** argument should be non-zero (**True**) if you're assigning a group to the layer but you don't want to affect the layer membership of shapes within that group. Otherwise, use 0 (**False**) to assign a single shape or a group and each of its members to that layer.

To remove a shape from a layer, use the **Remove** method of the **Layer** object. The arguments are the same for removing a layer as for adding one. For example:

```
layerObj.Remove shpObj, preserveMembersFlag
```

Adding Layers to and Deleting Layers from Pages and Masters

To add a layer to a page or master, use the **Add** method of the **Layers** collection of a **Page** object or **Master** object. For example, use the following statements to add a new layer named "Plumbing" to a page:

```
Set layersObj = pagObj.Layers
Set layerObj = layersObj.Add("Plumbing")
```

The name of the new layer must be unique to the page or the master. If it succeeds, the **Add** method returns a **Layer** object that represents the new layer.

To delete a layer from a page or master, use the **Delete** method of the **Layer** object. For example:

```
layerObj.Delete deleteShapesFlag
```

The **deleteShapesFlag** argument should be non-zero (**True**) to delete the shapes assigned to the layer. Otherwise, use 0 (**False**) to retain the shapes. The shapes' layer assignments are updated so that they no longer refer to the deleted layer.

Changing Layer Settings

You can change settings in the **Layer Properties** dialog box to make a layer visible or printable or to set its highlight color, among other things.

You change layer settings from a program by setting the formulas of cells that control these settings. To do this, use the **CellsC** property of a **Layer** object to get the cell that controls the setting you want to change, and then set the formula of that cell.

For example, to access the cell that contains the layer's name, use a statement such as the following:

```
Set layerCellObj = layerObj.CellsC(visLayerName)
```

> **Tip** You can also access layer settings by using the **CellsSRC** property of a **Shape** object that represents a page sheet. The **CellsSRC** property represents a ShapeSheet cell identified by section, row, and column indices. For details, see Chapter 17, *Automating Formulas*.

To determine whether a layer is visible, use statements such as the following:

```
If layerObj.CellsC(visLayerVisible).ResultIU = 0 Then
     text1.Text = "invisible"
Else
     text1.Text = "visible"
End If
```

To hide a layer:

```
Set layerCellObj = layerObj.CellsC(visLayerVisible)
layerCellObj.Formula = False or 0
```

The constants **visLayerName** and **visLayerVisible** are defined in the Visio type library. For a list of constants that control layer settings, see Appendix B, *ShapeSheet Section, Row, and Cell Indices*. For details about changing layer settings in Visio, see the Microsoft Visio Help (on the **Help** menu, click **Microsoft Visio Help**).

19

Automating Connections in a Visio Solution

Working with a Connect Object 386

Getting Information from a Connected Drawing 388

Iterating through the Connections on a Page: an Example 393

Creating a Connected Drawing from a Program 395

Connecting Shapes in a Flowchart: an Example 400

Connected drawings are among the most common and useful kinds of drawings you can create with Microsoft Visio. Connected drawings often illustrate relationships in a system, whether among people in an organization or stages in a manufacturing process. It's often easier to design relationships by diagramming them, and then use the diagram as a source of data about those relationships. In Visio, the act of connecting shapes is called *gluing* the shapes, and the connection between any two shapes is represented by a **Connect** object.

This chapter describes working with **Connect** objects and then using the properties of those objects to analyze a connected drawing. It also describes creating connected drawings by gluing shapes from your program.

Working with a Connect Object

A Microsoft Visio shape can be connected or glued to another Visio shape in a drawing. In the Visio object model, this relationship is represented by a **Connect** object. A **Connect** object represents a connection between two shapes in a drawing, such as a line and a box in an organization chart.

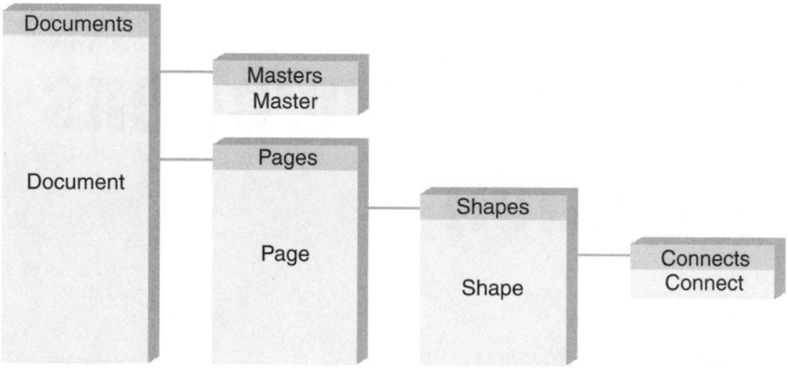

Figure 19-1 **Connect** object and related objects higher in the Visio object model.

Once you get a reference to a **Connect** object, you can find out which shapes are connected and how they are connected. You can also analyze directed graphs, such as flowcharts, or connected diagrams, such as organization charts, by getting properties of **Connect** objects for **Shape**, **Master**, and **Page** objects.

The **Connects** property of a **Page** object returns a **Connects** collection that includes a **Connect** object for every connection on the page. The **Connects** property of a **Master** object returns a **Connects** collection that includes a **Connect** object for every connection in the master.

A **Shape** object has two connection-related properties:

- A **Connects** property, which returns a **Connects** collection that includes a **Connect** object for each shape, group, or guide that shape is glued to.
- A **FromConnects** property, which returns a **Connects** collection that includes a **Connect** object for each shape, group, or guide glued to that shape.

For example, suppose a drawing contains two shapes named **A** and **B** and a one-dimensional (1-D) shape named **C** that connects **A** and **B**.

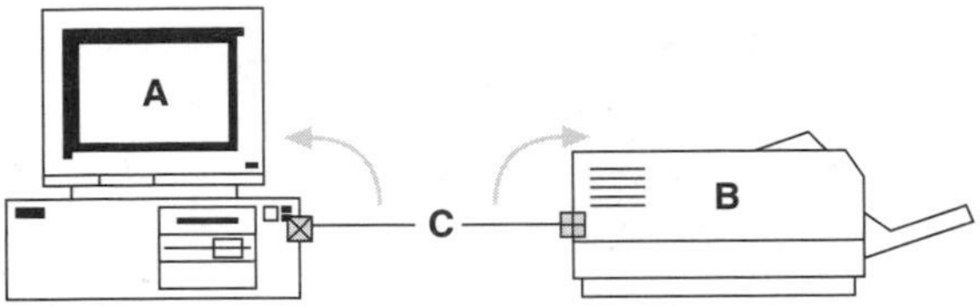

Figure 19-2 Two shapes connected by a 1-D shape.

The **Connects** collection for **A**'s **Connects** property is empty. The **Connects** collection for **A**'s **FromConnects** property contains one **Connect** object that represents **A**'s connection from **C**. **A** is not glued to any shape (**Connects** property), but **C** is glued to **A** (**FromConnects** property).

The **Connects** collection for **B**'s **Connects** property is empty. The **Connects** collection for **B**'s **FromConnects** property contains one **Connect** object that represents **B**'s connection from **C**. **B** is not glued to any shape (**Connects** property), but **C** is glued to **B** (**FromConnects** property).

The **Connects** collection for **C**'s **Connects** property contains two **Connect** objects: one representing **C**'s connection to **A**, and the other representing **C**'s connection to **B**. The **Connects** collection for **C**'s **FromConnects** property is empty. **C** is glued to **A** and **B** (**Connects** property), but no shape is glued to **C** (**FromConnects** property).

Or suppose a drawing contains four shapes named **A**, **B**, **C**, and **D**. Each shape has a control handle that is glued to a shape named **E**. In this case, shapes **A**, **B**, **C**, and **D** are connected to **E** directly via the control handle; the lines that show a hierarchical relationship between the shapes in this example are being drawn programmatically after the control handle is glued.

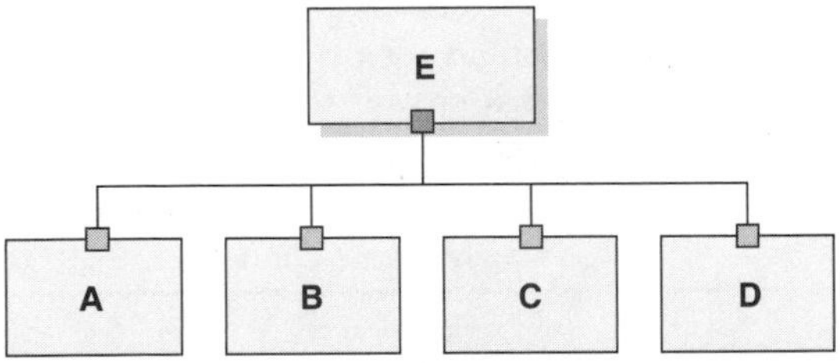

Figure 19-3 The **Connects** collection of **E** is empty, because it is not glued to **A**, **B**, **C**, and **D**—they are glued to **E**. The **Connects** collections of **A**, **B**, **C**, and **D** each contain one **Connect** object.

To get the **Connects** collection of shape **A**, get the **Connects** property of that **Shape** object. For example:

```
Set consObj = shpObj.Connects
```

The **Connects** collection of shape **A** contains one **Connect** object that represents **A**'s connection to **E**. This is also true of the **Connects** collections of shapes **B**, **C**, and **D**. The **Connects** collection of shape **E** is empty, because it's not glued to the other shapes—they are glued to it.

Summary of properties for determining connections

Object	Property	Returns
Shape, **Page**, or **Master**	**Connects**	A **Connects** collection that includes a **Connect** object for each shape that shape is glued to.
Shape	**FromConnects**	A **Connects** collection that includes a **Connect** object for each shape glued to that shape.
Connects collection or **Connect** object	**FromSheet**	The shape a connection or multiple connections originate from (the shape or shapes creating the connection).
Connects collection or **Connect** object	**ToSheet**	The shape one connection or multiple connections are made to (the shape or shapes receiving the connection).
Connect object	**FromPart**	The part of a shape a connection originates from (the part of the shape that creates the connection).
Connect object	**ToPart**	The part of a shape a connection is made to (the part of the shape that receives the connection).
Connect object	**FromCell**	The cell of a shape a connection originates from (the cell in the shape that creates the connection).
Connect object	**ToCell**	The cell of a shape a connection is made to (the cell in the shape that receives the connection).

Getting Information from a Connected Drawing

A **Connect** object has several properties that return information about the connection it represents. You can determine the shapes that are connected and the parts of a shape that are connected—for example, the top or side of a shape.

Determining Which Shapes are Connected

The **FromSheet** and **ToSheet** properties of a **Connect** object refer to **Shape** objects that represent the shapes that are connected. A shape is defined internally in Microsoft Visio in a sheet similar to the spreadsheet displayed for the shape in a ShapeSheet window. These properties derive their names from this internal sheet.

FromSheet returns the shape that creates the connection; **ToSheet** returns the shape the connection is made to (the shape that receives the connection).

For example, suppose a drawing contains two shapes named **Position** and **Executive**, and the **Position** shape is glued to the **Executive** shape with a control handle. The **Position** shape's **Connects** collection contains one **Connect** object, whose **FromSheet** property returns **Position** and whose **ToSheet** property returns **Executive**.

To find out what shapes are glued to a particular shape, use the **FromConnects** property, which returns its **Connects** collection. The **FromSheet** property of each **Connect** object in the collection identifies each shape that the shape of interest is glued to. Continuing the example from the previous section *Working with a Connect Object*, of the four shapes **A**, **B**, **C**, and **D**, each glued to **E**, the **FromSheet** property of each **Connect** object returned from the **FromConnects** property of **E** refers to **A**, **B**, **C**, and **D**.

> **Tip** When working with **Connect** objects in a collection returned by a shape's **Connects** property, you are typically looking for shapes a shape is connected *to*. The **ToSheet** property of each **Connect** object in the collection provides this information—the **FromSheet** property is always the same.

Determining Which Parts of Shapes are Connected

The **FromPart** and **ToPart** properties of a **Connect** object return integer constants that identify the general location of a connection on a shape. **FromPart** identifies the part of the shape from which a particular connection originates; **ToPart** identifies the part of the shape to which a particular connection is made. Constants for valid **FromPart** and **ToPart** values are defined in the Visio type library.

The following illustration shows the **FromPart** and **ToPart** values that would be returned to indicate the parts involved in typical connections in a drawing.

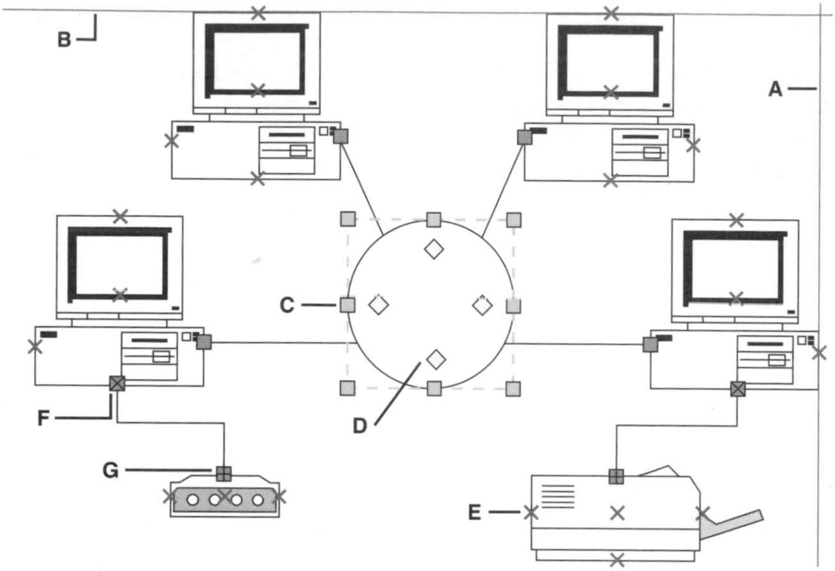

Figure 19-4 FromPart and **ToPart** values for typical connections in a drawing. (**A**) **visGuideIntersect** (if a 2-D shape is glued to the guide), **visGuideX** (if a control handle is glued to the guide), **or visConnectionPoint+***i* (if a 1-D shape is glued to the guide). (**B**) **visGuideIntersect** (if a 2-D shape is glued to the guide), **visGuideY** (if a control handle is glued to the guide), or **visConnectionPoint+***i* (if a 1-D shape is glued to the guide). (**C**) **visLeftEdge**. (**D**) **visControlPoint+***i*. (**E**) **visConnectionPoint+***i*. (**F**) **visBegin**. (**G**) **visEnd**.

The following table lists typical connections between shapes, and the constants for values returned by the **FromPart** and **ToPart** properties.

FromPart and ToPart constants for connections

Connection	FromPart constant	ToPart constant
Control handle glued to a connection point, guide, or guide point	**visControlPoint+***i*	**visConnectionPoint+***i* **visGuideX** **visGuideY**
1-D shape glued to a connection point	**visBegin** **visEnd**	**visConnectionPoint+***i*
2-D shape glued to a guide or guide point	**visRightEdge** **visLeftEdge** **visTopEdge** **visBottomEdge** **visMiddleEdge** **visCenterEdge**	**visGuideIntersect**

FromPart and ToPart constants for connections *(continued)*

Connection	FromPart constant	ToPart constant
1-D shape glued to a guide or guide point	**visBeginX** **visEndX** **visBeginY** **visEndY**	**visGuideIntersect**
1-D shape dynamically glued to a shape	**visBegin** **visEnd** ObjType cell for the 1-D shape must include **visLOFlagsRoutable** and/or GlueType cell must include **visGlueTypeWalking**.	**visWholeShape** To create dynamic or "walking" glue, the 1-D shape must connect to the pin of a shape that isn't a guide or a guide point.

For more details, see the **FromPart** and **ToPart** properties in the Microsoft Visio Developer Reference (on the **Help** menu, click **Developer Reference**).

Because a shape can have more than one control handle, **visControlPoint** is a base that represents the first control handle defined for a shape. If the value returned by **FromPart** is greater than **visControlPoint**, it represents the (*i*+1)th control handle for that shape. (To get *i*, subtract **visControlPoint** from the value returned by **FromPart**.) This is also true of **visConnectionPoint**—if the value returned by **ToPart** is greater than **visConnectionPoint**, it represents the (*i*+1)th connection point.

Gluing to a selection handle, vertex, or location within a shape automatically creates a connection point, which is why constants for these items are not defined. For details about the parts of a shape that can be glued, see *What Can Be Glued to What* in *Creating a Connected Drawing from a Program* later in this chapter.

Getting the Cells in a Connection

The **FromCell** and **ToCell** properties of a **Connect** object refer to **Cell** objects that represent the ShapeSheet cells involved in a connection. You can get or set the cell's formula, its result, or any other property of the **Cell** object and use it as you would any other **Cell** object—for example, as an argument to the **GlueTo** method.

Guidelines for Analyzing a Connected Drawing

When you are analyzing a connected drawing, you should keep the following in mind:

- Know what kinds of shapes the drawing contains.

  For example, does the drawing use 1-D shapes as connectors between 2-D shapes, or does it rely on control handles of 2-D shapes to draw lines from one shape to another? Are all lines between shapes instances of a connector master, or are some of them drawn with the **Line** tool?

- Know that connection data you gather from a drawing created with the mouse may have different connections than you might assume from looking at the drawing.

  For example, shapes have a stacking order on the page that can affect what a shape is actually glued to. If the user glues two or more shapes to the same point on another shape using the mouse, some shapes may actually be glued to other glued shapes instead of to the intended shape, as the following figure shows.

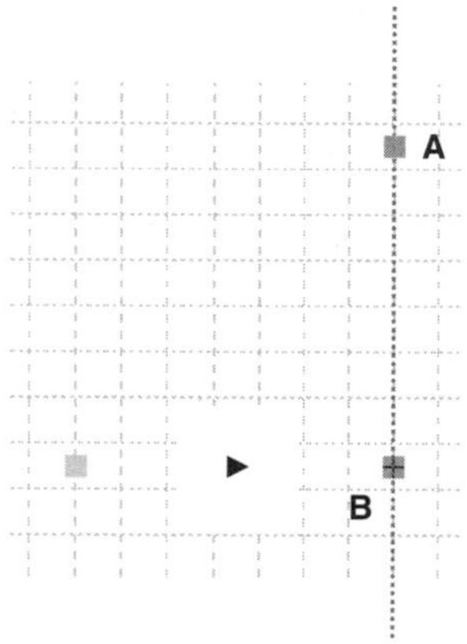

Figure 19-5 Resistor and diode shapes stacked in a certain order. The stacking order of shapes can affect their connections. (**A**) Because the resistor was glued first, it is glued to the guide. (**B**) When the diode is then glued, it may either be glued to the guide, or it may be glued to the resistor.

- Consider direction in the diagram; the parts of shapes that are glued might not correspond to directions that are indicated visually in a directed graph such as a flowchart.

  For example, you can glue either the begin point or the end point of a 1-D shape to another shape, and you can format either the begin point or the end point with an arrowhead. If you assume that an arrowhead in a drawing indicates an end point of a 1-D shape, you might not get an accurate analysis of the drawing.

For more details, see the **FromCell** and **ToCell** properties in the Microsoft Visio Developer Reference (on the **Help** menu, click **Developer Reference**).

Iterating through the Connections on a Page: an Example

The ShowPageConnections macro below iterates through the **Connect** objects for the first page in the active Microsoft Visio document. For each **Connect** object, ShowPageConnections retrieves the shapes that are connected (**FromSheet** and **ToSheet**) and the part of each shape that is connected (**FromPart** and **ToPart**). It then compares the values of **FromPart** and **ToPart** to each possible value, using the constants from the Visio type library, and displays the corresponding string, along with other data for the connection, in a listbox on a user form.

```
Sub ShowPageConnections ()
    'Pages collection of document
    Dim pagsObj As Visio.Pages
    'Page to work on
    Dim pagObj As Visio.Page
    'Object From connection connects to
    Dim fromObj As Visio.Shape
    'Object To connection connects to
    Dim toObj As Visio.Shape
    'Connects collection
    Dim consObj As Visio.Connects
    'Connect object from collection
    Dim conObj As Visio.Connect
    'Type of From connection
    Dim fromData As Integer
    'String to hold description of From connection
    Dim fromStr As String
    'Type of To connection
    Dim toData As Integer
    'String to hold description of To connection
    Dim toStr As String

    'Get the Pages collection for the document
    'Note the use of ThisDocument to refer to the current document
    Set pagsObj = ThisDocument.Pages
    'Get a reference to the first page of the collection
    Set pagObj = pagsObj(1)
    'Get the Connects collection for the page
    Set consObj = pagObj.Connects
```

```
        'Make sure the listbox is empty.
        UserForm1.ListBox1.Clear
        'Loop through the Connects collection
        For Each conObj In consObj
               'Get the From information
               Set fromObj = conObj.FromSheet
               fromData = conObj.FromPart
               'Get the To information
               Set toObj = conObj.ToSheet
               toData = conObj.ToPart
               'Use fromData to determine type of connection
               If fromData = visConnectError Then
                      fromStr = "error"
               ElseIf fromData = visNone Then
                      fromStr = "none"
               'Test fromData for
               'visRightEdge,visBottomEdge,visMiddleEdge,
               'visTopEdge,visLeftEdge,visCenterEdge, visBeginX,
               'visBeginY, visBegin, visEndX,
               'visEndY,visEnd
               ElseIf fromData >= visControlPoint Then
                      fromStr = "controlPt_" & CStr(fromData - _
                             visControlPoint + 1)
               Else
                      fromStr = "???"
               End If
               'Use toData to determine the type of shape the connector
               'is connected to
               If toData = visConnectError Then
                      toStr = "error"
               ElseIf toData = visNone Then
                      toStr = "none"
               ElseIf toData = visGuideX Then
                      toStr = "guideX"
               ElseIf toData = visGuideY Then
                      toStr = "guideY"
               ElseIf toData >= visConnectionPoint Then
                      toStr = "connectPt_" & CStr(toData - _
                             visConnectionPoint + 1)
               Else
                      toStr = "???"
               End If
               'Add the information to the listbox
               UserForm1.ListBox1.AddItem "from " & fromObj.Name & " " _
                      & fromStr & " to " & toObj.Name & " " & toStr
        Next
        UserForm1.Show
    End Sub
```

Creating a Connected Drawing from a Program

You create a connected drawing from a program by dropping masters on a drawing page and then gluing the shapes together. Gluing is a directional operation, so it's important to know what you have glued to what. After shapes are glued, you can move a shape that has other shapes glued to it without breaking their connections, but not vice versa. This is true whether you move the shapes from a program or in a Microsoft Visio drawing window. For example, suppose a rectangle has a line glued to it. Moving the rectangle does not break the connection—the line remains glued to the rectangle and stretches as needed. However, moving the line breaks the connection.

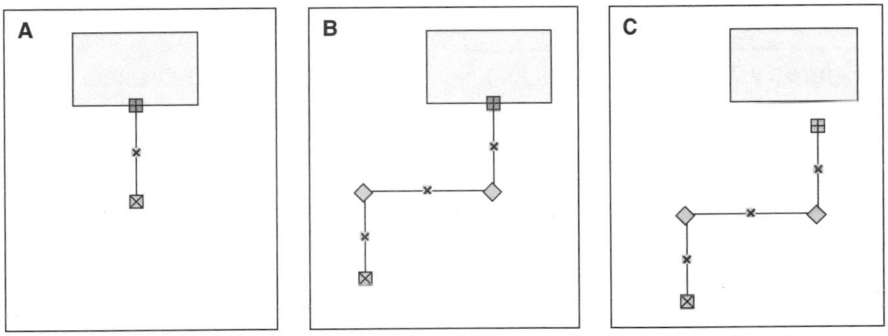

Figure 19-6 This drawing demonstrates moving connected shapes. The line is glued to the rectangle (**A**). If you move the rectangle (**B**), these shapes remain connected. If you move the line (**C**), the connection breaks.

To glue shapes from a program

1. Decide what shape you want to glue to another shape, what the other shape is, and where to connect the shapes.
2. Get a **Cell** object that represents the part of the shape (such as an end point, control point, or edge of the shape) that you want to glue to.
3. Use the **GlueTo** method to specify a part of another shape (such as a connection point, vertex, or selection handle), or the **GlueToPos** method to specify a location, to create the connection between the shapes.

What Can Be Glued to What

Only certain parts of shapes can be glued. For example, an endpoint of a one-dimensional (1-D) shape or a control handle of a two-dimensional (2-D) shape can be glued to a connection point, but a side of a 2-D shape can be glued to only a guide or guide point.

To use 1-D shapes to create a connected diagram, you glue the begin point and end point of each 1-D shape between two 2-D shapes, as shown in the following illustration.

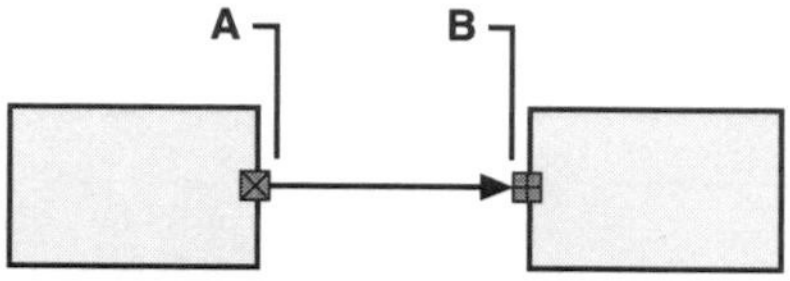

Figure 19-7 Cell references for begin and end points of a 1-D shape. (**A**) BeginX or BeginY. (**B**) EndX or EndY.

Another method for gluing one object to another is to create a master with a control handle that extends a line you can glue to another shape. As an example, the following illustration contains a shape that has a control handle that can be glued to another shape. The shape also has four named connection points, locations to which other shapes can be glued. The cell references you would use to glue these locations are shown in the following illustration.

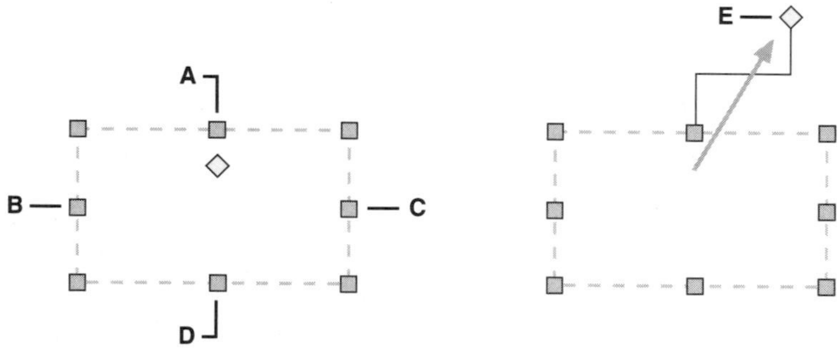

Figure 19-8 Cell references for the control handle and connection points. (**A**) Connections.top. (**B**) Connections.left. (**C**) Connections.right. (**D**) Connections.bottom. (**E**) Controls.X1.

Gluing to part of a shape represented by a pair of cells

Many points on a shape—control handles, connection points, end points, geometry vertices, and so on—are specified by two ShapeSheet cells, one for each of the *x,y* coordinates for the point. Whenever you glue to part of a shape represented by a pair of cells, you can specify either cell of the pair. For example, to indicate the first control handle on a shape, you can specify either Controls.X1 or Controls.Y1.

The following table lists the ShapeSheet cells that represent the parts of a shape you'll typically want to glue.

Typical cells for gluing parts of shapes

To glue this	Get one of these cells	And glue it to any of these cells in another shape
The begin point or end point of a 1-D shape	BeginX or BeginY EndX or EndY	Connections.X*i* or Connections.Y*i* Geometry.X*i* or Geometry.Y*i* AlignLeft, AlignCenter, AlignRight, AlignTop, AlignMiddle, or AlignBottom Angle
		PinX or PinY (to glue dynamically)
A control handle	Controls.X*i* or Controls.Y*i*	Connections.X*i* or Connections.Y*i* Geometry.X*i* or Geometry.Y*i* AlignLeft, AlignCenter, AlignRight, AlignTop, AlignMiddle, or AlignBottom
		PinX or PinY
The edge of a shape	AlignLeft, AlignCenter, AlignRight, AlignTop, AlignMiddle, or AlignBottom	Angle

For other details, see the **FromCell** and **ToCell** properties in the Microsoft Visio Developer Reference (on the **Help** menu, click **Developer Reference**).

Gluing to a selection handle

An alignment cell corresponds to the selection handle in the middle of the specified part of the shape. For example, AlignTop corresponds to the selection handle in the middle of the shape's top edge. Gluing to an alignment cell in a program is the same as gluing to the corresponding selection handle on the shape in a drawing window.

You don't actually glue to the selection handle itself—instead, you use the selection handle to create a connection point at that location on the shape. This is true whether you're gluing the shapes from a program or in a Visio drawing window. A row is added to the shape's Connections section to represent the new connection point.

Gluing to a guide or guide point

A guide is a line dragged out from a ruler in the Visio drawing window that you can use to align shapes. You can glue shapes to a guide, and then move the guide and the shapes with it. When you glue a 1-D shape to a guide, you can specify any cell in the guide. For example:

```
1DShp.Cells("BeginX").GlueTo  GuideShp.Cells("PinX")
2DShp.Cells("AlignLeft").GlueTo  GuideShp.Cells("PinX")
```

Gluing with Cell Objects

Once you've decided which part of the shape you want to glue to another shape, you get a **Cell** object that represents that part of the shape. To get a **Cell** object, get the **Cells** property of a **Shape** object and specify the name of the cell you want. For example, the following statement gets a **Cell** object that represents the *x*-coordinate of the first control handle of the shape represented by *shpObj1*:

```
Set celObj = shpObj1.Cells("Controls.X1")
```

If a point on a shape is represented by a pair of cells, you can specify only one cell of the pair. It doesn't matter which cell you specify. In the example above, Controls.Y1 would work equally well.

For details about working with **Cell** objects, see Chapter 17, *Automating Formulas*.

Gluing a Shape to Another Shape

You can use the **GlueTo** or **GlueToPos** method of a **Cell** object to glue a shape to another shape. With the **GlueTo** method, you specify a cell reference to a part of the other shape; the method then sets the formula of the **Cell** object to that cell reference. With the **GlueToPos** method, you specify a pair of decimal fractions relative to the other shape's width-height box. **GlueTo** or **GlueToPos** creates a connection point at that part of the shape or that location.

For example, the following statement uses **GlueTo** to glue the part of a shape represented by *celObj*—the control handle shown in the following illustration—to the shape represented by *shpObj2*, at that shape's fourth connection point, which has been renamed to Connections.bottom to create a more meaningful connection name.

```
celObj.GlueTo  shpObj2.Cells("Connections.bottom")
```

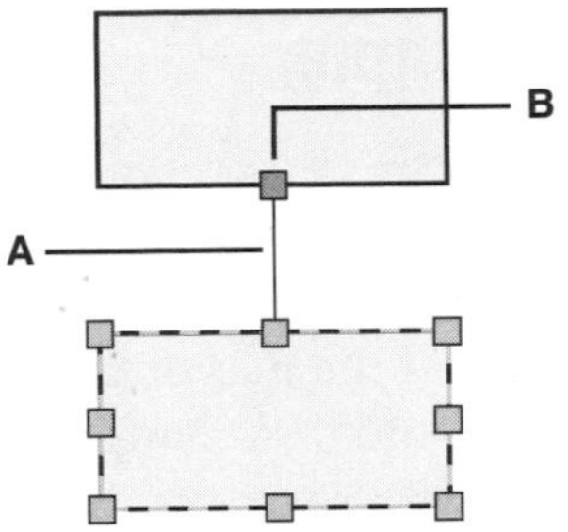

Figure 19-9 Gluing a control handle to a connection point with the **GlueTo** method. (**A**) *celObj* represents the control handle Controls.X1 of *shpObj1.* (**B**) *celObj.***GlueTo** *shpObj2.***Cells**("Connections.bottom") glues the control handle of s*hpObj1* to the connection point of *shpObj2* that has been named "bottom."

The following statement uses **GlueToPos** to glue the same shape to the center of *shpObj2*, creating a new connection point at that location. The location is specified as decimal fractions of the shape's width-height box, not as *x,y* coordinates. These fractions can be negative or greater than 1 to create a connection point outside the shape's width-height box.

```
celObj.GlueToPos shpObj2, .5, .5
```

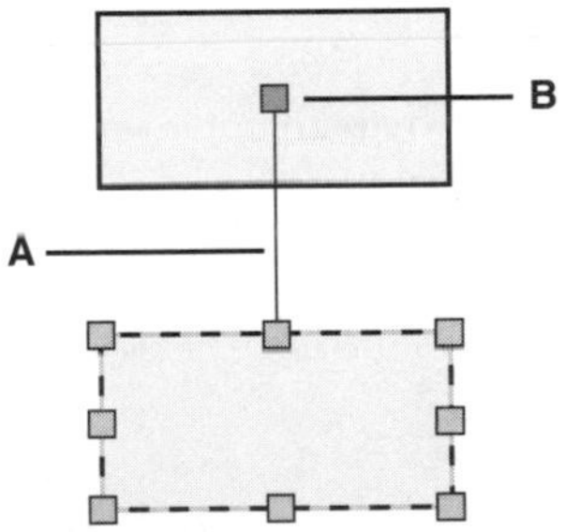

Figure 19-10 Gluing a control handle to a location with the **GlueToPos** method.
(**A**) *celObj* represents the control handle Controls.X1 of *shpObj1.*
(**B**) **GlueToPos***(shpObj2,.5,.5)* glues the control handle of *shpObj1* to the center of *shpObj2.*

Note To dynamically glue your shape, use the **GlueTo** method with the PinX or PinY cell as the cell you want to glue to. Gluing to PinX indicates a horizontal walking preference, and gluing to PinY indicates a vertical walking preference. All other cell references default to static glue. For details about static and dynamic glue, search the Microsoft Visio Help (on the **Help** menu, click **Microsoft Visio Help**).

Connecting Shapes in a Flowchart: an Example

The following Microsoft Visual Basic for Applications (VBA) procedure draws a simple flowchart on the Microsoft Visio drawing page based on data contained in an array that is passed as an argument to this procedure. The array is two-dimensional—the first element contains the name of the master, and the second element contains the shape's text. Before creating the flowchart, the procedure reads the array data and prints it to the **Immediate** window of the Visual Basic Editor.

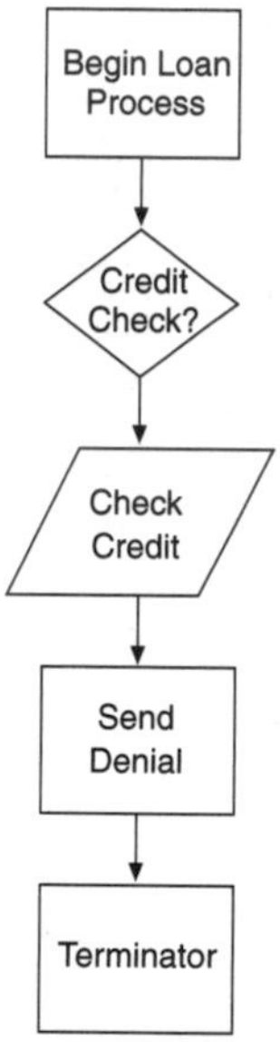

Figure 19-11 The flowchart created by CreateFlowchart.

```
Public Sub CreateFlowchart(arrFlowChart () As String)
    'Shape that you're connecting from
    Dim vPrevShape As Visio.Shape
    'Shape that you're connecting to
    Dim vNextShape As Visio.Shape
    'Shape representing the connection
    Dim vConnector As Visio.Shape
    'Reference to the flowchart master
    Dim vFlowChartMaster As Visio.Master
    'Reference to the connector master
    Dim vConnectorMaster As Visio.Master
    'The stencil containing the masters
    Dim vStencil As Visio.Document
```

```
'Master's PinX location
Dim dblXLocation As Double
'Master's PinY location
Dim dblYLocation As Double
'Begin cell for connector
Dim bCell As Visio.Cell
'End cell for connector
Dim eCell As Visio.Cell
Dim iCount As Integer

On Error GoTo eHandler
'Initialize X,Y location that will be passed to the Drop method
dblXLocation = 4.25
dblYLocation = 10.5
'Print array to Immediate window
For iCount = LBound(arrFlowChart) To UBound(arrFlowChart)
       Debug.Print arrFlowChart(iCount, 0) & " ": _
              arrFlowChart(iCount, 1)
Next
'Open Flowchart stencil
Set vStencil = Application.Documents.OpenEx _
       ("Basic Flowchart Shapes.vss", visOpenDocked)
'Add a shape to the drawing for each item in the array
For iCount = LBound(arrFlowChart) To UBound(arrFlowChart)
       'Get the master based on MasterName in the data array
       Set vFlowChartMaster = _
              vStencil.Masters(arrFlowChart(iCount, 0))
       'Add the shape to the page
       Set vNextShape = ActivePage.Drop(vFlowChartMaster, _
              dblXLocation, dblYLocation)
       'Set dropped shape text
       vNextShape.Text = arrFlowChart(iCount, 1)
       'Connect to previous shape dropped, if necessary
       If Not vPrevShape Is Nothing Then
              'Get connector master if necessary
              If vConnectorMaster Is Nothing Then
                     Set vConnectorMaster = _
                            vStencil.Masters("Dynamic Connector")
              End If
```

```
                'Add connector to the page (doesn't matter where _
                    for this example)
                Set vConnector = _
                    ActivePage.Drop(vConnectorMaster, 0, 0)
                'Connect begin point
                Set bCell = vConnector.Cells("BeginX")
                bCell.GlueTo vPrevShape.Cells("AlignBottom")
                'Connect end point
                Set eCell = vConnector.Cells("EndX")
                eCell.GlueTo vNextShape.Cells("AlignTop")
                vConnector.SendToBack
            End If
            Set vPrevShape = vNextShape
            Set vNextShape = Nothing
            'Set Y location for next shape
            dblYLocation = dblYLocation - 1.5
        Next
        Exit Sub
        eHandler:
        Debug.Print Error
    End Sub
```

20

Integrating Data with a Visio Solution

Associating Data with Shapes Using Automation 404

Visio Properties for Storing and Retrieving Data 406

Storing and Retrieving XML Data in Your Solutions 407

Writing Code to Extract Data from a Visio Drawing 410

Writing Code to Create a Visio Drawing from Data 414

Integrating a Visio Solution with a Database 418

If you're developing a solution that combines Microsoft Visio drawings with another source of data, such as a database, you'll be interested in the ways you can associate data with shapes and pages. Using custom properties and user-defined ShapeSheet cells, you can associate data with a shape; using a unique ID provides a way to establish a persistent link between a shape and external data associated with it. In addition, you can store data for documents, pages, masters, shortcuts, shapes, and text using a variety of different Visio properties.

This chapter also provides two code samples for extracting data from a drawing and creating a drawing from external data, two of the most common ways solution developers work with Visio and data from other applications. The two samples introduce some general approaches for integrating data with a Visio solution and are intended to give you a sense of the range of possible solutions you might create.

Associating Data with Shapes Using Automation

You can create custom properties as well as get and set custom property values exclusively from a program, or you can collect values filled in by the user of your Microsoft Visio solution. For example, you might provide masters that prompt the user to fill in certain data when a master is dropped in a drawing, and then use a program to gather that data from the user's drawings. To establish persistent links between data in a drawing and an external data source, you can use unique IDs associated with shapes and masters.

For details about creating user-defined cells and custom properties, see Chapter 7, *Enhancing Shape Behavior*.

Adding Custom Property and User-Defined Rows

Custom properties are a way to associate database-like fields with a shape or page, and are especially convenient if you plan to collect values entered by a user. For example, you might design a master to prompt a user to enter data when a shape is dropped on the page, and then use a Microsoft Visual Basic for Applications (VBA) program to gather the data that the user entered from the completed drawing.

The Value and Prompt cells in user-defined rows make it possible for you to store a value and reliably find it again. Because you can assign unique names to user-defined rows, it's unlikely that other programs will know about, much less attempt to write to, the cells in those rows. Scratch cells, in contrast, are likely to be used by many programs, so values you store in those cells can be overwritten when you least expect it.

You can add a custom property row or a user-defined row to a **Shape** object using the **AddNamedRow** method. If either the Custom Properties or User-Defined Cells section does not yet exist, the **AddNamedRow** method will add it to the ShapeSheet spreadsheet. For example, to add a user-defined row named Latitude to a shape:

```
shpObj.AddNamedRow visSectionUser, "Latitude", 0
```

This code is the equivalent of inserting a User-Defined Cells section in the ShapeSheet spreadsheet and replacing the default name of User_Row1 with User.Latitude. For example, to get the Value cell of the new Latitude row:

```
Set celObj = shpObj.Cells("User.Latitude")
```

Once you have a reference to the **Cell** object that is the Value cell, you can use the **Formula** property of that **Cell** object to get or set values. For example:

```
celObj.Formula = "48"
```

For details about the **AddNamedRow** method, see the Microsoft Visio Developer Reference (on the **Help** menu, click **Developer Reference**).

Generating and Using Unique IDs

Shapes and masters can have unique IDs that you can use to distinguish shapes in a drawing or to track the original source of a master. Sophisticated database solutions typically use unique IDs to create a persistent link between a shape or master and a record in an external database. Unique IDs allow applications to bind data to shapes more reliably than is possible with shape names and IDs.

A unique ID is stored internally as a 128-bit value and is passed as a null-terminated 39-character string, formatted as in the following example:

```
{2287DC42-B167-11CE-88E9-0020AFDDD917}
```

> **Note** If a shape has a unique ID, you can assume that no other shape in the same document has the same unique ID. The Visio engine generates unique IDs using the same technology that Automation uses to guarantee unique object IDs and never reuses them.

Unique IDs for shapes

By default, shapes do not have unique IDs; a program must generate them. To generate a unique ID for a shape, use the **UniqueID** property of a **Shape** object. For example:

```
IDString = shpObj.UniqueID(visGetOrMakeGUID)
```

If the shape already has a unique ID, this statement gets the ID; if the shape does not have a unique ID, the statement creates one.

To find out whether a shape has a unique ID, use the following statement. If the shape has no unique ID, this statement returns a null string ("").

```
IDString = shpObj.UniqueID(visGetGUID)
```

To delete a shape's unique ID, use the following statement:

```
shpObj.UniqueID visDeleteGUID
```

Some actions cause the Visio engine to delete a shape's unique ID automatically. If you cut a shape to the Clipboard and paste it once, or drag a shape to a different drawing window, its unique ID is preserved. However, if you paste the same shape from the Clipboard a second time or duplicate the shape by holding down CTRL and dragging, the new shape will not have a unique ID.

UniqueID and BaseID properties for masters

A master has both a **UniqueID** property and a **BaseID** property; both are automatically generated by the Visio engine when a new master is created.

A master's **UniqueID** cannot be deleted or reassigned, and changes only when you modify the master or assign a new **BaseID**. A master's **BaseID** does not change as a result of any user action, and provides a link to the original master that is more persistent than a master name or a **UniqueID**. You can change **BaseID**s using the **NewBaseID** property. For details, see the Microsoft Visio Developer Reference (on the **Help** menu, click **Developer Reference**).

You can pass a unique ID as an argument to the **Item** method of a **Shapes** or **Masters** collection. For example:

```
Set shpObj = shpsObj.Item("{2287DC42-B167-11CE-88E9-0020AFDDD917}")
```

Visio Properties for Storing and Retrieving Data

This section provides information about using properties for storing data from a Microsoft Visio drawing. The following table lists common properties that return strings and the maximum size of each string.

Properties for retrieving and storing text

Property	Object property applies to	Maximum size
Title, Subject, Author, Manager, Company, Category, Keywords, Description, HyperlinkBase, AlternateName	**Document**	63 characters each
Data1, Data2, Data3	**Shape**	Unlimited
Formula	**Cell**	Unlimited
FullName	**Document**	255 characters
Name	**Document**	255 characters
Name	**Layer, Master, Shortcut, Page, Shape, Style**	31 characters
NameID	**Shape**	36 characters
Path	**Document**	255 characters
Prompt	**Master, Shortcut**	255 characters
Text	**Shape, Characters**	Unlimited
UniqueID	**Master, Shortcut, Shape**	39 characters

The Visio engine returns both real numbers and integers as floating point numbers with 15 significant digits. To reduce the possibility of rounding errors in Microsoft Visual Basic or Microsoft Visual Basic for Applications (VBA), assign numbers to **Variant** or **Double** variables and store numbers in fields with the appropriate data type.

Storing and Retrieving XML Data in Your Solutions

Beginning with Microsoft Visio 2002, you can save Microsoft Visio drawings, stencils, and templates as XML (Extensible Markup Language) files and open them again in Visio without any loss of information. You can also include XML data from other applications within your XML data in Visio, provided the data contains well-formed XML that complies with the XML schema in Visio and the internal rules of Visio.

In a document, you can store and retrieve your solution data in XML through Automation. In a cell, you can store and retrieve your XML data as you would any other string value using the ShapeSheet spreadsheet or Automation.

> **Note** The three XML file formats in Visio correspond to the three types of Visio files: XML drawing files have the .vdx file name extension; XML template files have the .vtx file name extension; and XML stencil files have the .vsx file name extension. These files function in the same way as their binary counterparts (.vsd, .vst, and .vss, respectively).

For more details on the XML file format in Visio and how to work with the XML schema in Visio, see the XML for Visio Reference in the Microsoft Visio Developer Center on the MSDN Web site (msdn.microsoft.com/visio/).

Storing XML Data in and Retrieving XML Data from a Document

You can store and retrieve XML data at the document level (in a VDX, VTX, or VSX file) using the **SolutionXML** element contained immediately within the **VisioDocument** element. For example:

```
<VisioDocument>
    . . .
        <SolutionXML Name='SomeName' xmlns:x='y'><x:MyData>Data
            </x:MyData></SolutionXML>
    . . .
</VisioDocument>
```

A **VisioDocument** element can have zero or more **SolutionXML** elements, and each **SolutionXML** element must have a unique **Name** attribute. When you add a **SolutionXML** element to a Visio document, it is recommended that you use a namespace to mark non-Visio elements.

To access the **SolutionXML** element in a document at run time, you can use the **SolutionXMLElement**, **SolutionXMLElementCount**, **SolutionXMLElementExists**, and **SolutionXMLElementName** properties and the **DeleteSolutionXMLElement** method.

For example, you can create **SolutionXML** elements through Automation using code similar to the following:

```
docObj.SolutionXMLElement("SomeName") = _
    "<SolutionXML Name='SomeName' xmlns:x='y'> _
    <x:MyData>Data</x:MyData></SolutionXML>"
```

The string passed to the **SolutionXMLElement** property must match the **Name** attribute specified in the **SolutionXML** element.

For more details on the **SolutionXMLElement, SolutionXMLElementCount, SolutionXMLElementExists**, and **SolutionXMLElementName** properties and the **DeleteSolutionXMLElement** method, see the Microsoft Visio Developer Reference (on the **Help** menu, click **Developer Reference**).

For more details on the XML file format in Visio and how to work with the XML schema in Visio, see the XML for Visio Reference in the Microsoft Visio Developer Center on the MSDN Web site (msdn.microsoft.com/visio/).

Storing XML Data in and Retrieving XML Data from a Cell

You store XML data in cells using a string value within a **SolutionXML** element. Only A, B, C, or D cells in the Scratch section, or Value cells in the User-Defined Cells or Custom Properties sections of the ShapeSheet spreadsheet can accept XML data, and the XML must be well-formed.

When you work with XML data in cells through the ShapeSheet spreadsheet or Automation, you can retrieve your XML data as you would any string value in a cell.

Unlike document-level XML, **SolutionXML** elements maintained in a cell do not require a **Name** attribute. (In a cell, there are no uniqueness semantics for **SolutionXML** elements that use a **Name** attribute.) However, it is recommended that you supply a namespace to mark non-Visio elements within a **SolutionXML** element in a cell.

There are several legal ways that you can create a formula using the **SolutionXML** element. If a cell has a formula that matches one of the patterns shown here:

```
<SolutionXML> ... </SolutionXML>
```

```
<SolutionXML ... > ... </SolutionXML>
```

```
<SolutionXML ... />
```

and if the formula is well formed XML, for example:

```
    "<SolutionXML xmlns:x='y'><x:MyData>Data</x:MyData>
        </SolutionXML>"
```

or

```
    "<SolutionXML xmlns:x='y' x:MyData='Data'/>"
```

when the formula is saved as XML in Visio, it is saved as XML rather than as a parsed string, for example:

```
<User ID='2'>
    <Value Unit='STR'>
    <SolutionXML xmlns:x='y'><x:MyData>Data</x:MyData>
        </SolutionXML></Value>
    <Prompt>hello</Prompt>
</User>
```

If a cell contains XML, but it is not contained within a **SolutionXML** element, or if the XML is not well-formed, Visio will output a string value that is not recognizable as XML. For example, the formula of a Value cell in the User-Defined Cells section might be `"=<abc>"`. When Visio saves such a formula in XML it will generally output a string similar to that shown here:

```
<User ID-'2'>
    <Value Unit='STR'>&lt;abc&gt;</Value>
    <Prompt>Hello</Prompt>
</User>
```

> **Note** Visio treats cells with **SolutionXML** elements differently from other cells only when a document is saved in XML file format. When you work with XML data in cells through the ShapeSheet spreadsheet or Automation, you can store and retrieve your XML data as you would any string value in a cell.

For more details on the XML file format in Visio and how to work with the XML schema in Visio, see the XML for Visio Reference in the Microsoft Visio Developer Center on the MSDN Web site (msdn.microsoft.com/visio/).

Writing Code to Extract Data from a Visio Drawing

The shapes in Microsoft Visio drawings can contain a rich variety of information. Using Automation, you can write programs that extract information from a Visio drawing to use in another application. For example, you might want to use the shapes in a drawing to automatically generate sales orders. Or, you might extract information from the shapes in a flowchart to a spreadsheet to estimate the costs associated with a particular manufacturing process. You can also extract information about data types used in a solution, and protect data in a drawing from unplanned changes by saving a copy of the data in an external file.

No matter how you plan to use the data you extract from a drawing, the basic process for gathering it is the same. The code introduced in this sample outlines gathering data from a Visio drawing; what you do with the information you gather is dependent upon how your program interacts with other applications.

Extracting Data from a Drawing: an Example

Suppose you want to write an application that gathers information about the network components in a drawing to generate sales orders. A salesperson and a client might collaborate on a drawing that represents a new network system, as in the following illustration.

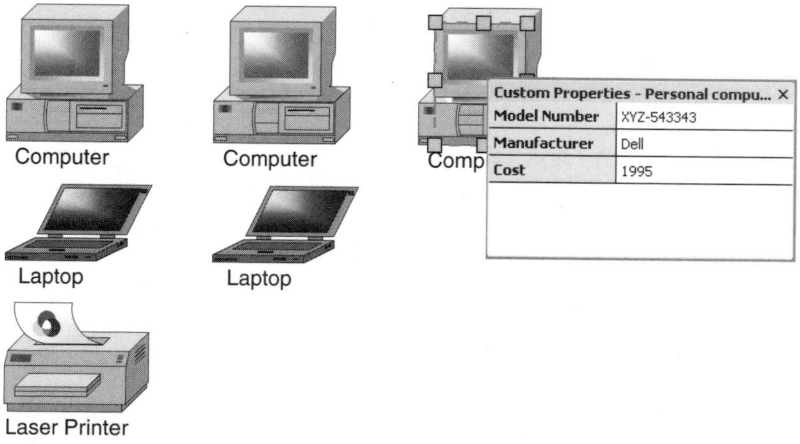

Figure 20-1 A Visio drawing with shape information that can be extracted.

You can write an Automation program that runs when the drawing is saved and that collects information about the shapes in the drawing and places it into an array. You could then write additional code that uses the data in the array to automatically generate an order for the specified components.

Model Number	Manufacturer	Cost
XYZ-543341	Dell	1995
XYZ-543342	Dell	1995
XYZ-543343	Dell	1995
ABC-499891	Dell	2150
ABC-499892	Dell	2150
ZWY-123121	Hewlet Packard	3200

Figure 20-2 Data about the shapes on the drawing page.

Using Microsoft Visual Basic for Applications (VBA), you could write code much like the following example that executes when the Visio drawing is saved. After defining variables and getting the **Shapes** collection associated with the first page in the drawing, this code defines the *OrderInfo* array to hold the data that will be gathered from the shapes in the collection. Each shape's name is identified and added to the array, along with information gathered about three custom properties for each shape: the part number, manufacturer, and cost. After this information is gathered for each shape on the page, the results are displayed in the **Immediate** window for verification. Finally, the data in the array is passed to another application or saved to disk as a text file.

For a detailed explanation of this code, see *Examining the Code for Extracting Data from a Drawing* later in this section.

```
Private Sub Document_DocumentSaved(ByVal doc As IVDocument)

    'Visio Page object
    Dim pagObj As Visio.Page
    'Visio Shapes collection
    Dim shpsObj As Visio.Shapes
    'Visio Shape object
    Dim shpObj As Visio.Shape
    'Visio Cell object
    Dim celObj As Visio.Cell
    'Array to hold purchase order info
    Dim OrderInfo() As String
    'Counter
    Dim iShapeCount As Integer
    'Counter
    Dim i As Integer

    'Get the active page.
    Set pagObj = ActivePage
    'Get the Shapes collection of the page.
    Set shpsObj = pagObj.Shapes
```

```
    'Total number of shapes.
    iShapeCount = shpsObj.Count

    'Set the array size to hold all of the shape information.
    '0-based array, 4 by total number of shapes.
    ReDim OrderInfo(3, iShapeCount - 1)

    'For each shape on the page, collect the Name, Part Number,
    'Manufacturer, and Cost.
    For i = 1 To iShapeCount
        'Get the i'th shape.
        Set shpObj = shpsObj(i)
        'Get the shape name.
        OrderInfo(0, i - 1) = shpObj.Name
        'Get the Part Number property, then get the value
        'as a string.
        If shpObj.CellExists("Prop.Part_Number", _
                visExistsLocally)Then
            Set celObj = shpObj.Cells("Prop.Part_Number")
            OrderInfo(1, i - 1) = celObj.ResultStr("")
        End If
        'Get the Manufacturer property, then get the value
        'as a string.
        If shpObj.CellExists("Prop.Manufacturer", _
                visExistsLocally) Then
            Set celObj = shpObj.Cells("Prop.Manufacturer")
            OrderInfo(2, i - 1) = celObj.ResultStr("")
        End If
        'Get the Cost property, then get the value.
        If shpObj.CellExists("Prop.Cost", visExistsLocally) Then
            Set celObj = shpObj.Cells("Prop.Cost")
            OrderInfo(3, i - 1) = celObj.ResultIU
        End If
        'Release Shape object.
        Set shpObj = Nothing
    Next

    'Print to Immediate window to verify data collection.
    For i = 0 To pagObj.Shapes.Count - 1
        Debug.Print OrderInfo(0, i) & "," _
            & OrderInfo(1, i) & "," _
            & OrderInfo(2, i) & "," _
            & OrderInfo(3, i)
    Next

    'Call a function to write data out to any external
    'data storage, and pass the array of collected data to
    'ExportData OrderInfo.

End Sub
```

Examining the Code for Extracting Data from a Drawing

The previous code sample can be broken into several distinct parts:

- Defining the variables and array that will contain the data.
- Looping through the shapes in the page's **Shapes** collection to gather data and place it into an array.
- Viewing the resulting array on the screen to verify data collection.
- Exporting the data to another application.

Defining variables

In the first section of the code, the **Dim** statement is used to define variables for the **Page** object, a **Shapes** collection, a **Shape** object, and a **Cell** object. In addition, an array called *OrderInfo* is defined, along with an integer for counting through the loop that follows.

Once the variables are defined, the page variable is set to the document's active page. The *shpsObj* variable defines a collection made up of all shapes on the active page, and *iShapeCount* tallies the number of shapes for which information will be gathered. Finally, the *OrderInfo* array defines an array to hold data about four properties for each shape contained in the **Shapes** collection for the page. If you were working in a document containing several pages, you could define a loop to increment through each page in the document. In that case, you could either expand the array to contain multiple **Shapes** collections, or create a different array for each page.

Using a loop to gather information about shapes

The next section of the code populates the *OrderInfo* array with information about all of the shapes on the page. The *iShapeCount* variable stores the number of shapes on the page; the counting integer is defined relative to this range. Using a **For...Next** statement, the integer starts with the first shape in the collection, gathers information about it, releases the shape, and then gathers information about the next shape, continuing until it reaches the last shape in the collection.

For each shape in the collection, this code adds four pieces of information to the array. The *shpObj.Name* property simply collects the name of the shape. The next three fields are drawn from custom property fields. The code first checks to see if the Prop.Part_Number, Prop.Manufacturer, and Prop.Cost cells exist; if they do, the *celObj* variable is assigned to each cell value in turn, and the resulting strings are added to the array. In this code, if a cell does not exist, the field is simply skipped. In a more complete solution, you might want the code to respond differently if the cells do not exist.

Verifying data collection

Using another **For...Next** statement, the next section of the code simply displays the information in the array for each shape in the **Immediate** window, separated by commas. Depending on the way you plan to use the information in the array, this can be a useful troubleshooting technique.

Exporting data to another application

This code sample doesn't actually include any code for exporting the data in the array to another application, as the approach will vary considerably depending on how the information will be used and which application you plan to work with.

Writing Code to Create a Visio Drawing from Data

Just as you can extract data from a Microsoft Visio drawing to use in another application, you can use data from other sources to create a diagram. For example, you might use information from a sales order for network components to generate an installation diagram, or you might extract data from an employee database to generate an organization chart.

However you plan to create the drawing, you need to make some important design decisions before you start coding:

- Determine whether your code creates a new drawing or assumes the user has already created one.
- Determine how the data source is selected: Is the data always drawn from the same location, or should it be selectable by a user?
- Decide how to choose which stencil contains the masters you plan to use in your drawing and how they map to the data you plan to use; you can design shapes for a new stencil as part of your solution.

The code sample in this section shows how you might create a simple diagram from the contents of a database.

Creating a Drawing from Data: an Example

Suppose you want to write an application that generates a network installation drawing from data imported from a sales order. When the sale is complete and the order is entered into a database (like the following illustration), an Automation program can extract records from the database and use them to create a drawing for an installation crew to use.

Hub / switch	Seattle
Personal computer	PC 1
Laptop	Department Laptop
PDA	Lab PC
Server	Group Server
Printer	Laser Printer

Figure 20-3 Records in a database.

In the example, the code associates a field in the database record with a shape on a particular stencil, and then drops instances of the shapes on a drawing page and adds information from other fields as custom properties of the shapes. The result is a drawing that configures the new items in a customer's network based on data entered by the salesperson.

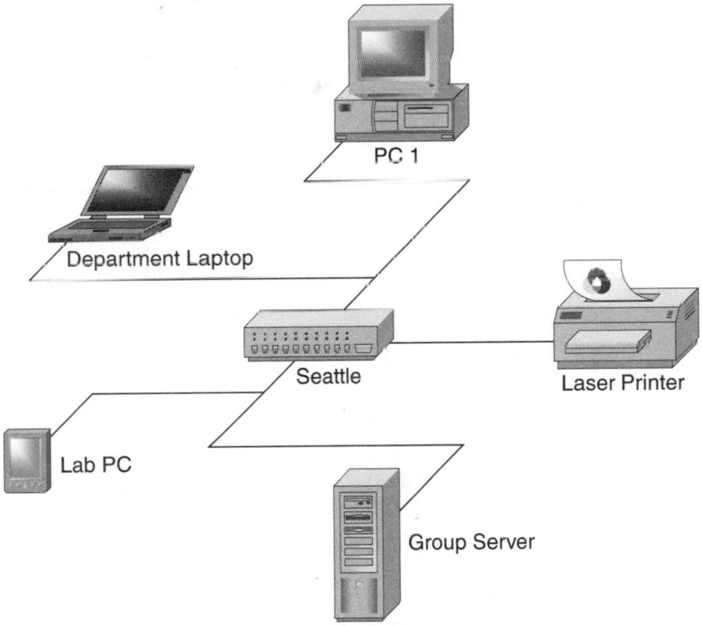

Figure 20-4 An installation diagram generated from database records.

Using Microsoft Visual Basic for Applications (VBA), you could write code much like the following example that creates a new drawing from a template that includes the stencil you want to use, and then populates it with shapes based on data read from the database. In this example, a hub shape is placed at the center of the page, and then nodes are connected to the hub in a circle. Each shape displays text, which in this example might include notes made by the salesperson about how the client wants a component to be configured.

For a detailed explanation of this code, see *Examining the Code for Creating a Drawing from Data* later in this section.

```
Public Sub CreateDrawing()

    Dim shpObjHUB As Visio.Shape
    Dim shpObjNodes As Visio.Shape
    Dim shpObjConnector As Visio.Shape
    Dim mstObjConnector As Visio.Master
    Dim mstObj As Visio.Master
    Dim stnObj As Visio.Document
    Dim dX, dY As Double
    Dim dDegreeInc As Double
    Dim dRad As Double
    Dim dPageWidth, dPageHeight As Double
    Dim i As Integer

    Const PI = 3.1415
    Const CircleRadius = 2

    Dim arrNetData() As String

    'Read data.
    InitData arrNetData

    'To place shapes in even increments around the circle,
    'divide 360 by the total number of items in the array.
    dDegreeInc = 360 / UBound(arrNetData)

    'Read the PageWidth and PageHeight properties.
    dPageWidth = ActivePage.PageSheet.Cells("PageWidth").ResultIU
    dPageHeight = ActivePage.PageSheet.Cells("PageHeight").ResultIU

    'Open the Basic Network Shapes 3D Stencil.
    Set stnObj = Application.Documents.OpenEx _
          ("Basic Network Shapes 3D.vss", visOpenDocked)

    'Process the hub shape.
    Set mstObj = stnObj.Masters(arrNetData(0, 0))
    Set shpObjHUB = ActivePage.Drop(mstObj, dPageWidth / 2, _
          dPageHeight / 2)

    'Set the text of the hub shape.
    shpObjHUB.Text = arrNetData(0, 1)

    'Get the Connector master.
    Set mstObjConnector = stnObj.Masters("Bottom to Top Angled")
```

```
    'Process the nodes.
    For i = 1 To UBound(arrNetData)
        Set mstObj = stnObj.Masters(arrNetData(i, 0))
        'Determine X, Y location for placement (in circle
        'around hub).
        dRad = (dDegreeInc * i) * PI / 180
        dX = CircleRadius * Cos(dRad) + (dPageWidth / 2)
        dY = CircleRadius * Sin(dRad) + (dPageHeight / 2)
        'Add shape to drawing in proper location.
        Set shpObj = ActivePage.Drop(mstObj, dX, dY)
        'Set shape text.
        shpObj.Text = arrNetData(i, 1)

        'Connect the current node to the hub.
        Set shpObjConnector = ActivePage.Drop _
            (mstObjConnector, 0, 0)
        shpObjConnector.SendToBack
        'Glue the begin point to the hub shape.
        shpObjConnector.Cells("BeginX"). _
            GlueTo shpObjHUB.Cells("Connections.X1")
        'Glue the end point to the node that was just added.
        shpObjConnector.Cells("EndX"). _
            GlueTo shpObj.Cells("Connections.X1")
    Next
End Sub
```

Examining the Code for Creating a Drawing from Data

The code sample in the previous section (*Creating a Drawing from Data: an Example*) can be broken into three distinct parts:

- Setting up the program
- Adding the hub shape to the page
- Adding the node shapes to the page and connecting them to the hub

Setting up the program

The first section of code defines the constants and variables the program will use. Next, the array containing the data that the drawing will be created from is defined and initialized. Finally, the page dimensions are determined (this information will be used later as the basis for centering the hub shape), and the stencil used by this drawing is opened. In a more sophisticated solution, you might design the code in such a way as to allow the user to choose which stencil to open. Alternatively, stencil information might be imported as part of the data, rather than hard-coded as it is here.

Adding the hub shape to the page

In this program, nodes are connected to a hub, which is centered on the document page. The next section of the code reads the imported array to identify which master to use for the hub shape, drops an instance of that master at the center of the page, and sets the text for the shape. Next, the connector shape is identified, though instances of it are not dropped on the page until the node shapes are added to the drawing.

Adding node shapes to the page and connecting them to the hub

The final part of this program contains a loop that matches a field in each record in the imported array with a master on the open stencil. Once the master has been identified, the placement of the shape instance is determined; shapes are added to the page in a circle around the hub. After the shape is dropped at the correct location, the connector shape identified above is added to the page. Its begin point is connected to the hub shape, and its end point to the new node shape. This process is repeated for each record included in the array, and results in the finished drawing.

Integrating a Visio Solution with a Database

Integrating a Microsoft Visio solution with a database requires planning to synchronize the drawings with the database. It's important to decide which database should be used, what should be changed and how, and when the changes should occur.

For example, you might develop a solution in which each master corresponds to a numbered part in a manufacturer's catalog. By storing a part number as a custom property of each master, it is easy to look up part information in a version of the parts catalog stored as a database. However, the correspondence between the database and drawings created from the solution is not necessarily one-to-one, because there might be 20 instances of a master in a drawing, all with the same part number. Deleting a shape in the diagram shouldn't delete that part from the database, but updating the database should identify components used in the drawing that are no longer available.

Alternatively, to check a drawing for correctness, a solution developer might build an external model of the components and their interconnections, and store the external model in a data repository or temporarily in memory. Because the model must represent both the inventory of the parts and their interconnections, it might be composed of multiple linked tables. In this model, each component in the drawing would need a unique identifier in addition to its part number, so that identical components in the drawing can be distinguished from each other in the model. It would make sense to synchronize the external model with the drawing in real time so that, as the user adds component shapes to the drawing, the solution could add a suitable node to the model, and behave similarly if the user deleted a shape or a connection.

Deleting a shape, however, will generally do more than simply delete a record in the table that records all the components; the table that records connections between components will have to be modified as well. In general, an action in the drawing corresponds to a transaction that must be performed on the database, not just a simple insertion or deletion of a record.

Similarly, in a department organization solution, deleting an employee from one manager's organization chart would not justify deleting the employee's record in the company's human resources database until the new organization has been created and approved by management (and perhaps not even then). Instead, the organization charts would be synchronized with a central data model that represents the reorganization as it is being designed.

After designing the interactions between a solution and a database, a solution can make changes by:

- Handling **ShapeAdded**, **ShapesDeleted**, **ConnectionsAdded**, **ConnectionsDeleted**, **TextChanged**, and other Visio events and updating the database as the user changes the drawing.
- Handling the **DocumentOpened** and **BeforeDocumentClose** events and performing batch updates or otherwise synchronizing the database when the user opens and closes the drawing.
- Creating an external program that queries the Visio drawing to extract the data when needed—for example, when the user requests it.
- Storing all the solution's data in an external database and using data associated with Visio shapes, such as a custom property, as a key attribute to access records in the external database.

The Database Wizard provided with Microsoft Visio can add user-defined cells and link custom property cells to database fields for simple solutions or for prototyping more complex solutions. You can use the DAO (Data Access Object) library provided by Microsoft to access databases through ODBC (Open Database Connectivity) or use the Jet database engine. Or, you might have the Visio solution call an Automation server that actually updates and synchronizes the database, which provides more control over the integrity of the database.

21

Handling Visio Events

An Event Overview 422

Writing Code Behind Events 423

Visio Event Objects 431

An event is an action or occurrence, often generated by a user, that your program might respond to. In Microsoft Visio, events can result from user actions such as opening or closing documents, dropping or deleting shapes on the drawing page, editing the text of shapes, and altering shape formulas. Knowing that such events have occurred can be extremely useful because it allows you to program your solution to respond to user actions that can otherwise be difficult to predict.

You can handle events either programmatically or by using Visio formulas. As with any Visio solution, you should start by putting as much of the functionality as possible in formulas. For details about handling events using formulas, see Chapter 7, *Enhancing Shape Behavior*.

Visio provides two separate ways to handle events from your program:

- In Microsoft Visual Basic for Applications (VBA) or Microsoft Visual Basic programs, the simplest approach is to use the **WithEvents** keyword to declare object variables that can receive events. This is called *writing code behind events*.
- You can create Visio **Event** objects that can run an add-on or advise your program that an event has occurred. This technique can be used from any development environment. (In versions of VBA or Visual Basic earlier than 5.0, this was the only means of handling Visio events through Automation.) You can also set event filters to tailor the events

that your solution listens to, and prevent many of the events that you want to ignore from entering the event queue.

For details about handling events in a C++ program, see Chapter 28, *Programming Visio with C++*.

An Event Overview

Earlier chapters in this guide describe how to control Microsoft Visio objects by using Automation to get and set properties and to invoke methods. This one-way communication has its limitations: Your program can tell a Visio instance what to do, but it cannot find out what is happening in a Visio instance without explicitly checking for each possible case. Events allow objects and their clients to engage in bidirectional communication.

Working with an object's events differs from working with an object's properties and methods in this key respect: Properties and methods are both defined *and* implemented by Visio; events are defined by Visio, however, you are responsible for writing the code to implement them.

The following illustration shows how your program calls Visio to implement properties and events, and how Visio calls your program to implement events.

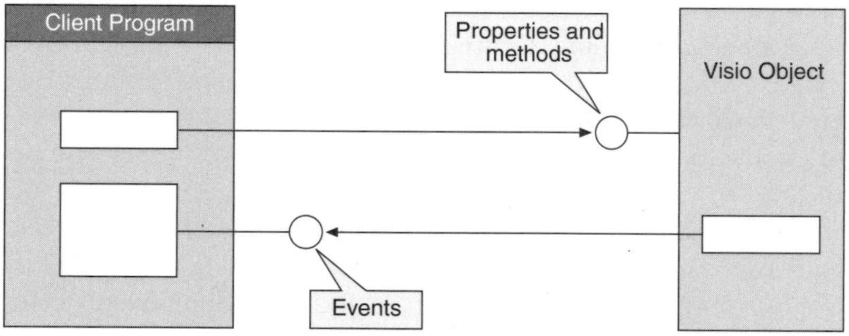

Figure 21-1 The interaction between Visio and your client program.

An event has both a subject and a source, which are typically different objects. The *subject* of an event is the object to which the event actually happens. For example, the subject of a **ShapeAdded** event is the **Shape** object that was added.

The *source* of an event is the object that produces the event. Most events have several potential sources. The source object you choose determines the *scope* in which the event fires—the higher the source object in the object hierarchy, the greater the scope. For example, if the source is a **Page** object, the **ShapeAdded** event fires whenever a shape is added to that page. If the source is the **Application** object, the **ShapeAdded** event fires whenever a shape is added to any page of any document that is open in the Visio instance.

Obviously, the more often an event fires, the more likely it is to affect the performance of your solution. Therefore, when you pick a source object, think first about the scope in which you want to handle the event.

> **Note** Beginning with Microsoft Visio 2002, you can use event filters to refine the events that you receive in your program. You can filter events by object, cell, ranges of cells, or command ID. For details about using event filters, see *Filtering Your Event Object* later in this chapter and see the method topics prefixed with **SetFilter** and **GetFilter** in the Microsoft Visio Developer Reference (on the **Help** menu, click **Developer Reference**).

The events that a source object can fire are called its *event set*. For Microsoft Visual Basic for Applications (VBA) or Visual Basic, these can be viewed in the Object Browser in the Visual Basic Editor. A Visio object that can source events will identify the members of its event set with a lightning bolt symbol. To search for events by object, by name, or by viewing a complete list of events, see the Microsoft Visio Developer Reference (on the **Help** menu, click **Developer Reference**).

Writing Code Behind Events

If you've written any Microsoft Visual Basic code, you've almost certainly written event procedures. An *event procedure* contains code that is executed when an event occurs. For example, a Visual Basic form with a button can have a procedure to handle the button's **Click** event. And writing code behind events in the Microsoft Visual Basic for Applications (VBA) environment in the Visio application is the same as writing code behind events in any other VBA host application; for example, any Microsoft Office application.

Every VBA project in Visio is set up to capture the events raised by the **Document** object associated with the project (**ThisDocument**). To respond to events raised by other Visio objects, you can declare object variables using the **WithEvents** keyword, which exposes all of the events defined for that particular object type, and provides skeleton event-handling procedures in your project. All you need to do is write code for the events you want to handle.

WithEvents object variables must be declared in class modules. You can declare them in the **ThisDocument** class, which is a default class module in every

Visio VBA project, or you can declare **WithEvents** object variables in a separate class module that you insert into your project.

Writing code behind events is also a way to handle the events raised by any Microsoft ActiveX controls that you have inserted into your project. For details on handling events for an ActiveX control, see Chapter 24, *Using ActiveX Controls in a Visio Solution*.

> **Note** Writing code behind events using the **WithEvents** keyword is a VBA and Visual Basic feature only. If you are programming in a different environment, see *Visio Event Objects* later in this chapter, or refer to your Component Object Model (COM) documentation for information on implementing interfaces that support COM-connectable objects.

All the information in this section also applies to a stand-alone Visual Basic project with the following exception: You need to set a reference to the Visio type library from your Visual Basic project. (In Visual Basic, click **References** on the **Projects** menu, and then select the Microsoft Visio 2002 type library.)

Handling Events Fired by ThisDocument

Every Visio VBA project contains a **ThisDocument** class module that responds automatically to the events raised by the **Document** object associated with your project.

For details about using the Visual Basic Editor, see Chapter 15, *Programming Visio with VBA*.

To create an event procedure in ThisDocument

1. Double-click **ThisDocument** in the **Project Explorer**, and the code window for your document opens. (If you don't see the **Project Explorer** in the Visual Basic Editor, click **Project Explorer** on the **View** menu.)

   The list box in the upper-left corner of the **Code** window is the **Object** box; the list box in the upper-right corner is the **Procedure** box.

2. Click **Document** in the **Object** box, and the event set for a **Document** object appears in the **Procedure** box.

3. Select an event from the **Procedure** box, and VBA creates an empty event procedure where you can write code to handle the event. Event procedures are always named *object_event*.

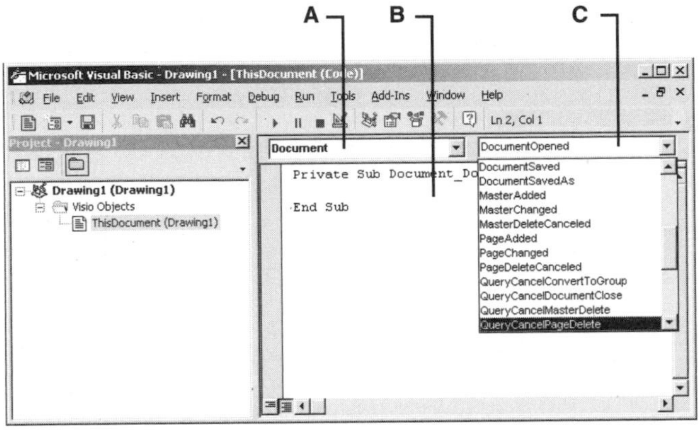

Figure 21-2 The **ThisDocument** code window. (**A**) **Object** box. (**B**) **Code** window for **ThisDocument** with a skeleton procedure. (**C**) **Procedure** box.The following example handles two events, **DocumentOpened** and **ShapeAdded**, to keep count of shapes (based on a master called Square) that are added to a drawing:

- The **DocumentOpened** event handler runs when a new drawing is based on the template that contains this code. The handler initializes an integer variable, *intSquares*, which is used to store the count.
- The **ShapeAdded** event handler runs each time a shape is added to the drawing page, whether the shape is dropped from a stencil, drawn with a drawing tool, or pasted from the Clipboard. The handler checks the **Master** property of the new **Shape** object and, if the shape is based on the **Square** master, increments *intSquares*.

```
'Number of squares added to drawing
Dim intSquares As Integer

Private Sub Document_DocumentOpened(ByVal Doc as IVDocument)
     'Initialize number of squares added
     intSquares = 0
End Sub

Private Sub Document_ShapeAdded(ByVal Shape As IVShape)
     Dim mastObj As Master
     'Get the Master property of the shape.
     Set mastObj = Shape.Master
     'Check whether the shape has a master. If not, the shape was
     'created locally.
     If Not ( mastObj Is Nothing ) Then
          'Check whether the master is "Square".
          If mastObj.Name = "Square" Then
               'Increment the count for the number of
```

```
                    'squares added.
                    intSquares = intSquares + 1
              End If
        End If
        MsgBox "Number of squares: " & intSquares, vbInformation
End Sub
```

To handle events fired by ThisDocument

1. Open the Visual Basic Editor by clicking the Visual Basic Editor button on the **Developer** toolbar. Or, on the **Tools** menu, point to **Macros**, and then click **Visual Basic Editor**.
2. In the **Project Explorer**, double-click **ThisDocument** to open its **Code** window.
3. Click **Document** in the **Object** box, and the events that get fired by a document will appear in the **Procedure** box.
4. Click the event you want to handle; Visio creates an empty event procedure for that event.
5. Fill in the event procedure with the code you want to execute when the event occurs.

Declaring an Object Variable Using the WithEvents Keyword

To handle events raised by Visio objects other than your project's document, you can use the VBA keyword **WithEvents** to declare an object variable for the Visio object whose events you want to handle. The following example describes setting up an object variable to handle the events raised by a **Page** object.

In **ThisDocument**, you declare an object variable using the **WithEvents** keyword and a Visio object type:

```
Dim WithEvents pageObj As Visio.Page
```

In addition to the usual access to an object's properties and methods, using the keyword **WithEvents** in this declaration gives the object variable the capacity to handle events fired by the **Page** object assigned to that variable. All events in the object's event set will be fired, and you provide code for the events that you want to handle.

By declaring this **WithEvents** variable as type *Visio.Page*, VBA can identify the type library (Visio) and the event set (Page) that it needs to capture. Now when you select *pageObj* in the **Object** box in the Visual Basic Editor, the **Procedure** box shows the events that are fired by the **Page** object.

For example, the following event procedure prints the names of shapes in the **Immediate** window whenever a shape is deleted from the active page of your project, which is represented by *pageObj*:

```
Public Sub pageObj_BeforeShapeDelete (ByVal Shape As IVShape)
    Debug.Print Shape.Name
End Sub
```

Before this procedure will run, however, you must connect the declared object (*pageObj*) with an instance of the object. Because this connection must be made before the **BeforeShapeDelete** event fires, you might put this statement in an event procedure for an event that you know will execute before **BeforeShapeDelete**, such as the document's **DocumentOpened** event. For example:

```
Private Sub Document_DocumentOpened(ByVal doc As IVDocument)
    Set pageObj = ActivePage
End Sub
```

When you are finished with an object reference it is a good practice to release the variable reference. This is often done in the **BeforeDocumentClose** event handler. For example:

```
Private Sub Document_BeforeDocumentClose(ByVal doc As IVDocument)
    set pageObj = Nothing
End Sub
```

For details about the **WithEvents** keyword, see your Visual Basic or VBA documentation.

To declare an object variable WithEvents in ThisDocument

1. Open the Visual Basic Editor and double-click the **ThisDocument** object in **Project Explorer**.
2. In the **Code** window, define an object variable using the Visual Basic keyword **WithEvents** in the **General** section of the module.
3. Click the object in the **Object** box, and the events that get fired by that object will appear in the **Procedure** box.
4. Click the event you want to handle; Visio creates an empty event procedure for that event.
5. Fill in the event procedure with the code you want to execute when the event occurs.
6. Set the object variable equal to an instance of the object.
7. Set the variable to **Nothing** when you're finished.

Defining a Class to Receive Events

You can streamline the process of handling events fired by a particular kind of Visio object by defining a class that contains your event variables and event-handling code. Writing code behind events in a class module works very much the same way as writing code behind events in **ThisDocument**. When you use a class module to receive events, however, you must create an instance of your class and connect it to a real object. (The **ThisDocument** object is instantiated and connected to the **Document** object associated with your project by default.)

When handling events in a separate class module, you write code in two places, your class module and your program.

- Your class module contains module-level **WithEvents** variable declarations, code inside of event procedures (code behind events), and code to bind your variable to Visio objects that fire events.
- Your program (often **ThisDocument**) contains module-level variable declarations of your class type, and code that creates and assigns an instance of your class to those variables.

Code in your class module

To add a class to your project, on the **Insert** menu, click **Class Module**. You can name this class whatever you want. Place all your event-handling code in this class. Let's say that you want to handle events from a Visio instance in your project—in this case, the source object is an **Application** object.

1. In your class module, declare a module-level **WithEvents** variable using the following statement:

   ```
   Dim WithEvents appObj As Visio.Application
   ```

2. After this variable is declared, *appObj* appears in the **Object** box in your class module, and when you select it, the valid events for that object appear in the **Procedure** box. Click an event in the **Procedure** box—an empty procedure is added to the class module, and you can write code behind the event you selected. For example, your solution may collect information about shapes in your drawing that it will process when the **NoEventsPending** event is fired.

3. You must associate your **WithEvents** variable with a real source object. To make the connection between a source object and the **WithEvents** variable, use the **Set** statement. The **WithEvents** variable is often assigned in the **Initialize** procedure of your class module and set to **Nothing** in the module's **Terminate** event.

   ```
   Set appObj = Application
   ```

Code in your program

Your event handler is in place, but nothing will happen until you define and create an instance of your class.

1. Add a reference to your class with the following declaration (usually module-level):

   ```
   Dim MyClass1 As MySinkClass
   ```

2. Create an instance of your class. For example, if we wanted to respond to events fired by the **Application** object as described in the previous topic, we could create an instance of the class module inside of the document's **DocumentOpened** event. To create an instance of your class module, use the **New** keyword:

   ```
   Set MyClass1 = New MySinkClass
   ```

   When you create an instance of your class, its **Initialize** event fires and the **WithEvents** variable is connected with a real object (see step 3 of the procedure in the previous section, *Code in your class module*). When you are finished with the instance of your class, release it by setting it to **Nothing**. This is often done in the **BeforeDocumentClose** event in your program:

   ```
   Set MyClass1 = Nothing
   ```

   For details about the **New** keyword, see your Visual Basic or VBA documentation.

To create a class module in your project to receive events

1. Insert a class module into your project.
2. Declare a module-level object variable using the **WithEvents** keyword inside your class module.
3. In the class module, click the object variable in the **Object** box, and the events that can be handled by that variable appear in the **Procedure** box.
4. Click the event you want to handle and provide code in the skeleton procedure.
5. Create an instance of your class module in your program.
6. Set the **WithEvents** variable to the source object whose events you want to receive.

Class Module that Responds to Events: an Example

The following example demonstrates a Visio project that uses a **WithEvents** variable to monitor events that are happening in a Visio instance. When this project is running, this event handler will display the document and shape name of any shape that is added to any document open in the Visio instance.

The project defines a class called *Listener*. In the *Listener* class, do the following:

- Declare a private **WithEvents** variable of type *Visio.Application*.
- Write code behind the application's **ShapeAdded** event.
- Connect the **WithEvents** variable with an **Application** object when the *Listener* class is instantiated. Then, release the connection when the class terminates.

```
'Code in the Class Module named Listener
Dim WithEvents m_app As Visio.Application
Private Sub Class_Initialize()
     Set m_app = Application
End Sub
Private Sub Class_Terminate()
     Set m_app = Nothing
End Sub
Private Sub m_app_ShapeAdded(ByVal Shape As IVShape)
     Debug.Print Shape.Document.Name; "/"; Shape.Name
End Sub
```

In **ThisDocument**, do the following:

- Define a variable of type *Listener*.
- Create an instance of *Listener* when the document enters run mode. Then, release the object when the document enters design mode or the document closes.

```
'Code in ThisDocument
Dim m_listener As Listener
Private Sub Document_RunModeEntered(ByVal doc As IVDocument)
     Set m_listener = New Listener
End Sub
Private Sub Document_DesignModeEntered(ByVal doc As IVDocument)
     Set m_listener = Nothing
End Sub
Private Sub Document_BeforeDocumentClose(ByVal doc As IVDocument)
     Set m_listener = Nothing
End Sub
```

Visio Event Objects

A Microsoft Visio **Event** object pairs an event with an action—either to run a Visio add-on or to notify an object in your program (also called a *sink object* or an *event sink*) that the event occurred. Your solution creates **Event** objects that describe the events you want to handle and tell Visio the action to take. When that event occurs, the **Event** object fires, triggering its action.

The first thing you must do is determine the type of **Event** object that your solution requires. What is your source object? What events do you need to receive? How will your solution respond to the events it does receive? Once you make these decisions, you create an **Event** object that runs an add-on or receives notifications.

> **Note** In versions of Microsoft Visual Basic and Microsoft Visual Basic for Applications (VBA) earlier than 5.0, this was the only way to create an event handler in the Visio application. If you are developing solutions in a language other than VBA, this is often the best technique. But if you are developing solutions in Visual Basic or VBA 5.0 or later, you might want to consider writing code behind events. For details about writing code behind events in Visio, see *Writing Code Behind Events* earlier in this chapter.

Defining Your Event Object

Before you create an **Event** object, you need to decide the following:

- The scope that the **Event** object should fire in.
- The event or events you want to receive.
- The action to perform when the event occurs—run an add-on or send a notification to an object in an already running program.

Determine the scope

The scope determines the source object whose **EventList** collection the **Event** object is added to. Any object that has an **EventList** collection can be a source of events. For performance reasons, add the **Event** object to the **EventList** collection of the *lowest* object in the hierarchy that can fire the **Event** object in the scope you want.

Indicate the event or events that will trigger an action

To indicate the event you want to handle, supply its *event code* to the **Add** or **AddAdvise** method. Event codes are prefixed with **visEvt** in the Visio type library. In some cases, an event code is a combination of two or more codes. For example, the event code for the **ShapeAdded** event is **visEvtAdd + visEvtShape**. In some cases, you can combine codes to indicate an interest in multiple events with a single **Event** object. For example, the event code **visEvtAdd + visEvtPage + visEvtShape** indicates that you're interested in both **ShapeAdded** and **PageAdded**.

When an **Event** object fires, the Visio engine passes the event code for the event that actually occurred, even if the **Event** object's event code indicates multiple events. To continue the last example, if a page is added, the Visio engine passes the event code **visEvtAdd + visEvtPage**.

Note Visual Basic and VBA report a run-time overflow error when performing statements using **visEvtAdd**. For example:

```
Set evt = evtList.AddAdvise(visEvtAdd + visEvtShape, _
    sinkObj, "", "")
```

The following factors cause this overflow condition:

- The first argument to the **AddAdvise** method is a 2-byte integer.
- Because **visEvtAdd** is declared as a member of an enumera tion in the Visio type library, it is treated as a 4-byte integer.
- The value of **visEvtAdd** is &H8000.
- Visual Basic and VBA do not support unsigned arithmetic.

Because **visEvtAdd** is a 4-byte value, which Visual Basic and VBA consider positive, **visEvtAdd + visEvtShape** is treated as 32768+64 = 32832, which is outside the range of legal values for a 2-byte signed quantity.

If **visEvtAdd** is explicitly declared as a 2-byte quantity with the value &H8000, Visual Basic and VBA consider it to be negative, and **visEvtAdd + visEvtShape** is treated as –32768+64 = –32704, which is in the range of legal 2-byte signed quantities.

To declare **visEvtAdd** as a 2-byte value in your program, add the following statement:

```
Global Const visEvtAdd% = &H8000
```

Decide the action to perform

The action determines which method you use to create the **Event** object, **Add** or **AddAdvise**. After you've decided what the source object should be, you can create the **Event** object by adding it to the **EventList** collection of the source object.

- To run an add-on or other external program, create an **Event** object using the **Add** method of the source object's **EventList** collection.
- To send a notification, create an **Event** object using the **AddAdvise** method of the source object's **EventList** collection. You must also tell Visio the object to notify. This will be a reference to your event sink.

For details on the **Add** and **AddAdvise** methods, see the Microsoft Visio Developer Reference (on the **Help** menu, click **Developer Reference**).

Filtering Your Event Object

Beginning with Microsoft Visio 2002, you can use event filters to refine the events that you receive in your program. You can filter events by object, cell, ranges of cells, or command ID. Event filtering allows you to tailor the events you listen to and prevents many of the events you don't want to hear from firing.

When an **Event** object created with the **AddAdvise** method is added to the **EventList** collection of a source object, the default behavior is that all occurrences of that event are passed to the event sink. The methods **SetFilterObjects**, **SetFilterSRC**, and **SetFilterCommands** provide a way to ignore (or pay attention to) selected events. Each method specifies an array and a **True** or **False** value indicating how to filter events for an object, a cell, ranges of cells, or for a command ID. Set the value to **True** to listen to events, or **False** to exclude events.

> **Note** If you set a filter to listen to specific events (by object, cell, ranges of cells, or command ID), only those events will fire.

For an event to successfully pass through an object filter, a cell range filter, or a command filter, it must satisfy the following criteria:

- It must be a valid object type, have a valid section, row, or cell reference, or have a valid command ID.
- If all filters are **True**, the event must match at least one filter.

- If all filters are **False**, the event must not match any filter.
- If the filters are a mixture of **True** and **False**, the event must match at least one **True** filter and not match any **False** filters.

Methods available for implementing event filters

Method	Description
SetFilterObjects	Provides a way to ignore or listen to selected events based on object type. One-dimensional array, 2 elements per object filter description (object type, True/False) Valid object types to filter on include: **visTypePage**, **visTypeGroup**, **visTypeShape**, **visTypeForeignObject** **visTypeGuide**, and **visTypeDoc**.
SetFilterSRC	Provides a way to ignore or listen to selected events based on a range of one or more cells. One-dimensional array, 7 elements per cell filter description (begin section, begin row, begin cell, end section, end row, end cell, True/False)
SetFilterCommands	Provides a way to ignore or listen to selected events based on a range of commands using command ID. One-dimensional array, 3 elements per command filter description (begin command, end comment, True/False)

The following example shows how you might create an event sink, get and set objects, and filter events that are passed to the event sink:

```
Option Base 1
Option Explicit

'Event sink
Dim vEventSink As adviseMe
Dim vEvent As Visio.Event

Public Sub SinkEvent()

'Get and set Event objects.

Dim vEventList As Visio.EventList

    'Get EventList collection for the document.
    Set vEventList = ActiveDocument.EventList
```

```
    'Add an advise sink.
    'adviseMe is a VB Class Module that implements
    'IVisEventProc to process events.
    Set vEventSink = New adviseMe

    'Add the cell changed event to the event list.
    Set vEvent = vEventList.AddAdvise(visEvtCell + visEvtMod, _
         vEventSink, "", "")
End Sub

Public Sub SetFilter()
    'Array for FilterObjects
    Dim arrFilterObjects(2) As Long

    'Array for FilterSRC
    Const maxSRCs As Integer = 1
    Dim arrFilterSRC(maxsrcs * 7) As Integer

    'Array for FilterCommands
    Dim arrFilterCommands(3) As Long

    'Set up an array of various objects to listen to.
    'Set up the FilterObject array to listen to Shape objects only.
    arrFilterObjects(1) = visTypeShape
    arrFilterObjects(2) = True

    'Set the filter for the event.
    vEvent.SetFilterObjects arrFilterObjects

    'Set up the FilterSRC array for specific cells to
    'pay attention to.
    'Listen to all cells in the Transform section
    'using visCellInval to say any cell.

    'Start cell of first range
    arrFilterSRC(1) = visSectionObject
    arrFilterSRC(2) = visRowXFormOut
    arrFilterSRC(3) = visCellInval

    'End cell of first range
    arrFilterSRC(4) = visSectionObject
    arrFilterSRC(5) = visRowXFormOut
    arrFilterSRC(6) = visCellInval

    'Receive events for the described range.
    arrFilterSRC(7) = True
```

```
        'Set the filter for the event.
        vEvent.SetFilterSRC arrFilterSRC

        'Set up the FilterCommands array to block cell
        'changed events caused by the Lay Out Shapes command.
        arrFilterCommands(1) = Visio.VisUICmds.visCmdToolsLayoutShapesDlg
        arrFilterCommands(2) = Visio.VisUICmds.visCmdToolsLayoutShapesDlg
        arrFilterCommands(3) = False

        'Set the filter for the event.
        vEvent.SetFilterCommands arrFilterCommands

End Sub
```

You can get the current status of an event filter using the methods **GetFilterObjects**, **GetFilterSRC**, **GetFilterCommands**.

For other details about using event filters, see the method topics prefixed with **SetFilter** and **GetFilter** in the Microsoft Visio Developer Reference (on the **Help** menu, click **Developer Reference**).

Getting Information about an Event Object

After you create an **Event** object, you can get information about it by querying its properties (as described in the Microsoft Visio Developer Reference). In addition, the **EventInfo** property of the **Application** object provides more information about certain events after they occur. For example, after the **ShapesDeleted** event fires, you can get the names of the deleted shapes from the **EventInfo** property.

Because there is only one **EventInfo** property for potentially many events, you must specify the event you want to handle when you get **EventInfo**. To do this, pass the event's sequence number (which Visio passes as the third argument when it calls **VisEventProc** on the corresponding sink object), or pass **visEvtIDMostRecent** for the most recent event. If there is no additional information for the event you specify, **EventInfo** returns an empty string.

For details about the information passed by a particular event, search for that event in the Microsoft Visio Developer Reference (on the **Help** menu, click **Developer Reference**).

Creating an Event Object that Runs an Add-on

An **Event** object that runs an add-on is created using the **Add** method of the **EventList** collection. To create an **Event** object that runs an add-on, you invoke the **Add** method with the following arguments:

- The event code for the event or events that you want to handle
- The action code **visActCodeRunAddon**
- The name of the add-on to run
- Optionally, a string of arguments to pass to the add-on when the **Event** object fires

When the **Event** object fires, Visio passes the argument string as command line arguments if the add-on is an EXE file, or as the *lpCmdLineArgs* field of the **VAOV2LSTRUCT** structure passed to an add-on implemented by a Visio library (VSL).

For example, the following code creates an **Event** object that runs an add-on called Showargs.exe and passes the string `"/args=Shape added!"` as a command line argument. The **Event** object is added to the **EventList** collection of the document.

```
Private Sub Form_Load()
    Dim eventsObj As Visio.EventList
    Dim docObj As Visio.Document

    'Create a new drawing.
    'A Visio instance has already been assigned to g_appVisio.
    Set docObj = g_appVisio.Documents.Add("")
    'Get the EventList collection of this document.
    Set eventsObj = docObj.EventList
    'Add an Event object that will run an add-on when the event _
    'fires.
    eventsObj.Add visEvtShape + visEvtAdd, visActCodeRunAddon, _
        "SHOWARGS.EXE", "/args=Shape added!"
End Sub
```

When a shape is added to any page in the document, the **ShapeAdded** event fires. The action the event triggers is to run the add-on Showargs.exe, which will identify the shape that was added along with the string `"Shape added!"`.

Persistence of an Event Object that Runs an Add-on

An **Event** object that runs an add-on can be stored with a Visio document if the source object has a **PersistsEvents** property of **True**. This is sometimes called *persisting an event*. An **Event** object can be stored with a document if it meets the following conditions:

- The **Event** object's action must be to run an add-on. **Event** objects that send notifications cannot be stored. If an **Event** object *can* be stored, its **Persistable** property is **True**.

- The **PersistsEvents** property of the event's source object must be **True**. Beginning with Microsoft Visio 2000, **Document**, **Page**, and **Master** objects can do this.

Whether a persistable **Event** object actually persists depends on the setting of its **Persistent** property. If the **Event** object is persistable, the Visio instance assumes that it should be stored with the document, so the initial value of its **Persistent** property is **True**. If you do not want the Visio instance to store the **Event** object, set its **Persistent** property to **False**.

> **Note** Before you attempt to change an **Event** object's **Persistent** property, make sure its **Persistable** property is **True**. Setting the **Persistent** property of a nonpersistable event causes an error.

Creating an Event Object that Sends a Notification

An **Event** object that sends a notification is created using the **AddAdvise** method of the **EventList** collection and can send a notification to a program that is already running. Creating this kind of **Event** object differs from creating one that simply runs an add-on in the following ways:

- You define an object in your program—not a Visio object—to receive the notification when it is sent. This kind of object is sometimes called a *notification sink* or *sink object*.
- You write an event procedure (**VisEventProc**) in your sink object to handle notifications when they are received.
- Your program creates instances of sink objects and the **Event** objects in the Visio instance at run time. Because this kind of **Event** object uses references, it cannot be stored with a Visio document and must be created each time the program runs.

The following diagram shows how a program interacts with objects in Visio to receive event notifications.

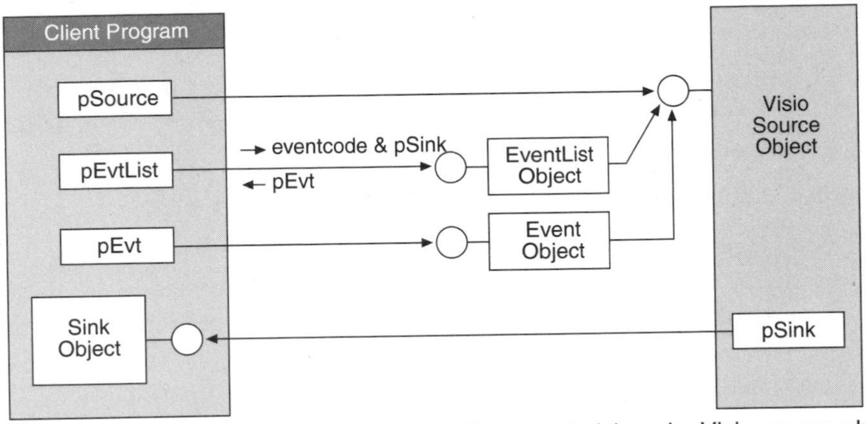

Figure 21-3 The interaction between a client event sink and a Visio source object.

In this diagram, *pSource* is a reference to the source object in the Visio instance. This is used to get a reference to the source object's **EventList** collection, which is assigned to *pEvtList*.

The program uses *pEvtList.AddAdvise* to create the **Event** object, which is assigned to *pEvt*. With **AddAdvise**, the program passes a reference to the sink object that the Visio instance sends the notification to when the **Event** object fires.

Define the sink object to receive notifications

A sink object is a non Visio object you define to receive the notifications that the Visio instance sends. At a minimum, the sink object must be programmable (that is, it must support the Automation **IDispatch** interface) and must expose an event procedure named **VisEventProc**. You can give the sink object whatever additional functionality makes sense for your program.

You can structure your solution in many ways. For example, you can create:

- One class for each event fired by a source object.
- One class to capture all the events fired by a single source object.
- One class to capture the events from multiple source objects.
- One class to handle a certain event fired from multiple source objects.

To create a sink object in VBA or Visual Basic

1. In your VBA project, on the **Insert** menu, click **Class Module**. Or, in your Visual Basic project, on the **Project** menu, click **Add Class Module**.
2. Name the new object. This is your sink object.

   Typically, you would set the object's **Public** property to **True**, but that isn't required. If you want, you can code predefined methods such as **Initialize** and **Terminate** or add your own methods to the class.

> **Note** Visual Basic projects that use the **AddAdvise** method must be set up as ActiveX EXE projects rather than a Standard EXE projects because they must expose public objects (sink objects). The **Instancing** property of classes that serve as sink objects should generally be set to **MultiUse**.

Write the VisEventProc event procedure

In your class module, write an event procedure called **VisEventProc** to handle notifications when they are received from Visio. Write code in the **VisEventProc** procedure in whatever way makes sense for your program. Visio does not require you to design your event handler in any particular way. You can choose to use any technique for branching within your procedure, and depending on the number and category of events your program will handle, you might define a different sink object for each event. When an **Event** object fires, the Visio instance calls the **VisEventProc** procedure for the corresponding sink object.

The **VisEventProc** procedure must be declared with the following parameters:

```
Public Sub VisEventProc( _
    'The event code of the event that caused the Event
    'object to fire.
    eventCode As Integer, _

    'A reference to the source object whose EventList
    'collection contains the Event object that fired.
    sourceObj As Object, _

    'The unique identifier of the Event object within its
    'EventList collection. Unlike the Index property, the
```

```
    'identifier does not change as objects are added or
    'removed from the collection. You can access the Event
    'object from within the VisEventProc procedure by using
    'source.EventList.ItemFromID(id).
    eventID As Long, _

    'The sequence of the event relative to events that have
    'fired so far in the instance of Visio.
    seqNum As Long, _

    'A reference to the subject of the event, which is the
    'object to which the event occurred.
    subjectObj As Object, _

    'Additional information, if any, that accompanies the
    'notification. For most events, this argument will be
    'Nothing.
    moreInfo As Variant) As Variant

End Sub
```

Note Beginning with Microsoft Visio 2000, **VisEventProc** is defined as a function that returns a value. However, Visio only looks at return values from calls to **VisEventProc** that are passed a query event code. Sink objects that provide **VisEventProc** through **IDispatch** require no change.

To modify existing event handlers so they can handle query events, change the **Sub** procedure to a **Function** procedure and return the appropriate value. For details about query events, see the **AddAdvise** method and event topics prefixed with **Query** in the Microsoft Visio Developer Reference (on the **Help** menu, click **Developer Reference**).

Create the Event object that sends the notification

Now that your program has defined your sink object, you will need to create **Event** objects to include in the **EventList** collection of the source object whose events you want to receive.

To create an Event object that sends a notification

1. Create an instance of your sink object.

   You can use the same instance of the sink object for multiple **Event** objects, or you can use more than one instance of the sink object.

2. Get a reference to the **EventList** collection of the source object in the Visio instance.

3. Use the **AddAdvise** method and provide the event code and a reference to the sink object.

   AddAdvise has two additional arguments. The third argument is reserved for future use and should be a null string (""). The fourth argument can be a string of arguments for the event handler. The Visio instance assigns these to the **Event** object's **TargetArgs** property. When your program receives a notification, **VisEventProc** can retrieve these arguments from the **Event** object that called it.

To define a sink object and set up event notification in your VBA or Visual Basic project

1. Insert a class module into your project.

2. In your class module, write an event procedure called **VisEventProc**.

   If you use the following **Implements** statement in your class module, you can click **IVisEventProc** in the **Object** box and then click **VisEventProc** in the **Procedure** box.

   ```
   Implements Visio.IVisEventProc
   ```

   For details about the **Implements** keyword, see your Visual Basic documentation.

3. In the **VisEventProc** procedure, write code to handle the notifications received from Visio in whatever way makes sense for your program.

4. In your program, create an instance of your class module.

5. Get a reference to the **EventList** collection of your source object.

6. Use the **AddAdvise** method of the **EventList** collection to create your **Event** object.

The VisEventProc Procedure: an Example

The following **VisEventProc** procedure uses a **Select Case** block to check for three events: **DocumentSaved**, **PageAdded**, and **ShapesDeleted**. Other events fall under the default case (**Case Else**). Each **Case** block constructs a string (*strDumpMsg*) that contains the name and event code of the event that fired. Finally, the procedure displays the string in a message box.

```
Public Sub VisEventProc(eventCode As Integer, _
    sourceObj As Object, eventID As Long, seqNum As Long, _
    subjectObj As Object, moreInfo As Variant) As Variant

    Dim strDumpMsg As String

    'Find out which event fired.
    Select Case eventCode
            Case visEvtCodeDocSave
                    strDumpMsg = "Save(" & eventCode & ")"
            Case (visEvtPage + visEvtAdd)
                    strDumpMsg = "Page Added(" & eventCode & ")"
            Case visEvtCodeShapeDelete
                    strDumpMsg = "Shape Deleted(" & eventCode & ")"
            Case Else
                    strDumpMsg = "Other(" & eventCode & ")"
    End Select

    'Display the event name and code.
    frmEventDisplay.EventText.Text = strDumpMsg
End Sub
```

For an example of a program that creates **Event** objects that might call this procedure, see *Event Objects that Send Notifications: an Example* later in this section.

Note Beginning with Microsoft Visio 2000, **VisEventProc** is defined as a function that returns a value. However, Visio only looks at return values from calls to **VisEventProc** that are passed a query event code. Sink objects that provide **VisEventProc** through **IDispatch** require no change.

To modify existing event handlers so they can handle query events, change the **Sub** procedure to a **Function** procedure and return the appropriate value. For details about query events, see the **AddAdvise** method and event topics prefixed with **Query** in the Microsoft Visio Developer Reference (on the **Help** menu, click **Developer Reference**).

Event Objects that Send Notifications: an Example

For example, let's say that when we created our sink object, we called the class module that we inserted into our project *CEventSamp*. The following code creates an instance of the sink object *CEventSamp* and creates **Event** objects to send notifications of the following events: **DocumentSaved**, **PageAdded**, and **ShapesDeleted**.

```
'Create an instance of the sink object class CEventSamp.
Dim g_Sink As CEventSamp
Dim docObj As Visio.Document

Private Sub Form_Load()
    Dim eventsObj As Visio.EventList

    'Create an instance of the CEventSamp class.
    'g_Sink is global to the form.
    Set g_Sink = New CeventSamp

    'Create a new drawing.
    'A Visio instance has already been assigned to g_appVisio.
    Set docObj = g_appVisio.Documents.Add("")

    'Get the EventList collection of this document.
    Set eventsObj = docObj.EventList

    'Add Event objects that will send notifications.
    'Add an Event object for the DocumentSaved event.
    eventsObj.AddAdvise visEvtCodeDocSave, g_Sink, "", _
        "Document Saved..."

    'Add an Event object for the ShapesDeleted event.
    eventsObj.AddAdvise visEvtCodeShapeDelete, g_Sink, "", _
        "Shape Deleted..."

    'Add an Event object for the PageAdded event
    eventsObj.AddAdvise (visEvtPage + visEvtAdd), g_Sink, "", _
        "Page Added..."
End Sub
```

When the **PageAdded**, **ShapesDeleted**, or **DocumentSaved event fires, the Visio instance calls VisEventProc** on the sink object g_sink. For an example of a corresponding **VisEventProc** procedure, see *The VisEventProc Procedure: an Example* earlier in this section.

Lifetime of an Event Object that Sends a Notification

Event objects created with the **AddAdvise** method persist until:

- The **Event** object is deleted with the **Delete** method.
- All references to the source object are released, including references that are held indirectly through a reference to the source object's **EventList** collection or to an **Event** object in the collection.
- The Visio instance terminates.

When the Visio instance terminates, it issues a **BeforeQuit** event, which the program should handle by releasing all its references to source objects or performing any other cleanup tasks. After the Visio instance issues **BeforeQuit**, it releases all its references to sink objects in the program.

22

Customizing the Visio User Interface

Using CommandBar Objects to Customize the Visio User Interface 448

Using Visio UIObject Objects to Customize the Visio User Interface 464

Using Custom User Interface Files 486

You can customize the Microsoft Visio user interface (UI) to make running your program easier or to simplify Visio for your users. For example, you might add a custom toolbar button or menu item that runs your solution, or remove tools and menu commands that you want to make unavailable while your solution is running.

This chapter discusses how to customize the Visio user interface from a program by accessing **CommandBar** objects or **UIObject** objects, or through a custom Visio user interface (VSU) file. For details about using the **Customize** command, see the Microsoft Visio Help.

You can modify the Visio user interface in any of the following ways:

- Use the **Customize** command (on the **Tools** menu, click **Customize**. Or, on the **View** menu, point to **Toolbars**, and then click **Customize**). Users can modify the user interface in this way, too, if they have access to the **Customize** command.
- Include code in your solution that accesses the Microsoft Office **CommandBar** objects.
- Include code in your solution that accesses the Visio **UIObject** objects.

- Create a VSU file that contains only menu and toolbar items specific to your solution and load this file each time your solution runs. A VSU file is a snapshot of your custom user interface, containing your custom user interface data. To make extensive changes to the Visio user interface, you can code your custom user interface changes in an external development environment and save a custom user interface file.

> **Tip** If your solution is an external program that uses the Visio engine as a component (as opposed to an add-on that runs within a Visio instance), you might want to conceal more than just the Visio menus and toolbars from your users. You can hide the Visio instance completely by setting the **Application.Visible** property to **False**. Window objects also have the **Visible** property, so you can hide just a window if necessary. For details about the **Visible** property, search the Microsoft Visio Developer Reference (on the Help menu, click **Developer Reference**).

Using CommandBar Objects to Customize the Visio User Interface

Microsoft Visio and other Microsoft Office applications share the same technology for creating menus and toolbars, and this technology is available to you through the Microsoft Office command bars object model. The command bars object model exposes a wealth of objects, collections, properties, and methods that you can use to show, hide, and modify existing command bars and command bar controls, and create new ones. In addition, you can specify a Microsoft Visual Basic for Applications (VBA) procedure to run when a user clicks a command bar button or to respond to events triggered by a command bar or command bar control.

Because the command bars object model is shared by Visio and all Office applications, you can write code to manipulate command bars that can be used in any custom Office application or Visio solution you develop. Everything the user can do in Visio using the **Customize** dialog box, you can also do in your solution code using the Office command bars object model.

> **Note** The topics in this section provide information on the basics of working with command bars in Visio. For other details about working with command bars, see "Working with Command Bars" in the *Microsoft Office XP Developer's Guide*.
>
> For details about the **CommandBars** collection and **CommandBar** and **CommandBarControl** objects, and their associated properties, methods, and events, see the *Microsoft Office Visual Basic Reference,* Microsoft Press, 2001.

Working with the Command Bars Object Model

Beginning with Microsoft Visio 2002, you can use Microsoft Office **CommandBar** objects to customize the Visio user interface. In Visio and Office applications, there are three kinds of **CommandBar** objects: toolbars, menu bars, and pop-up menus. Pop-up menus are displayed in three ways: as menus that drop down from menu bars, as submenus that cascade off menu commands, and as shortcut menus. Shortcut menus (also called "right-click menus") are menus that appear when you right-click an element in the application.

> **Note** Changes you make to the Visio user interface using Visio **UIObject** objects are still fully supported in Visio 2002. However, the Microsoft Office command bars object model offers a robust and viable alternative for customizing the Visio user interface for your solutions.

The command bars object model is straightforward to learn and to program with, and you can easily reuse your code in any Office solution. It also supports the creation of custom text boxes, combo boxes, and drop-down list boxes—objects that aren't supported in the Visio object model.

You work with the following collections and objects in the command bars object model: the **CommandBars** and **CommandBarControls** collections, and the **CommandBar**, **CommandBarButton**, **CommandBarComboBox**, **CommandBarControl**, and **CommandBarPopup** objects.

There are several differences between working with **CommandBar** objects and Visio **UIObject** objects:

- Unlike Visio **UIObject** objects, where menus and toolbars are separated into two groups containing different types of objects (menus and menu items, and toolbars and toolbar items), **CommandBar** objects are grouped into a single **CommandBars** collection, in which menus and toolbars are treated as the same kind of object. Similarly, menu items and toolbar items are treated as **CommandBarControl** objects.
- Changes that you make to the Visio user interface using **CommandBar** objects are made at the application level, not at the document level. And, unless you flag specific changes as temporary, the changes you make to the user interface persist between application sessions. Changes that you make to the Visio user interface using **UIObject** objects can be made at the application or document level, and these changes do not persist between application sessions.
- Changes you make to the Visio user interface using **CommandBar** objects are applied immediately to whatever command bars are currently active. If you use Visio **UIObject** objects to change the user interface, you typically start with a snapshot of the user interface, make your changes to that snapshot, and then apply the entire snapshot to the current user interface in one operation.

> **Note** To access **CommandBar** objects in Microsoft Visual Basic for Applications (VBA) or Microsoft Visual Basic, you must set a reference to the Microsoft Office 10.0 object library.

Creating a Command Bar

You create a command bar by using the **CommandBars** collection's **Add** method. The **Add** method creates a toolbar by default. To create a menu bar or pop-up menu instead, use the **msoBarMenuBar** or **msoBarPopup** constant in the **Add** method's **Position** argument.

You can create toolbars by using the **Customize** dialog box in Visio, or by accessing the Microsoft Office command bars object model. However, to create menu bars or pop-up menus, you must use **CommandBar** and **CommandBarControl** objects.

The following code sample illustrates how to create all three types of CommandBar objects:

```
Dim cbrCmdBar As CommandBar
'Create a toolbar.
Set cbrCmdBar = Application.CommandBars.Add(Name:= "MyNewToolbar")

'Create temporary toolbar that doesn't
'persist between application sessions.
Set cbrCmdBar = Application.CommandBars.Add(Name:= _
    "MyNewToolbar",Temporary:=True)

'Create a menu bar.
Set cbrCmdBar = Application.CommandBars.Add(Name:= "MyNewMenuBar", _
    Position:=msoBarMenuBar)

'Create a pop-up menu.
Set cbrCmdBar = Application.CommandBars.Add(Name:= _
    "MyNewPopupMenu", Position:=msoBarPopup)
```

After you have created a command bar, you can then add any controls that you want.

> **Note** To access **CommandBar** objects in VBA or Visual Basic, you must set a reference to the Microsoft Office 10.0 object library.

Specifying the context for displaying a command bar

The Visio object model partitions each collection of toolbars and menus into separate context sets, of which only one context can be active and visible at a given time (depending on what the user is doing and what window is currently active in Visio). Visio switches contexts frequently, such as whenever a new drawing opens or a user switches between open drawings.

Visio manages the display of command bars when switching between contexts. For example, if you define the context for a custom command bar to be the ShapeSheet window (**visUIObjSetShapesheet**), Visio automatically enables the command bar when the ShapeSheet context is active, and automatically disables the command bar when Visio switches to a different context such as the drawing window (**visUIObjSetDrawing**) or the Print Preview window (**visUIObjSetPrintPreview**).

Because Visio has multiple contexts, you need to define the context in which your command bar is available in Visio. You assign the context in which you want a command bar to appear using the **Context** property of the **CommandBar** object.

The **Context** property setting indicates the context that the command bar appears in and whether the command bar is visible or hidden when the context becomes active. The context number is a **String** value (for example `visUIObjSetDrawing` or `"2"`), which is followed by an asterisk if the command bar should be visible in that context while the context is active (for example, `visUIObjSetShapeSheet & "*" or "4*"`). For example, the **Standard** toolbar in the drawing window context typically returns a value of `"2*"`, whereas the **Action** toolbar typically returns a value of `"2"`.

> **Note** The default value for any new command bar that you create is `visUIObjSetDrawing` or `"2"`, which means that the command bar is hidden when the drawing window context becomes active.

The following are valid context settings for the **Context** property:

- **visUIObjSetDrawing** (2)
- **visUIObjSetStencil** (3)
- **visUIObjSetShapeSheet** (4)
- **visUIObjSetIcon** (5)
- **visUIObjSetPrintPreview** (7)

Attempting to set the **Context** property to any other value will fail. You can change the visibility for any command bar. However, you can only change the context number for custom command bars (not built-in command bars).

The following code samples demonstrate settings for the **Context** property of a command bar:

```
'Set the command bar to be enabled and visible
'when the drawing window context is active.
cbar.Context = Str(visUIObjSetDrawing) & "*"
```

```
'Set the command bar to be hidden (but enabled)
'when the ShapeSheet window context is active.
cbar.Context = visUIObjSetShapeSheet
```

Displaying a command bar

The best way to display a command bar in Visio is to use the **CommandBar** object's **Context** property. This approach allows you to reliably set the visibility of command bars in any context, regardless of what context is currently active in Visio.

You specify that a command bar is visible when the context becomes active by including an asterisk when you set the property, or specify that the command bar is hidden when the context becomes active by omitting the asterisk. For details on using the **Context** property, see *Specifying the context for displaying a command bar* earlier in this section.

Another way to show or hide a command bar is to use the **CommandBar** object's **Visible** property. However, you can only set this property for command bars that are in the current context, and therefore enabled. When using the **Visible** property, you should first determine if a command bar is enabled by querying the **Enabled** property of a **CommandBar** object.

For example:

```
'Display the command bar in the current context.
'Check the Enabled property before
'attempting to set the Visible property.
If cbar.Enabled = True Then
    cbar.Visible = True
End If

'Hide the command bar in the current context.
'Check the Enabled property before
'attempting to set the Visible property.
If cbar.Enabled = True Then
    cbar.Visible = False
End If
```

> **Note** Setting the **Visible** property of a command bar that is not in the current context results in an error.

Maintaining references to command bar controls when contexts change

Every time the context changes, Visio removes and then reapplies all custom user interface changes. To maintain references to command bar controls, you must assign a unique tag to each control using the **Tag** property. For example:

```
Public Sub Form_Load()
    With Application.CommandBars.Add"MyBar")
        With myBar.Controls.Add(msoControlButton)
            .Tag = "MyBar.MyControl"
        End With
    End With
End Sub
```

You also need to assign a unique tag to a command bar control if you will be using the **FindControl** method in your code, for example:

```
Public Sub DoSomething()
    Dim myControl As Office.CommandBar
    Set myControl = Application.CommandBars("MyBar"). _
        FindControl(Tag := "MyBar.MyControl")
    'Do stuff with myControl.
End Sub
```

The Microsoft Office dynamic-link library (MSO.dll) automatically hooks back into event handlers for command bar controls, provided the controls use the **Tag** property. The following code will continue to work after the context changes:

```
Private WithEvents myButton As Office.CommandBarButton
Public Sub Form_Load()
    With Application.CommandBars.Add("MyBar")
        Set myButton = .Controls.Add(msoControlButton)
        myButton.Tag = "MyBar.MyControl"
    End With
End Sub

Private Sub myButton_Click(ByVal Ctrl As Office.CommandBarButton, _
    CancelDefault As Boolean)
    'The button was pushed.
End Sub
```

> **Note** To access the **Tag** property and **FindControl** method of a **CommandBar** object in VBA or Visual Basic, you must set a reference to the Microsoft Office 10.0 object library.

Getting Information about Command Bars

The **CommandBars** property of the Visio Application object returns a reference to the **CommandBars** collection that represents the command bars in the container application.

The following code demonstrates using the **CommandBars** property to list the command bars in the current application:

```
Public Sub IterateCommandBars()
    Dim myCommandBars As CommandBars
    Dim myCommandBar As CommandBar
    'Get the set of CommandBars
    'for the application.
    Set myCommandBars = Application.CommandBars
    'List each CommandBar in
    'the Immediate window.
    For Each myCommandBar In myCommandBars
        Debug.Print myCommandBar.Name
    Next
End Sub
```

Deleting a Command Bar

Use the **Delete** method of the **CommandBars** collection to remove an existing command bar from the collection. You can delete toolbars and menu bars using the **Customize** dialog box in Visio or by using code. However, you can delete pop-up menus only by using code.

The following procedure illustrates one way to delete a **CommandBar** object:

```
Sub DeleteDrawingCommandBar()

    Dim cbars As CommandBars
    Dim cbar1 As CommandBar

On Error Resume Next

    'The gateway to the Microsoft Office command bars object model
    Set cbars = Application.CommandBars

    'Get the command bar named MyDrawingCommandBar
    'added by AddDrawingContextCommandBar().
    Set cbar1 = cbars("MyDrawingCommandBar")

    'Delete that command bar.
    cbar1.Delete

End Sub
```

An error occurs if the command bar does not exist. The procedure uses the **On Error Resume Next** statement to ignore this error because, if an error occurs, it means there is nothing to delete. An error also occurs if you try to delete a built-in command bar, such as the **Standard** toolbar, which cannot be deleted.

Working with Command Bar Controls

Each **CommandBar** object has a **CommandBarControls** collection, which contains all the controls (**CommandBarControl** objects) on the command bar. You use the **Controls** property of a **CommandBar** object to refer to a control on a command bar. If the control is of the type **msoControlPopup**, it also will have a **CommandBarControls** collection representing each control on the pop-up menu. (Pop-up menu controls represent menus and submenus and can be nested several layers deep.)

In this example, the code returns a reference to the **New** button on the **Standard** toolbar:

```
Dim ctlCBarControl As CommandBarControl
Set ctlCBarControl = _
    Application.CommandBars("Standard").Controls("New")
```

When you have a reference to a control on a command bar, you can access all available properties and methods of that control.

> **Note** When you refer to a command bar control by using the control's **Caption** property, you must be sure to specify the caption exactly as it appears on the menu.
>
> A more reliable way to identify specific controls is to use the **Tag** property. By using the **Tag** property, you don't need to worry about users renaming control captions, and it's easier to port your solution to different language versions.

Adding controls to a command bar

To add a control to a command bar, use the **Add** method of the **CommandBarControls** collection that specifies the type of control you want to create. You can add the following types of controls:

- Button (**msoControlButton**)
- Text box (**msoControlEdit**)
- Drop-down list box (**msoControlDropdown**)

- Combo box (**msoControlComboBox**)
- Pop-up menu (**msoControlPopup**)

The following example adds a button control to a command bar:

```
'Add a button to MyDrawingCommandBar
'that runs a VBA macro.
Set cbButton = cbar.Controls.Add(Type:=msoControlButton)
With cbButton
    .Caption = "VBA Macro"
    .TooltipText = "Click this button to run a VBA Macro"
    'Use the Tag property for context switching and
    'for use with the FindControl method.
    .Tag = "cbbVBAMacro"
    'Set the button face to use an internal icon.
    .FaceID = 7075
    'Use the OnAction property to run a VBA macro
    'contained in this document.
    .OnAction = "ThisDocument.HelloWorld"
End With
```

Using the OnAction property of a CommandBarControl object

Each **CommandBarControl** object in a **CommandBarControls** collection has an **OnAction** property, which specifies a procedure to run when a user clicks a button, displays a menu, or changes the contents of a combo box control.

In Visio, you can use the **OnAction** property to load a Component Object Model (COM) add-in, or to run a VBA macro, or a Visio add-on VSL (Visio library) in response to a user clicking a toolbar or menu item. (You do not need to write a handler for the **Click** event when you use the **OnAction** property.)

Use the following syntax to set the **OnAction** property to run a VBA macro or Visio add-on:

```
ctlButton.OnAction = "<ProjectName>!<MacroName>"

ctlButton.OnAction = "<MacroName|AddonName>"
```

For a COM add-in, the syntax for setting the **OnAction** property is:

```
ctlButton.OnAction = "!<ProgID>"
```

where *ctlButton* is the **CommandBarButton** object and *ProgID* is the programmatic identifier for the add-in. The programmatic identifier is the subkey that is created for the add-in in the Windows registry. You must set the **OnAction** property for any COM add-in you create that is loaded on demand. For details on implementing COM add-ins, see Chapter 23, *Using COM Add-ins in a Visio Solution*.

The following code demonstrates the various syntax options for the **OnAction** property:

```
'Runs a COM add-in that is registered for Visio.
MyCtlButton.OnAction = "!<MyAddin.VisioCOMAddin>"

'Runs the Hello World macro in the ThisDocument module
'of the Drawing1 project. Drawing1.vsd must be open.
MyCtlButton.OnAction = "Drawing1!ThisDocument.HelloWorld"

'Runs the Hello World macro in the active document.
MyCtlButton.OnAction = "ThisDocument.HelloWorld"

'Runs a Visio add-on named "My Organization Chart".
'Visio automatically looks at the Parameter property
'of the control to determine add-on arguments, if any.
MyCtlButton.OnAction = "My Organization Chart"
MyCtlButton.Parameter = "/FILENAME ""C:\Samples\My Organization _
    Chart Data.xls"""
```

The following code sets a button control's **OnAction** property to run a Visio add-on named "Hello World".

```
'Add a button to the command bar.
Set cbButton = cbar.Controls.Add(Type:=msoControlButton)
With cbButton
    .Caption = "Run Hello World add-on"
    .OnAction = "Hello World"
End With
```

Note To use the **OnAction** property in VBA or Visual Basic, you must set a reference to the Microsoft Office 10.0 object library.

You can also handle the **Click** event in response to a user clicking a command bar button. For details, see *Using the Click event procedure of a command bar button* later in this section.

Showing and enabling command bar controls

You specify whether a command bar control is shown on a command bar by using its **Visible** property. You specify whether a command bar control appears enabled or disabled (dimmed) by using its **Enabled** property. For example, the following two lines of code could be used to toggle the **Visible** and **Enabled** properties of the named controls:

```
Application.CommandBars("Menu Bar").Controls("Edit").Enabled = False

Application.CommandBars("Formatting").Controls("Font").Visible = False
```

> **Note** The **Enabled** and **Visible** properties differ in their behavior for custom controls versus built-in controls. For custom controls, **True** means always show or enable the control, and **False** means always hide or disable the control. For built-in controls, **True** means allow the command to determine the state of the control, and **False** means override the command's default behavior, thereby forcing the control to be hidden or disabled.

For details on using the **State** property of a control to toggle its checked or pressed state to represent a particular condition in the application, see "Visually Indicating the State of a Command Bar Control" in the *Microsoft Office XP Developer's Guide*.

Working with images on command bar buttons

Every built-in command bar button has an image associated with it. You can use these images on your own command bar buttons as long as you know the **FaceId** property value of the built-in button that contains the image. The values for the **FaceId** property range from zero (no image) to the total number of Microsoft Office button images (of which there are several thousand).

The following code sets a **CommandBarButton** object's **FaceId** property to a Visio macro icon:

```
'Add a button that runs a VBA macro
'to a command bar.
Set cbButton = cbar.Controls.Add(Type:=msoControlButton)
With cbButton
     .Caption = "VBA Macro"
     .TooltipText = "Click this button to run a VBA Macro"
     'Set the button face to use an internal icon.
     .FaceID = 7075
End With
```

To add a bitmap for the button face rather than using a built-in button image, set the **Picture** property of a **CommandBarButton** object. For more details, see the *Microsoft Office Visual Basic Reference*.

Writing Code for a Command Bar: an Example

The following example shows code for the **ThisDocument** object and a class module named **CommandBarEventHandler** that creates a command bar with three buttons. The example demonstrates how you might create and display a command bar with buttons, set various relevant properties such as the **Context** and **Position** properties of the command bar, and properties for button controls such as **Caption**, **TooltipText**, **Tag**, **FaceId**, and **OnAction**. It also includes code for handling the **Click** event of a button control and for deleting a command bar. This is the code for **ThisDocument**:

```
'Event handling class for CommandBarButtonClick events
Public myEventClass As New CommandBarEventHandler

'Adds a command bar that is available
'when a drawing window is active.
Sub AddDrawingContextCommandBar()

    Dim cbars As Office.CommandBars
    Dim cbar As Office.CommandBar
    Dim cbButton As Office.CommandBarButton

    'The gateway to the Microsoft Office command bars object model
    'is the CommandBars property of the Visio Application object.
    Set cbars = Application.CommandBars

    'Add a new command bar named MyDrawingCommandBar.
    'that only lasts through the current Visio
    'application session.
    Set cbar = cbars.Add(Name:="MyDrawingCommandBar", _
            Position:=msoBarTop, Temporary:=True)

    'Prevent users from modifying
    'the custom command bar.
    cbar.Protection = msoBarNoCustomize

    'Set the appropriate context and visibility
    'for the custom command bar.
    '* = visible in given context.
    cbar.Context = Str(visUIObjSetDrawing) & "*"

    'Add a button to MyDrawingCommandBar
    'that runs a VBA macro.
    Set cbButton = cbar.Controls.Add(Type:=msoControlButton)
    With cbButton
            .Caption = "VBA Macro"
            .TooltipText = "Click this button to run a VBA Macro"
```

```
        'Use the Tag property for context switching and
        'for use with the FindControl method.
        .Tag = "cbbVBAMacro"
        'Set the button face to use an internal icon.
        .FaceID = 7075
        'Use the OnAction property to run a VBA macro
        'contained in this document.
        .OnAction = "ThisDocument.HelloWorld"
End With

'Release this object.
Set cbButton = Nothing

'Add another button to MyDrawingCommandBar
'that loads a COM add-in.
Set cbButton = cbar.Controls.Add(Type:=msoControlButton)
With cbButton
        .Caption = "Run COM add-in"
        .TooltipText = "Click this button to run a COM add-in"
        'Use the Tag property for context switching and
        'for use with the FindControl method.
        .Tag = "cbbCOMAddin"
        'Set the button face to use an internal icon.
        .FaceID = 7075
        'Use the OnAction property to load a COM add-in.
        .OnAction = "!<MyAddin.VisioCOMAddin>"
End With

Set cbButton = Nothing

'Add another button to MyDrawingCommandBar
'that will be monitored by the event handling
'class for the Click event. Note that no OnAction
'property is used here.
Set cbButton = cbar.Controls.Add(Type:=msoControlButton)
With cbButton
        .Caption = "ClickEvent"
        .TooltipText = "Click this button to trigger event"
        'Use the Tag property for context switching and
        'for use with the FindControl method.
        .Tag = "cbbClickEvent"
        'Set the button face to use an internal icon.
        .FaceID = 7075
End With
```

```
    'Set a reference to the command bar button
    'in the event handling class.
    Set myEventClass.cbbMyButton = cbButton

End Sub

Private Sub HelloWorld()
    MsgBox "Hello World!"
End Sub

Sub DeleteDrawingCommandBar()

    Dim cbars As Office.CommandBars
    Dim cbar1 As Office.CommandBar

On Error Resume Next

    'The gateway to the Microsoft Office command bars object model
    Set cbars = Application.CommandBars

    'Get the command bar named MyDrawingCommandBar
    'added by AddDrawingContextCommandBar().
    Set cbar1 = cbars("MyDrawingCommandBar")

    'Delete that command bar.
    cbar1.Delete

End Sub
```

Following is the code for a class module named CommandBarEventHandler:

```
'This class can handle the Click event
'of one command bar button.
'Use the code to create an instance of this class
'and set a reference to the cbbMyButton object.

'Note the use of the WithEvents keyword.
Public WithEvents cbbMyButton As CommandBarButton

Private Sub cbbMyButton_Click(ByVal Ctrl As Office.CommandBarButton, _
    CancelDefault As Boolean)
    'Put event handling code here to handle
    'a click of the referenced command bar button.

    MsgBox "Button " & Ctrl.Caption & " was clicked."

End Sub
```

Using the Click event procedure of a command bar button

You can use command bar event procedures to run your own code in response to an event. In addition, you can use these event procedures to substitute your own code for the default behavior of a built-in control. For example, the **CommandBarButton** object exposes a **Click** event procedure that you can use to run code in response to an event:

```
'This class can handle the Click event
'of one command bar button.
'Use the code to create an instance of this class
'and set a reference to the cbbMyButton object.
Public WithEvents cbbMyButton As CommandBarButton

Private Sub cbbMyButton_Click(ByVal Ctrl As Office.CommandBarButton, _
    CancelDefault As Boolean)
    'Put event handling code here to handle
    'a click of the referenced command bar button.

    MsgBox "Button " & Ctrl.Caption & " was clicked."

End Sub
```

> **Note** For details on working with other events in the command bars object model, see "Working with Command Bar Events" in the *Microsoft Office XP Developer's Guide,* Microsoft Press, 2001.

Preventing Users from Modifying Custom Command Bars

To prevent users from changing your custom user interface—but allow them to perform normal customization of the built-in user interface—set the **Protection** property of the custom **CommandBar** object to **msoBarNoCustomize**.

```
Application.CommandBars("My CommandBar").Protection = _
    msoBarNoCustomize
```

Preventing Users from Modifying All Visio Command Bars

To prevent users from changing any built-in or custom command bar in Visio through the Visio user interface, set the **DisableCustomize** property of the **CommandBars** collection to **True**. For example:

```
'Prevents user's from customizing
'command bars through the user interface.
Application.CommandBars.DisableCustomize = True
```

> **Note** Be aware that setting the **DisableCustomize** property to **True** will prevent users from using the Visio user interface to modify all Visio menus or toolbars, including the custom command bars that you've created for a particular solution. However, you will still be able make changes to the user interface programmatically.
>
> This property setting does not persist between Visio application sessions, so you will need to set it and restore it for each Visio application session.

Using Visio UIObject Objects to Customize the Visio User Interface

You customize the Microsoft Visio user interface from a program by working with **UIObject** objects. Just as you get **Document** objects to work with open documents in a Visio instance, you get objects to work with the menus, toolbars, and accelerators in the Visio user interface.

The following illustration shows the **UIObject** objects in the Visio object model.

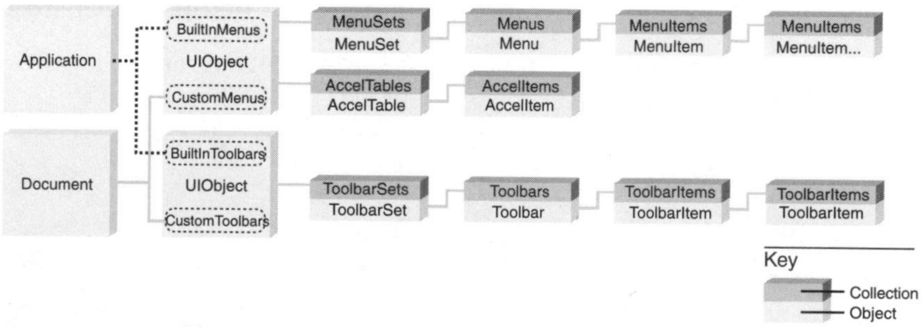

Figure 22-1 **UIObject** objects in the Visio object model.

Many objects in the Visio object model correspond to items you see in a Visio instance. For example, a **Menu** object can represent the **Visio Edit** menu, and a **MenuItem** object can represent the **Copy** command located on that menu, a custom item that runs a macro or add-on, or an anchor for a hierarchical menu (sometimes called a submenu).

> **Note** Beginning with Visio 2002, you can no longer customize the status bar in Visio using the **StatusBars** collection or **StatusBar** objects of the **UIObject** object. The **StatusBars** collection and **StatusBar** objects are no longer supported in Visio 2002. However, you can still show or hide the status bar using the **Application.ShowStatusBar** property.

UIObject objects differ from other objects in the Visio object model in that there is no single "**UIObject**" property that returns a **UIObject** object. Instead, the properties **BuiltInMenus**, **CustomMenus**, **BuiltInToolbars**, and **CustomToolbars** each return a **UIObject** object that represents a different part of the user interface (menus and accelerators in the case of **BuiltInMenus** or **CustomMenus**, and toolbars in the case of **BuiltInToolbars** or **CustomToolbars**).

To modify a copy of the built-in Visio user interface, use the **BuiltInMenus** or **BuiltInToolbars** property of the **Application** object to obtain a **UIObject** object. For example, to modify a copy of the built-in Visio menus and obtain a **UIObject** object that represents Visio menus and accelerators, start with this code:

```
Dim uiObj As Visio.UIObject
Set uiObj = Visio.Application.BuiltInMenus
```

To get a **UIObject** object that represents a copy of the built-in Visio toolbars, use this code:

```
Dim uiObj As Visio.UIObject
Set uiObj = Visio.Application.BuiltInToolbars(0)
```

To modify a custom user interface, use the **CustomMenus** or **CustomToolbars** property of the **Application** object or of any **Document** object to obtain a reference to the appropriate **UIObject** object. You should also use these properties to determine whether a custom user interface is in effect first.

For example, to get a **UIObject** object that represents the custom toolbars for the **Application** object:

```
Dim uiObj As Visio.UIObject
Set uiObj = Application.CustomToolbars
'Returns Nothing if the application has no custom toolbars.
```

To get a **UIObject** object that represents the custom menus for a **Document** object:

```
Dim uiObj As Visio.UIObject
Set uiObj = ThisDocument.CustomMenus
'Returns Nothing if document has no custom menus.
```

A **UIObject** object that represents menus (whether built-in or custom) has two properties that return collections: **MenuSets** and **AccelTables**. A **UIObject** object that represents toolbars (again, whether built-in or custom) has a **ToolbarSets** property that returns a collection.

> **Note** Unlike most other Visio object collections, collections that represent **UIObject** objects are indexed starting with zero (0). Specify an index of 0 with the collection's Item property to get the first item in any of the following collections: **AccelTables**, **AccelItems**, **MenuSets**, **Menus**, **MenuItems**, **ToolbarSets**, **Toolbars**, or **ToolbarItems**.

The **UIObject** branch of the Visio object model is fairly elaborate, so it's important to understand the various objects and their relationships to each other before attempting to customize them. The following topics in this section describe the hierarchy of objects that represent Visio menus, accelerators, and toolbars.

About Menu Objects

Different window contexts display different sets of menus, such as a drawing window, ShapeSheet window, or stencil window. For example, different menu items are displayed when a drawing window is active than when a stencil window is active. The following table lists the menu objects in the Visio object model.

Menu objects in the Visio object model

Object	Description
MenuSets	The collection of all possible Visio menu sets. To get a **MenuSets** collection, get the **MenuSets** property of a **UIObject** object that represents menus and accelerators.
MenuSet	The set of menus available in a given window context. For example, a **MenuSet** object could represent the set of menus available when a drawing window is active. To get a **MenuSet** object, use the **ItemAtID** property of a **MenuSets** collection and specify the ID of the context you want. For a table of contexts and other identifiers that can be used with **ItemAtID**, see the Microsoft Visio Developer Reference (on the **Help** menu, click **Developer Reference**). All **MenuSet** objects correspond to a given window context except for a **MenuSet** object that represents a shortcut menu (the menu that appears when you right-click something such as a shape, page, or stencil window, sometimes called a right-click menu or context-sensitive menu).

Note Beginning with Visio 2000, the **Position** property of a **MenuSet** object specifies whether the menu bar it represents is docked (left, right, top, or bottom) floating. The **RowIndex** property specifies where the menu bar appears relative to other bars displayed in the Visio window. For details about these properties, search for them by name in the Microsoft Visio Developer Reference (on the **Help** menu, click **Developer Reference**).

Menus	A collection of menus in a menu set. For example, the items in a **Menus** collection might represent the **File**, **Edit**, and **Tools** menus. To get a **Menus** collection, get the **Menus** property of a **MenuSet** object.
Menu	A menu. For example, the items in a **Menu** object that represents a **File** menu might be **Open**, **Close**, and **Edit**. To get a **Menu** object, use the **Item** property of a **Menus** collection with the index of the menu you want. **Menus** are indexed in the order they appear: from left to right or from top to bottom in a Visio instance. For example, in most window contexts, the **File** menu has an index of zero (0). To add a **Menu** object, use the **Add** or **AddAt** method of a **Menus** collection.

Menu objects in the Visio object model *(continued)*

Object	Description
MenuItems	A collection of menu items on a Visio menu. To get a **MenuItems** collection, get the **MenuItems** property of a **Menu** object.
MenuItem	A menu item, or command, on a Visio menu. To get a **MenuItem** object, use the **Item** property of the **MenuItems** collection with the index of the menu item you want. **Menu** items are indexed in the order they appear: from top to bottom on the menu. For example, the **Undo** command on the Visio **Edit** menu has an index of zero (0). To add a **MenuItem** object, use the **Add** or **AddAt** method of the **MenuItems** collection. The **CmdNum** property of a **MenuItem** object specifies a valid command ID, as declared in the Visio type library, or 0 if the item is a separator in a menu. If the menu item runs a program, its **AddonName** property specifies the name of a macro or program to run when the user chooses the menu item; its **AddonArgs** property specifies arguments to pass. If a Visio menu item has a hierarchical menu, then the **MenuItem** object that represents the hierarchical menu has a **MenuItems** collection with **MenuItem** objects. The **CmdNum** property of such a **MenuItem** object should be set to **visCmdHierarchical**, and the remaining properties and methods that can be used are: **Caption**, **Index**, **MenuItems**, **Parent**, and **Delete**. All other properties and methods will be ignored.

Beginning with Visio 2000, both **Menu** and **MenuItem** objects have the following method and properties:

- **IconFileName** method which specifies a custom icon file to be displayed for an item
- **FaceID** property which specifies an icon to be displayed with the item on the menu
- **Style** property which specifies whether to display the icon and text or text only
- **State** property which specifies whether the item appears "pressed" (if it has an icon) or checked (if it has only text)
- **Enabled** property that specifies whether the command is dimmed

For details about this method and these properties, search for them by name in the Microsoft Visio Developer Reference (on the **Help** menu, click **Developer Reference**).

About Accelerator Objects

An accelerator is a combination of keys that, when pressed, execute a command. For example, the accelerator for the **Copy** menu item is CTRL+C, and the accelerator for the **Paste** menu item is CTRL+V. The following table lists the accelerator objects in the Visio object model.

Accelerator objects in the Visio object model

Object	Description
AccelTables	The collection of all Visio accelerator tables. Different accelerators are used in different window contexts. To get an **AccelTables** collection, get the **AccelTables** property of a **UIObject** object.
AccelTable	The table of accelerators available for a given window context. The **AccelTable** objects exist only for window contexts, such as the drawing window, not for shortcut menus. To get an **AccelTable** object, use the **ItemAtID** property of an **AccelTables** collection and specify the ID of the context you want.
AccelItems	A collection of accelerators in an accelerator table. To get an **AccelItems** collection, get the **AccelItems** property of an **AccelTable** object.
AccelItem	A single accelerator item. Accelerator items, such as CTRL+C (**Copy**) and CTRL+V (**Paste**), are available when a drawing window is active. To get an **AccelItem** object, use the **Item** property of an **AccelItems** collection with the index of the menu you want.

Note Beginning with Visio 2000, the **AccelItem** object now has **AddonName** and **AddonArgs** properties. This means you can bind a Microsoft Visual Basic for Applications (VBA) macro or add-on to an accelerator. In earlier versions of Visio, only built-in commands could be bound to accelerators.

About Toolbar Objects

Different sets of toolbars are displayed in different window contexts. For example, when a ShapeSheet window is active, different toolbars are displayed than when a drawing window is active. The following table lists the toolbar objects in the Visio object model.

> **Tip** Beginning with Visio 2000, you can attach a custom toolbar to a Visio document by using the **Attach** button on the **Toolbars** tab in the **Customize** dialog box (on the **Tools** menu, click **Customize**). For more about creating and attaching toolbars, see the Microsoft Visio Help.

Toolbar objects in the Visio object model

Object	Description
ToolbarSets	The collection of all possible Visio toolbar sets. To get a **ToolbarSets** collection, get the **ToolbarSets** property of a **UIObject** object that represents toolbars. Use the **Application** object's **ShowToolbar** property to control whether Visio toolbars are visible.
ToolbarSet	The set of toolbars available in a given window context. For example, a **ToolbarSet** object could represent the set of toolbars available when a **ShapeSheet** window is active. To get a **ToolbarSet** object, use the **ItemAtID** property of a **ToolbarSets** collection and specify the ID of the context you want.
Toolbars	A collection of Visio toolbars in a toolbar set. To get a **Toolbars** collection, get the **Toolbars** property of a **ToolbarSet** object.
Toolbar	A Visio toolbar. To get a **Toolbar** object, use the **Item** property of a **Toolbars** collection with the index of the toolbar you want. Built-in toolbars are indexed by the order in which they would initially be docked in the Visio window if all built-in toolbars were visible. Custom toolbars are indexed in the order they are added to the collection. To add a toolbar, use the **Add** or **AddAt** method of a **Toolbars** collection. The **Caption** property of the **Toolbar** object represents the caption that appears on the hierarchical menu for the **Toolbars** menu item (**View** menu), or when the toolbar is floating.

Toolbar objects in the Visio object model *(continued)*

Object	Description

> **Note** Beginning with Visio 2000, the **Position** property of a **Toolbar** object specifies whether the toolbar it represents is docked (left, right, top, or bottom) or floating. The **RowIndex** property specifies where the toolbar appears relative to others displayed in the Visio window. For details about these properties, search for them by name in the Microsoft Visio Developer Reference (on the **Help** menu, click **Developer Reference**).

Object	Description
ToolbarItems	A collection of toolbar items in a Visio toolbar. To get a **ToolbarItems** collection, get the **ToolbarItems** property of a **Toolbar** object.
ToolbarItem	A control on a Visio toolbar. To get a **ToolbarItem** object, use the **Item** property of the **ToolbarItems** collection with the index of the toolbar item you want. **Toolbar** items are indexed in the order that they appear on the toolbar (left to right, or top to bottom, starting with index 0). To add a toolbar item, use the **Add** or **AddAt** method of a **ToolbarItems** collection.

> **Note** In Visio 2000, **ToolbarItem** objects have a **Style** property that specifies whether to display the icon and text or text only. **ToolbarItem** objects also have a **State** property that specifies whether the item appears "pushed" (if it has an icon) or checked (if it has only text). For details about these properties, search for them by name in the Microsoft Visio Developer Reference.

Planning User Interface Changes

As you begin designing your custom user interface, you need to answer the following questions:

- Will you be customizing a copy of the built-in Microsoft Visio user interface or an existing custom user interface? This determines how you obtain a **UIObject** object, change it, and how you restore the original interface when your solution finishes running.
- Should the custom user interface be available only for certain Visio documents, or for all documents in a Visio instance? This determines its *scope*, the context in which your custom user interface is available.
- Should the custom user interface be available only when a document is active, throughout a single Visio instance, or each time a user starts Visio? This determines its *persistence*, the length of time in which your custom user interface is available.

Customizing a copy of the built-in Visio UI versus an existing custom UI

Before you customize a Visio user interface, first determine whether the current user interface is the built-in Visio user interface or a custom user interface. If it's a custom user interface, good software design suggests that you should modify the existing interface for your solution and then restore it to its original condition, rather than starting from scratch with the built-in Visio user interface.

When you retrieve the built-in Visio menus or toolbars, you are actually retrieving a copy, or a snapshot, of the built-in Visio user interface that you can manipulate. The original built-in Visio user interface remains untouched, so you can restore it later. When you retrieve a custom user interface, you are retrieving the custom user interface that is currently active (including any custom toolbars the user might have added), not a copy.

To determine which user interface is in use, check the **CustomMenus** and **CustomToolbars** properties of all the **Document** objects in the **Documents** collection. Then check the same properties of the **Application** object. If an object is not using a custom user interface, both properties return **Nothing**, and you can simply retrieve a copy of the built-in Visio user interface.

If a custom user interface is already in use, you should decide whether you want to replace the custom user interface with your own, or just add your custom user interface items to it. If the custom user interface is attached to the document, you will probably want to apply changes to it directly. However, if the custom user interface is at the application level, you should use the **Clone** method to create a copy of that user interface, and apply your changes to the copy instead. Otherwise, those changes will still be visible after the user has closed the document.

The following example demonstrates how to retrieve the currently active user interface for your document without replacing the application-level custom user interface, if any. You would write additional code to add your custom user interface items.

```
'Check if there are document custom menus.
If ThisDocument.CustomMenus Is Nothing Then

    'Check if there are Visio custom menus.
    If Visio.Application.CustomMenus Is Nothing Then

        'Use the built-in menus.
        Set visUIObj = Visio.Application.BuiltInMenus
    Else
        'Use the Visio custom menus.
        Set visUIObj = Visio.Application.CustomMenus.Clone

    End If

Else
    'Use the file custom menus
    Set visUIObj = ThisDocument.CustomMenus
End If
```

For details about the **CustomMenus** and **CustomToolbars** properties, see the Microsoft Visio Developer Reference (on the **Help** menu, click **Developer Reference**).

Controlling the scope of your UI

Just as you can get a **UIObject** object from the **Document** or **Application** object, you can also apply your custom user interface changes to the **Document** or **Application** object by using its **SetCustomMenus** or **SetCustomToolbars** method. The scope you want determines the object to which you apply your changes.

You can choose to make your custom user interface available on an application or document level. To use a custom user interface regardless of which document is open, apply your custom user interface to the **Application** object.

To use a custom user interface on a document level, that is, while a document is active, apply your custom user interface to a **Document** object. This is the way you'll typically work when programming in Microsoft Visual Basic for Applications (VBA).

The following example shows how to set custom menus for the **ThisDocument** object:

```
Dim uiObj as Visio.UIObject

'Get a copy of the built-in Visio menus.
Set uiObj = Visio.Application.BuiltInMenus

... 'Make custom UI changes.

'Set custom menus for ThisDocument.
ThisDocument.SetCustomMenus uiObj
```

Controlling the persistence of your UI

The approach you use to customize the Visio user interface depends on the extent of the changes you intend to make and the development environment in which you are programming. Depending on the scope of your user interface changes, you might want your changes to persist while a document is active, throughout a single Visio instance, or each time the user starts Visio.

- UI persistence while a document is active

  A document can have a custom user interface that takes precedence over the Visio user interface (custom or built-in) while the document is active. For example, when a user creates a document from a particular template, you can add a toolbar button that runs a wizard to help the user create a drawing. As soon as the user closes the document, the Visio instance reverts to the previous user interface.

  When you are customizing the Visio user interface from VBA, you usually work on a document level; therefore, you can set the custom user interface for the **ThisDocument** object.

- UI persistence during a single Visio instance

  If you want your custom user interface to persist during a single Visio instance, set the custom user interface for the **Application** object from a VBA macro or stand-alone program.

- UI persistence each time the user starts Visio

  If you want your user interface changes to replace the Visio user interface on a more permanent basis, you can set the custom user interface for the **Application** object each time a user starts Visio, or create a custom user interface file.

After you create a custom user interface file, you apply it to the user interface by setting the **CustomMenusFile** or **CustomToolbarsFile** property for the **Application** object. Your custom user interface file loads each time the user starts Visio, until you specify a different file or restore the built-in Visio user interface. For details, see *Putting custom UI changes into effect* later in this chapter.

Making User Interface Changes

After you decide which **UIObject** object you want to work with and the scope and persistence of your custom user interface, you can begin to make the interface changes. To get to the item that you want to remove or to get to the location where you want to add an item, you must navigate the Microsoft Visio object model. To do this, first get a **UIObject** object; then a menu, accelerator, or toolbar; and then the specific items that you want to change. After you make your user interface changes, you must apply the customized **UIObject** object somewhere so that your user interface takes effect.

Getting a MenuSet, ToolbarSet, or AccelTable object

To get a **MenuSet**, **ToolbarSet**, or **AccelTable** object, use the **ItemAtID** property of the appropriate collection and specify the ID of the object you want. For a list of constants you can use with the **ItemAtID** property, see the Microsoft Visio Developer Reference (on the **Help** menu, click **Developer Reference**).

For example, the following code fragment uses the constant **visUIObjSetDrawing** to get a **MenuSet** object that represents the drawing window menus:

```
Dim uiObj As Visio.UIObject
Dim menuSetObj As Visio.MenuSet

'Get a UIObject object that represents a copy of the built-in
'Visio menus.
Set uiObj = Visio.Application.BuiltInMenus

'Get the drawing window menu set.
Set menuSetObj = _
    uiObj.MenuSets.ItemAtId(visUIObjSetDrawing)
```

The following example uses the constant **visUIObjSetShapeSheet** to get a **ToolbarSet** object that represents the **ShapeSheet** window toolbars:

```
Dim uiObj As Visio.UIObject
Dim toolbarSetObj As Visio.ToolbarSet
```

```
'Get a UIObject object that represents a copy of the built-in
'Visio toolbars.
Set uiObj = Visio.Application.BuiltInToolbars(0)

'Get the ShapeSheet window toolbar set.
Set toolbarSetObj = _
    uiObj.ToolbarSets.ItemAtID(visUIObjSetShapeSheet)
```

ID constants for window contexts

Constants that you can specify with the **ItemAtID** property for the most commonly used window contexts are listed in the following table and defined in the Visio type library. For lists of ID constants that represent shortcut menus, palettes, and pop-up windows available for **MenuSet**, **ToolbarSet**, and **AccelTable** objects, see the **SetID** property in the Microsoft Visio Developer Reference (on the **Help** menu, click **Developer Reference**).

ID constants that represent window contexts for the MenuSet, ToolbarSet, and AccelTable objects

ID constant	Context
visUIObjSetDrawing	Drawing window
visUIObjSetStencil	Stencil window
visUIObjSetShapeSheet	ShapeSheet window
visUIObjSetPrintPreview	Print preview window

Adding a menu and a menu item

After getting a **UIObject** object, you can add or remove items from the user interface. To add items, navigate the **UIObject** branch in the Visio object model to get the collection that contains the kind of item you want to add, and use that collection's **Add** or **AddAt** method.

The following example adds a new menu and menu item that are available when the Visio drawing window is active:

```
Dim uiObj As Visio.UIObject
Dim menuSetsObj As Visio.MenuSets
Dim menuSetObj As Visio.MenuSet
Dim menusObj As Visio.Menus
Dim menuObj As Visio.Menu
Dim menuItemsObj As Visio.MenuItems
Dim menuItemObj As Visio.MenuItem
```

```
'Get a UIObject object that represents a copy of the built-in
'Visio menus.
Set uiObj = Visio.Application.BuiltInMenus

'Get the MenuSets collection.
Set menuSetsObj = uiObj.MenuSets

'Get drawing window MenuSet object; get the context.
Set menuSetObj= menuSetsObj.ItemAtId(visUIObjSetDrawing)

'Get the Menus collection.
Set menusObj = menuSetObj.Menus

'Add a Demo menu before the Window menu.
'A menu without a menu item will not appear.
Set menuObj = menusObj.AddAt(7)
menuObj.Caption = "Demo"
```

The first half of this example assumes the **Window** menu is still in its initial position—eighth from the left on the menu bar. Adding or removing menus can change the position of other menus, however.

The second half of the example, shown below, adds a menu item to the **Demo** menu and sets the menu item's properties. For details, see *Setting properties of an item* later in this section.

The following sample code uses the **Add** method to add one item to the **Demo** menu that was added in the preceding sample code. When you add an item using the **Add** method, the item is added to the end of a collection. This example adds only one menu item, so its position is not an issue. However, if you were to add another item using the **Add** method, it would appear at the bottom of the menu. To control where a menu item appears, use the **AddAt** method and specify the ordinal position of the item.

> **Note** You can assign a keyboard shortcut to a menu item by preceding the intended shortcut character with an ampersand (&).

```
'Get the MenuItems collection.
Set menuItemsObj = menuObj.MenuItems

'Add a MenuItem object to the new Demo menu.
Set menuItemObj = menuItemsObj.Add
```

```
'Set the properties for the new menu item.
menuItemObj.Caption = "Run &Demo Program"
menuItemObj.AddonName = "Demo.EXE"
menuItemObj.AddonArgs = "/DVS=Fun"

'Tell Visio to use the new UIObject object (custom menus)
'while the document is active.
ThisDocument.SetCustomMenus uiObj
```

The last statement, *ThisDocument.SetCustomMenus uiObj*, tells the Visio instance to use the custom menus while the document is active. The custom user interface changes don't persist after the user closes the document.

Adding a toolbar and a toolbar button

You can add a custom toolbar button to one of the built-in toolbars or create an entire custom toolbar. The following procedure demonstrates how to add a toolbar button to a copy of the built-in toolbars for the drawing window context:

```
Sub AddToolbarButton( )
    'Object variables to be used in the program
    Dim uiObj As Visio.UIObject
    Dim toolbarSetObj As Visio.ToolbarSet
    Dim toolbarItemsObj As Visio.ToolbarItems
    Dim objNewToolbarItem As Visio.ToolbarItem

    'Get the UIObject object for the toolbars.
    Set uiObj = Visio.Application.BuiltInToolbars(0)

    'Get the drawing window ToolbarSet object.
    Set toolbarSetObj = _
          uiObj.ToolbarSets.ItemAtID(visUIObjSetDrawing)

    'Get the ToolbarItems collection.
    Set toolbarItemsObj = toolbarSetObj.Toolbars(0).ToolbarItems

    'Add a new button in the first position.
    Set objNewToolbarItem = toolbarItemsObj.AddAt(0)

    'Set the properties for the new toolbar button.
    objNewToolbarItem.ActionText = "Run Stencil Report Wizard"
    objNewToolbarItem.AddonName = "Stndoc.exe"
    objNewToolbarItem.CntrlType = visCtrlTypeBUTTON

    'Set the icon for the new toolbar button.
    objNewToolbarItem.IconFileName "dvs.ico"
```

```
    'Tell Visio to use the new custom toolbars while the
    'document is active.
    ThisDocument.SetCustomToolbars uiObj
End Sub
```

Here are some notes about the example:

Set toolbarItemsObj = toolbarSetObj.Toolbars(0).ToolbarItems. Built-in toolbars generally appear in the same order in the collection. In the case of the toolbar set for the drawing window context, the **Standard** toolbar is at index 0, and the **Format** toolbar is at index 1. The order in which toolbars appear in the collection does not always correspond to the order in which they appear on the screen, which can be changed by the user or by solutions that use the **RowIndex** property.

Set objNewToolbarItem = toolbarItemsObj.AddAt(0). Visio orders toolbar items horizontally, so this statement adds the **ToolbarItem** or button at the leftmost location on the toolbar if the toolbar is docked horizontally; this statement adds the **ToolbarItem** or button at the topmost location if the toolbar is docked vertically.

objNewToolbarItem.CntrlType = visCtrlTypeBUTTON sets the type of toolbar button to display. Visio includes other constants for built-in Visio toolbar buttons, but custom toolbar buttons can use only **visCtrlTypeBUTTON**, **visCtrlTypeSPLITBUTTON**, or **visCtrlTypeSPLITBUTTON_MRU_COMMAND**.

> **Note** The Microsoft Office command bars object model supports the creation of custom text boxes, combo boxes, and drop-down list boxes. For details, see *Using CommandBar Objects to Customize the Visio User Interface* earlier in this chapter.

objNewToolbarItem.IconFileName "dvs.ico" gets the file "dvs.ico" that contains the bitmap for the toolbar to display. Because no path to this file was given, Visio will search for it in folders along the user's **Add-ons** path, as specified on the **File Paths** tab of the **Options** dialog (on the **Tools** menu, click **Options**). Alternatively, you can specify a full path and file name to the icon file. It is also possible to use the **IconFileName** method to extract icon images from executable files. The icon file should contain a 16-by-16-pixel icon.

For details on the **IconFileName** method, see the Microsoft Visio Developer Reference (on the **Help** menu, click **Developer Reference**).

ThisDocument.SetCustomToolbars uiObj uses the custom toolbars while the document is active.

The following procedure demonstrates how to add a floating toolbar named "Test"; this floating toolbar cannot be docked but can be hidden in the drawing window context. The program first checks whether the Visio document or instance is using custom toolbars and assigns a **UIObject** object to the **uiObj** variable. The program then gets the **Toolbars** collection for the drawing window context, adds the new toolbar, and sets its properties.

```
Sub AddToolbar()
    Dim uiObj As UIObject
    Dim toolbarsObj As Toolbars
    Dim toolbarObj As Toolbar
    Dim toolbarItemsObj As ToolbarItems
    Dim toolbarItemObj As ToolbarItem

    'Check if the document has custom toolbars.
    If ThisDocument.CustomToolbars Is Nothing Then
        'Check if the instance is using custom toolbars.
        If Visio.Application.CustomToolbars Is Nothing Then
            'Use the built-in toolbars.
            Set uiObj = Visio.Application.BuiltInToolbars(0)
        Else
            'Use the application's custom toolbars.
            Set uiObj = Visio.Application.CustomToolbars.Clone
        End If
    Else
        'Use the document's custom toolbars.
        Set uiObj = ThisDocument.CustomToolbars
    End If

    'Get the Toolbars collection for the drawing window context.
    Set toolbarsObj = uiObj.ToolbarSets.ItemAtID( _
        Visio.visUIObjSetDrawing).Toolbars

    'Add a toolbar.
    Set toolbarObj = toolbarsObj.Add

    With toolbarObj
        'Set the toolbar's title.
        .Caption = "Test"
        'Position the toolbar floating at the
        'coordinates 300, 200.
        .Position = Visio.visBarFloating
        .Left = 300
        .Top = 200
        'Disallow docking.
```

```
            .Protection = Visio.visBarNoHorizontalDock _
                  + Visio.visBarNoVerticalDock
            'Make the new toolbar visible.
            .Visible = True
            'Allow the user to hide and show the toolbar.
            .Enabled = True
    End With
End Sub
```

Setting properties of an item

After you've added an item, you can set properties that define its behavior and appearance. For example, you can set the **Caption** property of a menu item to define the text that appears on the menu, or use the **FaceID** property or **IconFileName** method of a toolbar or menu item to specify what icon to display.

Two significant properties of a menu item or toolbar item are **CmdNum**, which specifies the ID of the command associated with the item, and **AddonName**, which specifies a program or macro to run when the user chooses the menu item or clicks the button. If the program takes command line arguments, they can be specified with the **AddonArgs** property. For details about the properties and methods of a particular item, search for that item in the Microsoft Visio Developer Reference (on the **Help** menu, click **Developer Reference**).

Caption specifies the text that appears on a menu or menu item. If you want to display the accelerator with the menu item, include it as part of the **Caption** property's text and insert two spaces between the "\a" and the accelerator text. For example:

```
"Open...\a  CTRL+O"
```

In this example, "Open..." is the menu item's caption; "CTRL+O" is the accelerator text; and "\a" left justifies the accelerator text. Adding the accelerator text to the **Caption** property doesn't add an accelerator, it simply displays it as part of the caption. You add accelerators by using the accelerator objects in the Visio object model.

You can also specify other properties, such as those in the following example:

```
menuItemObj.ActionText = "Run Demo 1"
'BACKSPACE key
accelItemObj.Key = 8
accelItemObj.Alt = True
```

ActionText specifies the text that appears on the **Edit** menu with **Undo**, **Redo**, and **Repeat** for a menu item. It also appears in any error messages or toolbar tool tips that might be displayed.

Key specifies the ASCII key code value for an accelerator. For example, the ASCII key code for the BACKSPACE key is 8, and the ASCII key code for the ESC key is 27. For details about ASCII key codes, see the Microsoft Platform Software Development Kit (SDK) in the MSDN Library. The **Alt**, **Control**, and **Shift** properties modify the **Key** for an accelerator. To set the properties for an accelerator, set any combination of modifiers to **True**, specify one key code, and set the item's **CmdNum** or **AddonName** property. To activate an accelerator command, press the combination of modifiers and the key that corresponds to the key code.

The **CmdNum** property specifies the command ID for an item. Every built-in Visio menu item and toolbar item represents a Visio command and has a command ID. For example, the command ID for **Show ShapeSheet** is **visCmdWindowShowShapeSheet**; the command ID for **Document Stencil** is **visCmdWindowShowMasterObjects**. For a list of valid command IDs, search for "visCmd" in the Visio type library in the **Object Browser** in the **Visual Basic Editor**.

> **Tip** If you want to hide the Visio user interface but not the Visio window, set the **ShowToolbar** or **ShowStatusBar** properties of the **Application** object to **False** to hide all toolbars or hide the status bar, respectively.

Removing items from a user interface

You can remove any item from the Visio user interface, whether the item is part of the built-in Visio user interface or a custom item you added. (As an alternative, if you want to make a toolbar or menu item temporarily unavailable, set its **Enabled** property to **False**; this dims the item.)

Removing an item doesn't remove the functionality of that item, just the access to that functionality. Other avenues, such as accelerators, may still be available. For example, if you remove the **Copy** command from the **Edit** menu, but not the accelerator (CTRL+C), a user can still use the copy functionality by pressing CTRL+C. You can remove the **Show ShapeSheet** command from the **Window** menu, but if the double-click behavior for a shape is to display the ShapeSheet window, that window still appears when that shape is double-clicked.

> **Tip** Every built-in Visio menu item and toolbar item represents a Visio command and has a command ID. If you want to remove one of these Visio items, you can identify it by its command ID. However, the **CmdNum** property of a custom menu item or toolbar item that runs a program or macro does not correspond to any Visio command ID, so when you want to delete the item, you cannot identify the item using its command ID. Instead, use the **Caption** property string of a custom menu or toolbar item to locate the item.

To remove an item, use the **Delete** method of that item. For example, the following statements remove the **Show ShapeSheet** menu item from the **Window** menu in the drawing window for the running Visio instance:

```
Dim uiObj As Visio.UIObject
Dim menuSetObj As Visio.MenuSet
Dim menuItemsObj As Visio.MenuItems
Dim i As Integer

Set uiObj = Visio.Application.BuiltInMenus
Set menuSetObj = _
    uiObj.MenuSets.ItemAtID(visUIObjSetDrawing)

'Get the Window menu.
Set menuItemsObj = menuSetObj.Menus(7).MenuItems

'Get the Show ShapeSheet menu item by its CmdNum property.
'This technique works with localized versions of Visio.
For i = 0 To menuItemsObj.Count -1
    If menuItemsObj(i).CmdNum = _
            visCmdWindowShowShapeSheet Then
            menuItemsObj(i).Delete
            Exit For
    End If
Next i

'Replace built-in Visio menus with customized set.
Visio.Application.SetCustomMenus uiObj
```

Removing a toolbar item

The following macro shows how to delete the **Spelling** toolbar button from the built-in **Standard** toolbar for the drawing window context:

```
Sub DeleteToolbarButton( )
    Dim uiObj As Visio.UIObject
    Dim toolbarSetObj As Visio.ToolbarSet
    Dim toolbarItemsObj As Visio.ToolbarItems
    Dim toolbarItemObj As Visio.ToolbarItem
    'Loop variable
    Dim i As Integer

    'Get the UIObject object for the toolbars.
    Set uiObj = Visio.Application.BuiltInToolbars(0)

    'Get the drawing window ToolbarSet object.
    Set toolbarSetObj = _
        uiObj.ToolbarSets.ItemAtID(visUIObjSetDrawing)

    'Get the ToolbarItems collection.
    Set toolbarItemsObj = toolbarSetObj.Toolbars(0).ToolbarItems

    'Get the Spelling ToolbarItem object.
    'Because this code gets the built-in Visio toolbars, you know
    'you'll find the Spelling toolbar item; if code got a custom
    'toolbar, it might not include the Spelling toolbar
    'item.
    For i = 0 To toolbarItemsObj.Count - 1
        'Get the current ToolbarItem object from the collection.
        Set toolbarItemObj = toolbarItemsObj(i)
        'Check whether the current toolbar item is the
        'Spelling button.
        If toolbarItemObj.CmdNum = visCmdToolsSpelling Then
            Exit For
        End If
    Next i

    'Delete the Spelling button.
    toolbarItemObj.Delete

    'Tell Visio to use the new custom toolbars while the
    'document is active.
    ThisDocument.SetCustomToolbars uiObj
End Sub
```

Removing an accelerator

The following macro shows how to delete the accelerator for the Visual Basic Editor from the drawing window context.

```
Sub DeleteAccelItem( )
    Dim uiObj As Visio.UIObject
    Dim accelTableObj As Visio.AccelTable
    Dim accelItemsObj As Visio.AccelItems
    Dim accelItemObj As Visio.AccelItem
    Dim i As Integer

    'Retrieve the UIObject object for the copy of the built-in menus.
    Set uiObj = Visio.Application.BuiltInMenus

    'Set accelTableObj to the Drawing menu set.
    Set accelTableObj = _
        uiObj.AccelTables.ItemAtID(visUIObjSetDrawing)

    'Retrieve the accelerator items collection.
    Set accelItemsObj = accelTableObj.AccelItems

    'Retrieve the accelerator item for the Visual Basic Editor by
    'iterating through the accelerator items collection and
    'locating the item you want to delete.
    For i = 0 To accelItemsObj.Count - 1
        Set accelItemObj = accelItemsObj.Item(i)
        If accelItemObj.CmdNum = Visio.visCmdToolsRunVBE Then
            Exit For
        End If
    Next i

    'Delete the accelerator.
    accelItemObj.Delete

    'Tell Visio to use the new custom menus while the
    'document is active.
    ThisDocument.SetCustomMenus uiObj

End Sub
```

Putting custom UI changes into effect

The final step in the process of customizing the Visio user interface is to set the custom user interface for an object, which applies your user interface to the Visio instance. The modifications your program makes to a **UIObject** object appear in the Visio instance after this step.

To put custom user interface changes into effect, use the **SetCustomMenus** or **SetCustomToolbars** methods of the **Document** or **Application** object and specify the **UIObject** object that represents your custom user interface.

For example, the following statement sets custom menus for a document:

```
ThisDocument.SetCustomMenus uiObj
```

To set custom toolbars for all documents in a single Visio instance, use this statement:

```
Visio.Application.SetCustomToolbars uiObj
```

If you directly change a **UIObject** object that represents the active custom toolbars or custom menus while a Visio instance is running, you must call the **UpdateUI** method of that **UIObject** object to make Visio display your changes.

For example:

```
'Get the UIObject object for the custom menus.
Set uiObj = Visio.Application.CustomMenus

...'Code changes to the custom interface.

'Update the custom interface with changes.
uiObj.UpdateUI
```

Using Custom User Interface Files

A Microsoft Visio user interface file (VSU) is a means of saving a custom user interface between Visio instances. If your solution makes extensive changes to the Visio user interface, and it's unlikely that your users will run other solutions that also make user interface changes, a VSU file might be a more efficient way of providing a custom user interface.

About Custom.vsu

Beginning with Microsoft Visio 2000, Visio uses a VSU file to preserve user customizations. The first time a user customizes the Visio user interface using the **Customize** command (on the **View** menu, click *Toolbars*), the Visio instance takes a snapshot of the user interface currently in effect (including customizations supplied by Visio solutions) and, when the user exits the Visio instance, stores it in a file called Custom.vsu in the user's profile folder.

If your solution employs a VSU file to supply a custom user interface, keep the following in mind:

- If a Custom.vsu file exists on a user's system, the **Application** object's **CustomMenus** and **CustomToolbars** properties return a **UIObject** object instead of returning **Nothing**. (In earlier Visio versions, **CustomMenus** and **CustomToolbars** returned a **UIObject** object only if the Visio user interface had been customized by a program that had used a VSU file.)
- A user's Custom.vsu file is a snapshot of whatever user interface is in effect when the user customized the user interface. If a solution customizes the Visio user interface, and the user then creates a custom toolbar, that user's Custom.vsu represents the solution's user interface plus the user's changes. If a solution then reloads its original VSU file, the Visio instance will appear to "lose" the user's customizations.
- If the Custom.vsu file is deleted, the Visio instance reverts to the built in user interface, and recreates the file the next time the user customizes the user interface.

Saving a Custom User Interface File

If you've made extensive user interface changes and intend to save your custom user interface to a VSU file, use the **SaveToFile** method of the **UIObject** object. For example:

```
uiObj.SaveToFile("c:\solutions\mytools.vsu")
```

Loading a Custom User Interface File

You can load a custom user interface file by setting the custom user interface for the **Application** object. You can also load a custom user interface file (VSU) when an event occurs, such as opening a document.

To load a custom user interface file for an **Application** object, set the following properties of the object to the name of the custom user interface file:

- **CustomMenusFile** Set this property for custom menus and accelerators.
- **CustomToolbarsFile** Set this property for custom toolbars and status bars.

For example, to load a custom user interface file each time the users starts Visio, use this statement:

```
Visio.Application.CustomToolbarsFile = "c:\solutions\mytools.vsu"
```

You need to set these properties for the **Application** object only once. These properties set the value of the **CustomMenusFile** and **CustomToolbarsFile** entries in the Microsoft Windows registry and tell Visio the location of the corresponding custom interface file. If a path is not specified, Visio looks in the folders along the Visio **Add-ons** path, specified on the **File Paths** tab (on the **Tools** menu, click **Options**). If the specified file cannot be located, or if the registry key is deleted or modified, Visio reverts to the built-in Visio user interface.

To load a custom user interface file when an event occurs, such as opening a document, put the code in the appropriate event for the **Document** object.

To load a custom user interface file each time a document is opened, use this statement in the **DocumentOpened** event procedure for the **Document** object:

```
ThisDocument.CustomMenusFile =  "c:\solutions\mytools.vsu"
```

If you are programming in an external development environment such as Microsoft Visual Basic, you can load a custom user interface file, make changes to it, and then save the changes to the file.

To load a custom user interface file, use the **LoadFromFile** method. For example:

```
UiObj.LoadFromFile "shortcut.vsu"
...'Make UI changes
uiObj.SaveToFile "c:\solutions\mytools.vsu"
```

Restoring the Built-in Visio User Interface

If your solution customizes the Visio user interface, it's a good idea to restore the original user interface when your solution finishes running. If your solution detected custom menus or custom toolbars on the user's system, or if the user might have customized the user interface while your solution was running, it should reverse its user interface changes by removing the items it added and restoring those it removed.

If you can be certain that no other customizations should be preserved, you can clear custom menus and custom toolbars to quickly restore the built-in Visio user interface. Clearing custom menus and toolbars does not erase a user's Custom.vsu file, but it does cause Visio to stop using it.

To restore the built-in Visio menus and accelerators, use the **ClearCustomMenus** method of the **Document** (or **Application**) object. To restore the built-in Visio toolbars, use the **ClearCustomToolbars** method of the **Document** (or **Application**) object. For example, to clear the custom menus for a **Document** object, use this statement:

```
ThisDocument.ClearCustomMenus
```

For example, to clear custom toolbars for the **Application** object, use this statement:

```
Visio.Application.ClearCustomToolbars
```

The next time the document is opened or a Visio instance is run, it uses the built-in Visio user interface.

23

Using COM Add-ins in a Visio Solution

Accessing COM Add-ins in Visio 491

Creating a COM Add-in for Visio 494

You can extend Microsoft Visio in a multitude of ways—using Microsoft Visual Basic for Applications (VBA) code, using a stand-alone executable, or using a Visio add-on (a Visio Solutions Library, or VSL).

And beginning with Microsoft Visio 2002, you can also extend Visio and build your custom solutions using Component Object Model (COM) add-ins.

A COM add-in is a dynamic-link library (DLL) that is specially registered for loading by Visio and other Microsoft Office or Office XP applications, and contains a COM object that implements the **IDTExtensibility2** COM interface. Because Visio and other Office applications support the COM add-in architecture, you can use the same tools to develop add-ins for other Office applications.

> **Note** A COM add-in also can be an ActiveX EXE file for Visual Basic. However, DLLs generally provide better performance than EXE files.

You have several options for creating your own COM add-ins:

- Use VBA with Microsoft Office Developer version 2000 or later.
- Use an external development tool, such as Microsoft Visual Basic or Microsoft Visual C++ (versions 5.0 or later).

Accessing COM Add-ins in Visio

You can access COM add-ins in Microsoft Visio through the **COM Add-Ins** dialog box, or through Automation using the **COMAddIns** property of a Visio **Application** object or the **COMAddIns** collection and **COMAddIn** object from the Microsoft Office 10.0 object library.

Viewing a List of Available COM Add-ins

You can view a list of the available COM add-ins in the **COM Add-Ins** dialog box in Microsoft Visio (on the **Tools** menu, point to **Macros**, and then click **COM Add-Ins**).

You can load (connect) or unload (disconnect) an add-in by selecting the check box next to it. Loading a COM add-in loads it into memory so you can work with it. Unloading an add-in removes it from memory; you cannot use the add-in until you load it again.

> **Note** To be able to load and run COM add-ins in Visio, you'll need to make sure that the **Enable COM add-ins** check box is selected on the **Advanced** tab in the **Options** dialog box (on the **Tools** menu, click **Options**).

To view the list of available COM add-ins

1. On the **Tools** menu, point to **Macros**, and then click **COM Add-Ins**.
2. To add a new COM add-in to the list, click **Add**.

   Clicking **Add** and selecting an add-in that does not appear in the list registers the add-in DLL (if it is not already registered) and adds the add-in to the list of available COM add-ins for Visio.
3. To remove a COM add-in from the list, click **Remove**.

   Removing an add-in deletes the registry key that contains the name and load behavior of the add-in. The Windows registry contains information about a COM add-in in two places:

   - As with any other COM DLL, the add-in DLL is registered as a unique object on the system.

- Additionally, information about the add-in is placed in another section of the registry to notify Visio (and other Office applications) that the add-in exists and should be used by Visio. This section is deleted when you remove an add-in from the list. The DLL itself remains registered, and if you add the add-in to the list again, the add-in's informational section is re-created in the registry.

> **Note** You can add only DLLs that are COM add-ins to the list of available add-ins in the **COM Add-Ins** dialog box. Only add-ins registered for the application you are working in can be registered.

Using the COMAddIns Property to Get Information about COM Add-ins

Use the **COMAddIns** property of an **Application** object for information about all COM add-ins currently registered in Microsoft Visio.

To get information about the object returned by the COMAddIns property

1. On the **Tools** menu, point to **Macros**, and then click **Visual Basic Editor**.
2. On the **View** menu, click **Object Browser**.
3. In the **Project/Library** list, click **Office**.

   If you do not see the Office type library in the **Project/Library** list, on the **Tools** menu, click **References**, select the **Microsoft Office 10.0 Object Library** check box, and then click **OK**.
4. Under **Classes**, examine the class named **COMAddIns**.

This following macro demonstrates using the **COMAddIns** property to list the COM add-ins registered with Visio:

```
Public Sub IterateCOMAddIns()
     Dim myCOMAddIns As COMAddIns
     Dim myCOMAddIn As COMAddIn

     'Get the set of COM add-ins
     Set myCOMAddIns = Application.COMAddIns

     'List each COM add-in in the
     'Immediate window
```

```
    For Each myCOMAddIn In myCOMAddIns
        Debug.Print myCOMAddIn.Description
    Next
End Sub
```

In addition to retrieving and changing information about COM add-ins using the **COMAddIns** collection and **COMAddIn** object, you can use the **COMAddIns** collection and the **COMAddIn** object to load and unload COM add-ins programmatically. For details about the **COMAddIn** object and **COMAddIns** collection, see the Microsoft Office Visual Basic Reference.

Creating a COM Add-in for Visio

You can create your own Component Object Model (COM) add-ins in essentially two ways:

- From within Microsoft Visio or a Microsoft Office application, use Microsoft Visual Basic for Applications (VBA) with Microsoft Office Developer (version 2000 or later).
- Use an external development tool, such as Microsoft Visual Basic or Microsoft Visual C++ (versions 5.0 and later).

> **Note** This chapter covers implementing COM add-ins using add-in designers in VBA and Visual Basic. For information about implementing COM add-ins in C++, see the Microsoft Developer Network (MSDN) Web site at msdn.microsoft.com.

Working with Add-in Designers

An *add-in designer* is file included with the template project that helps you create and register a COM add-in. You can create a COM add-in without including an add-in designer, but it simplifies the process of creating and registering the add-in. You can use an add-in designer to specify important information for your COM add-in:

- The name and description of the COM add-in
- The application the COM add-in will run in
- How the COM add-in loads in the application

Similar to forms in a Visual Basic or VBA project, an add-in designer has a user interface component and an associated class module. The user interface component is visible only to the developer at design time; it is never visible to the user when the add-in is running. You can think of the add-in designer as a sort of dialog box where you specify settings for an add-in.

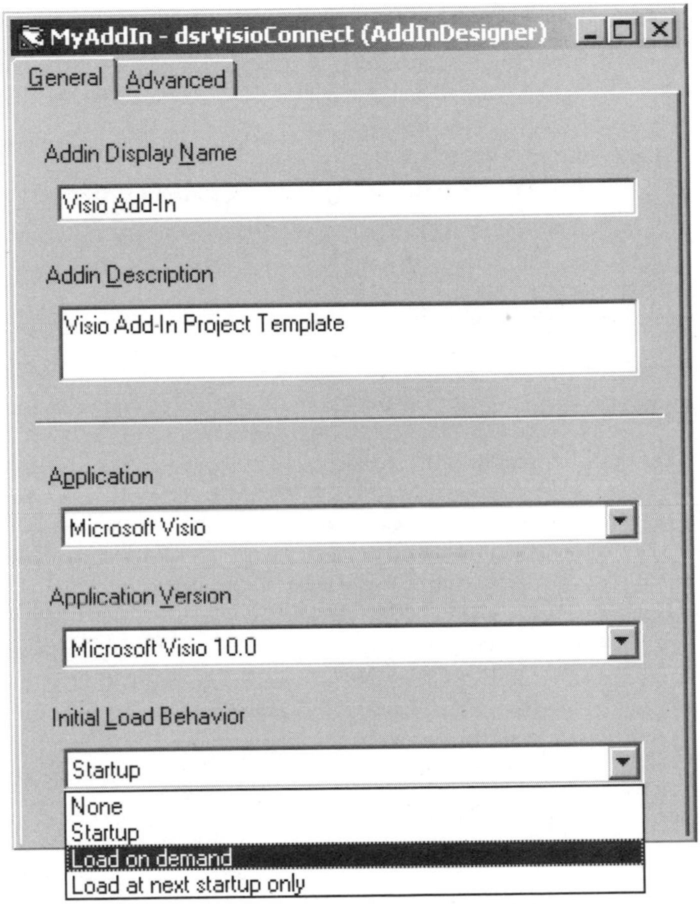

Figure 23-1 The Visio add-in designer template.

The class module contains the events that occur when the add-in is loaded or unloaded. You can use these events to integrate the add-in into the application.

When you compile your add-in, the information you provide to the add-in designer is used to properly register the DLL as a COM add-in. The add-in's name, description, and initial load behavior setting are written to the Windows registry. The add-in's host application reads these registry entries and loads the add-in accordingly.

> **Note** If you intend to create a COM add-in that works with more than one Office application, you will need to configure a designer for each host application. For more information on creating add-ins that work in multiple Office applications, see "Creating COM Add-ins for Multiple Applications" in the *Microsoft Office XP Developer's Guide,* Microsoft Press, 2001.

Configuring an add-in designer

To create your add-in, you first must specify the options you want on the **General** tab of the add-in designer, as described in the following table.

General tab options for the add-in designer

Option	Description
Addin Display Name	The name that will appear in the **COM Add-Ins** dialog box in Visio and Microsoft Office applications. The name you supply should be descriptive to the user. If the name will be taken from a resource file specified in the **Satellite DLL Name** box on the **Advanced** tab, it must begin with a number sign (#), followed by an integer specifying a resource ID within the file.
Addin Description	Descriptive text for a COM add-in, available from VBA in the **Description** property of the **COMAddIn** object. If the description is to come from a resource file specified in the **Satellite DLL Name** box on the **Advanced** tab, it must begin with a number sign (#), followed by an integer specifying a resource ID within the file.
Application	The application in which the add-in will run. This list displays applications that support COM add-ins.
Application Version	The version of the application in which the add-in will run.
Initial Load Behavior	The way that the add-in loads in the application. The list of possible settings comes from the Windows registry. Commonly used behaviors include **Startup** and **Load on demand**.

The **Advanced** tab of the add-in designer makes it possible for you to specify a file containing localized resource information for the add-in, and to specify additional registry data.

Advanced tab options for the add-in designer

Option	Description
Satellite DLL Name	The name of a file containing localized (translated) resources for an add-in; the file must be located in the same folder as the registered add-in DLL.
Registry Key for Additional Add-in Data	The registry subkey to which additional data is to be written.
Add-in Specific Data	The names and values to be stored in the registry subkey. Only **String** and **DWORD** type values are permitted.

Using add-in designers in VBA

One way to create your own COM add-ins in Microsoft Visio is to use VBA with Microsoft Office Developer (versions 2000 or later).

COM add-ins created with Office Developer are packaged as dynamic-link libraries (DLL files) and are registered so that they can be loaded by Office applications.

To add an add-in designer to your VBA project

1. On the **File** menu, click **New Project**.
2. In the **New Project** dialog box, select **Add-In Project**.

The add-in designer provides several properties that can be set to define the attributes of your add-in, including **Name**, **Description**, and **Load Behavior**. It also provides several events that can be used to add code, such as **OnConnection**, **OnStartupComplete**, and **OnDisconnection**.

The code you write for your COM add-in depends on what you want the add-in to do, as well as which application the add-in is for. Each of the applications that can use COM add-ins exposes its extensibility structure using its object model; you can view the object model for your particular application in the **Object Browser**.

Using the Visio add-in designer template in Visual Basic

If you plan to use Visual Basic, you can use the Visio add-in designer template to create your COM add-in. Files for the Visio add-in designer template are provided on the *Developing Microsoft Visio Solutions* CD. When you copy these files into your Projects folder for Visual Basic, the **Visio Addin** project becomes available to you in the **New Projects** dialog box.

Like the other add-in designers in Visual Basic or Office Developer, the Visio add-in designer template provides several properties that can be set to define the attributes of your add-in, including **Name**, **Description**, and **Load Behavior**. It also provides several events that can be used to add code, such as **OnConnection**, **OnStartupComplete**, and **OnDisconnection**.

To install the Visio add-in designer template for use in Visual Basic

1. Copy the following files from the *Developing Microsoft Visio Solutions* CD: VisioAddin.dsr, and Visio Addin.vbp.
2. Paste the files into the Projects folder in the following path on your hard disk: \Program Files\Microsoft Visual Studio\VB98\Template\Projects.

To use the Visio add-in designer template in Visual Basic

1. Open Visual Basic.
2. On the **File** menu, click **New Project**.
3. In the **New Projects** dialog box, choose **Visio Addin**.

   The Visio add-in designer template is added to your project. By default, the project is named **MyAddIn** and a designer class module named **dsrVisioConnect** appears in the project.

> **Note** You can choose the **Addin** project in the **New Projects** dialog box; however, it will contain code for developing a COM add-in for Visual Basic that you will need to edit to make the add-in work in Visio. If you use the Visual Basic **Addin** project, be sure to set a reference to the Microsoft Office 10.0 object library and use the **COMAddIn** object from the library.

The following code is provided for you in the Visio add-in designer template to help you get started:

```
Option Explicit

Public VisioApp As Visio.Application

'This method is called when Visio loads the add-in.
Private Sub AddinInstance_OnConnection(ByVal Application As Object, _
    ByVal ConnectMode As AddInDesignerObjects.ext_ConnectMode, _
    ByVal AddInInst As Object, custom() As Variant)

    On Error GoTo error_handler
```

```
    'Save the Visio instance.
    Set VisioApp = Application

    'Set a breakpoint and test various add-in
    'objects, properties and methods.
    Debug.Print VisioApp.ProductName

    Exit Sub

error_handler:
    MsgBox Err.Description

End Sub

'This method is called when Visio unloads the add-in.
Private Sub AddinInstance_OnDisconnection(ByVal RemoveMode As _
    AddInDesignerObjects.ext_DisconnectMode, custom() _
        As Variant)

    On Error Resume Next
    Set VisioApp = Nothing
End Sub
```

Specifying Load Behavior

When a COM add-in has been properly registered, it is available to whatever applications are specified in the add-in designers that the project contains. The registered COM add-in display name appears in the **COM Add-Ins** dialog box; if it does not, click **Add** to browse for the add-in DLL and add it to the list.

Selecting the check box next to an add-in in the **COM Add-Ins** dialog box loads (connects) the add-in and makes it available to the user; clearing the check box unloads (disconnects) the add-in, and it cannot be run.

As the developer, you specify the default setting for loading a COM add-in. You do this in the **Initial Load Behavior** list in the add-in designer.

Initial Load Behavior settings

Setting	Behavior
None	The COM add-in is not loaded when the application starts. It can be loaded in the **COM Add-Ins** dialog box or by setting the **Connect** property of the corresponding **COMAddIn** object. The value for **None** is 0.
Startup	The add-in is loaded when the application starts. Once the add-in is loaded, it remains loaded until it is explicitly unloaded. The value for **Startup** is 3.
Load on demand	The add-in is not loaded until the user clicks the button or menu item that loads the add-in, or until a procedure sets its **Connect** property to **True**. In most cases you won't set the initial load behavior to **Load on demand** directly; you'll set it to **Load at next startup only**, and it will automatically be set to **Load on demand** on subsequent starts of the host application. The value for **Load on demand** is 9.
Load at next startup only	After the COM add-in has been registered, it loads when the user runs the host application for the first time, and it creates a button or menu item for itself. Remember to set the **OnAction** property for any toolbar buttons or menu items that are created. When the add-in has been loaded once, its load behavior is changed to **Load on demand**. Each subsequent time the user starts the application, the add-in is loaded on demand—that is, it doesn't load until the user clicks the button or menu item associated with the add-in. The value for **Load at next startup only** is 16.

Writing Code in the Add-in Designer

After you have specified general information for a COM add-in in the add-in designer, you can begin writing code in the designer's class module. To view the add-in designer's class module, right-click the add-in designer in the **Project Explorer**, and then click **View Code** on the shortcut menu.

Code that is in the add-in designer handles the add-in's integration with the host application. For example, code that runs when the add-in is loaded or unloaded resides in the add-in designer's module. If the add-in contains forms, the add-in designer might contain code to display the forms.

Events for controlling your add-in

A COM add-in has events that you can use to run code when the add-in is loaded or unloaded, or when the host application has finished starting up or is beginning to shut down.

The events that are required for control of your COM add-in are available through the **IDTExtensibility2** interface, which provides a programming interface for integrating COM add-ins with their host applications.

Add-in projects in VBA or Visual Basic automatically implement the IDTExtensibility2 library in the add-in designer's class module.

To access these events in the add-in designer's class module, open the **Code** window for the add-in designer, and then select **AddinInstance** in the **Object** box. The events appear in the **Procedures/Events** box.

> **Note** This chapter covers implementing COM add-ins using add-in designers in VBA and Visual Basic. For information about creating a COM add-in from scratch, manually implementing the **IDTExtensibility2** interface, or the Microsoft Add-in Designer library (Msaddndr.tlb), see the Microsoft Developer Network (MSDN) Web site at msdn.microsoft.com.

Events in the IDTExtensibility2 interface

The **IDTExtensibility2** interface provides five events that you can use to manipulate your add-in and the host application: **OnConnection**, **OnDisconnection**, **OnStartupComplete**, **OnBeginShutdown**, and **OnAddInsUpdate**.

Events provided by IDTExtensibility2 interface

Event	Description
OnConnection	Occurs when the COM add-in is loaded (connected). An add-in can be loaded in one of the following ways: ■ The user starts the host application and the add-in's load behavior is specified to load when the application starts. ■ The user loads the add-in in the **COM Add-Ins** dialog box. ■ The **Connect** property of the corresponding **COMAddIn** object is set to **True**. For more information about the **COMAddIn** object, see the Microsoft Visual Basic Help.

Events provided by IDTExtensibility2 interface *(continued)*

Event	Description
OnDisconnection	Occurs when the COM add-in is unloaded. You can use the **OnDisconnection** event procedure to run code that restores any changes made to the application by the add-in and to perform general clean-up operations. An add-in can be unloaded in one of the following ways: ■ The user clears the check box next to the add-in in the **COM Add-Ins** dialog box. ■ The host application closes. If the add-in is loaded when the application closes, it is unloaded. If the add-in's load behavior is set to **Startup**, it is reloaded when the application starts again. ■ The **Connect** property of the corresponding **COMAddIn** object is set to **False**.
OnStartupComplete	Occurs when the host application completes its startup routines, in the case where the COM add-in loads at startup. If the add-in is not loaded when the application loads, the **OnStartupComplete** event does not occur—even when the user loads the add-in in the **COM Add-Ins** dialog box. When this event does occur, it occurs after the **OnConnection** event. You can use the **OnStartupComplete** event procedure to run code that interacts with the application and that should not be run until the application has finished loading. For example, if you want to display a form that gives users a choice of documents to create when they start the application, you can put that code in the **OnStartupComplete** event procedure.
OnBeginShutdown	Occurs when the host application begins its shutdown routines, in the case where the application closes while the COM add-in is still loaded. If the add-in is not loaded when the application closes, the **OnBeginShutdown** event does not occur. This event occurs before the **OnDisconnection** event. You can use the **OnBeginShutdown** event procedure to run code when the user closes the application. For example, you can run code that saves form data to a file.

Events provided by IDTExtensibility2 interface *(continued)*

Event	Description
OnAddInsUpdate	The **OnAddInsUpdate** event occurs when the set of loaded COM add-ins changes. When an add-in is loaded or unloaded, the **OnAddInsUpdate** event occurs in any other loaded add-ins. For example, if add-ins A and B both are loaded currently, and then add-in C is loaded, the **OnAddInsUpdate** event occurs in add-ins A and B. If C is unloaded, the **OnAddInsUpdate** event occurs again in add-ins A and B. If you have an add-in that depends on another add-in, you can use the **OnAddInsUpdate** event procedure in the dependent add-in to determine whether the other add-in has been loaded or unloaded.

For more information on each on these event procedures, see "Working with the IDTExtensibility2 Event Procedures" in the *Microsoft Office XP Developer's Guide*.

Hooking a COM Add-in into a Command Bar Control

If your COM add-in has a user interface, it must be integrated with the host application in some way so the user can interact with it. For example, the user interface for your COM add-in most likely includes a form. At some point, code in the add-in must be run to display the form.

One way to integrate your add-in with an application's user interface is to include code in the **OnStartupComplete** event procedure that creates a new command bar control (toolbar button or menu item) in the host application. When your add-in is loaded, the user can click the button or menu item to work with the add-in. You can use the **OnConnection** event procedure, but it does not guarantee that the command bar object has been loaded. Similarly, you can add code to unload your add-in in the **OnBeginShutdown** event procedure or the **OnDisconnection** event procedure.

The critical aspect of integrating an add-in through a command bar control is the process of setting up the event sink. You must create a command bar control that is event-ready, so its **Click** event is triggered when the user clicks the control. You can use the **WithEvents** keyword to create an event-ready command bar control.

If you set the load behavior for your add-in to **Load at next startup only**, you also must set the **OnAction** property for the command bar control. If you do not set the **OnAction** property, the add-in will load the first time the application starts. The next time you start the application, however, the load behavior for the add-in will be set to **Load on demand**, and the command bar control that you have created for the add-in will not load the add-in unless the **OnAction** property has been set.

Even if your add-in is not demand-loaded, it is a good idea to set this property in your code, in case you later change the load behavior for the add-in. The syntax for setting the **OnAction** property for a COM add-in is:

```
ctlButton.OnAction = "!<ProgID>"
```

where *ctlButton* is the **CommandBarButton** object and *ProgID* is the programmatic identifier for the add-in. The programmatic identifier is the subkey that is created for the add-in in the Windows registry. Each add-in designer or class module that implements the IDTExtensibility2 library in the COM Add-in project adds its own programmatic identifier to the registry, beneath the **AddIns** subkey for the host application in which it will run. The programmatic identifier for a COM add-in consists of the name of the project followed by the name of the add-in designer or class module (for example, MyCOMAddin.Connect).

To return the programmatic identifier for an add-in, you can use the **AddInInst** argument that is passed to the **OnConnection** event procedure. This argument provides a reference to the add-in designer or class module that the code is currently running in. The **AddInInst** argument is an object of type **COMAddIn**, which has a **ProgId** property that returns the programmatic identifier. Note that you must concatenate the !< and > delimiters before and after the programmatic identifier string to properly set the **OnAction** property.

> **Note** Because the **Tag** property provides you with additional information about the control, it is a good idea to set the **Tag** property for a command bar button that loads a COM add-in in any host application. For more details about the **Tag** property, see the Microsoft Office Visual Basic Reference.

Creating a command bar control

In some cases, you might want to provide access to your add-in through a menu command or toolbar, as described in the following procedure.

To create a command bar control that displays the add-in's form

1. In the add-in designer's module, use the **WithEvents** keyword to declare a module-level variable of type **CommandBarButton**. This creates an event-ready **CommandBarButton** object.

2. In the same module, create the **Click** event procedure template for the **CommandBarButton** object by clicking the name of the object variable in the **Object** box and then clicking **Click** in the **Procedure** dialog box.
3. Write code within the event-procedure template to open the form when the **Click** event occurs.
4. In the **OnConnection** event procedure, check to see whether the command bar control already exists, and return a reference to it if it does. If it does not exist, create the new command bar control, and return a reference to it. You must check whether the command bar control exists, so you do not create a new control each time your code runs.
5. When you create the new command bar control, do the following:
   - Set the **Tag** property for the **CommandBarButton** object to a unique string.
   - Set the **OnAction** property for the command bar control if the COM add-in is to be loaded on demand. If you fail to set the **OnAction** property, the command bar button will load the add-in the first time the application starts, but it will not load the add-in when the application is closed and reopened.
6. Within the **OnConnection** event procedure, assign the reference to the command bar control to the event-ready **CommandBarButton** object variable.
7. Add code to the **OnDisconnection** event to remove the command bar control when the add-in is unloaded.

Writing Code for a COM Add-in: an Example

The following example shows code for a COM add-in that loads when Visio opens (on **Startup**). The add-in then listens for the **DocumentOpened** or **DocumentCreated** events in Visio. When a user opens the specified Visio template or drawing created from the template, the add-in displays its user interface in a Visio stencil window. The code for the add-in lives in a designer file called VisioCOMAddin.dsr, which is based on the Visio add-in designer template.

```
Option Explicit

'Use WithEvents in the COM add-in to hook
'into the DocumentOpened and DocumentCreated
'Visio events in the application.
Public WithEvents g_VisioApp As Visio.Application
Public g_visWindow As Visio.Window

'This method is called when Visio loads the add-in.
Private Sub AddinInstance_OnConnection(ByVal Application As Object, _
    ByVal ConnectMode As AddInDesignerObjects.ext_ConnectMode, _
    ByVal AddInInst As Object, custom() As Variant)
    'Dim op_Win As Visio.Window
    Dim cbar As CommandBar
    On Error GoTo error_handler

    'Get the Visio instance.
    Set g_VisioApp = Application

    Exit Sub

error_handler:

    MsgBox Err.Description

End Sub

'This method is called when Visio unloads the COM add-in.
Private Sub AddinInstance_OnDisconnection(ByVal RemoveMode As _
    AddInDesignerObjects.ext_DisconnectMode, custom() As Variant)
    On Error Resume Next

    Set g_VisioApp = Nothing
    Set g_visWindow = Nothing
End Sub

Private Function AddStencilWindow() As Visio.Window
Dim op_Win As Visio.Window
On Error GoTo eHandler

    If Not g_VisioApp.ActiveWindow Is Nothing Then
        If g_VisioApp.ActiveWindow.Type = VisWinTypes.visDrawing Then
            'Add a dockable stencil window to the drawing window.
            Set op_Win = g_VisioApp.ActiveWindow.Windows.Add(, , _
                VisWinTypes.visDockedStencilAddon)
```

```
        Else
            'Add a nondockable stencil window to the application.
            Set op_Win = g_VisioApp.Windows.Add(, , _
                VisWinTypes.visStencilAddon)
        End If
    Else
        'Add a nondockable stencil window to the application.
        Set op_Win = g_VisioApp.Windows.Add(, , _
            VisWinTypes.visStencilAddon)
    End If

Set AddStencilWindow = op_Win

Exit Function

eHandler:
    Set AddStencilWindow = Nothing

End Function

Private Sub g_VisioApp_DocumentCreated(ByVal doc As Visio.IVDocument)
    'Add the stencil window add-in whenever a new document
    'is created from my template.
    Dim szTemplate As String
    'Get the template name; return the full path.
    szTemplate = doc.Template
    'Check for template name within the full path.
    If InStr(1, szTemplate, "COMAddin.vst", vbTextCompare) Then
        Set g_visWindow = AddStencilWindow
        If Not (g_visWindow Is Nothing) Then
            Dim myfrm As New frmMyForm
            LoadForm myfrm, g_visWindow.WindowHandle32
            'Pass the Visio instance to the form.
            Set myfrm.frmVisio = g_VisioApp
            'Display the form.
            ShowForm myfrm
        End If
    End If
End Sub

Private Sub g_VisioApp_DocumentOpened(ByVal doc As Visio.IVDocument)
    'Add the stencil window add-in whenever an existing document
    'based on my template opens.
    Dim szTemplate As String
    'Get the template name; return the full path.
    szTemplate = doc.Template
    'Check for the template name within the full path.
    If InStr(1, szTemplate, "COMAddin.vst", vbTextCompare) Then
```

```
                Set g_visWindow = AddStencilWindow
                If Not (g_visWindow Is Nothing) Then
                    Dim myfrm As New frmMyForm
                    LoadForm myfrm, g_visWindow.WindowHandle32
                    'Pass the Visio instance to the form.
                    Set myfrm.frmVisio = g_VisioApp
                    'Display the form.
                    ShowForm myfrm
                End If
        End If
End Sub
```

Making the DLL and Registering the COM Add-in

After debugging your COM add-in to your satisfaction, you can package it as a DLL.

To package a COM add-in as a DLL in VBA or Visual Basic

- On the **File** menu, click **Make *projectname*.dll**.

  The **Make Project** dialog box appears; you can enter a name for the DLL that is different from the suggested name.

  The process of making the DLL creates the COM add-in, registers it on the client computer, and makes the COM add-in available for use in Visio.

When you make the DLL, the information in the add-in designer is used to add a subkey to the Windows registry, indicating which applications can host the add-in. The COM add-in then appears in the **COM Add-Ins** dialog box in those applications for which it is registered.

Add-in registration

Before you can use a COM add-in in Visio, the add-in DLL must be registered, just as any other COM DLL on the computer. The DLL's class ID is registered beneath the HKEY_CLASSES_ROOT subtree in the Windows registry. The DLL can be registered on a user's computer by using a setup program, such as those created by the **Packaging Wizard** or by running the Regsvr32.exe command-line utility that is included with Microsoft Windows. Adding a COM add-in by using the **COM Add-Ins** dialog box also registers the DLL.

Registering the DLL beneath the HKEY_CLASSES_ROOT subtree informs the operating system of its presence, but additional information must be added to the registry for the add-in to be available to Visio. This is the information that you can specify in the add-in designer—the add-in's name, description, target application, target application version, and initial load behavior. The add-in designer makes sure this application-specific information is written to the correct place in the registry at the same time that the add-in DLL is registered. The **COM Add-Ins** dialog box displays the information contained in the subkey for the corresponding application.

This subkey must be added to the following registry subkey:

HKEY_CURRENT_USER\Software\Microsoft\Visio\Addins\ *YourProgId*

The new subkey itself must be the programmatic identifier of the COM add-in, which consists of the name of the project followed by the name of the class module or add-in designer (for example, MyCOMAddin.Connect).

The following table describes the entries that you can add beneath this subkey.

Entries for the subkey

Name	Type	Value
Description	**String**	Optional. Name to appear in **COM Add-Ins** dialog box.
FriendlyName	**String**	Optional. String returned by **Description** property.
LoadBehavior	**DWORD**	Required. Integer indicating load behavior: 0 (**None**), 3 (**Startup**), 9 (**Load on demand**), or 16 (**Load at next startup only**)

Distributing COM add-ins

If you are planning to distribute your COM add-in to other users, you must install all the necessary files on each user's system and register the add-in. How you do this depends on the environment in which you are developing the add-in.

Distributing COM add-ins created with Office Developer

If you are developing in Microsoft Office Developer (version 2000 or later), the easiest way to distribute a COM add-in is to create a setup program for the add-in. The user can install and register the add-in by running the setup program.

Before you can create the setup program, you must compile the COM add-in project to a DLL.

To create the setup program, run the **Packaging Wizard** on the add-in project that was compiled to a DLL. The **Packaging Wizard** creates a setup program that installs and registers the add-in DLL and any other necessary files, but not the code.

Distributing COM add-ins created with Visual Basic 6.0

If you are developing in Microsoft Visual Basic 6.0, the easiest way to distribute a COM add-in is to include the add-in designer in the add-in project and then create a setup program for the add-in. The user can install and register the add-in by running the setup program.

To create the setup program, run the Visual Basic 6.0 **Package and Deployment Wizard** on the add-in project. When the user runs the setup program, all the files required for the add-in to run will be copied to the user's computer and registered.

For more information about using the Visual Basic 6.0 **Package and Deployment Wizard**, see the documentation included with Visual Basic 6.0.

24

Using ActiveX Controls in a Visio Solution

Adding ActiveX Controls to a Visio Solution 512

Handling a Control's Events 517

Working with Controls at Run Time 517

Distributing ActiveX Controls in a Visio Solution 519

ActiveX Controls that Interact with Shapes: an Example 520

You can add ActiveX controls directly to Microsoft Visio drawings to make your Visio solution interactive. For example, you can add dialog box controls that are standard with the Microsoft Windows operating system, such as single-click buttons, check boxes, or list boxes. Or, you might add custom controls that you develop or purchase to incorporate more complex functionality, such as animation.

> **Note** ActiveX controls are supported in Visio 5.0 and later versions.

Adding ActiveX Controls to a Visio Solution

Using ActiveX controls in your Microsoft Visio solution allows you to create a user interface that is consistent with solutions based on other Microsoft Windows-based applications. Because the controls are on the drawing page, the user can work freely with both controls and Visio shapes in a drawing.

Working in Design Mode

To work with ActiveX controls in a Visio drawing, switch between design mode and run mode. In *design mode*, you can insert controls, move and size them, and set their properties. In *run mode*, you can use the controls—click a command button to run its **Click** event handler, for example. For other tasks, it doesn't matter whether Microsoft Visio is in design mode or run mode—all other Visio commands and tools work the same way in either mode.

The document's mode is synchronized with that of its Microsoft Visual Basic for Applications (VBA) project, so both the document and its project are always in the same mode. While a document is in design mode, none of its objects (including controls) issues events.

A Visio document opens in run mode by default, unless the macros in the document have been disabled. Macros are enabled or disabled depending on the security level setting for Visio and whether the VBA project has been digitally signed.

To switch to design mode, make sure the **Developer** toolbar is displayed. If the toolbar is not displayed, on the **View** menu, point to **Toolbars**, click **Developer**, and then click the **Design Mode** button on the **Developer** toolbar. The button inverts to indicate that Visio is in design mode.

> **Note** If the security level for Visio is set to **High**, only signed macros from trusted sources are allowed to run; all other macros are disabled. If the security level is set to **Medium** (the default setting in Visio), Visio prompts the user to enable or disable macros when a document with a VBA project opens. When a document opens with macros disabled, the document opens in design mode. The user cannot switch to run mode until the document is closed and reopened with macros enabled. To set the security level for Visio, on the **Tools** menu, point to **Macros**, and then click **Security**. On the **Security Level** tab, click **Low**, **Medium**, or **High**.
>
> To disable macros programmatically when a document opens, use the **visOpenMacrosDisabled** flag in the **OpenEx** method of a **Documents** collection.
>
> Visio also provides policy support for security, which allows an administrator to limit the security level that a user can set. For more details, see *Using Digital Certificates to Produce Trusted Solutions* in Chapter 15, *Programming Visio with VBA.*

Inserting a Control in a Drawing

Before you can insert an ActiveX control in a Visio drawing, the control must be installed on your system. Certain controls can also require that you have a design license to use them in applications that you develop.

You insert a control by selecting it in the **Control** dialog box, which lists all of the ActiveX controls installed on your system, including those installed by other applications. Such applications typically provide a run-time license for the ActiveX controls they contain. The run-time license entitles you to use those controls in the application that contains them but not to insert the controls in applications that you develop. To insert such controls in your applications, you need a design-time license. For details, see *Distributing ActiveX Controls in a Visio Solution* later in this chapter.

To insert an ActiveX control in a drawing

1. On the **Insert** menu, click **Control**. Or click the **Insert Control** button  on the **Developer** toolbar (to show the toolbar, on the **View** menu, click **Developer**).
2. In the **Control** dialog box, select a control; for example, you can select **Microsoft Forms 2.0 CommandButton**.

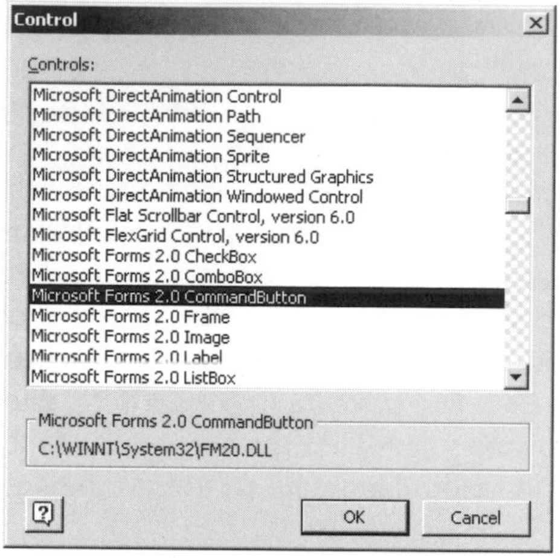

Figure 24-1 **Control** dialog box.

3. Click **OK** to insert the control on the drawing page.
4. Move and size the control as needed.

   A selected control has green selection handles, just like a selected shape, and you move and size the control the same way.

Figure 24-2 A selected control.

5. Edit the control and set its properties as needed.

   To edit a control, double-click it. A control activated for in-place editing in this way looks the same in Microsoft Visio as in any ActiveX container. To set a control's properties or write code for the control, right-click the control and point to the name of the control object on the shortcut menu. You can then select a command that allows you to modify the control using the Visual Basic Editor.

Figure 24-3 A control activated for in-place editing.

After you insert a control in a drawing, you can work with it in the same way as with a Visio shape. For example, you can cut or copy and paste the control, duplicate it with CTRL+drag, or make it into a master by dragging it to a stencil.

Tips for control developers

The first time you insert a control into a Visio drawing, VBA creates a "merged type library" for the control and stores it in your Temp folder in a file with an .exd file name extension. If you subsequently modify the control, delete the EXD file before attempting to insert the control again. If you receive an error message when you insert a control after modifying it, you can delete the cached EXD file to correct the problem.

If your control supports the **IClassFactory2** interface, Visio uses that interface when attempting to insert a new instance of that control. Therefore, the insertion succeeds only on systems in which the control is properly licensed. If your control does not support **IClassFactory2**, Visio uses the **IClassFactory** interface to instantiate the control, and licensing is not a consideration.

Setting the Tabbing Order of Controls

When Microsoft Visio is in run mode, pressing the TAB key moves the focus from one control to another on the drawing page. If you add more than one control to a drawing, you'll want the focus to move in a logical order.

The tabbing order of controls corresponds to the stacking order of the controls on the drawing page, starting with the backmost control. Initially, this is the order in which you inserted the controls in the drawing, with the most recently inserted control at the front.

To change the stacking order of controls relative to each other, use the following commands from the **Order** submenu on the **Shape** menu:

- **Bring to Front**
- **Send to Back**
- **Bring Forward**
- **Send Backward**

Using the Visio Ambient Properties in Controls

If you're developing ActiveX controls for use in Microsoft Visio, you can take advantage of the ambient properties that Visio defines. A control uses an application's ambient properties to maintain a consistent appearance with other controls in a document. For example, the **BackColor** property specifies the color of a control's interior.

To list the ambient properties defined by Microsoft Visio

- In the **Visual Basic Editor** window, right-click the **Object Browser**, click **Show Hidden Members** on the shortcut menu, and then select **IVAmbients** in the **Classes** list.

  Ambient properties are read-only.

Printing a Drawing Without its Controls

If you want the user to be able to print a drawing but not its controls, do one of the following:

- Select the controls, click **Behavior** on the **Format** menu, and under **Miscellaneous** select **Non-printing shape**.
- Assign all of the controls to the same layer and make that layer nonprinting.

  For details about layers, see Chapter 11, *Arranging Shapes in Drawings*.

Protecting Controls from Changes

When you distribute a solution that contains controls, you might want users to have the ability to edit the shapes in the drawing but not the controls. You can protect controls from user changes, even in design mode, by locking the shapes and protecting the document.

To protect controls from changes

1. Select the controls on the drawing.
2. On the **Format** menu, click **Protection**, and then select **From selection**.
3. On the **View** menu, click **Drawing Explorer Window**.
4. In the **Drawing Explorer**, right-click the document, click **Protect Document** on the shortcut menu, and then select **Shapes**.
5. Define a password in the **Protect Document** dialog box for added security.

   The user will be able to modify the drawing but not the controls.

Handling a Control's Events

After you add an ActiveX control to the drawing page, you can handle the various events issued by the control—for example, if you insert a command button, you can handle its **Click** event. You handle a control's events by writing event procedures in the Microsoft Visual Basic for Applications (VBA) project of the Microsoft Visio drawing that contains the control, just as you would handle a Visio event.

To write an event procedure for a control

1. In the Visual Basic Editor **Code** window for **ThisDocument**, select the control from the **Object** box.
2. Select the event you want to handle from the **Procedure** box.
3. Fill in the event procedure in the **Code** window.

For example, the following event procedure for a command button deletes a shape in the Visio drawing when a user selects the shape's name in a listbox control and clicks the command button:

```
Private Sub CommandButton1_Click( )
    Dim visShape As Visio.Shape
    If ListBox1.ListIndex >=0 Then
            Set visShape = _
                    ActivePage.Shapes(ListBox1.Text)
            visShape.Delete
    End If
End Sub
```

Working with Controls at Run Time

An ActiveX control typically exposes properties and methods you can use at run time to work with the control programmatically. For example, a listbox control has a **ListIndex** property that returns the index of the selected item and a **Text** property that returns the text of the item at that index.

About Control Names

A control has two names: a Microsoft Visio name and a Microsoft Visual Basic for Applications (VBA) name. Initially, these names are identical, consisting of the control type plus an integer that makes the name unique. For example, the first listbox control you insert into a drawing is given the name ListBox1, and you can use this name to refer to the control in both VBA code and in Visio. (Visio shapes follow a different naming convention. For details about the naming conventions, see Chapter 16, *Working with Visio Document, Page, and Shape objects.*)

Although initially set to the same value, the two names are programmatically distinct and cannot be used interchangeably.

- You use a control's VBA object name to refer to the control in VBA code. You change this name by setting the control's (**Name**) property in the VBA properties window in the Visual Basic Editor. You cannot use a control's VBA object name to get the corresponding **Shape** object from a Visio collection, such as the **Shapes** collection; instead, you must use the control's **Shape.Name** property—for example, **ListBox1.Shape.Name**.
- You use a control's Visio name to get the **Shape** object that represents the control from a Visio collection, such as **OLEObjects** or **Shapes**. You change this name by editing it in the **Name** box in the **Special** dialog box in Visio (select the control and click **Special** on the **Format** menu) or by setting the control's **Shape.Name** property in VBA. You cannot use a control's Visio name to refer to the control in VBA code.

> **Tip** For your own convenience, if you change one name from the default value, you might want to change the other name so that the control's VBA and Visio names are identical.

Getting a Control from the OLEObjects Collection

You can get the **Shape** object that represents a control from the **OLEObjects** collection of a Microsoft Visio **Document**, **Page**, or **Master** object. You can also get a control from the **Shapes** collection of a page or master. However, it's faster to use the **OLEObjects** collection because it contains only linked or embedded objects, whereas the **Shapes** collection also includes all of the linked or embedded objects plus the Visio shapes—potentially many more objects.

The **OLEObjects** collection contains an **OLEObject** object that represents each linked or embedded object in a Visio document, page, or master, plus any ActiveX controls. The **Object** property of an **OLEObject** returns a reference to the linked or embedded object that you can use to access the object's properties and methods.

You can retrieve a control from the **OLEObjects** collection by its index within the collection or by the name assigned to the control in Visio. Initially, this name is identical to the value of the control's VBA object name, as described in the previous topic, *About Control Names*. For example, the following statements get a shape named ListBox1:

```
Dim g_listbox As Object
Set g_listbox = _
    Document.OLEObjects("ListBox1").Object
```

If you want to perform the same operation on all controls, iterate through the **OLEObjects** collection and check the **ForeignType** property of each **OLEObject** object to see whether the **visTypeIsControl** bit is set. If **ForeignType** and **visTypeIsControl** are both **True**, the object is an ActiveX control.

Distributing ActiveX Controls in a Visio Solution

Microsoft Visual Basic for Applications (VBA) in Microsoft Visio provides the Microsoft Forms 2.0 ActiveX controls, which include standard dialog box controls, such as buttons, check boxes, text boxes, and combo boxes. You can distribute these controls most simply with a Visio solution, because they are included with Visio—no special installation or additional licensing is required.

You might acquire other controls by installing Microsoft Visual Basic or C++, downloading controls from the Internet, or buying third-party packages. Distributing a solution that contains such controls can be a little more complicated:

- Because the controls might not already be on the user's system, your solution's Setup program needs to check whether the control is already installed and, if not, install the control and register it on the user's system.
- Such controls typically come with a design-time license, so you can use them in your development projects, and the controls might require a run-time license for distribution.

For details about installing, registering, and licensing third-party controls, see the developer documentation provided with the control.

ActiveX Controls that Interact with Shapes: an Example

To understand how ActiveX controls can interact with Microsoft Visio shapes, consider the following example, which shows a drawing that contains a combo box control that lists the names of shapes in the drawing. The drawing also contains text boxes that display the text and certain custom properties of a selected shape, and a command button that updates a selected shape with new values in the text boxes. The drawing maintains a running total of cost and duration for all process flowchart shapes on the page, updating the totals as shapes are added, deleted, or changed.

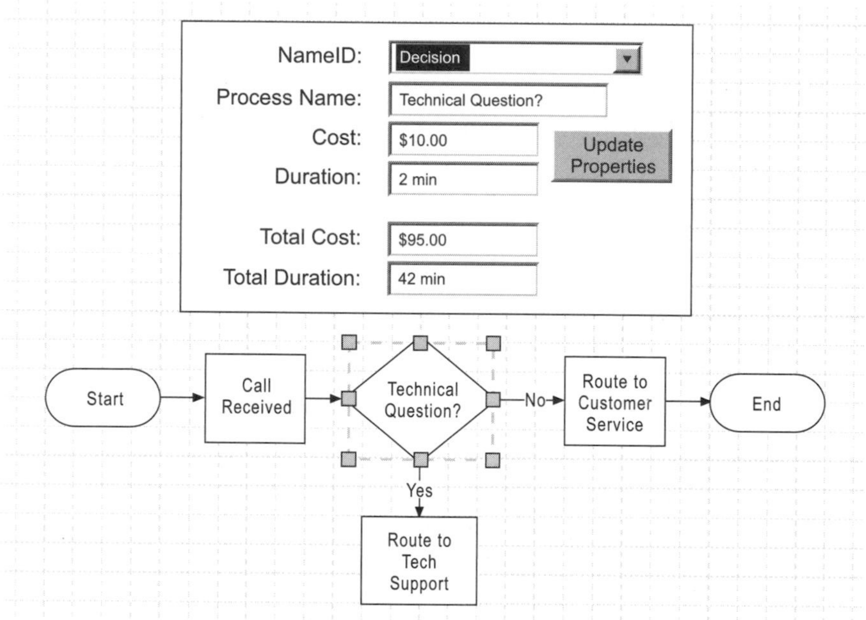

Figure 24-4 A drawing that uses ActiveX controls to interact with shapes.

The following code example shows a **ComboBox1_Change** event handler; this handler selects a shape in the drawing and displays its custom properties in the text boxes when the user highlights the shape's name in the combo box list:

```
Private Sub ComboBox1_Change()
    'The user has clicked on an item in the list box
    Dim strName As String
    On Error GoTo Ignore:

    If (bInComboBoxChanged) Then
        'Exit without doing anything; already responding to the
        'initial Change event
        Exit Sub
```

```
    End If

    'Set flag indicating the program is in the Change routine. If an
    'error occurs after this, it skips to the Ignore label,
    'after which the flag is reset.
    bInComboBoxChanged = True

    'Calling DeselectAll and Select on the Window object set
    'ComboBox1.Text (see theWindow_SelectionChanged). Save the
    'current text before callingDeselectAll,
    'so that we know which shape to select.
    strName = ComboBox1.Text

    'Select the item and get its properties
    ActiveWindow.DeselectAll
    ActiveWindow.Select ActivePage.Shapes(strName), visSelect

    With ActivePage.Shapes(strName)
        TextBox1.Text = .Text
        TextBox2.Text = Format(.Cells("prop.cost").ResultIU, _
              "Currency")
        TextBox3.Text = _
              Format(.Cells("prop.duration").Result _
                (visElapsedMin), "###0 min.")
    End With
    Exit Sub

Ignore:
    'Set flag indicating the program is NOT in the Change handler
    'anymore
    bInComboBoxChanged = False
End Sub
```

This handler does the following:

1. Clears the selection in the drawing.
2. Selects the shape whose name corresponds to the value of the **ComboBox1** control's **Text** property. If the drawing doesn't contain such a shape, the handler simply exits.
3. Sets the **TextBox1** control's **Text** property to the **Text** property of the shape.
4. Sets the **TextBox2** control's **Text** property to the value of the shape's **Cost** custom property, expressed as currency.
5. Sets the **TextBox3** control's **Text** property to the value of the shape's **Duration** custom property, expressed as minutes.

The global variable *bInComboBoxChanged* indicates whether the **ComboBox1_Change** handler is being called for the first time. Clearing the selection and selecting a shape triggers **Window_SelectionChanged** events. However, this example's handler for that event sets the **ComboBox1.Text** property, which triggers a **ComboBox1_Change** event and causes the **ComboBox1_Change** handler to run again. Because the handler sets *bInComboBoxChanged* the first time it runs, it can skip the selection operations the second time, preventing the program from entering a recursive loop.

It's also possible to prevent such loops by setting the **EventsEnabled** property of the **Application** object to disable event handling while the handler performs operations that would otherwise trigger events and cause handlers to run inappropriately. However, this approach is not recommended, because it disables *all* events for the instance of Visio, which might interfere with other solutions running on the user's system (especially if an error in your solution prevents it from reenabling events). Unless you are certain that your solution is the only one that will be handling Visio events, it's recommended that you use the global variable technique shown in the previous example.

25

Using the Visio Undo Manager in Your Program

The Visio Undo Manager 524

Creating Undo Scopes in Your Add-on 527

Creating Undo Units 528

Creating an Undo Unit that Maintains Non-Visio Data: an Example 531

Changes to a Microsoft Visio document can occur in one of two ways: through a user action in the user interface, or through an Automation program. A user can undo or redo the change in the user interface just as you can undo or redo changes in your program using the **Undo** or **Redo** method. Every Visio instance contains one Undo manager that tracks undoable and redoable actions across the application. An *undoable* action can be anything that modifies or changes the state of a document. The queues of undoable and redoable actions are called *stacks*.

The Visio Undo manager provides the flexibility to handle undoable actions as discrete actions, or to consolidate multiple undoable actions into a single unit that gets managed on the undo and redo stacks as a single undoable action. To do this, the Visio engine creates an *undo scope*.

Additionally, if your solution maintains a parallel or shadow model that represents data associated with the shapes in your drawing, you can create *undo units* to place on the Visio Undo manager to keep your data and drawings synchronized. Undo units contain the actions needed to undo or redo changes to a document.

> **Note** In versions earlier than Visio 2000, each individual action performed in an add-on was a single undoable action in Visio. If a user chose **Undo**, only the most recent action was undone.
>
> Beginning with Visio 2000, the sequence of actions performed by an add-on that is invoked from Visio is automatically managed as a single undoable action. If a user chooses **Undo**, all Visio-specific actions performed in the add-on are reversed. For details, see *How the Visio Undo Manager Works with an Add-on* later in this chapter.

The Visio Undo Manager

The Microsoft Visio engine creates an undo unit for every Visio command that changes the state of a document. An *undo unit* describes what has changed—it encapsulates all the information that's necessary to undo a change that a user doesn't want.

Every undoable action has a corresponding undo unit. For each undoable action that a user performs in the user interface, the Visio instance creates an undo unit that appears in the **Undo** list on the **Standard** toolbar.

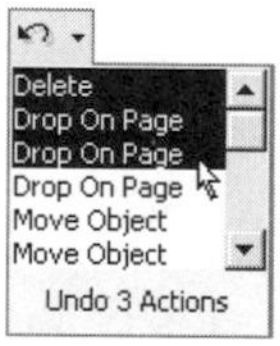

Figure 25-1 Example of list of undoable actions in the user interface.

Actions caused by running an add-on are handled differently from actions in the user interface. Users who run an add-on from the **Macros** submenu (on the **Tools** menu, click **Macros**) might think of that action as being similar to dropping a shape on a page—as a single undoable action. The user most likely expects to undo any add-on changes in a single action. For this reason, whenever an add-on is invoked from Visio, the add-on's undoable actions are consolidated inside an undo scope and are presented to the user as a single undoable action.

For details on creating your own undo scopes, see *Creating Undo Scopes in Your Add-on* later in this chapter.

An Undo/Redo Overview

Every Visio instance maintains one Undo manager to manage the undo and redo stacks. When a user clicks **Undo**, the Visio Undo manager takes the most recently added undo unit from the undo stack, and the undo unit carries out its actions and creates a corresponding object on the redo stack.

For example, if a user performs three actions on the drawing page, the Visio Undo manager would look something like the following illustration:

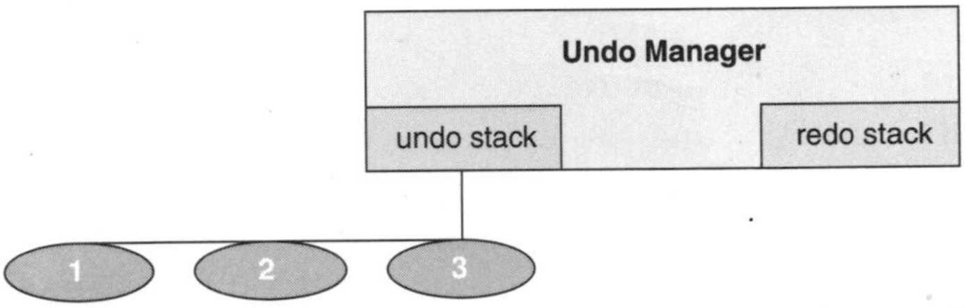

Figure 25-2 The state of the undo/redo stacks after three undoable actions.

If the user then clicks the **Undo** command, or your program invokes the **Undo** method of the **Application** object, the Visio Undo manager would appear as the following illustration shows:

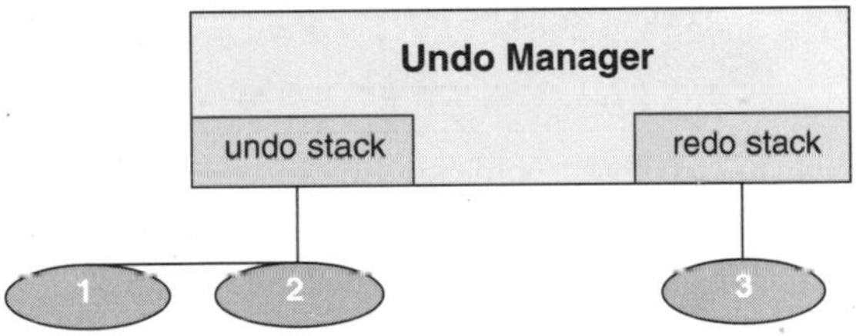

Figure 25-3 The state of the undo/redo stacks after one action is undone.

How the Visio Undo Manager Works with an Add-on

An add-on often performs multiple undoable actions—for example, it might change the fill of every shape on a page to blue. If a user didn't like this change and wanted to undo it, he or she would expect the **Undo** command to restore the drawing to its state before the add-on ran.

For this reason, the Visio engine consolidates the sequence of actions caused by an add-on into a single undoable action. Every time an add-on is invoked from a Visio instance, an undo scope begins. The undo scope ends when the add-on finishes. Everything inside of this scope is treated as a single undoable action.

For example, if an add-on executes three Visio commands, the undo stack would look like the following illustration after the add-on runs:

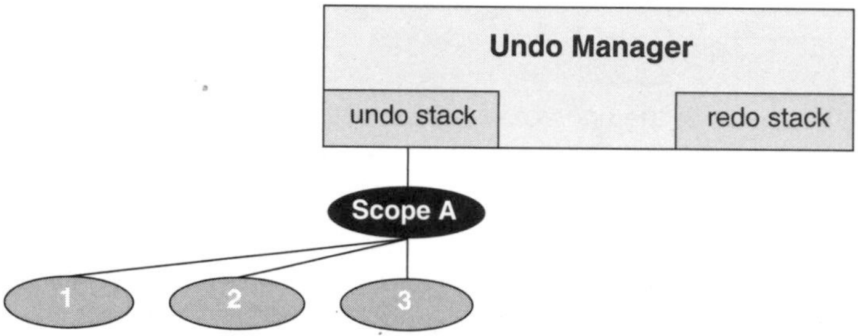

Figure 25-4 The state of the undo/redo stacks after an add-on is run that performs three undoable actions.

If the user then chose to undo the changes made by the add-on, the user would see a single command in the **Undo** list on the **Standard** toolbar and on the **Edit** menu, all three actions would be undone, and the undo queue would look like the previous illustration.

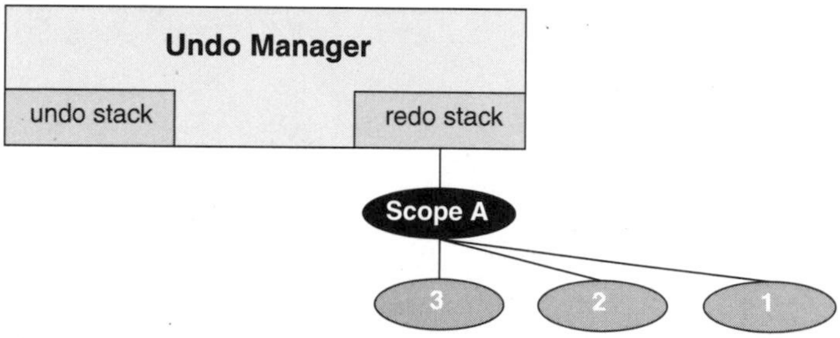

Figure 25-5 The state of the undo/redo stacks after choosing **Undo** for an add-on that performs three undoable actions.

> **Tip** When you include an undoable action inside an event handler, check the **Application** object's **IsUndoingOrRedoing** property first. You want to perform undoable actions only when this flag is **False**. If **IsUndoingOrRedoing** returns **True**, the event handler is being called as a result of an undo or redo action; if any undoable actions are performed, the redo stack is destroyed.

Creating Undo Scopes in Your Add-on

In some cases, the Microsoft Visio engine cannot automatically manage the undoable actions in an add-on. If an add-on is a stand-alone program, for example, Visio cannot detect when the add-on begins and ends. Or if a program is running modeless, Visio cannot be aware of all the operations that the add-on performs. For this reason, Visio provides mechanisms for you to create your own undo scopes.

In addition to consolidating operations into single undoable actions, you can also use undo scopes to determine if events that your program receives result from actions in the program itself. You can do this by creating undo scopes, and then checking each scope's ID inside your event handlers.

Creating an Undo Scope

To create an undo scope, use the **BeginUndoScope** and **EndUndoScope** methods of the **Application** object. You can create multiple scopes inside an add-on, and you can nest undo scopes inside each other.

The **BeginUndoScope** method opens a new scope and returns an ID for the scope. While the scope is open the Visio Undo manager gives it any new undo units that are added to the stack. The Visio engine also queues the **EnterScope** event so that later it can pass the scope ID and description to your program.

Consider the following guidelines when creating undo scopes:

- **BeginUndoScope** and **EndUndoScope** calls *must* be balanced.
- Undo scopes should be opened and closed within a function or subroutine. If you leave an undo scope open, user actions can get logged into the middle of the scope.

The **EndUndoScope** method takes an argument of **True** or **False**, which indicates whether you want to accept or cancel the changes made during the scope. You can use this as a technique for rolling back changes if you or your user decides to cancel your add-on.

For details about the **BeginUndoScope** and **EndUndoScope** methods, see the Microsoft Developer Reference (on the **Help** menu, click **Developer Reference**).

Associating Events with an Undo Scope

You can use an undo scope to determine whether events you receive are the result of an action taken by your add-on.

When you open an undo scope with the **BeginUndoScope** method, it returns a scope ID and fires the **EnterScope** event. When you close an undo scope with the **EndUndoScope** method, an **ExitScope** event fires. Any events caused when your undo scope is open fire between the **EnterScope** and **ExitScope** events.

When you receive events, you can use the scope ID to determine if an event is a result of an action taken in the undo scope.

To determine if your undo scope caused an event

1. Save the scope ID that is returned from the **BeginUndoScope** method in a program variable.
2. When you receive an event in your event handler, get the **IsInScope** property of the **Application** object, passing it the saved scope ID.
3. If the **IsInScope** property returns **True**, the event is a result of an action taken in your undo scope.
4. Create an event handler for the **ExitScope** event and clear your scope ID variable when the scope closes.

Creating Undo Units

If your solution maintains any type of parallel model that contains data associated with the shapes in your drawing, it is important that the model correctly represents the state of the drawing.

To ensure that your drawings and models remain synchronized, you can add undo units to the Microsoft Visio Undo manager. An *undo unit* is a Component Object Model (COM) object that supports the Visio **IVBUndoUnit** interface (or the **IOleUndoUnit** interface on an in-process COM object). It contains the actions needed to undo or redo changes to an external data source that reflect changes in the drawing.

The Visio **IVBUndoUnit** interface is designed to allow programmers using Microsoft Visual Basic for Applications (VBA) and Microsoft Visual Basic to create their own undo units for the Visio Undo manager. To create an undo unit, you must implement this interface, along with all of its public procedures, in a class module that you insert into your project. This section describes creating an undo unit by implementing the **IVBUndoUnit** interface in a VBA project.

For details about implementing interfaces in VBA or Visual Basic, search for the **Implements** keyword in your Visual Basic documentation. For details about **IVBUndoUnit**, see the Visio type library.

Creating an Undo Unit

You can take two approaches to creating an undo unit:

- You can create a single object that maintains its undone state.
- You can create two objects—one that encapsulates actions required to undo a change, and one that encapsulates the actions required to redo a change.

This topic and the next, *Creating an Undo Unit that Maintains Non-Visio Data: an Example*, describe a single undo unit that maintains its undo/redo state.

To create an undo unit

1. Insert a class module into your VBA project that implements the **IVBUndoUnit** class. This is your undo unit. To do this, use the **Implements** keyword:

   ```
   Implements Visio.IVBUndoUnit
   ```

   Inside this class module you must implement all of the public procedures of **IVBUndoUnit**. After you code the **Implements** statement, **IVBUndoUnit** will appear in the **Object** box in the code window.

2. Select **IVBUndoUnit** from the **Object** box.

   Skeleton procedures become available in the **Procedure** box for each of the procedures you must implement, as described in the following table.

IVBUndoUnit procedures

Procedure name	Description
Description	This property returns a string describing the undo unit. This string appears in the **Undo** list on the **Standard** toolbar.
Do	This method provides the actions that are required to undo and redo your action. If you are creating a single object for undoing and redoing, this procedure maintains your undo/redo state and adds an undo unit to the opposite stack. If the **Do** method is called with a **Nothing** pointer, the unit should carry out the undo action but should not place anything on the undo or redo stack.
OnNextAdd	This method gets called when the next undo unit in the same scope gets added to the undo stack. When an undo unit receives an **OnNextAdd** notification, it communicates back to the creating object that it can longer insert data into this undo unit.
UnitSize	This property returns the approximate memory size (in bytes) of the undo unit plus resources it has allocated. The Visio engine may use this memory size when deciding whether to purge the undo queue. This value is optional and can be zero (0).
UnitTypeCLSID	This property returns a string value that can contain a CLSID to identify your undo units. You can use the same CLSID for multiple undo units and use different values in the **UnitTypeLong** procedure. This value is optional and can be a **Null** or empty string.
UnitTypeLong	This property returns a **Long**, which you can use to identify your objects. This value is optional and can be 0.

Adding an Undo Unit in the Visio Undo Manager

At any location in your program where you perform an action in your parallel model, you should add an instance of your undo unit that can undo or redo your action. In this way, it will get called along with everything else in the undo stack if your add-on's changes get undone.

To add an undo unit in the Visio Undo manager

- Invoke the **AddUndoUnit** method of the **Application** object and pass it an instance of your undo unit class using the **New** keyword.

  For example, if the class module that you inserted into the project was named *MyUndoUnit*:

  ```
  Application.AddUndoUnit New MyUndoUnit
  ```

For details about the **New** keyword, see your Visual Basic documentation.

Creating an Undo Unit that Maintains Non-Visio Data: an Example

The following example demonstrates creating an undo unit that synchronizes a drawing and a parallel model—in this case, a simple variable called *m_nCount* that represents the number of shapes in the drawing. This variable is incremented each time a shape is added to the drawing.

The class module called **VBAUndoUnit** contains the logic to increment or decrement *m_nCount* if the **ShapeAdded** event subsequently gets undone or redone. **VBAUndoUnit** contains a flag to maintain its own undone state. The flag is initialized to **False** because this object is initially placed on the undo stack. After **VBAUndoUnit** gets called the first time, it carries out the undo logic, changes its undone state to **True**, and places itself on the redo stack.

The example uses the **Immediate** window in the Visual Basic Editor to display how this project keeps the drawing and the data synchronized.

The first block of code is contained in the **ShapeAdded** event handler in the **ThisDocument** class module. The program increments *m_nCount* by 1 and then adds the undo unit to the undo stack in the Visio Undo manager. Because the Visio engine automatically creates a scope when the event handler gets called, the undo unit will get executed if the user then decides to undo the shape that was just added to the drawing.

ThisDocument also contains procedures to increment and decrement the variable.

```
Private m_nCount As Long
Private Sub Document_ShapeAdded(ByVal Shape As IVShape)
    If Not Application.IsUndoingOrRedoing Then
           'Now you can perform undoable actions
           IncrementModuleVar
           Debug.Print "Original Do: GetModuleVar = " & GetModuleVar
           'Add an undo unit that undoes/redoes that action
           Application.AddUndoUnit New VBAUndoUnit
```

```
    End If
End Sub
Public Sub IncrementModuleVar()
    m_nCount = m_nCount + 1
End Sub
Public Sub DecrementModuleVar()
    m_nCount = m_nCount - 1
End Sub
Public Function GetModuleVar() As Long
    GetModuleVar = m_nCount
End Function
```

Here is the code inside **VBAUndoUnit:**

```
Implements Visio.IVBUndoUnit
Private m_bUndone As Boolean
    'm_bUndone is a flag that tells us whether an undo unit exists
    'on the undo or redo stack. When you first call
    'Application.AddUndoUnit, an instance of VBAUndoUnit is
    'placed on the undo stack. Then when undo occurs, the "Do"
    'method gets called and you toggle this flag and call
    'IVBUndoManager.Add to get an undo unit placed on the redo stack.
    'Then, the next time the Do method gets called, you toggle the
    'flag back again and call IVBUndoManager.Add again to get an undo
    'unit placed back on the undo stack. When an undo unit is on the
    'undo stack, m_bUndone should be False because it is not yet
    'undone. When your Do method gets called and the
    'undo unit is transferred to the redo stack, you toggle the flag
    'and m_bUndone will be True. You initialize m_bUndone as False
    'because the undo unit first exists on the undo stack.
    'During a rollback, (someone calls EndUndoScope(nID, *False*)),
    'VBAUndoUnit's Do method will get called with IVBUndoManager set
    'to Nothing. In that case, VBAUndoUnit cannot and should not
    'attempt to add an undo unit to the passed in Undo manager.
    'Always check for pMgr = "Is Nothing" inside of your Do method.
Private Sub Class_Initialize()
    Debug.Print "VBAUndoUnit created..."
End Sub
Private Sub Class_Terminate()
    Debug.Print "VBAUndoUnit purged..."
End Sub
Private Property Get IVBUndoUnit_Description() As String
    Debug.Print "VBAUndoUnit.Description"
    IVBUndoUnit_Description = "VBAUndoUnit"
End Property
Private Sub IVBUndoUnit_Do(ByVal pMgr As IVBUndoManager)
    'Undo or redo, according to the state flag:
    If (m_bUndone) Then
```

```
            'Redo the original action:
            ThisDocument.IncrementModuleVar
      Else
            'Undo the original action:
            ThisDocument.DecrementModuleVar
      End If

      'Toggle the state flag:
      m_bUndone = Not m_bUndone

      If Not (pMgr Is Nothing) Then
            'Add an an instance of VBAUndoUnit back to the opposite
            'stack
            pMgr.Add Me
            Debug.Print "VBAUndoUnit.Do called with an Undo manager"
      Else
            'Nothing left to do -- we are in a rollback and will most
            'likely soon be terminated...
            Debug.Print "VBAUndoUnit.Do called WITHOUT an Undo _
                  manager"
      End If
      'Confirm results of undo by printing the value of the
      'GetModuleVar variable
      Debug.Print "After VBAUndoUnit.Do - GetModuleVar = " & _
            ThisDocument.GetModuleVar
End Sub
Private Sub IVBUndoUnit_OnNextAdd()
      'OnNextAdd gets called when the next unit in the same scope gets
      'added to the undo stack.
      Debug.Print "VBAUndoUnit.OnNextAdd"
End Sub
Private Property Get IVBUndoUnit_UnitSize() As Long
      'UnitSize should return an approximate in memory size (in bytes)
      'of the undo unit itself plus anything it holds on to. This
      'allows Visio to use a memory size measurement to decide when to
      'purge undo.
      Debug.Print "VBAUndoUnit.UnitSize"
      IVBUndoUnit_UnitSize = 4
End Property
Private Property Get IVBUndoUnit_UnitTypeCLSID() As String
      'Return a CLSID string here if you think it's important to be
      'able to identify your units. If you have several different types
      'of units, you could return the same CLSID for all of them, but
      'choose different Long IDs for each.
      Debug.Print "VBAUndoUnit.UnitTypeCLSID"
      IVBUndoUnit_UnitTypeCLSID = Null
End Property
```

```
Private Property Get IVBUndoUnit_UnitTypeLong() As Long
    'Return a Long here if you want to identify your units. See
    'discussion in UnitTypeCLSID.
    Debug.Print "VBAUndoUnit.UnitTypeLong"
    IVBUndoUnit_UnitTypeLong = 0
End Property
```

26

Packaging a Visio Automation Solution

Installing a Visio Solution 536

Controlling when Your Program Runs 539

Distributing Your Program 544

If you're writing a program for others to use, you'll need to determine:

- The templates, stencils, and drawings that you'll distribute with your program.
- A Microsoft Visio file for storing your Microsoft Visual Basic for Applications (VBA) program.
- Where to install the files.
- How a user will run your program and what arguments might be passed to your program when it is run.
- Whether you need to create a Setup program that installs a stand-alone program, its related stencils and templates, and online Help in the appropriate folders.

This chapter discusses where to install various files to take advantage of the Visio default paths, some of the different ways a user can run your program, and considerations for distributing your program.

For details about creating Help files and Setup programs, see the documentation for your development environment. For details about associating Help with particular shapes, see Chapter 13, *Packaging Stencils and Templates*. Information about integrating the Answer Wizard into your Help files can be found in the Microsoft Visio Resource Kit, available from the Microsoft Visio Web site (http://www.microsoft.com/office/visio/).

Installing a Visio Solution

If you're providing your solution as a Microsoft Visual Basic for Applications (VBA) program, a Component Object Model (COM) add-in, or single executable (EXE) file, you might not need to create a Setup program to install it. However, if your solution includes one or more EXE files or DLLs, stencils, templates, or a Help file, a Setup program can assist the user to install your solution easily and accurately.

This section describes where to install your solution's files. For details about creating a Setup program, see the documentation for your development environment.

Specifying Visio File Paths and Folders

When installing your solution, install your program and Microsoft Visio files in folders in the appropriate path as specified on the **File Paths** tab (on the **Tools** menu, click **Options**).

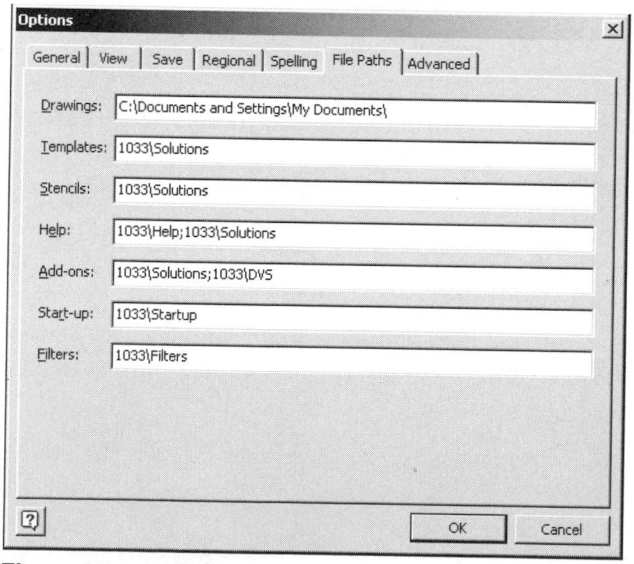

Figure 26-1 File Paths tab.

By default, the path containing the Solutions folder and its subfolders under the correct language folder for Visio is the specified path for templates, stencils, and add-ons. The path containing the Help folder under the correct language folder for Visio is the specified path for Help files. For example, to install templates that contain VBA macros, place them in the Solutions folder or any of its subfolders.

You might choose to install COM add-ins in the Solutions folder as well; however, the path in which you install COM add-ins is less important because Visio will look for COM add-ins based on where they are registered.

You can also change and add folders to the file paths to include custom folders you create. To indicate more than one folder in a path, separate individual items in the path string with semicolons. In the preceding figure, the add-ons path has been changed to "1033\Solutions;1033\DVS".

> **Note** If a path is not fully qualified, Visio looks for that folder in the folder that contains the Visio application files. For example, if the Visio executable file is installed in c:\Visio and the add-ons path is "Add-ons;d:\Add-ons", Visio would look for add-ons in both c:\Visio\Add-ons and d:\Add-ons and their corresponding subfolders.

Installation paths for your program's files

Install this file	In this Visio path
Program (EXE)	**Add-ons**
Visio library (VSL)	**Add-ons**
COM add-in (DLL)	Any path is allowed; the path information is determined by the registry settings.
Help (HLP or CHM) for programs or shapes	**Help**
Stencil (VSS or VSX)	**Stencil**
Template (VST or VTX)	**Template**

You can also find out what paths are in effect on the user's system by checking the following properties of an **Application** object: **AddonPaths**, **StartupPaths**, **DrawingPaths**, **StencilPaths**, **FilterPaths**, **TemplatePaths**, and **HelpPaths**.

Application object properties that correspond to File Paths tab settings

File Path field	Property
Drawings	**DrawingPaths**
Templates	**TemplatePaths**
Stencils	**StencilPaths**
Help	**HelpPaths**
Add-ons	**AddonPaths**
Start-up	**StartupPaths**
Filters	**FilterPaths**

For example, to get the **AddonPaths** property:

```
strPath = Visio.Application.AddonPaths
```

For more information about the **Application** object and its properties, see the Microsoft Visio Developer Reference (on the **Help** menu, click **Developer Reference**).

How Visio Searches File Paths

Files placed in the folders in a specified Visio path appear on selected menus and in dialog boxes in the user interface. By installing your solution files in folders in the appropriate Visio paths, you can take advantage of this behavior. When you use these paths, your solution files become available in the following ways:

- When Visio isn't running in developer mode, add-ons in folders in the Visio **Add-ons** path specified on the **File Paths** tab appear in the **Macros** dialog box and on the **Macros** submenu, along with VBA macros for the document that is open.

  When Visio is running in developer mode, add-ons in folders in the Visio **Add-ons** path specified on the **File Paths** tab appear in the **Run Add-on** dialog box (on the **Tools** menu, point to **Add-ons**, and then click **Run Add-on**) and on the **Add-ons** submenu.

> **Note** To run Visio in developer mode, click **Options** on the **Tools** menu, click the **Advanced** tab, select the **Run in developer mode** check box, and then click **OK**.

- Template files in folders in the Visio templates path appear in the **Choose Drawing Type** and **Open** dialog boxes, and on the **New** submenu on the **File** menu.
- Stencils in folders in the Visio stencils path are listed on the **Stencils** submenu on the **File** menu and in the **Open Stencil** dialog box.

Controlling when Your Program Runs

You can run a program in a number of ways depending on what type of program you write and where you install external program files. Here are some of your options:

Running a program when a Visio instance is started

To run your program every time Microsoft Visio is started, install your program's executable (EXE) or Visio library (VSL) file in the Visio startup folder specified on the **File Paths** tab (on the **Tools** menu, click **Options**).

To load a Component Object Model (COM) add-in when Visio is started, you must register it with a load behavior of **Startup**. When the add-in is loaded, it remains loaded until it is explicitly unloaded.

> **Note** When a COM add-in loads, it might not necessarily run until an event occurs that it is listening for. For more details on implementing COM add-ins, see Chapter 23, *Using COM Add-ins in a Visio Solution.*

Running a program from the Macros submenu or dialog box

To run your program—EXE or VSL file, or Microsoft Visual Basic for Applications (VBA) macro—from the **Macros** dialog box, install an external program's EXE or VSL file in the **Add-ons** path specified on the **File Paths** tab. All programs in this path appear in the **Macros** dialog box and on the **Macros** submenu along with any public VBA macros stored with the Visio document that is open.

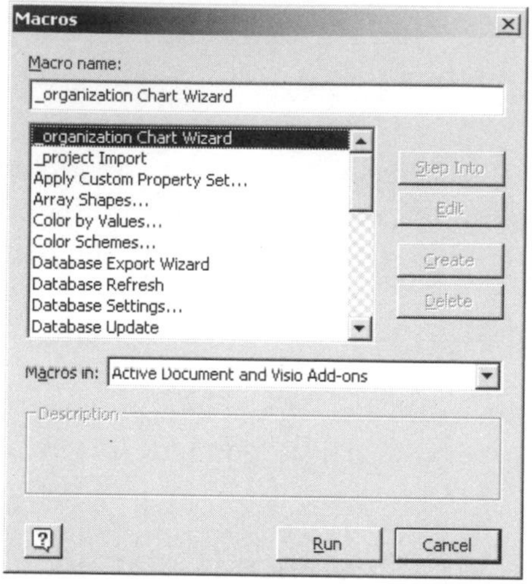

Figure 26-2 **Macros** dialog box.

Loading a COM add-in program from the COM Add-Ins dialog box

If you haven't set your COM add-in to load when Visio is started or to load on demand, you or your solution's users can load the COM add-in from the **COM Add-Ins** dialog box. Because the add-in must be registered, you don't need to specify a path for it. All registered COM add-ins appear in the **COM Add-Ins** dialog box (on the **Tools** menu, point to **Macros**, and then click **COM Add-Ins**).

> **Note** When a COM add-in loads, it might not necessarily run until an event occurs that it is listening for. For more details on implementing COM add-ins, see Chapter 23, *Using COM Add-ins in a Visio Solution.*

Binding a program to a cell in the Actions or Events section

You can run a program when a user right-clicks a shape and chooses a menu item, or when a shape event occurs, such as a double-click event. To run any program from a shape's shortcut menu, enter a formula that uses the Visio RUNADDON function in the Action cell of a row in the shape's Actions section, and enter the text of the menu item in the Menu cell. The RUNADDON function can run any add-on or macro in your VBA project.

Figure 26-3 An Action row in a shape's Actions section.

Unless you specify a full path, Visio looks for your program in the **Add-ons** path specified on the **File Paths** tab.

You can also set an action for a particular shape in the **Action** dialog box (available when the ShapeSheet window is active) by clicking in an Action cell and clicking **Action** on the **Edit** menu.

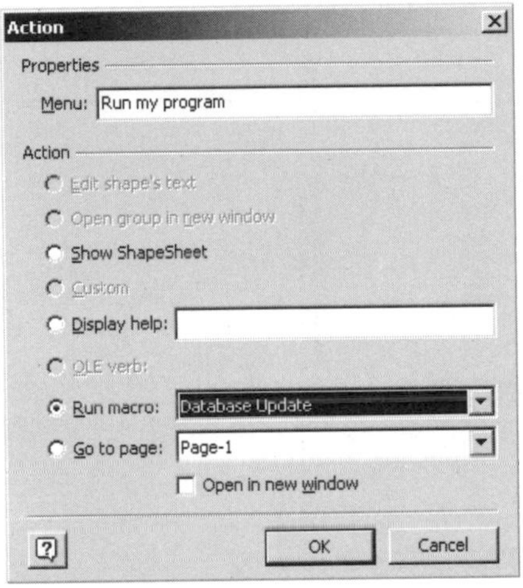

Figure 26-4 **Action** dialog box.

To pass command-line arguments to your program, use the Visio RUNADDONWARGS function—it is not used with VBA programs, only add-ons. For example, to run an external program named MyProg.exe:

```
= RUNADDONWARGS("MyProg.exe", "arguments")
```

To run your program when an Events cell gets evaluated, put the formula in the Events cell for the event that you want to trigger your program.

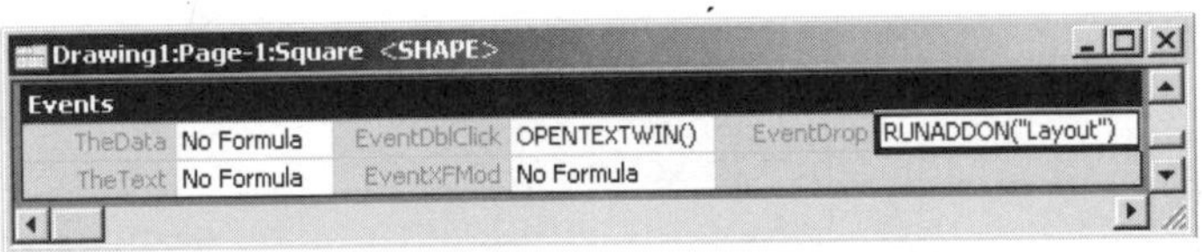

Figure 26-5 Events section in a ShapeSheet window.

For example, to run a VBA macro when the user drops a particular master in a drawing, put a formula such as the following in the EventDrop cell in the Events section of the master:

```
= CALLTHIS("Layout")
```

To run a VBA macro when a user double-clicks a particular shape, put the same formula in the EventDblClick cell in the Events section of the shape. Or set the double-click event for a particular shape by selecting a macro from the **Run macro** list on the **Double-Click** tab in the **Behavior** dialog box (on the **Format** menu, click **Behavior**).

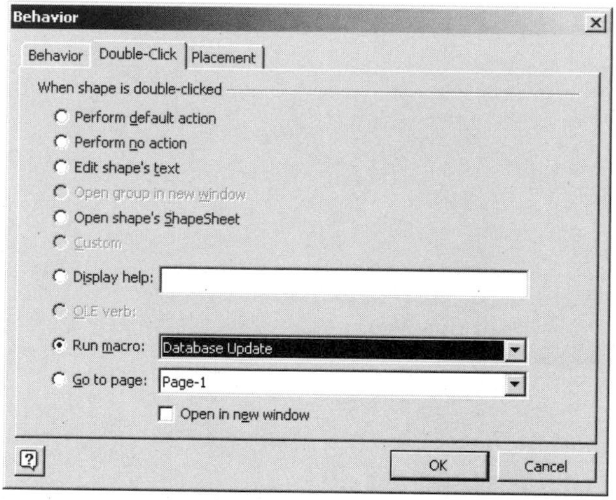

Figure 26-6 **Double-Click** tab in the **Behavior** dialog box.

For details about responding to events in the Events section, see Chapter 7, *Enhancing Shape Behavior.*

Running a program when the user chooses a menu command or toolbar button

You can add your own menu command or toolbar item to the Visio user interface and use it to run your program. For details, see Chapter 22, *Customizing the Visio User Interface.*

If you've created a toolbar button using the command bar object model and you want to load a COM add-in when a user clicks the button, you can use the **OnAction** property. (Setting the **OnAction** property allows Visio to load a COM add-in in response to a user clicking on a toolbar or menu item.) The syntax for setting the **OnAction** property for a COM add-in is:

```
ctlButton.OnAction = "!<ProgID>"
```

where *ctlButton* is the **CommandBarButton** object and *ProgID* is the programmatic identifier for the add-in. The programmatic identifier is the subkey that is created for the add-in in the Windows registry. You must set the **OnAction** property for any COM add-in you create that is loaded on demand. For more details on implementing COM add-ins, see Chapter 23, *Using COM Add-ins in a Visio Solution.*

You can also use the **OnAction** property to run a VBA macro or a Visio add-on VSL in response to a user clicking on a toolbar or menu item. You can set the **OnAction** property for a VBA macro or Visio add-on using the following syntax:

```
ctlButton.OnAction = "<ProjectName>!<MacroName>"

ctlButton.OnAction = "<MacroName|AddOnName>"
```

For example:

```
'Runs the Hello World macro in the ThisDocument module
'of the Drawing1 project. Drawing1.vsd must be open.
MyCtlButton.OnAction = "Drawing1!ThisDocument.HelloWorld"

'Runs the Hello World macro in the active document.
MyCtlButton.OnAction = "ThisDocument.HelloWorld"

'Runs a Visio add-on named "My Organization Chart".
'Visio automatically looks at the Parameter property
'of the control to determine add-on arguments, if any.
MyCtlButton.OnAction = "My Organization Chart"
MyCtlButton.Parameter = "/FILENAME ""C:\Samples\My _
    Organization Chart Data.xls"""
```

For more details on working with command bars, see Chapter 22, *Customizing the Visio User Interface.*

> **Note** To use the **OnAction** property in VBA or Visual Basic, you must set a reference to the Microsoft Office 10.0 object library.

Running VBA code inside of event-handling procedures

You can run VBA code by writing it in the **ThisDocument** class module under the appropriate event procedure. For example, to execute code when a document is opened, enter your code in the event procedure **DocumentOpened**.

Here are a few commonly handled document events: **BeforeDocumentClose**, **BeforePageDelete**, **BeforeShapeDelete**, **BeforeSelDelete** (before a set of shapes is deleted), **ShapeAdded**, **DocumentCreated**, **DocumentOpened**, **DocumentSaved**, and **DocumentSavedAs**.

For details about responding to object events, see Chapter 21, *Handling Visio Events*.

Distributing Your Program

The files you distribute to your users depend on the type of solution you create. Typically, if you create a Microsoft Visual Basic for Applications (VBA) program that is stored within a template, you'll distribute only the template and its stencils (and the files the VBA program references, if any). If you create an external program, you might need to distribute the executable (EXE) file, a template, and stencils. If you create an add-on or Component Object Model (COM) add-in, you might need to distribute only the EXE file or Microsoft Visio library (VSL) file, or COM add-in (DLL) file. You'll also need to be aware of copyright issues if you distribute Visio shapes, as described later in this chapter.

For details on distributing COM add-ins, see *Distributing COM Add-ins* in Chapter 23, *Using COM Add-ins in a Visio Solution*.

> **Note** Microsoft Office Developer (2000 and XP) and Visual Basic 6.0 provide wizards for packaging and deployment that can help you create a setup package you can then deploy to users. For information, see your Microsoft Office Developer or Visual Basic product documentation.

Distributing Microsoft VBA Programs

VBA programs are stored in a Visio template, stencil, or drawing. The only file you typically need to distribute is a template (VST or VTX) or drawing (VSD or VDX) and its stencils (VSS or VSX). If your VBA project references other Visio files, you need to distribute those also. There is no separate program file for a VBA program.

This illustration displays the possible elements of a VBA solution.

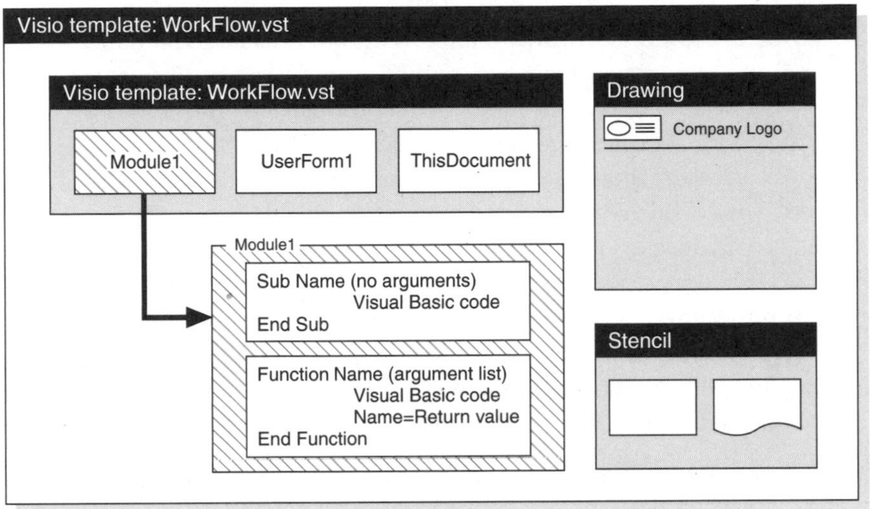

Figure 26-7 VBA solution and its elements: template, stencil, and VBA macros.

When a user creates a new document from a Visio file, Visio copies the VBA program to the new document and includes references to the same open stencils and other Visio files (if any).

Drawing File Size in a Microsoft VBA Solution

Determining where to store your VBA program can affect the size of the drawing file. You can store your program in a template, stencil, or drawing. Consider the following guidelines:

Although it's convenient to distribute, a template that contains a lot of VBA code can cause drawings to be much larger than necessary because the template's code is copied to each drawing created from the template. Such a template can also make a solution more difficult to maintain or upgrade, because each drawing has its own copy of the code.

If the purpose of the code is to help the user create a drawing, and it won't run again after that task is done, the template is probably still the best location for it. As an alternative, however, you can place the bulk of the code in a Visio stencil (VSS or VSX) and call it from the template. This helps conserve drawing file size and improves maintainability: You can simply distribute a new version of the stencil to upgrade your solution.

Using Universal Names in Your Solution

Beginning with Microsoft Visio 2000, any shape, master, page, style, row, or layer can be assigned a universal name in addition to its local name. A *local name* is a name, such as a shape name, that a user sees in the user interface. If your Automation solution will be localized (translated into another language), these names will often change for each location where they run.

Universal names are names that don't change when the solution is localized. Universal names do not appear in the user interface—only Automation clients can access Visio objects by their universal names. By using universal names in your source code, you can run your source code unchanged and avoid supporting multiple versions of your solution.

When an object is named for the first time, either in the user interface or through Automation, the universal name is set to the local name by default. After this original name is assigned, the following will apply:

- Any name changes that are made in the user interface affect only the local name.
- Universal names can be accessed or modified through the Automation interface only.

The properties and methods that you can use in your source code to refer to an object's universal name are found in the Visio type library with a suffix of "U."

To identify the properties and methods that reference universal names

1. In the **Object Browser**, select the class that you are working with; for example, **Page**.
2. In the list of class members, several properties and methods that will use the **Page** object's universal name are shown. For the **Page** object, they are: **DropManyU**, **GetFormulasU**, and **NameU**.

For details about using these properties and methods, see the Microsoft Visio Developer Reference (on the **Help** menu, click **Developer Reference**).

Important Licensing Information

The stencils, masters, and templates provided with Visio are copyrighted material, owned by Microsoft Corporation and protected by United States copyright laws and international treaty provisions.

As a solutions developer, you cannot distribute any copyrighted master provided with Microsoft Visio or through a Web-based subscription service, unless your user already has a licensed copy of Visio that includes that master, or your user has a valid subscription to the Web-based service, or you've signed an agreement that allows you to distribute individual masters to your users. This includes shapes you create by modifying or deriving shapes from copyrighted masters.

The Microsoft Visual Basic and C++ files of constants and global functions provided on the *Developing Microsoft Visio Solutions* CD are also copyrighted. You can include these files in your projects and use them to build executable programs. You cannot, however, distribute them to other developers unless they already have a licensed copy of the *Developing Microsoft Visio Solutions* CD that includes these files.

To copyright your original shapes, select a shape, click **Special** on the **Format** menu, and then enter copyright information in the **Copyright** box. After you enter copyright information in the **Special** dialog box, it cannot be changed in a drawing, stencil, or template file.

> **Note** For complete details about licensing of masters and Visio products, see the End User License Agreement for Microsoft Software that is included with Visio.

27

Programming Visio with Visual Basic

Getting a Visio Instance 550

Creating a Visio Document 555

Handling Errors in Visual Basic 556

Interpreting the Command String that Visio Sends to Your Program 558

Using the Visio Type Library in Visual Basic Projects 560

Earlier chapters in *Developing Microsoft Visio Solutions* focus on writing programs in the Microsoft Visual Basic for Applications (VBA) development environment within Microsoft Visio. This chapter focuses on specific issues related to writing external programs to control Visio using the Microsoft Visual Basic development environment.

For details about the Visio object model, which represents the objects, properties, and methods that the Visio engine exposes through Automation, see Chapter 14, *Automation and the Visio Object Model.*

Getting a Visio Instance

Any external program that controls Microsoft Visio through Automation must interact with a Visio instance. Depending on the purpose of your program, you might want to run a new Visio instance or use an instance that is already running.

Creating an Application Object

After you declare a Visio object variable for an **Application** object, you can use the **CreateObject** function in a **Set** statement to create the object and assign it to the object variable. You can then use the object variable to control the instance. For example:

```
Set appVisio = CreateObject("Visio.Application")
```

Creating an **Application** object runs a new Visio instance, even if other instances are already running.

You can also use the **CreateObject** function to create a Visio instance that is invisible. For example:

```
Set appVisio = CreateObject("Visio.InvisibleApp")
```

You can then use the **Application** object's **Visible** property to control whether the instance is visible.

> **Note** You can use the **InvisibleApp** object with *only* the **CreateObject** function. Attempts to use it with the **GetObject** function will fail. The **InvisibleApp** object is not available in versions of Visio earlier than Microsoft Visio 2000.

Getting an Application Object

You can use the **GetObject** function to retrieve an **Application** object for a Visio instance that is already running. For example:

```
Set appVisio = GetObject(, "Visio.Application")
```

Notice the comma, which indicates that the first argument to **GetObject**—a path to a file that is stored on the hard disk—has been omitted. The comma is required, because under some circumstances, **GetObject** takes a file name as its first argument. To retrieve a Visio instance, however, you must omit the file name argument or an error will occur. For details, see **GetObject** in your Microsoft Visual Basic documentation.

If more than one Visio instance is running, **GetObject** returns the active instance. When a program is run as an add-on or by double-clicking a shape, the active instance is the one that the program was run from. Otherwise, it is the instance that was most recently run or brought to the front. If no Visio instance is running, **GetObject** causes an error.

Releasing an Application Object

An application instance persists until you use the **Quit** method or a user closes the instance. You might want to include some error handling or use events to handle a user closing the instance, which can occur unexpectedly while your program is running.

Releasing an object in a program does not affect the corresponding object in the Visio instance. For example, releasing an **Application** object does not close Visio. The Visio application remains open, but your program no longer has access to it.

To release an **Application** object explicitly, set its object variable to the Visual Basic keyword **Nothing**. For example:

```
Set appVisio = Nothing
```

Don't release an object until you're finished using it. Once you release the object, the program can no longer refer to the corresponding object in the Visio instance. For example, if you release an **Application** object, the program can no longer use that variable to manipulate Visio, so it is unable to save or close the document or retrieve other objects from it.

To determine when to release objects from your program, you could write event handlers that release objects in response to events such as **BeforeQuit** or **BeforeDocumentClose**. For details on handling events, see Chapter 21, *Handling Visio Events*.

> **Note** If you are developing a COM add-in in Visual Basic, you do not need to call **CreateObject** or **GetObject** to get the Visio **Application** object. The **Application** object will be passed into the **OnConnection** method of your COM add-in. However, you'll need to save the **Application** object if you need to use it in your COM add-in. In the **OnDisconnection** method, you'll need to release the **Application** object by setting it to **Nothing**. For more details on implementing COM add-ins, see Chapter 23, *Using COM Add-ins in a Visio Solution*.

Using the Application Object in a Visual Basic Program: an Example

The following Visual Basic subroutine creates an **Application** object that runs a Visio instance and creates a drawing by opening a template and stencil. This subroutine follows these steps:

1. Creates a Visio instance.
2. Creates a new document based on the **Basic Diagram** template.
3. Drops an instance of the **Rectangle** master from the **Basic Shapes** stencil on the drawing page.
4. Sets the text of the rectangle shape on the drawing page to "Hello World!".
5. Saves the document.
6. Closes the Visio instance.

```
Sub HelloWorld ()
    'Instance of Visio
    Dim appVisio As Visio.Application
    'Documents collection of instance
    Dim docsObj As Visio.Documents
    'Document to work in
    Dim docObj As Visio.Document
    'Stencil that contains master
    Dim stnObj As Visio.Document
    'Master to drop
    Dim mastObj As Visio.Master
    'Pages collection of document
```

```
    Dim pagsObj As Visio.Pages
    'Page to work in
    Dim pagObj As Visio.Page
    'Instance of master on page
    Dim shpObj As Visio.Shape

    'Create an instance of Visio and create a document based on the
    'Basic Diagram template. It doesn't matter if an instance of
    'Visio is already running;the program will run a new one.
    Set appVisio = CreateObject("visio.application")
    Set docsObj = appVisio.Documents
    'Create a document based on the Basic Diagram template that
    'automatically opens the Basic Shapes stencil.
    Set docObj = docsObj.Add("Basic Diagram.vst")
    Set pagsObj = appVisio.ActiveDocument.Pages
    'A new document always has at least one page, whose index in the
    'Pages collection is 1.
    Set pagObj = pagsObj.Item(1)
    Set stnObj = appVisio.Documents("Basic Shapes.vss")
    Set mastObj = stnObj.Masters("Rectangle")
    'Drop the rectangle in the approximate middle of the page.
    'Coordinates passed with the Drop method are always inches.
    Set shpObj = pagObj.Drop(mastObj, 4.25, 5.5)
    'Set the text of the rectangle
    shpObj.Text = "Hello World!"
    'Save the drawing and quit Visio. The message pauses the program
    'so you can see the Visio drawing before the instance closes.
    docObj.SaveAs "hello.vsd"
    MsgBox "Drawing finished!", , "Hello World!"
    appVisio.Quit
End Sub
```

CreateObject is a Visual Basic function that creates an Automation object—in this example, **CreateObject** runs a new Visio instance and returns an **Application** object that represents the instance, which is assigned to the variable *appVisio*. The next six **Set** statements obtain references to the other objects that the program uses by getting properties of objects obtained earlier. Notice again the progression through the Visio object model from **Application** object to **Documents** collection to **Document** object to **Pages** collection to the **Page** object.

`Set docObj = docsObj.Add("basic diagram.vst")` uses the **Add** method to open a template and add it to the **Documents** collection. For details about adding **Document** objects, see *Creating a Visio Document* later in this chapter.

The statement *appVisio.Quit* uses the **Quit** method to close the Visio instance assigned to *appVisio*.

> **Note** This example does not explicitly release any of the objects used in the program by setting them to the Visual Basic keyword **Nothing** (Set appVisio = Nothing). It is good programming practice to explicitly release objects from your program when you are finished using them.

Working with an Instance's Window Handle

You can exert more control over a Visio instance by getting its window handle. After you get the window handle, you can manage the instance's frame window just as you would manage any other frame window from a Microsoft Windows application. For example, you might minimize the instance while your program is creating a complex drawing to save time repainting the screen.

The **Application** object's **WindowHandle32** property returns the window handle for the main, or frame, window of an instance. You can use **HWND** with standard Windows API calls to obtain other handles. For example, you can pass the window handle to **GetWindowTask** to get the Visio task handle.

For details about using Windows API calls, see your Microsoft Visual Basic documentation.

Interacting with Other Programs

While your program is running, you can find out which programs are available to the Visio engine, or install another program by getting the **Addons** collection of an **Application** object. This collection contains an **Addon** object for each program in the folders specified by the **Application** object's **AddonPaths** and **StartupPaths** properties or **Addon** objects that are added dynamically by other programs.

> **Note** To get a list with information on all COM add-ins currently registered in Visio, use the **COMAddIns** property. For details, see *Using the COMAddIns Property to Get Information about COM Add-ins* in Chapter 23, *Using COM Add-ins in a Visio Solution.*

By default, the programs represented by **Addon** objects are listed in the **Macros** dialog box and on the **Macros** submenu, along with VBA macros for the document that is open. When Visio is running in developer mode, the programs represented by **Addon** objects are listed in the **Run Add-on** dialog box (on the **Tools** menu, point to **Add-ons**, and then click **Run Add-on**) and on the **Add-ons** submenu.

You can add a program such as an EXE file by using the **Add** method of the **Application** object's **Addons** collection. The newly added program remains in the collection until the Visio instance is closed.

```
Set addonsObj = Visio.Application.Addons
Set addonObj = addonsObj.Add("c:\temp\myprog.exe")
```

Get the **Name** property of an **Addon** object to find out its name; get its **Enabled** property to find out whether it can be run. An EXE file is always enabled, but a program in a Visio library might not be. For details, see Chapter 28, *Programming Visio with C++*.

To run another program, use the **Run** method of the corresponding Addon object and include any necessary arguments or a null string ("").

For more details about **Addon** objects, their methods, and their properties, see the Microsoft Visio Developer Reference (on the **Help** menu, click **Developer Reference**).

Creating a Visio Document

After you get an **Application** object that represents a Microsoft Visio instance, the next step is to create or open a document.

To create a new, blank document

1. Get the **Documents** property of the **Application** object to get its **Documents** collection.
2. Use the **Add** method of the **Documents** collection to create the document.

   To create a new document without basing it on a template, supply a null string ("") as an argument to **Add**. For example, the following statement creates a new, blank document:

   ```
   Set docObj = appVisio.Documents.Add("")
   ```

A document created in this way has the Visio default drawing scale, styles, and other document settings. No stencils are opened.

To create a new document from a template

1. Get the **Documents** property of the **Application** object to get its **Documents** collection.
2. Use the **Add** method of the **Documents** collection to create the document.

   To base the new document on a template, supply the file name of that template as an argument to **Add**. For example, the following statement creates a new document based on the **Basic Diagram** template provided with Visio:

   ```
   Set docObj = appVisio.Documents.Add("Basic Diagram.vst")
   ```

If you don't specify a path with the template file name, the Visio engine searches the folders shown in the **Templates** box on the **File Paths** tab (on the **Tools** menu, click **Options**). To find out the current path settings, get the **Application** object's **TemplatePaths** property. For details about using the **File Paths** tab, see the Microsoft Visio Developer Reference (on the **Help** menu, click **Developer Reference**).

The **Application** object has a corresponding property for each of the fields on the **File Paths** tab in the **Options** dialog. For example, the **TemplatePaths** property corresponds to the **Templates** box on the tab. You can get any of these properties to find the current path, or you can set the property to change the path. For details, see the Microsoft Visio Developer Reference (on the **Help** menu, click **Developer Reference**).

Application object properties that correspond to File Paths tab settings

File Path field	Property
Drawings	**DrawingPaths**
Templates	**TemplatePaths**
Stencils	**StencilPaths**
Help	**HelpPaths**
Add-ons	**AddonPaths**
Start-up	**StartupPaths**
Filters	**FilterPaths**

In the previous example, the new document has the drawing scale, styles, and document settings defined in the **Basic Diagram** template. This template has a stencil—**Basic Shapes**—in its workspace, so creating the document also opens that stencil as read-only in a stencil window and adds the stencil file to the **Documents** collection of the instance.

Handling Errors in Visual Basic

When an error occurs during program execution, Microsoft Visual Basic generates an error message and halts execution. You can prevent many errors by testing assumptions before executing code that will fail if the assumptions aren't valid. You can trap and respond to errors by using the **On Error** statement in your program. For details about **On Error**, see your Visual Basic documentation.

This section specifically discusses running a Microsoft Visio instance from an external program. Errors can arise from a variety of situations. For details about common situations that errors can occur in, see *Handling Errors* in Chapter 15, *Programming Visio with VBA*.

If your program requires a running Visio instance, it's a good idea to make sure the instance is there. The following Visual Basic project writes code behind the **Click** event for two command button controls on a Visual Basic form.

```
'If you click this button, the process ID of the active
'Visio instance will be reported. You will receive a message
'that notifies you whether the GetObject function successfully
'returned an active Visio instance.
Private Sub Command1_Click()
    On Error Resume Next
    Dim appObj As Visio.Application
    Set appObj = GetObject(, "visio.application")
    If appObj Is Nothing Then
        MsgBox "There is no active Visio."
    Else
        MsgBox "ProcessID: " & appObj.ProcessID
    End If

End Sub

'If you click this button, a new (invisible) Visio instance
'is created and its process ID is reported. The instance is
'then made visible. You will receive a message that notifies
'you whether the CreateObject function successfully created a
'Visio instance. By creating an invisible Visio instance, the
'message box that contains the process ID remains visible
'until the user responds.
Private Sub Command2_Click()
    On Error Resume Next
    Dim appObj As Visio.Application
    Set appObj = CreateObject("visio.InvisibleApp")
    If appObj Is Nothing Then
        MsgBox "Failed creating Visio instance."
    Else
        MsgBox "ProcessID: " & appObj.ProcessID
```

```
            appObj.Visible = True
        End If
    End Sub
```

Interpreting the Command String that Visio Sends to Your Program

When an executable program (EXE) is run, it receives a command string from the environment that launched the program. The command string that the Microsoft Visio engine sends identifies the Visio environment as the environment that launched the program. You can use some of the values contained in the command string to retrieve certain objects in addition to arguments for the program. The values in the string depend on how the program was run—from the **Macros** submenu or from a formula, with arguments or without.

Running the Program from the Macros Submenu

If the program is run from the **Macros** submenu—the user chooses it from either the **Macros** submenu (on the **Tools** menu, click **Macros**) or the **Macros** dialog box—the command string that the Visio engine passes to the program looks like this:

```
"/visio=instanceHandle"
```

The significant portion of this command string is */visio,* which you can use to confirm that the program was run from the Visio engine and not some inappropriate environment. The Windows handle *instanceHandle* is the handle of the Visio instance that the program was run from.

Running the Program when a Formula is Evaluated

When a formula that uses the RUNADDON function is evaluated, the command string that the Visio engine sends to your program depends on the object that contains the formula. Following are examples of the command string that your program receives when a formula belonging to a shape, master, or style object is evaluated.

A shape formula that uses RUNADDON

If a shape formula uses a RUNADDON function to run a program when it is evaluated, the Visio engine sends a command string to the program, such as the following:

```
/visio=instanceHandle /doc=docIndex /page=pagIndex /shape=NameID
```

Various parts of the command string identify objects that contain the shape whose formula ran the program.

- *docIndex* is the index of the **Document** object.

  You can use this value to get the corresponding **Document** object from its collection. For example:

  ```
  Set docObj = appVisio.Documents.Item(docIndex)
  ```

- *pagIndex* is the index of the **Page** object.

  You can use this value to get the corresponding **Page** object from its collection. For example:

  ```
  Set pagObj = appVisio.Documents.Item(docIndex).Pages(pagIndex)
  ```

- *NameID* is the **NameID** property of the shape whose formula was evaluated.

  You can use this value to get the corresponding **Shape** object from its collection. For example:

  ```
  Set shpObj = appVisio.Documents(docIndex). _
          Pages(pagIndex).Shapes(NameID)
  ```

A master formula that uses RUNADDON

If the formula that was evaluated is in a master rather than in a shape on a drawing page, the command string looks like this:

```
/visio=instanceHandle /doc=docIndex /master=masterIndex /shape=NameID
```

- *masterIndex* is the index of the **Master** object.

  In this case, you would get the **Shape** object as follows:

  ```
  Set shpObj = appVisio.Documents(docIndex). _
          Masters(masterIndex).Shapes(NameID)
  ```

A style formula that uses RUNADDON

If the formula that was evaluated is in a style rather than a shape or a master, the command string looks like this:

```
/visio=instanceHandle32 /doc=docIndex /style=NameID
```

In this case, you would get the **Style** object as follows:

```
Set styleObj = appVisio.Documents(docIndex).Styles(NameID)
```

Running the Program with Arguments

If a cell formula uses a RUNADDONWARGS function to run the program, the command string includes the specified arguments:

```
/visio=instanceHandle /doc=docIndex /page=pagIndex
    /shape=Sheet.ID arguments
```

If a custom menu command or toolbar button's **AddOnArgs** property contains arguments, the command string looks like this:

```
/visio=instanceHandle arguments
```

The *arguments* string can be anything appropriate for your program. The entire command string is limited to 127 characters including flags (*/visio=*, */doc=*, */page=*, and */shape*, for example), so in practice the arguments should not exceed 50 characters. If the entire command string exceeds 127 characters, an error occurs and Visio will not run the program.

Running the Program from the Startup Folder

If the program is run from the Visio Startup folder, the command string also includes the flag */launch*.

```
/visio=instanceHandle /launch
```

Parsing a Command String

Parsing is the process of separating statements into syntactic units—analyzing a character string and breaking it down into a group of more easily processed components.

To retrieve and parse a command string, use the functions provided by your development environment for that purpose. In Microsoft Visual Basic, for example, use **Command** to retrieve the command string and string functions, such as **Mid** and **StrComp**, to parse it.

Using the Visio Type Library in Visual Basic Projects

The Microsoft Visio type library contains descriptions of the objects, methods, properties, events, and constants that the Visio engine exposes. You use the Visio type library to define Visio object types and constants in your program. Using Visio object types enables *early binding* and increases the speed of your program.

When programming with Visio 4.5 or later, you can set a reference to the Visio type library. To set a reference to the Visio type library in Microsoft Visual Basic, click **References** on the **Project** menu, and select the Microsoft Visio 2002 type library in the **Available References** list.

The Visio type library contains global symbolic constants defined for arguments and return values of properties and methods. Most arguments for properties and methods are numeric values. Using symbolic constants can make your code easier to both write and read.

For example, suppose you want to find out what type of window a **Window** object represents. The **Type** property of a **Window** object returns an integer that indicates the window's type. For example, if you set a reference to the Visio type library in your project, you can use the constant **visDrawing**, instead of 1, to check the window's type.

For a list of constants used by a particular method or property, look up the property or method in the Microsoft Visio Developer Reference (on the **Help** menu, click **Developer Reference**).

> **Note** Early versions of Visio did not include a type library, so all constants were defined in Visconst.bas. Visconst.bas is no longer required because the Visio type library contains global constants. The examples in this guide are provided with the assumption that you have a reference set to the Visio type library.
>
> If you use Visconst.bas instead of the Visio type library for some of your solution code, you cannot use Visio object types—you must use the generic *Object* variable type. For example, when defining variables, you must use `Dim docsObj As Object`, and not `Dim docsObj As Visio.Documents`. The constants in Visconst.bas are grouped by usage.

28

Programming Visio with C++

How Visio Exposes Objects 564

C++ Support in Visio 566

Handling Visio Events in C++ Programs 574

Visio Libraries 577

Any client that supports the Component Object Model (COM) can access and manipulate Microsoft Visio objects. Several development environments that are available commercially, such as Microsoft Visual Basic, conceal the details of COM, which appeals to many developers. But if you are prepared to work more closely with COM, you can use C or C++ to develop programs that control instances of Visio.

This chapter assumes that you are familiar with COM programming concepts, obtaining pointers to interfaces, and calling interface functions. It also assumes that you are familiar with the C++ programming language. For details about Automation, see the Automation documentation in the Microsoft Platform Software Development Kit (SDK) on MSDN (msdn.microsoft.com). For details about C++, see your C++ documentation.

This chapter discusses how Visio exposes objects to Automation in terms of COM. It describes basic support services provided by Visio; these services ease the task of developing C++ programs that control Visio instances. The chapter then explains how to develop a Visio library (VSL), a type of dynamic-link library (DLL) that a Visio instance loads at run time.

> **Note** Beginning with Visio 2002, you can build custom solutions using COM add-ins. For information on implementing COM add-ins in C++, see the Microsoft Developer Network (MSDN) Web site at msdn.microsoft.com.

For details about recompiling existing programs to use the new support services or about programming Visio with C, see the Readme.txt file located in \Libraries\C-CPP on the *Developing Microsoft Visio Solutions* CD.

How Visio Exposes Objects

The objects that Microsoft Visio exposes are Component Object Model (COM) objects. The concepts of an interface on an object and a reference to an interface are fundamental to understanding COM. If you use the C++ files provided with Visio and described later in this chapter, you won't need to program at this level. It can help, however, to have a general understanding of what's happening behind the scenes.

To illustrate an interface on an object and a reference to an interface, here is a simple example, expressed in pseudocode:

```
ipAppObj = <reference to an interface on a Visio Application object>
//Get documents collection
ipDocsObj = ipAppObj->Documents()
//Get first document
ipDocObj = ipDocsObj->Item(1)
```

Notice the similarities between the assignments in this example and object assignments in Microsoft Visual Basic. You can extrapolate from this example to use the Microsoft Visual Basic for Applications (VBA) programming information elsewhere in this guide. Given a reference to an interface on a **Document** object, the program can obtain, in like fashion, a reference to an interface on a **Page** object, and then a **Shape** object, and so on. The properties and methods provided by these objects are exactly the same as those discussed in earlier chapters of this guide.

The program state after this code executes is shown in the following illustration, which uses the common conventions for showing COM objects. The controlling program has obtained references to interfaces on three objects exposed by Visio. The arrows are the references, the circles are the interfaces, and the boxes inside the Visio instance are the objects.

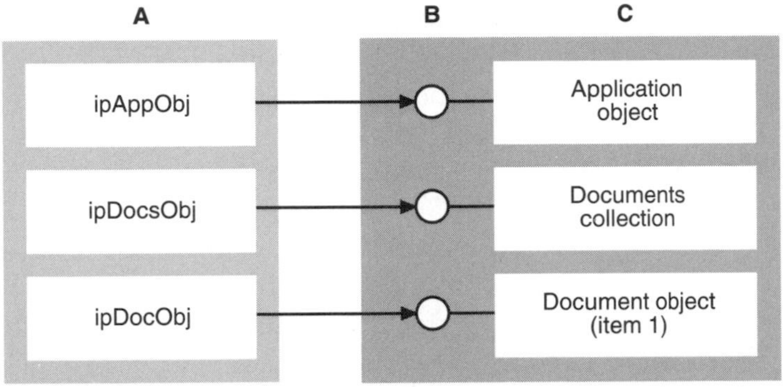

Figure 28-1 The program state after getting a **Document** object. (**A**) A program controlling a Visio instance. (**B**) COM interfaces. (**C**) An instance of Visio.

COM provides many kinds of interfaces, such as those that support persistent data storage. A COM interface pointer refers to data that represents the object that owns the interface. An interface also refers to an array of functions that perform the actions defined in that interface for that object. After you have a reference to an interface on an object, you can call the methods defined in that interface for that object.

The interfaces that Visio exposes are *dual interfaces*. In a dual interface, the first entries are identical to the entries in a standard **IDispatch** interface, the principal interface used to implement Automation. The **IDispatch** methods are followed by entries that correspond to the methods and properties exposed by the object. A dual interface has methods or properties that can be called either indirectly through **IDispatch** methods or directly through the "dual" methods.

IDispatch functions define a protocol that allows *late binding*—that is, binding that occurs at run time—between Automation controllers and Automation servers. However, if an Automation server provides a type library and implements dual interfaces (as Visio does), it enables *early binding*—that is, binding that occurs at compile time. This typically results in improved performance by the Automation controller, because the program makes fewer calls at run time to invoke a method. For details about **IDispatch** and dual interfaces, see the Automation documentation in the Microsoft Platform SDK on MSDN (msdn.microsoft.com).

C++ Support in Visio

The Automation interfaces on Microsoft Visio objects are defined in Visio.h, which is in \Libraries\C-CPP\Vao_inc on the *Developing Microsoft Visio Solutions* CD. This file contains a standard COM interface definition for each Visio object. To control a Visio instance through Automation from a C++ program, include Visio.h in your project source files.

Microsoft Visio also provides services in the form of wrapper classes that simplify programming Visio using C++. A *wrapper class* is so called because it encapsulates, or "wraps" the code involved in certain tasks, such as getting and releasing interface pointers and working with strings. The basic benefit of using these classes is that they keep track of **AddRef** and **Release** calls for you, using C++ constructors, destructors, and assignment operators. When appropriate, these wrapper classes also automatically wrap any arguments or return values with a wrapper class.

In addition to the files you'll use in your programs, the C-CPP folder on the *Developing Microsoft Visio Solutions* CD contains sample projects that illustrate the use of wrapper classes and event sinks. The Readme.txt file in the C-CPP folder gives more details on its contents and instructions on how to build the sample projects. You might find it helpful to study these projects before developing your own programs.

Using the Wrapper Classes

To use the wrapper classes, include Visiwrap.h in your project source files. This file is provided with Visio in the \Libraries\C-CPP\Vao_inc folder on the *Developing Microsoft Visio Solutions* CD. If you include Visiwrap.h, you do not need to include Visio.h explicitly, because Visiwrap.h includes it for you. The wrapper classes observe the following conventions:

- Wrapper class names use the **CVisio** prefix. For example, the wrapper class for a **Page** object is **CVisioPage**.
- Properties are accessed through methods that use the **get** prefix to read the property or **put** to set the property. For example, the methods for the **Name** property are **getName** and **putName**. (In Visio.h, the corresponding methods include an underscore between the prefix and the method name: **get_Name** and **put_Name**.) To find out what these methods do, see the **Name** property in the Microsoft Visio Developer Reference (on the **Help** menu, click **Developer Reference**).

A program that uses the Visio wrapper classes might include a code fragment similar to the following example. This program, from the sample Generic.cpp, creates a new document based on Sample.vst, drops two masters, and connects them. The function **vaoGetObjectWrap**, defined in Visiwrap.h, gets the Visio instance if one is running and, if not, runs an instance. For conciseness, error handling has been omitted.

This example also uses the helper classes **VBstr** and **VVariant**, which are defined in Helpers.h.

- **VBstr** A class that simplifies working with **BSTR** variables, which are used to pass strings through Automation.
- **VVariant** A class that simplifies working with **VARIANT** variables, which are the Automation counterparts of C++ unions.

```
HRESULT                hr= NOERROR;
CVisioApplication      app;
CVisioDocuments        docs;
CVisioDocument         doc;
CVisioPages            pages;
CVisioPage             page;
CVisioShape            shape;
CVisioShape            shape1;
CVisioMasters          masters;
CVisioMaster           master;
CVisioDocument         stencil;
CVisioCell             cell;
CVisioCell             cell1;

     ...
     if (VAO_SUCCESS != vaoGetObjectWrap(app))
            //Error handling
            goto CU;
     ...
     //Add a new document based on "sample.vst"
     //and get the drawing page
     hr= app.Documents(docs);

     //VBstr is the helper class for type BSTR
     hr= docs.Add(VBstr("sample.vst"), doc);

     hr= doc.Pages(pages);

     //VVariant is the helper class for type VARIANT
     hr= pages.Item(VVariant(1L), page);

     //Get the stencil and the first master to drop
     hr= docs.Item(VVariant("sample.vss"), stencil);
     hr= stencil.Masters(masters);
```

```
        hr= masters.Item(VVariant("Executive"), master);
        hr= page.Drop(master, 6.0, 6.0, shape);

        //Get the second master and drop it
        hr= masters.Item(VVariant("Position"), master);
        hr= page.Drop(master, 3.0, 3.0, shape1);

        //Connect the two shapes on the drawing page
        hr= shape.Cells(VBstr("Connections.X4"), cell);
        hr= shape1.Cells(VBstr("Controls.X1"), cell1);
        hr= cell1.GlueTo(cell);
...
}
```

Visiwrap.h includes Helpers.h, so if you're using the wrapper classes, you can use the helper classes also. For details about the helper classes, see the comments in Helpers.h.

The Interfaces Behind the Wrappers

The Visio.h file defines the objects exposed by Visio in standard COM interface declaration syntax. The wrapper classes defined in Visiwrap.h call the methods of these interfaces. For example, the following code fragment shows the beginning of the **CVisioApplication** wrapper class declared in Visiwrap.h. Notice the method declarations of **ActiveDocument**, **ActivePage**, and so on following the second VW_PUBLIC access specifier.

```
class FAR CVisioApplication : public CVisioUnknown
{
VW_PUBLIC:
    CVisioApplication( ) : CVisioUnknown( ) { }
    CVisioApplication(const CVisioApplication& other) : CVisioUnknown(other) { }
    CVisioApplication(const IVApplication FAR * other, BOOL
        bAssumeResponsibility= FALSE)
        : CVisioUnknown( ( LPUNKNOWN )other, bAssumeResponsibility ) { }
    const CVisioApplication FAR & operator=( const CVisioApplication FAR &other )
        { if ( &other != this )
            CopyIP( other.GetUnknown( ) );
            return *this; }
    const CVisioApplication FAR & operator=( const IVApplication FAR * other )
        { if ( ( LPUNKNOWN )other != GetUnknown( ) )
            CopyIP( ( LPUNKNOWN )other );
            return *this; }
    virtual ~CVisioApplication( ) { }
```

```
    IVApplication FAR * GetIP( ) const { return ( IVApplication FAR * )
        GetUnknown( ); }
    operator IVApplication FAR * ( ) { return ( IVApplication FAR * )
GetUnknown( ); }

//CVisioApplication method declarations
VW_PUBLIC:
    HRESULT ActiveDocument(CVisioDocument FAR &rWrap);
    HRESULT ActivePage(CVisioPage FAR &rWrap);
    HRESULT ActiveWindow(CVisioWindow FAR &rWrap);
    HRESULT Application(CVisioApplication FAR &rWrap);
    HRESULT Documents(CVisioDocuments FAR &rWrap);
...
```

The corresponding methods in the **Application** object interface are declared in Visio.h, as follows:

```
IVApplication : public IDispatch
{
    public:
    virtual /* [helpcontext][propget][id] */ HRESULT STDMETHODCALLTYPE
        get_ActiveDocument(
        /* [retval][out] */ IVDocument __RPC_FAR *__RPC_FAR *lpdispRet) = 0;

    virtual /* [helpcontext][propget][id] */ HRESULT STDMETHODCALLTYPE
        get_ActivePage(
        /* [retval][out] */ IVPage __RPC_FAR *__RPC_FAR *lpdispRet) = 0;

    virtual /* [helpcontext][propget][id] */ HRESULT STDMETHODCALLTYPE
        get_ActiveWindow(
        /* [retval][out] */ IVWindow __RPC_FAR *__RPC_FAR *lpdispRet) = 0;

    virtual /* [helpcontext][propget][id] */ HRESULT STDMETHODCALLTYPE
        get_Application(
        /* [retval][out] */ IVApplication __RPC_FAR *__RPC_FAR *lpdispRet) = 0;

    virtual /* [helpcontext][propget][id] */ HRESULT STDMETHODCALLTYPE
        get_Documents(
        /* [retval][out] */ IVDocuments __RPC_FAR *__RPC_FAR *lpdispRet) = 0;
    ...
};
```

Every object exposed by Visio has a similar declaration in Visio.h. Various macros in the declaration, which are not shown in this example, allow Visio.h to be included in either C or C++ source files.

Because every Visio interface derives from **IDispatch**, every Visio interface has the following methods:

- **QueryInterface**
- **AddRef**
- **Release** (for **IUnknown**)

These methods are followed by:

- **GetTypeInfoCount**
- **GetTypeInfo**
- **GetIDsOfNames**
- **Invoke** (for **IDispatch**)

For details about these standard COM methods, see the Automation documentation in the Microsoft Platform Software Development Kit (SDK) on MSDN (msdn.microsoft.com). The Visio **Application** object exposes the remaining methods (**get_ActiveDocument**, **get_ActivePage**, and so forth). These methods correspond to the methods and properties described elsewhere in this guide for use with Microsoft Visual Basic programs.

To learn more about a method, see the Microsoft Visio Developer Reference (on the **Help** menu, click **Developer Reference**). For example, to find more about the **get_ActiveDocument** method declared in the previous example, search for "ActiveDocument."

Obtaining a Visio Application Object

The sample program in Generic.cpp, which is shown in the section *Using the Wrapper Classes*, begins with the following code:

```
CvisioApplication  app;
if (VAO_SUCCESS != vaoGetObjectWrap(app))
    //Error handling
    goto CU;
```

This pebble starts the avalanche. To do anything with a Visio instance, you need an **Application** object, which is what **vaoGetObjectWrap** gets.

The **vaoGetObjectWrap** function calls the **vaoGetObject** function, which is declared in Ivisreg.h and implemented in Ivisreg.cpp. If you're not using the wrapper classes, you can call **vaoGetObject** directly. Look at the source code to see what **vaoGetObject** actually does.

The services defined in Ivisreg.h for working with a Visio instance are equivalent to those provided by the Visreg.bas file, which is supplied for use with Visual Basic. In particular, these files provide the necessary means to launch a new Visio instance or establish an **Application** object for the active Visio instance.

Values Returned by Visio Methods

Every method declared in Visio.h is specified to return an **HRESULT** that indicates whether the method executed successfully. The **HRESULT** returned by a method declared in Visio.h is passed along by the equivalent method of the corresponding wrapper class defined in Visiwrap.h.

If a method succeeds, it returns **NOERROR**. A common practice is to check a method's result by using **SUCCEEDED(*hResult*)**. The sample program includes a macro called **check_valid** to check the result of the method. This macro is shown later in this section.

Many methods also produce an output value that is independent of the **HRESULT** returned by every method. For example, the **ActiveDocument** method of the **CVisioApplication** wrapper class produces a reference to a **Document** object. By convention, a method's output value is written to the method's last argument. Thus the last argument passed to **ActiveDocument** is a reference to a **CVisioDocument** object, where the method can write a reference to the **Document** object.

To learn more about Visio methods, see the Microsoft Visio Developer Reference (on the **Help** menu, click **Developer Reference**).

Object reference return values

Many methods return an object reference as their output value. This value is really a COM interface pointer, which, like any interface pointer, must eventually be released.

- If you're using wrapper classes, the value returned is an object of another wrapper class—such as the **CVisioDocument** previously mentioned—in which the interface pointer is packaged. When the object goes out of scope, the Visio interface pointer it holds is automatically released.
- If you're not using wrapper classes, the interface pointer is held directly by your program, which must explicitly release the pointer at the appropriate time.

If a method that returns an object reference fails, the output value again depends on whether you're using wrapper classes.

- If you're using wrapper classes, you'll still get an object of the appropriate wrapper class, but the interface pointer held by the object is NULL. Calling the **IsSet** function on that object will return FALSE.
- If you're not using wrapper classes, the interface pointer is NULL, so you can simply check for that.

Even if the method succeeds, you might still need to check the output parameter. For example, if **ActiveDocument** is called when no documents are open, it returns an **HRESULT** of success and a NULL interface pointer (wrapped or not). The reasoning here is that an error did not occur—having no documents open is a perfectly valid state for which the caller should account. The various **Active*** methods behave in this manner, and you should verify that their output values are not NULL before proceeding. The various **Item** and **Add** methods, however, always return a non-NULL reference if they succeed.

The **check_valid** macro, defined in Generic.cpp, checks both possibilities. A function using **check_valid** must provide a **CU** label where it performs cleanup tasks.

```
#define check_valid(hr, obj)     \
if(!SUCCEEDED(hr) || !((obj).IsSet()))  \

goto CU;
```

String return values

Several methods return a string to the caller. The **Shape** object's **Name** property (**getName** of **CVisioShape** or **get_Name** of **IVShape**) is an example. All strings passed to or returned by Visio methods are of type **BSTR**, which consists of 16-bit (wide) characters in Microsoft Win32 programs. The Visio engine allocates the memory for the strings it returns, and the caller is responsible for freeing the memory.

The wrapper classes, defined in Visiwrap.h, take care of freeing memory for strings. If you do not use the wrapper classes, however, make sure that you call **SysFreeString** to free any string returned by a Visio instance.

Arguments Passed to Visio Methods

Passing arguments to Visio methods is straightforward:

- Integer arguments are declared as short or long, depending on whether they are 2-byte or 4-byte values.
- Floating-point arguments are declared as double.
- Boolean values are passed as short integers or as **VARIANT_BOOL**.
- Arguments that are object pointers, such as **BSTR** or **VARIANT**, merit further discussion.

Object pointer arguments

Some methods take object pointers, and some require a pointer to a specific type of Visio object. The **Cell** object's **GlueTo** method, for example, takes an argument that must refer to another **Cell** object.

Other methods that take object pointers are more lenient. For example, the **Page** object's **Drop** method takes a reference to the object to be dropped, because you might want to drop a master or a shape on a page.

The simplest way to pass an object pointer to a method is to pass a reference to an object of the appropriate wrapper class; for example, pass a reference to a **CVisioCell** object as an argument to the **GlueTo** method.

The interfaces defined in Visio.h declare object pointers as the corresponding interfaces. For example, Visio.h declares **GlueTo** as taking a pointer to an **IVCell** interface. Because the **Drop** method is not restricted to a particular object, Visio.h declares **Drop** to take an **IUnknown** interface, which means **Drop** takes a reference to any object. Internally, the **Drop** method determines what to drop by querying the object passed to it for an **IDataObject** interface. The interface you pass to **Drop** does not necessarily have to be an interface on a Visio object.

String arguments

Any string passed to a Visio instance must be of type **BSTR**. The helper class **VBstr**, defined in Helpers.h, is a convenient way to pass strings to Visio instances. **VBstr** allocates memory for the string when it is created and frees the memory when the **VBstr** is destroyed. If you don't use **VBstr**, make sure that you call **SysFreeString** to free the memory you have allocated for strings.

For example, the following statement uses a **VBstr** to pass a cell name to the **Cells** method of a **CVisioShape** object. In this statement, *cell* is a variable of type **CVisioCell**:

```
hr = shape.Cells(VBstr("Connections.X4"), cell);
```

VARIANT arguments

Some Visio methods take arguments that aren't constrained to a single type. For example, if you pass an integer 5 to the **Item** method of a **Documents** collection, it returns a reference to the fifth document in the collection. If you pass a string that is a document name to the same method, however, it returns a reference to a document of that name (assuming that the document is open).

COM defines a data structure known as a **VARIANT** for passing such arguments. The helper class, **VVariant** defined in Helpers.h, is a convenient way of passing a **VARIANT** to a Visio instance. For example, compare the following two statements:

```
hr = pages.Item(VVariant(1L), page);
hr = masters.Item(VVariant("Position"), master);
```

The first statement passes 1 (an integer) to the **Item** method of a **Pages** collection. The second statement passes `"Position"` (a string) to the **Item** method of a **Masters** collection. In these statements, *page* and *master* are variables of type **CVisioPage** and **CVisioMaster**, respectively.

Handling Visio Events in C++ Programs

One way to handle Microsoft Visio events in a C++ program is to use **Event** objects. An **Event** object pairs an event code with an action—either to run an add-on or to notify another object, called a *sink object*, whenever the specified event has occurred. For a discussion of how **Event** objects work and details about implementing them in Microsoft Visual Basic programs, see Chapter 21, *Handling Visio Events*.

The protocols the Visio engine uses to support the Visual Basic **WithEvents** style of event handling are the standard **IConnectionPoint** protocols provided by controls and used by control containers. As an alternative to using **Event** objects, a C++ program can receive events from a Visio instance using **IConnectionPoint** protocols, but it must implement the entire event-set interface declared for the type of Visio object from which it wants to receive events. For details about **IConnectionPoint** and related interfaces, see your Component Object Model (COM) documentation.

The topics in this section describe how to receive Visio events in C++ programs using **Event** objects that are established by calling **EventList.Add** or **EventList.AddAdvise**. Although this protocol is specific to Visio, a C++ program need not implement entire event-set interfaces; instead, the C++ program can register for just the events of interest rather than every event in an event set, which **IConnectionPoint** requires.

Implementing a Sink Object

You implement handling of Visio events in a C++ program in much the same way as in a Visual Basic program, with these exceptions:

- The sink object in your C++ program must be a COM object that exposes the **IDispatch** interface.
- The **IDispatch** interface must supply a method called **VisEventProc** that has the following signature:

```
STDMETHOD(VisEventProc) (
WORD           wEvent,        //Event code of the event that is firing
IUnknown FAR*  ipSource,      //Pointer to IUnknown on object firing the event
DWORD          dwEventID,     //The ID of the event that is firing
DWORD          dwSeq,         //The sequence number of the event
IUnknown FAR*  ipSubject,     //Pointer to IUnknown on event subject
VARIANT        VextraInfo     //Additional information (usually a context string)
);
```

When you call **AddAdvise** to create the **Event** object, you pass a pointer to the **IUnknown** or **IDispatch** interface on the sink object.

Using CVisioAddonSink

Beginning with Microsoft Visio 2000, instead of implementing your own sink object, you can use the **CVisioAddonSink** class provided with Visio. This class is declared in the file Addsink.h in \Libraries\C-CPP\Vao_inc on the *Developing Microsoft Visio Solutions* CD.

To use CVisioAddonSink

1. Include Addsink.h in your project source files. If you're using the wrapper classes defined in Visiwrap.h, skip this step.
2. Write a callback function to receive the event notifications sent to the sink object.
3. Call **CoCreateAddonSink** with a pointer to your callback function and the address of an **IUnknown** interface. **CoCreateAddonSink** creates an instance of a sink object that knows about your callback function and writes a pointer to an **IUnknown** interface on the sink object to the address you supplied.
4. Get a reference to the **EventList** collection of the Visio object that you want to receive notifications from.

5. Call the **AddAdvise** method of the **EventList** collection, obtained in step 4, with the **IUnknown** interface, obtained in step 3, and the event code of the Visio event that you're interested in. When the event occurs, the Visio instance will call your callback function.
6. Release the sink object when you're finished using it.

The sample program Generic.cpp uses **CVisioAddonSink** to handle two events: **DocumentCreated** and **ShapeAdded**. The program declares a callback function for each event. The signature of the callback function must conform to **visEventProc**, which is defined in Addsink.h. The following example shows one of the declarations. For the implementation of this function, see Generic.cpp.

```
HRESULT STDMETHODCALLTYPE ReceiveNotifyFromVisio (
IUnknown FAR*               IpSink,
WORD                        wEvent,
IUnknown FAR*               ipSource,
DWORD                       nEventID,
DWORD                       dwEventSeq,
IUnknown FAR*               ipSubject,
VARIANT                     eventExtra);
```

To create the sink object, the program gets the **EventList** collection of the **Application** object (represented by the **CVisioApplication** variable *app*), calls **CoCreateAddonSink** to create the sink object, and calls **AddAdvise** on the **EventList** collection to create the **Event** object in the Visio instance. The program sets a flag, *bFirstTime*, to ensure that the **Event** objects are created only once while the program is running. The ID of the **Event** object is stored in the static variable *stc_nEventID* for later reference. The **AddAdvise** call creates a second reference on the sink object, so the program can release *pSink*:

```
static long                 stc_nEventID = visEvtIDInval;
IUnknown FAR*               pSink = NULL;
IUnknown FAR*               pAnotherSink = NULL;
static BOOL                 bFirstTime = TRUE;
CVisioApplication           app;
CVisioEventList             eList;
CVisioEvent                 event;
...
if (bFirstTime && (SUCCEEDED(app.EventList(eList))))
{
    bFirstTime= FALSE;
    if (SUCCEEDED(CoCreateAddonSink(ReceiveNotifyFromVisio, &pSink)))
    {
        if (SUCCEEDED(eList.AddAdvise(visEvtCodeDocCreate,
            VVariant(pSink), VBstr(""), VBstr(""), event)))
        {
```

```
            event.ID(&stc_nEventID);
        }
        //If AddAdvise succeeded, Visio now holds a reference to
        //the sink object
        //via the event object, and pSink can be released
        pSink->Release();
        pSink= NULL;
    }
...
}
```

Event objects created with **AddAdvise** persist until the **Event** object is deleted, all references to the source object are released, or the Visio instance is closed. If your program needs to perform cleanup tasks before the Visio instance is closed, handle the **BeforeQuit** event.

If **CVisioAddonSink** is used in a Visio library (VSL), its unload handler must call **Event.Delete**.

For more information on Visio methods, events, and objects, see the Microsoft Visio Developer Reference (on the **Help** menu, click **Developer Reference**).

Visio Libraries

A Microsoft Visio library (VSL) is a special dynamic-link library (DLL) that is loaded by the Visio engine at run time. A VSL can implement one or more Visio add-ons, which are programs that use Automation to control Visio instances.

An add-on implemented by a VSL can interact with Visio objects in exactly the same fashion as an add-on implemented by an executable (EXE) file or code in a document's Microsoft Visual Basic for Applications (VBA) project, and a user can do exactly the same things. An add-on implemented in a VSL has performance and integration advantages over one implemented in an executable program—one reason being that a VSL runs in the same process as the Visio instance. You cannot, however, run a VSL from Windows Explorer as you can an executable program.

Visio recognizes any file with a .vsl extension in the **Add-ons** or **Start-up** path (**Options** dialog box) as a VSL. To install a VSL, copy the file to one of the folders specified in the Visio **Add-ons** or **Start-up** path. The next time you run a Visio instance, the add-ons implemented by that VSL are available to the instance.

The files you'll need to develop a VSL are provided in \Libraries\C-CPP on the *Developing Microsoft Visio Solutions* CD. This folder contains:

- Source and MAK files for a simple but functional VSL, described in Readme.txt in the C-CPP folder.

- The \Samples\MyAddon folder, which contains the file MyAddon.cpp, a shell for writing your own VSL.
- The Wizards folder, which contains two versions of a Microsoft Visual Studio **AppWizard** that generates MFC VSL projects: MFC5_VSL.awx for use with Microsoft Foundation Classes (MFC) version 5.0 and MFC4_VSL.awx for use with MFC version 4.x. The file Wizards.txt specifies the folders in which to copy the AWX files and recommends useful build and project settings.

Advantages of Visio Libraries

All else being equal, a VSL runs faster than an executable program. Because a VSL is a DLL, it is loaded into the process space of the Visio instance that is using the library. Calls from a VSL to a Visio instance do not cross a process boundary, as is the case when an executable program calls a Visio instance.

In addition, because a VSL runs in the same process as a Visio instance, it is much easier for it to open a dialog box that is modal to the process in which the Visio instance is running. When two executable files (an add-on and a Visio instance) are running, it is difficult for one to display a dialog box that is modal with respect to the other. An add-on executable program can display a dialog box, but the user can click the Visio window and change the Visio state while the dialog box is open.

It's also easier to add solution-defined windows as child windows of Visio windows using the **Add** method of a **Windows** collection. To do this, create an **HWND** and use the **WindowHandle32** from the window added with **Windows.Add** as the parent **HWND**. Using **HWND**s from different processes as parent windows doesn't work well, except in in-place containment scenarios.

The Architecture of a Visio Library

A VSL is a standard DLL that exports a required entry point with the prescribed name **VisioLibMain**.

A Visio instance loads a VSL using **LoadLibrary** and frees it using **FreeLibrary**. Unless your VSL is installed in a Visio Startup folder, your code shouldn't assume when the VSL will get loaded. A Visio instance loads non-startup VSLs only when it needs to do so. If a Visio instance does load a VSL, it does not call **FreeLibrary** on the VSL until the instance shuts down.

The file VDLLmain.c provides a default implementation for **DllMain**, which is the standard DLL entry point that Windows calls when it loads and unloads a DLL. The file Vao.c implements several other functions that you might find useful; some of these are mentioned in the paragraphs that follow.

Once a Visio instance has loaded a VSL, the instance makes occasional calls to the VSL's **VisioLibMain** procedure. One of the arguments the Visio instance passes to **VisioLibMain** is a message code that tells the VSL why it is being called. All Visio messages are defined in Vao.h.

The prescribed prototype for **VisioLibMain** can be found in Vao.h:

```
typedef WORD VAORC, FAR* LPVAORC;      //Visio add-on return code
typedef WORD VAOMSG, FAR* LPVAOMSG;    //Visio add-on message code

#define VAOCB __cdecl                  //Visio add-on callback procedure

//The prototype of VisioLibMain should conform to VAOFUNC
typedef VAORC (VAOCB VAOFUNC) (VAOMSG,WORD,LPVOID);
```

A typical **VisioLibMain** will look something like the following:

```
#include "vao.h"
VAORC VAOCB VisioLibMain (VAOMSG wMsg, WORD wParam, LPVOID lpParam)
    {
    VAORC result = VAORC_SUCCESS;
    switch (wMsg)
          {
          case V2LMSG_ENUMADDONS:
                //Code to register this VSL's add-ons goes here
                break;
          case V2LMSG_RUN:
                //Code to run add-on with ordinal wParam goes here
                break;
          default:
                //Trigger generic response to wMsg
                //Helper procedures VAOUtil_DefVisMainProc and
                //VLIBUTL_hModule are implemented in vao.c
                result = VAOUtil_DefVisMainProc(wMsg, wParam,
                      lpParam, VLIBUTL_hModule());
                break;
          };
    return result;
    }
```

This **VisioLibMain** specifically handles the V2LMSG_RUN and V2LMSG_ENUMADDONS messages. Other messages are deferred to **VAOUtil_DefVisMainProc**, a function that implements generic message responses. **VLIBUTL_hModule** evaluates to the module handle of the VSL.

Declaring and Registering Add-ons

When an instance sends the V2LMSG_ENUMADDONS message to a VSL's **VisioLibMain**, it is asking for descriptions of the add-ons implemented by the VSL.

The file Lib.c implements a sample VSL. In it, you can see source code demonstrating how a VSL registers add-ons. Two aspects are involved:

- Lib.c defines a data structure describing its add-ons.
- In response to the V2LMSG_ENUMADDONS message, Lib.c passes this data structure to the Visio instance that sent the message.

Lib.c implements one add-on. Near the top of the file is the following code:

```
#define DEMO_ADDON_ORDINAL 1
PRIVATE VAOREGSTRUCT stc_myAddons[] =
{
{
    DEMO_ADDON_ORDINAL,            //Ordinal of this add-on
    VAO_AOATTS_ISACTION,           //This add-on does things to Visio
    VAO_ENABLEALWAYS,              //This add-on is always enabled
    0,                             //Invoke on mask
    0,                             //Reserved for future use
    "VSL Automation Demo",         //The name of this add-on
    },
};
```

The **VAOREGSTRUCT** structure is declared in Vao.h. You'll find comments and declarations there that give more information on the various fields in the structure.

When a Visio instance tells a VSL to run an add-on, it identifies which add-on by specifying the add-on's ordinal, a unique value that identifies the add-on within the file. The **stc_myAddons** array declares one add-on whose ordinal is 1 (DEMO_ADDON_ORDINAL). If Lib.c implemented two add-ons instead of one, **stc_myAddons** would have two entries instead of one, and each entry would designate a unique ordinal.

The declared add-on is presented in the Visio user interface as "VSL Automation Demo." If you intend to localize your add-on, you wouldn't declare its name in the code as is shown here. Rather, you'd read the name from a string resource and dynamically initialize the **VAOREGSTRUCT**.

VAO_ENABLEALWAYS tells the Visio instance that this add-on should be considered enabled at all times. Other enabling policies can be declared. There are many add-ons, for example, that it makes sense to run only when a document is open. Such add-ons can declare an enabling policy of VAO_NEEDSDOC.

A Visio instance makes such add-ons unavailable when no documents are open. When such an add-on is run, it can assert that a document is open. Several static enabling policies similar to VAO_NEEDSDOC are declared in Vao.h.

Vao.h also contains a policy called VAO_ENABLEDYNAMIC. When a Visio instance wants to determine whether the add-on is enabled, it sends V2LMSG_ISAOENABLED to a dynamically enabled add-on. The add-on can claim to be enabled or disabled based on its own criteria.

The last aspect of **VAOREGSTRUCT** involves making an add-on run automatically when a Visio instance starts. To make an add-on implemented by an executable program run on startup, you simply place the executable file in one of the folders specified by the Visio **StartupPaths** setting.

For add-ons implemented in a VSL, those to be run on startup must also specify VAO_INVOKE_LAUNCH in the **invokeOnMask** member of their **VAOREGSTRUCT**. This constant allows a single VSL file to implement some add-ons that run automatically when a Visio instance launches, and some that don't.

By itself, **VAOREGSTRUCT** is just a data structure that doesn't tell a Visio instance anything. When a Visio instance sends V2LMSG_ENUMADDONS to a VSL, the library should respond by passing the Visio instance a pointer to the array of **VAOREGSTRUCTs**, discussed previously, so that the data they contain is available to the Visio instance. To do this, Lib.c makes use of a utility implemented in Vao.c. The code is as follows:

```
result = VAOUtil_RegisterAddons(
            ((LPVAOV2LSTRUCT)lpParam)->wSessID,
            stc_myAddons,
            sizeof(stc_myAddons)/sizeof(VAOREGSTRUCT));
```

For details about what this code does, look at the source code in Vao.c.

Running an Add-on

A Visio instance sends V2LMSG_RUN to a VSL when the VSL is to run one of its add-ons. The ordinal of the add-on to run is passed in the *wParam* parameter.

The Visio instance sends V2LMSG_RUN only if it has determined that the designated add-on is enabled, according to the enabling policy declared in the add-on's registration structure. If the add-on's enabling policy is VAO_ENABLEDYNAMIC, the VSL will already have responded with VAORC_L2V_ENABLED to the V2LMSG_ISAOENABLED message it received from the Visio instance.

In addition to the ordinal of the add-on to run, the Visio instance passes a pointer to a **VAOV2LSTRUCT** structure with the V2LMSG_RUN message. **VAOV2LSTRUCT** is defined as follows in the Vao.h file:

```
VAO_EMBEDDABLE_STRUCT
{

HINSTANCE       HVisInst;         //Handle of running Visio instance
LPVAOFUNC       lpfunc;           //Callback address in Visio
WORD            wSessID;          //ID of session
LPVOID          lpArgs;           //Reserved for future use
LPSTR           lpCmdLineArgs;    //Command line arguments

} VAOV2LSTRUCT, FAR* LPVAOV2LSTRUCT;
```

This structure gives the instance handle of the Visio instance sending the message, which is sometimes useful. (The **lpfunc** and **lpArgs** members are used by other functions in Vao.c.) In the **lpCmdLineArgs** member, the Visio instance passes an argument string to the add-on. This is the same string that the Visio instance would pass to an analogous add-on implemented as an executable program.

You'll sometimes be interested in the **wSessID** member, which is the ID the Visio instance has assigned to the "session" it associated with the V2LMSG_RUN it just sent. For example, you might use **wSessID** if your add-on initiates a *modeless* activity (an activity that doesn't terminate when the add-on returns control to the Visio instance).

Most add-ons will perform a modal action in response to V2LMSG_RUN: They receive the message, do something, and then return control to the Visio instance. Unless the add-on says otherwise, the Visio instance considers the session finished when it regains control from the add-on.

Pseudocode for this typical case would be:

case V2LMSG_RUN:

wParam is ordinal of add-on to run.

Execute code to do whatever it is the add-on with ordinal wParam does. This will probably involve instantiating Visio objects and invoking methods and properties of those objects. You can use the C++ support services discussed in the previous section just as if this code were in an EXE file.

if (operation was successful)

return VAORC_SUCCESS;

else

return VAORC_XXX; // See vao.h

Sometimes, in response to V2LMSG_RUN, an add-on may initiate an activity that doesn't terminate when the add-on returns control to the Visio instance. (Such activities are called modeless.) An add-on may, for example, open a window that will stay open indefinitely.

If your add-on implements a modeless activity, it should remember the session ID passed with V2LMSG_RUN. Pseudocode for such an add-on would be:

```
case V2LMSG_RUN:
        wParam is ordinal of add-on to run.
        Execute code to initiate modeless activity.
                For example, open a window and stash its handle.
        if (operation was successful)
                {
                stash lParam->wSessID where it can be looked up later.
                return VAORC_L2V_MODELESS;
                }
        else
                return VAORC_XXX;       // See vao.h
```

Note the return value of VAORC_L2V_MODELESS. This tells the Visio instance that the session still persists, even though the VSL has completed handling the V2LMSG_RUN message.

A modeless session initiated in this fashion persists until either the VSL ends the session or the Visio instance associated with the session terminates.

If the VSL ends the session (for example, perhaps the window it opened has been closed), it does so with the **VAOUtil_SendEndSession** function. The parameter *wSessID* contains the ID of the terminating session:

```
VAOUtil_SendEndSession(wSessID); //wSessID: ID of terminating session
```

When the Visio instance terminates, it sends V2LMSG_KILLSESSION to all extant sessions. With V2LMSG_KILLSESSION, the Visio instance passes a **VAOV2LSTRUCT** structure whose **wSessID** member identifies the ID of the session to terminate. The VSL should respond by terminating and cleaning up after the identified session.

Part 4

Appendixes

Appendix A Properties, Methods, and Events by Object

Appendix B ShapeSheet Section, Row, and Cell Indices

Glossary

Index

Appendix A

Properties, Methods, and Events by Object

The following is an alphabetic list of Microsoft Visio Automation objects. For details about an object, property, method, or event, see the Microsoft Visio Developer Reference (on the **Help** menu, click **Developer Reference**).

<Global>
<ThisDocument>
AccelItem
AccelItems
AccelTable
AccelTables
Addon
Addons
Application
Cell
Characters
Color
Colors
Connect
Connects
Curve
Document
Documents
Event
EventList
Font
Fonts
Hyperlink
Hyperlinks
Layer
Layers
Master
Masters
MasterShortcut
MasterShortcuts
Menu
MenuItem
MenuItems
Menus
MenuSet
MenuSets
MSGWrap
OLEObject
OLEObjects
Page
Pages
Path
Paths
Row
Section
Selection
Shape
Shapes
Style
Styles
Toolbar
ToolbarItem
ToolbarItems
Toolbars
ToolbarSet
ToolbarSets
UIObject
Window
Windows

Properties, Methods, and Events for the <Global> Object

Properties	Methods	Events
ActiveDocument ActivePage ActiveWindow Addons Application Documents VBE Windows		

Properties, Methods, and Events for the <ThisDocument> Object

Properties		Methods	Events
AlternateNames	Masters	Clean	BeforeDocumentClose
Application	MasterShortcuts	ClearCustomMenus	BeforeDocumentSave
AutoRecover	Mode	ClearCustomToolbars	BeforeDocumentSaveAs
BottomMargin	Name	ClearGestureFormatSheet	BeforeMasterDelete
BuildNumberCreated	ObjectType	Close	BeforePageDelete
BuildNumberEdited	OLEObjects	CopyPreviewPicture	BeforeSelectionDelete
Category	Pages	DeleteSolutionXMLElement	BeforeShapeTextEdit
ClassID	PaperHeight	Drop	BeforeStyleDelete
Colors	PaperSize	ExecuteLine	ConvertToGroupCanceled
Company	PaperWidth	FollowHyperlink	DesignModeEntered
Container	Password	OpenStencilWindow	DocumentChanged
ContainsWorkspace	Path	ParseLine	DocumentCloseCanceled
Creator	PersistsEvents	Print	DocumentCreated
CustomMenus	PreviewPicture	Save	DocumentOpened
CustomMenusFile	PrintCenteredH	SaveAs	DocumentSaved
CustomToolbars	PrintCenteredV	SaveAsEx	DocumentSavedAs
CustomToolbarsFile	PrintCopies	SetCustomMenus	MasterAdded
DefaultFillStyle	Printer	SetCustomToolbars	MasterChanged
DefaultGuideStyle	PrintFitOnPages	MasterDeleteCanceled	
DefaultLineStyle	PrintLandscape	PageAdded	
DefaultStyle	PrintPagesAcross	PageChanged	
DefaultTextStyle	PrintPagesDown	PageDeleteCanceled	
Description	PrintScale	QueryCancelConvertToGroup	
DocumentSheet	ProgID	QueryCancelDocumentClose	
DynamicGridEnabled	Protection	QueryCancelMasterDelete	
EmailRoutingData	ReadOnly	QueryCancelPageDelete	
EventList	RightMargin	QueryCancelSelectionDelete	
Fonts	Saved	QueryCancelStyleDelete	
FooterCenter	SavePreviewMode	QueryCancelUngroup	
FooterLeft	SnapAngles	RunModeEntered	
FooterMargin	SnapEnabled	SelectionDeleteCanceled	
FooterRight	SnapExtensions	ShapeAdded	
FullBuildNumberCreated	SnapSettings	ShapeExitedTextEdit	
FullBuildNumberEdited	SolutionXMLElement	ShapeParentChanged	
FullName	SolutionXMLElementCount	StyleAdded	
GestureFormatSheet	SolutionXMLElementExists	StyleChanged	
GlueEnabled	SolutionXMLElementName	StyleDeleteCanceled	
GlueSettings	Stat	UngroupCanceled	
HeaderCenter	Styles		
HeaderFooterColor	Subject		
HeaderFooterFont	Template		
HeaderLeft	Time		
HeaderMargin	TimeCreated		
HeaderRight	TimeEdited		
HyperlinkBase	TimePrinted		
ID	TimeSaved		
Index	Title		
InPlace	TopMargin		
Keywords	VBProject		
LeftMargin	VBProjectData		
MacrosEnabled	Version		
Manager	ZoomBehavior		

Properties, Methods, and Events for the AccelItem Object

Properties		Methods	Events
AddonArgs	Control	Delete	
AddonName	Key		
Alt	Parent		
CmdNum	Shift		

Properties, Methods, and Events for the AccelItems Collection

Properties	Methods	Events
Count	Add	
Item		
Parent		

Properties, Methods, and Events for the AccelTable Object

Properties	Methods	Events
AccelItems	Delete	
Parent		
SetID		
TableName		

Properties, Methods, and Events for the AccelTables Collection

Properties	Methods	Events
Count	Add	
Item	AddAtID	
ItemAtID		
Parent		

Properties, Methods, and Events for the Addon Object

Properties		Methods	Events
Application	Run		
Enabled			
Index			
Name			
ObjectType			

Properties, Methods, and Events for the Addons Collection

Properties		Methods	Events
Application	Item	Add	
Count	ObjectType	GetNames	

Properties, Methods, and Events for Application (InvisibleApp) Object

Properties	Methods	Events	
Active	AddUndoUnit	AfterModal	QueryCancelStyleDelete
ActiveDocument	BeginUndoScope	AfterResume	QueryCancelSuspend
ActivePage	ClearCustomMenus	AppActivated	QueryCancelUngroup
ActivePrinter	ClearCustomToolbars	AppDeactivated	QueryCancelWindowClose
ActiveWindow	ConvertResultDoCmd	AppObjActivated	QuitCanceled
AddonPaths	EndUndoScope	AppObjDeactivated	RunModeEntered
Addons	EnumDirectories	BeforeDocumentClose	SelectionAdded
AlertResponse	FormatResult	BeforeDocumentSave	SelectionChanged
Application	GetUsageStatistic	BeforeDocumentSaveAs	SelectionDeleteCanceled
AutoLayout	InvokeHelp	BeforeMasterDelete	ShapeAdded
AutoRecoverInterval	OnComponentEnterState	BeforeModal	ShapeExitedTextEdit
AvailablePrinters	PurgeUndo	BeforePageDelete	ShapeParentChanged
Build	QueueMarkerEvent	BeforeQuit	StyleAdded
BuiltInMenus	Quit	BeforeSelectionDelete	StyleChanged
BuiltInToolbars	Redo	BeforeShapeDelete	StyleDeleteCanceled
COMAddins	RenameCurrentScope	BeforeShapeTextEdit	SuspendCanceled
CommandBars	SetCustomMenus	BeforeStyleDelete	TextChanged
CommandLine	SetCustomToolbars	BeforeSuspend	UngroupCanceled
CurrentScope	Undo	BeforeWindowClosed	ViewChanged
CustomMenus	Visible	BeforeWindowPageTurn	VisioIsIdle
CustomMenusFile	WindowHandle32	BeforeWindowSelDelete	WindowActivated
CustomToolbars	Windows	CellChanged	WindowChanged
CustomToolbarsFile		ConnectionsAdded	WindowCloseCanceled
DefaultAngleUnits		ConnectionsDeleted	WindowOpened
DefaultDurationUnits		ConvertToGroupCanceled	WindowTurnedToPage
DefaultPageUnits		DesignModeEntered	
DefaultTextUnits		DocumentChanged	
DefaultZoomBehavior		DocumentCloseCanceled	
DeferRecalc		DocumentCreated	
DialogFont		DocumentOpened	
Documents		DocumentSaved	
DrawingPaths		DocumentSavedAs	
EventInfo		EnterScope	
EventList		ExitScope	
EventsEnabled		FormulaChanged	
FilterPaths		MarkerEvent	
FullBuild		MasterAdded	
HelpPaths		MasterChanged	
InhibitSelectChange		MasterDeleteCanceled	
InstanceHandle32		MustFlushScopeBeginning	
IsInScope		MustFlushScopeEnded	
IsUndoingOrRedoing		NoEventsPending	
Language		OnKeystrokeMessageForAddon	
LiveDynamics		PageAdded	
ObjectTypeOnDataChangeDelay		PageChanged	
Path		PageDeleteCanceled	
PersistsEvents		QueryCancelConvertToGroup	
ProcessIDPromptForSummary		QueryCancelDocumentClose	
ScreenUpdating		QueryCancelMasterDelete	
ShowChanges		QueryCancelPageDelete	
ShowMenus		QueryCancelQuit	
ShowProgress		QueryCancelSelectionDelete	

Properties, Methods, and Events for Application (InvisibleApp) Object *(continued)*

Properties		Methods	Events
ShowStatusBar	TypelibMajorVersion		
ShowToolbar	TypelibMinorVersion		
StartupPaths	UndoEnabled		
Stat	UserName		
StencilPaths	VBAEnabled		
TemplatePaths	VBE		
TraceFlags	Version		

Properties, Methods, and Events for the Cell Object

Properties		Methods	Events
Application	PersistsEvents	GlueTo	CellChanged
Column	Result	GlueToPos	FormulaChanged
ContainingRow	ResultForce	Trigger	
Document	ResultFromInt		
Error	ResultFromIntForce		
EventList	ResultInt		
Formula	ResultIU		
FormulaForce	ResultIUForce		
FormulaForceU	ResultStr		
FormulaU	Row		
InheritedFormulaSource	RowName		
InheritedValueSource	RowNameU		
IsConstant	Section		
IsInherited	Shape		
LocalName	Stat		
Name	Style		
ObjectType	Units		

Properties, Methods, and Events for the Characters Object

Properties		Methods	Events
Application	IsField	AddCustomField	TextChanged
Begin	ObjectType	AddCustomFieldU	
CharCount	ParaProps	AddField	
CharProps	ParaPropsRow	Copy	
CharPropsRow	PersistsEvents	Cut	
Document	RunBegin	Paste	
End	RunEnd		
EventList	Shape		
FieldCategory	Stat		
FieldCode	TabPropsRow		
FieldFormat	Text		
FieldFormula	TextAsString		
FieldFormulaU			

Properties, Methods, and Events for the Color Object

Properties		Methods	Events
Application	Index		
Blue	ObjectType		
Document	PaletteEntry		
Flags	Red		
Green	Stat		

Properties, Methods, and Events for the Colors Collection

Properties		Methods	Events
Application	Item		
Count	ObjectType		
Document	Stat		

Properties, Methods, and Events for the Connect Object

Properties		Methods	Events
Application	ObjectType		
Document	Stat		
FromCell	ToCell		
FromPart	ToPart		
FromSheet	ToSheet		
Index			

Properties, Methods, and Events for the Connects Collection

Properties		Methods	Events
Application	Item		
Count	ObjectType		
Document	Stat		
FromSheet	ToSheet		

Properties, Methods, and Events for the Curve Object

Properties		Methods	Events
Application		Point	
Closed		PointAndDerivatives	
End		Points	
ObjectTypeStart			

Properties, Methods, and Events for the Document Object

Properties		Methods	Events
AlternateNames	MasterShortcuts	Clean	BeforeDocumentClose
Application	Mode	ClearCustomMenus	BeforeDocumentSave
AutoRecover	Name	ClearCustomToolbars	BeforeDocumentSaveAs
BottomMargin	ObjectType	ClearGestureFormatSheet	BeforeMasterDelete
BuildNumberCreated	OLEObjects	Close	BeforePageDelete
BuildNumberEdited	Pages	CopyPreviewPicture	BeforeSelectionDelete
Category	PaperHeight	DeleteSolutionXMLElement	BeforeShapeTextEdit
ClassID	PaperSize	Drop	BeforeStyleDelete
Colors	PaperWidth	ExecuteLine	ConvertToGroupCanceled
Company	Password	FollowHyperlink	DesignModeEntered
Container	Path	OpenStencilWindow	DocumentChanged
ContainsWorkspace	PersistsEvents	ParseLine	DocumentCloseCanceled
Creator	PreviewPicture	Print	DocumentCreated
CustomMenus	PrintCenteredH	Save	DocumentOpened
CustomMenusFile	PrintCenteredV	SaveAs	DocumentSaved
CustomToolbars	PrintCopies	SaveAsEx	DocumentSavedAs
CustomToolbarsFile	Printer	SetCustomMenus	MasterAdded
DefaultFillStyle	PrintFitOnPages	SetCustomToolbars	MasterChanged
DefaultGuideStyle	PrintLandscape		MasterDeleteCanceled
DefaultLineStyle	PrintPagesAcross		PageAdded
DefaultStyle	PrintPagesDown		PageChanged
DefaultTextStyleDescription	PrintScale		PageDeleteCanceled
DocumentSheet	ProgID		QueryCancelConvertToGroup
DynamicGridEnabled	Protection		QueryCancelDocumentClose
EmailRoutingData	ReadOnly		QueryCancelMasterDelete
EventList	RightMargin		QueryCancelPageDelete
Fonts	Saved		QueryCancelSelectionDelete
FooterCenter	SavePreviewMode		QueryCancelStyleDelete
FooterLeft	SnapAngles		QueryCancelUngroup
FooterMargin	SnapEnabled		RunModeEntered
FooterRight	SnapExtensions		SelectionDeleteCanceled
FullBuildNumberCreated	SnapSettings		ShapeAdded
FullBuildNumberEdited	SolutionXMLElement		ShapeExitedTextEdit
FullName	SolutionXMLElementCount		ShapeParentChanged
GestureFormatSheet	SolutionXMLElementExists		StyleAdded
GlueEnabled	SolutionXMLElementName		StyleChanged
GlueSettings	Stat		StyleDeleteCanceled
HeaderCenter	Styles		UngroupCanceled
HeaderFooterColor	Subject		
HeaderFooterFont	Template		
HeaderLeft	Time		
HeaderMargin	TimeCreated		
HeaderRight	TimeEdited		
HyperlinkBase	TimePrinted		
ID	TimeSaved		
Index	Title		
InPlace	TopMargin		
Keywords	VBProject		
LeftMargin	VBProjectData		
MacrosEnabled	Version		
Manager	ZoomBehavior		
Masters			

Properties, Methods, and Events for the Documents Collection

Properties	Methods	Events	
Application	Add	BeforeDocumentClose	MasterDeleteCanceled
Count	GetNames	BeforeDocumentSave	PageAdded
EventList	Open	BeforeDocumentSaveAs	PageChanged
Item	OpenEx	BeforeMasterDelete	PageDeleteCanceled
ItemFromID		BeforePageDelete	QueryCancelConvertToGroup
ObjectType		BeforeSelectionDelete	QueryCancelDocumentClose
PersistsEvents		BeforeShapeDelete	QueryCancelMasterDelete
		BeforeShapeTextEdit	QueryCancelPageDelete
		BeforeStyleDelete	QueryCancelSelectionDelete
		CellChanged	QueryCancelStyleDelete
		ConnectionsAdded	QueryCancelUngroup
		ConnectionsDeleted	RunModeEntered
		ConvertToGroupCanceled	SelectionAdded
		DesignModeEntered	SelectionDeleteCanceled
		DocumentChanged	ShapeAdded
		DocumentCloseCanceled	ShapeChanged
		DocumentCreated	ShapeExitedTextEdit
		DocumentOpened	ShapeParentChanged
		DocumentSaved	StyleAdded
		DocumentSavedAs	StyleChanged
		FormulaChanged	StyleDeleteCanceled
		MasterAdded	TextChanged
		MasterChanged	UngroupCanceled

Properties, Methods, and Events for the Event Object

Properties		Methods	Events
Action	Index	Delete	
Application	ObjectType	GetFilterCommands	
Enabled	Persistable	GetFilterObjects	
Event	Persistent	GetFilterSRC	
EventList	Target	SetFilterCommands	
ID	TargetArgs	SetFilterObjects	
		SetFilterSRC	
		Trigger	

Properties, Methods, and Events for the EventList Collection

Properties	Methods	Events
Application	Add	
Count	AddAdvise	
Item		
ItemFromID		
ObjectType		

Properties, Methods, and Events for the Font Object

Properties		Methods	Events
Application	Index		
Attributes	Name		
CharSet	ObjectType		
Document	PitchAndFamily		
ID	Stat		

Properties, Methods, and Events for the Fonts Collection

Properties		Methods	Events
Application	ItemFromID		
Count	ObjectType		
Document	Stat		
Item			

Properties, Methods, and Events for the Hyperlink Object

Properties		Methods	Events
Address	NewWindow	AddToFavorites	
Application	ObjectType	Copy	
Description	Row	CreateURL	
ExtraInfo	Shape	Delete	
Frame	Stat	Follow	
IsDefaultLink	SubAddress		
Name			

Properties, Methods, and Events for the Hyperlinks Collection

Properties		Methods	Events
Application	ObjectType	Add	
Count	Shape		
Item	Stat		

Properties, Methods, and Events for the Layer Object

Properties		Methods	Events
Application	NameU	Add	
CellsC	ObjectType	Delete	
Document	Page	Remove	
EventList	PersistsEvents		
Index	Row		
Master	Stat		
Name			

Properties, Methods, and Events for the Layers Collection

Properties		Methods	Events
Application	Master	Add	
Count	ObjectType		
Document	Page		
EventList	PersistsEvents		
Item	Stat		
ItemU			

Properties, Methods, and Events for the Master Object

Properties	Methods	Events
AlignName	BoundingBox	BeforeMasterDelete
Application	CenterDrawing	BeforeSelectionDelete
BaseID	Close	BeforeShapeDelete
Connects	CreateShortcut	BeforeShapeTextEdit
Document	Delete	CellChanged
EditCopy	DrawBezier	CellChanged
EventList	DrawLine	ConnectionsAdded
Hidden	DrawNURBS	ConnectionsDeleted
Icon	DrawOval	ConvertToGroupCanceled
IconSize	DrawPolyline	FormulaChanged
IconUpdate	DrawRectangle	MasterChanged
ID	DrawSpline	MasterDeleteCanceled
Index	Drop	QueryCancelConvertToGroup
IndexInStencil	DropMany	QueryCancelMasterDelete
IsChanged	DropManyU	QueryCancelSelectionDelete
Layers	Export	QueryCancelUngroup
MatchByName	ExportIcon	SelectionAdded
Name	GetFormulas	SelectionDeleteCanceled
NameU	GetFormulasU	ShapeAdded
NewBaseID	GetResults	ShapeChanged
ObjectType	Import	ShapeExitedTextEdit
OLEObjects	ImportIcon	ShapeParentChanged
OneD	InsertFromFile	TextChanged
Original	InsertObject	UngroupCanceled
PageSheet	Layout	
PatternFlags	Open	
PersistsEvents	OpenDrawWindow	
Picture	OpenIconWindow	
Prompt	Paste	
Shapes	PasteSpecial	
SpatialSearch	ResizeToFitContents	
Stat	SetFormulas	
UniqueID	SetResults	

Properties, Methods, and Events for the Masters Collection

Properties	Methods	Events	
Application	Add	BeforeMasterDelete	QueryCancelConvertToGroup
Count	Drop	BeforeSelectionDelete	QueryCancelMasterDelete
Document	GetNames	BeforeShapeDelete	QueryCancelSelectionDelete
EventList	GetNamesU	BeforeShapeTextEdit	QueryCancelUngroup
Item		CellChanged	SelectionAdded
ItemU		ConnectionsAdded	SelectionDeleteCanceled
ItemFromID		ConnectionsDeleted	ShapeAdded
ObjectType		ConvertToGroupCanceled	ShapeChanged
PersistsEvents		FormulaChanged	ShapeExitedTextEdit
Stat		MasterAdded	ShapeParentChanged
		MasterChanged	TextChanged
		MasterDeleteCanceled	UngroupCanceled

Properties, Methods, and Events for the MasterShortcut Object

Properties		Methods	Events
AlignName	Name	Delete	
Application	NameU	ExportIcon	
Document	ObjectType	ImportIcon	
DropActions	Prompt	OpenIconWindow	
Icon	ShapeHelp		
IconSize	Stat		
ID	TargetDocumentName		
Index	TargetMasterName		
IndexInStencil			

Properties, Methods, and Events for the MasterShortcuts Collection

Properties	Methods	Events
Application	Drop	
Count	GetNames	
Document	GetNamesU	
Item		
ItemU		
ItemFromID		
ObjectType		
Stat		

Properties, Methods, and Events for the Menu Object

Properties		Methods	Events
ActionText	IsHierarchical	Delete	
AddonArgs	MDIWindowMenu	IconFileName	
AddonName	MenuItems		
BuiltIn	PaletteWidth		
Caption	Parent		
CmdNum	State		
CntrlType	Style		
Enabled	TypeSpecific1		
FaceID	TypeSpecific2		
HelpContextID	Visible		
HelpFile	Width		
Index			

Properties, Methods, and Events for the MenuItem Object

Properties		Methods	Events
ActionText	Index	Delete	
AddonArgs	IsHierarchical	IconFileName	
AddonName	MenuItems		
BeginGroup	PaletteWidth		
BuiltIn	Parent		
Caption	State		
CmdNum	Style		
CntrlType	TypeSpecific1		
Enabled	TypeSpecific2		
FaceID	Visible		
HelpContextID	Width		
HelpFile			

Properties, Methods, and Events for the MenuItems Collection

Properties	Methods	Events
Count	Add	
Item	AddAt	
Parent		
ParentItem		

Properties, Methods, and Events for the Menus Collection

Properties	Methods	Events
Count	Add	
Item	AddAt	
Parent		

Properties, Methods, and Events for the MenuSet Object

Properties		Methods	Events
BuiltIn	Position	Delete	
Caption	Protection		
Enabled	RowIndex		
Height	SetID		
Left	Top		
Menus	Visible		
Parent	Width		

Properties, Methods, and Events for the MenuSets Collection

Properties	Methods	Events
Count	Add	
Item	AddAtID	
ItemAtID		
Parent		

Properties, Methods, and Events for the MSGWrap Object

Properties	Methods	Events
Application		
hwnd		
lParam		
message		
ObjectType		
posttime		
ptx		
pty		
wParam		

Properties, Methods, and Events for the OLEObject Object

Properties		Methods	Events
Application	ObjectType		
ClassID	ProgID		
ForeignType	Shape		
Object	Stat		

Properties, Methods, and Events for the OLEObjects Collection

Properties		Methods	Events
Application	ObjectType		
Count	Stat		
Item			

Properties, Methods, and Events for the Page Object

Properties	Methods		Events
Application	AddGuide	GetFormulas	BeforePageDelete
Background	BoundingBox	GetFormulasU	BeforeSelectionDelete
BackPage	CenterDrawing	GetResults	BeforeShapeDelete
BackPageAsObj	Delete	Import	BeforeShapeTextEdit
BackPageFromName	DrawBezier	InsertFromFile	CellChanged
Connects	DrawLine	InsertObject	ConnectionsAdded
Document	DrawNURBS	Layout	ConnectionsDeleted
EventList	DrawOval	OpenDrawWindow	ConvertToGroupCanceled
ID	DrawPolyline	Paste	FormulaChanged
Index	DrawRectangle	PasteSpecial	PageChanged
Layers	DrawSpline	Print	PageDeleteCanceled
Name	Drop	PrintTile	QueryCancelConvertToGroup
NameU	DropMany	ResizeToFitContents	QueryCancelPageDelete
ObjectType	DropManyU	SetFormulas	QueryCancelSelectionDelete
OLEObjects	Export	SetResults	QueryCancelUngroup
PageSheet			SelectionAdded
PersistsEvents			SelectionDeleteCanceled
Picture			ShapeAdded
PrintTileCount			ShapeChanged
Shapes			ShapeExitedTextEdit
SpatialSearch			ShapeParentChanged
Stat			TextChanged
			UngroupCanceled

Properties, Methods, and Events for the Pages Collection

Properties	Methods	Events	
Application	Add	BeforePageDelete	QueryCancelConvertToGroup
Count	GetNames	BeforeSelectionDelete	QueryCancelPageDelete
Document	GetNamesU	BeforeShapeDelete	QueryCancelSelectionDelete
EventList		BeforeShapeTextEdit	QueryCancelUngroup
Item		CellChanged	SelectionAdded
ItemU		ConnectionsAdded	SelectionDeleteCanceled
ItemFromID		ConnectionsDeleted	ShapeAdded
ObjectType		ConvertToGroupCanceled	ShapeChanged
PersistsEvents		FormulaChanged	ShapeExitedTextEdit
Stat		PageAdded	ShapeParentChanged
		PageChanged	TextChanged
		PageDeleteCanceled	UngroupCanceled

Properties, Methods, and Events for the Path Object

Properties		Methods	Events
Application	Item	Points	
Closed	ObjectType		
Count			

Properties, Methods, and Events for the Paths Collection

Properties		Methods	Events
Application	Item		
Count	ObjectType		

Properties, Methods, and Events for the Row Object

Properties		Methods	Events
Application	Name	GetPolylineData	CellChanged
Cell	NameU	FormulaChanged	
CellU	ObjectType		
ContainingSection	PersistsEvents		
Count	Shape		
EventList	Stat		
Index	Style		

Properties, Methods, and Events for the Section Object

Properties		Methods	Events
Application	PersistsEvents	CellChanged	
Count	Row	FormulaChanged	
EventList	Shape		
Index	Stat		
ObjectType	Style		

Properties, Methods, and Events for the Selection Object

Properties	Methods	Events
Application	AddToGroup	
ContainingMaster	BoundingBox	
ContainingPage	BringForward	
ContainingShape	BringToFront	
Count	Combine	
Document	ConvertToGroup	
EventList	Copy	
FillStyle	Cut	
FillStyleKeepFmt	Delete	
Item	DeselectAll	
ItemStatus	DrawRegion	
IterationMode	Duplicate	
LineStyle	Export	
LineStyleKeepFmt	FitCurve	
ObjectType	FlipHorizontal	
PersistsEvents	FlipVertical	
Picture	Fragment	
PrimaryItem	Group	
Stat	Intersect	
Style	Join	
StyleKeepFmt	Layout	
TextStyle	RemoveFromGroup	
TextStyleKeepFmt	ReverseEnds	
	Rotate90	
	Select	
	SelectAll	
	SendBackward	
	SendToBack	
	Subtract	
	SwapEnds	
	Trim	
	Ungroup	
	Union	

Properties, Methods, and Events for the Shape Object

Properties	Methods	Events
Application	AddHyperlink	BeforeSelectionDelete
AreaIU	AddNamedRow	BeforeShapeDelete
CellExists	AddRow	BeforeShapeTExtEdit
CellExistsU	AddRows	CellChanged
Cells	AddSection	ConvertToGroupCanceled
CellsRowIndex	BoundingBox	FormulaChanged
CellsRowIndexU	BringForward	QueryCancelConvertToGroup
CellsSRC	BringToFront	QueryCancelSelectionDelete
CellsSRCExists	CenterDrawing	QueryCancelUngroup
CellsU	ConvertToGroup	SelectionAdded
Characters	Copy	SelectionDeleteCanceled
CharCount	Cut	ShapeAdded
ClassID	Delete	ShapeChanged
Connects	DeleteRow	ShapeExitedTextEdit
ContainingMaster	DeleteSection	ShapeParentChanged
ContainingPage	DrawBezier	TextChanged
ContainingShape	DrawLine	UngroupCanceled
Data1	DrawNURBS	
Data2	DrawOval	
Data3	DrawPolyline	
DistanceFrom	DrawRectangle	
DistanceFromPoint	DrawSpline	
Document	Drop	
EventList	DropMany	
FillStyle	DropManyU	
FillStyleKeepFmt	Duplicate	
ForeignData	Export	
ForeignType	FitCurve	
FromConnects	FlipHorizontal	
GeometryCount	FlipVertical	
Help	GetFormulas	
Hyperlinks	GetFormulasU	
ID	GetResults	
Index	Group	
IsOpenForTextEdit	HitTest	
Layer	Import	
LayerCount	InsertFromFile	
LengthIU	InsertObject	
LineStyle	Layout	
LineStyleKeepFmt	OpenDrawWindow	
Master	OpenSheetWindow	
MasterShape	Paste	
Name	PasteSpecial	
NameU	ReverseEnds	
NameID	Rotate90	
Object	SendBackward	
ObjectIsInherited	SendToBack	
ObjectType	SetBegin	
OneD	SetCenter	
Parent	SetEnd	

Properties, Methods, and Events for the Shape Object *(continued)*

Properties		Methods	Events
Paths	Shapes	SetFormulas	
PathsLocal	SpatialNeighbors	SetResults	
PersistsEvents	SpatialRelation	SwapEnds	
Picture	SpatialSearch	TransformXYFrom	
ProgID	Stat	TransformXYTo	
RootShape	Style	Ungroup	
RowCount	StyleKeepFmt	UpdateAlignmentBox	
RowExists	Text	XYFromPage	
RowsCellCount	TextStyle	XYToPage	
RowType	TextStyleKeepFmt		
Section	Type		
SectionExists	UniqueID		

Properties, Methods, and Events for the Shapes Collection

Properties		Methods	Events
Application	Item	CenterDrawing	
ContainingMaster	ItemU		
ContainingPage	ItemFromID		
ContainingShape	ObjectType		
Count	PersistsEvents		
Document	Stat		
EventList			

Properties, Methods, and Events for the Style Object

Properties		Methods	Events
Application	IncludesLine	Delete	BeforeStyleDelete
BasedOn	IncludesText	GetFormulas	QueryCancelStyleDelete
CellExists	Index	GetFormulasU	StyleChanged
CellExistsU	LineBasedOn	GetResults	StyleDeleteCanceled
Cells	Name	SetFormulas	
CellsU	NameU	SetResults	
Document	ObjectType		
EventList	PersistsEvents		
FillBasedOn	Section		
Hidden	Stat		
ID	TextBasedOn		
IncludesFill			

Properties, Methods, and Events for the Styles Collection

Properties		Methods	Events
Application	ItemU	Add	BeforeStyleDelete
Count	ItemFromID	GetNames	QueryCancelStyleDelete
Document	ObjectType	GetNamesU	StyleAdded
EventList	PersistsEvents	StyleChanged	
Item	Stat	StyleDeleteCanceled	

Properties, Methods, and Events for the Toolbar Object

Properties		Methods	Events
BuiltIn	Position	Delete	
Caption	Protection		
Enabled	RowIndex		
Height	ToolbarItems		
Index	Top		
Left	Visible		
Parent	Width		

Properties, Methods, and Events for the ToolbarItem Object

Properties		Methods	Events
ActionText	HelpFile	Delete	
AddonArgs	Index	IconFileName	
AddonName	IsHierarchical		
BeginGroup	PaletteWidth		
BuiltIn	ParentState		
Caption	Style		
CmdNum	ToolbarItems		
CntrlType	TypeSpecific1		
Enabled	TypeSpecific2		
FaceID	Visible		
HelpContextID	Width		

Properties, Methods, and Events for the ToolbarItems Collection

Properties		Methods	Events
Count	Parent	Add	
Item	ParentItem	AddAt	

Properties, Methods, and Events for the Toolbars Collection

Properties	Methods	Events
Count	Add	
Item	AddAt	
Parent		

Properties, Methods, and Events for the ToolbarSet Object

Properties	Methods	Events
Caption	Delete	
Parent		
SetID		
Toolbars		

Properties, Methods, and Events for the ToolbarSets Collection

Properties	Methods	Events
Count	Add	
Item	AddAtID	
ItemAtID		
Parent		

Properties, Methods, and Events for the UIObject Object

Properties	Methods	Events
AccelTables	LoadFromFile	
Clone	SaveToFile	
DisplayKeysInTooltips	UpdateUI	
DisplayTooltips		
LargeButtons		
MenuAnimationStyle		
MenuSets		
Name		
ToolbarSets

Properties, Methods, and Events for the Window Object

Properties		Methods	Events
AllowEditing	PageTabWidth	Activate	BeforeWindowClosed
Application	Parent	Close	BeforeWindowPageTurn
Caption	ParentWindow	DeselectAll	BeforeWindowSelDelete
Document	PersistsEvents	DockedStencils	OnKeystrokeMessageForAddon
EventList	Selection	GetViewRect	QueryCancelWindowCloseSelectionChanged
Icon	ShowConnectPoints	GetWindowRect	ViewChanged
ID	ShowGrid	Scroll	WindowActivated
Index	ShowGuides	ScrollViewTo	WindowChanged
InPlace	ShowPageBreaks	Select	WindowCloseCanceled
IsEditingOLE	ShowPageTabs	SelectAll	WindowTurnedToPage
IsEditingText	ShowRulers	SetViewRect	
Master	ShowScrollBars	SetWindowRect	
MasterShortcut	Stat		
MergeCaption	SubType		
MergeClass	Type		
MergeID	ViewFit		
MergePosition	Visible		
ObjectType	WindowHandle32		
Page	Windows		
PageAsObj	WindowState		
PageFromName	Zoom		

Properties, Methods, and Events for the Windows Collection

Properties	Methods	Events
Application	Add	BeforeWindowClosed
Count	Arrange	BeforeWindowPageTurn
EventList	BeforeWindowSelDelete	
Item	OnKeystrokeMessageForAddon	
ItemFromID	QueryCancelWindowClose	
ObjectType	SelectionChanged	
PersistsEvents	ViewChanged	
	WindowActivated	
	WindowChanged	
	WindowCloseCanceled	
	WindowOpened	
	WindowTurnedToPage	

Appendix B

ShapeSheet Section, Row, and Cell Indices

This appendix lists sections, rows, and cells that appear in the ShapeSheet window for shapes, styles, pages, and documents. It also lists the corresponding index constants that you can use in a program to access sections, rows, and cells with Automation, plus index constants you can use to access tab settings.

To find the value of a constant, use the **Object Browser** in the Visual Basic Editor. When a constant is selected in the **Members Of** list, the **Details** pane displays the value of the constant. To show the ShapeSheet window for an object, click the object, and then click **Show ShapeSheet** on the **Window** menu.

> **Tip** For quicker access to the ShapeSheet window, on the **Tools** menu, click **Options**. Click the **Advanced** tab, and then select the **Run in developer mode** check box under **Developer settings**. When you run in developer mode, the **Show ShapeSheet** command appears on an object's shortcut menu when you right-click the object.

Sections are listed alphabetically, and cells are grouped by section. In sections that have a variable number of rows, such as the Actions section, rows are indexed using the row constant as a base. To refer to a particular row, add an integer offset to the row index constant, starting with zero (0) for the first row. To reference a cell in a particular row, use the same integer in the cell name. For example, use Actions.Action[*i*].

For details about using cell references in formulas, see the Microsoft Developer Reference (on the **Help** menu, click **Developer Reference**). For details about accessing cells from a program, see Chapter 17, *Automating Formulas*.

Section, Row, and Cell Indices for Shapes

Section or row	Cell	Section index	Row index	Cell index
<no name>[1]	HelpTopic Copyright[2]	visSectionObject	visRowHelpCopyright	visObjHelp visCopyright
1-D Endpoints section[3]	BeginX BeginY EndX EndY	visSectionObject	visRowXForm1D	vis1DBeginX vis1DBeginY vis1DEndX vis1DEndY
Actions section	Actions.Action[*i*] Actions.Menu[*i*] Actions.C*i* Actions.D*i*	visSectionAction	visRowAction+*i*	visActionAction visActionMenuvisActionChecked visActionDisabled
Alignment section[4]	AlignLeft AlignCenter AlignRight AlignTop AlignMiddle AlignBottom	visSectionObject	visRowAlign	visAlignLeft visAlignCenter visAlignRight visAlignTop visAlignMiddle visAlignBottom
Character section	Char.Font[*i*] Char.Size[*i*] Char.FontScale[*i*] Char.Letterspace[*i*] Char.Color[*i*] Char.Style[*i*] Char.Case[*i*] Char.Pos[*i*] Char.Strikethru[*i*] Char.DblUnderline[*i*] Char.Overline[*i*] Char.Perpendicular[*i*] Char.Locale[*i*][5] Char.ColorTrans[*i*]	visSectionCharacter	visRowCharacter+*i*	visCharacterFont visCharacterSize visCharacterFontScale visCharacterLetterspace visCharacterColor visCharacterStyle visCharacterCase visCharacterPos visCharacterStrikethru visCharacterDblUnderline visCharacterOverline visCharacterPerpendicular visCharacterLocale visCharacterColorTrans
Connection Points section (non-extended row[6])	Connections.X*i* Connections.Y*i* Connections.DirX[*i*] Connections.DirY[*i*] Connections.Type[*i*] Connections.AutoGen[*i*]	visSectionConnectionPts	visRowConnectionPts+*i*	visCnnctX visCnnctY visCnnctDirX visCnnctDirY visCnnctType visCnnctAutoGen
Connection Points section (extended row[7])	Connections.X*i* Connections.Y*i* Connections.A*i* Connections.B*i* Connections.C*i* Connections.D*i*	visSectionConnectionPts	visRowConnectionPts+*i*	visCnnctX visCnnctY visCnnctA visCnnctB visCnnctC visCnnctD

Section, Row, and Cell Indices for Shapes *(continued)*

Section or row	Cell	Section index	Row index	Cell index
Controls section	Controls.X*i*	visSectionControls	visRowControl+*i*	visCtlX
	Controls.Y*i*			visCtlY
	Controls.XDyn[*i*]			visCtlXDyn
	Controls.YDyn[*i*]			visCtlYDyn
	Controls.XCon[*i*]			visCtlXCon
	Controls.YCon[*i*]			visCtlYCon
	Controls.CanGlue[*i*]			visCtlGlue
	Controls.Prompt[*i*][8]			visCtlTip
Custom Properties section	Prop.*Name*.Label	visSectionProp	visRowProp + *i*	visCustPropsLabel
	Prop.*Name*.Prompt			visCustPropsPrompt
	Prop.*Name*.SortKey			visCustPropsSortKey
	Prop.*Name*.Type			visCustPropsType
	Prop.*Name*.Format			visCustPropsFormat
	Prop.*Name*.Value[9]			visCustPropsValue
	Prop.*Name*.Invisible			visCustPropsInvis
	Prop.*Name*.Verify			visCustPropsAsk
Events section	TheData[10]	visSectionObject	visRowEvent	visEvtCellTheData
	TheText			visEvtCellTheText
	EventDblClick			visEvtCellDblClick
	EventXFMod			visEvtCellXFMod
	EventDrop			visEvtCellDrop
Fill Format section	FillBkgnd	visSectionObject	visRowFill	visFillBkgnd
	FillPattern			visFillPattern
	FillForegnd			visFillForegnd
	ShdwBkgnd			visFillShdwBkgnd
	ShdwPattern			visFillShdwPattern
	ShdwForegnd			visFillShdwForegnd
	FillForegndTrans			visFillForegndTrans
	FillBkgndTrans			visFillBkgndTrans
	ShdwForegndTrans			visFillShdwForegndTrans
	ShdwBkgndTrans			visFillShdwBkgndTrans
Foreign Image Info section[11]	ImgWidth	visSectionObject	visRowForeign	visFrgnImgWidth
	ImgHeight			visFrgnImgHeight
	ImgOffsetY			visFrgnImgOffsetY
	ImgOffsetX			visFrgnImgOffsetX
Geometry*i* section	Geometry*i*.NoFill	VisSectionFirst Component+*i*	visRowComponent	visCompNoFill
	Geometry*i*.NoLine			visCompNoLine
	Geometry*i*.NoShow			visCompNoShow
	Geometry*i*.NoSnap			visCompNoSnap
MoveTo row (in Geometry*i* section)	Geometry*i*.X*j*		visRowVertex+*j*	visX
	Geometry*i*.Y*j*			visY
LineTo row (in Geometry*i* section)	Geometry*i*.X*j*		visRowVertex+*j*	visX
	Geometry*i*.Y*j*			visY

Section, Row, and Cell Indices for Shapes *(continued)*

Section or row	Cell	Section index	Row index	Cell index
ArcTo row (in Geometry*i* section)	Geometry*i*.X*j* Geometry*i*.Y*j* Geometry*i*.A*j*		visRowVertex + *j*	visX visY visBow
Elliptical ArcTo row (in Geometry*i* section)	Geometry*i*.X*j* Geometry*i*.Y*j* Geometry*i*.A*j* Geometry*i*.B*j* Geometry*i*.C*j* Geometry*i*.D*j*		visRowVertex + *j*	visX visY visControlX visControlY visEccentricityAngle visAspectRatio
PolylineTo row (in Geometry*i* section)	Geometry*i*.X*j* Geometry*i*.Y*j* Geometry*i*.A*j*		visRowVertex + *j*	visX visY visPolylineData
NURBSTo row (in Geometry*i* section)	Geometry*i*.X*j* Geometry*i*.Y*j* Geometry*i*.A*j* Geometry*i*.B*j* Geometry*i*.C*j* Geometry*i*.D*j* Geometry*i*.E*j*		visRowVertex + *j*	visX visY visNURBSKnot visNURBSWeight visNURBSKnotPrev visNURBSWeightPrev visNURBSData
SplineStart row (in Geometry*i* section)	Geometry*i*.X*j* Geometry*i*.Y*j* Geometry*i*.A*j* Geometry*i*.B*j* Geometry*i*.C*j* Geometry*i*.D*j*		visRowVertex + *j*	visX visY visSplineKnot visSplineKnot2 visSplineKnot3 visSplineDegree
SplineKnot row (in Geometry*i* section)	Geometry*i*.X*j* Geometry*i*.Y*j* Geometry*i*.A*j*		visRowVertex + *j*	visX visY visSplineKnot
InfiniteLine row (in Geometry*i* section)	Geometry*i*.X1 Geometry*i*.Y1 Geometry*i*.A1 Geometry*i*.B1		visRowVertex	visInfiniteLineX1 visInfiniteLineY1 visInfiniteLineX2 visInfiniteLineY2
Ellipse row (in Geometry*i* section)	Geometry*i*.X1 Geometry*i*.Y1 Geometry*i*.A1 Geometry*i*.B1 Geometry*i*.C1 Geometry*i*.D1		visRowVertex	visEllipseCenterX visEllipseCenterY visEllipseMajorX visEllipseMajorY visEllipseMinorX visEllipseMinorY
Glue Info section	GlueType WalkPreference BegTrigger EndTrigger	visSectionObject	visRowMisc	visGlueType visWalkPref visBegTrigger visEndTrigger

Section, Row, and Cell Indices for Shapes *(continued)*

Section or row	Cell	Section index	Row index	Cell index
Group Properties section[12]	SelectMode	visSectionObject	visRowGroup	visGroupSelectMode
	DisplayMode			visGroupDisplayMode
	IsTextEditTarget			visGroupIsTextEditTarget
	IsSnapTarget			visGroupIsSnapTarget
	IsDropTarget			visGroupIsDropTarget
	DontMoveChildren			visGroupDontMoveChildren
HyperLinks section	Hyperlink.*Name*Description	visSectionHyperlink	visRow1stHyperlink+*i*	visHLinkDescription
	Hyperlink.*Name*.Address		visHLinkAddress	
	Hyperlink.*Name*.SubAddress		visHLinkSubAddress	
	Hyperlink.*Name*.ExtraInfo		visHLinkExtraInfo	
	Hyperlink.*Name*.Frame		visHLinkFrame	
	Hyperlink.*Name*.NewWindow			visHLinkNewWin
	Hyperlink.*Name*.Default			visHLinkDefault
Image Properties section[13]	Contrast	visSectionObject	visRowImage	visImageContrast
	Brightness			visImageBrightness
	Gamma			visImageGamma
	Blur			visImageBlur
	Sharpen			visImageSharpen
	Denoise			visImageDenoise
	Transparency			visImageTransparency
Layer Membership section	LayerMember	visSectionObject	visRowLayerMem	visLayerMember
Line Format section	LineWeight	visSectionObject	visRowLine	visLineWeight
	LineColor			visLineColor
	LinePattern			visLinePattern
	BeginArrow			visLineBeginArrow
	EndArrow			visLineEndArrow
	LineCap			visLineEndCap
	BeginArrowSize			visLineBeginArrowSize
	EndArrowSize			visLineEndArrowSize
	Rounding			visLineRounding
	LineColorTrans			visLineColorTrans
Miscellaneous section	NoObjHandles	visSectionObject	visRowMisc	visNoObjHandles
	NonPrinting			visNonPrinting
	NoCtlHandles			visNoCtlHandles
	NoAlignBox			visNoAlignBox
	UpdateAlignBox			visUpdateAlignBox
	HideText			visHideText
	ObjType			visLOFlags
	DynFeedback			visDynFeedback
	NoLiveDynamic			visNoLiveDynamics
	IsDropSource			visDropSource
	Comment			visComment

Section, Row, and Cell Indices for Shapes *(continued)*

Section or row	Cell	Section index	Row index	Cell index
Paragraph section	Para.IndFirst[*i*]	visSectionParagraph	visRowParagraph+*i*	visIndentFirst
	Para.IndLeft[*i*]			visIndentLeft
	Para.IndRight[*i*]			visIndentRight
	Para.SpLine[*i*]			visSpaceLine
	Para.SpBefore[*i*]			visSpaceBefore
	Para.SpAfter[*i*]			visSpaceAfter
	Para.HorzAlign[*i*]			visHorzAlign
	Para.Bullet[*i*]			visBulletIndex
	Para.BulletStr[*i*]			visBulletString
Protection section	LockWidth	visSectionObject	visRowLock	visLockWidth
	LockHeight			visLockHeight
	LockMoveX			visLockMoveX
	LockMoveY			visLockMoveY
	LockAspect			visLockAspect
	LockDelete			visLockDelete
	LockBegin			visLockBegin
	LockEnd			visLockEnd
	LockRotate			visLockRotate
	LockCrop			visLockCrop
	LockVtxEdit			visLockVtxEdit
	LockTextEdit			visLockTextEdit
	LockFormat			visLockFormat
	LockGroup			visLockGroup
	LockCalcWH			visLockCalcWH
	LockSelect			visLockSelect
Scratch section	Scratch.X*i*	visSectionScratch	visRowScratch+*i*	visScratchX
	Scratch.Y*i*			visScratchY
	Scratch.A*i*			visScratchA
	Scratch.B*i*			visScratchB
	Scratch.C*i*			visScratchC
	Scratch.D*i*			visScratchD
Shape Layout section	ShapePermeableX	visSectionObject	visRowShapeLayout	visSLOPermX
	ShapePermeableY			visSLOPermY
	ShapePermeablePlace			visSLOPermeablePlace
	ShapeFixedCode			visSLOFixedCode
	ShapePlowCode			visSLOPlowCode
	ShapeRouteStyle			visSLORouteSyle
	ConLineJumpDirX			visSLOJumpDirX
	ConLineJumpDirY			visSLOJumpDirY
	ConFixedCode			visSLOConFixedCode
	ConLineJumpCode			visSLOJumpCode
	ConLineJumpStyle			visSLOJumpStyle
	ShapePlaceFlip			visSLOPlaceFlip
	ConLineRouteExt			visSLOLineRouteExt

Section, Row, and Cell Indices for Shapes *(continued)*

Section or row	Cell	Section index	Row index	Cell index
Shape Transform section	PinX PinY Width Height LocPinX LocPinY Angle FlipX FlipY ResizeMode	visSectionObject	visRowXFormOut	visXFormPinX visXFormPinY visXFormWidth visXFormHeight visXFormLocPinX visXFormLocPinY visXFormAngle visXFormFlipX visXFormFlipY visXFormResizeMode
Tabs section	Tabs.*ci*[14] Tabs.*ci*[14]	visSectionTab	visRowTab + *i*	visTabStopCount[5] (*j**3) + visTabPos[15] (*j**3) + visTabAlign[15]
Text Block Format section	VerticalAlign TopMargin BottomMargin LeftMargin RightMargin TextBkgnd TextDirection DefaultTabStop TextBkgndTrans	visSectionObject	visRowText	visTxtBlkVerticalAlign visTxtBlkTopMargin visTxtBlkBottomMargin visTxtBlkLeftMargin visTxtBlkRightMargin visTxtBlkBkgnd visTxtBlkDirection visTxtBlkDefaultTabStop visTxtBlkBkgndTrans
Text Fields section[16]	Fields.Type[*i*] Fields.Format[*i*] Fields.Value[*i*] Fields.EditMode[*i*] Fields.UICat[*i*] Fields.UICod[*i*] Fields.UIFmt[*i*]	visSectionTextField	visRowField + *i*	visFieldType visFieldFormat visFieldCell visFieldEditMode visFieldUICategory visFieldUICode visFieldUIFormat
Text Transform section	TxtPinX TxtPinY TxtWidth TxtHeight TxtLocPinX TxtLocPinY TxtAngle	visSectionObject	visRowTextXForm	visXFormPinX visXFormPinY visXFormWidth visXFormHeight visXFormLocPinX visXFormLocPinY visXFormAngle
User-Defined Cells section	User.*Name*.Value[9] User.*Name*.Prompt	visSectionUser	visRowUser + *i*	visUserValue visUserPrompt

Footnotes

1. This section and its cells do not appear in the ShapeSheet window.
2. This cell can be written only once.
3. This section is present only for 1-D shapes.
4. This section is present only for two-dimensional (2-D) shapes that are glued to a guide.
5. This cell does not appear in the ShapeSheet window.

Footnotes *(continued)*

6. Non-extended rows have a row type of **visTagCnnctPt** or **visTagCnnctNamed**.
7. Extended rows have a row type of **visTagCnnctPtABCD** or **visTagCnnctNamedABCD**.
8. This cells appears only if the control has a tool tip (row type of **visTagCtlPtTip**).
9. This cell is the default and its name can be omitted from the cell reference.
10. This cell appears in the ShapeSheet window but is reserved for internal use.
11. This section is present only for linked objects, embedded objects, or Controls.
12. This section is present only for groups.
13. This section is present only for bitmaps.
14. The variable *c* represents a character and the variable *i* represents the row number.
15. The variable *j* represents a tab stop in this section.
16. This section is present only if you've inserted a field into the shape's text.

Section, Row, and Cell Indices for Styles

The following table lists sections, rows, and cells that are displayed in the ShapeSheet window for a style, with constants for the corresponding section, row, and cell indices.

You can reference many of the same sections and cells for a style that you can for a shape: Protection, Miscellaneous, Group Properties, Line Format, Fill Format, Characters, Paragraph, Tabs, Text Block Format, Events, Image Properties, and Shape Layout sections. For information on these sections and cells, see *Section, Row, and Cell Indices for Shapes* earlier in this appendix. You can also reference the section and cells shown in this table for a style.

> **Note** To show the ShapeSheet window for a style, open the **Drawing Explorer** (on the **View** menu, click **Drawing Explorer Window**), navigate to a style, right-click the style, and then click **Show ShapeSheet** on the shortcut menu.

Section or row	Cell	Section index	Row index	Cell index
Style Properties section	EnableTextProps EnableLineProps EnableFillProps HideForApply	visSectionObject	visRowStyle	visStyleIncludesText visStyleIncludesLine visStyleIncludesFill visStyleHidden

Section, Row, and Cell Indices for Pages

The following table lists sections, rows, and cells that are displayed in the ShapeSheet window for a drawing page or master, with constants for the corresponding section, row, and cell indices.

You can reference some of the same sections and cells for a page or master that you can for a shape: Actions, Custom Properties, Hyperlinks, Scratch, and User-Defined Cells sections. For information on these sections and cells, see *Section, Row, and Cell Indices for Shapes* earlier in this appendix. You can also reference the sections and cells shown in this table for a page.

> **Note** To show the ShapeSheet window for a page or master, make sure nothing is selected on the page, and then click **Show ShapeSheet** on the **Window** menu. If Visio is running in developer mode, you can right-click the page, and then click **Show ShapeSheet** on the shortcut menu.

Section or row	Cell	Section index	Row index	Cell index
Layers section	Layers.Name[*i*] Layers.Visible[*i*] Layers.Status[*i*][1] Layers.Print[*i*] Layers.Active[*i*] Layers.Locked[*i*] Layers.Snap[*i*] Layers.Glue[*i*] Layers.Color[*i*] Layers.NameUniv[*i*][1] Layers.ColorTrans[*i*]	visSectionLayer	visRowLayer + *i*	visLayerName visLayerVisible visLayerStatusvisLayerPrint visLayerActive visLayerLock visLayerSnap visLayerGlue visLayerColor visLayerNameUniv visLayerColorTrans
Page Layout section	PlaceStyle PlaceDepth PlowCode ResizePage DynamicsOff EnableGrid CtrlAsInput BlockSizeX BlockSizeY AvenueSizeX AvenueSizeY RouteStyle PageLineJumpDirX PageLineJumpDirY	visSectionObject	visRowPageLayout	visPLOPlaceSyle visPLOPlaceDepth visPLOPlowCode visPLOResizePage visPLODynamicsOff visPLOEnableGrid visPLOCtrlAsInput visPLOBlockSizeX visPLOBlockSizeY visPLOAvenueSizeX visPLOAvenueSizeY visPLORouteSyle visPLOJumpDirX visPLOJumpDirY

Section, Row, and Cell Indices for Pages *(continued)*

Section or row	Cell	Section index	Row index	Cell index
	LineToNodeX			visPLOLineToNodeX
	LineToNodeY			visPLOLineToNodeY
	LineToLineX			visPLOLineToLineX
	LineToLineY			visPLOLineToLineY
	LineJumpFactorX			visPLOJumpFactorX
	LineJumpFactorY			visPLOJumpFactorY
	LineJumpCode			visPLOJumpCode
	LineJumpStyle			visPLOJumpStyle
	LineAdjustFrom			visPLOLineAdjustFrom
	LineAdjustTo			visPLOLineAdjustTo
	PlaceFlip			visPLOPlaceFlip
	LineRouteExt			visPLOLineRouteExt
Page Properties section	PageWidth	visSectionObject	visRowPage	visPageWidth
	PageHeight			visPageHeight
	PageScale			visPageScale
	DrawingScale			visPageDrawingScale
	ShdwOffsetX			visPageShdwOffsetX
	ShdwOffsetY			visPageShdwOffsetY
	DrawingSizeType			visPageDrawSizeType
	DrawingScaleType			visPageDrawScaleType
	InhibitSnap			visPageInhibitSnap
Ruler & Grid section	XRulerOrigin	visSectionObject	visRowRulerGrid	visXRulerOrigin
	YRulerOrigin			visYRulerOrigin
	XRulerDensity			visXRulerDensity
	YRulerDensity			visYRulerDensity
	XGridOrigin			visXGridOrigin
	YGridOrigin			visYGridOrigin
	XGridDensity			visXGridDensity
	YGridDensity			visYGridDensity
	XGridSpacing			visXGridSpacing
	YGridSpacing			visYGridSpacing

[1]This cell does not appear in the ShapeSheet window.

Section, Row, and Cell Indices for Documents

You can reference some of the same sections and cells for a document that you can reference for a shape: Custom Properties, Hyperlinks, Scratch, and User-Defined Cells sections. For information on these sections and cells, see *Sections, Row, and Cell Indices for Shapes* earlier in this appendix. You can also reference the section and cells shown in this table for a document.

> **Note** To show the ShapeSheet window for a document, open the **Drawing Explorer** (on the **View** menu, click **Drawing Explorer Window**), right-click the document, and then click **Show ShapeSheet** on the shortcut menu.

Section or row	Cell	Section index	Row index	Cell index
Document Properties section	PreviewQuality PreviewScopeOutput Format LockPreview	visSectionObject	visRowDoc	visDocPreviewQuality visDocPreviewScope visDocOutputFormat visDocLockPreview

Tab Cells and Row Types

The tab settings for a shape's text are accessible from a program by section, row, and cell index. In Microsoft Visio, you can display and change tab settings by clicking **Text** on the **Format** menu, and then clicking **Tabs** or by using the Tabs section in the ShapeSheet window.

Section index	Row index	Cell index
visSectionTab	visRowTab + *i*	0 ... 180

The Tabs section contains a row for each set of tabs defined for the shape. Each row contains three cells for each tab stop defined in that row, up to 60 tab stops. Cells for the entire row are indexed starting with zero (0).

- The number of tab stops in a row is stored in cell **visTabStopCount**.
- The position of the *j*th tab stop (*j*>0) is stored in cell ((*j*-1)*3) + **visTabPos**.
- The alignment of the *j*th tab stop is stored in cell ((*j*-1)*3) + **visTabAlign**.

Tab stop	Index	Description
	0	Number of active tabs in the row
1	1	Position of the first tab
1	2	Alignment code for the first tab
1	3	Reserved
2	4	Position of the second tab
2	5	Alignment code for the second tab
2	6	Reserved
...	...	...
60	178	Position of the 60th tab
60	179	Alignment code for the 60th tab
60	180	Reserved

The number of tabs that can be set depends on the tab row type. You can change the row type by setting the **Shape** object's **RowType** property for the tab section and row to one of the row tag constants in the following table.

Constant	Description
visTagTab0	Zero tab stops
visTagTab2	Zero, one, or two tab stops
visTagTab10	Zero to 10 tab stops
visTagTab60	Zero to 60 tab stops

Glossary

1-D shape Either a straight line you draw using Microsoft Visio drawing tools or a shape that has a begin point and an end point, either of which can be glued between other shapes to connect them. A 1-D shape behaves like a line.

2-D shape A shape that has eight selection handles that you can use to resize the shape. Most closed shapes, such as rectangles and ellipses, are 2-D shapes. A 2-D shape behaves like a box.

Action 1. A user-defined menu item associated with a shape. When the shape is selected, the item appears on the shortcut menu and on the **Actions** submenu of the **Shape** menu. 2. A program or Microsoft Visio command that runs in response to an event.

Active document The document that is currently available for editing in an instance of Microsoft Visio.

Active page The drawing page that is currently available for editing in a Visio document.

ActiveX control An object you can place on a user form or drawing that has its own set of properties, methods, and events, such as a toolbar button.

Add-on A program that extends Microsoft Visio through Automation references to Visio objects, methods, and properties.

Alignment box The rectangle that appears around shapes and objects from other applications as you move them.

Anchor point A fixed point that anchors a "rubber-band" line, whose other end is connected to a control handle. Anchor points are visible only when live dynamics has been disabled for a document. When live dynamics is disabled, the rubber-band line stretches and shrinks to provide visual feedback as the user moves the control handle, but it does not affect the behavior of the control handle.

Anchored window A window that anchors to the inside edge of the drawing area. Anchored windows have an AutoHide feature so they can collapse or expand.

Angle of rotation The angle of the orientation of a shape's local coordinate system with respect to its parent coordinate system. The angle of rotation is specified in the Angle cell of the Shape Transform section.

Angular unit Unit in which angles are expressed in ShapeSheet cells.

Antiscaling Behavior in which a shape is not sized according to the drawing scale of a page. Visio automatically antiscales shapes when the drawing scale of the master exceeds the range of eight.

Argument A constant, variable, or expression passed to a procedure, such as a function.

Attribute An individual formatting element, such as line color, fill color, or line weight, that you can apply to shapes. A style can have more than one attribute.

Automation A means by which an application can incorporate or extend the functionality of another application by using its objects.

Background A page that appears behind another page in a drawing. Shapes on a background page are visible from the foreground page, but cannot be selected or edited unless the background page is first made active.

Begin point The selection handle at the beginning of a 1-D shape. The begin point is marked by an x.

Bitmap An image stored as a pattern of dots. A scanned photograph or graphic that you create in a paint program is stored as a bitmap.

Boolean value A data type with only two possible values—TRUE or FALSE. When numeric types are converted to Boolean values, zero (0) becomes FALSE and all other values become TRUE.

Bow The distance from the midpoint of a circular arc to the midpoint of the arc's chord.

Cell reference Used in formulas in a ShapeSheet spreadsheet to calculate the value of one cell on the basis of the value of another cell.

Center of rotation The point around which a shape or text block rotates. When you select a two-dimensional (2-D) shape with the **Rotation** tool, its center of rotation is marked by a circle with a plus sign inside it. By default, the center of rotation is at the center of the shape. You can move the center of rotation by dragging it with the **Rotation** tool. Also known as pin.

Chord A line that connects the endpoints of an arc.

Class module In a Microsoft Visual Basic or Visual Basic for Applications (VBA) project, a module containing the definition of a class (its properties and methods).

Client application In Automation, the application (such as your program) that uses the objects exposed by a server application, such as Microsoft Visio. The client application creates instances of the objects and then sets their properties or invokes their methods to make the objects serve the application.

COM (Component Object Model) add-in Compiled code that extends the functionality of Visio or any product that supports COM add-ins. A COM add-in is typically a dynamic-link library (DLL) that is specially registered for loading by Microsoft Visio and other Microsoft Office or Office XP applications.

Connection point A point on a shape to which a connector can be glued. You can create new connection points inside, outside, or on the perimeter of a shape using the **Connection Point** tool. Each of a shape's connection points is marked with a blue x when **Connection Points** is selected on the **View** menu.

Connector Any one-dimensional (1-D) shape that can be glued between two shapes in a drawing to connect the shapes. You can also use lines and other shapes you draw as connectors.

Control An object you can place on a user form or drawing that has its own set of properties, methods, and events, such as a toolbar button.

Control handle A handle that controls a shape's behavior in special ways. For example, you can create a control handle so the user can adjust the roundness of a shape's corners, reshape an arrow, or drag a connector directly out of a two-dimensional (2-D) shape.

Control point 1. The circular handle that appears on a line, arc, or spline (or a line, arc, or spline segment) when it is selected with the **Pencil** tool. You can drag a control point to change the curvature of an arc or ellipse. 2. A point that influences the curvature of a spline segment.

Control polygon A series of straight line segments that connect all the control points of a single spline.

Coordinates A pair of numbers that indicates the position of a point in relation to the origin of a shape, a group, or the page. The *x*-coordinate indicates the horizontal position, and the *y*-coordinate indicates the vertical position.

Custom color A color in a Visio drawing that is stored with a shape as an RGB or HSL value rather than as an index to the document's color palette. A custom color is saved only with the shape that it is applied to.

Custom property User-specified data associated with a shape. For example, a shape that represents an engine part could have custom properties that identify its part number, price, and number of items in stock.

Default units The units of measure used to display a value in a ShapeSheet cell if no units of measure are explicitly specified. Default drawing and page units are properties of a drawing page. Default angular and text units are application settings.

Design mode The state of Microsoft Visio in which you can insert ActiveX controls on a drawing page, move and size controls, and set their properties. The document's mode is synchronized with that of its Microsoft Visual Basic for Applications (VBA) project, so both the document and its project are always in the same mode. While a document is in design mode, none of its objects (including controls) issues events.

Digital certificate Security information entered into a program by the developer or by a third-party company that identifies the developer of a component as a trusted source. The main purpose of the digital certificate is to ensure that the public key contained in the certificate belongs to the entity to which the certificate was issued.

Digital signature Binary data that is calculated by applying an algorithm to the original data (in this case, the macro code) and a numeric private key. The private key has a corresponding public key. A digital signature can be used to prove that the data really is from the user or source that the digital signature claims it to be from.

Direction handle The handle that appears on a selected connection point to indicate its direction. The direction handle determines whether the shape rotates when it is glued to another shape.

Docked window A window that is fixed along the outside of any of the four borders of the drawing window.

Document sheet See Page sheet.

Document stencil A stencil that contains a copy of any master ever used on any page in the file. Masters on the document stencil are used to draw their instances in the drawing file. A document stencil is stored in a drawing or template file.

Domain of influence The portion of a spline, specified as a number of spline knots, whose curvature is influenced by a single control point.

Drawing All the shapes on a foreground page together with all the shapes on any assigned background pages.

Drawing file A file that stores one or more Visio drawings. Drawing files have the .vsd or .vdx file name extension. A drawing file can contain one or more pages. Every drawing file has its own stencil, called a document stencil, which contains all the masters you used on any of the drawing pages in that file, even if you deleted them from the drawing page. To view the document stencil, on the **File** menu, point to **Stencils**, and then click **Document Stencil**.

Drawing page The printable area in a drawing window that contains a drawing. A page can be either a foreground or a background page. Each page has a size, which usually corresponds to a standard paper size, and it has a scale.

Drawing scale The ratio of a page scale to a specified number of drawing units, such as 1 cm = 1 m.

Drawing unit Dimensions that reflect the actual size of objects represented by shapes in a Visio drawing. For example, in an architectural drawing that uses the scale 1 cm = 1 m, the drawing unit is meters.

Drawn shape A shape created using Microsoft Visio drawing tools.

Dynamic glue A type of glue behavior in which the endpoint of a connector can move from one connection point to another as the connected shapes are moved. Also called walking glue.

Eccentricity handle The circle that appears at each end of a dotted line when a control point of an elliptical arc is selected with the **Pencil** tool. Moving an eccentricity handle changes the angle and magnitude of an arc's eccentricity.

End point The selection handle at the end of a one-dimensional (1-D) shape. The end point is marked by a plus sign (+).

Endpoint Either of the square handles that appear at the beginning or end of a selected line, arc, or other one-dimensional (1-D) shape. The endpoint at the beginning of the shape (begin point) is marked by an x. The endpoint at the end of the shape (end point) is marked by a plus sign (+).

Enhanced metafile One of two metafile formats that is designed for applications written to run with the Win32 application programming interface (API). The enhanced metafile format is standardized, and pictures that are stored in this format can be copied from one Win32-based application to another. Because pictures in this format are truly device independent, they are guaranteed to maintain their shape and proportion on any output device.

Event An occurrence in an instance of Microsoft Visio, such as a change to a shape formula or the deletion of a page.

Event object A Visio object you create to handle Visio events. An **Event** object pairs an event with an action—either to run an add-on or to notify an object in your program that the event occurred. When the event occurs, the **Event** object fires, triggering its action.

Event procedure In a Microsoft Visual Basic or Visual Basic for Applications (VBA) program, code that is executed when an event occurs. For example, a button on a Visual Basic form usually has an event procedure to handle the **Click** event.

Event sink In a Visual Basic for Applications (VBA) program, a class that receives events fired by a particular kind of Visio object. In a stand-alone Visual Basic, C, or C++ program, an object that receives the notification sent by a Visio **Event** object and that enables two-way communication between a stand-alone solution and a Visio instance.

Explicit units Units of measure specified as part of a number-unit pair so that the result is always displayed using the units specified. For example, the value "3 mm" always appears as "3 mm" in a ShapeSheet spreadsheet.

Expression A combination of constants, operators, functions, and references to ShapeSheet cells that results in a value.

Field A placeholder in text that displays information, such as dimensions, dates, and times, in a specified format. A field might display the date and time a drawing is printed, a shape's angle of rotation, or the result of a formula you write. Fields are automatically updated when you change a drawing.

Fill The color and pattern inside a filled shape. The default fill in Microsoft Visio is solid white.

Floating window A window that can appear anywhere on the screen. A floating window is always on top of other windows.

Foreground page The top page of a drawing. Shapes on the foreground page appear in front of shapes on the background page and are not visible when you edit the background of the drawing.

Form A file in a Microsoft Visual Basic or Visual Basic for Applications (VBA) project with the file name extension .frm that contains user interface controls, such as command buttons and text boxes.

Format 1. To affect the appearance of a shape (such as the thickness and color of its lines, the color and pattern inside the shape, or its font) either by using a style or by applying individual attributes. 2. The appearance of a shape.

Format picture A character string that specifies the display format for the result of an expression, such as a custom property value or text field output. For example, the format picture "m/d/yy" causes a date to be displayed in the format "12/31/97."

Formula An expression that is entered in a ShapeSheet cell, which returns a value.

Formula bar The portion of a ShapeSheet window that you enter a formula in for the selected ShapeSheet cell. You can also enter formulas directly into a cell.

Function A procedure that takes arguments and returns a value. If a function takes no arguments, it must be followed by an empty set of parentheses (). Microsoft Visio includes mathematical, trigonometric, geometric, event, date and time, color, logical, statistical, and other functions.

Geometry An arrangement of vertices and segments that define a path.

Glue Shape behavior that causes one shape to stay connected to another, even if the shape to which it is glued moves. Gluing is a directional operation: If shape A is glued to shape B, shape B is not glued to shape A.

Grid Nonprinting horizontal and vertical lines displayed at regular intervals on the page. The grid makes it easier to align shapes and position them precisely.

Grid lines The faint vertical and horizontal lines that appear in the drawing window when the grid is turned on. You can use grid lines to help position shapes precisely.

Grid origin The point that defines the layout of grid lines on the drawing page. A vertical grid line and a horizontal grid line pass through the grid origin, and all other grid lines are drawn at specified intervals from these reference lines. By default, the grid origin is the lower-left corner of the drawing page.

Group A shape composed of one or more shapes. A group can also include other groups and objects from other applications. A group can be moved and sized as a single shape, but its members retain their original appearance and attributes.

Guide A reference line that can be dragged into the drawing window to help position and align shapes precisely. A horizontal guide is dragged from the horizontal ruler, a vertical guide from the vertical ruler.

Guide point A reference point that can be dragged into the drawing window to help position shapes precisely. A guide point is dragged from the upper-left corner of the drawing window, where the horizontal and vertical rulers meet.

Handle A control that appears when you select a shape. You can use handles to edit a shape. Handles vary according to the shape you select and the tool you use to select it. For example, when you select a shape with the **Pointer** tool, the shape displays selection handles that you can drag to change its size and proportions. When you select a shape with the **Rotation** tool, the shape displays rotation handles that you can drag to rotate the shape.

Height-based formula A formula whose value varies only with the height of the shape.

Implicit units Units of measure specified as part of a number-unit pair in which the result is displayed using a specified measurement system, which might not coincide with the units originally entered. For example, the expression "1 [in.,d]" specifies that the value is initially interpreted as 1 inch, but the *d* indicates that the result is displayed using the default drawing units of the current page. If the drawing units are centimeters, the ShapeSheet spreadsheet displays "2.54 cm."

Infinite line A line containing cells defining two points in the local coordinate space through which Microsoft Visio renders a line of indefinite length. Guides are defined as infinite lines.

Inherited formula A formula that is stored in a style or a master but used by an instance as if the formula were stored locally with the shape. A change to a formula in the style or master affects all shapes that inherit the formula and do not have an overriding local formula. A change to a style will overwrite a local formula unless you explicitly preserve local overrides.

Instance 1. A shape that is based on a master. 2. A running image of a Microsoft Windows-based application.

Internal units The units of measure that Visio uses internally to store dimensional values. These are inches for linear measurements and radians for angular measurements.

Knot A real number that marks the boundary between polynomial pieces on a spline.

Layer A named category of shapes. You can organize shapes in your drawing by assigning them to layers. You can selectively view, edit, print, or lock layers, as well as control whether shapes on a layer can be snapped to or glued to. Layers do not affect the stacking order of objects on a page.

Library The Microsoft Visio type library is a file that contains definitions of the objects, properties, methods, events, and constants that Visio exposes to Automation.

Local coordinates The coordinate system whose origin is the lower-left corner of a shape's width-height box. The geometry of a shape is expressed in local coordinates.

Local formatting Individual formatting attributes, such as line width, fill color, or font size, that you apply to a selected shape by using a command on the **Format** menu, such as **Line**, **Fill**, or **Text**. Local formatting is most useful when you want to give a unique look to one shape, or to just a few shapes. Changes to formatting in a style override local formatting unless you explicitly preserve local overrides.

Local formula A formula that is stored locally in a cell of a shape instead of being inherited from a master or a style. A local formula overrides changes to the corresponding cell in the master that the shape is an instance of. Also called local override.

Local name The name for any shape, master, page, style, row, or layer that a user sees in the user interface; objects also have a universal name that is visible to only Automation clients.

Local override See local formula.

Lock A setting that limits the ways that users can change a shape. For example, a lock on a selection handle prevents the user from resizing a shape using the selection handle.

Macro 1. A Microsoft Visual Basic for Applications (VBA) program that extends Microsoft Visio through Automation references to Visio objects, methods, and properties. 2. A procedure that takes no arguments and is contained within a module within a project stored in a Visio template, stencil, or drawing.

Master A shape on a stencil that you use over and over to create drawings. When you drag a shape from a stencil onto the drawing page, the shape becomes an instance of that master.

Master icon A representation of a master, which appears on a stencil. You select a master by clicking its icon.

Metafile An array of variable-length structures (called metafile records) that stores a picture in a device-independent format. Because a metafile is in a standard format, applications can exchange them and use them for image storage.

Method A procedure that acts on an object.

MDI frame window A multiple document interface (MDI) frame window has a sizing border, a title bar, a window menu, a minimize button, and a maximize button. In Microsoft Visio, the drawing window (including drawing windows created by add-ons), stand-alone stencil windows (including stencil windows created by add-ons), the ShapeSheet window and the icon editing window are MDI frame windows.

Modeless activity A program activity that does not terminate when control returns to Microsoft Visio. For example, an add-on may open a modeless window, which remains open after the add-on terminates.

Module In a Microsoftâ Visual Basicâ or Visual Basic for Applications (VBA) project, code that is a set of declarations followed by procedures. A standard module contains only procedure, type, and data declarations and definitions.

Multiplicity The number of times a spline knot is repeated.

Multishape A merged shape with multiple geometry sections that is designed to change its appearance based on its current setting (for example, a user might click a command on the shape's shortcut menu to show or hide part of the shape). Multishapes are created by using the **Combine** or **Join** command (on the **Shape** menu, point to **Operations**).

Nonperiodic spline A spline with defined endpoints. If a spline's begin point and end point coincide, the spline is closed.

Notification sink In a Microsoft Visual Basic for Applications (VBA) program, a class that receives events fired by a particular kind of Microsoft Visio object. In a stand-alone Visual Basic, C, or C++ program, an object that receives the notification sent by a Visio **Event** object and that enables two-way communication between a stand-alone solution and a Visio instance.

Number-unit pair An expression that includes a number and a corresponding dimension. For example, "1 cm" is a number-unit pair.

NURBS (Nonuniform rational B-spline) A commonly used way to represent curves, such as those drawn by the **Freeform** tool, mathematically.

Object A program element that a server application exposes via Automation to a client application. Objects in Microsoft Visio are hierarchically related as specified in the Visio object model.

Operator A symbol that denotes or performs a mathematical or logical operation.

Origin The (0,0) point of a Cartesian coordinate system. In Microsoft Visio, the origin is always the lower-left corner of the coordinate system of a shape, group, or page. Dimensions of a shape, such as its width and height, and the center of rotation are measured from its origin. The location of a shape in relation to its parent (a group or the page) is measured from the parent's origin.

Page The printable area in a drawing window that contains a drawing. A page can be either a foreground or a background page. Each page has a size, which usually corresponds to a standard paper size, and a scale, which Microsoft Visio preconfigures for particular drawing types.

Page coordinates The coordinate system whose origin is the lower-left corner of a drawing page.

Page scale The number of page units that represent the number of drawing units specified in the drawing scale. For example, if the drawing scale is 1 cm = 1 m, the page scale is 1 cm.

Page sheet A ShapeSheet spreadsheet that represents a page.

Page unit Dimensions that reflect the size of shapes as drawn on a Microsoft Visio drawing page. For example, in an architectural drawing that uses the scale 1 cm = 1 meter, the page unit is centimeters.

Parametric The ability of a shape in a Microsoft Visio drawing to adjust its geometry and other attributes according to the values of certain parameters.

Parent The next higher level in the coordinate system hierarchy. If a shape is a member of a group, its parent is the group. If a shape is not a member of a group, its parent is the drawing page.

Parent coordinates The coordinate system of a shape's parent. If the shape is in a group, the parent coordinate system is the group's local coordinate system. If the shape is not in a group, the parent coordinate system is the page coordinate system.

Path A series of contiguous line, arc, or spline segments. A shape can have more than one path.

Periodic spline A closed spline with no defined endpoints.

Persistence The lifetime of a variable, procedure, or object. For example, an object can persist while Microsoft Visio is running. An object that can store **Event** objects between Visio sessions is said to persist events.

Pin The point around which a shape or text block rotates. When you select a two-dimensional (2-D) shape with the **Rotation** tool, its pin is marked by a circle with a plus sign (+) inside it. A shape's pin expressed in parent coordinates (the PinX and PinY cells of the Shape Transform section) defines the shape's location on the drawing page. Also known as center of rotation.

Placeable shape A two-dimensional (2-D) shape that is set to work with routable connectors and automatic layout. If a shape is set as placeable, a routable connector can detect and avoid crossing through it. You can set a shape as placeable in the **Behavior** dialog box, by selecting **Lay out and route around** in the **Placement behavior** list. If you glue a routable connector, such as the dynamic connector, to a 2-D shape, Visio automatically sets the 2-D shape as placeable.

Polyline A contiguous set of line segments represented in a Microsoft Visio drawing by a PolyLine row in a shape's Geometry section. Lines represented as a PolyLine row are equivalent to lines represented as a sequence of LineTo rows, but a PolyLine row is more efficient. In Visio drawings, imported drawings often contain polylines.

Primary selection The first selected shape in a multiple selection, indicated on the drawing page by green selection handles. When a multiple selection is combined, the formatting of the primary selection is applied to the new shape. In a **Selection** object, the primary selection is the first item in the object's **Shapes** collection.

Procedure A named sequence of statements executed as a unit. For example, **Function**, **Property**, and **Sub** are types of procedures.

Procedure template The beginning and ending statements that are automatically inserted in the code window when you specify a **Function**, **Property**, or **Sub** procedure in the **Add Procedure** dialog box in the Visual Basic Editor.

Project In Microsoft Visual Basic for Applications (VBA), the code that you write that is saved with a Visio file. You can create only one project for a Visio document, but that project can consist of any number of modules, class modules, and user forms.

Property A named attribute of an object. Properties define object characteristics, such as size, color, and screen location, or the state of an object, such as enabled or disabled.

Range of eight A rule for handling instances whose scale is different from that of the drawing page. If the ratio of a master's drawing scale differs from that of the drawing page by less than a factor of eight, the instance is scaled appropriately for the drawing page. Otherwise, the instance is antiscaled.

Resize To change the dimensions of a shape.

Rotation handle A circular handle that appears at a corner of a shape's selection rectangle when you select the shape with the **Rotation** tool. Dragging a rotation handle changes the shape's angle of rotation.

Routable connector A one-dimensional (1-D) connector that automatically changes its path to avoid crossing through two-dimensional (2-D) placeable shapes that lie between the two shapes the connector connects. When you select a routable connector, it displays midpoints and vertices that you can drag to edit the connector's path manually.

Run mode The state of Microsoft Visio in which you can use Microsoft ActiveX controls that were inserted in design mode. For example, you can click a command button to run its **Click** event handler. A Visio document opens in run mode by default, unless the macros in the document have been disabled.

Scope The extent to which a variable, procedure, or object persists in a running program. The scope of an item typically depends on where it is declared. For example, the scope of a variable declared in a procedure is the procedure—when the procedure finishes executing, the variable goes out of scope.

ScreenTip Descriptive text that appears in a box when you pause with the mouse pointer over an item on the toolbar, a master icon on a stencil, or a control handle on a shape.

Segment An arc, straight line, or part of a spline.

Selection Shapes in a drawing that you have selected and can perform actions upon. Selected shapes have selection handles. Selection also refers to text selected in a text block. Selected text is highlighted when it is editable.

Selection handle A square handle that appears on a shape selected with the **Pointer** tool. Selection handles indicate that you can move or size the shape.

Selection net A means of selecting more than one shape at a time by dragging the **Pointer** tool to define a rectangular area that encloses all the shapes to be selected.

Selection rectangle The dotted line that surrounds selected shapes or objects from other applications when they are selected.

Server application An application that provides objects that can be controlled through Automation. A server application makes the objects accessible to other applications and provides, or exposes, the properties and methods that control them.

Shape 1. An open or closed object that is created using Microsoft Visio drawing tools or commands. 2. A grouped collection of shapes. 3. An instance of a master dropped in a drawing. 4. In a program, any item represented by a **Shape** object—a shape, group, guide, guide point, or page sheet of a drawing page or a master.

ShapeSheet spreadsheet The data that defines a shape, group, guide, guide point, or page. For example, a ShapeSheet spreadsheet describes a shape's dimensions, its angle and center of rotation, and the styles that determine the shape's appearance. ShapeSheet spreadsheets can contain formulas that define how the shape behaves when it is moved or sized and how it responds to events. The ShapeSheet spreadsheet is displayed in a ShapeSheet window, and it is accessible through the Visio Automation programming interface.

Sink object In a Microsoft Visual Basic for Applications (VBA) program, a class that receives events fired by a particular kind of Visio object. In a stand-alone Visual Basic, C, or C++ program, an object that receives the notification sent by a Visio **Event** object and that enables two-way communication between a stand-alone solution and a Visio instance. Also known as event sink, notification sink.

SmartShapes technology SmartShapes technology enables a shape's behavior to be customized with formulas in the ShapeSheet spreadsheet.

Snap The ability of shapes, guides, grid lines, and other elements in Microsoft Visio to pull shapes and other elements into position when they are moved and sized.

Spline A freeform curve that is based on a polynomial equation.

Spline knot A real number that marks the boundary between polynomial pieces on a spline.

Stacking order The order in which shapes overlap other shapes on the page and the order in which shapes are selected. You can change the stacking order of shapes by using commands on the **Shape** menu.

Stand-alone stencil A Microsoft Visio file with a .vss or .vsx file name extension that contains a collection of masters and is usually referred to simply as a stencil. Unlike a document stencil, a stand-alone stencil opens in a stand-alone window (not an anchored window) and usually does not have an accompanying drawing. You can't make stand-alone stencils float, or dock them to a side of the drawing window.

Static glue A type of glue behavior in which the endpoint of a connector remains fixed to a particular connection point, no matter how the shape it is glued to moves.

Stencil A collection of masters associated with a particular Visio drawing type, or template. By default, stencils that open with a template open in anchored windows, docked on the left side of the drawing window. You can make stencils in anchored windows float, or you can dock them on any side of the drawing window. You can open stencil files (.vss or .vsx files) independently of a template.

String A sequence of zero or more characters enclosed by quotation marks, for example, `"This is a string"`. Some user interfaces may automatically add and remove the quotation marks for better readability.

Style A collection of attributes that has a name and is saved with a template or drawing file.

Subdivision The divisions between grid lines and between intervals of the ruler. The options are **Fine**, **Normal**, and **Coarse**.

Subselect To select individual shapes within a group.

Template A Microsoft Visio file that opens one or more files and windows and can contain styles and settings for a particular kind of drawing; for example, the appropriate scale and grid. You can create a new drawing that has a template's styles and settings by opening the template file. Template files have the file name extension .vst or .vtx.

Text block The text area associated with a shape that appears when you click the shape with the **Text** tool or **Text Block** tool, or when you select the shape and start typing. You can size, move, and rotate a text block with respect to its shape's local coordinate system.

Tile 1. To print oversized drawing pages on multiple sheets of paper so they can be assembled into a complete drawing. 2. To arrange open windows side by side in the Microsoft Visio window.

Toolbar A row of boxes, buttons, and tools that appears below the menu bar in the Microsoft Visio window. To choose which toolbars you want to display and to create custom toolbars, on the **View** menu, point to **Toolbars**.

Type library A file that contains definitions of the objects, properties, methods, events, and constants that Microsoft Visio exposes to Automation.

Undo scope A sequence of undo units that are marked with a beginning and an end.

Undo stack A region of reserved memory where undo units are stored.

Undo unit An instance of a class that encapsulates the information that is necessary to reverse an action made by a user in the user interface or an Automation client.

Universal name The name for any shape, master, page, style, row, or layer used by Automation clients; objects may also have local names that are used in localized versions of an Automation solution. Universal names allow source code to remain unchanged for localized versions.

Unscaled drawing page A drawing page whose drawing scale is 1:1.

User form A file in a Microsoft Visual Basic or Visual Basic for Applications (VBA) project with the file name extension .frm that contains user interface controls, such as command buttons and text boxes.

Vertex One of the diamond-shaped handles that appear between two segments on a multiple-segment shape, or at the end of a segment. You can reshape a shape or connector by dragging its vertices.

Visio add-on See add-on.

Visio library A special dynamic-link library (DLL) that is loaded by Microsoft Visio at run time and can implement one or more Visio add-ons. A Visio library has the .vsl file name extension.

Visio type library A file that contains definitions of the objects, properties, methods, events, and constants that Microsoft Visio exposes to Automation.

Walking glue A type of glue behavior in which the endpoint of a connector can move from one connection point to another as the connected shapes are moved. More commonly known as dynamic glue.

Width-height box A rectangle orthogonal to a shape's local coordinate space with one corner at (0,0) and its opposite corner at (width,height).

Wizard An add-on that prompts the user for information to automate specific tasks.

Workspace list A list saved with a drawing, template, or stencil file that identifies the names of documents and windows to be opened, as well as the type, size, and location of the windows, based on their appearance when the file is saved.

XML (Extensible Markup Language) Extensible Markup Language (XML) is a meta-markup language that provides a format for describing structured data. XML provides basic syntax; all other elements are defined as needed. Microsoft Visio drawings, stencils, and templates can be saved in XML format with the file name extensions .vdx, .vsx, and .vtx, respectively.

Zero point 1. The location of the zero (0) on the horizontal or vertical ruler. 2. The point in the drawing window where the zero points of each ruler intersect. By default, the zero point is the lower-left corner of the drawing page.

Zoom The degree of magnification of a drawing in the drawing window. A zoom of 100% displays the drawing at the same size it will be when it is printed, unless you reduce or enlarge the printed output on the **Print Setup** tab in the **Page Setup** dialog box.

Index

Symbols

= (Equals sign) prefix to ShapeSheet formula 89
1-D Endpoints section 71
1-D shape connections
  automating 391
  connection points 176
  connectors 161
1-D shape formulas
  height-based 171
  smart formulas 165
1-D shape routing 165–166
1-D shapes
  behavior 34
  compared to 2-D 162
  converting 163
  described 161
  endpoints 35
  gallery 165
  gluing 396
  usability 162
1-dimensional line 163
128-bit value 336, 405
2-D shape connections
  automating 391
  connection points 176
2-D shapes
  behavior 34
  compared to 1-D 162
  converting 163
  described 161
  gluing 396
  placeable 165–166
  snap to grid 238
  usability 162
2-dimensional box 163
3-D boxes 127–129
32-bit color xxii

A

Accelerator object listing 469
Accelerators, deleting 485
AccelItem object 469
AccelItems collection 289
AccelTable object 469
AccelTables collection 289
Accept Dropped Shapes option 122
Access database 155
Action cell 143
Action command 142–143
Actions section 69, 71, 142, 149
ActionText property 482
Activate method 294
Active documents 326, 327
Active page 326
ActiveDocument property 327
ActivePage property 333
ActiveWindow property 315
ActiveX Automation controller 25
ActiveX controls 511
  adding 512
  ambient properties 516
  distributing 519
  getting 519
  handling events 517
  in design mode 515
  naming 518
  protecting 516
  run-time 517
  setting tabs 515
  with shapes 522
Add Control Handle To Shape option 188
Add method 334
Add Procedure dialog box 302
Add Shape To Groups On Drop Option 122
Add-In Manager 323
Add-ins 491
Add-ons
  creating undo scopes 527
  declaring 580
  registering 580
  running 581
  undoable action 523
  with Undo manager 526
AddAdvise method 433, 438, 441, 445, 577
Adding a Geometry section example 357
Adding menu items example 529
AddNamedRow method 405
Addon object 555

AddOnArgs property 560
AddonName property 482
AddonPaths property 538, 555
Addons collection 555
AddRef method 566, 570
AddRow method 355
AddSection method 355–356
Addsink.h 577
AddUndoUnit method 531
AlignBottom cell 397
AlignCenter cell 397
AlignLeft cell 397
Alignment boxes
  3-D box 129
  customizing 230, 247
  snap to grid 244
  updating 141
  with shapes 245–247
Alignment cell 397
Alignment section 71
AlignMiddle cell 397
AlignRight cell 397
AlignTop cell 397
All Styles list 209
Alt property 482
Ambient properties 516
Anchor points 140
ANG360( ) function 201
Angle cell, protecting 107
Angle field 105
Angle of rotation 84, 195
Angle values 74
Angled connectors 167–169
ANGTOPAR 177
Angular units 84
Angular values 201
Answer Wizard 536
Application object
  creating 550
  customizing 448
  getting 327, 551, 571
  in Visio object model 283, 286
  interfaces 448, 473
  properties 288
  references to 309
  releasing 551
Application object in Visual Basic example 427, 552
Application property 310
Arc tool 38, 109
Arcs
  controlling curves 108
  converting 113
  understanding 109
ArcTo row 110
Arguments
  functions 77
  object pointer 573
  passing 573
  running programs 560
  setting values 292
  string 573
  UniqueIDs 406
  VARIANT 574
Arithmetic operators 78
Arrays 367, 411
Arrow shapes 165
Arrow shapes example 13
Aspect ratio
  maintaining when resizing 169
Automation
  COM concepts 564–565
  connections 385
  described 283
  developers 19
  extracting 410
  in drawings 363
  library references 307
  programming for Visio application 295
  Reference (Visio) xxi
  server 15, 24
Automation and objects
  shapes 23, 403
  templates 23
  using 15
Automation in solutions
  implementing design 23
  integrating 24–25
  naming 546
  packaging 535
  programming languages 4, 14
  using 14
Available References list 307, 561

B

B-splines 115
BackColor property 516
Background pages 60, 378
Based On option 211
BaseID property 406
Basic Diagram template 556
BeforeDocumentClose event 419, 427
BeforeQuit event 445
BeforeShapeDelete event 18
Begin points 162
BeginArrow cell 223
BeginUndoScope method 528

BeginX and BeginY cells 123
BegTrigger cell 174
Behavior cells 139, 141
Bezier curves 338
Bitmaps 44
  editing 43
Bolt shape example 10
Boolean values 76, 154, 377, 407
Bows of arcs 108–109, 113
BSTR methods 572–573
Built-in Visio interface 473, 483, 489
Bus shape 165
Button 456

C

C-CPP folder 566
C/C++ programs
  controls 519
  copyright 547
  files on the Developing Microsoft Visio Solutions CD 566
  handling events 575
  programming 283, 564
Calculations for arc bows 113
Calculations for arc radius 113
CALLTHIS function 158
CanGlue cell 136, 139
Caption property 481
CD reference material xxiii
Cell object 15
  automating drawings 348
  error properties 316
  formulas 351
  in Visio object model 348
Cell object getting
  by index 349
  by name 349
  by row 349
  by section 349
  options 349
  shapes 398
Cell references
  control handles 138
  formulas 81
  in ShapeSheet spreadsheets 79
  nonstandard characters 83
  shape properties 13
  standard characters 82
  syntax 81, 82
  to other shapes 80
  within same shape 79
Cells
  formulas 76, 90, 348, 353
Cells, *continued*
  gluing 397
  in Events section 156
  locking 100
  scratch 89
  units of measure 84
Cells property
  formatting 330
  formulas 348
  getting 293, 349
CellsC property 383
CellSRC property 348, 361
CellsSRC property 384
Chair shape 136, 147
Change shape geometry example 147
Character Format section 185
Character section 71, 186, 194
Character string 405, 407
Characters property 340
Checked cell 143, 145
Checking command 145
CHM 538
Chords 109
Chr$ function 340
Circle shapes 109, 110, 111
Class module responding to events example 430
Class modules
  adding procedures 302
  code 428
  creating instances 429
  described 300
  handling events 428
  inserting 301
  transferring files 304
ClearCustomMenus method 489
Click event 460, 463
Clip art, importing 42
Closed shapes 33, 39
CLS 304
CmdNum property 482
CntrlType property 480
CoCreateAddonSink 577
Code
  copyright 54, 547
  digitally signing VBA projects 317
  examining 413
  extracting data 403, 410
  implementing 424
  protecting 317
  readability xxi
  transferring 27
  user interface 448
  writing 414, 549

Collections
  deleting objects 290
  iterating through 290, 361
  referring to objects 288
  verifying objects 316
Color indexes 219, 220
Color Palette command 221
Color Palette dialog box 220
Colors
  copying 221
  customizing 221
  defining HSL 219
  defining RGB 219
  managing 219
Colors collection 289
COM (Component Object Model) 284, 323
COM add-ins 26, 491
  loading 540
Combine command 41, 133, 148
Combine method 377
Combined shapes 119, 131
Combo box 456
Comma 551
Command bar buttons
  assigning images 459
Command bar controls 456
  adding 456
  coding 460, 463
  enabling 458
  properties 457
  showing 458
Command bar objects 448–449
  coding 460, 463
  creating 450
  deleting 455
  hiding 453
  protecting 463–464
  showing 453
Command button control 303
Command strings 558, 560
CommandBars property 455
Commands
  Combine 37
  Connect Shapes 166
  Fragment 37, 41
  Intersect 41
  Join 41
  Lay Out Shapes 165
  Lock Text 145
  Offset 41
  Operations 40
  Protection 72
  Section 69
Commands, *continued*
  shortcut menu 143
  Show Arms 149
  Subtract 41
  Trim 41
  Union 37
  Unlock Text 145
Component shapes
  3-D boxes 130
  parent pin 127
  protecting 131
  resizing 126
Compound object references 292
Concatenating 292
ConLineJumpCode cell 250
ConLineJumpDirX and ConLineJumpDirY cells 250
ConLineJumpStyle cell 250
Connect object, iterating 393
Connect object, working with 388
Connect Shapes command 166
Connected diagrams 388
  analyzing 392
  Automation 385
  creating 395–396
  getting information 389
  guidelines 392
Connecting shapes in flowchart example 400
Connection point tool 251
Connection points
  creating 179
  described 176
  directional editing 251
  inward 175
  inward/outward 176
  naming 180
  on grid lines 107
  outward 175
  types of 177
  understanding 175
  vectors 177
Connection points gluing 391, 396
Connection Points section 71, 79
Connections
  1-D and 2-D shapes 391
  analyzing 389–390, 392
  grouping effects 123
  in Visio solutions 385
  iterating 393
  working with 388
ConnectionsAdded event 419
ConnectionsDeleted event 419
Connector tool 166

Connectors
behavior of 250
defining glue behavior 173
gluing 173
layout options 248
routable and 1-D 165
creating 161, 167
Connects collection 388
Connects property 388
Consistency checklist testing 265
Constants
for connections 391
in library 561
Containers 80
ContainingMaster property 378
ContainingPage property 378
ContainingShape property 378
Context property 451, 453, 460
Contexts
switching 454
Visio user interface 451
Control dialog box 515
Control handles
behavior 140
cell references 138
described 137
on shapes 35
setting 141
shapes 136
text pins 188
Control handles
gluing cell pairs 397
Control point for arcs 110
Controller application 15
Controls
adding 303
ambient properties 516
at run time 517
customizing 511
distributing 519
handling events 517
in design mode 515
interacting shapes 522
naming 304, 518
protecting 516
setting tab order 515
stacking order 516
Controls adding 512
Controls for command bars 456
Controls section 35, 71, 136
Controls Toolbox 303
Convert To Group command 44
Converting shapes 1-D to 2-D 163
Coordinates
control handles 139
editing 74
flipping effect 104
for shapes 95
for vertices 95
height-based formulas 101
in text blocks 184
types of 95
zero point 96
Copy method 294, 339, 377
Copying shape elements 39
Copyright 54, 547
shapes 49
CorelDRAW! (.cdr) 43
Corners command 108
Count property 288, 290
CreateDrawing procedures 367
CreateObject function 27, 550, 553
Creating an undo unit example 531
Creating drawing from data example 414, 444
Currency property 155
Curves 108
Custom formula arrow example 103
Custom formulas 171
Custom line ends 231
Custom patterns
creating 223, 225
described 223
icons 225
inherited 224, 248
lines 229
Custom Properties
Dialog box 204
Section 71
Window 152
Custom Properties
adding 152, 403, 405
associating 149
defining 151–152
described 150
displaying 204
formats 154
getting cells 351
linking data 155
using 151
Custom properties for inventory control 151
Custom Scale option 256

Custom user interface
adding 448, 476, 512
comparing to Visio application 473
contexts 451
deleting items 483
described 486
designing 472
editing 475, 486
file 486, 488
hiding 482
loading 488
persistence 474
restoring 489
saving 487
scope of 474
toolbar buttons 479–480
working with 464
Custom.vsu 486
Customize dialog box 448
Customize Shape's Text option 188
CustomMenusFile property 488
Cut method 339, 377
CVisioAddOnSink helper class 577
CVisioApplication wrapper class 566
CVisioCell argument 573
CVisioDocument object 571
CVisioDocument wrapper class 569
CVisioMaster 574
CVisioPage 574

D

DAO (Data Access Objects) 24, 419
Data
custom linking 155
custom properties 150
exporting 414
extracting 410
integrating with programs 403
retrieving 407
storing 407
types 407, 410
verifying collection 414
with shapes 403
Data Access Objects (DAO) 24, 419
Data extracting 6, 24
Data saving
in other programs 411
storing 407
to disk 411
Data1, Data 2, and Data3 properties 341
Database Wizard 24, 155
Databases
custom linking 155
in Visio solutions 24
integrating solutions 419
Date or time property 154
Define Custom Properties dialog box 150
Define Styles command 210–211, 213, 216
Define Styles dialog box 210, 212, 217, 329
Degrees of angle 200
Delete method 339, 377, 383
Delete row command 74
DeleteSection method 359
DeleteShapesFlag argument 383
DEPENDSON function 157
Description box 313
Description property 328, 530
DeselectAll method 377
Design notes 263
Design-time license 519
Details pane, using 306
Developer
Reference (Visio) xxi
resources xxiv
toolbar 67
Developing Microsoft Visio Solutions on CD xxiii
Digital certificate and signatures 317
Dim statement 413
DisableCustomize property 464
Disabled cell 143, 146
Displaying pages 331
DistanceFromPoint 369
DLL 564, 578
DllMain 579
DLLs 25–26
Do procedure 530
Document
object formulas 348
Document master 11
Document object
comparing to 311
controlling scope 474
customizing 448, 466
described 286, 326
formulas 348
getting 327
in Masters collection 365
in Visio object model 286, 326
properties 288
ThisDocument 311
Document Properties section 71
Document property 288, 327, 329
Document stencils 12, 52
Document Stencil command 68

DocumentOpened event 419, 425
Documents
creating 556
editing 68
elements of 58
format of a Visio file 62
getting information 328
multiple pages 60
opening 59, 63
printing 330
saving 64, 299, 331
sharing data 403
Documents collection 286, 288–289, 311, 327, 364
Documents property 288
DontMoveChildren cell 124
Double variables 353, 407
DrawBezier method 338
Drawing development process 18
Drawing Explorer 209, 212
Drawing Explorer window 68
Drawing file document stencil 52
Drawing files
default styles 210
extracting data 6
validating model rules 7
working with objects 326
Drawing pages
arranging shapes 233
backgrounds 378
cell references 80
changing settings 381
editing objects 67
grids 237
guides 241
layering 381
reformatting shapes 213
styles 207
Drawing Scale section 256
Drawing scales
described 253
factors 256
in Masters 257
range of eight 257
setting up 256
testing 266
usability 255–256
Drawing shapes
closed 39
masters from 55
merging 40
repeating elements 39
Drawing tools
Arc tool 38
Described 37
Ellipse tool 38
Freeform tool 38
Line tool 38
Pencil tool 38
Rectangle tool 38
Drawing units 84, 253–254, 256
Drawing window, tiled view 73
DrawingPaths property 538
Drawings
connected 392
extracting data 410
file sizes 545
from masters 364
linking Help files 535
opening 59, 63
printing 330
saving 64, 299, 331
sharing data 403
with Automation 363
Drawings adding
ActiveX controls 511–512
controls 515
creating 345
pages 334
Drawings to specifications 12
DrawLine method 338
DrawNURBS method 338
DrawOval method 338
DrawPolyline method 338
DrawRectangle 338
DrawSpline method 338
Drop actions box 272
Drop method 339, 343, 366
Drop-down list box 456
DropMany method 366
DropManyU method 546
Dual interfaces 565
Duplicate method 339, 377
Duration property 154
DWG files 115
Dynamic Connector shape 165, 180–181
Dynamic connector tool 165
Dynamic connectors 169, 180, 250
Dynamic glue 173, 399
Dynamic intersection 181
Dynamic-link libraries (.dll) 25–26, 564, 578

E

Early binding 561, 565
Eccentricity handles 35
Eccentricity of arcs 35, 111–112
EditMaster command 56, 69
Edit menu 56
Edit Text Of Group option 189
EditPattern command 225
Ellipse tool 38
Elliptical arcs 108–109, 111–113
Enable Live Dynamics feature 140
Enabled property 453, 458, 469, 483
Encapsulated PostScript (.eps) 43
EndArrow cell 223
Endpoints 35, 162, 172
EndTrigger cell 174
EndUndoScope method 528
EnterScope event 528
Equals sign prefix to ShapeSheet formula 89
Equipment rack shapes example 12
Error function 316
Error handling 315, 557
Error property 316
EVALTEXT function 192
Event
  BeforeShapeDelete event 18
  ShapeAdded 17
Event filters 433
Event formulas
  described 156
  optimizing 159
  simulating 157
Event handlers 425, 522
Event object
  add-on runs 437
  creating 441
  defining 431
  filter 433
  notifying 438, 445
  performing 433
  persisting 437
  properties 422, 436
  query 441
  scope 431
EventDblClick cell 156
EventDrop cell 156
EventInfo property 436
EventList collection 431, 433, 577
EventList.Add 574
EventList.AddAdvise 574
Events
  class module code 428
  defining a class 428
Events, *continued*
  fired by 424, 426
  handling 422
  implementing code 424
  initializing 429
  paired with actions 431
  persistence 437
  procedures 517, 425
  protocol 574
  receiving 295
  running 544
  section 71, 156–157
  verifying 528
Events with undo scope 528
EventsEnabled property 522
EventXFMod cell 156–157, 174, 177
Examples
  1-D shapes 164
  adding a Geometry section 357
  adding a new menu and menu item 529
  Application object in Visual Basic 427, 552
  arrow shapes 13
  change shape geometry 147
  Class module responding to events 430
  connecting shapes in flowchart 399
  creating 3-D box group 128
  creating an undo unit 531
  creating drawing from data 414, 444
  custom formula arrow 103
  custom properties for inventory control list 151
  equipment rack shapes 12
  extracting data from drawing 410
  field sales automation 8
  First Sub procedure in module 299
  floor plan 336
  getting layer objects 382
  Hello World program 345
  iterating through connections 393
  iterating through Pages collection 379
  kitchen island group 125
  monitoring power consumption 16
  moving plan for office 6
  network equipment shapes 12
  placing shapes in drawings 367
  reorganizing office 6
  resizing an arrow 100
  security system 9, 24
  swimming pool shape 255
  totaling values and monitoring events 16
  word balloon with control handle 141
Excel 287
EXD files 515
Executable (.exe) files 25, 437, 538

Existing Visio Shapes, adapting 45
ExitScope event 528
Export File command 304
Export File dialog box 317
Extracting data from drawing example 410

F

Features, new xxi
Field codes 341
Field dialog box 204
Field sales automation example 8
File paths 537
File Paths dialog box 280
File Paths tab 539
Files
  format of a Visio file 62
  moving templates 280
  opening 63
  read-only 64
  saving 64
  searching paths 539
  write-only 64
Fill Format section 71, 75
Fill patterns 226
Fill Style box 210
FillBkgndTrans cell 222
FillForegnd cell 84–85, 222
FillForegndTrans cell 222
Filling shapes 39, 133
FillPattern cell 223
FillStyle property 341
FillStyleKeepFmt property 342
Filter events 433
FilterPaths property 538
First Sub procedure in module example 299
Fixed grids 238, 240
Fixed list property 154
Flip Horizontal and Flip Vertical
  commands 104–105
Flipping
  effect on coordinates 104
  protecting from 107
  shapes 103
FlipX and FlipY cells 76, 103, 196
Floor plan examples 336
Flowchart stencil 213
Folders, installing solutions in 537
Font section 186
Font Size Changes With Shape option 193
Fonts
  resizing 190, 193
  resizing formulas 194
  resizing with shapes 189
  TrueType 218
For loops 290
For statement 290
For...Next statement 413
Foreign Image Info section 71
ForeignType property 519
Format cell 204
FORMAT function 85, 203
Format menu 108, 131
FORMATEX function 201–202
Formatting
  applying 209
  consistent results 216
  grouped shapes 131
  instance of masters 215
  preserving 219
  protecting 342
  results 200
  strings 202
  text 185
Formula
  angled connectors 167, 169
  readability xxi
  shortcuts 144
Formula bar 67, 76
Formula property 351
FormulaForce property 293, 353
Formulas
  and geometry 93, 96
  automating 92
  connection points 177
  controlling location 94
  controlling recalculation 90
  counterrotating 194
  designing 86
  dimmed commands 146
  editing 66–68, 77, 212
  elements of 76
  entering 76
  for arcs 108, 113
  for control handles 136
  for moving shapes 99, 354
  for shapes 13, 21
  for units 83–84
  handling events 422
  height-based 100
  identifying 87
  in automated drawings 348
  in Event section cells 156

Formulas, *continued*
in Geometry section 102
in grids 240
in groups 121–122
in labeled cells 69
in pages 333
in user-defined cells 88
inherited 362
protecting 90, 131, 143, 204, 353
resizing 126, 193
results 200, 353
smart 165, 377
text block testing 206
Formulas To Display command 75
Fragment command 41
Fragment method 377
Freeform tool 38
FreeLibrary function 579
FRM 304
FromCell property 391
FromConnects property 388
FromPart property 391, 393
FromSheet property 389–390, 393
FullName property 328
Function procedure 302
Functions
CALLTHIS 158
DEPENDSON 157
GOTOPAGE 158
in formulas 77
OPENFILE 158
OPENSHEETWIN() 158
OPENTEXTWIN() 158
performing actions 158
PLAYSOUND 158
RUNADDONWARGS 159
RUNDADDON 159
SETF 159

G

GDI Plus xxii
Generate Icon Automatically From Shape Data 273
Generic.cpp 566, 571
Geometry
formulas 87
of shapes 10
rows 98, 356
Geometry section
adding 70, 356
ArcTo row cells 111
control handles 139
described 71
filling shapes 133
Geometry section, *continued*
formulas 95–96, 102, 130
groups 40
merged shapes 119, 131, 148
paths 94
revising objects 45
shape considerations 32
GeometryCount property 361
GetFormulasU method 546
GetIDsOfNames method 570
GetObject 27
GetObject function 551
GETREF function 91
GetResults method 353
Getting layer object example 382
GetTypeInfo method 570
GetTypeInfoCount method 570
GETVAL function 91
GetViewRect method 369
GetWindowTask property 554
Global constants 305
Global object
described 309
getting 327
in Visio object model 286
using 309
Global variables 287
Glue 161, 172
shapes 174
Glue Info section 71, 174
Glue To Shape Geometry 179
GlueTo method 391, 395, 573
GlueToPos method 395
Gluing
behavior 173
connected drawings 395
connections 176, 391
guide points 398
guides 244
pair of cells 397
rules 396
selection handles 397
shapes 172, 392, 397, 399
specifying 175
GOTOPAGE 158
Graphic
files 42–43
images, importing 42
objects 43
Gravity formulas 195
GRAVITY function 194
Grid & Ruler section 72

Grids
designing 237
displaying 238
fixed 238, 240
hiding 238
points 107
setting grid units 239
spacing 238
storing formulas 240
variable 238, 240
Group
command 40, 121
membership 61
method 343
Group Properties section 71, 124
Grouped shapes and objects 36, 40, 122, 338
Groups
adding 122, 343
alignment boxes 128, 246
changing 122
characteristics 120
connections effects 123
controlling behavior 123–124
controlling selection 124
controlling shape text 189
creating and controlling 121
formulas for shapes 122
merged shapes 119
mode settings 125
performance testing 263
protecting formatting 131
resizing 126
revising 46
selection 124
vs. merged shapes 120
when to use 120
GUARD function
90, 100, 117, 131, 152, 192, 204, 219, 293, 353
Guide points
changing 242
connections 391
creating 242
described 241
gluing 398
Guides
connections 391
creating 242
described 241
displaying 243
gluing 398
hiding 243
in grouped shapes 243
manipulating 242
Guides, *continued*
positioning 243
rotating objects 243
selecting 242
snapping disabled 243
GUIDs 405

H

Height
cells 76, 79
values 74
Height-based
formulas 100–101, 103
shapes 94, 101, 103
Hello World program example 345
Hello.vsd 311, 327, 346
Help
context IDs 268
files 263, 538
HTML Help (.chm files) 268
online xxiii
HelpPaths property 538
HideText cell 204
HitTest 369
HLP 268, 538
HPJ 268
HRESULT 571
HSL color values 222
Hub shape 418
Hyperlinks collection 289
Hyperlinks section 71

I

iClassFactory2 interface 515
Icon editing window 273
IconFileName property 469
iConnectionPoint protocols 574
Icons 56
iDataObject interface 344
Identifying formulas 87
iDispatch interface 565
Ignore events 433
Image Properties section 72
Immediate window 414
Implements statement 442
Import File command 304
Importing graphic images 42
IncludesFill property 330
IncludesLine property 330
IncludesText property 330

Index
getting cells 349
getting shapes 335
Index for objects 288–289
Infinite lines 241
Inherited
data 362
formulas 13, 75, 87, 131, 211, 362
InitWith procedure example 16
Insert Row command 143
Insert row command 74
Insert Section dialog box 69
Installing
files in folders xxiii
stencils and templates 280
Instance of masters
assigning to layers 236
behavior 11
creating 52
layering 235
reformatting 215
Instance of Visio application
creating 550
handling errors 557
in Application object 556
in Visio object model 286
retrieving 551
running other programs 550
window handle of 554
Integrated development environment (IDE) 295
Interaction Style option 163
Interface
controls 303
functions 564–565, 569
pointer 565, 571
Intersect command 41
Invalid object reference errors 292
Invisible cells 134, 154
Invoke method 570
InvokeHelp method 268
InvokeOnMask 581
IOLEUndoUnit 529
IpArgs member 582
IpCmdLineArgs 582
Ipfunc member 582
IsDropSource cell 122
IsDropTarget cell 122
iShapeCount variable 413
IsInScope property 528
IsSet function 572
IsUndoingorRedoing property 527
Item method 336
Item property 288
ItemAtID property 468
Iterating
through collections and rows 361
through connections example 393
through Pages collection example 379
IterationMode property 376
IUnknown interface 577
IVBUndoUnit 529, 530
Ivisreg.cpp 571
Ivisreg.h 571

J

Join command 41, 133

K

Key property 482
Keywords Property 328
Kitchen island group example 125

L

Labels 154
Late binding 565
Lay Out Shapes command 167, 248, 250
Layer dialog box 237
Layer index 381
Layer Membership section 72, 236
Layer object
getting 382
identifying 382
Layer Properties dialog box 235, 381, 383
LayerCount property 382
Layers
assigning 234
assigning masters to 236–237
assigning shapes to 234, 236
changing settings 383
described 61, 234, 381
identifying 381–382
optimizing 235
removing 235
working with 381
Layers collection 381
Layers section 72
Level text block, width 198
Level text formulas 197
Libraries 25–26, 305–308, 578
dynamic-link 578
Line dialog box 232
Line ends 223, 225
Line Format section 72, 75
Line Patterns
colors 230
scaled option 230

Line segments
  converting 113
  editing 113
Line Style box 210
Line styles 208
Line tool 38
LineColorTrans cell 222
LinePattern cell 223
LineStyle property 341
LineStyleKeepFmt property 342
LineWeight cell 208, 211
Live dynamics 140
LoadFromFile method 488
LoadLibrary function 579
Local
  formulas 75, 87
  name 79, 546
  variables 287, 302
Local coordinates 95, 98, 123
Local formatting 208
Lock cells 100
Lock Project For Viewing option 317
Lock protection, shape features 116
Lock Text command 143, 145, 146
LockCalcWH cell 113, 129, 138, 141
LockFormat cell 109, 131, 204, 219
LockGroup cell 122
LockHeight cell 126, 169
Locking
  project 317
  shape behavior 116
  shape formatting 131
  shapes 100, 107
  text 143
LockMoveX and LockMoveY cells 100
LockRotate cell 100, 107
Locks
  for group formats 131
  for shape feature 116
  for shapes 107
LockTextEdit 145
LockTextEdit cell 204
LockVtxEdit cell 169
LockWidth cell 117, 126
LocPinX and LocPinY cells 98, 106
LOCTOPAR formulas 177
Logical operators 78
Loops 290, 361, 413

M

Macro description 313
Macros 26
  deleting 484, 485
  running, 313, 539, 558
Macros dialog box 313, 558
Macros menu 314
Master design 21
Master drawing window 56
Master formula, evaluating 559
Master icons 57, 265, 273
Master object 286
  adding layers 383
  copyright 54
  creating 343
  deleting layers 383
  dropping on page 364, 366
  formulas 66, 67, 348
  getting 365
  patterns 223
  reformatting 214
Master Shortcut Properties dialog box 272
Master shortcuts 271
Masters
  adding custom properties 152
  assigning to layers 234, 236
  automating drawings 11, 364
  BaseIDs 406
  cleaning up 272
  consistency of 264, 265
  control handles 136
  copyright of 54
  creating 51–52, 55, 343
  creating for grids 238
  custom properties 152
  dropping on page 366
  editing 56, 69, 189, 272
  from other programs 55
  getting 365
  group behavior 36
  Help files 268
  layering 61, 235
  naming 265, 272
  packaging 261
  range of eight rule 258
  reusing 52
  setting units 239
  testing 264, 265
  text in 184
  UniqueIDs 406
  verifying items 265
  working with layers 381
  working with scales 253, 257, 259–260, 266–268
Masters collection 289, 365
Masters property 365
Mathematical operators 77
MAX function 194

Measuring units, setting up 256
Member shapes 126, 130–131
Members in groups 125
Members Of list 306
Menu cells 144
Menu command to run programs 542
Menu items 476
Menu object 468
Menu object listing 466
MenuItem object 468
MenuItems collection 289
Menus, adding 476
Menus collection 289
MenuSet object 468
MenuSets collection 289
Merged shapes
  when to use 120
Merging shapes 40, 119–121, 131, 133–134, 148–149
Metafiles
  editing 43
  imported 44
Methods
  declaring variables 293
  invoking 295
  return values 292
  using 294
Micrografx Designer (.drw) 43
Microsoft Access 155
Microsoft Excel 287
Microsoft Office 295
Microsoft Office command bars object model, 448–449
Microsoft SQL Server 155
Microsoft Visio Developer Center, xxiv
Microsoft Visio Developer Reference, xxiv
Microsoft Windows 218
Mid function (Visual Basic) 560
MIN function 194
Miscellaneous section 72
Modeless activity 582
Modeling with Visio application
  described 5
  real-world examples 8
  validating 7
Module-level variables 287
Modules 300–304
Monitoring Events and Totaling Values
  VBA Val function 16
Monitoring power consumption example 16
Moving office plan example 6
MSDN Web site (for Visio developers) xxiii
MsgBox statement 302
Multidimensional units 84
Multiple Geometry sections 115
Multishapes 119, 131
MyAddon.cpp 578
Myprog.exe 157

N

Name property 328, 330, 336
NameID property 336
NameU property 546
Naming
  masters 265
  styles 217
Nested groups 124, 126
Network equipment shapes example 12
New keyword 531
New Master dialog box 56
New Stencil command 53
NewBaseID property 406
No Style style 217
NoAlignBox cell 248
NoCtrlHandles cell 141
Node shapes 418
NOERROR result 571
NoFill cell 133
NoLine cell 133
Non-Printing Shape option 516
Nonuniform rational B-spline (NURBS) 115
Normalized angles 200
NoShow cell controls 149
NoShow cells 134
NoSnap cells 179
Nothing variable 291
Notification sinks 438, 442
Nudge subroutine 354
Nudge.exe 354
Null string 328, 331, 353, 405, 545, 555
Number property 154
Number-unit pairs 83, 86, 203
Numbers 83, 407
NURBS 115

O

Object Browser 306
Object formulas
  displaying 66, 67
  editing 66
Object linking and embedding 286
Object model (Visio) 284, 286
Object pointer arguments 573

Object references
  concatenating 292
  getting 286–287
  in Visio object model 287
  releasing 287
  restricting scope 292
  return values 571
  to collections 288
  to object variables 292
Object types in libraries 308
Object variables 287, 291–293, 426, 427
Objects
  CreateObject 27
  declaring 570
  default property 15, 294
  error properties 316
  GetObject 27
  gluing 396
  in collections 286
  in groups 36
  in pseudocode 565
  location 94
  moving formulas 99
  properties 288
  releasing 291
  vaoGetObject 27
ObjType cell 166
ODBC (Open Database Connectivity) 24, 419
Offset command 41
OLEObjects collection 519
On Error statement 315, 557
OnAction property 457, 460
OneD property 407
Online Help xxiii
OnNextAdd procedure 530
Open DataBase Connectivity (ODBC) 155
Open dialog box 277, 343
Open group command 47
Open shapes 33
Open Stencil dialog box 54, 68, 214
OPENFILE function 158
OPENSHEETWIN ( ) function 158
OPENTEXTWIN ( ) function 158
Operations command 40
Operations submenu 224, 248
Operators 78
Order of evaluation (for events) 78
Order of pages 236, 335, 379
OrderInfo array 411, 413
Organization chart stencil 396
Overlapping shapes 41

P

Padlock handles 75
Page coordinates 95, 123, 369
Page Layout section 72
Page object 15
  adding layers 383
  described 332
  formulas 348
  getting 333
  in drawings 364
  in Visio model 286, 326
  removing layers 383
Page Properties section 72
Page property 331
Page rotation 105
Page Setup dialog box 95
Page units 84–85, 254
PageHeight cell 367
Pages
  adding 334
  adding custom properties 152, 405
  analyzing connections 392
  changing settings 381
  collection 289, 332
  displaying 331
  editing formulas 68
  grid design 237
  guides 241
  hub shapes 418
  layering 61, 235
  layout options 248
  overview 60
  printing 330
  saving 331
  scaled pages 256
  turning 331
Pages property 288
PageSheet property 333, 348, 381
PageWidth cell 367
pagIndex 559
Paragraph section 72, 186
Parametric shapes 10
Parent coordinates 95, 98, 123
Parsing 560
Paste method 339
Paste Shortcut command 271
Path property 328
Paths
  described 94
  installing files 538
  merged shapes 133
  pencil tool 37
  routable connectors 167
  searching files 539

Pencil tool 38, 45, 75
Persistence of user interface 474
PersistsEvents property 437
Pictures, importing 42
Custom properties for inventory control
  list example 128
Pattern Properties dialog box 226
Persistable property 437
Persistent property 437
Pie wedge shape 165
Pin
  coordinates 98
  customizing 230
  flipping effects 104
  formulas 66
  moving around 99, 106, 127, 232
  rotating effects 105
  text blocks 184
  text control handle 188
PinX and PinY cells 74–75, 98–100, 106
Pipe shapes 171
Placeable shapes 165
Placing shapes in drawings example 367
PLAYSOUND function 158
Policy settings 322
Pop-up menu 456
Portable code 262
Portable drawings 11
Position property 460
Precedence order in formulas 78
Preserve Local Formatting option 219
PreserveMembersFlag argument 382
Print dialog box 330
Print method 330
Private procedures 302
Procedures
  naming 302
  type of 302
Programming for Visio application 295
Programs
  binding 542
  copyright information 264
  creating 395, 535
  distributing 544, 545
  exporting data 414
  for setup xx
  handling errors 557
  handling events 422
  importing shapes 42
  in Automation 15
  installing 536
  instance of Visio application in 550
  interacting 15, 555
Programs, *continued*
  intrepreting commands 558
  migrating 27
  setting up code 417, 561
  using wrapper class 566
  writing 429, 549
Programs running
  at startup 539
  evaluating formulas 559
  from Macros menu 558
  from Startup folder 560
  in context 315
  options 539
  with arguments 560
Project Explorer 304, 311
Project Explorer window 298
Project Properties window 297
Project/Library box 306–307
Prompt box 272
Prompt cell 351, 405
Properties
  custom 150
  dialog box 152
  default for objects 294
  references to objects 288
  retrieving 407
  storing 407
  using 292
Property procedure 302
Proportions
  maintaining when resizing 170
Protect Document command 280
Protect Document dialog box 516
Protecting
  controls 516
  formulas 90, 100, 353
  group editing 122
  group formatting 131
  local formats 219
  local formatting 342
  program code 317
  read-only files 55
  row type 113
  shape geometrics 32
  shape resizing 126
  stencils 280
  styles 219
  templates 280
  text block width 190
  text editing 189
  text values 204

Protecting shapes
  from flipping 107
  from rotating 107
  from scaling 260
Protection cells 75
Protection dialog box 116
Protection property 460, 463
Protection section 72
Public procedures 302

Q

Query events 441
QueryInterface method 570
Quit method 551
Quotation marks 89, 91, 154, 159, 340, 351

R

Range of eight rule 258
Read-only files 59, 64, 280, 328
Read-only property 293, 407
Read-write files 64
Read-write properties 293
Readme.txt 564, 578
Recalculation control 90
Rectangle shapes 38, 108
Rectangle tool 38
Redo method 523
Redo stack 525
Redoable action 523
Reference material
  CD xxiii
  Help xxiii
  Web xxiv
References
  failing 572
  invalid 292
  migrating 27
  objects 571
  Visio library 561
Release calls 566
Release method 570
Remove
  action 317
  method 382
Remove From Group command 122
Remove Unreferenced Layers option 235
Reorder Pages dialog box 379
Reorganizing office example 6
Reposition Only option 126
ResizeMode cell 125–126
Resizing
  arc bows 110
  basing on text value 192
  custom formulas 130
  custom sizing 194
  group behavior 125
  in one direction 126
  protecting proportions 101
  protecting text 190
  text amount 192
  using coordinates 95
Resizing an arrow example 100
Resizing mode settings 126
Result property 353
ResultInt property 353
ResultIU property 353
Results
  replacing formulas 353
  using shape operations 41
ResultStr property 353
Retrieving objects 288
Return string 407
Return values 293, 316
Reverse Ends command 206
RGB color values 222
Road sign shape 189
Rotating
  1-D shapes 35
  2-D shapes 35
  protecting from 107
  shapes 103, 105
  text block 194
Rotation in the Protection dialog box 107
Rotation tool 35, 105–106
Routable connectors 167
RouteStyle cell 167
Row tag constants 356
RowCount property 361
Rows
  adding 355
  deleting 359
  iteration loop 361
  unable to delete 356
  working with 355
RowsCellCount property 361
Rubber band line 140
Ruler & Grid dialog box 238
Ruler & Grid formulas 238
Ruler & Grid section 72
Rulers 95, 238, 242
Run In Developer Mode option 67–69, 178
Run mode 513
Run-time license 515

RUNADDON function 159, 542, 559
RUNADDONARGS function 158
RUNADDONWARGS function 542, 560

S

S-connector 165
Save method 331
SaveAs method 331
Saved property 328, 331
SaveToFile method 487
Scale With Group option 126
Scaled drawings 60
Scaled option 225, 227
Scanned images 42
Scope of procedures 302
Scratch cells 88, 89
Scratch section 72, 88–89, 129
ScreenTips 136
Search text box 306
Section command 69
Section controls 70
Sections dialog box
  adding 69, 355
  deleting 359
  displaying 69
  working with 355
Security settings 318, 322
Security system example 9, 24
Segments 359
Select method 376–377
Select mode settings 125
SelectAll method 377
Selection handles 35, 75, 397
Selection object 286, 343, 375–378
Selection property 376
SelectMode cell 124
SETF function 143, 146, 158–159
SetFilterCommands 433
SetFilterObjects 433
SetFilterSRC 433
Shape
  formulas 75
  resizing 94, 126
Shape bounding box 180
Shape cell references 79–80
Shape control handles 136, 139
Shape design
  components 6
  planning 21
  to specifications 12
  using Automation 23
Shape distribution
  packaging 261–262
  performance 263
Shape formulas 100
Shape geometry 115
  anchor points 140
  described 94
  formulas 93, 96
  hiding 134
  optimizing 115
  shortcut commands 147
Shape groups 36, 40, 121–122, 243
Shape IDs 80
Shape layers 61, 233–234, 236
Shape Layout section 72
Shape object 15
  adding rows 355
  adding sections 355
  adding user-defined rows 405
  analyzing connections 389
  as part of group 338
  assigning layers 382
  described 334
  deselecting 377
  editing 359
  formulas 348
  getting 335
  in Visio model 286, 326
  in windows 376
  operation results 41
  performing on 377
  properties 288, 292, 337, 340, 405
  removing layers 382
  selecting 375, 377
  UniqueIDs 405
Shape properties 13, 150, 288
Shape protecting 116, 131
Shape testing 206, 264, 268, 270
Shape Transform section 72, 96, 98, 126, 192
Shape-record connection 155
ShapeAdded event 17, 419, 425, 531
ShapeFixedCode cell 181
ShapePlowCode cell 250
ShapeRouteStyle cell 167, 174, 250
Shapes
  3-D box 128
  adding 340, 376
  adding connection points 178
  adding control handles 136
  adding custom properties 152
  aligning 241
  anatomy 13, 32
  antiscaling, 257

Shapes, *continued*
attributes 13
automatic layout 248
behavior 11
behavior enhancements 135
behavior of 250
changing 338
color 219, 222
components 11
connecting 123, 176, 388, 418
controlling curves in 108
conversions 44
coordinate system 95
copying 339
copyright 49, 264
creating 10, 31, 338
customizing 262
cutting 339
deleting 339
designing 262–263
determining connections 389–390
determining scope 378
developing 13, 19
displaying 73
drawing 37
dropping on page 364
duplicating 339
dynamic connectors 180
flipping 103, 106
formulas 87
gluing 173, 392, 395, 397
grouping and ungrouping 121
handles 34
hiding 134
importing 42
inheriting formulas 87
interacting 522
layering 235
layout options 248
limiting text 192
linking data 403
locking 100, 107
merging 119, 132–133, 148
modeling 5
moving 74, 94, 99, 354
optimizing 115
performance 263
planning 262
positioning 98, 367
protecting 219, 260, 342
reformatting 213
removing 376
resizing 189, 194

Shapes, *continued*
revising 45
rotating 103, 106
rounding corners 108
scaling 266
selecting 375
snap to grid 237, 239
styles 212, 341
transparent color 222
ungrouped 49, 121
units of measure 84
using loops 413
width 201
Shapes and stencils, planning 21
Shapes and templates, automating 23
Shapes collection 289, 334–335, 338, 413
Shapes getting
by ID 336
by index 335
by name 335
by property type 337
Shapes property 288
Shapes text block 183–185
ShapesDeleted event 419
ShapeSheet cell references 79
ShapeSheet formulas 10, 13, 83, 150
ShapeSheet Reference (Visio) xxi, 4
ShapeSheet sections 69–70
ShapeSheet spreadsheets 10, 13
ShapeSheet window 10, 13, 44, 73, 138, 185
displaying 66, 69
editing 66, 68, 76
ShdwBkgndTrans cell 222
ShdwForegndTrans cell 222
Shorcut command, dimming 146
Shortcut menus 142–143, 144, 147, 542
Show Arms command 149
Show Document Stencil command 54
Show Hidden Members command 516
Show ShapeSheet command 67, 69
ShowInMenu macro 314
ShowPageConnections macro 393
Sink object 431, 433, 438, 442, 575, 577
Size & Position window 105
SmartShapes symbols 13
Snap
to alignment box 107
to grid 237
to shape geometry 179
Snap & Glue command 39
Snap & Glue dialog box 175, 177
Software Development Kit (SDK) 564–565

Solution design
- creating 10
- implementing 23
- in drawings 6
- usability 19
- Visio objects 15

Solutions
- conserving 545
- distributing 544
- file folders 537
- file paths 537
- installing 536
- integrating 24, 403, 419
- migrating 27
- packaging 261, 535
- performing in other systems 263

Sounds, playing 158
Source code 54, 547
Spatial relationship properties 369
SpatialNeighbors property 369
SpatialRelation property 369
SpatialSearch property 369
Special dialog box 518
Splines 33, 38
Stand-alone programs 25
Stand-alone stencils 52
Standard toolbar 37
Startup folder 560
StartupPaths property 538, 555
State property 469
Static glue 173
Static variables 302
StatusBarItems collection 289
StatusBars collection 289
Stencil design 21
StencilPaths property 538

Stencils
- adding new masters to 55
- cleaning up 274
- color 221
- conserving 545
- copyright 54
- creating 51–54
- custom patterns 223
- document 12
- editing 214
- file 326
- file formats 62
- getting 364
- Help files 269
- installing 280
- layering 235
- making editable 56

Stencils, *continued*
- migrating 27
- opening 54–55, 59, 64, 68
- packaging 261, 535
- performing 263
- protecting 280
- saving 64, 299
- stand-alone 214
- styles 216
- testing 264, 274–276

StrComp function 560
String arguments 573
String property 154
Strings 202, 572
Style command 208
Style dialog box 209, 217
Style formula, evaluating 559
Style object formulas 348
Style Properties section 72
Style property 469
StyleKeepFmt property 342

Styles 209
- attributes 208
- color 219
- consistency 216
- copying 211
- creating 210, 330
- defaults 210
- defining 208, 218
- described 208
- editing 68, 210, 212
- fills 208
- for corners 108
- guidelines for 212
- identifying 341
- in stencils 214, 216
- in templates 22, 216
- in text 208
- inherited 211
- lines 208
- managing 207
- naming 217
- removing 216
- understanding 208

Styles collection 289, 329
Styles property 329, 341
Sub procedure 302
Subject matter experts 19
Subject property 328
Subtract command 41
SUCCEEDED result 571
Summary tab 276
Swimming pool shape example 255

Syntax for cell references 81–82
SysFreeString 572–573
System architects 19

T

Tab setting 515
Tabs section 72, 186
Tag property 454, 460
TargetArgs property 441
Template design 22–23
TemplatePaths property 538, 556
Templates
  benefits 12
  cleaning up 276
  color 221
  conserving 545
  consistency 216
  copyright 54
  creating 51–52, 57, 59, 556
  deleting 276
  elements of 58
  file 326
  grids 237, 239
  guides 241
  installing 280
  migrating 27
  moving files 280
  multiple pages 60
  opening 64
  packaging 281, 555
  performing 263
  placeable shapes 167
  planning 22
  protecting 280
  saving 59, 299
  scaling 60, 257
  styles 216
  testing 277, 279
Testing
  custom formulas 263
  different scales 267
  handling errors 557
  master scales 266
  read-only stencils 275
  read-only templates 279
  return values 316
  same size scales 266
  shape Help 270
  stencils 274–275
  templates 277, 279
  verifying objects 316
Testing in Open dialog box 277, 343
Text
  adding 340
  attributes 185
  behavior of 183
  fonts 186
  formatting 185, 203
  formulas 189, 190, 192, 200, 204
  in data fields 341
  in groups 189
  output 202
  positioning 187
  protecting 143
  resizing 189, 192–194
  rotating 194–196
  sizing 192, 200
  styles 208
Text Block Format section 72, 186, 204
Text block tool 187
Text blocks
  amount of text 192
  coordinates 184
  designing 183
  displaying format results 200
  leveling 198
  offsetting 200
  positioning 187
  resizing 189, 190–191
  restricting 190
  rotating 195–196
  testing 206
Text box 456
Text box control 303
Text designing 184
Text dialog box 185
Text Fields section 72, 200–201
Text property 340, 407
Text strings 154
Text Style box 210
Text tool 189
Text Transform section 73, 185
TextBkgndTrans cell 222
TextChanged event 419
TEXTHEIGHT function 189, 192
TextStyle property 341
TextStyleKeepFmt property 342
TEXTWIDTH function 189, 192
TheData cell 156
ThePage shape 80
ThePage!DrawingScale formulas 260
ThePage!PageScale formulas 260
TheText cell 156
ThisDocument object 296, 301, 309, 311, 424–426
Tile command 73

Tiled patterns, designing 227
Title property 328
ToCell property 391
Toolbar buttons
  adding 479
  deleting 484
  to run programs 542
Toolbars
  adding 480
Toolbars collection 289
ToolbarSets collection 289
Tools
  Arc 35
  Ellipse 38
  Freeform 35
  Line 35
  Pencil 35
  Pointer 35
  Rectangle 38
  Rotation 34
TooltipText property 460
ToPart property 391, 393
ToSheet property 389–390, 393
Totaling values and monitoring events example 16
Transistor symbol 106
Transparency cell 222
Transparent colors 222
Triggering events 91, 431
Trim command 41
Trusted source 317
Turning pages 331
TxtAngle cell 185, 200
TxtHeight cell 185, 191, 200
TxtLocPinX and TxtLocPinY cells 185
TxtPinX and TxtPinY cells 185, 195, 200
TxtWidth cell 185, 198, 200
Type libraries 305–307, 561
Type property 337

U

UIObject object
  editing 475
  listing 464
Undo manager 523, 525–526, 529, 531
Undo method 523
Undo scope
  associating events 528
  creating with add-ons 527–528
  described 523
  verifying 528
Undo stack 525
Undo unit 523–524, 529, 531
Undoable action 523
Ungroup command 49, 121
Union command 41, 133
Union method 377
Unique IDs
  as arguments 406
  generating 405
  shape objects 405
UniqueID property 336, 405–406
Unitless cells 84
Units of measure 76, 84–85, 89, 239
UnitSize procedure 530
UnitTypeCLSID procedure 530
UnitTypeLong procedure 530
Universal name 79, 546
UpdateAlignBox cell 141, 247
UpdateUI method 486
URL for Microsoft Visio Developer Center xxiv
Usability
  design 19, 262
  drawing scales 255
  naming conventions 264
  of masters 264
  shape behavior 262
USE function 223
Use Group's Setting option 126
User forms 300, 303–304
User interface
  adding user forms 303
  persistence 474–475
User-defined cells 351
User-Defined Cells section
  adding cells 88
  described 73
  naming conventions 79
  scratch section 88
User-defined rows 405
User.Prompt cell 89

V

V2LMSG_ENUMADDONS message 579
V2LMSG_ISAOENABLED message 581
V2LMSG_RUN message 581
Value cells 351, 405
Values
  declaring variables 293
  editing 74
  flipping effects 104
  multidimensional units 84
  returned by Visio methods 571
  rotating effects 105
Valve shapes 171
Vao.h 580
VAO_ENABLEALWAYS 580

VAO_ENABLEDYNAMIC 581
VAO_INVOKE_LAUNCH 581
VAO_NEEDSDOC 581
vaoGetObject function 27, 571
vaoGetObjectWrap function 566, 571
VAOREGSTRUCT 581
VAOUtil_DefVisMainProc 579
VAOV2LSTRUCT 581
Variable grids 238
Variable list property 154
Variables
  data type 293
  declaring 302
  defining 413
  objects 291
  objects described 287
  static 302
  text block formulas 190
VARIANT arguments 574
Variant data type in Visual Basic 293
VBAUndoUnit 531
VDLLmain.c 579
VDX 63, 407
Vector-based graphics 42–43
Vectors, non-zero 177
Vertices
  closing 39
  described 93
  effects of moving shapes 35
  shape geometry 94
  start and end points 163
  x and y coordinates 95
Vertices for 3-D box 128
visActCodeRunAddon constant 437
visBegin constant 390
visCentimeters constant 353
visConnectionPoint constant 391
Visconst.bas 27, 305, 561
visControlPoint constant 391
visDeselect constant 376
visDrawingUnits constant 353
visEnd constant 390
VisEventProc method 438, 440, 575
visEvtAdd constant 431–432, 436, 438
visEvtIDMostRecent constant 436
visEvtPage constant 432, 438
visEvtShape constant 432, 438
visFieldCodes constant 341
visGetGUID constant 336, 405
visGuideX and visGuideY constants 390
Visible property 453, 458
Visio Automation Reference xxi
Visio Developer Center xxiv
Visio Developer Reference xxi
Visio document
  components 62
Visio file paths 280
Visio folders, installing solutions in 537
Visio libraries (.vsl) 25, 287, 305–306,
    578–579, 581
Visio object model 4, 283–284, 288, 388, 466
Visio object types 287
Visio ShapeSheet Reference xxi
Visio solutions xix
Visio type libraries 305–308
Visio.h 566, 570–571
VisioLibMain function 579
Visiwrap.h 566
visLayerName constant 384
visLayerVisible constant 384
visLeftEdge constant 390
visPageUnits constant 353
Visreg.bas 358
visRightEdge constant 390
visRowVertex 358
visSectionCharacter constant 356, 359
visSectionFirstComponent constant 356
visSectionLastComponent constant 356
visSectionObj constant 359
visSectionParagraph constant 356, 359
visSectionTab constant 356, 359
visSectionTextField constant 356, 359
visSelect constant 376
visTagArcTo constant 356–357
visTagComponent constant 356–357
visTagEllipse constant 356–357
visTagEllipticalArcTo constant 356–357
visTagInfiniteLine constant 356–357
visTagLineTo constant 355–357
visTagMoveTo constant 356–357
visTagNURBSTo constant 356–357
visTagPolylineTo constant 356–357
visTagSplineBeg constant 356–357
visTagSplineSpan constant 356–357
visTypeDoc constant 337
visTypeForeignObject constant 337
visTypeGroup constant 337
visTypePage constant 337
visTypeShape constant 337

Visual Basic
  code protection 317
  COM add-ins 491
  controls 519
  error functions 316
  handling errors 557
  migrating 27
  overflow reports 432, 438
  releasing objects 291
  sink objects 440
  Variant data 293
  writing event code 424
Visual Basic Editor
  Add-In Manager 323
  navigating in project 298
  running code 313
  saving projects 299
  setting options 297
  starting 297
  using 296
Visual Basic for Applications (VBA)
  Add-In Manager 323
  Automation compared to 14
  class modules 296
  COM add-ins 491
  creating projects 300
  customizing 297
  developing in 295
  digitally signing VBA projects 317
  disabling project creation 299
  distributing code 23, 545
  enable 299
  environment 296
  event code 424
  exporting files 304
  finalizing project 317
  handling events 422
  importing files 304
  inserting custom objects 301
  macros 26
  managing 316
  migrating from Visual Basic 27
  overflow reports 432, 438
  running code 313
  running instances 309
  sink objects 440
  using Object Browser 306
  writing 549
Visual Basic IDE 295
Visual Basic programming for
    Visio application 283–284, 295
VLIBUTL_hModule 579
VSD 63
VSL 25, 299, 538, 578–579, 581
VSS 52, 299, 538
VST 59, 64, 299, 538
VSU 448, 487
VSX 52, 64, 407
VTX 59, 64, 407
VVariant helper class 566, 574

W

WalkPreference cell 174
Wall shape 165
Web site for Microsoft Visio 322, 536
Width
  formulas 94, 96, 130
  values 74
Width cell 79–80, 83
Width-height box 184
Window object 286, 331, 343, 376–377
Window testing, other systems 276
WindowHandle32 property 554
Windows .DLL 25–26
Windows desktop,
  running Visio application from 25
Windows Explorer,
  running Visio application from 25
WindowsHandle32 property 578
WinHelp (.hlp files) 268
WithEvents (VBA keyword) 422, 424, 426
Word balloon shape 138
Word balloon with control handle example 141
Workspace 59
  list 274, 280
  saving 64
Wrapper classes 566

X

X and Y cells 102
X, Y coordinates 95, 111, 115, 179
XBehavior and YBehavior cells 139, 141, 188
XDynamics and YDynamics cells 139, 140, 188
XGridDensity and YGridDensity cells 238
XGridSpacing and YGridSpacing cells 238
XML
  solution data 407
  storing in cell 407
  storing in document 407
XML file format 407
XML for Visio 407

Z

Zero points 96

Power Strip

The power strip is used to expand the number of available electrical outlets. A power strip also provides protection against electrical surges and spikes, which are sudden increases in voltage significantly above the designated level of an electrical circuit. For example, in normal household and office wiring in the United States, the standard voltage is 120 volts. If a power surge or spike causes the voltage to rise above 120, a power strip prevents the increased voltage from destroying your computer or other sensitive electrical equipment. Power strips protect against normal power fluctuations as well as abnormal fluctuations resulting from lightening strikes or other aberrant power occurrences.

Tools are central to the progress of the human race. People are adept at building and using tools to accomplish important (and unimportant) tasks. Software is among the most powerful of tools moving us forward, and Microsoft is proud to create tools used by millions worldwide and to contribute to continuing innovation.

Proof of Purchase

Use this page as proof of purchase if participating in a promotion or rebate offer on this title. Proof of purchase must be used in conjunction with other proof(s) of payment such as your dated sales receipt—see offer details.

Developing Microsoft® Visio® Solutions

0-7356-1353-2

CUSTOMER NAME

Microsoft Press, PO Box 97017, Redmond, WA 98073-9830

MICROSOFT LICENSE AGREEMENT

Book Companion CD

IMPORTANT—READ CAREFULLY: This Microsoft End-User License Agreement ("EULA") is a legal agreement between you (either an individual or an entity) and Microsoft Corporation for the Microsoft product identified above, which includes computer software and may include associated media, printed materials, and "online" or electronic documentation ("SOFTWARE PRODUCT"). Any component included within the SOFTWARE PRODUCT that is accompanied by a separate End-User License Agreement shall be governed by such agreement and not the terms set forth below. By installing, copying, or otherwise using the SOFTWARE PRODUCT, you agree to be bound by the terms of this EULA. If you do not agree to the terms of this EULA, you are not authorized to install, copy, or otherwise use the SOFTWARE PRODUCT; you may, however, return the SOFTWARE PRODUCT, along with all printed materials and other items that form a part of the Microsoft product that includes the SOFTWARE PRODUCT, to the place you obtained them for a full refund.

SOFTWARE PRODUCT LICENSE

The SOFTWARE PRODUCT is protected by United States copyright laws and international copyright treaties, as well as other intellectual property laws and treaties. The SOFTWARE PRODUCT is licensed, not sold.

1. **GRANT OF LICENSE.** This EULA grants you the following rights:

   a. **Software Product.** You may install and use one copy of the SOFTWARE PRODUCT on a single computer. The primary user of the computer on which the SOFTWARE PRODUCT is installed may make a second copy for his or her exclusive use on a portable computer.

   b. **Storage/Network Use.** You may also store or install a copy of the SOFTWARE PRODUCT on a storage device, such as a network server, used only to install or run the SOFTWARE PRODUCT on your other computers over an internal network; however, you must acquire and dedicate a license for each separate computer on which the SOFTWARE PRODUCT is installed or run from the storage device. A license for the SOFTWARE PRODUCT may not be shared or used concurrently on different computers.

   c. **License Pak.** If you have acquired this EULA in a Microsoft License Pak, you may make the number of additional copies of the computer software portion of the SOFTWARE PRODUCT authorized on the printed copy of this EULA, and you may use each copy in the manner specified above. You are also entitled to make a corresponding number of secondary copies for portable computer use as specified above.

   d. **Sample Code.** Solely with respect to portions, if any, of the SOFTWARE PRODUCT that are identified within the SOFTWARE PRODUCT as sample code (the "SAMPLE CODE"):

      i. **Use and Modification.** Microsoft grants you the right to use and modify the source code version of the SAMPLE CODE, *provided* you comply with subsection (d)(iii) below. You may not distribute the SAMPLE CODE, or any modified version of the SAMPLE CODE, in source code form.

      ii. **Redistributable Files.** Provided you comply with subsection (d)(iii) below, Microsoft grants you a nonexclusive, royalty-free right to reproduce and distribute the object code version of the SAMPLE CODE and of any modified SAMPLE CODE, other than SAMPLE CODE, or any modified version thereof, designated as not redistributable in the Readme file that forms a part of the SOFTWARE PRODUCT (the "Non-Redistributable Sample Code"). All SAMPLE CODE other than the Non-Redistributable Sample Code is collectively referred to as the "REDISTRIBUTABLES."

      iii. **Redistribution Requirements.** If you redistribute the REDISTRIBUTABLES, you agree to: (i) distribute the REDISTRIBUTABLES in object code form only in conjunction with and as a part of your software application product; (ii) not use Microsoft's name, logo, or trademarks to market your software application product; (iii) include a valid copyright notice on your software application product; (iv) indemnify, hold harmless, and defend Microsoft from and against any claims or lawsuits, including attorney's fees, that arise or result from the use or distribution of your software application product; and (v) not permit further distribution of the REDISTRIBUTABLES by your end user. Contact Microsoft for the applicable royalties due and other licensing terms for all other uses and/or distribution of the REDISTRIBUTABLES.

2. **DESCRIPTION OF OTHER RIGHTS AND LIMITATIONS.**

   - **Limitations on Reverse Engineering, Decompilation, and Disassembly.** You may not reverse engineer, decompile, or disassemble the SOFTWARE PRODUCT, except and only to the extent that such activity is expressly permitted by applicable law notwithstanding this limitation.
   - **Separation of Components.** The SOFTWARE PRODUCT is licensed as a single product. Its component parts may not be separated for use on more than one computer.
   - **Rental.** You may not rent, lease, or lend the SOFTWARE PRODUCT.

- **Support Services.** Microsoft may, but is not obligated to, provide you with support services related to the SOFTWARE PRODUCT ("Support Services"). Use of Support Services is governed by the Microsoft policies and programs described in the user manual, in "online" documentation, and/or in other Microsoft-provided materials. Any supplemental software code provided to you as part of the Support Services shall be considered part of the SOFTWARE PRODUCT and subject to the terms and conditions of this EULA. With respect to technical information you provide to Microsoft as part of the Support Services, Microsoft may use such information for its business purposes, including for product support and development. Microsoft will not utilize such technical information in a form that personally identifies you.
- **Software Transfer.** You may permanently transfer all of your rights under this EULA, provided you retain no copies, you transfer all of the SOFTWARE PRODUCT (including all component parts, the media and printed materials, any upgrades, this EULA, and, if applicable, the Certificate of Authenticity), **and** the recipient agrees to the terms of this EULA.
- **Termination.** Without prejudice to any other rights, Microsoft may terminate this EULA if you fail to comply with the terms and conditions of this EULA. In such event, you must destroy all copies of the SOFTWARE PRODUCT and all of its component parts.

3. **COPYRIGHT.** All title and copyrights in and to the SOFTWARE PRODUCT (including but not limited to any images, photographs, animations, video, audio, music, text, SAMPLE CODE, REDISTRIBUTABLES, and "applets" incorporated into the SOFTWARE PRODUCT) and any copies of the SOFTWARE PRODUCT are owned by Microsoft or its suppliers. The SOFTWARE PRODUCT is protected by copyright laws and international treaty provisions. Therefore, you must treat the SOFTWARE PRODUCT like any other copyrighted material **except** that you may install the SOFTWARE PRODUCT on a single computer provided you keep the original solely for backup or archival purposes. You may not copy the printed materials accompanying the SOFTWARE PRODUCT.

4. **U.S. GOVERNMENT RESTRICTED RIGHTS.** The SOFTWARE PRODUCT and documentation are provided with RESTRICTED RIGHTS. Use, duplication, or disclosure by the Government is subject to restrictions as set forth in subparagraph (c)(1)(ii) of the Rights in Technical Data and Computer Software clause at DFARS 252.227-7013 or subparagraphs (c)(1) and (2) of the Commercial Computer Software—Restricted Rights at 48 CFR 52.227-19, as applicable. Manufacturer is Microsoft Corporation/One Microsoft Way/Redmond, WA 98052-6399.

5. **EXPORT RESTRICTIONS.** You agree that you will not export or re-export the SOFTWARE PRODUCT, any part thereof, or any process or service that is the direct product of the SOFTWARE PRODUCT (the foregoing collectively referred to as the "Restricted Components"), to any country, person, entity, or end user subject to U.S. export restrictions. You specifically agree not to export or re-export any of the Restricted Components (i) to any country to which the U.S. has embargoed or restricted the export of goods or services, which currently include, but are not necessarily limited to, Cuba, Iran, Iraq, Libya, North Korea, Sudan, and Syria, or to any national of any such country, wherever located, who intends to transmit or transport the Restricted Components back to such country; (ii) to any end user who you know or have reason to know will utilize the Restricted Components in the design, development, or production of nuclear, chemical, or biological weapons; or (iii) to any end user who has been prohibited from participating in U.S. export transactions by any federal agency of the U.S. government. You warrant and represent that neither the BXA nor any other U.S. federal agency has suspended, revoked, or denied your export privileges.

DISCLAIMER OF WARRANTY

NO WARRANTIES OR CONDITIONS. MICROSOFT EXPRESSLY DISCLAIMS ANY WARRANTY OR CONDITION FOR THE SOFTWARE PRODUCT. THE SOFTWARE PRODUCT AND ANY RELATED DOCUMENTATION ARE PROVIDED "AS IS" WITHOUT WARRANTY OR CONDITION OF ANY KIND, EITHER EXPRESS OR IMPLIED, INCLUDING, WITHOUT LIMITATION, THE IMPLIED WARRANTIES OF MERCHANTABILITY, FITNESS FOR A PARTICULAR PURPOSE, OR NONINFRINGEMENT. THE ENTIRE RISK ARISING OUT OF USE OR PERFORMANCE OF THE SOFTWARE PRODUCT REMAINS WITH YOU.

LIMITATION OF LIABILITY. TO THE MAXIMUM EXTENT PERMITTED BY APPLICABLE LAW, IN NO EVENT SHALL MICROSOFT OR ITS SUPPLIERS BE LIABLE FOR ANY SPECIAL, INCIDENTAL, INDIRECT, OR CONSEQUENTIAL DAMAGES WHATSOEVER (INCLUDING, WITHOUT LIMITATION, DAMAGES FOR LOSS OF BUSINESS PROFITS, BUSINESS INTERRUPTION, LOSS OF BUSINESS INFORMATION, OR ANY OTHER PECUNIARY LOSS) ARISING OUT OF THE USE OF OR INABILITY TO USE THE SOFTWARE PRODUCT OR THE PROVISION OF OR FAILURE TO PROVIDE SUPPORT SERVICES, EVEN IF MICROSOFT HAS BEEN ADVISED OF THE POSSIBILITY OF SUCH DAMAGES. IN ANY CASE, MICROSOFT'S ENTIRE LIABILITY UNDER ANY PROVISION OF THIS EULA SHALL BE LIMITED TO THE GREATER OF THE AMOUNT ACTUALLY PAID BY YOU FOR THE SOFTWARE PRODUCT OR US$5.00; PROVIDED, HOWEVER, IF YOU HAVE ENTERED INTO A MICROSOFT SUPPORT SERVICES AGREEMENT, MICROSOFT'S ENTIRE LIABILITY REGARDING SUPPORT SERVICES SHALL BE GOVERNED BY THE TERMS OF THAT AGREEMENT. BECAUSE SOME STATES AND JURISDICTIONS DO NOT ALLOW THE EXCLUSION OR LIMITATION OF LIABILITY, THE ABOVE LIMITATION MAY NOT APPLY TO YOU.

MISCELLANEOUS

This EULA is governed by the laws of the State of Washington USA, except and only to the extent that applicable law mandates governing law of a different jurisdiction.

Should you have any questions concerning this EULA, or if you desire to contact Microsoft for any reason, please contact the Microsoft subsidiary serving your country, or write: Microsoft Sales Information Center/One Microsoft Way/Redmond, WA 98052-6399.

PN 097-0002296